Principles of
Catholic Theology

BOOK 3

Principles of Catholic Theology

Book 3, *On God, Trinity, Creation, and Christ*

THOMAS JOSEPH WHITE, OP

The Catholic University of America Press
Washington, D.C.

Contents

Principles of
Catholic Theology

On Wisdom, Mystery, and
the Trinity

The human being is a truth-seeking animal, one that inevitably desires happiness and spiritual repose. It is also a being capable of desiring perspective on human experience, understanding of why all things are, and what one may rightly hope for from life. Religious traditions of course seek to address questions of ultimate explanation. They seek to pass beyond the domains of what can be known by natural reason, or human philosophy, to reach out to the encounter with the transcendent and absolute truth, so as to orient all of human existence toward its true homeland or finality. Catholic Christianity can be thought about in this way, insofar as it addresses directly our human hope for an ultimate explanation and fulfillment. At the same time, Christianity also speaks of a higher form of truth, one that is "super"-natural or above nature, one that heals and elevates our nature into a higher sphere. The supernatural life of grace introduces us into genuine and immediate friendship with God, albeit in the darkness of faith, and in the expectation of hope and charity, infused theological virtues that are a gift of God. These gifts place us in immediate and intimate contact with God in himself, in his Trinitarian life. They also introduce us into a new

Originally published in *The Thomist* 87, no. 4 (2023): 659–82. Used with permission.

communion with other human beings, one that stems from the person of Christ, the God-man, and that configures us to Christ in his life of grace. This life stems from his Incarnation, passion, and resurrection. It also, in turn, configures us to his human fullness of grace, his death, and his glorified humanity. With Christ, we discover the Holy Trinity, in view of living in communion with the Holy Trinity, we are configured to Christ.

Principles of Catholic Theology is a multi-volume set of theological writings on the truth of Catholic Christianity. The first book is concerned with the nature of theology, and the second with the rational credibility of Christianity. Both of these prior volumes already identify the mystery of the Most Holy Trinity as the central mystery of the Christian faith, seconded only by that of the Incarnation. It is in virtue of the fact that God has become human that the human race has come to know God in God's very life, as Father, Son, and Holy Spirit, so that the two mysteries inevitably implicate one another. Who God is as Trinity is revealed to us in the Incarnation, and the Incarnation of the Son of God in human history introduces us to the inner mystery of God as Trinitarian. Therefore, we turn to the topics of the Trinity and Christology in this volume.

Here in the Introduction to Book 3, I would like to reflect briefly on theology as "wisdom" insofar as it seeks knowledge of the Trinity and of all things in light of the Trinity. This is fitting since this volume contains chapters that reflect extensively on the nature of God, the mystery of the Holy Trinity, the Creation that comes forth from God, and the Incarnation of the Son of God. These reflections are a precursor to the subsequent volume, Book 4, which is concerned with the Church, Mariology, Grace, and Nature.

My aim in this introductory reflection is to contextualize the *reprise* of Thomistic reflection on the divine nature and the Holy Trinity in the wake of developments in modern theology, especially in light of the proliferation of modern historical studies (biblical, patristic, and medieval), ecumenical concerns, and in the wake of important developments in modern Trinitarian theology. How might one envisage today in a Thomistic lens the tasks and responsibilities of a revitalized Trinitarian theology, one that is open to a sense of mystery, responsible toward historical sources, engaged in genuinely Catholic ecumenism, and conversant with problematics in modern theology? I cannot treat this question comprehensively in one opening reflection, as indeed the whole of this volume is intended in some sense as a response to the interrogation. However, we can at least allude thematically to various challenges that the question raises and indicate various ideas that any comprehensive answer to it must include. By setting out in this way, we can invite the reader to think in a more considered way about both the promise and the challenge of theological scholasticism when one appeals to its principles within the context of contemporary Catholic theology.

ON WISDOM AND MYSTERY

Defined in a very general way, a mystery is something that awakens our intellectual desire for greater understanding, explanation, and contemplation—not only because it is imperfectly understood by us, but also because it is super-intelligible, that is to say, transcending our limited capacities for understanding precisely because it is something intrinsically profound in intelligibility, and even inexhaustibly so. The signs in us of the perception of mystery are intellectual wonder and loving admiration, in the sense that when we come to know better something that is intrinsically mysterious, we also grow in admiration and wonder. We can speak in this sense of the "mystery of life" because even as we come to understand the intelligibility, beauty, and goodness of human existence, we also wonder at and admire many elements of it that exceed our comprehension.

This all being said, the New Testament employs the term "mystery" in a very distinct sense. St. Paul speaks of this mystery in Col. 1:25–28, and correlates it to the notion of wisdom:

> I became a minister according to the divine office which was given to me for you, to make the word of God fully known, the mystery hidden

for ages and generations but now made manifest to his saints. To them God chose to make known how great among the Gentiles are the riches of the glory of this mystery, which is Christ in you, the hope of glory. Him we proclaim, warning every man and teaching every man in all wisdom, that we may present every man mature in Christ.

This text suggests several interconnected senses of mystery: (1) God in himself: the eternal Father who is revealed in his Son and in his Spirit; (2) The Incarnation of the Son and the filial adoption in grace that is communicated by God to the saints; (3) The glory of beatitude that results from this filial adoption, for which we hope in this life.

Speaking in more formal theological language, then, we can speak of the mystery of God that is unveiled to us in the Incarnation of the Word made flesh, and that is communicated to us by the life, death, and resurrection of Jesus Christ, in the Holy Spirit. Of course, this process of communication occurs principally through the Church, her liturgy, and her sacraments, but it is also something that has the power to possess our entire life in both its contemplative and active dimensions, as a journey into God.

It is significant that Paul purposefully aligns this sense of the encounter with the mystery of God (the inner life of the Father, his Son, and the Holy Spirit) with the quest for wisdom. He indicates here simultaneously the fulfilment of both the ancient Hebraic-biblical concept of wisdom (the creation as an emanation from the uncreated wisdom of God), and that of Hellenistic philosophy (the rational and contemplative search for ultimate explanation), while claiming that what both initiate and aspire to imperfectly is only found perfectly and gratuitously in the revelation of the Father, made known to us in the Son made man, Jesus Christ, and in the Spirit.

Both patristic and scholastic authors of East and West made generous use of this Pauline coordination of the twin notions of mystery and wisdom.[1] The search for wisdom terminates in the encounter

---

1. Just to take one prominent example, consider Gregory of Nyssa in *Against Eunomius* 3.2, where he seeks to coordinate an analysis of God's pre-existent wisdom with

with the mystery of God, and God alone can fulfill by grace the interminable human desire for contemplation and for perfect understanding of what is ultimate in the order of being. Far from being a divisive idea, this notion found in Aquinas's thought provides a sound basis for a historically inclusive and broad-minded ecumenism of East and West.

That being said, there are notions specific to the Thomistic tradition for thinking about wisdom in distinct ways, as (1) philosophical, (2) theological-doctrinal, and (3) mystical. The three are irreducibly distinct but also inseparable within a unified Christian life. This distinction of forms of wisdom is not arbitrary, for reasons that I take to be indisputable. Evidently, we wish to affirm that there is an incomprehensible mystery at the ground of all being that we rightly name the Holy Trinity, and that our genuine knowledge of this mystery is imperfect but nevertheless real. Furthermore, let us grant that this knowledge is dynamically unitive, that is to say, related to ongoing growth in the love of God and a contemplative desire for the vision of God, as indeed it should be. The affirmation of a genuine philosophical wisdom regarding God is implied necessarily by this idea, since what we receive in faith (the direct encounter with the wisdom of God in Christ, and the mystery of the Trinity) cannot be sheerly external or unnaturally violent with regard to our native desire to know the truth about being. Just because we are capable of grace, so too we must be capable of asking the question of what is ultimately underived in reality. The mystery of the Trinity can only be revealed to a created being that is personal, one that is intellectual and freely loving, capable of understanding even philosophically that life is wondrous or "mysterious," and that the "mystery" of being (its

---

the mystery of the Incarnation as a manifestation of divine wisdom. Similar examples abound, many of which are at least remotely similar to ideas one finds in Aquinas. See also *Against Eunomius* 2.1, 2.2, 2.6, 2.11, which clearly denote the central mystery as that of the Holy Trinity, but see it as something manifest in the "mysteries" of the Incarnation, the Cross, and the communication of grace to human persons. *Nicene and Post-Nicene Fathers*, vol. 5, trans. H. C. Ogle and H. A. Wilson; ed. P. Schaff and H. Wace (Buffalo, NY: Christian Literature Publishing Co., 1893).

beauty and goodness) can be contemplated, and not merely comprehended or dominated by human cognition. The human quest for explanatory wisdom is one that ascends toward what is "above" the human intellect, as explanatory of all else yet incomprehensible in itself, and this is the sign also (for theologians) that we are able to receive from God, without violence to our nature, something we could not procure by our own powers or understand merely on our own terms: the epiphany of the inner life of God. Consequently, there exists something like an innate aspiration to philosophical wisdom that is proper to our rational nature, no matter how much we may ignore it or thwart it, individually or collectively.

Nevertheless, this cannot be all, since we already now possess, by divine revelation, true knowledge of what and who God is in himself, as Father, Son, and Holy Spirit. This insight into the mystery of God in himself occurs by grace and within faith, but it truly does attain in faith to the *res* or inner reality of God in himself (cf. Aquinas, ST I-II, q. 1, a. 1). Even if we see through a glass darkly, we do see, and this insight of faith receives its focus from scripture, read within sacred tradition, including in the most important references of conciliar definitions or dogmatic enunciations. These doctrines matter precisely because they allow us to focus our gaze, through scripture and the liturgy, above the horizon of merely natural knowledge, so as to see out into the mystery of God in himself, as he has revealed himself to us, in the prophecies of Israel, and in the apostolic teaching, concerning the human life, death, and resurrection of God incarnate. Theology, then, has an inward contour and "scientific" integrity as a body of knowledge regarding the mystery of God as best we can come to know it in this life, over time. This "science" is sapiential because it seeks to pass through arguments and explanations into contemplation of the mystery of God in himself, by way of greater understanding, always in the service of love and unitive contact with the Holy Trinity.

As this last comment intimates, theology, when practiced well in the Church, must be open to mysticism, that is to say, to a greater experiential and non-experiential union with God that anticipates the higher mode of knowledge of God that will come to fruition after this life. In our current, embodied state as rational animals, we only come to know God as sensate, culturally-linguistic creatures who think abstractly, who are dependent upon the visible historical mediations of the Church, her language, liturgy, and traditional notions, as well as the sacraments (mysteries) instituted by Christ himself for our sanctification. Nevertheless, through all these, we *tend* toward a higher mode of union. This occurs through love, yes, but also in special forms of knowledge, which can be called mystical, since they incline our being and our spiritual powers more deeply into anticipatory eschatological union with the mystery of God even in this life.

On this point, Aquinas appeals in particular to the significance of the gifts of the Holy Spirit.[2] These seven gifts are given in baptism as a dimension of grace, along with the theological virtues of faith, hope, and love. Prior to the gifts, the three theological virtues of faith, hope, and love already are infused habits that orient us in this life toward a stable and ever-growing contemplative union with God.[3] These theological virtues are intrinsically oriented toward and come to fruition in the beatifying vision of God in the life to come.[4] What the gifts of the Holy Spirit add to this, however, is the mode of perfection and intensification of the exercise of the theological virtues. With them, we see better or more deeply, and we are able to love more profoundly, by unitive intensity. Here we can mention only two that pertain especially to contemplation: understanding (*intellectus*) and wisdom (*sapientia*), both of which have mystical connotations. "Understanding" for Aquinas is likened by similitude, in the supernatural order, to Aristotle's notion of *nous* or insight, from the *De Anima* III, 6.[5] The Holy Spirit can elevate the gaze of the intellect *through* scripture and ecclesiastical doctrine (as well as liturgical prayer) into a deeper gaze upon the reality of the mystery

---

2. See *Summa theologiae* I-II, q. 68. [*Summa Theologica*, trans. English Dominican Province (New York: Benziger, 1947).]

3. ST I-II, q. 62.

4. See ST II-II, q. 1, a. 1; q. 4, a. 1; q. 17, a. 2; q. 23, aa. 1, 6 and 8.

5. ST II-II, q. 8, a. 1.

of Christ and of the Trinity. The Spirit alights upon the soul to elevate it into friendship with God in a special way that cannot be maintained by the soul's own power, but that is a sheer gift. This gift can in turn leave an abiding impression upon the soul and perhaps also augment the intensive perfection of the habit of faith over time, in a general way, so that the agency of the gifts translates into a more intensive spiritual savoring or touching of the soul with God by union, over time.[6] Likewise, the movement of the mind that is given by this form of insight is also often accompanied by a deeper union of love with the mystery known (in *sapiential* charity). This *sapientia* is something Aquinas compares by similitude with Aristotle's notion of connatural love: we become like our friends because our will becomes conformed over time to theirs and theirs to ours, in a shared life. This in turn affects our judgments about how to live wisely in accord with love.[7] So too, in a shared life with God the Father, and by friendship with Christ, the soul becomes conformed more perfectly by love and sound judgement to the eternal Word made flesh, by the inward promptings of the Holy Spirit, who resides within the saints of God's Church (John 14:23–26).

All of this suggests that the mystics (who live by the inward promptings of the Holy Spirit in an especial way) need to refer themselves to the scriptural, liturgical, and doctrinal teaching of the Church as a precondition for their lives in Christ. They remain "accountable" to the common faith of the Catholic Church and the official theological instances of the articulation of the faith. Indeed, they depend upon the Church so that they can find God in all of his truthfulness and live by the objective contours of the apostolic teaching of Christ. Simultaneously, members of the theological guild also seek unitive love with Christ and can find inspiration and challenge from the mystical authors. Historically speaking, the greatest

---

6. See ST II-II, q. 8, aa. 6–8.

7. ST II-II, q. 23, a. 5; q. 45, aa. 1, 2, and 4. In q. 23, a. 5 Aquinas references Aristotle on the notion of conformity to friends in various forms of common life in *Nicomachean Ethics* VIII, 12. See also *Nicomachean Ethics* I, 3 as it pertains, seemingly, to ST II-II, q. 45, a. 2, as well as ST I, q. 1, a. 6, ad 3.

of theologians have typically had a profound inner life, even if the ecclesial service of theology is distinct in its objectives (but never separated!) from personal search for union with God, and from other modes of service to the Church. The philosophers are invited by both to remain existentially attentive to yet-more-ultimate explanations of the mystery of life received from divine revelation, while those who are granted the grace of faith still remain accountable to the tasks of serious human reasoning, including philosophical reasoning about God which must be learned from the philosophical, scientific, and historical disciplines.

ON CATHOLIC *SACRA DOCTRINA,* HISTORICAL GENEALOGY, AND THOMISM

On the view of theology I have just indicated, the theologian should seek to understand and explain the Christian faith in fidelity to scripture, tradition, and the magisterium in such a way as to remain open to the use of natural philosophical resources (including knowledge stemming from thorough historical study and the modern sciences), and should do so while remaining open to and oriented toward experiential and interior union with God. Perhaps some might conclude (erroneously) that based upon these Thomistic criteria, it would be true to say that only those who are Thomistic might be considered genuine Catholic theologians. However, Aquinas affirms something contrary to this in the first *quaestio* of the *Summa theologiae* (ST I, q. 1), where he considers *sacra doctrina* as both a science and wisdom of God, the Holy Trinity. There, he observes that the first principles of the science of theology are derived from scripture as it is read by the Church collectively and as she enunciates them, especially in the Nicene creed. (He says something very similar in the *Compendium of Theology.*)[8] Aquinas also notes in the same *quaestio* that theology is sapiential, that is to say,

8. See Thomas Aquinas, *Compendium of Theology,* trans. C. Vollert (St. Louis & London: Herder, 1947), c. 246.

oriented toward contemplative union with God, and that it must respect the integrity of philosophical arguments (especially regarding God and human nature) and may make use of them within theology, as a higher science may integrate the principles and conclusions of a lower science into itself.[9] We should note that on this view, anyone engages in genuine theological discourse who, first, takes his or her starting points from the understanding of revelation that is safeguarded by the Church, her tradition, and her pronouncements, and who, second, seeks also to be attentive to the inherent exigencies of natural reason (philosophical, scientific, historical) and the unitive or mystical aspirations of theology. Therefore, any exercise in "Thomistic" theology must, by Aquinas's own criteria, assume that there are non-Thomistic theologies, and that Thomistic contributions to the theological search for God take place within a wider ecclesiastical estuary of theological traditions and spiritual practices that seek genuine knowledge and love of the Trinity.[10]

This perspective, however, does not lead to relativism in regard to the various schools of theology, or at least, it need not and should not. There is a native impulse in human nature toward school-thought, and indeed, we find schools of religious thought not only in Catholic Christianity but also in other ecclesial Christian traditions (for example, Palamitism, or Reformed scholasticism) and indeed in non-Christian religious traditions (for example, theistic Vedantism, or Hanafism in Sunni Islam). The specific character of a Catholic school of theology stems from the fact that it seeks a particular way of combining (1) a responsible reception and interpretation of Catholic doctrinal intellectual traditions with (2) a profound and truthful philosophical vision of God, creation, and humanity and (3) an orientation toward the practical spiritual life of union with God. It must do so inevitably while also (4) engaging constructively and respectively with other ecclesiastical schools and their great

---

9. ST I, q. 1, aa. 1, 5, and 6.

10. I discuss this idea at further length in *Principles of Catholic Theology*, Book 1, *On the Nature of Theology* (Washington, DC: The Catholic University of America Press, 2023).

figures to seek to negotiate what either should be retained or disputed in regard to their alternative or convergent theological or philosophical assertions.

Theological schools of the kind just designated are numerous, but to name some, we might mention Augustinianism, Cappadocianism, Coptic Cyrillianism, versions of Byzantine scholasticism (such as that found in Maximus, Damascene, or Palamas), Bonaventurianism, Thomism, Scotism, Suarezianism, Rahnerianism, or the thought of the Communio school characterized by influential modern figures like De Lubac, Ratzinger, and Von Balthasar. Many other instances could be named.

At this juncture, it is helpful to make two important observations. First, virtually everyone who, over time, promotes a unified vision of Christian theology tends toward participation in a certain school of thought. Certainly, those just listed are highly defined, and *many, if not most,* theologians might refuse to avail themselves of explicit alignment with any of them. But just to the extent that a person is committed to normative doctrinal claims and associated ways of interpreting these claims theologically, however apophatically, in alignment with a series of judgments about philosophy, history, and the spiritual life, one is acquiring a kind of universal view of theology, its inward contours and possibilities, as a science and as a wisdom. Even those who advance the position that "most or all classical schools over-interpret on their own terms the doctrines of the faith in ways that are epistemologically unwarranted" fall back inevitably upon more fundamental views that they do think must be maintained based on the force of tradition, liturgy, personal spiritual intuitions, or other adjacent criteria. Minimalistic schools are not only still schools but are, in fact, often aligned to form a kind of socially interminable pressure point upon more maximalist schools to seek uniformity of a more generic kind against what are perceived as the dangers of too highly specific (i.e., epistemologically unwarranted and potentially divisive) forms of theological reasoning. There can be good ecclesiological reasons for this, but the dynamic can also arise for other reasons, including intellectual haziness, spiritual fear of the unknown, or the triumphalist or jingoistic desire to be right. Advancing *something like* the thought of a school, thus, is in some ways inevitable, but it is also important to note here a second point. To advance theologically *in a school* as a kind of sub-tradition within the Christian intellectual tradition does not imply that one advocates for the eradication of a plurality of schools or approaches to theology, nor should one imagine that it must be thus. Clearly, there are things that everyone needs to agree upon, and there are also contributions specific theologians make within the tradition that become virtually normative within the common doctrine of the Church, such as Cyril's teaching on the hypostatic union or Aquinas's teaching on the Eucharist, in the Catholic tradition. Nevertheless, there is always a de facto pluralism of theological traditions in the Church, and this has to be taken into account by all who seek to find unity and truth in Catholic theological work. At the same time, precisely because there is also a common ground of unity in theological science, it is possible to seek greater unity and consensus by privileging certain doctors or references (like the thought of Augustine or Aquinas) as potential sources of convergence or as figures who help us make discernments. This process will lead to inevitable disagreements, but that is fine. The Church contains internal theological disagreements and regulates these "from above" over time by way either of clear magisterial pronouncements or by way of practical magnanimity by permitting her children to seek the truth through a plurality of intellectual traditions and by way of a spiritual competition of arguments in the shared holy pursuit of the undifferentiated truth.

What should we say in this light about historical genealogy? Is it licit for a Thomist, or anyone else for that matter, to read figures such as Athanasius, Gregory of Nazianzus, Augustine, Dionysius, or, for that matter, Aristotle, as teachers whose doctrines provide a possibility for or even an anticipation of the theological teachings of Thomas Aquinas? And can one justifiably make use in turn of Aquinas's

"Thomistic principles" in order to make discernments about the value of ideas found subsequently in historical figures like Luther, Kant, Hegel, Bulgakov, or Rahner?

Here, we may make four brief observations.

First, in any historical genealogy that is to be placed in the service of theology, there is an irreducible role for historical accuracy. Some historical interpretations contradict express evidence, while others do not, and some interpretations of historical texts are more probable or reasonable than others. Sometimes, however, texts are themselves inherently vague or open to various subsequent contrasting interpretations. Augustine provides a famous instance of this, as does Aristotle. There are many contestable forms of Aristotelianism and of Augustinianism.[11] Likewise, a figure like Augustine makes some affirmations that should be re-interpreted or rejected in light of the subsequent Catholic magisterium. But one can interpret texts while still maintaining a passion for historical accuracy that allows the diversity and convergence of distinct theological authors and traditions to come to the fore, and while still seeking a greater unity in the faith among the great figures of the past.

Second, we inevitably select a limited number of sources in any genealogy, which already shows a set of value judgments about what matters most, and in any historical study we tell, we provide normative views of what has emerged as the most important theological result of past developments. In short, no genealogy ever has been or ever could be innocent of theologically normative judgments, even if every genealogy also should seek to be historically accurate.

---

11. Many of Aquinas's readings of Aristotle are *both* highly contestable *and* textually defensible, whereas the same can be said of alternative readings of Aristotle found in Averroes, a point of which both Aquinas and his contemporaries were very aware. The texts of Aristotle are often in mere obediential potency to Thomism, historically considered. And this can be said in other ways of the texts of Augustine or Dionysius. Generally speaking, it is not wise to wager against Aquinas in his interpretation of ancient texts, as he can provide surprisingly plausible readings, even by the standards of contemporary historiography. Anecdotally, my Anglican tutor in Oxford, a classicist who had no ideological inclinations in this regard, once told me that he was inclined to think that Aquinas had provided some of the clearest and best commentaries on Aristotle ever to exist.

Third, the very idea that some notions are true and that some schools of thought are preferable (in their principles, analysis, conclusions, or spiritual practice) inevitably leads to normative views of genealogy. Everyone has ideas of what really matters most in theological history, and these do not arise from one's historical attention to texts per se, but from one's view of what is true about reality, especially in regard to God, Christ, and divine revelation. However, here a subtle point emerges. Many past figures and their theological texts are in partial or complete obediential potency to a variety of subsequent readings. One can read Aristotle, Augustine, or Dionysius, for example, in the way Aquinas does or in the way Bonaventure does. The point is not primarily about which of these two great medieval doctors reads these three past figures more accurately (though this also matters), but about the *two distinct synthetic, doctrinal ways* that each of them appropriated past masters and their insights, restating them in (arguably) yet more profound and novel ways than had existed hitherto. One observes in this process of interpretation and synthesis, as well as original actualization, that there is both fidelity to the past and a newly emergent, developmental vitality of insight. Accordingly, one can seek to appropriate Aquinas or Bonaventure today as various theologians do, such as Scheeben, Rahner, Ratzinger, or a variety of contemporary Thomists.

What emerges from this historical process is a diversity of "collections" of wisdom traditions in the Church. Again, this should lead not to relativism but to more intensive, if respectful, debate. In fact, one must debate about the truth (historical, theological, philosophical, spiritual, and moral) precisely to help adjudicate and advance the insight and spiritual acumen of the life of the Church from within. The ancients debated. The medievals did so. And the moderns continue to do so. So, a theology that is primarily either didactic or spiritual in aspiration must also be at times polemical or dialectical in orientation so as to seek to provide new pathways toward the truth and new ways of advancing the theological heritage of traditions respectfully and rightly received from the past. In all of this, we should also mention the ecumenical context of Catholic theological work. The search for the truth in Catholic theology also presupposes a common conversation with all baptized Christians regarding the truth of Christianity and a common baptismal life of shared discipleship of all those who seek to know and love God the Holy Trinity, in whom we share a common baptism, and a common ecclesial existence.

ON KNOWING AND EXPERIENCING THE TRINITY IN HISTORY

This brings me to the final point, which is less methodological and more formally doctrinal. It is concerned with our knowledge and experience of the mystery of the Trinity within the economic sphere of human history. I take it that the eternal processional life of the Holy Trinity is the ontological pre-condition for the temporal missions of the Son and of the Holy Spirit. The Son can only be sent into the world by the Father because he is, first and foremost, the eternally begotten Son and Word of the Father. The Holy Spirit can only be sent into the world by the Father and the Son because he is the eternally spirated Spirit of the Father and the Son (proceeding through and from the Word). The eternal relations of origin precede the missions ontologically and are not constituted by the latter. The missions, however, do manifest, or render present within history, the very persons in their eternal mutual relations. As Aquinas notes, a mission just is an eternal procession with the addition of an external effect.[12] When the eternal Word becomes flesh, it is the very *Word* who becomes flesh, that is to say, he who is eternally from the Father, as his only-begotten Son.

In addition to this statement about the ontological priority of the processions to the missions, I would like to add a statement about the *epistemological* priority of the processions to the missions for us

12. See ST I, q. 43, a. 2, ad 3.

in our coming to understand the Trinity. It is undoubtedly true that we only come to know the persons of the Father, Son, and Holy Spirit personally, even quasi-experientially (through the illumination of faith, hope, and love), *because* the Father has first sent the Son and the Spirit into the world. The Trinitarian missions are the presupposition of our coming to know the Trinitarian God in himself. Nevertheless, it is only when we gain understanding or insight in faith that Jesus Christ is true God and true man, and that in his person he is uncreated, eternally begotten of the Father, God from God, light from light, true God from true God, that we can in turn also understand *who* has been sent, and *what* is present among us. Namely, we can come to understand that it is the eternal Son and Word of the Father who is present among us, and that he is God and Lord. And it is only really when we first come to understand this that we can, in turn, understand that the Word is hypostatically distinct from the Father (a distinct divine person) and that he is one in being and nature with the Father, just as it is only when we come to understand that the Holy Spirit is an eternal person distinct from the Father and the Son, who is also Lord and God, (worshipped and glorified) that we come in turn to understand that the Father, Son, and Holy Spirit are each personally distinct and that they are each truly the one God.

To begin to think like this is made possible by the primary principles of insight into scripture's most basic "givens," which are expressed in creedal understanding. It is from these most basic insights that there begins to emerge Trinitarian reflection, including the clear distinction (originating first with Augustine, based on his reading of scripture) of eternal processions and temporal missions.[13] It is not an accident that the clear theological distinction of eternal processions and temporal missions first arose conceptionally *after* the Council of Nicaea and within the context of anti-Arian polemics by pro-Nicene thinkers. It is the very admission that the Son and the

---

13. Augustine sets out to develop the distinction in *The Trinity*, books 1–4 [trans. E. Hill, ed. J. E. Rotelle (Hyde Park, NY: New City Press, 1991).] For a thematic consideration of Augustine's notion of divine sending, see Lewis Ayres, *Augustine and the Trinity* (Cambridge: Cambridge University Press, 2010), 181–87, 233–50.

Holy Spirit are each truly God and are truly personally distinct from the Father that gives rise to the eventual intelligibility of the doctrine of the temporal missions and not the inverse.

Furthermore, we do not come to know the Holy Trinity only by way of the historical life, death, and resurrection of Jesus Christ. These mysteries *do* constitute the central and most essential way we come to know the Holy Trinity, coupled with the revelation of the sending of the Holy Spirit upon the Church at Pentecost. However it is important to note that we *also* come to know the Trinity by: (1) the teachings of the Old Testament, which the Fathers rightly noted contains a great deal of proto-Trinitarian revelation that is brought to completion and explicit clarity by the New Testament revelation, (2) the verbal teachings of Jesus regarding the Father, himself, and the Holy Spirit, and not merely his passion and resurrection, (3) the teachings of the apostles, whose inspired words need not and do not always correspond precisely to closely parallel antecedent words or actions of Christ, (4) the sacraments and liturgical traditions of the Church, which are of apostolic origin or derivation, (5) the theological, spiritual, and mystical writings of the saints, who typically assimilate the revelation most intensively, and finally (6) creation itself insofar as it can be "reread" in light of divine revelation to give us some insight into the Trinitarian Creator, who has created all things in the intelligibility of his Word and the goodness of his Holy Spirit.

Given what has just been stated, it seems to me necessary to affirm, even today in light of the prevalence of metaphysical skepticism on all sides, that the human person, with the help of God's grace, can reflect in coherent and true ways on the immanent life of God, based on what God has revealed about himself in these various formats. Here, I would defend the significance and centrality of the divine names (the attributes rightly ascribed by analogical reasoning to the divine nature, such as simplicity, goodness, eternity, and so on) and the notion of eternal relations of origin in God (from the Cappadocians and Augustine).

One could just stop there, and many do, resulting in a highly apophatic but still distinctly Trinitarian theological form of reflection. One can note that there is a unity of three persons who are distinguished by relations of origin of some pre-existent, eternal kind that we know only very imperfectly. This minimalistic standpoint is entirely permissible, doctrinally and historically speaking, but if we survey the Catholic doctors of the Church, including most Eastern fathers, it is not a majority standpoint. It is also anything but a *required* standpoint as if one were obliged to reject the explorations of Athanasius, Damascene, Anselm, Bonaventure, or Aquinas in order to remain theologically more insightful than they were. (We may think helpfully here about what Chesterton said regarding the democracy of the dead.)

I am in the camp of those, then, who think it is possible and salutary to go further than the so-called "minimalists" by considering anew the medieval Western exploration of Augustine's psychological analogy (the twin eternal processions of the Son and Spirit as pertaining to a similitude of knowledge and love respectively). Indeed, I argue in this volume, as I have elsewhere, that this similitude is of significant importance for Trinitarian theology. It provides us with a privileged theological analogy by which to think of the inner life of God that has been revealed to us in Christ. And it is only if we have some way of understanding the immanent eternal life of God as a truth of revelation (no matter how apophatically, how opaquely) that we can coherently articulate a notion of the God of revelation: the Trinity of persons who are the one God, according to an order or *taxis* of relations, Father, Word, and Spirit. Simply to affirm the reality of eternal relations of origin and to enshrine it in a series of metaphors is permissible, but it is also intellectually and mystically anemic. Anselm, Bernard, Bonaventure, Albert, Aquinas, Catherine of Siena, Scheeben, Newman, Elizabeth of the Trinity, Ratzinger, and many others think that we can see further here, with the use of the psychological analogy, and I accept to follow them in this.

The aim here is definitively not to construct some scholastic fortress of all too human logic in which to imprison a mystery, but merely to articulate better our revealed and mysterious knowledge of God the Holy Trinity, one that is real. I take it that Aquinas does this with his proper theological analogies of eternally generated *Verbum* and eternally spirated *Amorem*. These, in turn, help us gain insight into the persons themselves, disposing us theologically to the reception of the gifts of understanding and wisdom which I have mentioned above, that impel us toward yet deeper intuitive and loving union with God. Mysticism without intellectual content is as dangerous a thing as arid speculation without love. It is, in fact, one very distinct thing to point back to a number of profound theological texts, patristic or modern. It is quite another thing to say something that is true in a constructive way, one which is consistent with sound natural reasoning and that is intrinsically open to and at the service of the inner spiritual life of Christian believers.

Let me complete this section with a few more punctuated thoughts that are logically related.

First, given what I have said above, the question Karl Rahner poses of whether it is sheerly impossible for the Father or the Holy Spirit to become incarnate is of some real consequence. Rahner famously claimed that only the Son can truly become incarnate because he alone is the Word who communicates God to creatures.[14] Medieval scholastics, by contrast, argued that each of the three persons has the divine omnipotent capacity to become human, but that only the Son fittingly becomes human. They did note, then, that it was not impossible for there to have been an alternative economy, one that never has come to pass, in which the Father or Spirit became human.

What is at stake in this question is, I think, something more than human fantasies about possible worlds, or a logical game about human ways of conceiving the divine essence and the divine will.

14. See Karl Rahner, *The Trinity*, trans. J. Donceel (London: Continuum, 2001), 28–30, contrasted with Aquinas, ST III, q. 3, aa. 5 and 8. See also the important speculative and historical consideration of this question by Dominic Legge, *The Trinitarian Christology of St. Thomas Aquinas* (Oxford: Oxford University Press, 2017).

Instead, the argument touches upon the very nature of God and the mystery of the Trinity in itself. Consider in this regard that the very mystery we celebrate and reverence is a mystery of the free expression of God in history and of the gratuitous initiative of God to save us by his own designs of wisdom and love through the sending of his Son in our flesh. It is also a mystery of God in himself, of God who reveals himself as Father, Son, and Holy Spirit, three who are one in their transcendent Lordship and in all that pertains to the nature of God. But if the Holy Trinity really is revealed in the Incarnation of the Son as one God in three persons, and if God freely undertakes this initiative gratuitously (by his omnipotent goodness), then it follows necessarily that this omnipotent goodness is present equally and identically in all three persons, who are Father, Son, and Holy Spirit. Indeed, one of the first things we must conclude from the Incarnation is that the Father has the loving power to effectuate the Incarnation by sending the Son into the world. Thus, even though only the second person has become incarnate due to divine fittingness, it is also true that the Father and the Spirit possess the same power to effectuate the mystery of the Incarnation as does the Son, and indeed, they must, precisely because he has become incarnate and because he who has become incarnate is one in being, essence, and power with them. However, precisely because this last statement is true, *it necessarily follows that the Father and the Holy Spirit possess the power to incarnate by love.* Indeed, to deny this claim is very close, if not equivalent, to the denial of the unicity of the three persons, insofar as they all possess one incomprehensible and transcendent nature in common as God. If the Son reveals to us that he is one of the Trinity, crucified (cf. John 8:28), he can only do so because there is a ground of unity that he shares with the Father and the Holy Spirit, present precisely in the human crucifixion of the second person.

Why in the world, then, would Rahner argue that only the Son has the power or capacity to incarnate and that the Father and the Spirit do not? The answer is, I think, quite simple. Rahner interprets

the notion of "Word" to be attributed to the eternal Son principally (and not secondarily, as the scholastics did) so as to denote the
Son's relation to creatures.[15] "Word" thus signifies principally and
primarily the Father communicating himself to what is not God
and within that which is not God by taking up a created human nature. The Word is identifiable as Word even eternally only in virtue
of his capacity for incarnation in a created nature. This position is
evidently very close to that of Hegel and has unambiguous Sabel-
lian overtones. The eternal Word is always, already by definition, for
communication, for incarnation, and for God's self-communication
to human nature. Thus, the Word as Word from all eternity is always, already "on the verge" of the economy, as the almost necessary moment of God's Trinitarian self-revelation in what is not God.
As Rahner also notes logically, then, if God creates, he must incarnate in human nature, and the human being simply is what God creates when he wishes to create in order to realize perfectly his own
self-communication.[16] Humanity appears, then, as a moment within the temporal unfolding of the life of God, who eternally expresses himself in his Word by way of incarnation. The immanent Trinity
just is the economic Trinity, and the economic Trinity just is the immanent Trinity. Of course, Rahner does not posit this divine unfolding in history as something necessary in the way that Hegel does, but
he does remove the conditions of possibility for any real intelligibility of the immanent Trinity apart from, transcendent of, or antecedent to this historical life of divine self-expression. The Trinity that
transcends the economy of human divinization becomes literally unthinkable, or something very close to it. This produces a very unhap-
py result for modern Trinitarian theology, first because it mitigates

15. See Rahner, *The Trinity*, 29–33, contrasted with Aquinas in ST I, q. 34, a. 3.
16. Rahner, *The Trinity*, 32–33: "Human nature in general is a possible object of the
creative knowledge and power of God, because and insofar as the Logos is by nature the
one who is 'utterable' (even into that which is not God); because he is the Father's Word,
in which the Father can express himself, and, freely, empty himself into the non-divine;
because, when this happens, that precisely is born which we call human nature ... Man is
possible because the exteriorization of the Logos is possible."

too greatly against the possibility of knowledge of the eternal God in himself, second, because it conceives of God principally under the optics of historical becoming, and third because it breaks too radically with fifteen hundred years of antecedent Trinitarian theology, whether intentionally or not.

What, then, about the Barthian or Balthasarian counter-alternative? Kenoticism without Hegelianism is certainly possible. Martin Luther and John Calvin provide us with non-trivial instances of it in early modernity, and there are early modern Catholic notions of the passion of Christ as an intra-divine dereliction that complement their conceptions. Barth clearly aspires to this possibility of a non-Hegelian kenoticism in *Church Dogmatics* IV, 1, in which he seeks to develop an alternative expression of kenotic Trinitarian Christology, one that does not historicize God, or oblige God to sunder or surrender divine natural properties as a condition for the Incarnation.[17] To do so, he decides to place the preconditions for kenosis (God's human Incarnation, suffering, and death) in the eternal life of God himself, so that what happens to Christ in time, in the dereliction and descent into hell on the Cross is expressive by analogy or similitude of what God always already was and is, in the eternal life of the Father and the Son. Hans Urs von Balthasar also follows in this path, albeit with greater indebtedness to the implausible Sophia ontology of Sergius Bulgakov.[18] God, then, is timeless and eternal, transcendent of history, for both Barth and von Balthasar. Yet there exists something in God's eternal processions that anticipates or provides the foundation for Christ's human obedience, suffering, death, and descent into hell.[19] These latter human actions are not

---

17. See the profound analysis of the problems arising from Hegel in 19th century Lutheran kenoticism in Karl Barth, *Church Dogmatics* IV, 1, pp. 179–210. [Trans. and ed. G. W. Bromiley and T. F. Torrance, 4 vols. (Edinburgh: T. & T. Clark, 1936–1975).]

18. See in this regard Hans Urs von Balthasar, *Theo-Drama: Theological Dramatic Theory, IV: The Action, Action*, 313–15; 323–38, which follows Bulgakov and goes beyond Barth toward a more radical form of intra-Trinitarian kenosis. [Trans. G. Harrison, *Theo-Drama: Theological Dramatic Theory, IV: The Action* (San Francisco: Ignatius Press, 1994).]

19. See, for example, the vivid series of statements about intra-Trinitarian kenosis made in *Theo-Drama* 4, 331: they begin from eternally kenotic generation and spiration,

identical with the eternal life of the Trinity and do not constitute it, but they do present a similitude of it in human form. The humanity of God crucified is the living icon, to so speak, of the eternal processional life of God.

The inevitable question that arises here, however, is whether Barth and von Balthasar glide inadvertently (despite their clear affirmations and intentions to the contrary) toward a reductively univocal conceptualization of the divine and human natures and the two wills of Christ. For now, there is obedience not only in Christ as man, but also in the eternal life of God, and also something like suffering or separation, or kenosis, or self-emptying, or a history of mutual freedom and consent. Are we confronted here with radical new insights, never before evoked so clearly by the Catholic intellectual tradition, or are we dealing with creative modern theological thought experiments, ones that may entail problematic anthropomorphic depictions of the inner life of God? In the wake of precedent theological tradition, it is not only fair to ask the question, but even morally incumbent to do so.

There are pathways toward differentiated consensus that are available. The two natures and the two wills of Christ are not only distinct (as Barth and Von Balthasar each affirm). They are also

---

as anticipatory of the kenosis of God in the creation of human freedom, in the covenant with Israel, in the Incarnation, and in the Cross and resurrection. On p. 333, Von Balthasar writes: "... if Jesus can be forsaken by the Father, the conditions for this 'forsaking' must lie within the Trinity, in the absolute distance/distinction between the Hypostasis who surrenders the Godhead and the Hypostasis who receives it. And while the distance/distinction between these two is eternally confirmed and maintained ('kept open') by the Hypostasis who proceeds from them [the Holy Spirit], it is transcended in the Godhead that is the absolute gift they have in common." This statement provides an emblematic example of the ambiguity that can be present in some of Von Balthasar's writing. It is possible to read such a statement as a traditional restatement of Trinitarian processional eternity, in which the three persons partake equally and identically of the Godhead, and the various forms of Trinitarian benevolence or kenosis are various expressions of eternal Trinitarian interpersonal communion and divine self-communication. But it is also equally plausible to read the same passage as the positing of an eternal kenotic life in God that redefines each and every traditional notion in light of the separation of the Cross so that the economic human expression of the Son's suffering is appropriated so as to radically re-configure all previous theological discourse.

similar and dissimilar, or analogous (which, again, they both affirm). The question is how one can come to an understanding of the various ways in which the human actions and sufferings of Christ resemble, by proper similitude, his eternal person and the divine nature. To respond to this query, I maintain the importance of the instruments of the tradition, such as the Dionysius-Thomistic notion of analogical predication, the appeal to a theology of the divine names or attributes of the one divine nature, the use of the notion of eternal relations of origin, and the carefully constructed analogical similitude of the psychological analogy: all of these have an essential role to play in adjudicating how to address this issue, namely of how the human life and death of Christ reveal to us the inner mystery of the Trinity.

Note that in making this appeal to a traditional set of theological notions, I am not appealing to distinctly Thomistic ideas. The principles mentioned are, in fact, widely common to the classical tradition, both east and west, and I presuppose that Thomas Aquinas provides only one highly coherent and insightful form of thinking so as to maintain and advance theological understanding of these principles. Meanwhile, I think it is fair to say, as a point of textual accuracy, that Barth and von Balthasar are immeasurably learned men, but they have little time for the systematic use of the traditional notions just mentioned.[20] Despite my admiration for them each, I consider this to be an objective and significant deficiency in their thought. In fact, they each combine what one might characterize as a powerful dose of apophatic insistence on the unknowability of the divine essence with a vivid Christological, human-centered depiction of the epiphany of the inner life of God. This results in a historicization of God that is possibly more profound than that of Rahner, since now the inner life of the eternal Son is only 'envisagable' in a cruciform way. One can note that this is true even while maintaining, as mentioned

20. Perhaps I should be convinced otherwise on this point, but what I read in Von Balthasar, *Theo-Logic* II: *Truth of God*, trans. A. J. Walker (San Francisco: Ignatius, 2004), 125–70 seems to remove any doubt about his speculative convictions in this regard.

above, that for these authors, what is revealed in the Cross and descent into Hell is what is always, already eternally true in God. The paradoxical tensions that emerge from this position are genuinely intriguing and perhaps even more profound than those of any other school of thought that has hitherto emerged. However, like many others in the theological guild, I still fail to find them persuasive.

All of this being said, my own very limited theological reflection on the Trinitarian revelation of Christ, his Incarnation, human action, suffering and death, and resurrection can be read as a kind of Thomistic homage to Barth and von Balthasar, even if it is genuinely polemical in many respects. I am undertaking, in what I hope is a respectful way, to re-envisage in Thomistic terms what I think their theologies rightly aspire to, and to do so in a way that few Thomists before me have sought to do. How is it, after all, that the mysteries of the life of Jesus reveal the Most Holy Trinity? How is the Trinity made known to us in the suffering, death, descent into hell, and resurrection of Christ? If one does not follow the path of Barth and von Balthasar past Golgotha, what other paths might be available to encounter that event, even ones from which we might eventually gain a better perspective into the mystery of God crucified? And how can the mysteries of the life of Christ place us, thus, in direct contact with the inner mystery of the Holy Trinity and invoke in us a development of contemplative knowledge and love in the service of union with God?

Beauty and goodness in our world are a manifestation of an uncreated beauty and love, and it is true that only a participation metaphysics of *esse* can fully acknowledge this, as both Thomas Aquinas and von Balthasar assert. But this means that there has to be a sense of what God is immanently, as he is in himself, as a precondition or a dimension of our understanding of what derives from God, and as a condition for our understanding of God as he is present in the world, in the missions of the persons-in-procession, manifest in Christ. This new presence of God in his Son, incarnate, crucified, and resurrected, is beautiful and good, and is an invitation to mystical experience here below of the inner life of God. It is one that concords with doctrinal truth and with an aspiration even to know God more perfectly in the beatific vision and in the fullness of filial adoption by grace. My aim in seeking to study the economic mission of the Son incarnate in Trinitarian terms, then, is not something stemming simplistically from a rejection of the modern Germanic theological tradition. Rather, it is an acceptance of Barth's and von Balthasar's new questions and invitations, reconceived in Thomistic terms. In that sense, it is an homage to their aspirations, if not to the thought-form of either as such.

CONCLUSION

The attentive reader will conclude from this introduction that this volume of theological essays seeks to reassert or at least reconsider the importance of Thomistic theology for the practice of contemporary Catholic theology. This undertaking does not deny that there is a genuine polyphony of theological voices and schools of thought that unfolds within the one common life of the Church. Indeed, the tradition has its place in this common life, and indeed I believe we can even still speak rightly when we denote Thomas Aquinas as a "common doctor" within the Catholic intellectual tradition. Even for those who conscientiously choose not to follow him consistently, presumably in the name of a wider universalism of investigation, it can be readily noted that his thought has the power to preserve many key insights that we have received down through the ages and to explain and advance understanding of core principles of Christian philosophy and of Catholic theology, understood as *sacra doctrina*, that is to say, as both science and wisdom. Modern Thomists provide us with a range of resources to think about how this process of reflection might continue in our own historical epoch as we encounter new questions or advances from various modern scientific, philosophical, theological, or historical domains. It is helpful in this regard to have people in the Church and in the theological guild, who maintain a deeper historical and contemporary intellectual commitment to the study and promotion of Thomism. However, Aquinas can also only function as a common doctor (in the qualified and nuanced way I am alluding to) if his thought is employed by his students and disciples as a vehicle for conversation and common truth-seeking, not only with those who learn consistently from his insights, but also and perhaps especially with all those who participate in the wider search for Christian wisdom, both Catholic and non-Catholic. I hope that this third volume of *Principles of Catholic Theology* can be one example of such a form of conversation in the search for common truth in the Catholic theological tradition. For indeed, if we can speak together constructively regarding God, the very mystery of the Holy Trinity, then it would seem that we should be able, in turn, to speak together regarding everything else, as seen in light of God. This Catholic or universal aspiration would seem to be a very salutary and indeed necessary one for all theologians, united across their distinct traditions, within the *kairos* to come. It is also one in which the appeal to scholastic theology more generally, and to Thomistic theology specifically, should continue to have a constructive and definitive place. After all, everything that rises must converge.

PART I

On God, Trinity,
and Creation

1

Monotheistic Rationality and Divine Names

Why Aquinas's Analogy Theory Transcends Both Theoretical Agnosticism and Conceptual Anthropomorphism

I

In the age of high scholasticism, the summit of philosophical thought was seen to reside in the demonstrative knowledge that we might have of God, and in the speculative contemplation of the attributes of God: properties such as divine simplicity, perfection, goodness, immutability, eternity, and so forth. This medieval vision of philosophy presumes, of course, that we might derive knowledge of God from creatures, positive knowledge that is both demonstrative and, in a sense, contemplative. But is this claim true? Do creatures bear any relation of similitude to God, from which we might perceive truths about God himself? If so, *in what way* do the ontological characteristics of creatures (their perfections and limitations) allow us, or not allow us, to speak of what God is and of what God is not? From creatures, how can philosophy offer names for God? As a way

Originally published in *God: Reason and Reality, Basic Philosophical Concepts Series,* ed. Anselm Ramelow (Munich: Philosophia Verlag GmbH, 2014), 37–80. Used with permission.

of entering into the question, I would like to consider briefly the basic answer offered by Aquinas and some objections to that solution. This sets the stage for thinking more deeply about how we might name God philosophically.

In the *Summa theologiae*, Aquinas broaches this topic quite early on, in question 4, article 3 (where he asks, "Whether any creature can be like God?"). There, he makes a fundamental distinction between what he elsewhere terms "univocal agents" and "non-univocal" or "equivocal" agents.[1] Let us be clear: we are speaking here of univocity and equivocity as something that pertains not only to our logical designations about reality (how we name reality), but also as something proper to the reality itself, characterizing the being of things. Univocal agents, then, for Aquinas, are those who transmit that form or essence of being that they themselves possess to the realities they act upon. Their very natures are transmitted to the other: so a parent communicates human life to his or her child, and both the parent and the child possess the same (essentially identical) human nature. Both are equally human, univocally speaking.

By contrast, the light and warmth of the sun do not make the creatures of the earth to be sunlight or to partake as such of the processes of fusion reaction that are characteristic of the nature of a star. They do, however, transmit effects of the sun from which there accrues a certain likeness between the light and warmth of the earth and that of the sun itself. This is an equivocal agency because the two realities remain distinct in species or nature. And so it would be equivocal to say that the earth is a sun (because the two are not of the same species), but we can, Aquinas says, attribute a likeness of genus to the two entities, invoking a commonly shared quality: the earth and the sun are both warm bodies, albeit of specifically different kinds and to differing degrees, but in a common genus.

---

1. This precise terminology is employed in *Summa Contra Gentiles* I, cc. 29, 31, but the same conceptual analysis and examples used there are presented again here, and later in *ST* I, q. 13, a. 2 as well, to articulate how we speak of God analogically. See the analysis of this conceptual distinction in Aquinas by Norman Kretzmann, *The Metaphysics of Theism* (Oxford: Oxford University Press, 1997), 147–57.

But God is not a generic kind of reality among others, a being among other beings, as we will have occasion to return to later. So, how might we speak of him? And, here, Aquinas posits a famous theorem: "If there is an agent not contained in any *genus*, its effects will still more distantly reproduce the form of the agent, not that is, so as to participate in the likeness of the agent's form according to the same *specific or generic* formality, but only according to some sort of analogy; as existence is common to all. In this way all created things so far as they are beings, are like God, as the first and universal principle of all being … God is essential being, whereas other things are beings by participation."[2] So, for St. Thomas, the philosopher is capable of the rational consideration of the attributes of God by recourse to a process of analogical naming.

Historically, there are positions that take Aquinas's understanding of the analogical naming of God to be problematic by way of mutually opposed extremes. For some, his theory of naming God is too weak and fails to offer a sufficiently strong sense of names that can carry over from creatures to God in 'precisely the same sense,' i.e., univocally. One must make use of univocal predication to safeguard true knowledge of God. This is the view of Duns Scotus, and today, it is championed by some analytic philosophers of religion, such as, perhaps most notably, Richard Swinburne.[3] In his book *The Coherence of Theism*, Swinburne offers an univocalist account of God's attributes in

---

2. *ST* I, q. 3, a. 4, corp. and ad 3.

3. See, for example, Scotus, *Ordinatio*, I, d. 3, q. 1, no. 25–26, on the univocal concept of being, an idea he received in part from Avicenna. [Edition from *Opera omnia*, ed. C. Balić and others (Rome: Typis Polyglottis Vaticanis, 1950–2013).] On the Scotist doctrine of univocal predication of divine attributes more generally, see Olivier Boulnois, *l'Être et représentation* (Paris: Presses Universitaires de France, 1999), and "La destruction de l'analogie et l'instauration de la métaphysique," in *Sur la connaissance de Dieu et l'univocité de l'étant*, texts of John Duns Scotus (Paris: Presses Universitaires de France, 1988), 11–81; Richard Cross, *Duns Scotus* (Oxford: Oxford University Press, 1999), 33–39, *Duns Scotus on God* (Aldershot and Burlington: Ashgate, 2005), 251–54. Richard Swinburne appeals to and interprets Scotus in order to articulate aspects of his own theory of religious language, especially in *The Coherence of Theism* rev. ed. (Oxford: Clarendon Press, 2010), ch. 5. There are further qualifications and applications of the doctrine in *Revelation* (Oxford: Clarendon Press, 1992), ch. 3, and *The Christian God* (Oxford: Clarendon Press, 1994), ch. 7.

which he ascribes to God such properties as beliefs, real relations to creatures, existence in time, and being a "substance," presumably in a larger genus with other substances.[4] These are all ascriptions Thomists find anthropomorphic. For others, meanwhile, Aquinas's theory of analogical naming is too strong or too ambitious and fails to acknowledge the radical limitations of all our attempts to describe or prescribe notions for the divine, even when an analogical distance is acknowledged. The radical equivocity of all our names for God recalls to us the truth of the unspeakable and incomprehensible transcendence of God: the divine darkness. This is the view of Heidegger, who builds upon the Kantian prohibition of classical arguments for the existence of God and who labels such scholastic thinking "onto-theology."[5] Today, this view is most eloquently represented by Jean-Luc Marion. He appeals to Dionysius the Areopagite's radical apophaticism in order to develop a phenomenological ontology of divine love and the consideration of the creation as a gift.[6] Marion wishes to approach the mystery of God by means of the philosophical mystery of the goodness and 'givenness' of reality without recourse to causal argumentation derived from a metaphysical consideration of the being of things.[7] Marion gives a rhetorically potent label to this latter form of reflection, especially when it seeks to speak of God: that of "conceptual idolatry."[8] And in his early work, Marion suggests this ascription could be given even to the work of Aquinas himself.[9]

4. See, for example, Swinburne, *The Coherence of Theism*, ch. 10 and 12.

5. See in particular Martin Heidegger, "The Onto-theo-logical Constitution of Metaphysics," in *Identity and Difference*, trans. J. Staumbaugh (New York: Harper and Row, 1969), 42–74. The notion of ontotheology in the work of Immanuel Kant appears most importantly in *The Critique of Pure Reason*, trans. N. K. Smith (London: Macmillan, 1990), II, III, 7.

6. See, for example, Jean-Luc Marion, *The Idol and the Distance*, trans. T. A. Carlson (New York: Fordham University Press, 2001); *God without Being*, trans. T. A. Carlson (Chicago and London: University of Chicago Press, 1991); *Being Given: Toward a Phenomenology of Givenness*, trans. J. L. Kosky (Stanford: Stanford University Press, 2002).

7. See Marion, *God without Being*, ch. 6; *Being Given*, books III–V.

8. On this idea, Jean-Luc Marion, "De la 'mort de Dieu' aux noms divins: l'itinéraire théologique de la métaphysique," in *l'Être et Dieu*, ed. D. Bourg (Paris: Cerf, 1986), 113.

9. In *God without Being*, 29–32, 73–83, Marion underscores both difficulties and promising possibilities in Aquinas's analogical approach to metaphysical thinking about

In the face of these criticisms, the fundamental question is, simply: is Aquinas's account of the analogical naming of God true, and is it helpful to us today in seeking to talk about the mystery of God philosophically? In what follows, I will consider the topic briefly from five distinct but interrelated viewpoints that follow upon one another by logical succession. To consider Aquinas's procedure of divine naming, I will discuss his "analogical" appropriations of Aristotle, Proclus, and Maimonides respectively. The first section, then, (II) will consider the use St. Thomas makes of Aristotle for what Bernard Montagnes terms "predicamental" or, as termed here, "horizontal analogy," that is to say, analogical significations of being to diverse modes of *created* being. Meanwhile, Aquinas's use of Proclus (III) allows us to consider the background of a theory of "transcendental analogy," or significations posed *of God*, derived from creatures.[10] The consideration of Aquinas's critique of Maimonides on divine naming (IV) allows us to see how these forms of analogical signifying steer away from any radically apophatic or even agnostic approach to the divine. What, then, is divine naming as an analogical procedure? This will be considered in the fourth section (V). Last, I will discuss the ways analogical naming of God is intrinsically open (but in qualified ways only) to the notion of attributions of names based on divine revelation (as in Christian Trinitarian theology) as well as metaphorical terms for God (as is frequent in the Biblical tradition) (VI). The divine names are complementary to human metaphorical speaking about God and to the mystery of divine revelation regarding the inner life of God. These succinct considerations will allow us to conclude by thinking about the Judeo-Christian tradition and the philosophical rationality of offering divine names for God.

God. Aquinas is not seen to escape entirely from the dangers of ontotheology. Subsequently, however, he argues that Aquinas's thought does not represent a species of ontotheological thinking. See Jean-Luc Marion, "Saint Thomas d'Aquin et l'onto-théo-logie," *Revue Thomiste* 95 (1995): 31–66.

10. On the distinction of predicamental and transcendental analogy in Aquinas, see Bernard Montagnes, OP, *La doctrine de l'analogie de l'être d'après Saint Thomas d'Aquin* (Louvain: Publications Universitaires; Paris: Béatrice-Nauwelaerts, 1963); Cornelio Fabro, *Participation et causalité selon saint Thomas d'Aquin* (Paris-Louvain: Publications Universitaires de Louvain, 1961).

II

Let us begin by thinking about the origins of the theory of the transcendentals, as it first began to emerge in Aristotle's thought. Aristotle famously differed with Plato regarding the nature of the good, or whether the good has a form in which all other goods participate. In the *Republic*, Plato had offered a theory of the latter: of the good as a transcendent essence or form —an Idea —from which all other realities derive their intrinsic goodness.[11] Aristotle, with his well-known phrase, "Plato and the truth I love both but the truth more," parted company with Plato in Nicomachean Ethics Book I, chapter 6, and provided an alternative understanding of the good, not as a form, but as a reality or property said analogically by proportionality across a spectrum of categories, or predicamental modes of being.[12] That is to say, realism regarding our immediate experiences provides us with evidence of a complex world, Aristotle's diverse categorical modes of being, in which there are irreducibly diverse genera of beings: substances, their natures, quantities, qualities, relations, habits, actions, passions, time, place, environment, position.[13] None of these categories is finally utterly reducible to one another, whether ontologically, logically, experientially, or linguistically. Our ordinary language and implicit phenomenological experiences suggest a diversity of 'folds' to reality that the intellect can then trace out conceptually. But the good is said of all these categories, not in a specifically or generically unified way (as

11. Plato, *Republic* VI in 505a2–507b10; 511b3–e; 533b–c; 541°. All translations of Plato are taken from *Complete Works*, ed. J. M. Cooper, trans. G. M. A. Grube (Indianapolis, IN: Hackett, 1997).

12. Aristotle, *Nic. Ethics* I, 6, 1196b24–26, 27–28: "But of honor, wisdom, and pleasure, just in respect of their goodness, the accounts are distinct and diverse, the good, therefore, is not something common answering to one Idea ... Are goods one, then, by being derived from one good or by all contributing to one good, or are they rather one by analogy?" (All translations of Aristotle are taken from *The Complete Works of Aristotle*, 2 vols., ed. J. Barnes, [Princeton: Princeton University Press, 1984].)

13. Aristotle appeals to the ontologically primary character of the categorical modes of being in multiple places in his corpus. See, for example, *Categories, Physics*, Book I; *Metaphysics*, Books IV and V.

in the case of a form), but only in an analogical way, according to proportion. A is to B as C is to D.[14] A good *time* to play American football is different from a good *place* to do so. The *substantial* goodness of a human person insofar as he or she exists is distinct from his or her moral goodness (based on *operative* actions or qualities). (A human being who does great wrong is good in his substantive being, but not in his moral life.) An appropriate *quantity* of wine is distinct from an appropriate *quality*. A good *sweater* is distinct from a good *parent*, and so on. The good is said in many ways because the goodness of the things themselves is realized according to a spectrum of similitudes or in analogical fashion.

When Aquinas takes up this idea from Aristotle, he explicitly relates it to his understanding of the analogical significations of not only the good, but of being, truth, and unity as well.[15] These notions, often referred to as transcendentals, are called such because they span across or transcend the multiple categories, and so each of them can only be denoted in analogical ways. So, the being of a substance (such

14. Aristotle, *Nic. Ethics* I, 6, 1196a23–29: "Further, since things are said to be good in as many ways as they are said to be (for things are called good both in the category of substance, as God and reason, and in quality, e.g., the virtues, and in quantity, e.g., that which is moderate, and in relation, e.g., the useful, and in time, e.g., the right opportunity, and in place, e.g., the right locality and the like), clearly the good cannot be something universally present in all cases and single; for then it would not have been predicated in all the categories but in one only."

15. Aquinas, *Commentary on the Nicomachean Ethics*, I, lec. 6, n. 80: "To understand [Aristotle's criticisms of Plato's Idea of the Good] we must know that Plato held the 'ideal' to be the 'ratio' or nature and essence of all things that partake of the idea. It follows from this that there cannot be one idea of things not having a common nature. *But the various categories do not have one common nature, for nothing is predicated of them univocally. Now good, like being with which it is convertible, is found in every category.* Thus the *quiddity or substance*, God, in whom there is no evil, is called good; the *intellect*, which is always true, is called good. In *quality* good is predicated of virtue, which makes its possessor good; in *quantity*, of the mean, which is the good in everything subject to measure. In *relation*, good is predicated of the useful which is good relative to a proper end. In *time*, it is predicated of the opportune; and in *place* of a location suitable for walking, as in a summerhouse. *The same may be said of the other categories.* It is clear, therefore that there is not some one good that is the idea or the common 'ratio' of all goods. Otherwise good would not be found in every category but in one alone." [Emphasis added.] Trans C. I. Lintzinger, *Commentary on the Nicomachean Ethics* (Chicago: Henry Regnery, 1964). This text resonates with the basic text of Aquinas on the transcendentals as such, *De Ver.*, q. 1, a. 1.

as being human) is distinct from the being of a property such as a quality (like being musical). The unity of an operation (like sight) is different from the unity of a place (such as the parking lot). Truth statements about what is the case that concern relations ("... that is his father ...") are different from truth statements that concern passions ("... he is currently undergoing surgery ..."). In short, the transcendental notions are both grounded in the multiplicity of the ontological character of reality and are said analogically of that reality.[16]

The upswing of this fact is two-fold. First, for Aquinas, it follows necessarily not just for God but even for ordinary realities that surround us: there are certain non-trivial features of these realities that we *cannot* speak of in purely univocal terms, and to do so would represent a serious misunderstanding of the structure of reality as well as the logic of realistic predication.[17] As Cajetan rightly noted against Scotus, the significations of the good for Aquinas take on their common meaning, or offer a readily identifiable common core only in an analogically unified way: transcendental notions (such as goodness or being) are intrinsically analogical notions, not univocal ones.[18] Goodness, then, for St. Thomas, can be defined in a unified fashion as that perfection of finality or actuation by which a thing or property becomes in some way appetible or desirable. Accordingly, it is what is good that we desire.[19] Ontologically, however, the

16. For further evidence of this view in Aquinas, see his *Commentary on Aristotle's Metaphysics*, trans. J. P. Rowan (Notre Dame, IN: Dumb Ox Books, 1995), IV, lec. 2; XII, lec. 4.

17. For the logically adjacent criticisms of the Platonic forms in Aquinas, see *De Ver.*, q. 10, a. 6; SCG II, c. 26; III, c. 24, 69; *In Div. Nom.* V, lec. 2.

18. See the study of Cajetan's critique of Scotus on this point by Joshua P. Hochschild, *The Semantics of Analogy: Rereading Cajetan's De Nominum Analogia* (Notre Dame: Notre Dame University Press, 2010). Hochschild makes the point I am emphasizing ontologically in semantic terms: P. 174: "... Cajetan's analysis of what a proportionally unified concept entails for the rest of logic confirms the importance of context, and the necessary role of judgment, in the use and interpretation of analogical terms. Cajetan, apparently unlike some of his contemporaries, does not hold that words have fixed semantic properties independently of their role in sentences; rather they must be understood and analyzed in light of propositional and inferential context."

19. See *ST* I, q. 5, a. 1; *De Ver.* q. 21, a. 1. Aquinas appeals for his definition of the good in the first of these texts to Aristotle's *Nic. Ethics* I, 1,1094a3.

realization of this perfection takes on different forms and only appears mysteriously in and through a diversity of forms: the perfection of a degree of human love simply is formally distinct from the perfection of the art of playing the violin: a good friend, a good violinist. To try to reduce this commonality to a generic form is to rob the notion of the good of its intrinsic flexibility and to obscure the perception of the irreducibly ontologically complex realization of the good.

Second, we can already conclude, even from talking about intra-worldly realizations of being or of the good, that God cannot be signified univocally, or under the sign of a common form shared with creatures, no matter how carefully qualified. For, as Aquinas notes in the *Summa Contra Gentiles* I, 32, if the goodness of God could be signified, for instance, in univocal continuity with goodness as it is realized in this world, then goodness would have a formal constitution. It would be a species of thing or something specific, common to a multiplicity of realities. But if it were a given species or genus, then it would not be applicable to all the other genera or species of beings, but only to one.[20]

However, God is not in any one genus of being, for, if he were, he would be a subsidiary member of the larger collection of beings who participate in the being common to all creatures and would not

---

20. See SCG, I, c. 32, para. 2 and 4: "An effect that does not receive a form specifically the same as that through which the agent acts cannot receive according to a univocal predication the name arising from that form. Thus, the heat generated by the sun and the sun itself are not called univocally hot. Now, the forms of the things God has made do not measure up to a specific likeness of the divine power; for the things that God has made receive in a divided and particular way that which in Him is found in a simple and universal way. It is evident, then, that nothing can be said univocally of God and other things … Moreover, whatever is predicated of many things univocally is either a genus, a species, a difference, an accident, or a property. But, as we have shown, nothing is predicated of God as a genus or a difference; and thus neither is anything predicated as a definition, nor likewise as a species, which is constituted of genus and difference. Nor, as we have shown, can there be any accident in God, and therefore nothing is predicated of Him either as an accident or a property, since property belongs to the genus of accidents. It remains, then, that nothing is predicated univocally of God and other things." *Summa contra Gentiles* I, trans. A. Pegis (Garden City, NY: Doubleday, 1955).

be the author of every genus of existent realities.[21] Just because God exists, therefore, as the author of all created beings, and therefore of all genera of beings, he cannot partake univocally of a specific or generic attribute in common with other similar kinds of realities.

Likewise, if goodness did pertain to God univocally, it would be applicable to other realities only metaphorically. Why? Because God alone would be good, and other realities would be so only equivocally speaking, as in a Manichean vision of reality. That is to say, due to his essentially unique, univocal possession of goodness, such goodness would be incommunicable to others who do not share in the divine essence. Or the inverse: some species of created reality known to be good univocally could alone be designated as the good, and God could only be said to be so equivocally in comparison with that reality. It is as if we were to say only the lion is specifically good, and everything else is good insofar as it resembles the lion. So, God, Mother Theresa, or one's best friend may be said to be good insofar as they are like the lion. But to say that God is a lion is a metaphor since there are features of the essence of being a lion that cannot be attributed to God. For example, God —as the cause of every genus of being—is himself without matter or dependence upon physical causality of any kind. This differentiates him from an animal such as a lion. But just as the lion's nature is not capable of signifying God *per se*, so neither could goodness if it were identified with any particular created essence. In the case of the lion, the differentiation from the divine essence is most easily demarcated by appeal to the matter of the being in question. In the case of other creatures, some form of complexity would intervene that would inevitably differentiate that being from God essentially. This is true, for example, even in spiritual creatures such as human beings, or angels (presuming they exist) since in these beings, there is still a difference between the nature of the reality and its existence: the things that exist as creatures do not exist by virtue of their very nature or essence. Rather they

21. See SCG I, c. 25, para. 1–3.

are given being or receive their being from others.[22] But this is not so in the case of God. The existence of God is identical with his essence.[23] He thus surpasses every genus of creaturely being and cannot be termed, therefore, through the univocal appeal of the former in order to signify what he is.

The irony is that by beginning with the insistence on univocity in order to maintain continuity between our creaturely significations and God, we end up with an implicit turn toward radical equivocity that makes it impossible to signify God except by way of creaturely anthropomorphism. This can occur in a metaphorical way when God is depicted problematically in terms of the material forms of things in this world. It can occur in a more metaphysically sophisticated way by employing what are essentially human spiritual modes of being to designate God without accounting for the transcendent alterity of the divine attributes and the analogical significations of these names when used rightly of God. And so, we end up like Richard Swinburne ascribing to God changing beliefs, existence in time, or a host of other anthropomorphic properties. Is this not something akin to what Marion deems 'conceptual idolatry'? Univocal name-giving readily begets equivocity theory as a reaction. In reality, however, univocity theorists, to the extent that they avoid this form of problematic thinking, make implicit use of purely analogical concepts to discuss the divine names, at least insofar as they speak truthfully of God.

III

Up to this point, we have considered the ways that transcendental properties or names such as being or goodness are ascribed analogically across the horizontal trajectory, so to speak, of intra-creaturely reality, i.e., the categorical modes of being in this world. However, there is another, more ultimate sense in which they must be said

22. Aquinas, *De Ente et Essentia*, IV-V.
23. *ST* I, q. 3, a. 4; SCG I, c. 22.

analogically as well, of the first cause of creation. That is to say, in the passage from creatures to God, which Montagnes and others have termed "transcendental analogy." As a way of understanding this form of thinking, it is useful to consider briefly Aquinas's criticisms of Neoplatonist divine naming manifest in the way he intreprets Proclus's *Book of Causes*, and Dionysius' *Divine Names*.

In relating his understanding of divine names to the work of Proclus in the *Book of Causes*, Aquinas wishes to refute any notion that God is simply to be identified with the common being or goodness that stands at the heart of reality. In doing so, he makes clear his rejection of Neoplatonist emanationist schemas, which posit an underlying unity between the world and God (or seem to). God is not the common being that stands at the heart of reality and in which everything else participates 'formally,' so to speak.[24] To think this way is possible only if one confuses our intellectual abstract notion of being or of the good with a formal content in reality itself, an error of Plato perpetuated by his disciples.[25] Rather, what one must rightly do is appeal to the notion of God as the transcendent and unique *author* of the common being and goodness of created reality. It is this idea—which one finds in Proclus—that Aquinas does appreciatively receive from the Neoplatonic heritage: God alone subsists of himself and, in his simplicity, is identical with his own existence and goodness.[26] By contrast, all created reality participates in existence and goodness that it receives from God, and does so only insofar as God is the cause and origin of all that proceeds from him. Consider in this respect Aquinas's commentary on proposition 4 in the *Book*

24. See the commentary on the *In de Causis, A Translation and Analysis of Thomas Aquinas' Expositio Super Librumde Causis*, trans. Elizabeth Anne Collins-Smith (Austin, TX: UT-Austin Diss., 1991) lec. 3, 4, 24.

25. *In de Causis*, lec. 6; *In de Div. Nom.*, V, lec. 2; SCG I, 26; *De Subst. Separ.* cc. 1 and 6.

26. *In de Causis*, lec. 21: "Now he proves that God is firstly and maximally simple, by reason of unity: for God is most greatly one since he is the first unity just as he is also the first goodness; and simplicity pertains to the definition of unity. For that which is one, not aggregated from many is called 'simple.' Whence God, insofar as he is firstly and maximally one, he is also firstly and maximally simple." [Trans. Elizabeth Anne Collins-Smith, 1991.] Compare Aquinas's similar language in his own treatment of divine simplicity in *ST* I, q. 3, a. 7.

of Causes: "The first of created things is being, and no created thing is before it." St. Thomas interprets it by recourse to Proposition 138: "Of all the principles which participate in the divine character, the first and highest is being":

> Now, what is common to all the distinct intelligences is first created being. Regarding this, he presents the following proposition: *The first of created things is being, and there is nothing else created before it.* Proclus also asserts this in Proposition 138 of his book, in these words: "Being is the first and supreme of all that participate what is properly divine‖ and of the deified ... Dionysius did away with the order of [platonic Ideas], maintaining the same order as the Platonists in the perfections that other things participate from one principle, which is God." Hence, in Chapter 4 of *On the Divine Names*, he ranks the name of good in God as the first of all the divine names and shows perfections from God that things participate, he puts being first. For he says this in Chapter 5 of *On the Divine Names*: "Being is placed before the other participations" of God "and being in itself is more ancient than the being of *per se* life, than the being of *per se* wisdom, and than the being of *per se* divine similitude."[27]

Consequently, Aquinas says, there results a similitude or analogy in the order of being between creatures and God that is derivative from this unique 'transcendent' form of causality, a form of causality that is proper to God alone. God alone creates all that exists, and so it resembles him, but only analogically as an entirely unique kind of cause.[28]

How, then, should we speak about the analogy between creatures and God? Here is the key to divine naming, the process that undergirds our speculative contemplation of the divine attributes. On this central point, Aquinas appropriates the thought of Dionysius the Areopagite and employs the latter cautiously to interpret Proclus's ideas about divine causality in a distinctly Christian monotheistic way.[29]

---

27. Proposition 4 in *Commentary on the Book of Causes*, trans. Vincent A. Guagliardo, OP, Charles R. Hess, OP, Richard C. Taylor (Washington, DC: The Catholic University of America Press, 1996).

28. See the very similar doctrine of *ST* I, q. 13, a. 2.

29. See the discussion of this issue by Jan Aertsen, *Medieval Philosophy and the Transcendentals: The Case of Thomas Aquinas* (Leiden: Brill, 1996), 165–70.

Aquinas argues that just because there is a unique, analogical causal resemblance that stems from creation, the human mind may ascend from the perfections found in creatures to the analogical consideration of the attributes of God. This form of thinking, however, must be three-fold. First, because creatures exist and are good and so forth, God can be said to exist and be good analogically, *per viam causalitatis*, by way of causality. In so far as God is the cause of creatures, their perfections must resemble him. If they have being or are good, then he must have being and be good, yet in a more perfect way, as the cause is greater than the effects. Second, however, we must just as soon affirm negatively (*per viam remotionis* or *negationis*) that God is not existent or good in the way creatures are, and so his divine essence is utterly incomprehensible and unknown. We name him in darkness. For the cause utterly transcends the effects. And yet we also, lastly, can and must affirm that God is existent and good *per viam eminentiae*, by way of preeminence, for whatever the unknown and unknowable existence and goodness of God are, they are superabundant and exceed in perfection anything we can or do know in this world.[30]

Notice two things about this procedure: first of all, it elicits from the intelligence a constructive response of philosophical reason regarding the project of divine naming that is both rational and nuanced, which terminates in a positive form of knowledge. The mind is invited to affirm of God certain perfections that it must, in turn,

---

30. See *ST* I, q. 12, a. 12. "Our natural knowledge begins from sense. Hence, our natural knowledge can go as far as it can be led by sensible things. But our mind cannot be led by sense so far as to see the essence of God because the sensible effects of God do not equal the power of God as their cause. Hence, from the knowledge of sensible things the whole power of God cannot be known, nor, therefore, can His essence be seen. But because they are His effects and depend on their cause, we can be led from them so far as to know of God "whether He exists," and to know of Him what must necessarily belong to Him, as the first cause of all things, exceeding all things caused by Him. Hence, we know of His relationship with creatures in so far as He is the cause of them all; also, that creatures differ from Him, inasmuch as He is not in any way part of what is caused by Him; and that creatures are not removed from Him by reason of any defect on His part, but because He super-exceeds them all." The basic text of Dionysius from which the three-fold *viae* are taken is *De divinis nominibus*, c. 7, 3.

also qualify negatively, as well as super-eminently. However, these qualifications build upon and perfect a fundamentally kataphatic or positive set of significations.[31] God truly is simple, good, wise, eternal, immutable, and so on. In saying such things, we speak truly of God. The life of the intellect is thus carried over in darkness, as it were, toward a light that is hidden yet whose hidden richness and intellectual attraction is divined through the search for the truth about our ontological origins. Against Swinburne, this model of divine naming is both analogical and adequate: that is to say, it speaks coherently and truly of God as he is in himself, without falling into the anthropomorphisms of univocity.

Second, this procedure seems to place our conceptual gaze upon God at a two-fold distantiation from anything like the 'conceptual idolatry' that Marion would seek to ward off. For, on the one hand, even 'univocal perfections' that we attribute to human beings, such as wisdom, cannot be attributed to God in the way categorical properties are attributed to other persons: for God is not wise by way of a quality that is attributed to his substance (as in a human person), but due to his simplicity, God simply is his wisdom.[32] This means, however, that to say that God is wise is absolutely true, but it is also, in some real sense, incomprehensible.[33] That God is wise is something we know to be the case, but what the divine wisdom is itself remains unknown.[34] The mind rests in a positive intellectual judgment, albeit indirect and analogical, of something that pertains truly to God. God is wise, and the mind can rest in this truth. But this is also a rest as in darkness.

---

31. *ST* I, q. 13, aa. 2–3, 6, 11.
32. *ST* I, q. 3, a. 6; q. 13, a. 2.
33. *ST* I, q. 3, prol.; q. 13, a. 3.
34. *ST* I, q. 12, aa.1 and 12; q. 13, a. 6.

IV

Aquinas's articulation of the divine names of God gives adequate sense to the utter transcendence of God. Does this same procedure veer too inordinately, however, toward the equivocations of agnosticism? To consider the question, let us compare aspects of Aquinas's thought on divine naming with that of Maimonides, who died just a generation before Aquinas began teaching. Like Aquinas, Maimonides offers only *a posteriori* arguments for the existence of God. He is wary of any direct ideational intuitions of the divine, as we find in the ontological argument. Rather, he seeks to derive from the transient and finite entities of the world we perceive, considered as effects, knowledge of the necessary existence of a transcendent cause of the world that exists without ontological change or limitation of power.[35] Nevertheless, for Maimonides, such argumentation is not intended to terminate in any form of positive contemplation or consideration of the attributes or names of God, but only in what we might call a radically apophatic form of equivocity: God cannot be named from this world except negatively.[36] Famously, Maimonides claims that divine names can be taken in two ways. First, they may signify not what God is in himself, but only likenesses of effects derived from God with effects produced by creatures. Thus, to say, for instance, that God is wise is to say that God is the cause of beings that are themselves wise and that he acts through his effects as does one who is wise. However, this does not entail that we might properly attribute to God wisdom in and of himself. Maimonides affirms the opposite. Second, to attribute to God a name is to affirm only that the negation of that name cannot be ascribed to God. To say that God is living, for example, is only to say that we cannot ascribe to God the mode of being proper to non-living things.

While Maimonides does clearly affirm some form of speculative,

---

35. See *Guide for the Perplexed*, II, c.1.
36. *Guide for the Perplexed*, I, cc. 52–59.

demonstrative knowledge of God, his philosophy foreshadows in certain respects that of Immanuel Kant. Our demonstrations of the existence of God amount to something akin to a heuristic exercise in rehearsing the possibility of meaning in the universe. But they allow us to say nothing of God in himself. The potential idolatry of the gentile philosophers is displaced by a practical study of the moral law: a turn toward the primacy of practical intellect in the wake of speculative apophaticism. This, at any rate, is one way to read Kant and Maimonides in light of one another (by way of a Kantian intensification of Maimonidian apophaticism). Such a reading is of some influence among modern Orthodox Jewish intellectuals deeply influenced by Kant's treatment of the religious limitations of speculative reason, figures such as Joseph Soloveichik and David Novak.[37]

Aquinas offers a number of points of response to Maimonides's arguments. His simplest and strongest argument is the following: if all our language concerning God were simply utterly equivocal, we would be incapable of saying anything about God at all, whether positive or negative, even by way of demonstration. "... all our knowledge of God is taken from creatures, so that if there were agreement in name alone, we would know nothing of God save some empty words with nothing to underwrite them. It would also follow that all the demonstrations concerning God advanced by the philosophers would be sophistical. For example, if it were said that whatever is in potency is reduced to act by a being in act, and from this it were concluded that God is being in act, since all things are brought

---

37. Soloveichik was trained in Neo-Kantian theory under Herman Cohen and criticized the causal metaphysics of Maimonides from this perspective, reinterpreting Talmudic observances in light of Kantian anthropology. The speculative antinomies of our inherent 'agnosticism' thus open the path to resolution of acute existential human questions only by means of religious faith. Soloveichik locates the resolution of the mystery of being human in the observances of the Torah. See his *The Halakhic Mind* (New York: The Free Press, 1986), esp. 92–97; and *Halakhic Man* (Philadelphia: The Jewish Publication Society, 1983), esp. 128–37. For the thinking of David Novak on this subject, see in particular, *The Natural Law in Judaism* (Cambridge: Cambridge University Press, 2008); *Talking with Christians: Musings of a Jewish Theologian* (Grand Rapids: Eerdmans, 2005).

into existence by him, there would be a fallacy of equivocation."[38] Accordingly, we would be unable to say truly that God is pure act.

Likewise, if God is spoken of from his effects only by comparison with the effects of creatures and not in himself, then we may say God is fire in that he cleanses us like fire cleanses physically, or that he is wise because he creates order just as wise persons are the source of order in human dealings. But this criterion is so thin that it allows us to equate the application of terms such as fire and wisdom to God with equal and undifferentiated validity. In short, if Maimonides is correct, there is no differentiation possible between rigorously analogical names for God, such as divine simplicity, goodness, wisdom, and so forth, and merely metaphorical names, such as fire, lion, or husband.[39]

Again, if there were no difference between saying that "God is alive" and saying that "God is not a non-living thing," then there would be no difference between saying "God is alive" and saying that "God is a lion." For a lion is not a non-living thing. The differentiations between God and creatures must be identified not only through the elaboration of purely negative differences, but also through the articulation of positive differentiations within creatures and between creatures and God.[40]

Aquinas's responses to Maimonides predict in interesting ways the consequences of radical equivocity theory. They show prefigurations of the kind of post-modernist forms of divine naming we see arise in the wake of Kant and Heidegger: if we relegate the project of divine naming to the purely equivocal, the philosophical rationality of the Judeo-Christian tradition necessarily becomes unstructured. Our discourse about God loses its grounding in our more proximate and logically prior forms of explanation and demonstration. Consequently, we can no longer justify sufficiently what we say of God

---

38. *De Potentia Dei* in *Thomas Aquinas: Selected Writings,* trans. Ralph McInerny (London: Penguin Books, 1998), q. 7, a. 7. See likewise SCG I, c. 33.

39. *De Potentia Dei,* q. 7, a. 5.

40. *De Potentia Dei,* q. 7, a. 5.

philosophically and why we do so. Speculative reason consequently has little to contribute regarding what we might or might not say regarding God. The process of divine naming thus descends into a field where metaphor and analogy stand shoulder to shoulder and become indifferentiated. Two possibilities then emerge. One is that divine naming becomes an exercise in an insufficiently structured form of intuitive description, merging images, univocal names, and analogies, all jumbled together, without sufficient discrimination or rigorous justification. We see this arguably in the writings on the divine in the late Heidegger, in Marion's philosophy of God, and in the event ontology of thinkers like Barth and Balthasar. The other possibility is that divine naming is interpreted as the rhetorical exercise of the author, a sophistical and arbitrary imposition of discourse by the will to power. So, then, the name of God has to be the subject of a never-ending deconstructionist critique that seeks to explain why or why not certain metaphors or names are oppressive or liberating in given cultural and political contexts. This is the intellectual backdrop to the religious pluralist and feminist forms of critical skepticism with regard to the classical monotheistic tradition that used to be prevalent in American religious studies departments. How to adjudicate between either of these options is, it seems to me, impossible unless we first solve the speculative problem that lies behind their mutual development.

Leave it to say that when divine naming is rightly oriented, no matter by how many important apophatic qualifications, it is necessarily also always analogical in orientation. The knowledge of what God is not, is in some way grounded in and presupposes some form of kataphatic or positive knowledge of God by way of causal similitudes, insofar as God is the creative author of the reality from which we begin to know him and name him.

A last but not unimportant comparison of Aquinas and Maimonides should be mentioned with regard to the divine name given in Exodus 3:14–15. The name of God in his singularity given in Ex. 3:15 (*YHWH*) is uttered under the euphemism of "*Kyrios*" in the Greek

Septuagint, and "Lord" in English. It seems to be interpreted in meaning or explicated by Exodus itself in 3:14 with the theological gloss: "I am He who is," or perhaps "I will be who I will be." Aquinas follows Maimonides (*Guide for the Perplexed* 1.60–62), as well as Origen and Jerome, in distinguishing between *YHWH* (from Exod. 3:15) and "I am He who is" (Exod. 3:14) as distinct divine names. Nevertheless, Aquinas also interprets the names as inseparable and mutually related.[41] In his metaphysical exegesis in *ST* I, q. 13, a. 9 and a. 11, ad 1, he identifies the Tetragrammaton as the divine name that signifies the incommunicability of the divine nature in its individuality, just as a singular name signifies the incommunicability of the individual human being (like Paul or Rebecca.) This contrasts with the name "God," which signifies the nature (a. 8), and the name "He who is," which signifies the uniqueness of the perfection of God as *Ipsum esse subsistens*: subsistent being in itself (a. 11). Although these signifying terms are diverse, their multiplicity is derived from our human manner of knowing God based upon terms drawn from creatures, creatures that are themselves complex. For as *ST* I, q. 3 (esp. aa. 3–4) has already made clear, in material creatures there is a real distinction between individuality and nature, as well as between essence and existence, but there is no real distinction in God between either nature and individual, or essence and existence. Therefore, while we may rightly designate God in various senses (as existence, deity, or individual) under these terms, in their ultimate ontological ground, they signify He who is absolutely simple. By consequence, the multiplicity of terms can be seen only as complementary and interrelated within a larger biblical and metaphysical framework of apophatic and kataphatic approaches to naming God. In short, when we say God is he who is, or is the divine nature, or is this singular personal God: the Lord, we are saying three different things and signifying God in three different ways, as existence itself, as he who has the divine nature, and in his personal singularity. But these three are in God himself, truly one.

---

41. See Armand Maurer, "St. Thomas on the Sacred Name 'Tetragrammaton,'" *Mediaeval Studies* 34 (1972): 275–86.

The point of this particular reflection, however, is to underscore that Aquinas thinks that the philosopher *qua* philosopher can identify a certain analogy even for the naming of God in his singular personal individuality. That is, the philosopher can at least conceive of the possibility of giving a personal name to God, as we might give the name Paul or Rebecca to another. At the same time, however, due precisely to the apophatic and indirect form of our natural knowledge and naming of God, the awareness or knowledge of "who God is" personally in himself is utterly inaccessible to us.[42] Consequently, while we can speak, with Maimonides, of the philosophical "mystery," so to speak, of the individual name of God or his personal identity, this is something that is not naturally disclosed to us. We stand naturally upon a precipice in darkness, looking out into the divine possibility: the possibility that God should, from the other side of the gulf of unknowing, address us personally, as a Thou: as he did to Moses in the desert, as "I am He who is." And as he did, for Christians, in the human flesh of Christ, the God-man: As Jesus says in the Gospel of St. John, invoking the divine name: "For when you have lifted me up, [upon the cross] then you will know that I am." (John 8:28) Sinai and Golgotha speak the divine name to us in a new and hitherto unknown way, to communicate to us the singularity and identity of He who is, and who approaches us personally, through the encounter of revelation. But even within the realm of philosophical divine naming alone, we do have a certain analogy from which to 'anticipate' this pure possibility or reason: that of the personal disclosure of God's individual singularity, in and through experiential contact.

V

What, then, is divine naming as an analogical procedure? How does Aquinas himself employ words and concepts to signify the divine? We have looked at various examples above. In various texts, however, Aquinas focuses specifically on the theoretical issue of how

---

42. Cf. *ST* I, q. 12.

divine naming functions through analogical significations of the divine nature. And, here, he famously gives two diverse and potentially competing answers to the question. The first is from *De Veritate* q. 2, a. 11 (circa 1256 AD), while the second is from *Summa theologiae* I, q. 13, a. 5 (circa 1266 AD). In the first text, Aquinas develops the idea of an "analogy of proportionality" between creatures and God. This form of analogy implies a likeness between the properties of two things without implying any necessary causal relation between the two things. So, for instance, we can see that the human eye perceives and that, analogically speaking, the human mind perceives. Yet this need not imply that the sensate powers of physical sight depend upon mental insight, or vice versa. Correspondingly, one might speak of human wisdom or of divine wisdom, and in doing so, one is speaking analogically, by proportionality. There is something in common between creaturely wisdom and the wisdom of God, but the latter is also utterly different from and disanalogous to human understanding. The divine wisdom, meanwhile, has in itself no "real relation" to human wisdom, meaning that it has no ontological relativity to human creaturely modes of being. The divine wisdom of God is not determined in its very existence in any way by causal dependence upon creatures, nor is it to be grouped in any way within a common genus of wisdom that might conceptually inscribe modes of wisdom both finite and infinite. The analogy of proportionality is meant to safeguard the absolute transcendence and alterity of God with respect to creatures.

In the later text (ST I, q. 13, a. 5), Aquinas characterizes the analogy between creatures and God by what he terms an analogy of attribution *ad alterum*: the analogy between the Creator as cause and his creaturely effects. Here, the order of thinking starts from the side of creatures: we approach the mystery of God philosophically only by beginning with the creaturely realities we experience immediately. The arguments for the existence of God are *a posteriori* demonstrations, by which we argue from the inherent ontological dependencies we see in creatures (in their 'chains' of mutual interdependence and contingency) to the necessity existence of a transcendent, creative cause.[43] Because creatures exist, God must exist. The cause is known only through its effects (indirectly and inferentially), but it is also truly known so, however imperfectly.

It follows from all this, however, that we can posit necessarily a similitude between the effects and the cause because every created effect must in some way resemble its transcendent cause.[44] Consequently, all created effects are *related* to their transcendent cause, and their properties can be traced to Him by way of this causal similitude and this corresponding relational dependency. The "analogy of attribution" between creatures and God, therefore, is not one that refers to God linguistically as an analogate term within a broader set, as if God were a species of being within a larger genus, or a mere member of *ens commune*, one present in the total set of created beings. Rather, the analogical names we derive from creation for the sovereign and transcendent Creator all refer to him as in darkness, as to that lodestar from which all things proceed, and in whom all perfections must be present in simplicity and perfect actuation, but who himself rests above the mere modes of being of finite effects. God can be spoken of using terms derived from creatures (through a process of refinement or purification), and so words like "simplicity," "perfection," "goodness," "eternity," "wisdom," and so on can be attributed to Him, based on the relation between creatures and God. But what is God's very perfection or goodness or wisdom is something that remains inscrutable and incomprehensible. We speak the truth of God, but as in the summit (or abyss) of a philosophical "mystery"

43. On the demonstrations for the existence of God in Thomas Aquinas, see Edward Feser, *Aquinas: A Beginner's Guide* (Oxford: Oneworld Press, 2009); John Wippel, *The Metaphysical Thought of Thomas Aquinas* (Washington, DC: The Catholic University of America Press, 2000); Rudi Te Velde, *Aquinas on God* (Aldershot: Ashgate, 2006); Thomas Joseph White, OP, *Wisdom in the Face of Modernity. A Study in Thomistic Natural Theology* (Naples, FL: Sapientia, 2009).

44. See on this principle in Aquinas, John Wippel, "Thomas Aquinas on Our Knowledge of God and the Axiom that Every Agent Produces Something Like Itself," in *Metaphysical Themes in Thomas Aquinas II* (Washington, DC: The Catholic University of America Press, 2007), 152–71.

that is grounded in rational deliberation but also rationally indissoluble.

Many modern commentators on Aquinas have posited that these two texts are basically opposed on some level and denote mutually incompatible approaches to the offering of divine names.[45] The earlier Aquinas sought to underscore the primacy of the Aristotelian "analogy of proportionality," while the later Aquinas focused upon a more Platonic form of analogical thinking (analogy of attribution *ad alterum*) that saw all beings as derived from (participating in) the transcendent gift of being from God. Aquinas the Aristotelian cedes (in part at least) to Aquinas the Neoplatonist. This genealogical reading of Aquinas has its intellectual attractions, but it also seems to overstate implausibly the developmental aspect of Aquinas's metaphysical thinking over the course of ten years. More fundamentally, it certainly seems possible to read the two texts as basically compatible with one another. On this reading, each underscores a distinct aspect of the process of analogical naming of God: the reality of inherent similitude of attributes and the causal dependency or relationality of creatures upon the Creator. On this reading, the analogy of attribution is that which underscores the radical dependence of all creatures upon God: just as they depend upon Him for their very being in act (*actus essendi*), so also God is utterly transcendent of the creaturely realm, and in him the act of being is identical with his very essence. He does not receive existence or being in act from others but is himself the utterly unique giver of the gift of creation. Thus, God is simultaneously present in all his creation, but also utterly hidden, as the cause is obscure to the effects that are incapable ontologically of representing him adequately. That being said, however, when we turn to speak of what God is in himself, independently of creatures, and from before the dawn of creation, He has in himself certain perfections that are to be attributed to Him inherently.

45. See most influentially Bernard Montagnes, *La doctrine de l'analogie de l'être d'après Saint Thomas d'Aquin.*

If we say, for instance, that God is wise, or good, or simple, or eternal, we speak truly of that which God is in himself. And so the analogy of proportionality (A is to B as C is to D) underscores not relational dependence and similitude of effects that depend upon the cause, but the inherent likeness of creatures to God *by way of attributes found analogously in each.* The qualities of wisdom found in human beings are in some way inherent to them, just as the substantial wisdom of who God is is inherent to God and identical with God's very essence. Thus, God truly is wise, and Socrates is truly wise, in two utterly differentiated ways.

The first form of analogy helps us to safeguard causal dependency and therefore to underscore the transcendence of God. It serves as a caution against univocity, and if we lose sight of it, we will risk falling into the dangers of an overly optimistic kataphaticism. The wisdom of God and the wisdom of Socrates may be known truly under a common analogical concept, but that concept needs to be differentiated internally by the rigors of apophatic purification. The distance between the two wisdoms is one that is underscored by remembrance of the unique character of the *actus essendi* of God: God is his wisdom and gives existence to all other beings, and by that very measure he remains incomprehensible and intellectually incircumscribable. The second form of analogy safeguards the capacity of analogy to name the intrinsic properties or attributes of God and serves as a caution against equivocity and radical apophaticism. The cause is not comprehended in its effects, but the inherent deity of God may truly be signified by divine naming, however imperfectly and indirectly. Not only is God truly wise, good, simple, etc., but God is all these things in an incomprehensible form of perfection that utterly exceeds that of being found in creatures. Divine naming therefore is not an agnostic procedure, but speaks under the veil of darkness into the very life of God.

VI

The view of analogical names for God that we have been considering is based, in fact, upon claims of natural reason, whether those claims are universally accepted or not. This admission, however, leaves open the question of knowledge of God by way of divine revelation. Or does it? Does the theory of analogical naming, as I have presented it, leave room open to the grace of divine revelation? Or is such theory opposed implicitly to the real possibilities of human religion and divine revelation, such that once it is developed to its logical end, reason may no longer become truly receptive to Biblical thinking? In this case, it would be a kind of "religion within the limits of analogical reason." And certain Reformed and Lutheran critics (such as Karl Barth and Eberhard Jüngel) have argued in diverse ways that this is the case for Aquinas's thought.[46] We should consider, then, how the analogical naming of God is intrinsically open (but in qualified ways only) to the notion of attributions of names based on divine revelation, as one finds in Christian Trinitarian theology. And also (but distinctly!), how does it permit but also qualify the use of metaphorical terms for God, as is frequent in the Biblical tradition?

The first question, it must be noted, is not about Biblical *metaphors* but rather about *proper analogies that are specific to divine revelation alone* and not proper to philosophical theology. What would be examples of these? The two most evident that stem from Christian claims of divine revelation are those which denote Jesus of Nazareth as the Son of God and as the Word (taking the latter in the conceptual sense of *logos, verbum,* not in the sensible sense of the spoken word) of God. It is evident that the patristic and scholastic theological tradition took these divine names to be known only through divine revelation but also to be something other than mere metaphors.

---

46. On the criticisms of Barth and Jüngel, see Thomas Joseph White, "How Barth Got Aquinas Wrong: A Reply to Archie J. Spencer on Causality and Christocentrism," *Nova et Vetera* (English edition) 7, no.1 (2009): 241–70.

That is to say, orthodox Christian doctrine affirms that there is a real distinction of persons in the Most Holy Trinity, such that the eternal Son of God is intemporally begotten of the Father, as the *Logos* of the Father. The analogies of Son and Word here are mutually correlative and, in a sense, mutually correcting.[47] The analogy of generation implies a real begetting and a real distinction of persons that is constitutive of the very life of God. The analogy of the *Logos* implies that the begetting is wholly immaterial and purely spiritual. Because the begetting in question is non-material, it cannot be represented or ever conceived merely in terms of temporal becoming and the historical development of physical bodies. Rather, it must be thought out along the lines of the inner image of God, which we find in the spiritual soul of human beings in terms of the procession of conceptual thought and spiritual wisdom from the subject of the human person. As the human concept is secreted immaterially from the human intellect by way of abstraction, so analogously, the eternal *Logos* proceeds from the Father immaterially. However, because there is a begetting of distinct persons in God, the immaterial procession in God is utterly different from the procession of a concept from the mind of a single person. The Son is truly distinct from the Father personally, even as his *Logos* or eternal truth. Furthermore, human thoughts are merely the changing contingent properties of the human subject (accidents of a substance, and ontologically flimsy accidents at that), while the *Logos* is not a characteristic or accidental property of the Father, but possesses in himself the very being and incomprehensible essence of the Father. He is substantially identical with the Father in essence, "God from God, light from light, true God from true God," as the Nicene creed states. All that is in the Father, then, is in his eternally begotten *Logos:* The Father and the Son, with the Holy Spirit, simply *are* the one God.

One has no reason to know about the inner Trinitarian life of God apart from the encounter with divine revelation in the person of Christ. And so correspondingly, if one does have reason to believe

47. *ST* I, q. 27, aa. 1–2; q. 34, a. 2.

in this mystery, it is in virtue of the grace of supernatural faith and not apart from it. Is such belief, however, consonant with the vision of analogical divine names that has been described above, or is it not? From a Thomist point of view, the answer is that it most certainly is and that this should be accepted from the beginning as a theological principle of faith. Supernatural faith and human reason (when each is rightly understood in and through an unending historical process of mutual purification) do not contradict and may be accepted as presenting distinct but compatible and interrelated truths.[48] On this view, if the exponent of Christian doctrine is to hold that Jesus Christ is both God and man, and is the person of the *Logos* made flesh (John 1:14), then he must also hold that Jesus, insofar as he is God, is one in being with the Father. (John 1:1–3). But if this same Christian thinker is also committed to the kind of robust philosophical account of God I have alluded to above, then there is also the necessity to qualify or understand the divinity of Christ in light of the divine names that are appropriately given to the one God, in keeping with philosophical reason. Actually, this is said too abruptly since the Scriptural revelation itself gives approbation to a host of divine names that might "overlap" with those articulated in philosophy. In the Bible, after all, God is revealed as being unique and one, sovereignly good, wise, eternal, alive, omnipresent, Himself love, just, and so forth. Therefore, to think about these names is not only to think of God philosophically. Rather, philosophical reflection can come to the aid of theological reflection as a "subordinate science" as a way to seek further clarity and depth of understanding of what divine revelation has already given. Consequently, we might say that sacred theology can seek rightly to understand as deeply as possible not only the truth that the Father, Son, and Holy Spirit are one in being and yet distinct persons, but also that the divine life and essence of the Father, Son and, Holy Spirit is itself simple, perfect, good, eternal, infinite, one, life itself, and so on.

---

48. This is the view of the First Vatican Council, *Dei Filius* (1870).

On this view, what is not permitted is that we might import univocal conceptions of deity into the life of the divine persons such that philosophical irrationalities are introduced into Trinitarian doctrine. It is perfectly and necessarily true to say that philosophical reason cannot demonstrate or disprove the existence of the Holy Trinity, for natural reason, by its own powers, simply cannot attain the divine essence directly, but only names God indirectly from creatures. It cannot, thus, demonstrate or disprove that God is essentially a Trinity of persons. For philosophy attaining even to its summit, "what" God is in himself immediately remains veiled. But it is true to say that philosophical reason can detect and diagnose serious philosophical irrationalities when they are introduced into theological reasoning and can, by that same measure, seek to safeguard not only the prerogatives of enlightened reason, but also the prerogatives of a sound Christian doctrine of God. If, for example, a narrative of kenotic historical development is introduced into the life of God, such that the Son is differentiated from the Father personally and "formally" in and through his historical existence in time as human, then the temporality of history is introduced into the very constitution of the life of God and the distinction of the Trinitarian persons. By this same measure, however, the unity and the transcendence of God as Creator both risk being undermined by what, following Marion, we might call another *distinctly theological* species of conceptual idolatry. In this case, the mystery of God's wholly other incomprehensibility is obscured artificially.[49] Philosophy, then, also has a necessary role *within* theology that dignifies that theology while also respecting the primacy of the principles of faith that it serves. A healthy philosophical reason aids in the protection of human religious thinking from intellectually problematic forms of anthropomorphism and from intra-worldly projective schemes of conceptuality transferred problematically onto the life of God. Philosophy

---

49. This argument is presented in more detail in Thomas Joseph White, "Kenoticism and the Divinity of Christ Crucified," *The Thomist* 75, no. 1 (2011): 1–42.

"helps us keep ourselves from idols" (I John 5:21). It also helps us see how a truly profound presentation of Trinitarian faith that takes divine transcendence seriously may speak to the profound longing of human reason to have a deeper understanding of the inner life of God. Just as philosophy trails off into the sublime unknowing of the immanent essence of God and only approaches God in darkness, so also the revelation of the Trinity, truly received in supernatural faith, 'answers' structurally to the natural desire to know the first cause of created reality.[50] In this way, revelation truly unveils the mystery of God, not in philosophical terms alone, but in the new luminous light and deep obscurity of faith. If that faith is presented in philosophically-informed ways, it shows the deep solidarity between our natural aspiration to know the names of God by the pathways of metaphysical reflection and ascent and the supernatural gift of knowledge of the inner life of God by way of the revelation in Christ and the descent of the living God into human flesh and history.

In light of the first topic of revealed analogies, we can consider the issue of metaphor more succinctly. Aquinas notes rightly at the beginning of the *Summa theologiae* that Biblical theology is immersed in metaphorical expressions for God and his provident activities.[51] Does the analogical study of the divine names rule out the use of such ascriptions? Clearly not: consideration of the love of God is not opposed to the consideration of God's jealousy. Think of parallels: justice and anger, divine power and the warring arm of God, the life of God and God as a vine who gives sustenance to Israel, the just and merciful decisions of God and the portrait of God as "turning his face" away or towards us. The real question is not whether the two modes of signification are compatible. In fact, what was said above about the potential for aphilosophical conceptual idolatry would apply here all the more intensively: without analogical thinking of the divine names, the use of metaphors could quickly become

---

50. *ST* I, q. 12, a. 1.
51. *ST* I, q. 1, a. 9.

insufficiently intellectually structured. God could be envisaged only under the idioms of matter, a veritable "ontic being among beings," in the worst of the Heideggerian senses of that prescription. A naïve literalism can, therefore, also be fraught with the dangers of a naïve idolatry.

The real question, rather, is: If one does possess both natural and supernatural ascriptions of divine names that are proper and not metaphorical (such as divine simplicity, goodness, unity, but also Sonship, *Logos*, etc.), *then why might there be any need for metaphorical ascriptions at all?* What, in fact, do they contribute to the rest?

One initial and evident answer is that they condescend to our ordinary human ways of coming to understand any subject matter (including God) through the medium of the sensible and representative images and symbols. Thinking of God under the images of his physical world, through the poetry of divine revelation, is not anti-philosophical or anti-theological. On the contrary, this manner of proceeding is integral to and compatible with the human way we think in general about all the things that we consider. Indeed, it is true to say this in a variety of disciplines: the modern sciences, ordinary philosophical analysis, contemporary ethical argument, and political and legal theory. All of these disciplines make great use of metaphors, and it is inevitable that one should grasp an intelligible subject matter through this irreducibly human way of representing reality. To do less would be inhuman, and God comes to human beings through the medium of human knowledge and culture. In doing so, He sanctifies and elevates linguistic metaphorical modes of knowing and signifying to a new plane (in Biblical revelation), but in a way that is consistent with our natural way of being.

Likewise, we can also say that metaphors touch upon the embers of the human heart in ways that ennoble and speak more deeply to human affectivity and so to the holistic composite of the human subject, as both body and soul, mind and symbol, passions and rationality. Metaphorical knowledge illustrates or symbolizes actively, so to speak, the life of grace working among human beings, making the goodness and reality of God *tangible* in ways that mere conceptuality alone could not do adequately. In this sense, the metaphorical incarnation of the scriptures is itself a preparation for and foreshadowing of the ontological incarnation of God in human flesh and the presence of the activity of God in the sacramental liturgy of the Catholic faith.

The more subtle issue, however, pertains to the richness of symbols, precisely as a form of intellection. For metaphorical knowledge is sometimes more crude than knowledge that is uniquely conceptual. However, it is also capable of suggesting a plenitude of conceptual depth and plurality in a way that merely conceptual thought is not. To say that Christ is a source of divine grace is itself consonant with the teaching of John 15:5: "I am the Vine and you are the branches." For Christ is the source of divine life, both by virtue of his divinity and through the medium of his human nature, through which he freely gives grace to human beings.[52] To say this alone, however, about the image of the vine is also incomplete. For this *image* also simultaneously *represents* something about the way God works *progressively* in creatures (like viniculture), from within (like sap), and in multiple ways (in a diversity of branches). It suggests by analogy with the growth of plant life on a spiritual plane that God is the resplendent uncreated wisdom who is the source of the progressive divine illumination of the human mind, that he is the uncreated fire of charity who is the inspiration of the movements of growth in charity in the human heart. It suggests that God acts in view of the growth in the "life" of virtue of human beings, even in view of their redemption (the fruit of the vine), which opens up the question of the final state of the soul after death, and that of the final state of the "vine" of human history. In short, the metaphor, which is very basic or very material, in this case, is also simultaneously suggestive of a depth and wealth of theological conceptuality.

We can finish with a thought regarding the philosophical and

---

52. *ST* III, q. 8, a. 1.

theological comparison of religions. The poetic heritage of the Western theological canon (from, say, the Bible to John of the Cross) should be studied simply out of respect for the mature desires of human rationality, if for no other reason. It also serves, however, as a basis for dialogue with the poetic traditions of the RigVeda, the Buddhist canon of sermons, the Confucian philosophy of the political significance of ritual, and the Daoist philosophy of nature. That is to say, it serves as a necessary partner to the high speculation of the Judeo-Christian tradition (in scholastic theology, for instance), which has built so extensively upon the foundation of Scriptural names of God. But it also can serve as a medium for interaction with the highly speculative reflection of other traditions, through the medium of their own symbolic and representative forms of thought, as well as in keeping with the consideration of their ontological and ethical concepts.

The theological study of divine names and the genuine openness to intellectual universality are not, therefore, rightly juxtaposed or contrasted, but are, in fact, deeply interrelated. The capacity to understand all things in light of God invites the mind to a more universal horizon and makes possible the hope of a true intellectual unity, so that the quest for universal truth is not one that occurs in vain or against the backdrop of the void. The deepest capacity to accept and admire the distinction and qualities of the variety of creatures can be found within the aspiration to the knowledge of God. This knowledge invites one to a profound form of respect and gradual, responsible critical judgment regarding the profound values and truths present in the patrimonies of human religious and philosophical reflection.

VII

What might we conclude from these arguments? First, that the analogical use of language is grounded in our ordinary linguistic practices and analysis of common place entities. Speaking analogically about the existence, unity, and goodness of created realities entails a process of conceptual unlearning and relearning of the range of meanings of various terms so as to come to an analogically unified grasp of the ontological complexity of reality. Second, the causality of God is unlike any other, such that when we speak of God, we are necessarily obliged to qualify our language at various removes and by a relatively ornate process of speculative reflection so that we might speak of God rightly and well. And even when we do so, when we do signify God in what he is, we do so non-comprehensively and apophatically, as speaking of a mystery that infinitely surpasses us, even as it is in some real sense intellectually accessible to us. Third, the philosophical articulation of names for God need not be the arbitrary imposition of a pseudo-rational rhetoric nor a mere exercise of intellectual false hope. On the contrary, the speculative impulse to seek to understand something of God is the most noble aspiration of the human intellect and is the 'place' where our mind might also naturally encounter the philosophical *question* (itself philosophically unanswerable) of the possibility of divine self-disclosure. That is to say, of divine revelation. That divine revelation itself, meanwhile, elicits the use of a healthy and sound philosophical form of reflection, such that ontological thinking should exist even within the practice of theological reasoning itself. Lastly, however, philosophical and theological traditions do well to enrich themselves by a deep immersion in the poetic and metaphorical traditions of the Bible, as well as the broader traditions of human literature and religious reflection.

The perspective of this chapter, of course, is set at odds with the tendencies of the contemporary university, which is structured culturally in view of the values of pragmatic liberal pluralism and the axiomatic acceptance of rational heterogeneity. However, the attempt to underscore the existential centrality of knowledge of God is perhaps more pertinent to that very same university than might initially be evident. For historically, the rational search for understanding about God was at the center of the university and gave inward rational unity or teleological orientation to the whole edifice of scientific learning. I am referring to the vision of the medieval university at its origins, but we might apply this classical insight to the heart of the contemporary world by a kind of inversion. What happens when we take away the reference point of God as an object of human investigation? Surely, the post-modern fracturing of the distinct scientific discourses in contemporary academic culture is in part related to this noteworthy philosophical absence. Might one not be so bold as to suggest a correspondence between the forgetfulness of philosophical theology and the obscurity of the unity of modern learning?

Of course, what is said here provocatively of philosophical theology might perhaps be stated with even more certainty with regard to philosophy *tout court*. For it is, above all, philosophy that gives unity to all other forms of knowledge and brings them all into one ultimate form of organized discourse, and without this, the universality of the university is endangered. The question, however, is: can philosophy really do this without talking about God? According to Aquinas, we know created realities first in our natural order of understanding, but we understand them best only in light of the attributes of God, the first principle and final end of all things. In His light alone do we grasp the meaning of all lesser, created lights. Modern secularized philosophy departments are busy working to protect themselves from the aggressive claims of neuroscience on the one hand and the relativizing hermeneutical stances of post-modern literature on the other. Philosophy is often seen trying to reassert its right to exist or its relevance, as it stands between an empiricist reductionism on the one hand and a rationalist relativism on the other. But the way of reassertion of philosophy's irreducible splendor and unifying role even in the heart of the contemporary academy comes in part through the reassertion of philosophy's capacity to seek God and to speak rationally and truthfully about God. It is this that gives ultimate light to the unity of all natural learning. In this task, the multiform reflections of Thomas Aquinas on the analogical naming of God are an inestimable resource, and one of perennial value.

2

Divine Simplicity

INTRODUCING DIVINE SIMPLICITY

The topic of divine simplicity encompasses several central questions. For example, is God's essence ontologically composite, and if so, in what way, or if not, how does God differ from creatures? Does God have a physically composite body or distinct spiritual faculties, such as an intellect distinct from his will? Are his attributes (such as power, wisdom, and goodness) formally distinct or really identical? Does God receive his existence from another or from himself, similarly to creatures? Does God have accidental properties that characterize him, such that he is subject to historical change in non-essential ways? Answers to such questions have obvious implications for any Christian doctrine of the Trinity since they directly affect how one understands both the distinction and unity of the trinitarian persons. Are the persons of the Trinity distinguished by being different persons of the same essential kind who are not identical in individual being (like three human persons), or are they identical in individual being and essence, and thus non-composite in a way that is utterly distinct from human persons? Do they have distinct accidental properties while sharing in one divine essence

Originally published in the *St Andrews Encyclopaedia of Theology*, ed. Brendan N. Wolfe et al., www.saet.ac.uk.

and individual being so that each person can develop natural properties as God that the other two persons do not have? Or are their qualities (like power, wisdom, and goodness) really identical with their essence, so that they are really distinct only in virtue of their intra-trinitarian relations of origin, even while being one as God?

Such questions have a medieval scholastic feel to them, but as we shall see below, they also have roots in biblical notions about God from the Old and New Testaments, especially as the Bible was interpreted in the patristic era, in which manifold reflections about divine simplicity arose, especially in the context of trinitarian theology.

In modern continental trinitarian theology, the topic of divine simplicity is largely either ignored or thoroughly reconceptualized. There are several reasons for this. First, a common strand of modern theology (represented by figures like Albrecht Ritschl and Adolf von Harnack) considers classical divine attributes (such as simplicity and impassibility) to originate primarily from Hellenistic metaphysical speculation alien to the Judaic and biblical world of thought, and thus extrinsic to the enlightened prerogatives of a modern, historically informed theology. Second, major figures of the 'trinitarian renewal' of the twentieth century, such as Karl Barth, Sergius Bulgakov, Karl Rahner, and Hans Urs von Balthasar, provide no thematic treatment of divine simplicity, despite its presence in patristic theology and in various conciliar definitions. This silence stems not from ignorance but from a selective decision to relinquish the use of some (but not all) classical metaphysical themes in light of the just-mentioned genealogical claim. They each seek in various ways to respond to challenges to divine simplicity enunciated by modern secular philosophers with innovative theological proposals that do not rely on seemingly questionable pre-modern philosophical ideas about the divine essence. This modern strategic rethinking of trinitarian theology is coupled with the decision to appropriate apologetically some categories of post-Hegelian philosophical ontology that depict God in event-orientated, historical terms. Thus, such modern trinitarian theologies typically depict God, his deity, and the trinitarian persons in great part in relation to the economy of creation and salvation, and therefore, in dynamic terms not fully compatible with the classical ideas pertaining to notions of trinitarian simplicity and immutability. Finally, some analytic theists, while open to a host of classical questions, consider the doctrine of divine simplicity unsustainable since they believe that it entails either that God's attributes (such as goodness or eternity) be considered in a reified way as identical with his essence, and thus God is transformed into an abstract entity, or they fear that a God who is simple can neither know, love, nor respond dynamically to the real world of change, freedom, and history that characterizes creation, and human beings especially.

This chapter seeks to show that the neglect of divine simplicity by modern theology is unjustified since the doctrine of simplicity is arguably of biblical provenance and is essential in patristic and medieval theology to a coherent account of the intra-trinitarian life of God. Classically, the doctrine serves as a logical condition of possibility for a coherent idea of the Trinity as Creator, who can know and love the world in the most perfect of ways precisely in virtue of God's transcendent divine simplicity. In light of these considerations, I argue that the doctrine of divine simplicity can and should be considered a constitutive element in any comprehensive theological treatment of the Christian doctrine of God.

BIBLICAL TOPICS THAT POINT TOWARD THE IMPLICIT SCRIPTURAL ORIGINS

The notion of God's simplicity as a first principle of reality is first discussed explicitly not in the Bible but in Graeco-Roman philosophical literature, including in the work of Aristotle[1] and Plotinus.[2] By contrast, the notion of divine simplicity is not mentioned

---

1. Aristotle, *Metaphysics*, 12.7.1072a 32–34.
2. Plotinus, *Enneads*, trans. G. Boys-Stones, J. M. Dillon, L. P. Gerson, R. A. H. King,

explicitly in either the canon of the Old or New Testament. In his discussions of divine simplicity, Aristotle is concerned to show that the first principle in all of reality is purely actual, not characterized by material potency, and that God's eternal intellectual life is non-compositional, distinct from the kind of historically developmental, abstract, and rationally discursive knowledge that characterizes human beings. Plotinus is concerned, similarly, with the maximal perfection of the One, the first principle of all things that are found in the world, upon which all others depend, insofar as they are derived from what is primary. For Plotinus, causal derivation implies ontological composition, while primacy implies simplicity.

Notions such as these originating from Hellenistic philosophers were taken up and employed in selective ways by Christian patristic and medieval authors. However, it is problematic to presume for this reason that early Christian theological notions of divine simplicity are primarily of Hellenistic origin or are specifically philosophical in content. One may argue, as patristic and medieval authors did themselves, that their theological treatment of the topic derives principally from notions of God conveyed within biblical literature. Here this chapter proceeds not chronologically but thematically and will mention briefly five biblical notions that implicitly require recourse to topics involving divine simplicity.

First, there is the question of the individual unity or multiplicity of deities in Old Testament literature. Clearly, the proponents of mature Judaism, exemplified in the post-exilic Second Temple period, posited the reality of one God alone as the true and unique God.[3] They came to do so against the backdrop of various competing forms of religiosity, Near Middle Eastern or Graeco-Roman, some of which envisaged divinity in pluralistic form, in pantheons

---

A. Smith, and J. Wilberding (Cambridge: Cambridge University Press, 2019), 1.6.1, 5.4.1, 5.9.3, 5.9.14.

3. Richard Bauckham, *Jesus and the God of Israel: God Crucified and Other Studies on the New Testament's Christology of Divine Identity* (Grand Rapids: Eerdmans, 2008).

or by means of polytheism. For Old Testament authors to depict God as one and unique, they needed implicit recourse to the notion of God's nature, or deity, as instantiated only in God individually. While there are many humans and many angels, there is only one Lord of Israel.[4] There is only one God, the Creator.[5] This is a classical way of thinking precisely of divine simplicity.

Second, the question arises in the analysis of Old Testament literature of whether the ancient Hebrews or some of their members envisaged their deity under corporeal terms. Visions of YHWH that suggest corporeality[6] may well be read metaphorically or be interpreted as anthropomorphic visions of God accommodated to human understanding. However, some scholars have proposed that at least some strands of Old Testament literature indicate belief in a localized, corporeal deity.[7] My aim here is not to offer justification to such views, but only to note that such historical questions inevitably touch upon the topic of God's composition as a being, and thus affect our judgments about the simplicity of the divine nature. Did some ancient Hebrews believe that YHWH had a physical body, and in this case, is God an ontological composite of natural form and bodily matter? By contrast, if one can plausibly read such texts as metaphorical, does this mean the divine nature is non-composite in the senses previously indicated (non-material) and thus simple when contrasted with physical bodies?

Third, there is the question of YHWH's relationship with the angels in Old Testament literature and the development of the angelology of later Judaism.[8] Some scholars claim that in some texts, 'the LORD, YHWH' may be read as one or merely the first among the 'sons of God,' where the latter phrase may indicate either angelic

4. Deut 6:4.

5. Exod 3:14–15; Isa 45:5–13; Ps 102:24–25.

6. Exod 24:9–11; Ezek 1:4–28.

7. James Barr, "Theophany and Anthropomorphism in the Old Testament," *Vetus Testamentum* Sup 7 (1959): 31–38. Mark Smith, *Where the Gods Are* (New Haven: Yale University Press, 2016).

8. Serge-Thomas Bonino, *Angels and Demons: A Catholic Introduction*, trans. M. J. Miller (Washington, DC: The Catholic University of America Press, 2016).

beings or a consortium of deities.[9] Others read passages of these kinds as indicating by ancient metaphorical discourse the uniqueness and superiority of the LORD of Israel among all the other supposed Gods or among all the angels whom the nations take to be gods.[10] In either case, the interpretation of biblical texts rests upon implicit notions of individual uniqueness of YHWH, the LORD, as one who has a nature distinct from and transcendent of the angelic host and the supposed gods worshipped problematically by non-Israelite peoples.

Fourth, there is the theme of the God of Israel as the unique creator of all that exists in creation, evidenced in Second Isaiah (45:14–25) and in the final redaction of Genesis 1–2, as well as in the scribal literature of the Second Temple period.[11] God alone creates and gives being to all that is, to all that is not God. In this case, existence or being pertains to created things in a way that is different from the way it pertains to God, who simply exists eternally, while other things come into being due to the initiative and sustaining activity of the Creator. In short, at least some biblical texts affirm that the world is created by the one God of Israel.[12] In this case, God's being is not causally dependent in the way that the being of creatures is. Therefore, God does not exist in the way created realities exist, and his being is not composite as theirs is, by subjection to a 'complex composition' of potential and actual existence, such that they have potency to be or not be. God simply is.

Finally, we can indicate a theme that is proper to the New Testament and that has to do with the implicit but clear denotation (at least in some books of the New Testament) that both Jesus and the Spirit are divine and one with God, the Father of Jesus Christ.[13] If there is a real distinction of persons in God—the Father is eternally

---

9. Mark Smith, *The Origins of Biblical Monotheism: Israel's Polytheistic Background and the Ugaritic Texts* (Oxford: Oxford University Press, 2003).

10. Patrick D. Miller, *The Religion of Ancient Israel* (Louisville: Westminster John Knox, 2000).

11. Walter Brueggemann, *Theology of the Old Testament: Testimony, Dispute, Advocacy* (Minneapolis: Fortress, 2012), 145–51. Sir 16:26–30; Wis 7:22–30.

12. Ps 96:5; Ps 148:2–5; Jer 10:12–13; Isa 66:2; Neh 9:6; Prov 3:19; Job 33:4.

13. Phil 2:6–11; Gal 4:6; Rom 8:9–10; John 1:1–3; John 16:13.

distinct from his Son and Word, who are in turn distinct from the Holy Spirit (or Paraclete)—and yet God is also one, one is led to question precisely how these two assertions can coincide. Orthodox Christianity of the fourth century employed the *homoousios* (literally: of the same substance or essence) formula at Nicaea to convey the unity of essence (or consubstantiality) common to the persons, indicated as truly distinct hypostatic subjects. However, it follows from such a formulation (which has a basis in the teaching of the New Testament regarding the divinity of Christ and the Spirit) that the Trinity is ontologically simple in a way three human persons are not, since three human beings may have one nature or kind but are three individual substances, whereas the three persons of the Trinity are one in being and substance and not merely one in natural kind. Here, the divine simplicity pertains essentially and inalienably to a coherent doctrine of the Holy Trinity as such.

PATRISTIC EXPOSITIONS

Irenaeus

Patristic reflections on divine simplicity are numerous. Here this chapter considers three particularly noteworthy cases that build by logical congruity on the notions enunciated above. The first pertains to the work of Irenaeus. In *Against Heresies*, Irenaeus famously engages critically with Valentinus's theology of the divine *pleroma* (plenitude of divine being), which he analyses based upon his reading of the *Gospel of Valentinus*.[14] In doing so, he notes a fundamental incongruity in the thought of the Gnostic author. On the one hand, Valentinus espouses a doctrine in which the material world is ontologically deficient or evil, derived from a pre-cosmic, primal fall in the *pleroma*. The deity, split by inward schism, gives rise to the material world. On the other hand, Valentinus also considers the

---

14. Irenaeus. *Against Heresies*, in *Ante-Nicene Fathers*, vol. 1, ed. A. Roberts and J. Donaldson (Peabody, MA: Hendrickson Publishers, 2004). Book II 2.13.8.

membership in that *pleroma* to be pluralistic and multiple, in a way that is most readily conceivable and imaginable in material terms, so that one element of the deity (*Sophia*) can break corporate communion with others. Irenaeus notes that God is the Creator and author of complex material realities, which are good in themselves, but that in contrast to them, he is not composite in a material way. The three agents of salvation—the Father, his Word, and his Spirit—are one and are spiritual or immaterial, not physical and composite. Therefore, their 'plurality' or distinctiveness does not imply composition and multiplicity of the kind found in created material realities.[15] The God of the Old Testament is God the Creator and is also God the Father, Son, and Holy Spirit. This God is one and is without material parts.

Cappadocians

A more developed teaching on divine simplicity in the Holy Trinity emerges in the thought of the Cappadocian fathers, Basil the Great, Gregory of Nazianzus, and Gregory of Nyssa. The Cappadocians were confronted with the objections of Eumonius and other fourth-century Anomoeans who denied the divinity of the Son and the Spirit. Eunomius argued that the Father alone was God and that his essence was characterized by unbegottenness, such that anything begotten was not of the essence of God.[16] Therefore, the begotten Son is not truly one in essence with the Father (as Nicaea had asserted). To counter this idea, these fathers developed the notion of relational identity in the trinitarian persons, whereby the Son and the Spirit are distinguished from the Father because they derive from him by way of relations of origin (in eternal begetting and spiration respectively). However, the Son and the Spirit receive

15. Michel René Barnes, "Irenaeus' Trinitarian Theology," *Nova et Vetera* (English edition) 7, no. 1 (2009): 67–106.

16. Lewis Ayres, *Nicaea and its Legacy: An Approach to Fourth-Century Theology* (Oxford: Oxford University Press, 2004), 144–49. Gregory of Nazianzus. "Oration 29" in *Nicene and Post-Nicene Fathers*, vol. 7. ed. and trans. C. G. Browne and J. E. Swallow (Peabody, MA: Hendrickson Publishers, 1994), no. 11.

from the Father all that pertains to the essence of the divine nature such that they are truly equal and identical to him in being.[17] In this respect, the Trinity is simple (non-composite) because the Son and the Spirit as hypostatic persons are identical in being and essence with the Father, not inferior or alien in any respect.[18] As a culturally proximate influence, Plotinus had argued for the simplicity of the first principle in the deity, the One, from whom *Nous* and *Psyche* derive and who are ontologically subordinate to the One.[19] The simplicity of the One implies the subordination and inequality of the *Nous* and *Psyche*. But in the Cappadocian affirmation of divine simplicity, the notion is affirmed precisely to alleviate or render impossible any inequality of the persons, therefore underscoring their real identity as each being the one God. Consequently, their view is non-hierarchical and is monotheistic, in a decidedly trinitarian-biblical way, that contrasts markedly with a prominent strand of non-biblical Hellenistic philosophy of the time. The doctrine of divine simplicity as it emerges in the Cappadocians, then, is distinctly Christian and theological in character.

Augustine

A final example, and the one that is historically of greatest influence in Western theology, pertains to the work of Augustine of Hippo. In the fifth book of his work *The Trinity*, Augustine is concerned to respond to Arian criticisms of trinitarian faith, most notably to the idea that the Son and Spirit must be inferior to the Father.[20] There, he posits that the Son and Spirit are identical with the Father in essence and are wholly and truly God. They are distinguished from the Father only by relations of origin, not properties pertaining to the divine nature.[21] However, Augustine continues in this argument

---

17. Gregory of Nazianzus. "Oration 31" in *Nicene and Post-Nicene Fathers*, no. 9.
18. Gregory of Nyssa. 'Against Eunomius' and 'Not Three Gods.'
19. Plotinus, *Enneads*, 5.4.1, 6.9.4.
20. Augustine. *The Trinity*. V, 1, 6.
21. Augustine. *The Trinity*. V, 1, 6.

to specify that properties of the divine nature (wisdom, goodness, etc.) are not merely accidents or potential properties of the substance of the godhead but are somehow mysteriously identical with the godhead. God does not merely have wisdom or goodness but is subsistent wisdom and goodness. This subsistent wisdom and goodness are proper to all three persons, so that the Father does not become wise by generating the Son or good and loving by spirating the Spirit. Rather, the Father communicates all that he subsists in as God, in his eternal wisdom and goodness, to the Son and to the Spirit, by generation and spiration respectively. Here, one can mark a new development in the patristic reflection on divine simplicity that posits a non-composition of substance and property in God's essence. Augustine invokes this negation of composition to underscore the distinctive unity and identity of being present in the three persons who are the one God. The three persons are not distinguished by any individual properties or accidents pertaining to the divine nature, but each possesses that nature in its fullness and singularity of being. They are each the one God.

MEDIEVAL THEOLOGIANS

Doctrinal Background to Medieval Theories of Divine Simplicity

Medieval Christian theological reflections on divine simplicity are manifold and, in fact, extremely diverse. The treatment of the topic by various well-known theologians is far from homogeneous. On the contrary, it is often indicative of ideas proper to a given thinker. However, parameters of unity were provided by several factors. One of these was the thought of Augustine on divine simplicity, which acted as a proximate inspiration for most Western theologians. Likewise, there were two important public debates in the twelfth century regarding trinitarian theology that led to ecclesiastical formulations of a doctrine of divine simplicity. The first of these had to do with the claims of Gilbert of Poitiers (d. 1154), which were rejected by the Council of Reims in 1148. Gilbert noted that the essence of the three persons in God must be one and the same since they are each the one God. He concluded from this, however, that the relations of origin between the persons must be something distinct from their essence since the essence unites them, but the relations distinguish them. He concluded that there must be a distinction between each of the persons and their relative properties since each person is essentially God and is related to others only accidentally.[22] According to this view, relations are accidental to the substance of a trinitarian person, much as they would be in human persons. God the Father is not identical with his paternity or his relation to his Son. Rather, he merely possesses paternity while sharing the essence of God with the Son. In this way of thinking, the three persons of the Trinity are conceived of as relatively similar to three human beings identical in essence (as human) and related merely by accidents or properties (as in a father and son relation, for example). This position was criticized by Bernard of Clairvaux and condemned by the Council of Reims because it failed to acknowledge the simplicity of the divine nature of the Trinity along the lines indicated by Augustine.[23] On Augustine's view the relations of the persons are not accidental additions to a substance but pertain in some mysterious way to the very substance of the divine persons.

This Augustinian medieval idea of the Trinity is apophatic in many respects since it implies that the divine communion of persons in God is utterly dissimilar to the relations of human persons. However, it does also suggest that we can think of the persons in the Trinity by analogy with created persons if we take divine simplicity (and thus divine transcendence) into account. Such an idea was developed more expressly at the Fourth Lateran Council in 1215, which

22. Gilbert of Poitiers, *Expositio in Boecii de Trinitate* in *The Commentaries on Boethius by Gilbert of Poitiers*, ed. N. Haring (Toronto: PIMS, 1966), 1.5, nos. 42–43. Gilles Emery, *The Trinitarian Theology of Saint Thomas Aquinas*, trans. F. Murphy (Oxford: Oxford University Press, 2007), 90–91.

23. G. R. Evans, *Bernard of Clairvaux* (Oxford: Oxford University Press, 2000), 75–77, 123–27.

took issue with the theology of Joachim of Fiore (d. 1202). Joachim had written against Peter Lombard, who had affirmed in his writings that one may not say that the essence of God begets or spirates. By error, Joachim believed that this claim implied that Lombard was treating the essence in God as a kind of additional fourth subject, really distinct from the three persons who are subject to begetting and spiration. He responded by affirming that the essence of God begets and spirates and, in doing so, attributed processional activities to the essence of God. On this view, the persons seem to each have distinct *essential* attributes that differentiate them, such as natural begetting or natural being begotten. Therefore, they seem to have essential differences (that is to say differences of essence), and so to be united as one only morally or ethically as in a communion of human persons who are not truly consubstantial. Joachim may have wished to indicate that the eternal processions of the trinitarian persons just are what God is (the processional life of Father, Son, and Spirit). However, in the process, he affirmed that the essence itself differentiates in composite ways due to the divine processions. The Fourth Lateran Council rejected this view by explicitly appealing to the simplicity of the divine nature.[24] The Trinity is more dissimilar than similar to a communion of created persons. The Father, Son, and Holy Spirit are distinguished only by relations of origin, but these are not properties or accidents. The whole substance of the godhead is communicated from the Father to the Son by eternal generation and from the Father and the Son to the Holy Spirit by eternal spiration. Thus, each person possesses the fullness of the deity in its perfection and simplicity, and each person is truly the one God.

Theologians in the medieval Catholic Church saw rightly that both of the problematic positions noted above fail to understand sufficiently the implications of the doctrine of divine simplicity. If the nature of God is simple, then there cannot be personal relations

---

24. Fourth Lateran Council, *Decrees of the Ecumenical Councils*, ed. Norman P. Tanner (London: Sheed & Ward; Washington, DC: Georgetown University Press, 1990).

in God that are extrinsic to his essence. Nor can God's nature be subject to diverse composite activities of self-differentiation, like begetting and spirating. The three persons are distinct, but they are also truly one in essence because each person of the Holy Trinity partakes fully of the one divine nature of God.

Thomas Aquinas on Divine Simplicity

Aquinas treats the doctrine of divine simplicity in multiple places in his corpus, but this chapter concentrates on his mature positions presented in the *Summa theologiae* (*ST*), especially *ST* I, q. 3, as well as in the treatment of trinitarian relations and persons in qq. 28–29, which, it shall be argued, is a logically related topic. In *ST* I, q. 3, Aquinas discusses various forms of ontological composition that pertain to creatures or logical complexity that pertains to our way of thinking conceptually about creatures, and he systematically denies that such forms of composition pertain to the divine nature. He thus denies that our logical conceptions of composition can be rightly ascribed in a literal way to God. It is important to note that in this context (*ST* I, q. 3), Aquinas is reflecting on the mystery of the divine essence, which Christian theology claims is proper to all three trinitarian persons (*homoousios*). Therefore, his reflections on divine simplicity are organically related to a broader vision of trinitarian theology that is being explored. Here, four of the principal forms of composition in creatures and non-composition in God that Aquinas treats will be noted, all of which have some foundation in the biblical and patristic material noted above, and all of which have consequences for Aquinas's understanding of the Trinity.

Form and Matter

Following Aristotle, Aquinas thinks that every physical, material being that humans experience in the cosmos is a form-matter composite.[25] 'Form' in this context designates the substantial determination

---

25. Aquinas, *De Principiis Naturae*, in *Opuscula Philosophica*, ed. R. Spiazzi (Rome: Marietti, 1954), cc. 3–8.

of a given thing such that it has a nature of a given kind and properties that are specific to that nature. The form of an orange tree, for example, is its genus and species. Each tree falls within the genus of vegetative living things and additionally within the species of trees that produce a distinctive kind of fruit according to its organic constitution and material properties. Understood in this way, the form of a physical reality accounts for its nature, properties, and sameness of kind, relative to others. Matter, meanwhile, denotes the physical component parts of a natural form, as well as the radical potency present in and through all the material parts, such that every physical reality is potentially subject to indefinite transformation by substantial corruption and the subsequent generation of new forms. Even though it is always subject to potential transformation, the matter of any given reality is also always actuated by the natural form such that all the material parts are organized and arranged as parts of a given kind of thing, and they express the nature and properties of that form, in and through their material configurations. The material body of a hound is different from the material body of a human being, a fir tree, or a lake.

In virtue of these two principles, which are always present and mutually implicated in all material bodies, every physical reality we come to know is ontologically composite. Why, then, would we not ascribe a similar kind of ontological composition to God? Aquinas gives several reasons.[26] One is that any material thing is inevitably subject to passive change due to the action upon it by other realities and, therefore, is a reality caused by and ontologically dependent upon other realities. However, God the Creator is, by biblical definition, the one who gives being to all created realities. It is he who causes them to be, and not the inverse. Consequently, the divine nature cannot be a material thing, one that depends for its being on others. Likewise, Aquinas thinks that God is pure actuality, a plenitude of being that is transcendent and incomprehensibly

26. *ST* I, q. 3, a. 2.

perfect, and that gives being to all others, so his being is not subject to the potentiality of becoming more perfect. If he were material, this would be the case, as he would be continually subject to the potency of alteration for an ameliorated state. Thus, the divine nature is not a material body.

Arguments of this kind lead Aquinas to affirm that God is simple in a way material beings are not since he is not a composite of form and matter. We should note the principally apophatic character of this affirmation. God's nature cannot be imagined, represented sensibly, or conceived of after the fashion of any of the material bodies that we continually experience. He is the author of the physical cosmos and is even intimately present to all he creates as its transcendent author, but he is not a material being and, in this sense, is unimaginable.

Evidently this understanding of God aligns closely with the biblical and patristic notion we explored above, that God is not a material body. The idea also has trinitarian consequences. If the nature of God common to all three persons is not material, then the distinction of persons in God cannot take place in virtue of a material distinction of the divine nature, as if one person were to have some composite part of the deity and another person were to have another part. Instead, one must find alternative analogies to conceive of the distinction of persons in God, based on immaterial procession, so as to think about the eternal generation of the Word and the eternal spiration of the Holy Spirit. Classically, this is done by appeal to the analogy from human acts of the mind, that is to say, by conceiving of the Son analogically as the *Logos* or immaterial Word of the Father, who proceeds from the Father by similitude to a human act of immaterial understanding, and by conceiving of the Spirit analogically as Love, who proceeds from the Father and the Son by similitude to a human act of immaterial willing or of love.[27]

---

27. *ST* I, q. 27.

Essence and Individual

The second negation of composition in God follows closely from the first. Every material thing we encounter is an individual of a given kind. A given human being, such as St. Paul, is not identical with human nature as such but is one individual having human nature. The world we experience consists of a variety of such kinds of beings, such as humans, horses, trees, and so forth, each of which kind is instantiated not in a platonic idea but only ever in a multiplicity of concrete individuals. Therefore, when we think of what is essential to an individual being (such as a human being), we may define the essence by reference to both the form and matter if the latter is considered abstractly and universally as a necessary constituent of the nature of such things. That is to say, each human being consists essentially of both form and matter, of soul and individual body, not merely of the soul. But the individual matter of Paul is not essential to any other human being, nor could it be.[28] It is human to have an individual body, then, but it is not essential to us as humans to have the body of another individual human distinct from ourselves. Given this way of thinking about the essences of individuals we experience in the material world, is it also then possible to think of God along these lines? Is God (the Lord God of Israel) one god among others, an individualized divine nature who shares the same nature and properties with other such beings but who is individually distinct from the other gods?

Aquinas argues that this cannot be the case.[29] God is not composed of matter and form, so he is individuated by his form alone. Otherwise stated, God is unique in virtue of his individual deity. He is the one God because he alone has the nature of God. Evidently, this medieval scholastic idea aligns quite closely with the modern historical question we noted above pertaining to the development of Israelite religion. How, historically speaking, did the ancient

28. *ST* I, q. 75, a. 4; *SCG* II, c. 54.
29. *ST* I, q. 3, a. 3.

Israelites come to believe that YHWH is the one true God? That question is genealogical and is related to ancient claims of prophetic revelation, while the question we are treating here is metaphysical and has a philosophical dimension. Ultimately, however, the two topics are deeply related since the genealogical question seeks to resolve the question of when and how the people of Israel came to the conviction of something like the idea formulated by Aquinas and other theologians in a more theoretical mode, namely that God alone is God, that he alone possesses the nature and attributes of the one God and Creator of all things.

This idea also has trinitarian consequences since it suggests that if the three persons each possess the divine nature in its fullness, then they are not three individual beings, each having the divine nature in the same way three human persons have human nature, that is to say as distinct substances. Rather each has the fullness of the divine nature within his person, and thus they are each the one God since there is no composition of nature and individual in God. The three persons are 'consubstantial.'

Essence and Existence

Aquinas posits a real distinction in all created beings of essence and existence (or *esse* in Latin).[30] Essence, for Aquinas, signifies the nature of a given thing. In material beings, the essence consists of both form and matter, where the latter is conceived of abstractly in universal terms. For example, it is not essential to all human beings to have the body of a given individual like Paul, nor could it be, but it is essential to all human beings to have a physical body as well as a soul. Therefore, the whole form-matter composite pertains to the essence of what it is to be human. In angelic realities, which are wholly immaterial, the essence pertains to the form alone, as each angel has a unique nature in virtue of its immaterial form and not in virtue of an immaterial body.

---

30. *De Ente et Essentia*; SCG II, c.52–54; *Quaestiones disputatae de potentia Dei*, q. 7, a. 2.

Esse signifies the act of being, or singular existence, of a given individual substance.[31] Each individual material essence (a human being or a horse or a tree) has an individual existence. This is true as well of each immaterial being (or angel); its existence is unique. Existence is thus common to all things in a way essence is not since the many created realities in the world are of many different natural kinds (essences), but they all have existence in common. At the same time, existence is proper to each individual reality in a wholly unique way, as the singular existence of the archangel Gabriel is distinct from that of a man, a pine tree, or a blade of grass. No created reality is the cause of its own existence. Instead, we see that all realities around us, including ourselves, come into and can go out of existence, and they are both given existence and sustained in being due to the causal activity of others. Nothing in creation exists merely by nature due to the kind of essence it has, such that it would exist by sheer primal necessity. Aquinas famously relates essence and existence in creatures to one another as potency is related to act. Each individual essence can be or not be, and thus is either in mere potency to exist or does truly exist. However, even when creatures do actually exist, they have the latent potency within them not to exist in virtue of their created status.

Aquinas argues that this kind of composition of essence and existence that is found in all created realities cannot obtain in God or his divine nature.[32] In differentiation from creation, God the Creator does not receive his being from another and is not caused to be. He simply is from all eternity and is the cause of all else that is. He communicates existence to others from the abundance of his own infinite and perfect being, but his being is not received from, ontologically enriched by, or dependent upon, his interactions with his creatures. If this is the case, then God is incomprehensibly different from his creation. His divine essence alone exists by nature and is

31. *De Ente et Essentia*, c.2, 5; *Quaestiones disputatae de potentia Dei* q. 7, a. 2, ad 9.
32. *ST* I, q. 3, a. 4.

ontologically necessary in a way no created reality can be. His essence also contains the plenitude of all existence since he is being essentially, in all that pertains to being, and all that comes to exist in creation comes from his prior actuality and perfection and is a merely participated and imperfect expression of God's transcendent nature.[33] In God, there is no ontological composition of essence and existence.

Evidently, this idea is deeply related to the Old Testament notion we touched upon above, regarding the idea that the God of Israel alone is the Creator of all that is, 'he who is,'[34] the one who gives being to all things. It also touches upon the idea in trinitarian theology that the Father, Son, and Holy Spirit each possess the plenitude of divine *esse* and that they all, therefore, give rise together to all that exists apart from God. In short, all acts of the Holy Trinity *ad extra* ('outside' of God) in the creation and the redemption, are works of all three persons, since all three possess the one essence of God and thus the one divine existence.[35] They each possess that plenitude from which all things proceed and come forth in being and by which all things are sustained in being. On this view, which is related logically to the doctrine of divine simplicity in the aforementioned respect, it is the Trinity that creates, sustains, and redeems all things in creation, and never merely one of the persons acting alone, as if the Father might act divinely as God and Lord, without the Son or the Spirit. The unity of trinitarian action and the doctrine of divine simplicity are deeply interrelated ideas.[36]

Substance and Accident

The final composition we will consider in this context pertains to substance and accidental property. As Aquinas notes, created realities are complex ontologically since they are each composed of substance

33. *ST* I, q. 13, a. 11.
34. Exod 3:14–15; Isa 45; John 8:58.
35. *ST* I, q. 42.
36. *ST* I, q. 11, a. 3.

and accidents. That is to say, they have unity as individual substances (like a singular tree or a human), and they also have properties such as a given quantity, qualities, relations to other things around them, and so forth. Human qualities such as intelligence or moral excellence are not identical with the whole human substance (as if a person were his or her act of understanding or volition) but characterize human beings as important properties.

Following Augustine, Aquinas argues that this kind of ontological composition does not exist in the divine nature.[37] One reason has to do with act and potency argumentation. A given substance that has accidental qualities is in ontological potency to have or not have the qualities in question, especially if these qualities emerge and develop dynamically. The divine nature, however, is not in potency to further development through a historicity of divine becoming and does not depend upon any other reality causally so as to develop in being (for example, through interaction with creation). Instead, what we call God's 'essence' entails a numinous plenitude such that God is perfect in being from all eternity to all eternity.[38] A similar argument follows from the negation of the real distinction of essence and existence in God. If God possesses essentially, or by nature, the fullness of existence and communicates being to all others as Creator, then God does not develop in existence progressively, as he would if he had something like the equivalent of accidental properties as they are found in human beings.[39]

On this view, we may still affirm (along with Aquinas and other like-minded medieval theologians) that God actively knows and loves all that exists in the creation. Indeed, Aquinas argues at length that all that exists in creation comes forth into being from the knowledge and love that characterize the divine essence.[40] Nevertheless, such knowledge and love of the divine nature are not like human

37. *ST* I, q. 3, a. 6.
38. *ST* I, q. 4.
39. *ST* I, q. 3, a. 6.
40. *ST* I, qq. 14, 19, 20.

understanding and loving, at least in that they are not enriched or historically qualified positively in a developmental fashion by engagement with creation. Rather, God creates out of the plenitude of eternal contemplation and love that characterizes his very nature as God.[41] Were this not the case and were God to learn experimentally from creation and grow in moral virtue through his engagement with it, then creation would in some sense, actively qualify and cause God to be, and the two would necessarily exist within a larger co-constituting system, an idea that stands in tension with traditional biblical and patristic notions of Creator and creation.

As we have noted above, Augustine argues in a similar vein that God is not wise or good by qualification but that God is his goodness and wisdom. This idea has consequences for trinitarian theology in several ways. First, it means that one cannot differentiate the persons in God by appeal to distinct natural characteristics, as if God were powerful only in his paternity, wise only in his filiation, and good only in his spiration. Instead, all three persons partake of the plenitude of the divine essence and, therefore, also partake of the plenitude of all divine 'qualities,' which are mysteriously identical with the essence of God.[42] The Father, Son, and Holy Spirit possess in equal and identical measure the power, wisdom, and goodness of God that characterize his essential life.[43] Second, the divine attributes, such as wisdom and goodness, must also be in some real sense identical with one another. What we perceive in creation as distinct features of human beings, such as knowledge and love, can and must be ascribed to the divine nature, but what we signify when we indicate them in God is something that is mysteriously one in God himself.[44] The divine simplicity, perfection, goodness, eternity, power, and so forth are identical in God, yet each of these terms helps us indicate more clearly what God is, even if his essence

41. *ST* I, q. 14, a. 8 and q. 20, a. 2.
42. *ST* I, q. 42, aa. 1 and 4.
43. *ST* I, q. 39, aa. 7–8.
44. *ST* I, q. 13, aa. 2 and 4.

remains beyond our plenary comprehension. Finally, on this view, the persons in the Trinity cannot be distinguished by various qualities or accidental properties they acquire due to their respective actions in the economy of creation and salvation.[45] For example, the Father is not differentiated from the Son by his unique qualifying action of creation, and the Son is not differentiated by his unique action of redemption or Incarnation. Rather, the divine persons are at the origin of all that occurs in the economy of creation, and they act in virtue of the essence they share as the one God. That action does not re-qualify or enrich them collectively or individually but is the expression of the plenitude of trinitarian life that they possess inalienably from eternity.

Trinitarian Persons and Divine Simplicity

Aquinas's theology of divine simplicity has a direct bearing on the way in which he conceives of the distinction of trinitarian persons. If the three persons are each the one God and subsist as the one God, then the real distinctions that obtain between them do not derive from the divine nature which they share but from the two processions of generation and spiration and from the relations of origin that these processions instantiate. The Father eternally begets the Son as his Word and, in so doing, communicates to the Son all that he is and has as God.[46] The Father and the Son eternally spirate the Holy Spirit as their reciprocal Love and, in so doing, communicate to the Spirit all that they have and are as God.[47] The Son is thus related to the Father eternally as the one he originates from, and the Spirit likewise to the Father and the Son. Like other scholastics, such as Albert the Great and Bonaventure, Aquinas argues that the relations of origin in the Holy Trinity are not accidental properties of the persons but are mysteriously subsistent.[48] The

---

45. This viewpoint contrasts notably with Karl Rahner, *The Trinity*, 24–30.
46. *ST* I, q. 27, a. 2; qq. 33–34.
47. *ST* I, q. 27, aa. 3–4; qq. 36–38.
48. *ST* I, q. 29, a. 4. Bonaventure, *Commentaria in quatuor libros Sententiarum*. 4 vols.

Father is his paternity; he is a principle of origin of the Son and the Holy Spirit in all that he is, as font of the Trinitarian life. The Son is his filiation; he is from the Father and for the spiration of the Spirit in all that he is as Word. The Spirit is his spiration; he is from the Father and the Son in all he is.[49] Each person is truly God (having in himself the plenitude of the divine essence), and each person possesses his deity in a particular personal mode. He is God in either a paternal, filial, or spirated way.[50] Such notions follow directly from the two-fold affirmation that (1) the divine essence is simple in the ways indicated above and (2) the three persons are one in essence (consubstantial, *homoousios*), in accord with the formulation of the Nicene Creed.[51]

This view of the trinitarian persons underscores both the relational primacy of the Father and the radical egalitarianism that obtains in God. The Father is the principle and font of trinitarian life, but he is not greater in nature or ontological stature than the Word or the Spirit, even if these two derive from him originally. Indeed, they receive eternally from him all that he is as God, in the simplicity and plenitude of his divine being and life. This affirmation does not negate or eclipse the real distinction of the persons in God or the inter-personal reality of their communion or their relationships with creatures by grace. On the contrary, this way of indicating personal distinction in God augments a sense of their communion as mutual indwelling. The inter-personal communion of the Trinity implies a singular, shared, mutual essence of the one God present in all three persons.[52] This means that by perichoresis, or mutual indwelling, the whole of 'what'

(Ad Claras Aquas, Quaracchi: Prope Florentiam Ex Typographia Collegii S. Bonaventurae, 1882–89) d. 26, a. un, q. 3. Gilles Emery, "La relation dans la théologie de saint Albert le Grand," in *Albertus Magnus: Zum Gedenken nach 800 Jahren: Neue Zugänge, Aspekte und Perspektiven*. ed. Walter Senner, OP (Berlin: Akademie Verlag, 2001), 455–65.

49. *ST* I, q. 33, a. 2.

50. Gilles Emery, "The Personal Mode of Trinitarian Action in Saint Thomas Aquinas," *The Thomist* 69, no. 1 (2005): 31–77.

51. Gilles Emery, 'Essentialism or Personalism in the Treatise on God in St. Thomas Aquinas?' *The Thomist* 64, no. 4 (2000): 521–63.

52. *ST* I, q. 42, a. 5.

the Father is, is in the Son and the Spirit, and the whole of 'what' the Son is, is in the Father and the Spirit, and the whole of 'what' the Spirit is, in his divine plenitude, is in the Father and the Son. This mutual indwelling is also accomplished from and in the living and eternal 'cycle' of trinitarian processions so that the Father is in the Son and Spirit insofar as he communicates to them to be from him all that they are as God, yet in personal distinction. They likewise only have in themselves all that the other two do, either as one who receives all that he is from the Father and gives it to the Spirit with the Father (in the case of the Son) or as one who receives all that he is from the Father and the Son (in the case of the Spirit).

The distinction of persons in their self-communication to creatures by grace is also underscored by this doctrine of divine simplicity since it allows one to appreciate that when all three persons each act distinctly, they also always act with the other two. All actions of the Father, while paternal in mode, also imply common action of the Son and Spirit respectively, who act in their own irreducibly distinct personal modes of action. When one person is active in his distinctness, the other two must also be active in their relative modes of distinctness. If the Father communicates grace to a human person, in his distinctive mode as Father, then the Son also does so with him, in his distinctive mode as the begotten Son of the Father, and the Spirit in his distinctive mode as the spirated Love of the Father and the Son. Each person is truly God, so that when we commune by grace with Jesus Christ, who is the Son of God, we also commune with one who, as God and Lord, is in perfect communion with the Father, indeed one in being with the Father, in the sense just indicated. In other words, communion with one person is always communion with that person in his personal action, but it is also communion with the other two persons in their personal action, so that the reciprocity of interpersonal relationship with one person of the Trinity that grace effectuates in us, implicates personal relationship with the whole Trinity, as a communion of persons, and without conceiving of the latter in any way as a mere abstract essence.

Alternative Medieval Concepts

As noted above, the treatment of divine simplicity in Western medieval scholasticism is far from homogeneous. Although Aquinas's conception of divine simplicity has been historically influential, alternative conceptions exist that have had similarly important influence in the Western theological tradition. Though they are each Franciscans, the distinctive and, in some sense, incompatible conceptions of John Duns Scotus and William of Ockham each deserve particular consideration in this respect.

Scotus's conception of divine simplicity can be helpfully contrasted with that of Aquinas in two ways. First, Scotus posits, in keeping with Augustine and Aquinas, that God's essence and nature is simple, in the sense that it is non-composite and individually unique. However, he retains what has come to be called 'a formal distinction' of the attributes of the one God. Aquinas held that our diverse ways of indicating God through divine names or attributes is semantically meaningful since each name denotes something true about God. Terms such as divine wisdom, goodness, justice, mercy, and so on each say something true of God. However, these terms denote what is truly one and identical in God's own essence, not formally or essentially distinct. What we call God's wisdom, goodness, justice, and mercy are truly one in God's own life and nature.[53] Scotus, meanwhile, predicates these terms to God while underscoring that the attributes they specify in God are formally distinct and not reducible to one another specifically in the eternal life of God. He does not predicate that they are accidental to one another, nor does he claim that they are properties of the essence. Like Augustine and Aquinas, he denies this kind of composition in God, but his notion of simplicity is more 'complex' than that of Aquinas because he believes that the language we use for God's essence when we employ terms for God must correspond in a partially univocal way to the

---

53. *ST* I, q. 13, aa. 2–4.

very reality of God's essence, and since we use distinct terms and each is posited univocally and truly of God in some sense, these distinctions in speech must correspond to something formally distinct in the nature of God.[54] Scotus wants to underscore the harmony between our way of speaking of God and the very nature of God that we denote rightly in our speech.

This view of simplicity has significant consequences in Scotus' treatment of the trinitarian persons. Unlike Aquinas, who seeks to distinguish the persons of the Trinity primarily by reference to their relations of origin, Scotus distinguishes the persons in part by recourse to the notion of distinct eternal natural actions of the person of the Father. Insofar as the Father naturally produces thought through the essential activity of understanding, so he produces an immaterial Word (analogous to a concept) that is his natural offspring. This Word is infinite in perfection and consequently is a personal reality (since any reality that is infinite in perfection must be personal). Insofar as the Father naturally loves, through the essential activity of loving, he spirates the Spirit who is Love. This Love is infinite in perfection and, consequently, is a personal reality. The formal distinction of understanding and love that is applicable to God according to the distinction of attributes of the divine essence thus plays an important role in trinitarian theology. The Father is characterized by formally distinct natural actions that produce distinct persons. The logic of Scotus' position permits him to claim overtly that once one has identified the formally distinct attributes of the essence of God and the naturally distinct operations that they imply, which are infinite in perfection, one can, in turn, demonstrate rationally by philosophical argument that there are eternal personal processions in God of Word and Love. While Aquinas argues that natural reason cannot demonstrate the existence of the Trinity as the mystery of the inner life of God (and so this has to be revealed to be

54. Duns Scotus, John. 1950–2013. *Opera omnia*. Edited by C. Balić and others. Rome: Typis Polyglottis Vaticani, *Ordinatio* 1.8.1.4, nos. 192–93 [*Opera omnia*, 261–62 (vol. 4)]. Cross, *Duns Scotus on God*, 107–11, 235–40.

known), Scotus argues that there is some real possibility of natural knowledge of the trinitarian processions, based on his doctrine of formal distinction, and his mitigated reception of the doctrine of divine simplicity.[55] Scotus' theology thus appears less apophatic than that of Aquinas, suggesting a marked confidence in the natural dispositions of human reason to attain understanding about God's inner life as Trinity, as reflected both in the doctrine of univocal divine names and the theory of formal distinction.

Ockham's position on divine simplicity is, in many respects, the inverse of Scotus's. Ockham posits that there is such a marked notion of divine simplicity that obtains when one thinks of God that it is difficult to entertain the very notions of eternal processions and distinction of persons in God. If God is simple, how can God be understood as a Trinity? Ockham problematizes the traditional Augustinian notion of a 'psychological similitude' that conceives of the two processions of the Word and Spirit by comparison to human mental acts of understanding and love, respectively. This similitude is not intelligible for Ockham, in light of the doctrine of divine simplicity, except as something akin to a metaphor.[56] The reason is that everything that is found in one divine person is found in another if they are truly one in essence, and the activities of understanding and will are proper to each person, so they cannot be distinguished by such activities. The Church affirms that there is a distinction of persons in God according to relation of origin, and so Ockham derives a way to affirm nominally a set of propositions about the Trinity that are logically consistent. He is reticent, however, about our capacity to attain any true knowledge of the eternal processions of the Trinity in this life (whether analogically or univocally). This reservation is related to his notion of divine simplicity.

---

55. Duns Scotus, John. 1950–2013. *Opera omnia, Ordinatio* 1.2.2.1–4, nos. 221–22, 226, 355–56 [*Opera omnia*, 2:259–63, 336]. Cross, *Duns Scotus on God*, 132–42, 153–55.

56. William of Ockham. *Opera theologica*. Vols. 1–10 (St. Bonaventure, NY: Franciscan Institute Publications, 1967–86.). d. 2, q. 1 [*Opera Theologica* [*oTh.*] 2]; d. 1, q. 6 [*oTh.* 1]; d. 7, q. 2 [*oTh.* 3]; Russell L. Friedman, *Medieval Trinitarian Thought from Aquinas to Ockham*. Cambridge: Cambridge University Press, 2010), 124–31.

Another alternative is presented by the fourteenth-century Byzantine theologian, Gregory Palamas, who distinguishes between the essence and energies of God. This distinction has applications in Gregory's theology of grace and divinization. By God's gift, human beings are invited to participate in the energies of God, but they are not able to apprehend or enjoy any immediate spiritual communion with his essence, even in heaven. They do participate in the life of God in himself but under a condition.[57] This view is influential with some Eastern Christians and can be associated logically with those who are critical of the *Filioque*, the affirmation of the procession of the Spirit from the Father and the Son. Some Western theologians like Augustine, Anselm, and Aquinas (in differing ways) distinguish the Son from the Spirit based on relations of origin, and so they underscore that there must be a relation of origin of the Spirit from the Son. Eastern theologians inspired by Palamas, who posit a highly qualified concept of divine simplicity, may accept the Cappadocian notion of the generation of the Son from the Father and of the procession of the Spirit from the Father without feeling constrained by the Western concept of the doctrine of simplicity to resolve the question of the relation of the Son to the Spirit (the relation of origin between them).[58] Therefore, they may argue that the absence of distinction between essence and energies in Western theology (and the corresponding notion of God's essence as non-composite) is logically related to the Western affirmation of the *Filioque*. Furthermore, some argue (paradoxically) that the Western concept of simplicity leads to pantheism since it somehow implies that God's essence is identical with his energies, and thus, God is identical with his activity in the world.[59] This latter claim seems to brazenly ignore clear conceptual arguments to the contrary.

57. Gregory Palamas, *The Triads*, trans. N. Gendle (Mahwah: NJ: Paulist Press, 1983), 93–112.

58. George C. Papademetriou, *Introduction to St. Gregory Palamas* (Brookline, MA: Holy Cross Orthodox Press, 2004), 77–94.

59. Vladimir Lossky, *The Mystical Theology of the Eastern Church* (Yonkers, NY: SVS Press, 1997), 73–75.

Classical Reformation Notions

Neither Martin Luther nor John Calvin produced extensive reflections on the concept of divine simplicity. Luther does insist thematically on God's hiddenness and his inaccessibility to all merely human modes of knowledge, which some see as implying a notion of divine simplicity.[60] Calvin, meanwhile, unambiguously underscores God's simplicity in the context of his discussions of the equality, unity, and real distinction of the trinitarian persons.[61] Their respective presentations of trinitarian theology are often modest when it comes to reflection on the inner life of the processions of the persons, a reserve that is perhaps indicative of a measured acceptation of the trinitarian reserve of Ockham mentioned above. Instead of focusing on the immanent life of the Trinity, their theologies indicate truths of revelation manifest especially in light of the Incarnation, life, atonement, and resurrection of Jesus of Nazareth. However, later Protestant scholastic theology, particularly in the Reformed tradition, made appeal to the notion of divine simplicity in a more thematic fashion, and the idea is present in various confessional decrees in the Lutheran, Reformed, and Anglican traditions respectively, such as those of the Augsburg Confession, the Belgic Confession, the Thirty-Nine Articles of Religion, the Westminster Confession of Faith, the Savoy Declaration, and the Second London Confession of Faith. These statements typically underscore, at the very least, that the divine nature is non-bodily (without parts) and one, in addition to being good, infinite, eternal, and characterized by activities of knowledge and love that are not historically complex and developmental in the way those of human beings are.

---

60. See John W. Hoyum, "Luther and Some Lutherans on Divine Simplicity and Hiddenness," *Lutheran Quarterly* 34, no. 4 (2020): 390–409.

61. John Calvin, *Institutes of the Christian Religion*, trans. F. L. Battles (Philadelphia: Westminster, 1961), I, ch. 13, 2.

MODERN TRENDS

Spinoza and Hegel

The seventeenth-century philosophy of Baruch Spinoza presents a potential challenge to theories of divine simplicity, particularly through its contestation of traditional theistic notions of God. Interpretations of Spinoza's *Ethics* are famously controverted. However, it is clear that he posits in the *First Part* that God is best understood uniquely by recourse to philosophy (and not revelation), and that God is defined as the causal source of the natural world, to whom all entities or characteristics of nature are attributed as properties are attributed to a solitary substance.[62] Furthermore, the natural world emerges from God by necessity and is, in a sense, identical with God as a single subject to whom an infinite number of properties found in nature may be attributed, realities studied by the natural sciences and rational philosophy.[63] Whether Spinoza is a pantheist or an atheist, his decision to redefine 'God' in naturalistic terms effectively renders the first principle co-extensive with the material cosmos. Spinozist metaphysics thus posits a universe that is one, but that is not simple. Nature is a unity of parts that can be explained by recourse to a unified system of causal necessities studied by scientifically informed natural philosophers. We might speak here of a total unity of composition that is transparent to reason and thus, in a sense, comprehensively simple, both ontologically and logically. This last point is important since Spinoza wishes to reject systematically any recourse to supernatural revelation in order to explain the world; natural reason suffices to understand everything. One can argue, however, that the problem then emerges of what is primary: the reason of the universe that informs matter, or the materiality of the universe that gives rise to mind. Nature, or 'God,' seems somehow to consist in both.

---

62. Baruch Spinoza, *Ethics: Proved in Geometrical Order*, trans. M. Silverthorne (Cambridge: Cambridge University Press, 2018) *First Part*, propositions 1–15.
63. Spinoza, *Ethics*, propositions 16–18.

In the nineteenth century, Hegel, inspired by Spinoza, seeks to provide a post-Enlightenment metaphysical analysis of world history that is philosophical and all-comprehensive. But he takes a different approach to Spinoza, making use both of dogmatic Christian resources, as well as pre-modern philosophical resources, such as the thought of Aristotle. From Aristotle, Hegel takes up the notion of God as thought thinking itself and the conception of teleology, which Spinoza rejected. However, he reinterprets these Aristotelian notions historically and sees God's own intellectual actualization as occurring in and through the history of created reality, not only in the physical cosmos and animal life, but especially in the spirit and culture of human persons (art, politics, religion, and philosophy).[64] The composite unity of God and the world that one finds in Spinoza's naturalism is thus rethought in historical terms by appeal to an immanentistic dynamic, the unfolding of divine spirit in and through the history of the human spirit. Furthermore, this understanding of God is interpreted in overtly trinitarian terms. The traditional doctrinal depictions of God as Father, Son, and Holy Spirit are religious representations of an earlier stage of human reflection, one that comes to maturity when recast in distinctly philosophical terms. The Father represents divine Spirit prior to the unfolding of the history of the world, while the Son represents eternal Spirit in its free self-emptying identification with the contrary attributes of finitude and temporality, as well as subjection to non-being. God the Holy Spirit represents the reconciliation of the dialectical movement in God to self-identify with God's contrary, and so, historical Spirit that is not merely finite or infinite, temporal or eternal, but all these things simultaneously, reconciled within the context of a greater teleological whole. God will become all in all and, in so doing, will become God's plenary self. This final state concludes with the emergence within history of a human culture of rational perfection, one

---

64. Georg W. F. Hegel, *The Phenomenology of Spirit*, trans. T. Pinkard (Cambridge: Cambridge University Press, 2018), 454–67.

that attains a rational coherence with God (the immanent and transcendent principle of all history).[65] Hegel thinks that this age of the Spirit is manifest in modern society through liberal democratic freedom, where Enlightenment philosophical education is placed at the service of international order. This 'end of history' is the age of the Holy Spirit.

The First Vatican Council

The First Vatican Council re-affirmed the Catholic Church's theological commitment to a doctrine of divine simplicity in 1870 in the dogmatic constitution *Dei Filius*.[66] In historical context, this document seeks to exclude a pantheistic conception of the deity or the cosmos associated at the time with the philosophies of Spinoza and Hegel. In doing so, it sought to underscore the continued philosophical viability of classical metaphysics and the theological normativity of classical conceptions of the Trinity inherited from thinkers like Augustine and Aquinas. As we have noted above, various classical scholastic schools in the Western and Eastern traditions promoted diverse accounts of the simplicity of the divine nature of the Trinity. The Council was not seeking to adjudicate between various patristic traditions or scholastic schools but instead sought to affirm in a general way the classical affirmation of the mysterious transcendence, eternity, and immutable identity of the one God over and against competing conceptions of God as historical or ontologically composite with creation. This Catholic restatement of the mystery of divine transcendence is closely related logically to the claim of the council that belief in God is reasonable and that God's existence can be demonstrated by natural reason. The human person is orientated by its intellectual nature toward an encounter with the transcendent mystery of God. Accordingly, modern and contemporary

---

65. Georg W. F. Hegel, "The Consummate Religion," in *Lectures on the Philosophy of Religion, The Lectures of 1827*, vol. 3, edited by P. C. Hodgson, translated by R. F. Brown, P. C. Hodgson, J. M. Stewart (Berkeley: University of California Press, 2006), 426–90.
66. First Vatican Council. *Dei Filius*, chapter 1.

Catholic authors from a variety of schools have sought to present anew, explain, and defend a vibrant notion of divine simplicity.[67] Contemporary Protestant philosophers and theologians have often followed suit by seeking to underscore the essential role that the affirmation of divine simplicity plays in classical Reformed notions of God as transcendent Creator and as Trinity.[68]

Modern Continental Trinitarian Trends

In mainstream modern continental theology, however, alternative trends have emerged. One might summarize this situation by arguing that divine freedom has come to play the role in modern trinitarian theology that divine simplicity plays in classical trinitarian thought. Hegel's understanding of the Trinity is a remote influence in this respect. For Hegel, as we have noted, the Trinity is a pre-Enlightenment dogmatic religious representation that can be reconceptualized philosophically so as to indicate the ontological process that is at the heart of reality. That is the process of the diremption of absolute spirit by which God self-identifies freely with contraries to God's own self and eventually achieves reconciliation with God's self in and through a historical process of development. God, represented as Father, is impassible, eternal, and infinite,

---

67. Scheeben, *Handbook of Catholic Dogmatics*, vol. II; Reginald Garrigou-Lagrange, *De Deo Uno* (Paris: Desclée et Brouwer, 1938); Gilles Emery, *The Trinitarian Theology of Saint Thomas Aquinas* trans. F. Murphy (Oxford: Oxford University Press, 2007); Eleonore Stump, *Aquinas* (London: Routledge, 2006); Te Velde, *Aquinas on God: The 'Divine Science' of the* Summa Theologiae; Juan José Herrara, *La simplicidad divina según santo Tomás de Aquino* (Salta, Argentina: Ediciones de la Universidad del Norte Santo Tomás de Aquino, 2011); Thierry-Dominique Humbrecht, *Trinité et Création au Prisme de la Voie Négative chez Saint Thomas d'Aquin* (Paris: Parole et Silence, 2011); Serge-Thomas Bonino, *Dieu, 'Celui Qui Est': De Deo ut Uno* (Paris: Parole et Silence, 2016). See also the Thomistic reflections of Norman Kretzmann, *The Metaphysics of Theism: Aquinas's Natural Theology* in Summa Contra Gentiles I (Oxford: Clarendon Press, 1997).

68. See, for example, James E. Dolezal, *God without Parts: Divine Simplicity and the Metaphysics of God's Absoluteness* (Eugene: Pickwick Publications, 2011); Steven J. Duby, *Divine Simplicity: A Dogmatic Account* (London: Bloomsbury T&T Clark, 2016); Adonis Vidu, *The Same God Who Works in All Things: inseparable Operations in Trinitarian Theology* (Grand Rapids: Eerdmans, 2021).

while God represented as Son is subject in his very deity to temporality, finitude, death, and non-being. The Holy Spirit represents a new configuration of deity in which these two polarities of God explored in divine freedom achieve a new synthesis of greater rational plenitude, in and through the history of God's being as finite, as absolute spirit within temporal human historical spirit.

Modern trinitarian theologians typically disavow the rationalism and pantheistic tendencies of Hegel and maintain the transcendence of God as Creator and redeemer, as one who gives being to all things and redeems all things in Christ out of the plenitude of his pre-existent, eternal life, and inalienable creative power. However, in their 'corrective' to Hegel, they also typically affirm that God, in his transcendence, does have the freedom to identify with or to subject himself to his ontological contrary, without ceding his eternal and divine identity.[69] Thus, for thinkers like Moltmann and Jenson, God can be subject to historicity, passibility, or suffering even within his own being and essence as God (particularly in the Incarnation), and, in doing so, achieves a kind of di-polarity of freedom. He is free to exist simultaneously as eternal and temporal, impassible and suffering, immutable and mutable, and so forth.[70] Evidently, this kind of historical vision of God as freely kenotic and as able to exist in distinct modes is a vision of God as ontologically composite and not simple, at least not in the ways envisaged above. More moderate versions of this thesis affirm that God's human mode of being in the Incarnation, in which the Son as man is humanly subject to the Father in obedience, suffering, and death, are indicative of di-polar modes of being in the Trinity that pre-exist the human modes and that are analogous to them. So Barth posits a divine obedience in God of the Son to the Father that is constitutive of the life

---

69. Thomas Joseph White, *The Trinity: On the Nature and Mystery of the One God* (Washington, DC: The Catholic University of America Press, 2022), 397–99, 555–58.

70. Robert Jenson, *Systematic Theology* I (Oxford: Oxford University Press, 1997), 66; Jürgen Moltmann, *The Crucified God: The Cross of Christ as the Foundation and Criticism of Christian Life*, trans. R. A. Wilson and J. Bowden (San Francisco: Harper and Row, 1974), 202–4.

of God from all eternity, thus indicating a kind of composite nature in God, wherein God as Father has natural qualities of willing distinct from and juxtaposed to, those of the Son.[71] Bulgakov and von Balthasar, meanwhile, posit an eternal kenosis in God that precedes and is the exemplar for the kenosis of the passion, wherein the Son undergoes human death freely.[72] The Son, in his eternity, is subject as God to a mystery of self-emptying, mirrored by the Father's eternal self-emptying in generating the Son. The Spirit emerges from the two as the fruit of this mutual communion of free self-diremption.[73] If such ideas are to be taken as something more than metaphorical depictions of the divine processions, then they would seem to entail states of potency and actuation that are really distinct from one another in God and that are present in the divine nature as it unfolds in a 'pre-history', one that constitutes the distinct persons eternally as they undergo the fluctuations of their various natural modes of being. Under such conditions, one can speak of an eclipse or of a conceptually strategic abandonment of the theology of divine simplicity in modern mainstream continental trinitarian theology.

It should be noted in this context that the thinkers mentioned above are seeking to conserve many traditional Christian ideas regarding the mystery of the Trinity and to do so by translating the doctrine into a modern intellectual idiom, making use of (and reacting against) certain versions of post-Enlightenment ontology. They are beholden in this respect to various continental ontologies, but not in an uncritical way. They accept elements of Spinoza's and Hegel's break with pre-modern forms of metaphysics and embrace their notion of the world and human culture as an unfolding and evolving process from and in God. They also maintain Hegel's strategy of

71. *Church Dogmatics*, 4 vols., ed. and trans. G. W. Bromiley, T. F. Torrance (Edinburgh: T. & T. Clark, 1936–75) (hereafter *CD*), IV:1, Section 59: 157–357, especially 177–201.

72. Sergei Bulgakov, *The Lamb of God*, trans. B. Jakim (Grand Rapids: Eerdmans, 2008), 98–99; Hans Urs von Balthasar, *Theo-Drama*, vol. 4, 319–33.

73. Hans Urs von Balthasar, *Theo-Drama: Theological-Dramatic Theory*, vol. 3, *The Dramatis Personae: Persons in Christ*, trans. G. Harrison (San Francisco: Ignatius Press, 1992), 183–91, 521–23.

rehabilitating teleology and placing it in God (by positing the realization of act-potency composition in God), and like him, they also
seek to identify who God is by focusing on the unfolding dynamic of
God in history. However, they distance themselves, in part at least,
from the pantheistic connotations of Spinoza and Hegel, and argue
instead that creation depends utterly upon God for its being, even if
God determines himself freely in relation to the creation. What unfolds in the economy of trinitarian creation and redemption then
(the historical dynamic of the so-called economic Trinity) corresponds to the pre-existent and final teleological life of God (the uncreated, eternal dynamism of the immanent Trinity).

Some Analytic Objections
and Responses

Modern analytic philosophers who are theists sometimes object to
the doctrine of divine simplicity for a variety of reasons. Some, such
as Alvin Plantinga, note that the notion of simplicity entails that all
the divine attributes are identical with the essence of God.[74] They
object to this idea because they think that it naïvely reifies human,
abstract notions, such as goodness or wisdom, so as to identify them
mistakenly with the essence of God. This way of thinking would misguidedly project onto God a merely human abstract, logical way of
thinking, one analogous to the Platonic theory of forms, which projects universal human concepts problematically onto individuals and
onto the causal structure of reality. Understood in this way, divine
simplicity is a construct of human logic and has no place in realistic
discourse pertaining to God. Second, some philosophers worry that
the notion of subsistent relations in trinitarian theology is incoherent since relations, as they understand them, are either mere properties or are abstract entities (relation-sets of human logic) and not
something real in themselves. Richard Swinburne, for example, depicts the three persons of the Trinity as three perpetually co-existent

74. See Alvin Plantinga, *Does God Have a Nature?*, (Milwaukee: Marquette University Press, 1980).

individual centers of consciousness related to one another by causal origin and by a moral consensus of cooperation.[75] This vision of the Trinity is ontologically complex on many levels. Finally, and most commonly, many analytic theists worry that the notion of the divine simplicity is incompatible with a God who knows and loves, and who stands in real relation to his creation, makes choices, adjusts or responds to human behavior, and so forth. All engagements of God with creatures by way of knowledge and love must entail change in God, and thus invite us to disavow the doctrine of divine simplicity. William Hasker writes against the doctrine of divine simplicity for this reason, arguing that God must alter internally and perhaps develop in perfection over time based upon his real relations with creation.[76]

While a thorough consideration of such positions exceeds the scope of this essay, it should be noted that proponents of the classical doctrine of divine simplicity have developed a variety of responses to such objections. Here, we may indicate briefly some of their arguments. First, in response to Plantinga, it has been pointed out that the concepts we use to denote God's essence, such as goodness and wisdom, are abstract, but the process by which we qualify such concepts analogically so as to rightly denote God in himself entails that we acknowledge God's singular transcendence and distinctiveness as one who is the author of all that exists and therefore as one who is not caused and composite in the ways creatures are. The doctrine of simplicity then entails a careful analysis of the conditions under which it is permissible and even required to use property terms abstractly to denote the individual personal being of God, much as one may denote atomic structures in matter under the rubric of waves and particles simultaneously, while accepting the limitations of language and human concepts when doing so.[77] Second, the attribu-

75. Swinburne, *The Christian God*, 125–91.

76. William Hasker, "Is Divine Simplicity a Mistake?," *American Catholic Philosophical Quarterly* 90, no. 4 (2016): 699–725.

77. Eleonore Stump, "Simplicity and Aquinas's Quantum Metaphysics," in *Die*

tion of relations to the persons of the Trinity in a subsistent mode is based on the idea that mutual relativity emerges from the simultaneity of action and passion.[78] As the Father eternally begets the Son, so the Son is begotten of the Father, and in this respect, they are mutually related to one another in all that they each are in an ontologically reciprocal way. This idea in itself is not incoherent, and therefore its use is logically consistent with the simultaneous affirmations that God is one and that there are real relations in God. The fact that we never encounter such substantial relations in any created reality only serves to underscore the radical transcendence, alterity, and incomprehensibility of the trinitarian communion of persons, but it does not make that communion wholly unintelligible to us. The notion of subsistent relations is an analogical one that takes created relations and created substances and transposes something of each onto God by similitude while simultaneously respecting the greater dissimilitude of God with respect to each. The doctrine of divine simplicity plays a helpful role in this process since it invites one to acknowledge that each divine person is the one God, even while being distinct from the other two persons by relations of origin.[79] Third, it is true that affirmations of divine simplicity of the kind noted above do entail the negation of compositions of act and potency in God such that God's life would change progressively or develop qualitatively in virtue of his engagements with creatures. It does not, however, entail the negation of the ascription of choice to God, in relation to creatures, or of knowledge of creatures in God.[80] It does ensure that when theologians speak of God knowing the world or loving the world or choosing to act in this or that way, they do so while recognizing that God's knowledge and decrees stem from and express

Metaphysik des Aristoteles im Mittelalter: Rezeption Und Transformation, ed. Gerhard Krieger (Berlin: De Gruyter, 2016), 191–210.

78. Emery, The Trinitarian Theology of Saint Thomas Aquinas, 78–102.

79. Thomas Joseph White, "Divine Simplicity and the Holy Trinity," International Journal of Systematic Theology 18, no. 1 (2016): 66–93.

80. SCG III, c. 10–23.

his purely actual plenitude of perfection and fullness of existence.[81]
In this sense, God's knowledge, love, and choice-making for creation
stem from within his eternity and encompass an eternal awareness of
all that is in creation, in its temporality and development. His action
in the world stems from his perfection, that always already 'encompasses' all created historical being. This does not mean God cannot
'react' to creatures in new temporal initiatives, but only that when
he does so, such actions occur mysteriously in light of God's eternal
knowledge and love of himself and of the whole of his creation.[82]
Nor need this view lead to the denial of free will in creatures, since
God's creative knowledge is the source of the real and historically
contingent freedom of creatures, which God in his simplicity sustains in being, and protects in his providence.[83]

CONCLUSION

The controversies over divine simplicity are of conceptual importance. Although some may discount any appeal to this traditional
idea, it arguably arises within Christian history as a way to reflect on
themes in biblical literature. The mystery of God, the divine nature,
is not a composite body, an individual of a given kind who shares in
deity with others, a being who receives existence from others or participates in being, or a substance subject to historical alterations under the influence of actions effectuated by others. When promoters
of the notion of divine simplicity deny such compositions of God,
they wish to underscore his transcendence and numinous alterity so
as to indicate obliquely in human language him from whom all created things proceed and have being, and who is not himself created.

---

81. Michael J. Dodds, *The Unchanging God of Love: Thomas Aquinas and Contemporary Theology on Divine Immutability* (Washington, DC: The Catholic University of
America Press, 2008), 161–237.

82. Eleonore Stump, *The God of the Bible and the God of the Philosophers* (Milwaukee: Marquette University, 2016).

83. Dodds, *The Unchanging God of Love*, 170–83; Bonino, *Dieu, 'Celui Qui Est': De
Deo ut Uno*, 289–96, 676–82.

The doctrine is deeply related to the notion of divine unity since it is employed to underscore God's essential perfection, fullness of being, and immutable identity, attributes in virtue of which God is eternally unique and one in his incomprehensible existence.

Such ideas also have profound consequences for one's theological reflection on the mystery of the Trinity. As patristic and scholastic authors have underscored, the nature of God is present in its fullness in each person of the Trinity so that each is personally the one God. Therefore, the three persons are not distinguished by nature or by properties of the divine nature. Rather, they are rightly distinguished, on this view, by relations of origin through eternal generation and spiration. This understanding of the Trinity entails the idea that the three persons are each truly distinct, but also each equally and identically God, so that what results from the affirmation of divine simplicity is, arguably, a highly coherent notion of trinitarian monotheism. Each person can be understood as possessing a distinct personal mode of subsistence, or personal way of being God, in virtue of the relations of origin, even while having the fullness of the deity as the subsistent God. Therefore, each divine person exists only ever in real relation to the others even while also possessing in himself all that pertains to the others as God, in virtue of the divine essence that is common to the three.

Promoters of the doctrine of divine simplicity hold diverse views and sometimes draw divergent conclusions from appeal to the notion. Critics of the notion are equally diverse and continue to raise a variety of excellent challenges to the idea. This all being said, the notion of divine simplicity is at the center of ancient biblical and patristic thinking about the Trinity and is at the core of a great deal of traditional theological thinking. Those who reject the idea sometimes generate very original theologies of God, but also ones often riddled with significant conceptual difficulties. For these various reasons, the notion of divine simplicity will continue to be a mainstay consideration of Christian theology, especially in reflections pertaining to the Trinity, the doctrine of God, reasonable biblical interpretation, and the role of philosophical theology within Christian theology. Having recently been subject to a historical eclipse, the doctrine of divine simplicity seems to be re-emerging gradually in contemporary theology and shining anew, like the risen Son, who is eternally simply one in being with his Father and the Holy Spirit.

3

Divine Simplicity and the Holy Trinity

THE CHALLENGE OF DIVINE SIMPLICITY

The doctrine of divine simplicity is central to traditional Christian reflection about the mystery of God the Holy Trinity. The notion is influential in the work of Athanasius and the Cappadocian Fathers, as well as in the writings of Hilary and Augustine. It is present in the great scholastic doctors, such as Bonaventure, Albert, Aquinas, and Scotus (albeit in various ways). And it is a doctrinal teaching of the magisterium of the Catholic Church, both at the Fourth Lateran Council (1215), where the teaching is connected to the affirmations of the non-similitude of God and creatures (the analogy of being: in response to Joachim of Fiore), and at the First Vatican Council (1869–70), which affirms the transcendence of God as Creator (with respect to forms of pantheism derived from Spinoza and Hegelian notions of the historicization of deity).[1]

Originally published in the *International Journal of Systematic Theology* 18, no. 1 (2016): 65–93. Reprinted by permission of the publisher.

This chapter was written for the 2015 Classical Theism Project of the Philosophy Department of the University of St. Thomas (Minnesota). The funding source for the workshop was the John Templeton Foundation. I am grateful to Professors W. Matthews Grant and Eleonore Stump for their helpful comments on earlier drafts of this chapter.

1. Fourth Lateran Council, Denzinger, 800 and 805; First Vatican Council, *Dei Filius*, Denzinger, 1001; see also the condemnation of unitarianism, which contains the important insistence on the unity of the divine essence, by Pius V in the Constitution

The doctrine of divine simplicity has its noteworthy defenders in modern and contemporary theology, including within the realm of analytic philosophy.[2] It also has received intense scrutiny or criticism, especially within analytic theist circles.[3] More commonly, however, it has simply been ignored, particularly in the continental theological projects that remain of acute influence.[4] Nevertheless, ignorance of history is never good counsel. Consider in this respect two influential theological projects of the twentieth century, both controversial and both opposed by extremes, but which illustrate in similar ways the need for a doctrine of divine simplicity.

On the one hand, stands the representative trinitarian theology of Karl Barth. Barth's complex reflection defies any formulaic summaries, but it is quite clear that in his mature work, he habitually speaks of the Trinity by employing the language of single subject agency. God is he who expresses himself both in terms of his mode

Cum quorumdam hominum, August 7, 1955 (Denzinger 1880) (references are to the 43rd edition of Denzinger, *Compendium of Creeds, Definitions, and Declarations on Matters of Faith and Morals*, ed. P. Hünermann, R. Fastiggi and A. Nash (San Francisco: Ignatius Press, 2012)). A pertinent historical analysis is offered by Gilles Emery, "The Immutability of the God of Love and the Problem of Language concerning the 'Suffering of God,'" in *Divine Impassibility and the Mystery of Human Suffering*, ed. J. Keating and T. J. White (Grand Rapids: Eerdmans, 2009), 27–76.

    2. Matthias Scheeben, *Handbook of Catholic Dogmatics*, vol. II: *Doctrine about God or Theology in the Narrower Sense*, trans. M. J. Miller (Steubenville, OH: Emmaus Academic, 2022); Garrigou-Lagrange, *De Deo*; Kretzmann, *The Metaphysics of Theism: Aquinas's Natural Theology in* Summa Contra Gentiles I; Gilles Emery, *La théologie trinitaire de saint Thomas d'Aquin* (Paris: Cerf, 2004), G. Emery, *The Trinitarian Theology of Saint Thomas Aquinas*; Eleonore Stump, *Aquinas*; Te Velde, *Aquinas on God: The 'Divine Science' of the* Summa Theologiae; Juan José Herrara, *La simplicidad divina según santo Tomás de Aquino*; Thierry-Dominique Humbrecht, *Trinité et Création au Prisme de la Voie Négative chez Saint Thomas d'Aquin*.

    3. See, for example, Alvin Plantinga, *Does God Have a Nature?* (Milwaukee: Marquette University Press, 1980); Christopher Hughes, *On a Complex Theory of a Simple God: An Investigation in Aquinas' Philosophical Theology* (Ithaca and London: Cornell University Press, 1987); Swinburne, *The Christian God* (Oxford: Clarendon Press, 1994); William Hasker, *Metaphysics and the Tri-Personal God* (Oxford: Oxford University Press, 2013).

    4. I take it as a point of fact that there is no substantive historical and speculative engagement with the doctrine of divine simplicity in the work of Karl Barth, Karl Rahner, Wolfhart Pannenberg, Hans Urs von Balthasar or Walter Kasper. Barth does formulate some passing objections to the doctrine, some of which I will note below.

of being as Father and in his mode of being as Son.[5] Simultaneously, Barth conceptualizes the distinctions of persons in terms of
differentiated property terms: the Father is 'one who commands'
while the Son is 'one who obeys.'[6] Here, we can see two valid concerns: to maintain an acute insistence on the singularity and unity of the one God and to maintain the idea that the Holy Trinity
is revealed in and through the economy of salvation by the actions
and words of Christ who is obedient to the Father. But critical questions have been raised. Is the three-fold personal character of the
Trinity sufficiently underscored? Many critics claim that it is not.[7]
If the 'modes of being' of God as Father and Son are distinguished
by distinct properties (commandment/obedience), then the persons seem to be differentiated by natural properties rather than relational notions such as generation and spiration. Does this practice
maintain sufficiently the unity of the divine nature and will in God,
especially if the Father and Son are said to be one in essence (and

---

5. See, for example, Barth's claim that:

God is God in these two modes of being [as Father and Son] which cannot
be separated, which cannot be autonomous, but which cannot cease to be different. He is God in their concrete relationships the one to the other, in the
history which takes place between them. He is God only in these relationships
and therefore not in a Godhead which does not take part in this history, in the
relationships of its modes of being, which is neutral toward them ... The true
and living God is the One whose Godhead consists in this history, who is in
these three modes of being [as Father, Son and Spirit] the One God, the Eternal, the Almighty, the Holy, the Merciful, the One who loves in His freedom
and is free in His love.

CD, IV:1, 203.

6. CD IV:1, 200–1:

We have not only to deny but actually to affirm and understand as essential to
the being of God the offensive fact that there is in God Himself an above and a
below, a prius and a posterius, a superiority and a subordination ... His divine
unity consists in the fact that in Himself He is both One who is obeyed and
Another who obeys.

These two interconnected themes of uni-personal identity and intra-trinitarian obedience are especially forcefully summarized in CD IV:2, 43–4.

7. Including those most influenced by Barth: Moltmann and Balthasar, who clearly
wish to accentuate the distinction of personal subjects in God.

thus share all the same divine properties)? Some theologians have argued that Barth's theology is problematic in this respect.[8] In fact, the two issues noted here in Barth's trinitarian theology are perhaps interrelated. Barth does not locate personal distinction explicitly in relations of origin and relational notions like generation and spiration. Consequently, how can he understand God as three other than by assigning a differentiation of natural properties to persons within the Godhead? In any event, reasonable questions arise regarding both the plenary acknowledgement of the three persons and of the one divine nature, as understood in this influential theology.

Consider on the other extreme the analytic trinitarian theology of Richard Swinburne.[9] Swinburne understands the *homoousios* formula of Nicaea primarily in terms of a common essence or nature that is shared by the three persons of the Holy Trinity without implying an individual unity of being or substance.[10] He wishes especially to defend the rational intelligibility of the real distinction of the three persons of the Holy Trinity. Consequently, he affirms that the three persons are distinct individuals who are united in essence in that they each share in common the perfection of the divine nature.[11] Consequently, they are each unique subjects of

---

8. See, for example, Guy Mansini, "Can Humility and Obedience be Trinitarian Realities?," in *Thomas Aquinas and Karl Barth: An Unofficial Catholic–Protestant Dialogue*, ed. B. L. McCormack and T. J. White (Grand Rapids: Eerdmans, 2013), 71–98; Thomas Joseph White, *The Incarnate Lord: A Thomistic Study in Christology* (Washington, DC: The Catholic University of America Press, 2015), 277–307.

9. See especially in this regard, Swinburne, *The Christian God*, 125–91.

10. Swinburne, *The Christian God*, 164:

A monadic property of a divine individual G1 would be one which belonged to him, quite apart from his relations to anything else ... For just because the possession of a monadic property does not consist in any relation to other individuals, and so does not carry any consequences for other individuals, it would seem that any other individual of the same kind could have it.

11. Swinburne, *The Christian God*, 177:

The first divine individual is the one who actively causes another divine individual and, in co-operation with him, a third divine individual. The second divine individual is the one who actively causes only one further divine individual and that in co-operation with another divine individual. The third divine individual is he who is the active cause of existence (either by himself or in co-operation) of no other individual.

consciousness, understanding, and decision-making who are united in intellect and will only insofar as each decides to act always only in perfect concord and moral union with the two others.[12] Commentators have not failed to note that this conceptual portrait of the Holy Trinity comes precipitously close to tri-theism.[13] In seeming contrast to Barth, Swinburne clearly affirms the reality of three personal subjects in God and is unambiguous in maintaining the singularity of the nature common to the three persons. However, it seems he is less successful than Barth in preserving the truth that the three persons who share a common nature are *one in being*. Barth is arguably less clear about the identity of nature and the threeness of the persons, but he is quite clear about the oneness of being of the Holy Trinity.

Behind both these conceptions, there is a shared premise: that a modern re-articulation of the doctrine of the Holy Trinity need not have recourse to the traditional understanding of divine simplicity. For Barth, this decision is primarily theologically motivated, based upon his rejection of traditional metaphysical categories (which he terms the 'analogy of being').[14] For Swinburne, the decision is

12. Swinburne, *The Christian God*, 175:

Each of the postulated divine individuals would be omnipotent in the sense that each could at any period of time do anything logically possible—for example, bring it about that the earth moves round the sun in a clockwise direction. But the omnipotence of each individual is limited by his perfect goodness, and if one individual has promised the other individual that he will not perform actions (when there is not a unique best action) in this area (e.g. the area of movements of heavenly bodies), then his perfect goodness limits his omnipotence so that he does not do such an act. Thus each of two individuals with the [same] divine properties can be omnipotent.

13. Although this criticism is widespread, one can find a typical instance of it in Edward C. Feser, "Swinburne's Tri-Theism," *International Journal for Philosophy of Religion* 42, no. 3 (1997): 175–84.

14. See CD II:1, 332–5, where Barth discusses the doctrine of divine simplicity critically as a derivation of 'the platonic-aristotelian idea of being' (p. 334). Barth claims that we know naturally less of divine unity and simplicity than classical monotheism has claimed, and that we know God truly in his multiple divine attributes and historicity as a result of revelation. The passage suggests a typical Barthian dialectic between purely equivocal ascriptions for God (on a natural or philosophical level) and almost univocal ascriptions that are given uniquely christologically (by revelation). Barth does affirm a

philosophically motivated, based on the claim that certain classical notions of divine simplicity are inherently problematic.[15] However, the problems in each of these (conceptually contrasting) theologies arise due precisely to the absence of a doctrine of divine simplicity. This is true in Swinburne, particularly with regard to his rejection of the traditional affirmation that *in God, there exists no composition of nature and individual.* This is true in Barth, particularly with regard to his inattention to the traditional affirmation that *in God, there exists no composition of substance and property (or accident).* If these affirmations of divine simplicity are true, then, *pace* Barth, there can exist no differentiation of natural properties between the Father and the Son (such as commandment and obedience), and, *pace* Swinburne, there can exist no differentiation of nature and singularity of being (i.e., the three persons just are the one being who is God).

Barth is clearly correct to affirm that the three persons are one in being. Swinburne is clearly correct to affirm that they are truly distinct persons who share one and the same nature. We cannot clarify rightly, however, how both these affirmations are true if we do not engage with the problem of divine simplicity. Why? Because we cannot understand rightly what it means to say that God is one unless we clarify how the unity of God differs from or is like that of creatures. Unity occurs in creatures insofar as they are unified composites. In what way, then, is the one God like or unlike the composite creatures he has made? To ask this question is to ask the question of divine simplicity. This, in turn, has consequences for how we understand the eternal processions and relations of the persons in God. Aquinas argues that there is in God no real distinction of form and

---

qualified doctrine of divine simplicity in *CD* II:1, 444–61, which he interprets in terms of the unity of God as Creator: 'God Himself in His being for Himself is the one being which stands in need of nothing else and at the same time the one being by which everything else came into being and exists' (458). This unity is made known to us, however, uniquely due to the elective action of the trinitarian God: 'In face of the cross of Christ it is monstrous to describe the uniqueness of God as an object of 'natural' knowledge' (453).

15. See, in particular, Swinburne, *The Christian God*, 151–69.

matter, essence and individual, essence and existence, or substance and property. If this is the case, and if God the Father communicates to the Son and to the Spirit (with the Son) his very essence (as the *homoousios* formula of the Nicene-Constantinopolitan creed affirms), then we must say that the Father differs from the Son and the Spirit only according to relations of origin. Relationality, in this case, is not a natural property of the persons, but is 'subsistent.' Or we might say that the Father is eternally subsistent as one who is ever relational *toward* the Son and Spirit. He does not choose to generate or spirate the persons of the Son and the Holy Spirit, but he is the personal act of generation and co-spiration. This is likewise true of the other persons of the Trinity in their inherent relationality. Due to the mystery of divine simplicity, then, we ought to speak about the trinitarian persons as 'subsistent relations,' in order rightly to maintain a sense of their real personal distinctiveness and their authentic unity of being.

If this line of argument is correct, the doctrine of divine simplicity matters greatly for trinitarian theology, and needs to be recovered in depth, in view of a deeper reflection on the balance and coherence of trinitarian thought. I will argue for this position below in three stages. First, I will consider briefly key aspects of Aquinas's doctrine of divine simplicity. I will then draw some conclusions from this about the philosophical rationality of belief in the Holy Trinity. Finally, I will consider what the implications of a doctrine of divine simplicity are for understanding the trinitarian processions and the distinction of the persons in God as 'subsistent relations.' This will allow us to return briefly to some of the dilemmas that are present in the modern debates on trinitarian theology (both continental and analytic) and suggest theological points of reference that might be gained from the consideration of Aquinas's trinitarian theology.

AQUINAS ON DIVINE SIMPLICITY

In considering Aquinas's account of divine simplicity, there are two Thomist presuppositions that should be kept in mind. First, our knowledge of God's simplicity is derived indirectly from the consideration of his created effects, whether in the order of nature or of grace. We come to know God a posteriori, passing from effects to their primary cause, and not by some kind of apriorist intuition or immediate conceptual grasp.[16] This is significant because it means that whatever God's simplicity is, it is not identical with something intuited immediately from various forms of simplicity in creatures. Second, the notion of simplicity as a divine attribute for Aquinas is strongly characterized by apophatic qualifications. Here, some nuance is important. Against Maimonides, Aquinas clearly does think that the attribution of simplicity denotes *positively* something that is true of God's very being.[17] However, we do not perceive directly the reality that we denote positively.[18] We can only craft notions of divine simplicity by comparisons made with created realities. The qualified notion of simplicity that we formulate to speak of God, then, stems in large part from *negations of compositions* found in creatures that must be made when we speak of the mystery of God. Such thinking entails assignations of unity or identity in God of what is distinct in creatures (for example, the idea that God just is his existence or is *esse* in God's very essence or is *id quod est*). Such thinking, while ultimately always positive in ascription, is also

---

16. *ST* I, q. 2, a. 1; q. 12, aa. 12–13.

17. *ST* I, q. 13, a. 2: 'these names *signify the divine substance*, and are predicated *substantially* of God, although they fall short of a full representation of Him'. See also *ST* I, q. 13, a. 5 and Aquinas, *De Potentia Dei*, in *Quaestiones Disputatae*, vol. II, ed. R Spiazzi (Rome: Marietti, 1965), q. 7, a. 7 (hereafter *De Pot.*). I have formulated criticisms of what I take to be an exaggerated apophaticism in prominent strands of modern Thomism in White, *Wisdom in the Face of Modernity: A Study in Thomistic Natural Theology*, ch. 8. Especially helpful on the subject of Aquinas and the primacy of affirmative significations of divine names is the work by Thierry-Dominique Humbrecht, *Théologie négative et noms divins chez Saint Thomas d'Aquin* (Paris: J. Vrin, 2005).

18. *ST* I, q. 13, a. 3.

always partially apophatic in method, since we ascribe to God in his incomprehensibility and transcendence a way of being that is unlike that of any composite reality we experience directly.

I will begin, then, with a key text from Aquinas's mature work: the six series of negations identified in his treatment of divine simplicity in question 3 of the *Summa theologica, prima pars*. Here, Thomas considers various kinds of ontological composition that arise in creatures and the impossibility of their presence in God. These can be grouped into four headings for the sake of economy: material composition, the distinction between essence and individual, the distinction between essence and existence, and the distinction between substance and property (or accident). These groupings correspond to articles 2, 3, 4, and 6 of question 3. We can consider each of these briefly and, in doing so, note various ways of thinking about God (some quite influential or well-known) that Aquinas's philosophy of divine simplicity implicitly disavows.

Material Composition

It is quite clear that there are physical realities in the world. What physical realities are is far more difficult to determine. We need not embark here, however, on a full-scale consideration of mereological problems (the metaphysical topic of whole and parts) in order to note three most basic things.[19] First, there are all around us entities, physical beings, that are in some way unified, or one. We distinguish natural beings from one another, and for the sake of argument, it need not matter at how micro or macro a level we do this, be it with regard to quarks, aardvarks, or stars. There are unified, singular beings. Second, the various natural realities that exist around us have determinations of natural kind: they can be named according to stable properties that inhere in them, by which we can rightly

---

19. For helpful presentations of Aquinas's hylomorphism see, in particular, Stump, *Aquinas*, 191–216; David S. Oderberg, *Real Essentialism* (London: Routledge, 2008); Jeffrey E. Brower, *Aquinas's Ontology of the Material World: Change, Hylomorphism, and Material Objects* (Oxford: Oxford University Press, 2014).

catalogue them according to universal modes. Stars are not human beings, are not singular water molecules, and so forth. Third, each thing we might consider in its unity and natural kind is also a thing composed of material parts, divisible, even indefinitely and infinitely so, according to quantity and material potency. The star can implode, the human being can be harmed or killed by violence, the atom can be split, and so on. If we acknowledge these three affirmations, and we would be wise to do so, then it is not difficult to accept some variant of the form–matter distinction. There exists, in every physical reality we can observe, a unifying form of a given kind (however vague and generic we want to make this designation, such as non-living physical being, living physical being, rational animal, and so forth). There is also in each physical being a composition of material parts and a deep-down indetermination of material potency (signaled by the infinite quantitative divisibility of the reality). We could even go so far as to say that the natural form of each thing is substantial in kind: the form gives substantial determination to all the material parts, providing to each reality its unity as a composite whole.[20] Consequently, there is in every physical being, as a material being with a given form and ontological unity, a real composition of form and matter.[21]

Why should we not attribute this kind of composition to God? Consider two reasons. First, it must be the case that any physical thing having material parts is subject to alteration or change, *and thus ontological determination*, due to the action of another. What exists in anything that exists materially can be and is regularly determined by other agents. But God, if God truly exists, is the giver of being to all other realities (the Creator of all that is). He cannot receive any motion or change from another that would cause God to become something new or to become new under some aspect. This would make his being, or some aspect of it, dependent upon others

---

20. On substantial form, see Aquinas, *De Principiis Naturae*, cc. 14–17

21. Aquinas, *De Principiis Naturae*, cc. 3–8. See the discussion in Bower, *Aquinas's Ontology of the Material World*, 21–7.

and caused by them in some way. But that would simply mean that God would not exist or that we would not yet be thinking in truth about God, as he who alone, unilaterally, gives being to all things (and does not in any way receive his being from them).[22]

A simpler but more technical way of saying this is to underscore that there is no act–potency composition in God and that the materiality of any form–matter composite constitutes a kind of potency.[23] This truth is apparent on a most basic, visceral level when we consider merely the material divisibility of any body. It can be divided and subdivided infinitely. In fact, one might reasonably argue that there are not absolute simples on the level of material parts, necessarily, in that we could always subdivide some material smallest part into something yet smaller, based simply on the material potency and divisibility always residual in every material thing. God, however, is the first, wholly non-contingent cause of all that exists and the first mover who is unmoved or unchanged by all that he gives being and motion to. By this very fact, we may say with certitude that God is not a form–matter composite. God is 'form' or divine nature without a material substantiation.[24]

Notice some truths that follow from this. God is wholly un-envisageable. There is no representation of the divine nature accessible to the human senses. No natural reality that we know in ordinary experience can be compared with God conceptually in a

22. *ST* I, q. 3, a. 2.

23. *ST* I, q. 3, a. 2: 'matter is in potentiality. But we have shown (*ST* I, q. 2, a. 3) that God is pure act, without any potentiality. Hence it is impossible that God should be composed of matter and form.' For recent explanations of this distinction, see Lawrence Dewan, "St. Thomas, Metaphysical Procedure and the Formal Cause," in *Form and Being* (Washington, DC: The Catholic University of America Press, 2006), 167–74; David S. Oderberg, "No Potency without Actuality: The Case of Graph Theory," in *Contemporary Aristotelian Metaphysics,* ed. T. E. Tahko (Cambridge: Cambridge University Press, 2012), 207–28.

24. *ST* I, q. 3, a. 2: "every agent acts by its form; hence the manner in which it has its form is the manner in which it is an agent. Therefore whatever is primarily and essentially an agent must be primarily and essentially form. Now God is the first agent, since He is the first efficient cause. He is therefore of His essence a form; and not composed of matter and form."

merely univocal way because our ordinary concepts of natural realities (essences) are derived from sensate individuals, and God is not one of these. When we speak of God's natural form or activity, we speak in a way analogous to substantial form as we might consider it in creatures, but also in utter distinction from them. Here, the Hebraic revelation and the heritage of classical metaphysics coincide profoundly. 'You shall make no graven images' (Ex. 20:4). Biblical apophaticism is philosophically reasonable.[25] If God were to take upon himself one of the 'forms' of the world, becoming human, for example, he could not do so in such a way as to confuse the divine nature with the human form or human nature. There would have to be two natures in the personal presence of God made human. Not that we can show by this fact that God has become human.

It also follows, significantly, that God is not in history in the sense that he does not undergo historical change in his divine essence. The doctrine of divine simplicity excludes philosophies of divine becoming, whether in the sophisticated conceptual mode from Heraclides to Hegel or in the dramatic mythological mode from the ancient Eastern world epoch of the *Bhagavad-Gita* to the modern Western world epoch of the *Book of Mormon*.[26] God is not a body subject to historical evolution or material endurance through diverse temporal states.[27] If God were to become a subject of history by becoming human, it would make no sense to say that this would entail a historicization of the divine essence, as if the divinity could itself become material. Rather, if God has become subject to history, we might say that he lives within time and experiences history uniquely by virtue of his human nature but not by virtue of his divine nature.

25. See the Eastern Christian argument to this effect by John Damascene, *The Orthodox Faith I*, in *Nicene and Post-Nicene Fathers*, vol. 9, ed. Philip Schaff and Henry Wace, trans. S. D. F. Salmond (Oxford: James Parker, 1899), cc. 3–4.

26. I am assuming that Hegel has a concept of historicized divinity. See on this point, Cyril O'Regan, *The Heterodox Hegel* (Albany, NY: State University of New York Press, 1994), 63–80.

27. See the helpful analysis of this point by Kretzmann, *The Metaphysics of Theism*, 113–38.

By virtue of his divine nature, God causes to be all that exists in its being and historical becoming.

Essence and Individuation

It follows from the first stage of our argument that we must now negate any composition in God of nature or essence and individuation. This argument can be stated in the following way. First, consider that individuals as we encounter them are diverse material entities, instantiations of various kinds of things. There are thousands of orange trees in fields in California and Florida. Yet, each tree is a material individual having what we might call the designate matter of that individual—roughly the material quantity of an extended body: 'this orange tree here.' The natural form of the tree is individuated by matter, according to Aquinas.[28] However, formally speaking, the trees are all the same *kind* of thing, some species of orange tree. Similarly, each human individual partakes of the formal nature of humanity, but no human individual can simply say, 'I am man.'[29] To cite Aquinas:

> Consequently, humanity and a man are not wholly identical; but humanity is taken to mean the formal part of a man, because the principles whereby a thing is defined are regarded as the formal constituent in regard to the individualizing matter. On the other hand, in things not composed of matter and form, in which individualization is not due to individual matter—that is to say, to 'this' [designate] matter— the very forms being individualized of themselves—it is necessary the forms themselves should be subsisting 'supposita' [the subsistent individual]. Therefore 'suppositum' and nature in them are identified. Since God then is not composed of matter and form, He must be His own Godhead, His own Life, and whatever else is thus predicated of Him.[30]

28. Aquinas, *De ente et essentia*, in *Opuscula Philosophica*, ed. R. Spiazzi (Rome: Marietti, 1954), c. 4 (hereafter *De Ente*). See on this point, Wippel, *The Metaphysical Thought of Thomas Aquinas*, 351–75.

29. Not even Jesus Christ: Pontius Pilate's *ecce homo* refers to Christ as the exemplary cause of the human race, due to his moral beauty, not the formal cause, due to his singularity of being.

30. *ST* I, q. 3, a. 3.

Notice what is suggested by this argument. God, in his simplicity, is not a kind of thing, at least in the way we usually come to talk about kinds of things in ordinary human experience, always in contact with material individuals of various kinds.

It follows from this that definitions of God, which begin from univocal terms drawn from material individuals, are destined to be false starting points, potentially idolatrous concepts. God is not 'a mind' or 'a person' or 'a sentient being' or anything at all that we might objectify in ordinary universal terms, because all these supposedly apriorist nominal definitions are drawn from ordinary natural kinds through typical universal abstractions from individuals. Not that we cannot talk about God analogously from things we know more proximately, but we cannot do so in any way that denotes God as one kind of thing among others or like others, as if God were an individual included in a larger natural set. When an analytic theist says something like, 'let us suppose that God is defined as an acorporeal mind with infinite power,' then a problematic conception has already been engaged.

Various kinds of questions still remain even after we negate the composition of essence and individuality in God, and these issues are not trivial in kind. First, Aquinas, as is well known, argues that angels or separated substances are individuated not by their matter (since they are immaterial), but by their form alone.[31] Consequently, each angel is its own species. There are a multiplicity of pure spirits, but each has a distinct essence, having its own unique degree of perfection in natural knowledge and love. Metaphorically speaking, the angels are like snowflakes, each being a unique, crystalline formation of pure spirit. Again, it is as if Noah's ark had only one animal of each kind: a single genus but diverse species.[32] But does

---

31. *ST* I, q. 50, aa. 2 and 4. See the analysis by Serge-Thomas Bonino, *Les anges et les démons: Quatorze leçons de théologie* (Paris: Parole et Silence, 2007), 115–33.

32. If the non-rational animals are really diverse in species: Aquinas, *De Ente* c. 4 suggests that the differences among them are only accidental, not essential, a theory with potential repercussions for the metaphysical analysis of biological evolution. See in this regard, Lawrence Dewan, "The Importance of Substance," in *Form and Being*, 96–130.

the argument of Aquinas that we have just restated above allow us to distinguish sufficiently, then, God from the separated substances (presuming for philosophical purposes that angels exist)? After all, there is no distinction of essence and individual in the angels either, since each angel is individuated by its essence. Angels are not God, however. The angels might each have their own species, but they are grouped at least in a generic commonality as created separated substances, and surely the simplicity of God the Creator is other than theirs.

Second, this issue touches upon thorny questions regarding Aquinas's own interpretation of Aristotle. Aristotle, in *Metaphysics* XII, 8, seems to discuss the possibility of something like 54 or 56 separated substances, each not-individuated by matter. But is God, as pure act, who is mentioned in *Metaphysics* XII, 6–7 and 9–10, other than these separated substances? Aquinas thinks that Aristotle does have arguments in favor of the uniqueness of God as distinct from these separated substances and reads these passages accordingly.[33] This is a possible reading based on Aristotle's notion of God as pure act and the seeming uniqueness that accrues to God alone by virtue of his pure actuality. The separated substances of *Metaphysics* XII, 8 are clearly in potentiality, at least with respect to place, and so seem to be characterized by a composition of act and potency of some sort. They also seem to be perfected only by contemplating another (God). One might argue, then, that Aristotle understands there to be one God alone who is pure actuality and the primary actuating cause of all others. If this is true, then he has achieved some real if imperfect knowledge of the God of monotheism.[34] However, even

33. See, in particular, Aquinas, *In duodecim libros Metaphysicorum Aristotelis expositio*, ed. M. R. Cathala and R. Spiazzi (Rome: Marietti, 1964), XII, 7, para. 2529–35; 8, para. 2544–50; 9, para. 2555; 11, para. 2614–16 (hereafter *Comm. on Metaphysics*).

34. Even if it is true, this does not mean that Aristotle understands God very perfectly. He might still deny, for example, that God knows truly the world that depends upon him. He has no explicit concept of God as Creator and as omnipotent with respect to his creation. See on this issue the contrasting views of Joseph Owens, *The Doctrine of Being in the Aristotelian Metaphysics: A Study in the Greek Background of Medieval Thought*

if Aquinas's reading were to be accepted, one must be able to take further steps in the argument. It is not enough to show that God, as pure act, transcends all composition of essence and suppositum. Something more is needed in order to differentiate God from angelic being or separated substances.[35]

A third problem is the following: God is the Creator, who gives being to all that is not God. But if that is the case, then we must be able to talk about what is utterly different and unique about God as one who does not receive being from others but who is the unique transcendent author of being in others, unlike them in this ultimate and fundamental respect. For all these reasons, we need to affirm a deeper form of non-composition than the two considered thus far.

Essence and Existence

This brings us to the famous topic. Aquinas affirms that there exists in every created substance a real distinction between essence and existence. By essence, I mean the formal nature of a given thing— be it a form in matter (such as a human nature: the human being is essentially an embodied rational animal) or an immaterial form (the hypothetical separate substances: essentially immaterial).[36] By existence, I mean not only the mere fact of a thing existing but the act of being of a given thing, what Aquinas terms the *actus essendi*. Every reality we normally experience is able to be or not be, or is in potency to existence.[37] No natural reality that we consider exists by

---

(Toronto: PIMS, 1951), and Enrico Berti, "Unmoved Mover(s) as Efficient Cause(s) in Metaphysics Λ 6," in *Aristotle's Metaphysics Lambdai*, ed. M. Frede and D. Charles (Oxford: Oxford University Press, 2000), 181–206.

35. My point here is not that Aquinas's interpretation of Aristotle on God is necessarily correct, but that from within the internal logic of his own thinking, one needs to differentiate God clearly from Aristotelian separated substances.

36. See Aquinas, *De Ente*, cc. 1–3.

37. Aquinas, *De Ente*, c. 3 and *De Pot.* q. 7, a. 2, ad 9:

Being [*esse*], as we understand it here, signifies the highest perfection of all: and the proof is that act is always more perfect than potentiality. Now no signate form is understood to be in act unless it be supposed to have being. Thus we may take human nature or fiery nature as existing potentially in matter, or as existing in the power of an agent, or even as in the mind: but when it has being

the sheer fact of the kind of nature that it possesses as if existence were essentially constitutive of that reality: 'It is simply of the nature of this tree here, unlike all other trees that it always exists because the actuality of being is intrinsic to it essentially.' Such is not the case, even with respect to human beings or angels. And why is this? It is because of the distinction of potency and act in any created thing with respect to existence.[38] The act of being of a given thing is not identical with its essence or nature. For any created entity, 'to be or not to be' really is the question.

We might say, likewise, that each thing that exists receives its existence from others and thus partakes or participates in existence.[39] Each created reality has being and participates in being, but is not itself being. This fundamental ontological potency (or non-necessity) in all things points toward God, the first cause of all that exists: himself un-derived Being, 'He Who is' (Ex. 3:14–15). Accordingly, Aquinas also negates any composition of *esse* and *essentia* in God.[40] Unlike the angels, who receive their existence from another, the unique first cause of all, the Creator, is being by nature. It is of the essence of God to exist. He is an 'infinite sea' of subsistent being, in the words

---

it becomes actually existent. Wherefore it is clear that being [*esse*] as we understand it here is the actuality of all acts, and therefore the perfection of all perfections. Nor may we think that being, in this sense, can have anything added to it that is more formal and determines it as act determines potentiality: because being in this latter sense is essentially distinct from that to which it is added and whereby it is determined. But nothing that is outside the range of being can be added to being: for nothing is outside its range except non-being, which can be neither form nor matter. Hence being is not determined by something else as potentiality by act but rather as act by potentiality: since in defining a form we include its proper matter instead of the difference: thus we define a soul as the act of an organic physical body. Accordingly this being is distinct from that being inasmuch as it is the being of this or that nature. For this reason Dionysius says (*Div. Nom.*, v) that though things having life excel those that merely have being, yet being excels life, since living things have not only life but also being.

38. For a contemporary explanation and defenses of the Thomist "real distinction," see Lawrence Dewan, "St. Thomas and the Distinction between Form and Esse in Caused Things," in *Form and Being*, 188–204.

39. Aquinas, "Exposition of *On the Hebdomads of Boethius*," in *Selected Writings: Thomas Aquinas*, ed. and trans. R. McInerny (London: Penguin, 1998), c. 2.

40. *ST* I, q. 13. a. 4.

of Aquinas.[41] Thus, there is not the radical composition of creature-ly being in him that is found in all others, including Aristotle's separated substances, in whom there is composition of potency and act, at least with regard to place, as well as spiritual perfection of operation. The Creator alone is wholly un-derived in his ineffable existence, and all else that is is utterly and totally derived, dependent upon God for all that it is and possesses, in complete ontological dependence upon the sovereign first cause.

Notice two important truths that follow from this. First, if what Aquinas says is correct, then God is not a member of the sum of all beings, which Aquinas calls *ens commune*.[42] God is not rightly called an entity in the ordinary sense because every created entity (*ens*) is a composite being, an essence partaking of *esse*. God can be designated as an *ens* only analogically, as 'a being' who is uniquely subsistent existence. Nor can God be the being within all beings, the participated common being of all things. For God is not a being or the sum of being, but the transcendent origin and giver of all being. This is yet another reason why he cannot be named univocally by a strict transference of the names of created beings to God. Indeed, we must say that God is *not* in a genus of being. It is an error to speak of him as if he were a type or particular subset of being because God is the cause of every genus of being. To be in a genus is to be limited in being vis-à-vis all other genera, and God cannot be subject to the potentiality of limitation that one finds necessarily in any finite essence.[43] Each creature has a genus, but God has none. Furthermore, even typical use of analogical terms that we employ *among creatures* will not work when applied to God. For example, we ascribe the transcendental notions (being, unity, truth, and goodness) analogically to distinct generic categorical modes of being. The existence of a given quality is both like and unlike the existence of a given quantity. The unity of substance is like and unlike the unity of a given relation.

41. *ST* I, q. 13, a. 11.
42. *ST* I, q. 3, a. 4, obj. 1 and resp. 1.
43. See the interrelated arguments to this effect in Aquinas, *SCG* I, cc. 22, 25.

A good quantity of a given reality is different from a good quality of that same reality. Such transcendental terms are applied to diverse genera of beings analogically, not univocally.[44] So here, we naturally employ already distinctly analogical notions for created realities.[45] However, God is not a member of the transcendentals—the range of *ens commune*, common being, to which we attribute the analogical terms being, unity, truth, and goodness. Why? Because God is the transcendent cause of all that we ascribe these names to, he who gives them their *esse*, or act of being.[46] So God can be named analogically from creatures, as goodness, truth, unity, and so on, but only if we take into account the negation of the real distinction that applies to him alone, making our ascriptions of being to him unique among all others.[47]

If all this is true, then Aquinas's account of God basically avoids the critique given of metaphysics as ontotheology typically presented by many Heideggerians (like Jean-Luc Marion), as well as the criticisms of metaphysics as idolatry presented by theologians like Karl Barth and Eberhard Jüngel.[48] God's being is not intelligible as a member of a larger ontic system of beings, nor is he one specific or generic kind of being within a larger set. To think either of these things would entail that God is somehow within the set of created entities, even if one were to claim that he supposedly has various specifying properties that mark him out as divine. To approach thinking about God this way is to err quite seriously.

44. See Aquinas on the strictly analogical knowledge of the transcendentals in *Comm. on Aristotle's Metaphysics*, IV, 1, para. 529–47; *Commentary on the Nicomachean Ethics*, I, 6, para. 74–82.

45. See Aquinas, *Truth*, trans. R. Schmidt (Chicago: Henry Regnery, 1954), q. 1, a. 1 (hereafter *De Ver.*).

46. See Aquinas, *Comm. on Metaphysics*, prologue and *ST* I, q. 4, aa. 1–2.

47. See the helpful analysis of this point by Eleonore Stump in her essay, "Simplicity and Aquinas's Quantum Metaphysics."

48. See, for example, Jean-Luc Marion, *God without Being*; I analyze in some detail the objections of Barth and Jüngel in this respect in White, *The Incarnate Lord*, ch. 3.

Substance and Accident

Lastly, if all we have said is true, then it follows that there can be no distinction in God between substance and accidental properties. We see this distinction in all the realities that surround us as soon as we acknowledge that there are substantially unified wholes. A given tree is a substance having various properties: a given quantity, various qualities, relations to other realities, a setting in time and place, and so on. Ordinary reality is complex this way, downright baroque, or at least gothic in its complexity.[49] This cannot be true of God. Why? First, any accidental property added to the essence of God would denote an additional actuality to which God was essentially in potentiality. God would be potentially qualified in his essence for this or that qualitative accident. So God's own essence would be composite, having in it both potentiality and actuality, but God, who is the first cause of all secondary dependent beings, is pure actuality.[50] Second, if God were to have accidental properties inherent in his essence, then there would be actual existence of accidents that did not pertain to him essentially, just as in human beings, the activity of willing or thinking is a mere accidental property of our substance (and not what we are essentially) even if it is quite important to our personal identity. (After all, we continue to exist as human beings even when we are asleep.) But God is his existence, and so there can be no delimitation of the plenitude of being present in him essentially. Consequently, God possesses infinite existence essentially as the unique giver of all being to all limited, finite creatures:

> What is essential is prior to what is accidental. Whence as God is absolute primal being, there can be in Him nothing accidental. Neither can He have any essential accidents (as the capability of laughing is an essential accident of man), because such accidents are caused by

49. On the ten categories as signifying really distinct modes of being, see Aquinas, *Comm. on Metaphysics*, V, 9, para. 889–94.

50. *ST* I, q. 3, a. 6.

the constituent principles of the subject. Now there can be nothing caused in God, since He is the first cause. Hence, it follows that there is no accident in God.[51]

Traditional affirmations about God follow from what has been said. Namely, that God simply is each of his properties or that these so-called properties are ascribed to God analogically in such a way as to make clear that they are only subsistent in God. God simply is his wisdom, his goodness, his intellect, his will, and so forth.[52] Thus, the Thomist would not be able to say, with Swinburne, that God possesses omnipotence or perennial existence as a property of his being, as the kind of entity that God is.[53] Nor would he or she be able to say that more than one individual subject would be able to share these divine properties (like omniscience or omnipotence) while remaining distinct as entities but identical in properties (as Swinburne says of the Father, Son, and Holy Spirit.)[54] These ideas constitute a form of strong conceptual anthropomorphism. Further, if Aquinas is correct, then what we know of God's goodness, wisdom, perfection, and so forth are distinct titles drawn from creatures and rightly all attributed to him analogically, but they are also purely and simply identical in God himself. Whatever God's simplicity is, and we have no direct, immediate experience of it, it is identical with God's perfection, goodness, and so forth.[55] So

51. *ST* I, q. 3, a. 6.
52. *ST* I, q. 6, a. 3; q. 16, a. 5; q. 18, a. 3; q. 19, a. 1.
53. See Swinburne, *The Christian God*, 126–49, 156–58.
54. Swinburne, *The Christian God*, 172:

Each individual would be bringing about many good states, within himself, in relation to the other individual, and creating and sustaining without. Since each would recognize the other as having the divine properties, including perfect goodness, it is plausible to suppose that each would recognize a duty not to prevent or frustrate the acts of the other, to use his omnipotence to forward them rather than frustrate them.

55. *ST* I, q. 13, a. 4:

our intellect, since it knows God from creatures, in order to understand God, forms conceptions proportional to the perfections flowing from God to creatures, which perfections pre-exist in God unitedly and simply, whereas in creatures they are received and divided and multiplied. As therefore, to the

Scotus's idea that there are formal distinctions of divine attributes in God, implying some kind of real ontological distinctiveness of attributes not merely in our way of thinking of God but in God himself, is a rationally objectionable form of high conceptual anthropomorphism as well.[56] It is the case that our ascriptions of attributes drawn initially from creatures can, when highly qualified, denote what God is in himself *substantialiter*.[57] It is true to say that God is good, or wise, or one. However, such ascriptions are qualified by the three-fold Dionysian *viae*: God is said to be good as the cause of good realities. God is not good in the way created realities are. God is good in a superabundant and transcendent way, of which we have no immediate experience.[58] This last qualification (marked by apophaticism) leaves space open for the Thomist claims that what the attributes all signify in their conceptually diverse richness just is the one God in his pure actuality and simplicity.

Lastly, we might note that if Aquinas is right, then God does not possess indeterminancy of intellect and will, as would any creaturely person in a state of potency as to thinking and choosing. What God is eternally is his act of self-contemplation and the non-egotistical love of his own infinite goodness.[59] Whatever God knows or freely

---

different perfections of creatures, there corresponds one simple principle represented by different perfections of creatures in a various and manifold manner, so also to the various and multiplied conceptions of our intellect, there corresponds one altogether simple principle, according to these conceptions, imperfectly understood. Therefore although the names applied to God signify one thing, still because they signify that under many and different aspects, they are not synonymous.

56. For a helpful presentation of Scotus' position, see Richard Cross, *Duns Scotus on God*, 103–14.

57. *ST* I, q. 13, a. 2; Aquinas, *De Pot.* q. 7, a. 5:

the idea of negation is always based on an affirmation: as evinced by the fact that every negative proposition is proved by an affirmative: wherefore unless the human mind knew something positively about God, it would be unable to deny anything about him. And it would know nothing if nothing that it affirmed about God were positively verified about him. Hence following Dionysius (Div. Nom. XIII) we must hold that these terms signify the divine essence, albeit defectively and imperfectly.

58. Aquinas, *De Pot.* q. 7, a. 5, ad 2; *ST* I, q. 12, a. 12; q. 13, a. 1.

59. Aquinas, *SCG* I, cc. 44–88.

chooses to create, he does so only out of his knowledge of himself and out of the love of his own goodness. This knowledge and love of creatures has no medium other than that of the divine essence and implies no change in God. In other words, God knows all that he creates insofar as he knows himself, and he is, in his very being and essence, the cause of all that exists. In loving himself, God wills that all other realities exist. Consequently, God chooses to create out of his eternal and infinite actual self-determination and not out of any kind of cognitive or moral indetermination. This is true even as God freely creates effects that are purely contingent and that participate in their own finite, imperfect way, in God's own eternal goodness. If we take this line of thinking, then various forms of neo-Molinism are rightly to be avoided. There is no middle science. God is not learning from the world, reacting to it, or altering his being in relation to it. God is the giver of being 'all the way down,' and all that exists other than God exists as pure gift, as the uniquely participated actuality of existence that is given to creatures.

SIMPLICITY AND PHILOSOPHICAL DEMONSTRATION OF THE TRINITY

As a transition to the second part of this chapter, let us return to the mystery of the Holy Trinity and make two points pertinent to the relation between the doctrine of divine simplicity and the theological dogma regarding trinitarian persons. Each of these points touches in some way deeply upon the relationship between philosophy and theology as distinct but interrelated sciences.

First, it follows from Aquinas's account of divine simplicity that the mystery of the Holy Trinity is one that can in no way be demonstrated to exist by recourse to philosophical argumentation. This is the case for two reasons. First, the Holy Trinity is the cause of the world as Creator, and the works of creation are works of all three persons by virtue of that which they possess in common, namely the divine wisdom, goodness, and power that pertain to the divine essence. Since we know a cause from its effects and since the effects of creation spring from a unique, singular divine cause, then these effects only tell us that God exists and is one and simple. They do not reveal to us as such that God is Trinity.[60] For that, we would have need of revelation through the divine missions of the eternal Son made man and the sending of the Holy Spirit.[61]

Second, we cannot have recourse to demonstrations of the Holy Trinity based on the essential attribute of divine goodness, as Richard of St. Victor and others have claimed, wherein they make appeal to the notion of interpersonal communion as a feature of perfection.[62] The argument somewhat simplified is as follows: perfection for all persons is attained or exists only through mutual communion with other persons, for it is proper to the person to love and to be loved by another person. But God is personally perfect in his goodness. Therefore, God must possess personal communion within God's own self. There must exist a communion of persons in God.[63]

We should affirm the major, but we should also qualify. Perfection

---

60. *ST* I, q. 32, a. 1; Aquinas, *De Ver.* q. 10, a. 13; Aquinas, *Commentary on Boethius' De Trinitate*, in *Thomas Aquinas: Faith, Reason and Theology*, trans. and ed. Armand Maurer (Toronto: PIMS, 1987), q 1, a. 4. For a helpful exposition and defense of Aquinas's position, with reference to a variety of medieval and modern views to the contrary, see Matthias Scheeben, *The Mysteries of Christianity*, trans. C. Vollert (New York: Crossroad, 2006), 25–48.

61. *ST* I, q. 43.

62. See Richard of St Victor, *On the Trinity*, trans. C. P. Evans in Coolman and Coulter, *Trinity and Creation*, III.

63. Swinburne offers a version of this argument as a reason for the belief that there are only three divine individuals who are omnipotent, rather than a multitude:

> Is there an overriding reason for a first divine individual to bring about a second or third or fourth such? I believe that there is overriding reason for a first divine individual to bring about a second divine individual and with him to bring about a third divine individual, but no reason to go further. If the Christian religion has helped us, Christians and non-Christians, to see anything about what is worthwhile, it has helped us to see that love is a supreme good. Love involves sharing, giving to the other what of one's own is good for him and receiving from the other what of his is good for one; and love involves co-operating with another to benefit third parties. This latter is crucial for worthwhile love (Swinburne, *The Christian God*, p. 177)

for persons is attained only through mutual communion of persons, *for all created persons*, precisely because they are composed of act and potency in the order of being and specifically in their spiritual operations of intellect and will. Human beings and angels become more perfect in the order of accidental operation through the knowledge and love that they gain of others by progressively experiencing what it means to love and to be loved. This cannot be true of God, and, in fact, if it were, then God would not be pure actuality and would not only not be the Creator, but would also not be perfectly one, *actus purus*. The argument from interpersonal communion is an argument that implicitly denies the reality of biblical monotheism. It risks to promote a form of Marcionite theology that fails to do justice not only to philosophical reason but also monotheistic faith in the authentic revelation of the one God in the Old Testament as the premise of the truth of the New Testament.

A second main point is that, based on Aquinas's analysis of divine simplicity, not only can the mystery of the Holy Trinity not be proven, it also can in no way be disproven. Why is this? Because the essence of God, as we have described it above, is entirely inaccessible to us in any immediate way and is only known indirectly through the medium of creatures that are God's created effects. We can speak absolutely truly of God in a mediated analogical fashion, based upon a careful series of negations of compositions we find in creatures. And we can say many very important non-trivial things about what God is in himself, including the things we have said here about divine simplicity. But what we cannot do is know in a direct way what the simplicity of God is in itself. Consequently, if the Thomist metaphysician who is agnostic regarding the mystery of the Holy Trinity studies that doctrine, he or she cannot say whether it is true or not. It is a mystery given to us to know by the gift of divine revelation and the illumination of faith and not by way of the gift of created being as such. This is good news: it shows the gratuity of the supernatural revelation.[64] In revealing himself as Trinity, God is truly sharing his own

---

64. A point on which Barthians and Thomists ought to agree, and in which both are

life with us, inviting us into something that completely transcends the ordinary range of our natural knowledge and its limited capacities. However, God is also not revealing anything that contradicts or confounds our human reason. On the contrary, emphasis on the divine simplicity elicits increased awareness of the transcendence of God with respect to his creation. Increased awareness of the transcendence of God can in turn deepen the natural desire to want to know God immediately, even if this desire cannot be achieved or fulfilled by any natural capacity or action.[65] Thus, the revelation of the Trinity may be said rightly to answer to an innate natural desire of the human heart that philosophically derived knowledge itself can never quench or fulfill. Likewise, revelation of the mystery of God the Holy Trinity is not something violent or extrinsic to human reason, but something that awakens, elevates, and fulfills the deepest natural human desire for truth concerning who God is.

THE SIMPLICITY OF THE HOLY TRINITY: SUBSISTENT RELATIONS AND MODES OF SUBSISTENCE

Affirmation of the simplicity of God co-exists, then, with the possibility of belief in the revelation of the Holy Trinity. But how does the affirmation of the simplicity of God affect or qualify one's doctrinal understanding of the Holy Trinity? Briefly stated, this theoretical stance has two very important consequences in trinitarian theology. The first pertains to the notion of subsistent relations, and the second to personal modes of subsistence.

---

in concord with the teaching of Vatican I, and the modern Catholic magisterium. See the articulation of this idea by Scheeben in *The Mysteries of Christianity*, 43–48.

65. On the controversial topic of the natural desire to see God in Aquinas, I offer a restatement of one version of the traditional Thomist interpretation in Thomas Joseph White, "Thomas Aquinas and the Paradigm of Nature-Grace Orthodoxy," *The Thomist* 78, no. 1 (2014): 247–89.

Subsistent Relations

If the Father, Son, and Holy Spirit are all the one unique God, then each person possesses in himself the fullness of the deity and simply is God. How, then, might we distinguish the three persons? Only by way of the relations of origin: the Son or *Logos* originates eternally from the Father as the immaterial generation of wisdom that comes forth from the Father. The Spirit originates eternally from the Father and the Son as the immaterial spiration of love shared by the Father and the Son. This is already the answer given in the fourth century in response to Neo-Arianism, by the Cappadocians in the East, and by Augustine in the West. In medieval Western theology, however, reflection on this topic became more acute in the thirteenth century in reaction to the twelfth-century theory of Gilbert of Poitiers (d. 1154), which was condemned by the Synod of Reims in 1148 and listed by Lombard in his *Sentences* as a heretical opinion.[66]

Gilbert held in effect that the essence of the three persons must be one and the same (if they are the one God), but that, therefore, the relations of generation and spiration that obtain between them must be 'extrinsic' or ontologically 'external' to their essence, since the shared essence is what unites the persons but the relations are what necessarily distinguish the persons from one another. This led him, in turn, to hold that there is a distinction between each of the persons and their relative properties since each person is a given individual who is God *essentially* 'prior to' the fact of being related to the others (i.e., the relations are accidental). Consequently, the Father is not his paternity nor the Son his filiation. Rather, paternity is a property of the Father. Filiation is a property of the Son. When Bernard of Clairvaux sided polemically against this theory, he did

---

66. Gilbert of Poitiers, *Expositio in Boecii de Trinitate*, I, 5, nn. 42–3; II, 1, n. 37; and Peter Lombard, *The Sentences*, trans. Giulio Silano (Toronto: PIMS, 2007–10), I, d. 33, c. 1. For the discussions of Gilbert and Joachim of Fiore that ensue below, I am deeply indebted to Emery, *The Trinitarian Theology of Saint Thomas Aquinas*, 89–96, 145–47.

so by invoking the doctrine of divine simplicity: the relations cannot be 'accidental' to what the persons of the Trinity are. Evidently, Gilbert's theory leans strongly toward the affirmation of the persons of the Trinity as three individual beings who each share the same common nature but who are related to one another by accidental properties, somewhat similar to what we would find in three human beings. We should note in passing that this model bears striking similarities to that proposed by Richard Swinburne, a point we will return to below.

It was Albert the Great and Thomas Aquinas who responded to this theology in the thirteenth century by formulating the notion of 'subsistent relations' to speak about the persons of the Holy Trinity. The notion of subsistent relation has no pure analogue in our ordinary human experience of created realities but has nothing about it that is inherently incoherent. Rather, it is an analogical notion specific to the faith, not unlike notions such as the *homoousios* of Nicaea, the 'hypostatic union' at Ephesus and Chalcedon, or that of 'transubstantiation' employed to speak about the Eucharist at Lateran IV.

Relation, as Aquinas notes, denotes two things: the existence in a subject (relations are normally properties of a given subject) and being toward another or in connection with another (relations form from one thing being connected to or toward another). It is in only the latter sense that the term 'relation' is suitable to speak about the persons of the Trinity since there is no composition of substance and property in God.[67] Thus if we affirm there to be real relations in God, each relation must be personally 'subsistent,' not accidental. Here, Gilles Emery speaks of Aquinas's theory of trinitarian 'redoubling.'[68] We must think of each person under a two-fold aspect: as relationally only ever 'toward' the other two persons and simultaneously as one who possesses the plenitude of the divine essence,

67. *ST* I, q. 28, aa. 1–3; q. 29, a. 4.
68. See G. Emery, "Essentialism or Personalism in the Treatise on God in Saint Thomas Aquinas." See a helpful illustration in *ST* I, q. 40, a. 1.

substance, and existence. The Father is only ever toward the Son and Spirit, as the one who generates the Son and spirates the Spirit with the Son. Thus, the Father simply is his paternity. And at the same time, the Father is truly God, possessing in himself the plenitude of the divine essence, power, goodness, existence, and so forth.

However, all that is in the Father is received by the Son by generation, and all that is in the Father and the Son is received by the Holy Spirit by spiration. Thus, the mutual indwelling of the persons (their 'perichoresis') is implied by their unity of essence.[69] The Son contains in himself all that the Father is and that the Spirit is, and so likewise for the Spirit: he contains in himself all that is in the Father and in the Son. Each divine person is intelligible to us only if we think of him as always only relative to the other persons, but we must also think of each person as essentially God, as the subsistent one who is, who possesses in himself the plenitude of being and of the divine essence. There is nothing of what it means to be 'God' found in the Father that is not found in the Son and the Spirit, since he communicates all that he is as God to the Son and the Spirit. Likewise, there is nothing in the Son that is not in the Spirit and the Father and nothing in the Spirit that is not in the Father and the Son. Thus each person is a subsistent relation: a term that has no pure analogue to anything in the created order, and yet a term that applies truly to the persons of the Trinity, as rightly understood by a theology informed by the ontology of divine simplicity.[70]

Personal Modes of Subsistence

A second main point stands in seeming contrast to the one just made. The divine essence is only intelligible for us as the deity of the three subsistent persons of the one God. Therefore, we may

69. *ST* I, q. 42, a. 5. The grounds of perichoresis are found in the unity and singularity of divine essence. The latter does not result from the perichoresis but is the foundation for it.

70. Can we say, then, that there are distinct individuals in God? Only qualifiedly. There are distinct individual persons or hypostases in God, but there is not a distinction or multiplicity of individual substances. See *ST* I, q. 39, a. 2.

speak of the attributes of the one God (God's simplicity, goodness, perfection, power, and so forth) *only insofar as these attributes are found in three subsistent modes.*

Aquinas formulated this notion of subsistent modality in part in response to the problematic theories of Joachim of Fiore (d. 1202), which were condemned at the Fourth Lateran Council in 1215. Joachim reacted against Peter Lombard, who had claimed that we must not say that the essence of God begets or spirates, but only that the persons beget or spirate. Joachim took this to suggest that the essence was being reified as a kind of fourth entity in the Trinity alongside the three persons and so sought instead to claim that the essence begets and that the essence spirates.[71] He seemingly wished to say that the relational processions of the Trinity just are the essence of God, but by virtually equating essence with processional relations, he evacuated his theology of any way of speaking of *that by virtue of which the persons are one* (i.e. the divine essence). As Lateran IV noted, his theory inadvertently made the unity of the persons the result or effect of a relational communion between the persons, not something present in the persons by virtue of an identical being and essence.[72]

Although Joachim's theology is quite different from that of Barth,

71. See Emery, *The Trinitarian Theology of Saint Thomas Aquinas*, 145–47.

72. Lateran IV, c. 2 (Denzinger 803):

Joachim asserts that [Peter Lombard] does not teach a Trinity but a quaternity of God, that is, three persons and that common essence as a fourth. Joachim clearly professes that there is no such reality that is Father, Son, and Holy Spirit; there is no essence or substance or nature, though he agrees that Father, Son, and Holy Spirit are one essence, one substance, and one nature. But this unity he conceives, not as true and proper, but, so to say, as collective and by similitude, just as many people are called one nation and many faithful one Church ... To support this doctrine, he relies mainly on the word that Christ spoke in the Gospel about the faithful: 'I will, Father, that they be one in us as we are one ... (John 17:22ff.) ... When [however] he who is the Truth prays to the Father for his faithful ... the word 'one' as applied to the disciples is to be taken in the sense of a union of charity in grace but in the case of the Divine Persons, in the sense of a unity of identity in nature ... For between Creator and creature no similitude can be expressed without implying greater dissimilitude [*non potest tanta similitudo notari, quin inter eos maior sit dissimilitudo notanda*].

there is a noteworthy point of comparison. If, for example, we read Barth in *Church Dogmatics* IV:1 to affirm in the strongest sense that the persons of the Father and the Son are distinguished by virtue of their relations of commandment and obedience, then it is the case that essential properties of God differ in the Father and in the Son, and so they are distinguished by diverse actions that occur within the life or essence of God. Essence begets essence insofar as there is commandment and obedience in the divine nature, which, after all, is something Barth affirms explicitly.[73]

Aquinas formulated the notion of the subsistent mode of being of the divine essence precisely so as to speak positively to the understandable concern of Joachim, without losing sight of the principle of eternal unity in the Holy Trinity. It is true that God simply is the eternal subsistent relationship of the three Persons. We can say in this sense that God is 'essentially' the trinitarian communion of persons.[74] However, when we speak (1) of the Son being begotten of the Father and (2) of the Son being one in essence with the Father (*homoousios*), we utter two distinguishable truths (at least according to our human way of understanding the mystery), both of which are necessary for a proper understanding of God. Joachim's theory fails to acknowledge the necessity of this conceptual and linguistic complexity in our matter of thinking about God.[75] However, we can, from

---

73. *CD* IV:1, p. 201:

We have to reckon with such an event even in the being and life of God Himself. It cannot be explained away either as an event in some higher or supreme creaturely sphere or as a mere appearance of God. Therefore we have to state firmly that, far from preventing this possibility, His divine unity consists in the fact that in Himself he is both one who is obeyed and Another who obeys.

See also *CD* IV:2, 84–86, e.g.,85: 'it is indeed a part of the divine essence to be free for this decree and its execution, to be able to elect and determine itself to this form'. Notice that the divine nature (and not merely personal modes of being) has become the agent that freely self-determines into two modes, as the Father who commands and the Son who obeys.

74. *ST* I, q. 28, a. 2.

75. *ST* I, q. 39, a. 5:

Concerning this, the abbot Joachim erred in asserting that as we can say "God begot God," so we can say "Essence begot essence": considering that, by reason of the divine simplicity God is nothing else but the divine essence. In this he

this irreducible linguistic duality that is proper to our abstract knowledge of God, construct, in turn, a third form of speech that serves to strengthen our sense of the trinitarian character of all truths said of the divine essence. This is the notion of a *personal mode of subsistence*.

If, as we have said above, the persons of the Holy Trinity are best understood by us through the use of analogical concepts as 'subsistent relations,' and if the divine essence of God truly is simple (at least in the ways we have characterized it above apophatically), then we must also say that there are three personal modes of subsistence of the divine essence in God.[76] For example, in the Father, the goodness of God subsists in a paternal mode, that is to say, as pertaining to one who eternally begets the Son and Spirit. This same goodness subsists in a filial mode in the Son, as the Son's goodness that he receives from all eternity from the Father as his begotten *Logos* and as the goodness of him who spirates the Spirit with the Father. This same and identical divine goodness subsists eternally in the Holy Spirit uniquely in a spirated mode, as the eternal goodness of one who proceeds from the Father and the Son as their mutual love. In each case, we are speaking about the unique divine goodness of the one God that pertains to his deity, and that is shared in equally and

---

was wrong, because if we wish to express ourselves correctly, we must take into account not only the thing which is signified, but also the mode of its signification ... Now although 'God' is really the same as 'Godhead,' nevertheless the mode of signification is not in each case the same. For since this word 'God' signifies the divine essence in Him that possesses it, from its mode of signification it can of its own nature stand for person. Thus the things which properly belong to the persons, can be predicated of this word, 'God,' as, for instance, we can say "God is begotten" or is "Begetter," ... The word 'essence,' however, in its mode of signification, cannot stand for Person, because it signifies the essence as an abstract form. Consequently, what properly belongs to the persons whereby they are distinguished from each other, cannot be attributed to the essence. For that would imply distinction in the divine essence, in the same way as there exists distinction in the *supposita*.

Strikingly, if one substitutes the name of Barth for Joachim and the notion that "God obeys God" for the notion that "God begot God," the analysis of Aquinas seems to apply to Barth's theology in relevant ways.

76. See, on this topic, Emery, "The Personal Mode of Trinitarian Action in Saint Thomas Aquinas."

identically by the three persons. However, we are also speaking of the goodness of the Father, Son, and Holy Spirit, who each possess the deity in a personal way, or we might say, who each are the one God ever only in a personal subsistent mode of being.

The use of a theory like this, taken from Aquinas, would allow us to speak of the divine will in the Father and in the Son in terms that are not wholly different from Barth's. The divine will is present in the Father in a paternal mode and is communicated to the Son by way of generation. The divine will is present in the Son in a filial mode, as received from the Father. Understood in this way, the personal mode in which the Son possesses the will of God from all eternity is relationally receptive as regards the Father, even if the Son is 'light from light' or 'pure act from pure act.' The Son is omnipotent and so, in Aquinas's view, unable to obey the Father by virtue of his deity as God. Christ is able to obey the Father uniquely by virtue of the Incarnation. Obedience is a property of his human nature alone.[77] But the human obedience of Christ is the obedience of his person, and so it expresses in a human way *the personal subsistent relation* he has toward the Father from all eternity, as God, in his filial mode of being as Son. Consequently, the eternal mode of being of God the Son can be revealed to us in and through the human obedience of Christ, his human self-offering to the Father, especially in his suffering, dereliction, and death, and in his receiving and sending the Holy Spirit. In a Thomistic account of the economy of salvation, the human life of Christ does render manifest in history the eternal life of the Holy Trinity. Who God truly is eternally is revealed to us in and through the human life, obedience, and suffering of Christ. However, we only understand this rightly if we maintain a proper sense of the distinction of natures in Christ, including a sense of the simplicity of the divine nature of Christ as God, which he shares in with the Father and the Holy Spirit.

---

77. *ST* II-II, q. 20, aa. 1–2.

CONCLUSION: SIMPLICITY MATTERS

It should be clear from the considerations offered above that *any notion* of divine unity is predicated upon *some account* of divine simplicity. When we seek to say how the persons of the Trinity are one, we inevitably must speak by comparative similitude with creatures. As the Fourth Lateran Council notes, however, the unity of the persons of the Holy Trinity is more unlike than like to that which is found between created persons (the famous *maior dissimilitudo in tanta similitudine*). The unity of persons of the Holy Trinity should not be equated in kind with that which we find in the communion of created persons in the Church; else we fall into a patent form of ecclesiocentric idolatry (in which the Church problematically re-conceives both God and herself according to false theological projections). To avoid such patent anthropomorphism, we stand in need of a doctrine of divine simplicity.

Swinburne clearly wishes to insist upon at least a simplicity of essence. The three persons are the one God, and thus, they each possess the one divine essence. But since his theology allows for a composition of essence and individual substance, as well as a distinction of essence and property in the persons of the Trinity, his theory seems to make the unity of being tenuous at best (as if we were dealing with three individual beings), and the relations of the three persons somehow extrinsic or external to the persons. Analytic commentators who are critical of Swinburne in this respect but who also retain his rejection of divine simplicity typically seek to affirm the singularity of nature in God. To do so, however, they are obliged to distinguish properties *within the divine nature* as pertaining more properly to one person than to another. Thus, William Hasker conceives of the persons as three streams of life within one subsistent nature and posits accordingly a real distinction between the nature and the three persons.[78] Interestingly, what results is a position not

78. Hasker, *Metaphysics and the Tri-Personal God*, 243–44:
The constituted kind ... *is divine Trinitarian person*; the constituting kind ... is divine mind/soul or concrete divine nature. The divine nature constitutes

wholly unlike that of Barth, which we noted above. A diversity of properties of the divine nature has to do the 'work' of differentiating the persons, and so the persons are, in a sense, recipients or properties of the divine nature, which self-deploys in three modes.

In contrast with Swinburne, Barth clearly wishes to insist upon the non-composition of being and essence. There is only one God. However, the elements of his thought taken over from Hegelian actualistic ontology seem to import a kind of history into God, one of commandment and obedience, which may or may not be essentially related (from all eternity) to the historical economy of creation. If one places any strong accent upon these historicizing elements in Barth's thought, then the unity of being in God seems to be qualified as that of a composite essence, in which diverse actualistic states of nature take place in different persons of the Trinity. But in this case, there is a real distinction of substance and natural property in God (since one person can possess properties of the divine nature that the others do not have). As a consequence, the divine unity seems to be attenuated. Interestingly, many of Barth's disciples (such as Jürgen Moltmann, Hans Urs von Balthasar, and Robert Jenson) have distanced themselves from his theology by affirming more clearly a real distinction of persons. However, by retaining the actualistic, historicizing ontology of essence as the principle of personal differentiation, they have made the unity of God more obscure or tenuous. This is most acutely expressed in Moltmann's *The Crucified God*, where the obedience of the Son that distinguishes him from the commanding Father leads him to the cross, where he is annihilated in death and non-being, with Hegel's speculative Good Friday (in which atheism is true for a moment) taking place within the life

---

the divine Trinitarian persons when *it sustains simultaneously three divine life-streams*, each life-stream including cognitive, affective, and volitional states. Since in fact the divine nature does sustain three life-streams simultaneously, there are exactly three divine persons ... We shall say, then, that the one concrete divine nature sustains eternally the three distinct life-streams of Father, Son, and Holy Spirit, and that in virtue of this the nature constitutes each of the persons although it *is not identical* with the persons.

See also 214–37. For Hasker's critique of Swinburne, see 147–54.

of God, but only in the second person.[79] Although the metaphysics differs remarkably from that of Swinburne, it is interesting that Moltmann also approaches from a contrary direction the cliff of absolute tri-theism.

Clearly, what is lacking in all this is a theology of divine simplicity. Swinburne's concern for a definition of personhood is seemingly too univocal as attributed to God since, in reality, there does not obtain in God a distinction of individual and nature as there does in human persons, and Swinburne's theology does not account for this adequately. Barth's concern for the trinitarian revelation of God in history is too univocal as well. The Son's human actions do reveal to us his eternal will as God that he receives from the Father eternally. But in reality, the Son's human actions, though they are actions of God the Son, are not identical in their natural form of being (as pertaining to a created human nature) with the characteristics of the divine nature of the Son. The Word of God incarnate subsists in two natures precisely so that he can reveal his divine life to us in and through his human life and actions, but not so as to confuse the characteristics of our humanity with those that pertain to the deity of God. The obedience of Christ reveals to us the *personal relativity* of the Son to the Father, even as it pertains naturally only to his humanity.

---

79. Moltmann, *The Crucified God: The Cross of Christ as the Foundation and Criticism of Christian Life*, 243, 246–47:

The Son suffers dying, the Father suffers the death of the Son ... The Fatherlessness of the Son is matched by the Sonlessness of the Father, and if God has constituted himself as the Father of Jesus Christ, then he also suffers the death of his Fatherhood in the death of the Son. Unless this were so, the doctrine of the Trinity would still have a monotheistic background ... The content of the doctrine of the Trinity is the real cross of Christ himself ... Only if all disaster, forsakenness by God, absolute death, the infinite curse of damnation and sinking into nothingness is in God himself, is community with this God eternal salvation, infinite joy, indestructible election and divine life ... If one describes the life of God within the Trinity as the 'history of God' (Hegel), this history of God contains within itself the whole abyss of godforsakenness, absolute death and the non-God ... To think of 'God in history' always leads to theism and to atheism. To think of 'history in God' leads beyond that, into new creation and *theopoeisis*.

Though this passage is extravagantly wild, consider the possible parallels to Barth's more sober rendering in *CD* IV:2, 108–14.

A theology of divine simplicity allows us to maintain the partial truths of both Barth and Swinburne, while avoiding the problem areas of their respective theologies. With the Fourth Lateran Council, we should say that the unity of the three persons is both like and unlike that which is found in creatures. We can understand the transcendence and dissimilitude the divine essence of the Trinity best if we take seriously the traditional doctrine of divine simplicity, and, in turn, allow this to influence our understanding of the relations of the trinitarian persons.

Presumably, the more general point is clear. The affirmation of divine simplicity does not enter into trinitarian theology primarily as a philosophical or metaphysical theory. Nor is it 'merely' a doctrine of the Catholic faith. It is an unequivocally biblical teaching clearly contained in Scripture. Why is this the case? Because the doctrine of the Holy Trinity is itself of biblical origin, and the affirmation of the mystery of the Holy Trinity logically implies the notion of divine simplicity necessarily. If God the Holy Trinity is the Creator of the world and is truly one in being and essence, then the three persons who are each the unique God do not receive their being from others as creatures do. In the generation of the Son and the spiration of the Spirit, it is the very being and essence of the deity that is communicated. Nor, then, do the three persons share a common nature only (like human persons) but also possess a unique and undivided existence. They are each the one unique God in whom there is no distinction of individual being and natural kind. Nor do they each have personal properties composed of material parts, like those of physical creatures. They do not merely share common properties or attributes, but each possesses the plenitude of the divine nature, from which they are able to create all the perfections of creatures, which the latter possess as a created gift. God, then, is utterly distinct from all creatures, as one who is non-composite and transcendent in an uncreated and tri-personal way. To say all this is just to say that God the Holy Trinity is simple. We can affirm this basic truth of biblical revelation without adopting Aquinas's *particular understanding* of divine simplicity. However, Aquinas offers us an account of divine simplicity that is deeply consonant with scriptural faith and sacred tradition, and which has an immediate viability and attractiveness within a contemporary theological context.

To say that the doctrine is biblical does not exclude it as a truth of philosophical reason. Biblical revelation is conceived in relation to natural reason not only dialectically but also constructively. Grace does not destroy nature but heals and elevates it. Theology does not do away with philosophy but purifies it from within. The mystery of the Holy Trinity does not evacuate the metaphysics of divine simplicity but invites us to consider it anew, ever more profoundly. For the one God of Israel is also the God of Christianity, and in a certain way also the God of the philosophers. This is not a new idea. Moses on Mount Sinai looked into the incomprehensible darkness of God. It is said by the Church Fathers (Gregory of Nyssa in particular) that he perceived therein the mystery of the Holy Trinity, as the Lord, He Who Is, the Creator of all that exists, in whom there is no composition of nature and being.[80] If we would wish to encounter this God ourselves, after the example of Moses, we would do well to follow the thought of Thomas Aquinas, for he too ascends to the heights of that mountain.

80. Gregory of Nyssa, *The Life of Moses*, trans. A. Malherbe and E. Ferguson (New York: Paulist Press, 1978), I, c. 46; II, 22–26, 174.

4

The Modes of Subsistence of Trinitarian Persons

In his work from 1981, *After Virtue*, Alasdair MacIntyre noted that important intellectual advances from the past can be lost or forgotten. Intellectual traditions do not always evolve homogeneously toward perfection by an arc of inevitable rationality. Instead, the world of understanding is one of contestation, discussion, and sometimes arbitrary resolution or chance forsaking. Successful traditions of human inquiry can be abandoned for reasons having little to do with their explanatory efficacy, due in part to political and cultural circumstances that are unforeseen and unmasterable. On this view, traditions of successful rationality are fragile, not inevitable. MacIntyre's key example pertains to virtue ethics, a tradition that he believes provides more explanatory power for human moral life than other currently available traditions of reason but which, in fact, receded from use in the modern period in the wake of rising tides of deontology and utilitarianism. Like Elizabeth Anscombe and Servais Pinckaers before him, MacIntyre proposed a project of retrieval

Originally published in *Une théologie à l'école de saint Thomas d'Aquin: Hommage au prof. Gilles Emery OP à l'occasion de ses 60 ans*, ed. N. Awais, B.-D. de la Soujeole, and D. Rey-Meier (Paris: Cerf and Studia Friburgensia, 2022), 205–26.

of principles of Thomistic virtue ethics, an undertaking that has achieved marked academic and cultural success in recent decades.[1]

Gilles Emery's work in Trinitarian theology has inaugurated a project of renewal that is somewhat similar in intellectual stance as well as consequence. Emery is an expert in the study of medieval Trinitarian theology, and the thought of Aquinas in particular, and in this sense differs methodologically from MacIntyre. His work, however, has created the conditions for a *ressourcement*–a retrieval and new application in contemporary circumstances–of classical Trinitarian theology. In this chapter, I would like to focus on just one instance of this work, namely, his treatment of the modes of subsistence of the Trinitarian persons, and to note contemporary applications of the idea that I take to be significant.[2] The Thomistic idea of modes of subsistence in Trinitarian persons is one that appeals to the three distinctive ways (modes) in which each of the divine persons is God, based on the distinction of the relations of origin of the three persons. The Father, Son, and Holy Spirit are each truly God, according to an order of procession that exists in the very life of God. Therefore, each of them is God in a distinctive relational way, and this relational way or mode of being characterizes the deity we ascribe to each. The Father is God as unoriginate source of the Trinity, while the Son is true God as the begotten Word of the Father, and the Spirit is God as the spirated love of the Father and the Son.

This idea of distinct personal modes of divine being in God has consequences for the way we understand the simultaneous unity and personal distinctiveness of the three persons in their common action. Trinitarian actions of creation, redemption, and sanctification effectuated in creatures imply a common action of the three as the one God and a revelatory structure of personal action in which each is active in a given mode or personal way of agency. It is this

---

1. Alasdair MacIntyre, *After Virtue* (South Bend, IN: Notre Dame University Press, 1981).

2. See Gilles Emery, "The Personal Mode of Trinitarian Action in Saint Thomas Aquinas."

idea that I would like to explore below, especially as it helps us analyze alternative approaches to Trinitarian persons and economic actions developed by modern theologians like Karl Rahner and Jürgen
Moltmann. These latter theologians, in two different ways, seek to
define the persons in God by their distinct relations to creation and
their distinct actions in the economy of salvation. The relations of
the persons to the economy, I will argue, thus become in some way
constitutive of the distinction of persons in God. Aquinas's modal understanding of divine personhood, meanwhile, allows him to
maintain a contrary view, which is more appealing. On this view,
which Emery has highlighted, the unified action of the Trinity in the
economy is truly revelatory of the eternal relations of the Trinitarian persons and thus manifests the distinct persons in their communion and personal activity. Their economic action also reveals their
transcendent unity as the one God. This action of the Trinity in
the economy is not constitutive, however, of the eternal life of God
nor of the persons in their distinctness. The persons of the Trinity
truly reveal and communicate themselves to us in the economy by
grace so that we come to understand and possess them as they are in
themselves. They do so, however, without newly defining themselves
or evolving internally as a result of this process. The notion of the
subsistent modes of being of God in the unity of Trinitarian action is
a keystone, then, of a theology that seeks to successfully maintain a
balance between both the transcendence of the Trinity with respect
to the creation and the intimate presence of the Trinity with respect
to creatures by grace.

TRINITARIAN RELATIONS
AND PERSONAL MODES OF
BEING GOD

The Thomistic idea of modes of subsistence in Trinitarian persons
is one that appeals simultaneously to three ideas. First, there is
that of Trinitarian processions as consisting of reciprocal relations,

secondly that of divine simplicity (the complete possession of the divine essence by each person), and thirdly, that of the persons as subsistent relations. I will present each of these ideas briefly and then, in light of them, explore the notion of personal modes of subsistence.

Reciprocal Relations in Trinitarian Life

Catholic Christianity classically confesses that there are three truly distinct persons in God: the Father, Son, and Holy Spirit, who are consubstantial (one in being and essence) such that each of the persons is truly and completely the one God. Since the 4th century, in the wake of the Arian controversy, theologians have distinguished the persons in God principally by appealing to the notion of relations.[3] The persons are distinguished by intra-divine relations of origin, in which the Son is begotten of the Father by way of eternal generation, and the Spirit proceeds from the Father by way of eternal spiration. In the generation of the Son and in the spiration of the Spirit, the Father communicates to the derivative persons all that pertains to him as God, the plenitude of the divine essence, so that each of them is truly and completely God, or as the Nicene creed says of the Son, "God from God, light from light, true God from true God."[4]

Augustine famously explored developments of this idea in his *The Trinity* by suggesting that one could draw an analogy from relational origins of knowledge and love in acts of the mind of human persons to discuss the relative origin of the Son as Word and the Spirit as love.[5] On this view, one could understand the Son as the

---

3. See the helpful study of this period by Khaled Anatolios, *Retrieving Nicaea: The Development and Meaning of Trinitarian Doctrine* (Grand Rapids, MI: Baker Academic, 2018).

4. Thus, the phrasing of the Council of Nicaea, *Decrees of the Ecumenical Councils*. See the idea expressed clearly in early pro-Nicene orthodoxy by Gregory of Nazianzus, *Oration 29*, n. 16, in *On God and Christ. The Five Theological Orations and Two Letter to Cledonius*, trans. Frederick Williams and Lionel Wickham (Yonkers, NY: St. Vladimir's Seminary Press, 2002).

5. Augustine, *The Trinity* IX, 1, 8.

eternal Word of the Father, derivative of the Father's eternal act of self-knowledge, and the Spirit as the eternal love of the Father and the Son, derived from and expressive of the mutual love of the two.[6]

Aquinas brings to the analysis of Trinitarian relations his own reflection based on Aristotelian ideas about the ontology of relations.[7] In created things, real relations imply two terms that are reciprocal or relative to one another. Such relations emerge either from reciprocal action and passion or in relative quantity. In the quantitative realm, which does not apply to God as such, one can identify real relations of height, depth, weight, and so on, based on comparative quantity. In actions that create effects, there is a real relation of the agent and the patient. This can be true in the immaterial realm. When the human mind is actively generating a concept of something known, the concept is being passively begotten of the human mind. When one person begins to love another by an inclination of the will, he does so under the experiential effect or ontological imprint of the other person whose personal goodness draws forth the will to love.

The notion of reciprocal relation is especially useful in Trinitarian theology, as Aquinas notes, because it allows one to formulate an analogical notion for persons in God, in whom there is real distinction without substantial differentiation.[8] In the created realm, a given substance can relate to itself and so accrue distinctions of reciprocity without multiplying beings. Simply stated, a human being can know conceptually and love voluntarily, and these actions imply real relations but do not imply distinct substances. The act of knowing is immanent within the knower, and the act of loving (even if one loves another person) is an act occurring immanently within a given person, tending toward the other.

Such notions can only be applied to Trinitarian persons by

---

6. *The Trinity,* V, 3–4; XV, 5.

7. *ST* Ia, q. 13, a. 7 and q. 28, a. 1; Id., *In Meta.* V, lect. 17, 1001–32.; *Commentary on Metaphysics.* For historical background and conceptual discussion of real relations in the Trinity in Aquinas, see Gilles Emery, *The Trinitarian Theology of St. Thomas Aquinas,* 78–102.

8. *ST,* Ia, q. 28, a. 2.

analogy. Most significantly, as we will note in a moment, there are no accidents or non-substantial properties in God. God is his wisdom and his love. Consequently, any relational derivation in God is substantial in kind. The eternal Word of the Father possesses in himself the plenitude of the divine nature and life, while a human concept does not possess the fullness of a human being within it. The eternal Spirit of love possesses in himself all that is in the Father and the Son as God, while any human love is only a characteristic or aspect of a person, not his or her very substance. What the notion of reciprocal relations does provide, however, is a nuanced but clear analogy for the life of eternal reciprocity in God. The Son is eternally derived from the Father as his begotten Word, by a procession we can compare by similitude to the act of immaterial conceptual understanding in a human being, while the Spirit is eternally derived from the Father and the Word as the immanent term of their mutual love, by a procession we can compare by similitude with the human volitional spiration of love.[9] These two processions are constituted by—or we might say eternally sustained within—the reciprocal relations of generation and spiration.[10] The Son receives all that he has from the Father, and the Father gives all that he has as God to the Son. The Spirit receives all that he has from the Father and the Son as from one principle, and they communicate to him all that they have as God.[11] Therefore, there is an eternal relation of the Father to the Son and of the Son to the Father, expressed in the procession of begetting, and an eternal relation of the Father and Son to the Spirit and of the Spirit to the Father and the Son expressed in the procession of spiration. The life of the Holy Trinity is a relational life of mutual communication and reception and thus is also an unfathomable mystery of eternal communion.[12]

---

9. *ST*, Ia, q. 34, a. 1; q. 37, a. 1–2.

10. *ST*, Ia, q. 40, a. 1–4.

11. *ST*, Ia, q. 36, a. 4.

12. On Trinitarian perichoresis as related to the relations of the persons, see *ST*, Ia, q. 42, a. 5.

Divine Simplicity

To this first idea of relational identity of persons in God, we can add a second, that of divine simplicity. Several diverse patristic and medieval theories of simplicity preceded Aquinas', and his treatment collects various prior reflections on divine simplicity into a thematic unity, evidenced especially in *Summa theologiae* I, q. 3. For the purposes of our argument, it is especially important to consider *ST* I, q. 3, aa. 3, 4, and 6. In these articles, Aquinas denies that there exist in the divine nature various kinds of compositions found in creatures. In article 3, he argues that there is no real distinction of nature and individual in God, as one commonly finds in material creatures. Whereas a human being or an orange tree is one of millions of such kinds of substances, there is only one who is God, who possesses the entire divine nature. In a. 4, Aquinas notes that God is unlike all creatures, material and immaterial, in that he does not receive his being from another, and that, therefore, there obtains no real distinction in him of essence and existence. Unlike all derivative realities that are given being, God exists by nature. It is of his essence to be, and he, therefore, possesses in himself the plenitude of all that pertains to being. In article 6, Aquinas notes that the divine nature cannot be a composite of substance and property. Such a composition would imply that God might develop progressively from potency to act through the actuation of his properties—namely, the accidental activities of knowledge and love—so as to evolve in perfection. Rather, God's knowledge and love are subsistent and pertain to him essentially. God is his knowledge and love. He possesses in himself from all eternity the unfathomable fullness of perfect knowledge and love by nature.

These reflections are each pertinent for the Trinitarian account of relations we have alluded to above since they each color the way one understands the relational identity of the persons derived from the Father. If, in fact, the Son and the Spirit are one in essence with the Father, and if there is only one God, then they are not three gods, but the one God subsisting in three modes based on relational derivation. If the divine essence of God implies in itself the plenitude of existence and simply is this fullness of being, then the Son and the Spirit who proceed from the Father simply possess in themselves all that God is in his plenitude of existence, though they receive all that they are as God from the Father. If the divine nature is not constituted by a distinction of substance and properties, then the Son and the Spirit do not have distinct natural attributes or properties that the Father does not have (or vice versa). Rather, each of the persons possesses all that pertains to God's divine essence: divine knowledge, love, power, and so forth, as each is wholly and truly the one Lord.

Persons as Subsistent Relations

These two reflections on persons as relational and on the simplicity of the divine nature lead logically to a third Thomistic consideration: that pertaining to the Trinitarian persons as subsistent relations.[13] Aquinas made a major contribution to Trinitarian thought by his reflection on this concept. Basically, if the persons are distinguished by their relations of origin and thus characterized by relationality, and at the same time, there are no properties or accidents in God distinct from essence (such as properties of relations that we find in creatures), then the relations in God are not accidental but substantial. That is to say, in dissimilitude to human persons who have real relations to others as properties of their substance, the Trinitarian persons are relational in all that they are. The Father is always already characterized in all that he is by his relations of generation and spiration. His paternity is not a property of his person; rather, he is his paternity. The Son is one who is from the Father in all that he is, as one eternally begotten, and relationally active with the Father, as from one principle, in the spiration of the Spirit. The Spirit is always from the Father and the Son in all that he is, as their mutually spirated love.

Gilles Emery has noted helpfully that this way of thinking of

---

13. See on this topic, *ST*, Ia, q. 29, a. 4.

divine persons, as relations that are subsistent rather than accidental, leads to a twofold consideration of each person that he terms "reduplication."[14] Simply stated, we can only think of each Trinitarian person as both relational in all that he is and subsistent God (i.e., as one possessing the plenitude of the divine essence.) The Father is the eternal principle of the Son and Spirit, innascible in his very person, and he is truly the one God, possessing the plenitude of the divine essence, eternal life, wisdom and love, divine power, and so forth. The Son is the eternally begotten Word of the Father who also possesses in himself the identical divine perfection, eternal life, wisdom, and love, etc., but as one who has all he is as God from the Father. The Spirit is the eternally spirated love of the Father and Son, immanently present within them as the mutual term of their reciprocal love, possessing in himself the plenitude of the divine essence, eternal life, wisdom and love, as from the Father and Son as a unique principle. Each person is truly God, and each person is relationally constituted or distinguished in virtue of his relation of origin.

Trinitarian Monotheism and Modes of Subsistence

The vision of Trinitarian theology that Aquinas's theory of persons as subsistent relations gives rise to is one that is radically egalitarian. Each of the persons is equally and identically God because each of the persons truly possesses unequivocally all that pertains to the divine essence. Therefore, there is only one God. At the same time, the persons are truly distinct and intelligibly distinguishable in virtue of their relational modes of subsistence, as each either is the originator of or originates from another or others. In this sense, Aquinas's theological vision is one of irreducible Trinitarian monotheism. There is only one God, and that one God is truly three distinct persons who are one in being and essence.

From this standpoint, it is clear why and how we can speak of

14. See the proposals of Gilles Emery, "Essentialism or Personalism in the Treatise on God in St. Thomas Aquinas?."

three personal modes of subsistence in God or of three distinct modes of subsistence in God. We mentioned above that each of the three persons can best be named under a twofold conceptual moniker by reduplication as (a) relational and (b) subsistent God. It follows from this line of thinking that each person is truly God in a distinct mode or way of being, depending on his relational origin. The Father is God and Lord in an unoriginate way, as the eternal principle and origin of the Son and Spirit. The Son is God in an eternally begotten way, as the Word of the Father. The Spirit is God in a spirated way, as one who is the mutual love of Father and Son. The deity or divine essence of God exists, then, in three modes.[15] To say this is not to reduce the distinct persons in God to a mere unitarian modalism, as if God were really only three distinct natural modes of being and not three truly distinct persons. On the contrary, the modal distinction in question presupposes the affirmation of real personal distinctions in God. There are only three modes of being God, we might say, because there are truly three persons in God. Just as the Father, Son, and Spirit are each equally and identically powerful, wise, and good, in virtue of their common deity, so they are all also powerful, wise, and good in distinctly personal ways in virtue of their relational origins which give rise to distinct modes of subsistence.

15. For texts where Aquinas clearly states as much, see *De Potentia*, q. 2, a. 1, ad 13; a. 5, ad 5; q. 3, a. 15, ad 17 and q. 9, a. 5, ad 23. See also G. Emery commenting on these texts, "The Personal Mode of Trinitarian Action in Saint Thomas Aquinas," 56: "A precision should be made: in the Trinity, the personal distinction does not modify the divine being or nature as such, or the power of acting, or the action. But the three persons are distinct under the aspect of the mode of being of the divine essence in them and, consequently, under the aspect of the mode of acting corresponding to the mode of being. The distinction of these modes concerns, therefore, the proper relation of the person, that is, the intra-Trinitarian relationship of person to person according to origin. Each person exists and acts in accordance with his relation to the other persons. This mode of being and of acting expresses the order (*ordo*) of the persons since the real plurality of the divine persons rests in this order. For Thomas Aquinas, indeed, the personal distinction is not based solely on the difference of origin of the Son and the Holy Spirit (generation and spiration), nor even on the mode of the procession of the Son and Holy Spirit (mode of nature or intellect, mode of will or love), but on the order of origin within the Trinity: the Son has his existence from the Father, the Holy Spirit has his existence from the Father and the Son."

To underscore this last point, we can appeal to what I have termed the "mode of subsistence" of the divine persons. This term provides us with a way of underscoring the idea of personal identity in God by averting not primarily to the divine nature subsisting in three modes (as I have done in the previous paragraph) but by averting to the three persons as persons, each being God in a distinct way. If we think of the Father as a divine person, distinct from the Son and the Spirit, we must take into account his paternal principality, as the origin of all Trinitarian life, and of all that comes forth from the Trinity in creation. He is the one from whom the Word and Spirit issue forth by eternal procession, in whom all things are made. So too, then, if we think of him as God, we must consider him as one having the plenitude of the deity that he eternally communicates fully to the Son and the Spirit by generation and spiration, respectively. So then, by consideration of these ideas taken together (distinct personhood and plenitude of deity), we may consider the Father's identity in virtue of his distinct mode of subsistence. He is the one who is God in a paternal and principal way, eternal font of the Son and the Spirit. The Son is he who is God in a begotten mode, as the eternally generated Word of the Father, who possesses the godhead from another, which we can understand by a similitude taken from intellectual procession. The Father, in knowing himself perfectly from all eternity, expresses himself in the generation of his begotten Word, who contains in himself the plenitude of the Father's wisdom and being. The Spirit is he who is God in an eternally spirated mode as one who is breathed forth from the Father and the Son, which we can understand by a similitude taken from the voluntary procession of love, which tends to the good of the other. The Spirit is the impression of mutual love who comes from the Father and the Son, in whom they express the totality of their nature and being.[16] Each of the persons in his relational mode of being has a distinctive personal identity as God in virtue of the relations of origin characteristic of that person.

16. *ST* Ia, q. 37, a. 1.

ECONOMIC APPLICATIONS

What we have said up to now may seem irrelevant to a theology of the divine economy, one that would take seriously the mysterious activity of the distinct persons of the Trinity both in our creation and in the drama of redemption, in which the Son becomes human and the Spirit is sent forth upon the apostolic Church at Pentecost to sanctify humanity. This is far from the case, however. Here we can consider briefly three concrete applications of the principles enunciated above that facilitate a correct understanding of the divine economy (God active in creation and redemption) as wholly Trinitarian in form: the unity of all divine action *ad extra*, Trinitarian missions and grace, and the distinction of natures in the Incarnate Word. We can then compare the Thomistic vision we are exploring with two alternative modern views of the issues under consideration.

Unity and Personal Character of All Divine Action

A first and most important general application of the theology we have been exploring above is concerned with all action of the Holy Trinity *ad extra* or outside of God. When God creates and sustains all things in being or acts within creation by the communication of grace in view of the redemption and sanctification of creatures, God acts as Trinity. In all such action, the three persons are implicated in their unity, in virtue of the shared being and essence that they possess as God. Simultaneously, however, such Trinitarian action, not despite but precisely because it is the action of all three persons in their natural unity, is also the action of each distinct person in accord with his mode of subsistence.

We can illustrate the idea briefly by appeal to the notion of Trinitarian creation. It is not merely the Father who creates, but the Trinity, and so the act by which God communicates being to creatures is an act of the Son and Spirit just as much as it is an act of the Father.[17]

17. *ST*, Ia, q. 45, a. 6, resp.

God's active communication of being to all things that are not God occurs in virtue of the divine essence and life of God, namely his infinite perfection, goodness, wisdom, power, and so forth. This act is also, however, a personal act of the Father who has desired to give being to all things as one who is wholly and uniquely unoriginated, the principle and font of Trinitarian life, from whom all things come forth.[18] The Father has created us in his Word, the principle of intelligibility in all things, in whom all that is made is made (John 1:1–3), and the Father has created us in his Spirit, the uncreated gift of the Father and Son, in whom and from whom the gift of being is given to all creatures by love. Accordingly, creatures bear ontological notes of Trinitarian resemblance, vestiges of the persons, in accord with their own respective modes of being.[19] Creatures bear an imperfect resemblance to the Father in virtue of their substantial autonomy, which they receive from the Father in his subsistent primacy. Creatures bear an imperfect resemblance to the begotten Word as derivative realities marked by species and intelligibility. They come forth from the Father pregnant with inner meaning and truth, in virtue of their very being. Creatures bear an imperfect resemblance to the Spirit of love as realities that have a relation to order. They are all inclined to achieve perfections and to communicate the good. The Holy Spirit is a person who is uncreated love, who gives the gift of being to all created realities so that they, in turn, might be inclined to the order of love.[20] Of course, all three persons author the creation actively but because they all act together, the creatures that emanate forth from them bear imperfect similitudes in particular ways to each of the persons from whom they originate.

Trinitarian Grace and Missions

A second application of the notion of persons as distinct subsistent modes of being is evident in the consideration of the economy of

18. *ST*, Ia, q. 45, a. 6, ad 2.
19. *ST*, Ia, q. 45, a. 7.
20. *ST*, Ia, q. 45, a. 7.

grace. We can consider this reference both in terms of efficient causality and final causality. Efficient causality here refers especially to the Trinity as source of all grace, while final causality refers especially to our human possession and enjoyment of the uncreated persons by knowledge and love, as an ultimate effect of grace.

To the first of these two considerations: The Holy Trinity is the source of the diffusion of all grace. Based on the principles of common action enunciated above, it is clear that this activity occurs in virtue of the divine nature common to the three persons. Indeed, grace is itself rightly understood as a participation in the divine nature.[21] Simultaneously, however, the gift of grace is also wholly personal in origin. The Father personally communicates grace to intellectual creatures (angels and human beings) so as to adopt them as children of God, sons in the Son. He sends the Son and Spirit into the world by way of their divine missions, so as to render them present in the world in new ways, both invisibly and visibly, culminating in the Incarnation and in Pentecost.[22] Yet the divine sending of the Son and the Spirit into the world on the part of the Father is also a collaborative personal work of the Son and of the Spirit respectively, who each will personally to be sent on mission, that is to say, who will as God to be present and active in creation in a new way in virtue of their personal activity in the communication of grace.[23] In his visible mission, the Son himself personally communicates grace and enlightens human persons, introducing them into the inward contours of his own mystery. The Holy Spirit also personally gives grace, enlightens, communicates charity and other gifts, and sanctifies. Each of these actions are only ever actions of the persons as such, not of an impersonal divine nature. However, these same actions are never actions of only one of the persons. They always implicate the persons in their natural unity, mutual indwelling, and communion. When the Holy Spirit sanctifies, he does so as the Spirit

21. See 2 Pet 1:4, and Aquinas's commentary in *ST*, Ia-IIae, q. 110, a. 3, as well as his reflection in a. 4.

22. *ST*, Ia, q. 43, a. 1, 2, and 7.

23. *ST*, Ia, q. 43, a. 3, 5, and 6.

of the Father and the Son, eternally proceeding from them as love and sent into the world by them to do their work. By working in the world actively he not only renders himself present, but also renders the Father and Jesus Christ present, and they act with him and in him.[24] The communication of divine life is a Trinitarian act even as it is also a person-specific act, in which the subsistent mode of being of each person is made manifest and magnified by their common action in the economy of grace.

In the order of final causality, a different result obtains from our considerations. We have noted that all three persons communicate grace, even when each of them does so personally. Such grace can effectuate, however, a deeper intimacy and understanding of only one of the persons, precisely as something willed by all three. For example, the Holy Trinity may wish to reveal the Son of God in particular to someone. "And in the synagogues immediately [Saul] proclaimed Jesus, saying, 'He is the Son of God'" (Acts 9:20). In this case, the origin of the grace can be said to be from the Father, Son, and Holy Spirit, in truly distinct personal modes of action, but the final effect terminates in the union of the creature with one person in particular. A person can receive the grace of understanding and insight so as to know Jesus Christ personally in a much more profound way. However, this same dynamic can and often does occur with respect to each person, so that a human being who first comes to discover Jesus

---

24. Thomas Aquinas, *Super Ioan.* In *Commentary on the Gospel of St. John*, vol. 2 (Petersham, MA: St. Bede's Publications, 2000), XIV, lect. 6, 1957: "Now the Son comes in the name of the Father not because he is the Father, but because he is the Son of the Father. In a similar way, the Holy Spirit comes in the name of the Son not because he was to be called the Son, but because he is the Spirit of the Son: 'Anyone who does not have the Spirit of Christ does not belong to him' (Rom 8:9); 'God has sent the Spirit of his Son into our hearts' (Gal 4:6), because he is the Spirit of his Son, and not because he was to be called the Son: 'he predestined [them] to be conformed to the image of his Son' (Rom 8:29). The basis for this is the consubstantiality of the Son with the Father and of the Holy Spirit with the Son. Further, just as the Son, coming in the name of the Father, subjects his faithful to the Father—and 'has made them a kingdom and priests to our God' (Rev 5:10)—so the Holy Spirit conforms us to the Son because he adopts us as children of God: 'You have received the spirit of adoption, by which we cry out 'Abba! Father'' [Rom 8:15]."

Christ can be enlightened progressively with regard to the Father's personal presence and identity, and so grow to love the Father more deeply. Or a person can receive the grace to know and understand the Holy Spirit specifically as an inward teacher and guide, uncreated gift, and friend. Furthermore, the three persons in themselves are mutually related. So, an illumination that makes one more aware of the very person of Jesus Christ also inevitably draws one closer to the Father of our Lord Jesus Christ (2 Cor. 11:31), and to the Holy Spirit who is the Spirit of the Son (Gal. 4:6). Here we should also make brief mention of exemplary causality since our conformity to a given person in the order of grace, to his personal mode of being, must also carry with it some degree of spiritual conformity to the other persons. If the final effect of grace is to draw us into union with Jesus Christ, in his filial mode of being, so too it must draw us into relative connection with the Father as our Father, and with the Spirit of Christ whom he sends upon the Church, so that she might share in his Spirit, the Spirit of his Father.

Incarnation and the Distinction of Natures

A final application of the notion of subsistent modes of Trinitarian persons pertains to the mystery of the Incarnation. We have noted above that the persons of the Trinity act collectively in all works of God outside of God, but that the terminative effect of their collective action can draw a human being into a personal knowledge of one person in particular. In this example, they collectively will a distinctive final effect that pertains to one Trinitarian person as such. The Incarnation presents us with a unique example of this truth. Aquinas logically underscores that the Incarnation, in which the Son of God personally takes on a human nature, body and soul, is a work of all three persons of the Holy Trinity. Only the Son is human, but the three persons are the transcendent source and ground of the effectuation of the mystery. The Incarnation of the Son is willed by the Father, Son, and Holy Spirit, as efficient source.[25] The

25. *ST*, IIIa, q. 3, a. 1 and 4.

terminative effect of their action is hypostatic: The Trinitarian persons desire that the Son should become human, subsisting personally in a human nature.[26]

A number of significant consequences follow from this claim, some of which should be stated briefly in this context. First, it is clear on this view that only the second person of the Trinity is human, not the Father or the Holy Spirit. Consequently, anything that Jesus Christ does or is subject to as man, either actively or passively, is properly ascribed to him personally and is not rightly ascribed to the Father or the Spirit.[27] When the child Jesus is born of Mary, it is the eternal Word who is born in a cave in Bethlehem, not the Father or the Holy Spirit. This is likewise the case when Jesus preaches, walks from town to town in Galilee, or is tortured and crucified, dies, and is buried. All such actions and sufferings are rightly attributed to God because the Word and Son is himself God.[28] They are not accurately attributed, however, to the other two persons of the Trinity.

Second, when the Son acts not only as man but also as God, he only ever acts with the Father and the Spirit. If, for example, Jesus of Nazareth touches the eyes of a man born blind and heals him, his human gestures and words pertain to him alone as the Incarnate Son, but his divine action and the miraculous effect of his divine compassion and omnipotence pertains also to his Father who works with him and in him, and to the Holy Spirit who is within him, working with him and from him.[29]

Third, whether Jesus Christ acts or suffers in characteristically human ways (as when he walks, sleeps, or is crucified), or acts in both divine and human ways simultaneously (when he teaches divine truth with authority or heals miraculously), he does so as the eternal Son of the Father. Therefore, he acts or suffers personally in virtue of his subsistent mode of being, proper to him as a Trinitarian

---

26. *ST*, IIIa, q. 2, a. 2.
27. *ST*, IIIa, q. 16, a. 2.
28. *ST*, IIIa, a. 4.
29. *ST*, IIIa, q. 19, a. 1.

person. Simply stated, the one who acts or suffers is the Son. His personal mode of being God is filial and is identical with his personal mode of being human. The man Jesus is human in a mysteriously filial way, so that his human actions and gestures indicate his personal identity as the Son. By this very fact it follows that all his human actions and sufferings or his theandric (divine-human) actions, are indicative of his personal relation to his Father and to the Holy Spirit and so reveal, however obliquely, the presence and activity of these other two persons in his human life and ministry. If Jesus heals a man born blind, he does so as the Son of the Father, as one wholly relative to his Father, and his action reveals the hidden presence and activity of his Father, who is the unoriginate principle of the action, as well as that of their common Spirit, who is active with them as their mutual love. If Jesus freely suffers crucifixion, even unto death, he does so as the Son sent by the Father, revealing the will of the Father to redeem humanity and the will of the Son to do so with and for his Father, and in doing so to send the Spirit upon humanity.[30] So, too, the Spirit who inspires Jesus' human heart and mind to embrace the mystery of the Cross does so in view of his own desire to act upon humanity in light of the crucifixion. The Spirit wishes to communicate the grace of Christ to all human beings as One who is the love of the Father and the Son.[31] He reveals himself at Pentecost when he is sent by the Father and by Jesus Christ upon all humanity.

ALTERNATIVES

At this point it is helpful to consider two influential counter-alternatives to the views we have been proposing, one developed by Karl Rahner and the other by Jürgen Moltmann. We can begin with Rahner, whose views are especially influential and are articulated

---

30. *ST*, IIIa, q. 47, a. 2–3.

31. On the Holy Spirit as the source of Christ's habitual grace and gifts as man, see *ST*, IIIa, q. 7, a. 13, as well as q. 7, a. 5–6, all of which have implications for the way in which one should interpret q. 8, a. 1 and 3 on Christ as head of the Church and of all human beings. The Spirit of the Son distributes the grace of Christ to all who receive it.

clearly in his well-known work *The Trinity*.[32] In that work, Rahner elaborates a number of theses that break decisively with the tradition we have been exploring above.

First, Rahner claims that traditional Catholic scholastic theology has focused unhelpfully on a non-personalist *de Deo ut uno* treatise concerned with divine attributes of the divine nature, to the exclusion of a more experientialist and pastoral consideration of the Trinitarian persons in their economic activity.[33] Likewise, he bids farewell to the idea of a systematic treatment of the immanent Trinity based on the analogy from acts of the human soul (the psychological analogy).[34] These choices signal that he is poised to move all substantive discussion of the distinction of persons in God from the plane of theoretical consideration of the immanent life of God to the realm of the economic activity of the Trinity. The *Grundaxiom* has decisively epistemological connotations in this regard: the only way we know the Trinity itself is from the consideration of the Trinity in the economy.[35]

This initially ambiguous proposal begins to emerge in its greater novelty when we consider the ontological implications of Rahner's formulation. Central to his presentation of Trinitarian theology is the claim that the Incarnation just is what happens when God communicates himself outside of himself, an idea he joins with the proviso that human nature emerges from God only ever in view of this act of incarnation.[36] God can freely create, then, it seems, but if he does so, he will create a world of human beings and will himself become

32. Karl Rahner, *The Trinity*. See also the earlier developments in this regard in Rahner's essay "Remarks on the Dogmatic Treatise 'De Trinitate,'" in *Theological Investigations* Vol. 4, trans. K. Smith (London: Darton, Longman, & Todd, 1967) originally published in German in 1960.

33. Rahner, *The Trinity*, 10–21.

34. See Rahner, *The Trinity*, 19, 46–48, 115–20.

35. Rahner, *The Trinity*, 21: "The Trinity is a mystery of *salvation*, otherwise it would never have been revealed ... We must point out in *every* dogmatic treatise that what it says about salvation does not make sense without referring to this primordial mystery of Christianity." Similarly, p. 22: "The 'economic' Trinity is the 'immanent' Trinity and 'immanent' Trinity is the 'economic' Trinity."

36. Rahner, *The Trinity*, 32–33.

human so as to express himself in what he formerly was not. It is of essential importance to this schema that only the Son can become incarnate, precisely because he is the communicable Word of the Father, the divine mode of self-communication expressed in creatures by way of incarnation. This may seem like merely a repetition of a medieval Scotistic theme on the Incarnation as the term of creation, now repurposed for modern uses. However, what Rahner in fact affirms more or less explicitly is that the Son is naturally distinct from the Father and the Spirit eternally in virtue of a pre-existent relation that he has to creatures. Only he from all eternity, in virtue of his personal identity, can become human.[37] Clearly, this is something neither Scotus nor Aquinas would ever have said. This idea is of course the opposite of that which we have been exploring in this chapter, since it suggests that the Son as Son has distinct natural capacities or potencies as God toward creatures that the other two persons do not have. In this case, there is no wholly common natural identity of the three persons based on a corresponding theology of divine simplicity (all that is in the Son is in the Father and the Spirit).[38] There is no personal distinction expressed in three distinct modes of subsistence of the one divine nature. Instead, the personal distinctions in God correspond to natural distinctions in God. What Aquinas has united in his theology, Rahner has sundered. Where Aquinas posits three distinct personal modes of subsistence of the one God, we enter with Rahner into the territory of three personal agents having distinct natural properties based on their real relations to creatures.

Nor is this interpretation mere conjecture since this is the accompanying proposal that Rahner makes expressly in his work. He takes issue with the traditional claim that the divine persons cannot have "real relations" with creatures (i.e., they cannot become

37. The argument is given in Rahner, *The Trinity*, 26–33. The Son alone can be human based on his unique ontological relation to creation as the principle of divine self-communication.

38. It is because of the simplicity of God that one must affirm that each of the persons has the power to become human, even if it is more fitting that the Son become human based on his filial mode of subsistence. See *ST*, IIIa, q. 3, a. 5 and 8.

ontologically relative to and determined by creatures).[39] Rahner affirms the inverse and, perhaps more significantly, claims that each person of the Trinity can and must have distinct real relations to creatures, precisely as a condition for there to be authentic experiential engagement of Trinitarian persons, each in their uniqueness, with created persons.[40] Consequently, what we arrive at is the idea that the economic Trinity (which is seemingly just what God 'really is') consists of three persons who are each subject individually to distinctive *natural* determinations through their historical relations with creatures. This suggests that there could be three distinct sets of nature-determinations, each set proper to a given person, which develop economically in each person based on independent real relations with creatures. If one follows this line of thinking, then there are three natural sets of properties or activities in the three persons that are not wholly overlapping or identical.

Rahner himself did not develop this idea in greater detail, but those inspired by his *Grundaxiom* would do so, sometimes in critical engagement with his own theological positions, which they considered to be incomplete. A famous case is presented in the work of Jürgen Moltmann, whose view we can consider as our second example.[41] Moltmann complains, somewhat understandably, that Rahner enunciates principles he fails to follow through on in a sufficiently systematic way.[42] What would it mean for our theology of the Trinity

39. Rahner, *The Trinity*, 34–38.

40. See, for example, Rahner, *The Trinity*, 64 and 102: The Word "just is" the self-expression of the Father, which is always, already *both* immanent in God (communication of what the Father is to us in his Word) *and* his self-expression in what is not God (in creation and the human nature of Christ). God *freely* chooses to self-communicate, but he also seems somehow to determine himself eternally in his identity as Father, Word, and Spirit for and in relation to the creation. See also Rahner, *The Trinity*, 13–14: "Today's theology hardly ever sees any connection between the Trinity and the doctrine of creation. This isolation is considered legitimate since the 'outward' divine operations are 'common' to the three divine persons, so that the world as creation cannot tell us anything about the inner life of the Trinity."

41. See especially Jürgen Moltmann, *The Trinity and the Kingdom: The Doctrine of God*, trans. M. Kohl (San Francisco: Harper and Row, 1981).

42. See especially Moltmann, 144–48, where he claims Rahner and Barth advanced,

if each of the persons were to have real relations to creation that are distinct in form? Moltmann argues that in the mystery of creation, each person of the Trinity must relate really (by ontological alteration) to creation in distinct ways, and so, also as a result of creation, each person of the Trinity begins to relate to each other in a new way, altering dynamically the very life of God.[43] The creation occurs only when the Father first makes room in his own self and being (the divine nature of the Father) for the creation by limiting his infinite power (making it really relative to creation), and the Son, in turn, reciprocates this gesture in a distinctive way.[44]

Moltmann presents similar ideas in regard to the crucifixion. He claims, famously, that the Son suffers death and non-being not only in his human nature but in his very person and divine nature. Moltmann follows Hegel in affirming that death occurs in God himself.[45] The Father, meanwhile, experiences mourning and suffering of a distinctively paternal sort, suffering divinely in a way that is distinct from the divine suffering of the Son.[46] The Father and the Son, then, each have a distinctive mode of being God, as in Aquinas, but there corresponds to this in each of them distinct natural non-identical modes of being God, determined by their distinct relations to creatures. Moltmann goes so far as to say that one of the persons can experience death (in crucifixion) while another does not,

---

in effect, an implicit form of modalism, suggesting that the logic of the *Grundaxiom* can be taken up and followed through on in a new way.

43. Moltmann, 80–83.

44. Moltmann, 111: "If we think about this external state of affairs, transferring it by a process of reflection to the inner relationship of the Trinity, then it means that the Father, through an alteration of his love for the Son (that is to say through a contraction of the Spirit), and the Son, through an alteration in his response to the Father's love (that is, through an inversion of the Spirit) have opened up the space, the time and the freedom for that 'outwards' into which the Father utters himself creatively through the Son. For God himself this utterance means an emptying of himself—a self-determination for the purpose of a self-limitation. Time is an interval in eternity, finitude is a space in infinity, and freedom is a concession of the eternal love. God withdraws himself in order to go out of himself." See also, Moltmann, *God in Creation: A New Theology of Creation and the Spirit of God* (Minneapolis: Fortress, 1993), 86–88.

45. Moltmann, *The Trinity and the Kingdom*, 81–88.

46. Moltmann, 89–90.

underscoring the natural polarity that can exist in God, across the spectrum of persons: this spectrum transcends the distinction between being and non-being.[47] Now the economic Trinity is a Trinity in whom the persons are distinguished by diverse natural properties accrued in virtue of their individual relations to the history of creation and redemption, and even in a certain sense, existence and non-existence.[48] Moltmann is helpfully clear about the fact that his proposals are meant directly to undermine traditional notions of divine unity, of an abstract monotheism that he thinks is devoid of credibility.[49] The three persons in God are distinct not only in relation but also in subsistent divine properties and thus possess a quasi-substantial autonomy with respect to one another. Their unity is social rather than consubstantial, analogous to that of three distinct human persons who live and develop together by a shared history, in which they cooperate with one another through their mutual engagements within the economy.

Clearly, what we have just sketched out briefly above is a vision of the Trinity very different from that presented in previous sections. There are several motivations subjacent to this new articulation of Trinitarian theology. Despite their noteworthy differences, Rahner and Moltmann are united in their wish to provide Christian theology with a vision of the Trinity in which the persons are seen to be actively engaged with and reactive to the world. They both wish also to distance themselves (in differing ways) from the legacy of classical philosophical metaphysics as it traditionally plays a role within Trinitarian theology, especially in the treatment of attributes of the divine nature. They also wish to underscore the personal and experiential character of our understanding of the Trinity within a lived

47. See Jürgen Moltmann, *The Crucified God: The Cross of Christ as the Foundation and Criticism of Christian Theology*, 235–52. At 243: "The Son suffers dying, the Father suffers the death of the son. The grief of the Father here is just as important as the death of the Son. The Fatherlessness of the Son is matched by the Sonlessness of the Father, and if God has constituted himself as the Father of Jesus Christ, then he also suffers the death of his Fatherhood in the death of the Son."

48. Moltmann, *The Trinity and the Kingdom*, 112–13.

49. See the thematic argument in Moltmann, *The Crucified God*, especially 219–52.

history with God, in which we come to know who God is precisely as he engages with us in that history. In addition, Moltmann, in particular, wishes to rethink radically the doctrine of the distinction of natures in Christ so as to apply to the Son as God (in his divine nature) the very features of passivity, suffering, and death associated with his human life. In this way, he hopes to demonstrate the personal way in which God is present to his creatures, living in solidarity with them in suffering.[50]

However, there are ironies that emerge with regard to the aims of both Rahner and Moltmann. They each wish to underscore God's genuine solidarity with us in economic history, his relation to us in a tri-personal way, and the distinctive features proper to each person in virtue of his shared history with us. But they do so just to the extent that they each pursue a line of argument that distinguishes the persons in virtue of their distinct economic *natural* actions or passions; they also define the persons in God in non-unified, essentially differentiated ways.[51] In short, they threaten to undermine genuine monotheism as a constituent aspect of Trinitarian doctrine, just as they threaten to jettison any internal content of the formula *homoousios* as pertaining to a unified and singular essence of God common to the three persons. In reacting to the one extreme of a non-personalistic monotheism in textbook scholasticism (real or imagined), one risks running headlong into a non-monotheistic social trinitarianism in which the unity of the persons is no longer fully intelligible. Or alternatively, one can fall into a modalism that would distinguish three irreducible natural states in God corresponding to three persons, but that would not maintain a sufficiently clear distinction of persons who share a common nature. God would

---

50. See Moltmann, *The Crucified God*, 267–78.

51. This is why Rahner's decision not to call the three hypostases "persons" but "modes of subsistence" for fear of anthropomorphism (Rahner, *The Trinity*, 103–15) is in fact a differentiation of the hypostases based on natural features. He clearly believes there to be three persons in God but wants to differentiate them primarily through distinct natural activities. His decision to not call the three "persons" then is not necessitated by the principles of his thought mentioned above, but it is consistent with them in its own way.

become a historical process consisting in diverse natural forms of self-differentiation.

Furthermore, "from him who has not, even what he has will be taken away" (Matt. 13:12). The supposed strength of this alternative approach is that it allows one to underscore how the Trinity is truly present to creatures, such that the persons can act and react in personally singular ways in historical self-constitution or self-distinction by their engagement with human persons. However, it is important in this regard to recall that God the Creator is uniquely present to all that exists (omnipresent), because the Creator alone gives being in its totality, and he alone does so to all that exists.[52] In virtue of his solitary communication of being to all that is, God is closer to creation than it is to itself, without thereby identifying himself with creation.[53] God is in all his creation, and creation is mysteriously in God, but the two are also always distinguishable.[54] It is this omnipresence of transcendent causality that allows God to communicate grace to intellectual creatures in all times and places since he alone is already present to them as Creator, in all that they are, including in their innermost spiritual life of knowledge and love. Consequently, only if the Trinitarian persons each truly possess the fullness of the godhead by which being is given to the world are they also each able to communicate grace personally to each rational creature in history and, more generally, to render themselves personally present to all that exists as Trinitarian persons, in any circumstance. Accordingly, if one abandons a traditional theology of the divine nature as emblematically represented by the *de Deo ut uno* treatise, one will effectively jeopardize realistic understanding of the real presence of the Trinitarian persons to all human persons in the economy as well.

Finally, if the human nature of Christ exerts a relative action upon the deity of Christ such that his deity is redefined by the

52. *ST,* Ia, q. 8, a. 1 and 4.
53. *ST,* q. 45, a. 5; q. 8, a. 3.
54. *ST,* q. 4, a. 2; q. 8, a. 2.

historical human experiences he undergoes, then God, in his divine essence, is not truly distinct from, nor transcendent to the world and to the horrors of the worst human suffering. Rather, he is in fact defined precisely, essentially, and in some sense, eternally, by historical suffering in his Trinitarian self-differentiation of persons. In this case, the Incarnation is not the revelation of God's historical solidarity with us in human suffering, which reveals his transcendent Trinitarian love and its capacity to remake all things. Instead, the Incarnation is the occasion for our human suffering to reconstitute or remake the Trinitarian persons in their mutual relations and personal-constitutions so that our human suffering is hypostasized eternally.[55]

What are the advantages of the view we have underscored in the first part of this chapter in contradistinction to the one just sketched out? First, the classical understanding of Trinitarian persons as subsistent relations avoids the twin errors of modalism and of subordinationism, so as to underscore that there are three truly distinct persons in the Trinity who are each truly and completely the one God. Second, by its understanding of the doctrine of the simplicity of the divine nature, this theology makes clear that all that is in the Father is in the Son and in the Spirit, but by an order of procession. The twin processions of generation and spiration are presented by analogy with human acts of intellection and love so as to make clear that there is a distinct analogy for the immanent life of the Trinity that does not depend upon God's historical outward action with us. The immanent Trinity as a mystery is genuinely intelligible by theological analogy and is in no way an incoherent notion. Third, the

---

55. Moltmann, *The Trinity and the Kingdom*, 81: "The Son suffers death in this forsakenness. The Father suffers the death of the Son. So, the pain of the Father corresponds to the death of the Son. And when in this descent into hell the Son loses the Father, then in this judgment the Father also loses the Son. Here, the innermost life of the Trinity is at stake. Here, the communicating love of the Father *turns into infinite pain* over the sacrifice of the Son. Here, the responding love of the Son becomes *infinite suffering* over his repulsion and rejection by the Father. What happens on Golgotha *reaches into the innermost depths of the Godhead, putting its impress on the trinitarian life in eternity*." Emphasis added.

view we have presented underscores that while each of the persons is truly God, they are each also God in a distinctly subsistent mode or personal way based on the relations of origin. Therefore, they are only intelligible as personal agents, even when they act together in concord in virtue of their shared divine essence and life. In fact, it is precisely because of their consubstantiality that the three persons can be present in their modal uniqueness as persons and can act genuinely as persons always in concert with the others. When the Father acts and reveals himself in the economy, he acts with the Son and Spirit and, in so doing, also reveals them personally, in communion with himself. This facet of classical Trinitarian thought seems to address adequately, in fact, the worries of a theologian like Rahner regarding personal experience of the Trinity without without incurring the metaphysical liabilities of his novel thought form. Finally, this Thomistic understanding of the personal mode of subsistence of the Trinitarian persons allows one to understand, at least in part, how the Son of God can mysteriously reveal his personal identity as Son in his human nature, with its specific finite limitations, actions and sufferings, while acting always in concord with the Father and the Spirit as Lord. The Son reveals himself in our human form and in our flesh without undermining or negating the real distinction of his godhead and his humanity, of the divine and human natures of his one personal subject. We can and must maintain, then, that he truly reveals his filial mode of subsistence in our human flesh, even in his suffering and death, but we can and must do so while maintaining the Chalcedonian affirmation of the real distinction of the two natures of Jesus.

CONCLUSION

Contemporary students of the thought of St. Thomas Aquinas sometimes juxtapose two distinct ways of approaching his thought, commonly signified under the monikers of "Thomasian" and "Thomist." The former category refers to the historical and textual study of

Aquinas as a thinker within his original context, as a receiver and interpreter of antecedent patristic and medieval Christian tradition, who was conversant with Neoplatonic, Arabic, and Aristotelian trends of thought and who engaged in dialectic in the midst of the great university debates of his age. The latter category refers to those who seek to extract principles from Aquinas's thought that may serve the test of time and acquire a perennial or longstanding value in and through a tradition of ongoing inquiry and debate internal to the Thomistic tradition and by engagement externally with alternative viewpoints, Christian or non-Christian. There is no doubt that when contemporary scholars receive and interpret the intellectual heritage of Aquinas, these two trends of appropriation do really exist. At the same time, however, theoretical pathways between each of these approaches are always manifold and indeed inevitable. Ideally, the two approaches function in tandem by what might be characterized as a virtuous circle of mutual support. If the study of Aquinas in his historical context is to achieve a true depth and desirable level of universal interest to all comers for all ages, it must engage with perennial and profound questions of philosophy and theology, not only as they manifest themselves in Aquinas's historical thought, but also as they manifest themselves in the wider world of human inquiry. And if Thomism is to be a genuine study of reality that appeals to principles found in Aquinas's own thought, then it must not only seek the accountability of accuracy and true understanding of St. Thomas' textual self-expression. It must also ever seek to understand the historical thought of Aquinas better by taking into account the nuances of what he was saying in his given context and over the course of his own life as a theologian and saint. The best Thomasian is also a kind of Thomist, and the best Thomist is a kind of Thomasian.

The idea we have appealed to in this chapter, underscored by the scholarship of Gilles Emery, is indicative of the organic unity and non-competitiveness of these two vital approaches to the thought of St. Thomas. Understanding his work on the persons of the Holy Trinity in its own historical context and form of development serves as an excellent resource for speculative contemplation of the mystery of God. Engagement with our contemporaries who seek God and who seek to speak of God intelligibly should invite us to return to Aquinas and the Thomistic tradition with renewed interest and vigor so as to think more deeply about what the Catholic Church actually confesses and teaches with regard to the very reality of God in himself, Father, Son, and Holy Spirit. In this ongoing work of research and contemplation, it is of essential importance that Trinitarian theologians take into account Aquinas's treatment of the Trinitarian persons as personal modes of subsistence of the one God. As we enter discussions surrounding the use of this idea, it becomes clear that what is at stake is nothing less than the truthful and coherent confession of the Christian notion of God.

5

The Holy Spirit

In considering the mystery of God the Holy Spirit theologically, we will begin with a brief examination of the biblical revelation of the person and mission of the Spirit in the divine economy. This leads us to a reflection on the Holy Spirit as the eternal, uncreated love of the Father and the Son, who is the ground of our creation and sanctification. From this, an analysis of the controversy surrounding the Spirit's procession from the Son necessarily stands in order, followed by a consideration of ecumenical prospects for convergence between Eastern and Western Christians on the doctrine of the Holy Spirit. We conclude with reflections on the Holy Spirit as the uncreated soul of the Church.

FROM THE SPIRIT OF THE LORD TO
THE SPIRIT OF CHRIST

Christian theology takes its point of departure from the divine revelation given in and through salvation history. Within this history, faith perceives a divine economy in which God freely manifests his hidden identity to us and simultaneously communicates to

Originally published in *Oxford Handbook of Catholic Theology*, ed. Lewis Ayres and Medi Ann Volpe (Oxford: Oxford University Press 2019), 183–97.

the human race a participation in his divine life. Just as the Incarnation of the Son of God is foreshadowed in the Old Testament but only comes to full light in the New, so likewise, the Holy Spirit is unveiled progressively in and through the economy as a person distinct from the Father and the Son.

In the faith of ancient Israel, God's identity and action are personified by recourse to the notion of the 'Spirit of the Lord' and the 'Spirit of God.' The Spirit of God is present at the time of the original creation, undertaking the work of ordering the world.[1] Likewise, the Spirit of the Lord who revealed his Name to Moses[2] also inspires Moses and the elders of Israel as the oracles and guardians of divine law.[3] More generally, throughout the Old Testament, he is the principal agent who dispenses divine prophecy, inspires judges, and anoints kings.[4] He descends in a particular way upon the Messianic figure of Isaiah 11:2 ('the Spirit of the Lord is upon me ...") and inspires him to bring consolation to the people of Israel.[5] In the eschatological prophecies of Ezekiel and Joel, it is said that the end times will be those in which the Spirit of God writes not on tablets of stone but directly upon all the human hearts of the elect.[6] These various prophecies (messianic anointing, eschatological indwelling) will be fulfilled in Christ and the life of the apostolic Church.

While the Holy Spirit is known in the Old Testament only through personifications of divine activity, he is revealed in the New Testament as a distinct person whose work and activity accompany that of Jesus Christ. The missions of the Son and the Spirit are seen to be intimately interrelated. In the Synoptic Gospels, the Holy Spirit is at the origins of Christ's virginal conception in the womb of the Virgin Mary.[7] He descends upon the adult Christ in his baptism and

---

1. Gen. 1:2.
2. Exod. 3:14–15.
3. Num. 11:25–29.
4. Judg. 3:10; 1 Sam. 10:6; 1 Sam. 16:13; Ezek. 11:5.
5. Isa. 40:1→Phil. 2:1.
6. Ezek. 11:19; 36:26; Joel 2:28–32→Acts 2:14–33.
7. Matt. 1:20; Luke 1:35.

drives him out into the desert to fast and pray.[8] The Spirit accompanies Jesus in his public life by signs and wonders,[9] and enables him to fulfill the prophecies of Isaiah that confirm him as the Messiah.[10] In dying, Christ crucified gives up his Spirit to the Father.[11] As the risen Lord, he announces to the disciples that when he has ascended to the Father, the Holy Spirit will be sent upon the apostolic Church to inspire and guide her membership.[12]

The Gospel according to St John contains complementary ideas: on the night before he suffers, Jesus promises the disciples that the Father will send the Holy Spirit upon them in his name[13] and that he too will send the Spirit upon them "from the Father," calling him the "Spirit of truth who proceeds (*ekporeuetai*) from the Father."[14] The night of the resurrection, Christ fulfills this promise by "breathing" the Holy Spirit upon the apostles, so that they might forgive sins.[15] Analogously, St. Paul speaks about the Holy Spirit as the agent of our sanctification and filial adoption.[16] "God has sent the Spirit of his Son into our hearts crying out, *abba*, Father."[17] Consequently, the Holy Spirit is also the "Spirit of Christ"[18] and the "Spirit of Jesus."[19]

If we consider the development from the monotheism of the Old Testament to that of the New, we can identify a movement from discourse about the 'Spirit of the Lord' to that of the 'Spirit of Christ.' The Christological monotheism of the New Testament that affirms the divinity of Christ (his unity with the Father) also portrays the Holy Spirit as being sent from Christ. In this way, it underscores not

---

8. Matt. 3:16–4:1; Luke 3:22; 4:1.
9. Luke 3:16; 4:14.
10. Luke 4:18 and Acts 10:38→Isa. 11:2.
11. Luke 23:46.
12. Acts 1:8; 2:33.
13. John 14:25–26.
14. John 15:26, see also 16:7.
15. John 20:22–23.
16. Rom. 8:14–16.
17. Gal. 4:6.
18. Rom. 8:9.
19. Phil. 1:19.

only the divinity of Christ[20] but also the inseparability of the missions of the Spirit and the Son, who work in union, both being sent into the world by the Father.

A SPIRIT WHO IS LOVE

Christian theological reflection concerning the deity of the Holy Spirit came into its maturity in the fourth century AD. In the face of Arian Christologies of the early fourth century (that denied the divinity of Christ), St Athanasius of Alexandria posited a central theological argument for the divinity of Christ that was to influence later thinking concerning the Holy Spirit. In his *Orations Against the Arians*,[21] he argued, in effect, that human salvation consists of union with God (divinization or *theosis*) and that this grace is attained by virtue of the Incarnation. Because God became human, human beings can be united to God. If Christ is not God, then the universe is not saved by one who is himself a union of God and man and is inevitably left only to its own finite, non-divine resources and initiatives. Given the divine transcendence of the Father, self-divinization is not possible for creatures. Christ, to be the savior who unites us to God, then must truly be both God and man. Athanasius applies very similar arguments to show the divine status of the Spirit in his *Letters to Serapion*.[22] Soon afterward, the Cappadocian Fathers built on Athanasius's reasoning. Against neo-Arians who claimed the Spirit was a creature of the Father, they noted that the Spirit is the source of divinization and that his work is integral to the salvific agency of the Son.

---

20. Larry W. Hurtado, *Lord Jesus Christ: Devotion to Jesus in Earliest Christianity* (Grand Rapids, MI: Eerdmans, 2003).

21. 1.38–40, 2.20–21, 3.12. A good selection of texts may be found in Khaled Anatolios, *Athanasius* (London: Routledge, 1998).

22. Athanasius and Didymus, *Works on the Spirit: Athanasius's Letters to Serapion and Didymus the Blind's On the Holy Spirit*, trans. Mark DelCogliano, Andrew Radde-Gallwitz, and Lewis Ayres (Crestwood, NY: St Vladimir's Seminary Press, 2001).

… The Godhead of the Holy Spirit can be proved thoroughly scriptural … Christ is born, the Spirit is his forerunner; Christ is baptized, the Spirit bears him witness; Christ is tempted, the Spirit leads him up; Christ performs miracles, the Spirit accompanies him; Christ ascends, the Spirit fills his place. Is there any significant function belonging to God, which the Spirit does not perform? Is there any title belonging to God, which cannot apply to him, except "ingenerate" and "begotten'? … The Spirit it is who created and creates anew through baptism and resurrection. The Sprit it is who knows all things, who teaches all things … He makes us his temple, he deifies, he makes us complete … All that God actively performs, he performs.[23]

Accordingly, in the reformulation of the Nicene Creed in the ecumenical council of Constantinople (381 AD), the Holy Spirit was confessed as the "Lord and giver of life, who proceeds from the Father, who with the Father is worshipped and glorified." The Holy Spirit is the Creator himself, one with the Father and the Son, and with them, he is the principal agent of our salvation.

A second decisive contribution of the Cappadocians came when they articulated the distinction of the divine persons by using the notions of generation and procession. Because the Father and the Son are one in being, they are identically God in all things (divine wisdom, love, power, and so forth). Consequently, they can be distinguished only because the Son is eternally begotten of the Father and eternally receives the divine nature or essence from the Father. By considering the distinctness of Son and Spirit *only* from the perspective of their relations to the unoriginate Father, we avoid dividing the divine attributes. The Holy Spirit, then, is distinguished from the Father and the Son because he proceeds eternally from the Father, and because unlike the Son, he is not begotten as the Father's Word.[24] In this way the Cappadocians also rightly emphasized the paternal monarchy of the Father as the font or origin of Trinitarian life in God, from whom the Son and the Holy Spirit originate in their distinctness.

---

23. Gregory Nazianzen, *Or.* 31.29 in *On God and Christ,* 139–40.
24. See Gregory Nazianzen, *Or.* 29.2; 31.9.

Third, this insight was coupled with another of equal importance regarding the monotheistic character of Trinitarian faith. St. Gregory of Nyssa in his *To Ablabius: On Not Three Gods,* emphasizes that there is a two-fold division of terms or names that can be ascribed to God: some proper to a unique person (Father, Word, Holy Spirit) and others equally and identically attributable to each person (divine life, simplicity, goodness, and so forth). Each of the persons has to be considered in a two-fold way: (1) as giving or receiving his divine life to or from another, and (2) as possessing the fullness of the divine nature. The distinction of the person of the Holy Spirit is upheld by recourse, then, to his relation of origin from the Father. His divinity and Lordship, meanwhile, are underscored by the attribution to him of the fullness of the divine nature, a nature he receives from the Father, but which he also possesses equally with the Father and the Son.

A generation after the Cappadocians, St. Augustine of Hippo articulated the fundamental principles of Nicene theology in distinctive ways, contributing significant insights of his own. In particular, he noted that the principal scriptural analogy for the Son is that of the Word, a notion that pertains to intellect. The uncreated Word is also Wisdom begotten from the unbegotten Father, both the Wisdom of God (1 Cor. 1:24) and sharing in the unique divine Wisdom. If God is spirit, however, then there must also be an analogical resemblance between the Holy Spirit and something in the spiritual souls of human beings—one other than that pertaining to the intellectual generation of the Word. And so, Augustine introduces the complementary notion of love or will, a term that can be attributed analogically to God as well. The Holy Spirit is the uncreated charity of the Father and the Son, a person who is substantial love.[25] Just as the Son is wisdom begotten from the Father in his wisdom, so the Holy Spirit is spirated love, who proceeds from the Father who is love.

Augustine insists on the paternal monarchy of the Father as the

---

25. See Augustine, *The Trinity,* 9.3.3.

unique primary origin of the Word and the Spirit.[26] However, he also sees an order emergent in the mystery of the processions of the Word and the Spirit. Just as in the human being, spiritual love can only proceed forth in the will as a result of knowledge (because we can only love what we first know), so in the life of God, the Spirit who is love must proceed forth from divine knowledge. He is, therefore, the Spirit of both the Father and the Word: a love who comes forth from wisdom. The human being as a knowing person capable of loving is a created image of God as the uncreated Father who creates all things in his Word and loves them in his Spirit of charity.[27] In considering the procession of the Holy Spirit more closely, then, Augustine builds on an idea that is found in other Latin authors, such as St. Hilary[28] and St. Ambrose[29]: the Holy Spirit proceeds eternally from the Father and the Son. The Father, in generating the Word, gives to the Word all that he possesses, including the power to spirate, or breathe out, the Spirit, from himself as Son, but also with the Father. In fact, the Father and the Son spirate the Spirit *as one principle* or source of the Spirit.[30] The Spirit, then, is the shared love of the Father and the Son, their mutual communion-in-love who is a person.

> As then holy scripture proclaims that charity is God, and as it is from God and causes us to abide in God and him in us, and as we know this because he has given us of his Spirit, this Spirit of his is God charity. Again, if there is nothing greater than charity among God's gifts, and if there is no greater gift of God's than the Holy Spirit, what must we conclude but that he is his charity which is called both God and from God? And if the charity by which the Father loves the Son and the Son loves the Father inexpressibly shows forth the communion of them both, what more suitable than he who is the common Spirit of them both should be distinctively called charity?[31]

---

26. Augustine, *The Trinity*, 15.3.5.
27. *The Trinity*, 15.6.9–10.
28. Hilary, *The Trinity*, 2.29; 8.20; 12.56.
29. Ambrose, *On the Holy Spirit*, 1.11.
30. Augustine, *The Trinity*, 5.14.15.
31. *The Trinity*, 15.19.37.

One can object that there is a problem with Augustine's ambitious use of this psychological analogy to speak of the persons of the Trinity because terms proper to the divine nature (i.e., wisdom and love) are being attributed to singular persons in a distinct way. What Augustine has discerned, however, is that love, for instance, can be attributed to the Holy Spirit as a term proper to the divine nature (the divine love common to the Father, Son, and Spirit) *or as a relational term* used to denote the reception of the divine nature from another. His presentation of the Spirit as the personal love of the Father *and the Son* shows us why there can only be a difference between the Son and the Spirit if the difference is conceived uniquely in terms of the relations of origin. The Son comes forth from the Father alone, the Spirit from the Father and the Son, and as the love who is a fruit of their relatedness. However, these differences do not cancel out the mystery of divine unity and identity. The wisdom and love that are common to all three persons are in the Father who is unbegotten, in the Son as begotten Word, and in the Spirit as love spirated forth from the Father and the Son. By his theology of the procession of the Holy Spirit, Augustine maintains the Cappadocian understanding of the distinctions of persons by recourse to a theory of relations of origin and in fact deepens their insight through his understanding of the Spirit proceeding from the Son. Yet this also leads to a deeper sense of the monotheistic character of the Trinitarian faith. Because the persons are *only* distinguishable by means of relational terms, they are, therefore, otherwise utterly identical in essence, wisdom, love, power, and so forth. This profound understanding of the unity of the persons was bequeathed to the subsequent theological heritage of Western Christianity. As we will see, Augustine's ideas will be further developed by Thomas Aquinas in his theological reflections on the Holy Spirit.

THE FILIOQUE AND ST. THOMAS AQUINAS

The Western Christian tradition continued to develop the ideas of Augustine and other patristic authors who affirmed a procession of the Holy Spirit from the Father and the Son as one principle. Progressively, this view became normative in Western theological and doctrinal thinking and, from the sixth century onward, began to appear in creedal formulations in the Latin-speaking Church. When the "Filioque" clause was originally added to the Nicene–Constantinople Creed ('He proceeds from the Father *and the Son*'), it was intended to underscore the divinity of the Son in his unity with the Father in all things over and against various heresies (such as Arianism and Adoptionism). However, it also represented a doctrinal development in the Western Church's thinking regarding the mystery of God in himself. By the eighth century, this development was, at times, fiercely contested by some ecclesiastical authorities in the east. Popes and Western councils of this era gave increasing approbation to the doctrine.[32] As the Church in the West began to employ the Filioque in councils and creedal statements, the doctrine took on an increasingly symbolic role as the nexus for the treatment of three controversial issues: (1) the doctrinal unity of the Eastern and Western Churches regarding the doctrine of God, (2) the overarching doctrinal and juridical authority of the pope, and (3) the political unity of the Christian empire. In later disputes between East and West, theologians readily distinguished these three issues conceptually, but existentially, they have remained deeply intertwined for centuries. Subsequent to "the schism of 1054," the Catholic Church continued to teach the doctrine of the Filioque and elevated it to the status of a dogma at the Second Council of Lyon (1274) and again at the Council of Florence (1438–45). Although these councils were aimed at the reconciliation of East and West,

---

32. Robert M. Haddad, "The Stations of the Filioque," *St. Vladimir's Theological Quarterly* 46, no. 2 (2002): 209–68. Henry Chadwick, *East and West: The Making of a Rift in the Church: From Apostolic Times Until the Council of Florence* (Oxford: Oxford University Press, 2003).

their language regarding the spiration of the Spirit from the Father and the Son "as from one unique principle" was to gain little approbation in the Eastern Christian world.

We will return later to the possibility of an ecumenical convergence of the Orthodox and Catholic Churches in discussions regarding the Holy Spirit's procession. Here, however, it is helpful to consider two arguments from St. Thomas Aquinas (1225–74) in support of the doctrine of the Filioque, as well as his reflections on the relational character of the Spirit as love. Aquinas's arguments in these matters touch upon the very nature of Trinitarian theology as such, and they invite us to probe more deeply the way theological language can and should be used to describe rightly the mystery of God.

A first argument of Aquinas stems from his understanding of the correlation between divine missions and divine processions. Just as the persons in God proceed eternally from one another, so likewise the Son and Spirit are sent from the Father into the world in their missions to save and divinize the human person. What is the difference between a procession and a mission? The former is eternal and is constitutive of the identity of God as such. The latter, according to Aquinas, is simply the procession itself, rendered present to the creation in a new way by grace. "[A divine mission] includes the eternal procession, with the addition of a temporal effect."[33] The Holy Spirit proceeds from the Father and the Son eternally but is sent on mission temporally into the world to save and divinize, being present in the world in a new way, as he who is from the Father and the Son. The idea being expressed here is of decisive importance: nothing that arises in the economy adds anything or alters anything that is proper to the divine identity of God as such. Rather, the opposite is the case: by means of the divine missions, God, in his immutable perfection, invites spiritual creatures to participate in his uncreated life, a life characterized eternally by the processions of the Word and the Spirit.

33. *ST* I, q. 43, a. 2, ad 3.

It follows from this line of thinking that *no new relations* between the persons who are God can arise in virtue of the economy alone. The missions are not the occasion for an evolution within the divine life of God, nor do creation and salvation history enrich the pure actuality and infinite perfection of God in any way. Therefore, if there are relations between the persons *ad intra* that are truly revealed *in the economy* by Scripture, then these same relations *must be constitutive of who God is eternally* and cannot be an addition or alteration of God for the sake of the economy, as if the work of salvation in turn invited God into some form of development. But such a personal relation is precisely what is revealed in John 15:26, where Christ promises to send the Spirit upon the apostles. For only if the Spirit is eternally relative to the Son as one who proceeds from him personally (by a relation of origin) can Christ, in turn, promise as the Son made man to send the Spirit upon the Church economically.[34] Otherwise, there transpires by virtue of the creation and the economy a "new relation" of the Spirit to the person of the Son, one that must necessarily introduce change into the very identity of God.

Of course, one can object that this is precisely what transpires in the economy. The idea of a historical becoming of the Trinity is not unheard of in modern Protestant theology, where it is most often invoked to assert that the event of the crucifixion enters into the very being and relations of the persons of God.[35] Modern Orthodox thinkers such as David Bentley Hart, however, rightly criticize such historicizations of the divine as problematic human projections. Hart introduces a soteriological dimension to the argument: only if God is immutably and impassibly himself in utter transcendence of his creation can he, in turn, save the creation precisely as the God of love who is not subject to evil but who is free from any alteration to his goodness by the vicissitudes of history.[36] Such an

---

34. *In Ioan.* 15, lec. 5, 2061.
35. See Jüngel, Moltmann, Jenson, and others.
36. David Bentley Hart, *The Beauty of the Infinite: The Aesthetics of Christian Truth* (Grand Rapids, MI: Eerdmans, 2003).

idea converges felicitously with the reasoning of Aquinas. The Holy Spirit in the economy is revealed in his goodness and love as one sent by the Son to save us from death. This revelation of the Spirit of Christ in time is not a modalist façade that corresponds only to God's outer activity. Rather, it unveils the inner essence of the living God as such, as he who transcends creation as its Creator and who alone can overcome the threats of suffering, death, and non-being, conforming man to the divine life in the process. But if the personal relation of the Spirit of love to Christ the Savior is unveiled in time, it must also be grounded in the very mystery of God himself, such that the Spirit originates from the Son eternally. To say otherwise is to surrender God's transcendent mystery to the immanent world of human history, allowing the human tribulation that called forth the divine missions to obscure the eternal identity of God and his victory of impassible love.

A second argument of Aquinas pertains to the analogical character of speech concerning God. St Thomas notes that all analogical attributions of natural terms to the mystery of God are drawn from the generic categories that constitute all human conceptual speech. That is to say, following Aristotle's *Categories*, we can ascribe terms to realities around us that denote individuals, essences, qualities, quantities, relations, action, receptivity, time, place, position, and environment. Yet, with regard to God, some of these generic terms are inapplicable. God is not determined by time and place but is ineffably eternal and omnipresent. He is not determined by quantity or passive potency because he is not a body but the author of all physical beings and is himself a pure actuality of subsistent wisdom and love. If we ascribe to God an essential nature (*ousia, essentia*), qualities (wisdom, love, power, and so forth), or actions (creation, salvation), then these terms must pertain to the divine essence and life as such, which are common to the three persons. Consequently, the only term of our categorical mode of understanding that can be employed to denote the distinction of persons in God is that of the relation. It is because the Son possesses all that the Father has (all that is proper to the divine essence, its qualities, actions, and so forth) that he can be distinguished only by his relation of origin as the Word who is eternally begotten from the wisdom of the Father. If the Spirit proceeds only from the Father, then, and not from the Son, he is distinguished from the Father by his relation of origin but is in no way distinguishable from the Son.[37] Consequently, if there is to be a theological intelligibility to the real distinction between the Son and the Spirit, then one of the two must originate from the other. Scripture denotes for us which option conforms to revelation: the Spirit proceeds from the Father and the Son. He is distinct from the Father and the Son not because he differs in essence, qualities, or action but because he alone proceeds relationally from both the Father and the Son as from one principle.

It could be argued that St Thomas's reasoning amounts to a form of rationalism that would seek to trap human reflection on the mystery of the Triune God within the constraints of an Aristotelian conceptualization of reality. In truth, however, what he is demonstrating is much more profound. For as in his broader doctrine of analogical predication concerning God, Aquinas is advancing between two extremes: one of an apophaticism that would employ terms for God only equivocally so that no speech we could use would be capable of signifying the mystery of God and another extreme of univocity in which we would be able to understand God's inner mystery adequately by recourse to our ordinary human understanding and terms.[38] The notion of analogy allows one to claim that the Holy Spirit is truly—although very imperfectly—intelligible as a person distinct from the Father and the Son (due to our analogical application of the notion of relations of origin). Yet the Holy Spirit is also a person in a wholly other way from created human persons because he partakes fully of the ineffable divine essence of God, and three persons who are one in being is something wholly transcendent of

37. ST I, q. 36, a. 2; In Ioan. 15, lec. 5, 2064.
38. See ST I, q. 13, a. 5.

our ordinary experience and concepts. His mystery is accessible to human thought in faith, but only indirectly and as encompassed by mystery. Were we to deny that there is a relation of origin between the Son and the Spirit, we would be obliged into one of two quandaries: either the two divine persons are differentiated by some other term (such as nature, quality, or action) in which case one is subordinate to the other and Christian monotheism is implicitly undermined, or their distinction as persons who both proceed from the Father is literally inconceivable so that the distinct mystery of the Trinity is at base unintelligible—purely extrinsic to human understanding—and it cannot be assimilated by human thought, even when addressed by divine revelation. The first extreme is that of Aetius and Eunomius, the neo-Arian opponents of the Cappadocians who claimed that human concepts were adequate to define and understand the mystery of God the Father. Since his essential deity was seen to exclude any notion of procession or relation, the Son and Spirit could not be understood to be God. The other extreme is that of an apophatic Christian agnosticism that would minimize the intelligibility of the Trinitarian mystery to such a degree as to render its theological meaning intrinsically obscure. (Thomists would tend to see this tendency manifest in the theology of Photius, with his seeming refusal to speculate on the eternal relation of the Spirit and the Son.) In fact, a fair analysis of Aquinas's argumentation can lead to the coherent claim that he is a true inheritor of the Cappadocian understanding of the Triune God, in that he successfully safeguards the two-fold truth of the distinction of persons by recourse to the relations of origin (generation and spiration), and that of the monotheistic character of the three persons due to their equal possession of the ineffable divine essence. Because the Spirit proceeds from the Father and the Son, he is truly distinguishable from each relationally, and because he is identical with them in all else, he is truly the one God of Israel and in no way a subordinate principle. All that is proper to the Father as God is equally proper to the Son and to their Spirit. There is nothing found within the Father or the Son that is not also found within the Spirit, who is God. And yet the Father is the unique source of the whole Trinitarian life that he communicates to the Son and the Spirit.

Aquinas's acute sensitivity to this patristic habit of thought challenges him, in turn, to deepen thinking regarding the Augustinian 'psychological analogy,' so as to emphasize that the Son, who is the Word, and the Spirit, who is charity, are denoted by these proper terms (Word, Love) only because the terms themselves are subject to being used to denote relations of origin, and not merely essential terms (attributes common to the three persons). So, for instance, the Son is called the Word of the Father not because he is in any way the source of the Father's wisdom (the essential wisdom of God) but because he is the immanent expression of the Father's wisdom, analogous to an interior word of the human mind that is expressive of a mental concept. The human word that expresses thought inwardly is relative to the mind and its concepts from which it proceeds so that the analogical use of the notion "word" to describe the Son is a relational concept.[39] Similarly with love: the Spirit is described as the Love of the Father and the Son not by recourse to an essential notion (because God is subsistent love by nature, and this love is equally common to the three persons) but a relational notion. How, then, can love be relational if it proceeds from one who loves in view of the other who is loved and loves in return? St. Thomas here employs the analogy of the voluntary "inclination" or "impulse" towards the person loved that love implies in the one who loves.[40] The Holy Spirit is a person who proceeds as the relational love of the Father for the Son and of the Son for the Father. Consequently, he is the expression of a two-fold immanent inclination of the Father toward the Son and of the Son toward the Father, eternally spirated forth from both "simultaneously" as an expression of mutual love. This procession of love is immanent to the Father and the Son in their unity, and so it

39. SCG 4, 11.
40. SCG 4, 19; Emmanuel Durand, *La périchorèse des personnes divines: Immanence mutuelle, Réciprocité et communion* (Paris: Cerf, 2005).

proceeds from both of them as from one source. At the same time, the begotten Son also receives from the unoriginate Father the gift of spirating the love of the Spirit, insofar as he receives all that he has from the Father.[41] It is true to say, then, both that the Spirit proceeds from the Father through the Son and that the Spirit is their mutual bond of love.

ECUMENICAL PROPOSALS

Orthodox theologians have always recognized that the Filioque theology of the West has called for some form of response from within the Eastern tradition. Classically, such a response takes one of three forms. First, there are those who have rejected the notion unequivocally as a doctrinal error, insisting upon the irreducible truth of the generation of the Son from the Father and the spiration/procession of the Spirit from the Father (and not the Son). Photius's theology could be seen as representative of this view. The monarchal primacy of the Father is preserved through a respect for the mystery of God that does not seek to resolve the question of the eternal relation between the Son and the Spirit. A second tendency (less common but historically enduring) has been to show a qualified sympathy for the Western doctrine, understanding a potential convergence between the Filioque and the classical Eastern idea that the Spirit proceeds from the Father "through the Son." Among the more pre-eminent defenders of this position is St. Maximus the Confessor (c.580–662).

However, the third and most prominent trend is that envisaged by historical figures such as Gregory of Cyprus (1241–90) and St. Gregory Palamas (1296–1359), and which is articulated in modern Orthodox theology by such seminal figures as Vladimir Lossky and Dumitru Stăniloae. This position, generally speaking, tends to maintain that the doctrine of the Filioque, as conceived in the

41. *ST* I, q. 36, a. 3.

Augustinian tradition, is problematic. One reason for this is that it introduces the idea that a hypostatic property of the Father (his being the unique source of Trinitarian life) is communicable to the Son with regard to the Spirit. But what is shared by the persons is the divine nature and life, not personal properties as such, so that if the Father gives the power of spiration to the Son, he does so by virtue of their shared divine nature. This, however, seems to make the divine essence the source of the spiration of the Spirit. Therefore, either the Spirit must also possess the power to spirate himself since he, too, is God by nature (which is an absurd idea), or he proceeds from the divine essence of the Father and the Son as a creature (which is blasphemous). At the same time, this Palamite tradition tends to see positive value in the Filioque doctrine insofar as the doctrine challenges or invites Orthodox thought to consider the eternal and temporal relations of the Spirit and the Son. Orthodox theologians tend, therefore, to distinguish the Spirit's relation to the Son (1) in the eternal mystery of God and (2) in the divine economy. In the eternal life of God, the Spirit proceeds forth from the Father to rest upon the Son as the resplendence or glory of the Son, who is the recipient of the Father's eternal love. In the economy, the Spirit is sent by the Father upon the Church *through* the Son made man, who is the principle of divinization of creatures within the economy. The Son and the Spirit thus work together to sanctify human beings, and the Spirit within the economy is the Spirit of the Son. Yet both persons come forth uniquely from the Father who sends the Spirit upon the Son and sends him into the world as the Spirit of his Son.

The Romanian theologian Dumitru Stăniloae writes:

> The Father does not beget the Son, and does not cause the Spirit to proceed as two separate actions, as two Persons who remain separated; but the begetting and the procession, although distinct, are united. Consequently the Person of the Son and the Person of the Spirit also remain united, or interior, to one another ... [T]hough the Spirit's manifestation is by the Son, his coming into existence is not by the Son, even if he is united to the begetting of the Son ... [T]he shining

out from the Son marks a progress in the existence which the Spirit receives from the Father, one might say a fulfilment, the achievement of the end for which he came into existence.[42]

Such a view suggests points of convergence with the Latin tradition. Arguably, however, its criticism of the Filioque fails to recognize that there is nothing incoherent or contradictory with the idea of the Son partaking personally in a personal characteristic that the Father has (as the source of the Spirit) and that this is precisely what would distinguish him from both the Father (who unlike him is the unbegotten source of the Spirit) and the Spirit (who unlike him proceeds from both the Father and the Son). Furthermore, there is a theological ambiguity to the notion that there exist new relations between the persons either (1) at the *term* of the intra-Trinitarian processions rather than at their origins or (2) arising in the economy or through divine agency *ad extra* that are distinct from the eternal relations of God in himself. Such ideas risk to straddle the theologian with either modalist ideas of a God distinct in revelation from what he is in himself, or of a subordinationism in which the Spirit and Son do not partake fully of a perfection of their relations except through an intra-divine becoming, or by virtue of their presence in creaturely history. After all, to whom is the Spirit being manifest? What kind of new perfection does such manifestation entail?

Contemporary Catholic-Orthodox discussions of the Eastern and Western positions of thought on this matter have led to a number of healthy clarifications. On the one hand, the Catholic Church has insisted in recent decades that Eastern Churches in communion with Rome should not be obliged to mention the Filioque in the recitation of the creed. This suggests that the Western Church does not see the explicit acceptance of the doctrine as a condition for Church

42. Dumitru Stăniloae, "The Procession of the Holy Spirit from the Father and His Relation to the Son, as the Basis of Our Deification and Adoption," in *Spirit of God, Spirit of Christ*, ed. L. Vischer (London/Geneva: SPCK/World Council of Churches, 1981), 183–84.

unity, so long as the Filioque is not deemed heretical in the East but is at least given warrant as a legitimate theological opinion or way of approaching the mystery of God. Orthodox leaders are often willing to work towards this form of consensus through theological dialogue. Similarly, the Catholic Church has emphasized in her universal *Catechism of the Catholic Church* (*CCC*) that the Father "as the principle without principle, is the first origin of the Spirit, but also that as Father of the only Son, he is, with the Son, the single principle from which the Holy Spirit proceeds."[43] This idea is given further expression in the Pontifical Council for Promoting Christian Unity's 1995 document "The Greek and Latin Traditions Regarding the Procession of the Holy Spirit." Here, an ecumenical interpretation of the Filioque is presented (taken from Maximus the Confessor's *Letter to Marinus*), which has recourse to the idea of perichoresis, the indwelling of the Son in the Father. One can affirm that the Father is the unique source of the Spirit, but it must be added that he is so precisely *as* Father, that is to say, as the eternal Father of his only-begotten Son and Word. Consequently, the Son is present in the Father from whom the Spirit proceeds. "The Spirit does not precede the Son, since the Son characterizes as Father the Father from whom the Spirit takes his origin, according to the Trinitarian order. But the spiration of the Spirit from the Father takes place by and through (the two senses of *dia* in Greek) the generation of the Son, to which it gives its Trinitarian character." This interpretation of the doctrine of the Filioque is meant to converge with classical Cappadocian and Palamite assertions that the Spirit proceeds from the Father through the Son. Exploratory formulations such as these invite Catholic and Orthodox interlocutors alike to consider ways that the Filioque can be seen as a legitimate theological development compatible at base with the insights of the Eastern Christian tradition.[44]

---

43. *Catechism of the Catholic Church*, 2nd ed. (Vatican City: Libreria Editrice Vaticana, 1997), 248 (hereafter *CCC*).

44. Jean-Miguel Garrigues, *L'Esprit qui dit "Pere!": L'Esprit-Saint dans la vie trinitaire et le probleme du filioque* (Paris: Tequi, 1981).

If both sides are willing to seek ways of understanding positively each other's interpretations of the eternal and temporal relations of the Son and Spirit, the Filioque dispute can become the occasion for a deepening understanding of Trinitarian life as it is manifested in the life of Jesus Christ. In the formulation of the *Catechism*: "This legitimate complementarity provided it does not become rigid, does not affect the identity of faith in the reality of the same mystery confessed."[45] Indeed, it can enrich our understanding of that reality.

THE HOLY SPIRIT AS THE UNCREATED SOUL OF THE CHURCH

In the Nicene Creed, the doctrine of the Holy Spirit is mentioned just before that of the Church, signifying that the mystical body of Christ is sustained and upheld in being and in grace by the indwelling work of the Holy Spirit. The Church is united by the graces of faith, hope, and love, as well as sacramental grace, virtues, and charisms that are present in her living members. But this created grace that sanctifies Christ's faithful is also ultimately the fruit of the Holy Spirit himself, who animates the body of Christ from within, unifying and enlivening that body as an uncreated living principle. The Church lives by the Spirit of Christ as her soul in view of her union with the Father. "The Holy Spirit is likened to the heart [of the Church], since he invisibly enlivens and unifies the Church."[46] From this basic thought, three ideas follow.

First, the Church is present in the world not only visibly but also invisibly there where the Holy Spirit is at work preparing and leading souls to the encounter with Christ. This work of the Spirit is universal in scope, present throughout history, and throughout the comprehensive diversity of human cultures. Yet this universal activity is

45. CCC 248.
46. ST III, q. 8, a. 1, ad 3.

also always a preparation for the uniquely saving Gospel of Christ, and thus, it attains its apotheosis only in the ecclesial realization of visible unity that is centered in Christ and made possible by his sacramental economy. Theologically speaking, the signs of the Spirit acting in non-Christian persons and cultures are discerned most certainly there where the work of grace becomes manifest by way of a free decision for life in the Church. At the same time, his work is presumed to be universal in scope and cannot be reduced to what is given to human sight or measured in visible results. Consequently, the mission of the Church implies vigorous and intelligent proclamation of the Gospel *and* dialogue that seeks to understand in depth the virtues, values, and insights of interlocutors of non-Christian identity. This two-fold approach to evangelization seeks to be faithful simultaneously to the universal work of the Spirit and the Christological and ecclesiological concentration of his activity.

Second, the Holy Spirit is the uncreated charity of the Father and the Son, and consequently, his special note of presence in the visible Catholic Church is that unity that is obtained only through mutual love.[47] This principle has to characterize every other note of ecclesial unity, be it the unity that arises from sacramental regeneration and communion, liturgical worship, doctrinal fidelity to the truth, or juridical and religious obedience. Without the inner animating dynamic of the love of God and neighbor, the life of the Church would wither into nothingness. However, the Church is continuously renewed by the Holy Spirit such that the sacramental and liturgical life of the Church is sustained by an interior love. Her obedience to God and her teaching and proclamation are expressions of the "Spirit of truth"[48] who guides her interiorly and who is himself an inextinguishable source of love for all mankind. "By this will all men know that you are my disciples, if you have love for one another."[49]

Last, the work of the Holy Spirit in the Church is eschatological

---

47. Charles Journet, *L'Eglise du Verbe Incarné*, vol. II. *La structure interne de l'Eglise: Le Christ, la Vierge, l'Esprit Saint* (Paris: Saint-Augustin, 1999).

48. John 15:26.

49. John 13:35.

in orientation. Ecclesial unity in the Spirit in this life is anticipatory of a mystery that is coming to be. It will take on perfect expression in the life of heaven, where it is consummated in the beatific vision by means of the light of glory. The *Apocalypse* ends with a vision of heaven in which the Spirit inspires the Church inwardly to loving communion with Christ as the eternal bridegroom.[50] Theologically speaking, this entails the elevation of human souls to the vision of God face to face, by which they encounter the Father directly in the gaze upon his uncreated Word and perceive all things (incomprehensively) in him. This also entails the radical outpouring of the Spirit who is love into the hearts of all the blessed so that animated by the Spirit, they might love with the measure of charity that this vision affords them, a love that unites them forever with God in his love for himself, and with one another in friendship. This mystical life in the Spirit is anticipated even now in the Church through loving worship, the practice of virtue, and the experience of charity. In the life of the world to come, it will blossom as the human will comes to rest in that personal love of the Father for the Son and of the Son for the Father, a love who is the Holy Spirit of God.

50. Rev. 22:1–5, 17.

6

Beauty, Transcendence,
and the Inclusive Hierarchy
of Creation

Interpreters of Thomas Aquinas have long argued about whether he holds that beauty is a "transcendental," that is to say, a feature of reality coextensive with all that exists, like unity, goodness and truthfulness.[1] In the first part of this chapter, I will argue that Aquinas can be read to affirm in an implicit way that there is beauty in everything that exists. He also affirms clearly that this beauty derives from God, who is uncreated beauty. In the second part of the

Originally published in *Nova et Vetera* (English edition) 16, no. 4 (2018): 1215–26.
1. A helpful survey of modern scholarly opinions is presented by Jan Aertsen in *Medieval Philosophy as Transcendental Thought: From Philip the Chancellor (c.a. 1225) to Francisco Suárez* (Leiden: Brill, 2012), 161–76. J. Maritain argues that beauty is a transcendental in *Art and Scholasticism with Other Essays*, trans. J. F. Scanlan (New York: Scribner's, 1939.) Étienne Gilson speaks of *pulcrum* as "the forgotten transcendental" in *Elements of Christian Philosophy* (New York: Doubleday, 1960), 159–63. Wippel does not include beauty in his account of the transcendentals in Aquinas, in *The Metaphysical Thought of Thomas Aquinas*, 192–94. Jan Aersten himself seems to be of two minds. In his earlier work, *Medieval Philosophy and the Transcendentals: The Case of Thomas Aquinas*, 335–59, he speaks of beauty as a kind of transcendental, while in the later work noted above, he expresses reticence. See also the brief but insightful interpretation of Pasquale Porro, *Thomas Aquinas: A Historical and Philosophical Profile*, trans. J. Trabbic and R. Nutt (Washington, DC: The Catholic University of America Press, 2016), 203–4, who treats beauty as a transcendental in Aquinas's thought.

chapter, I will consider what it might mean from a Thomistic point of view to speak of a transcendent divine beauty and what it cannot mean philosophically speaking, given Aquinas's other metaphysical commitments, particularly with respect to his doctrine of divine simplicity. In the final part of the chapter, I hope to treat the question of how the beauty of the creation both manifests and conceals divine beauty and to give special attention to the topic of the hierarchy of perfections in creatures (as being, living and intellectual). My argument will be that Aquinas's hierarchical understanding of reality is inclusive in character so that an order of political and religious ethics derives from the natural order of beauty. The world's natural beauty ought to be respected and cared for in ways that acknowledge the intrinsic ontological integrity of all lesser realities but also their inclusion within an order that sustains rational creatures and their reference to the divine.

BEAUTY AS A TRANSCENDENTAL FEATURE OF REALITY

The notion of a transcendental feature of being has its proximate origins in the 12th century theories of Philip the Chancellor, who first composed a treatise on the subject. However, the remote origins of the notion can certainly be found in Aristotle's *Metaphysics*, where there are overt discussions of the fact that unity, truth, and goodness are features of reality that are co-extensive with being.[2] Aristotle sought to identify in the *Categories* and in *Metaphysics* IV and V the categorial modes of being that are irreducibly diverse genera

2. The study of notions "convertible" with being has its prehistory in the philosophies of Aristotle and Plato (See, for example, *Republic* 507b; *Sophist* 245c–255e, 260a; *Metaphysics* C, 2, 1003b23–1005a18; K, 3, 1061a15–17; *Nic. Ethics* I, 6, 1196a23–34). Avicenna spoke in different places of being (*esse*) as *res, aliquid, bonum, verum,* and *unum* (*Metaphysics* I, c. 4, 27 and 30; c. 5, 31–34; c. 8, 55–56; IV, c. 3, 212). The first systematic treatment of the topic, however, was presented by Philip the Chancellor in his *Summa de bono* (ca. 1225–1228), at Paris, and the topic was subsequently explored by Alexander of Hales and Albert the Great. For studies on the transcendentals, see particularly Aertsen, *Medieval Philosophy and the Transcendentals* and *Medieval Philosophy as Transcendental Thought.*

of being. These are the distinct ontological features of reality: substances, natures, quantities, qualities, relations, habits, actions, passions, time, place, and position. For example, all substances have diverse qualities and quantities, but none of them is merely identical with its qualities or quantities, nor are quantity and quality reducible to one another. The categories are properly basic features of reality, then. However, Aristotle also sought to identify features of being that "transcend" the diverse genera and that are found in all that exists, albeit in analogically diverse ways, not in generically or specifically identical modes. For example, one may speak of a good quality, such as human affability, as distinct from a good quantity, such as a sufficient amount of water, a good place, such as where we plan to meet, or substantial goodness, such as that of the intrinsic goodness of any human being. In each of these cases, one discovers ontologically distinct forms of goodness, just as one also encounters distinct forms of unity, truth (inherent intelligibility in things), and being. These transcendental modes of being are designated in analogical ways, not univocally, because they are not proper to any particular species of being or genera of being. Rather, they are common to every genus and, therefore, "transcend" the specifications of any one univocal designation. We cannot rightly say, for example, that only trees exist, that only substances have unity, or that goodness is always a quantity. Every genus of thing exists since being is common to all. Every genus is characterized by unity in some sense, as when we speak of one quality or one quantity or one place. Goodness is not reducible to one genus of being, like quality or quantity, but is analogically common to every genus of being.

Aquinas has distinct textual accounts of what he takes to be the core transcendental notions. For the most part, they seem conceptually coherent with one another. In the famous text of *De Veritate* q. 1, art. 1, he names as transcendental notions *ens, res, unum, aliquid, verum,* and *bonum.* The logic of the distinctions is presented with admirable clarity. Being [*ens*] can be considered either per se or with respect to another. If per se, then one can think of the "content" of

FIGURE 6.1

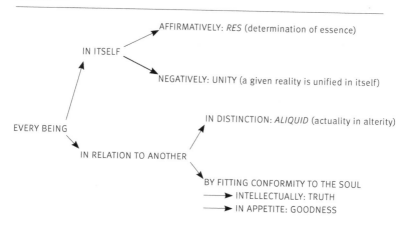

what exists either positively (as *res* or "a determinate reality") or negatively (as *unum*: that which is indivisible). If a given being is considered with respect to another being, then it can be considered either in distinction from it (as *aliquid* or "something actually other") or by fitting conformity to the soul (*convenientia*). If the latter is the case, this can be considered two ways, either with respect to intellect (*verum*, all that is, is somehow true) or with respect to appetite (*bonum*, all that is, is somehow good).[3]

What does this analysis mean concretely? Consider the example of a large oak tree. That tree has a given natural form or inherent determination of essence as a tree of a given kind. It has a unity as well that marks it off ontologically from other realities around it. It is inherently intelligible as an actually existing reality in distinction from others (*aliquid*) and in relation to them. Its being has an intrinsic intelligibility such that we can study and understand it. It also has an intrinsic goodness, especially when the tree flourishes, such that we

3. The figure above is indebted in part to that presented by Aertsen in *Medieval Philosophy as Transcendental Thought*, 222.

could speak about whether the tree is healthy and robust or whether it is still growing to its perfection. All of these features of being apply not only to the whole substance of the tree in its unity and totality but also to the diverse categorial properties or modes of being, such as the tree's particular quantity, qualities, relations, time and place, and so forth. The tree's quantitative parts have a given determination, unity, intelligibility, and so forth, but so do the tree's qualities and its relations to its surroundings. The being, unity, truth, and goodness of the tree are features we find "throughout" its ontological constitution, both in its form and material elements, in its substance and in its diverse properties.

Aquinas offers an epistemological analysis of the natural unfolding of our concepts of being in *Summa theologiae* I, q. 5, a. 2. The account complements the ontological reflections of *De Veritate* q. 1, a. 1 that we have been exploring above. In this context, at the start of the *Summa*, Aquinas is considering the goodness of God, after having considered God's being or existence, and prior to the consideration of God's unity and living activity as a mystery of truth. His treatment of divine attributes, then, does not follow the same order as his treatment of the transcendental notions. But he notes all the same even here that our notions of being and of actuality both precede our notion of goodness since the knowledge of the latter presupposes the knowledge of the former.

> In idea being is prior to goodness. For the meaning signified by the name of a thing is that which the mind conceives of the thing and intends by the word that stands for it. Therefore, that is prior in idea, which is first conceived by the intellect. Now the first thing conceived by the intellect is being; because everything is knowable only inasmuch as it is in actuality. Hence, being is the proper object of the intellect, and is primarily intelligible; as sound is that which is primarily audible. Therefore in idea being is prior to goodness.[4]

4. *ST* I, q. 5, a. 2. We should note that "actuality" is listed here as a transcendental feature of being. Aquinas, commenting on Metaphysics H, 8, 1050b5–16, notes that actuality and potentiality are modes of being that apply not only to movement (capacity to move versus actual movement) but also to the existence (*esse*) of substance. *In IX Meta.*, lec. 9, 1869 (ed. Marietti, 450): "Sed id quod possibile est esse, contingit non esse in actu.

We find another account of the ontological order of transcendental notions presented in *De Veritate* q. 21, a. 1. In the first *quaestio*
of this book (q. 1, a. 1), Aquinas was considering the transcendental
notion of truth. Here he is considering the transcendental notion
of goodness.[5] He reiterates the idea of truth and goodness as concepts that denote being insofar as it is relational. He adds, however, some important qualifications. "Truth" denotes being insofar as
it is capable of *specifying* the intellect that understands it, perfecting it in this way. The notion of *species* here recalls the idea of *res*: all
that exists insofar as it exists implies some kind of interior ontological determination capable of informing our intellectual knowledge
by its intrinsic intelligibility or truthfulness. The water molecule, for

---

Manifestum est ergo, quod illud quod possibile est esse, contingit esse et non esse. Et sic
potentia simul contradictionis est, quia idem est in potentia ad esse et non esse." "But
what is capable of existing may possibly not be actual. Hence it is evident that what is
capable of existing may either exist or not exist; and thus the potency is at one and the
same time a potency for opposite determinations, because the same thing is; in potency
both to existence and non-existence" (See also lec. 3, 1805; lec. 5; 1825, lec. 9, 1868–71).
Consequently, Aquinas sees that for Aristotle the question of the actuality and potentiality in the being of the substance reveals a capacity of an essentially determined being
to exist or not exist, and it will eventually be seen that this leads us back to a necessarily
existent being in whom the substance and being in act (or *ousia* and *energeia*) are absolutely one (*In XII Meta.*, lec. 5, 2494; lec. 7, 2524–27). Translation taken from Aquinas,
Commentary on Metaphysics.

5. *De Veritate*, q. 21, a. 1: "The true and the good must therefore add to the concept
of being, a relationship of that which perfects. But in any being there are two aspects to
be considered, the formal character of its species and the act of being by which it subsists in that species. And so a being can be perfective in two ways. (1) It can be so just
according to its specific character. In this way the intellect is perfected by a being, for it
perceives the formal character of the being. But the being is still not in it according to its
natural existence. It is this mode of perfecting which the true adds to being. For the true
is in the mind, as the Philosopher says; and every being is called true inasmuch as it is
conformed or conformable to intellect. For this reason all who correctly define true put
intellect in its definition. (2) A being is perfective of another not only according to its
specific character but also according to the existence which it has in reality. In this fashion the good is perfective; for the good is in things, as the Philosopher says. Inasmuch
as one being by reason of its act of existing is such as to perfect and complete another, it
stands to that other as an end. And hence it is that all who rightly define *good* put in its
notion something about its status as an end. The Philosopher accordingly says that they
excellently defined good who said that it is 'that which all things desire'" (Translation
from Aquinas, *Truth*). See the pertinent remarks of Aertsen in *Medieval Philosophy as
Transcendental Thought*, 230.

example, has an intrinsic determination that is different from that of a mouse, the color blue, one's relation to one's aunt, or the capacity to play the violin. Truth declines transcendentally across these distinct ontological categorial modes of being (substances, essences, qualities, quantities, relations, habits, etc.). When we know the truth about such dimensions of being, it perfects our intellect.

Meanwhile, goodness denotes the perfective character of existence not insofar as it is assimilated to understanding but insofar as one being draws another toward its intrinsic perfection. Here too, the notion is nuanced. Goodness pertains to a perfection intrinsic to a given reality itself, insofar as that reality flourishes and reaches its perfection. But goodness is also defined relationally. It is something perfective of other realities around it, either by becoming an end pursued or a good means toward an end.[6] Implicit in this idea is the understanding that good realities can be mutually perfective. If one being attains a perfection that is appetible to another, it can in turn contribute to the perfection of the other in its own species. The examples could be diverse. The mature rabbit can help perfect the mature wolf. But we may also say that the perfect math professor conveys wisdom that perfects in turn the student, or the friend who loves according to virtue and with genuine personal love of another, invites the friend who is loved to a reciprocal love of the other that is virtuous and perfective and in turn perfecting.

The relational characteristics of being as both true and good are grounded for Aquinas, then, in the things themselves, by virtue of their being. In this line of thinking, we do not ever say correctly that a human being *truly* is a professional chess player or *truly* is acting in a morally just way in the midst of a genocide simply due to our relational apprehension of him or our attraction to his moral qualities, but *also always more fundamentally* because these ascriptions are characteristic of his being as such, of what he really is in himself.

Evidently, none of the analysis of Aquinas discussed thus far

---

6. *De Veritate* q. 21, a. 1, corp.

contains any mention of beauty. He does not list it as a transcendental term in his texts on transcendental notions. Perhaps then one should simply exclude it from any textually responsible Thomist account of his teaching on this subject. However, at least two well-known texts should give us reason to pause before reaching such a conclusion. One is found in his *Commentary on Dionysius' Divine Names*, cap. 4, lec. 5. The other is in his discussion of the beauty of the eternal Son of God in a discussion of the Holy Trinity in the *Summa theologiae* I, q. 39, a. 8.

In the first of these texts, Aquinas is commenting on Dionysius. The extended text is analytically dense and quite remarkable. Aquinas is discussing the ways in which one might say that God is beautiful and in what ways one might not say so. I will return to his topic below. Here, however, it is pertinent to consider Aquinas's discussion of the presence of beauty in all that exists. He makes six main points.[7] First, all beauty comes from God insofar as God is the cause

---

7. *In Divinis Nominibus* cap. 4, lec. 5, para. 348–49: "pulchrum de Deo dicitur secundum causam [...]. Dicit ergo primo quod ex pulchro isto provenit esse omnibus existentibus: claritas enim est de consideratione pulchritudinis, ut dictum est; omnis autem forma, per quam res habet esse, est participatio quaedam divinae claritatis; et hoc est quod subdit, quod singula sunt pulchra secundum propriam rationem, idest secundum propriam formam; unde patet quod ex divina pulchritudine esse omnium derivatur. Similiter etiam dictum est quod de ratione pulchritudinis est consonantia, unde omnia, quae, qualitercumque ad consonantiam pertinent, ex divina pulchritudine procedunt; et hoc est quod subdit, quod propter pulchrum divinum sunt omnium rationalium creaturarum concordiae, quantum ad intellectum; concordant enim qui in eamdem sententiam conveniunt; et amicitiae, quantum ad affectum; et communiones, quantum ad actum vel ad quodcumque extrinsecum; et universaliter omnes creaturae, quantamcumque unionem habent, habent ex virtute pulchri." "The beautiful is said of God according to cause [...]. He [Dionysius] says therefore first that from the Beautiful esse [existence] comes to all existing things: for it is clear from the consideration of beauty, as was said; but every form, through which a thing has esse, is a certain participation of the divine brightness; and this is what he adds, that singulars are beautiful according to a proper notion, i.e., according to a proper form; whence it is apparent that from the divine Beauty the esse of all things is derived. Similarly, also it was said that consonance is from the notion of beauty; whence all things, which pertain to consonance in any way, proceed from the divine Beauty. And this is what he adds, that because of the divine Good there is concord of all rational creatures with respect to intellect: for they agree who come together in the same opinion and friendship with respect to affection; and communication with respect to act, or something extrinsic; and universally all creatures, whatever unity they have,

of all that exists. Second, he gives a first definition of beauty. Beauty can be defined ontologically as the splendor (*claritas*) that results from form. Everything has a formal determination of some kind insofar as it has existence (*esse*). Therefore, insofar as anything exists (and has some formal ontological content) it has some degree of beauty. Third, the splendor of the form in created things is a participation in the divine splendor from which it originates. The divine nature is the transcendent exemplar of beauty in diverse finite created realities. Fourth, then, (and perhaps most importantly) "*ex divina pulchritudine esse omnium derivatur*": literally, the existence of everything originates from divine beauty. Fifth, a second definition of beauty is considered. Beauty can be defined ontologically as a property of being that emerges from proportion or harmony (*consonantia*). For example, authentic relationships of personal friendship imply spiritual harmony or concord and are beautiful and noble in this respect. Sixth, then, the concord or beautiful harmonies we find in the created order are expressive of the wisdom of God, who is the author of creation.

Evidently, if the *existence* of everything derives from divine beauty, and if everything that has existence is in some way beautiful by virtue of its intrinsic form, then it would seem to follow logically that beauty, for Aquinas, is a characteristic of being that is coextensive with all that exists. We see a similar idea expressed in the aforementioned passage of the *Summa theologiae*. Here, however, Aquinas gives a more synthetic definition of beauty in things that combines both the definitions found in our previous discussion (*claritas* and *proportio*), but also adds a third, *integritas*: ontological integrity or wholeness.

> Species or beauty has a likeness to the property of the Son. For beauty includes three conditions, "integrity" or "perfection," since those things which are impaired are by the very fact ugly; due "proportion"

they have from the power of the Beautiful" (*Cosmic Structure and the Knowledge of God: Thomas Aquinas' In Librum beati Dionysii de divinis nominibus expositio*, English trans. H. C. Marsh (Ann Arbor, MI: UMI Diss., 1994), 361–62).

or "harmony"; and lastly, "brightness" or "clarity," whence things are called beautiful which have a bright color.[8]

Aquinas is discussing essential attributes of God that might be appropriated to one person of the Holy Trinity more fittingly than another. The Father, Son, and Holy Spirit are all beautiful because God is beautiful in essence, and the three persons are each the one God. However, we can appropriately attribute beauty to the Son in a fitting way because the Son derives eternally from the Father as the eternally begotten Word and Wisdom of the Father, through whom all things are made. Beauty tracks onto the notions of integrity or specific determination, of proportion or harmony, and of splendor. The Son is the eternal Word of the Father who has in himself all that is in the Father (the "species" of the divine essence that he receives from the Father) and who exists in eternal harmony with the Father, as the splendor of the Father.

The implication of this point of view is readily apparent. God is essentially beautiful, and God has created all that exists in light of the eternal Word and Wisdom of God, who is the Son. Consequently, all that exists and that derives from God is in some way beautiful. The beauty in things themselves has a three-fold foundation. Most fundamentally, there is the integrity or wholeness of a thing. A given tree is beautiful because it is integral, having all its limbs, leaves, and flowers, having reached its maturity and magnificence. Second, there is proportionality. A tree is beautiful because of the proportions that emerge from the perfection of its form. The quantitative arrangement of the branches in proportionate arrangement to one another is beautiful, but so are the arrangements of the colors of the trunk, leaves, and flowers, which are harmonious in qualitatively as well as quantitatively proportionate ways. Most ultimate in the order of beauty is splendor. When the form is integral and perfect and expresses itself through the right proportion of harmonious perfections of quality and quantity, what emerges is an innate splendor or

8. *ST* I, q. 39, a. 8.

clarity of form. A tree that is beautiful has a splendid magnificence that derives from its ontological perfection, its integrity, and harmonious proportions.

We should note that this idea of beauty can clearly pertain to spiritual realities or activities as well as physical or material things. Clearly, this must be the case because it is a perfection susceptible of being ascribed to God and to the divine nature. We can easily consider examples from human agency. The virtuous person who is truly temperate has a temperance that is integral or whole (both across diverse cases of temperance and across time, perduring in character). The beauty of the virtue is exhibited in the spiritual harmony it evokes in a person's reasonable actions, as he is proportionately temperate in relation to diverse conditions and persons so as to exhibit friendliness, thoughtfulness, justice, and affability. (Temperance is ultimately at the service of justice and charity). In a most beautiful case, temperance makes a person more spiritually beautiful or radiant, as a person who lives in reasonable ways in the service of love in his thinking and acting toward others and toward God. The point in giving this example is to make clear in a simple way that beauty is defined by Aquinas in such a way that it can readily be considered co-extensive with all that exists—both material and immaterial—a transcendental feature of reality.

If this is the case, we must ask, in turn, what exactly is the relationship between truth, goodness, and beauty? We should note that Aquinas's definition of beauty grounds the attribute in the given form or species of a thing. This seems closely aligned with the transcendental notion of *res* (intrinsic determination) and that of truth (the intellectual grasp of the species or form of a thing). Beauty has its foundation in the truth of a reality as formally determined in some way. Furthermore, beauty has some likeness to the transcendental goodness since both of them attract another in a relational way. Goodness denotes a perfection in things that can in turn perfect others in accord with their own end. What is good can become a goal that another reality pursues so as to flourish. Beauty denotes something else that is analogous. It attracts admiration and love, but of a given kind. Its goodness is intellectual or contemplative in nature. Beauty is the splendor of the species or form, and its attraction is that of the truth or formal determination of a reality insofar as it has the power to garner our admiration. In other words, when beauty does attract, whether intellectually or sensibly, it does so by virtue of the splendor of the form, which is capable of eliciting the appetite. We might say that beauty is the goodness of the truth of a thing, the delightfulness (or appetibility) of its intelligibility. To state things in this fashion is to place emphasis on the formal determination as the key element rather than the splendor, a decision which gives primacy to the truth of the beautiful reality and only secondarily emphasizes its goodness. However, we could also say that beauty is the species or formal determination of goodness. This way of speaking places emphasis on the goodness of beauty but notes that it implies formal determination (and thus a truth) of a definite kind. This is why beauty invites admiration, while goodness perfects. Goodness is grounded in final causality, while beauty is grounded in formal causality. Beauty has the power to hold our gaze. Goodness has the power to give our lives ultimate purpose or meaning. The two are not to be confused, even if they are often found together.

Does this analysis suggest then that beauty is a "blended transcendental," a mere combination of truth and goodness, or something that results from the two of them? If so, is the denotation of beauty as a transcendental something gratuitous since it is a notion contained implicitly in those of *verum* and *bonum*? The concept of beauty as we have defined it here is co-extensive with being and does arise implicitly from an enriched consideration of truth and goodness, in their relationship to one another. Beauty is the attractive appeal of the form, and so a particular kind of goodness of intelligibility embedded in the ontological truth of things. But the concept adds something essential to our concept of truth and goodness as such since beauty is a distinctive feature of reality and one that any robust metaphysical analysis of being needs to take account of. Aquinas's definition is powerful precisely because it allows us to truly distinguish truth, goodness, and beauty, which remain irreducibly distinct features of reality, and to see their interrelation as dimensions of being. Far from being gratuitous, this metaphysical reflection provides an organically united conceptual analysis of very elevated topics that are of central importance to human understanding.

THE BEAUTY OF GOD

Clearly, Aquinas affirms that God is beautiful, but what can it mean to say this? St. Thomas typically avoids offering any definition of God in his writings and instead makes thematic appeal to the three-fold *via* taken from Dionysius the Areopagite in his *On the Divine Names*, c. 7, 3. God is known *per viam causalitatis* as the transcendent cause of creatures. Because creatures must in some way resemble their cause as his effects, certain attributes of creatures that imply no intrinsic imperfection (such as being, unity or goodness) may be ascribed to God in an analogical way. However, due to God's utterly ineffable and transcendent manner of existing, these attributes must be thought of *per viam negationis*, or *remotionis*, that is to say, by negating or removing from them all that pertains necessarily to creaturely imperfection. Finally, *per viam eminentiae*, these analogical ascriptions given to God may be thought to exist in him in an all-surpassing, preeminent way, not found in any creaturely form.[9]

According to this way of thinking, creatures do resemble God as

9. *ST* I, q. 12, a. 12: "From the knowledge of sensible things, the whole power of God cannot be known; nor therefore can his essence be seen. But because they are his effects and depend upon their cause, we can be led from them so far as to know of God whether he exists, and to know of him what must necessarily belong to him, as the first cause of all things, exceeding all things caused by him. Hence, we know of his relationship with creatures in so far as he is the cause of them all; also, that creatures differ from him, inasmuch as he is not in any way part of what is caused by him; and that creatures are not removed from him by reason of any defect on his part, but because he super-exceeds them all" (Translation slightly modified). Note that just after this text Aquinas proceeds to clarify (in q. 13) the analogical character of the knowledge this way of thinking permits. For similar texts, employing the triple viae, see *SCG* I, c. 30; *In Divinis Nominibus*, c. 7, lec. 4; *De potentia Dei*, q. 7, a. 5, ad 2.

the effects of the Creator resemble their cause by similitude. Therefore, they allow us to signify positively what he is essentially by analogy. However, this process of signifying must be qualified by a series of well-thought-out negations since God is also in many respects unlike or dissimilar to his created effects. Our names for God, then, can be true and accurate, but they do not suggest any *immediate* or direct apprehension of what God is in himself. The essence of God is truly signified by our use of the divine attributes, but God's divine nature remains incomprehensible.[10]

Aquinas defines beauty in creatures by noting three characteristics: the integrity of the form, its emergent properties of proportion or harmony, and its expressive splendor. He also makes clear in his *Commentary on the Divine Names* that these notions can be employed analogically to speak about the uncreated beauty of God. However, when considering this procedure in accord with the three-fold *viae* mentioned above, one must take into account foremost Aquinas's doctrine of divine simplicity, which surely is of consequence for thinking about any attribution of beauty to the divine essence.

In *Summa theologiae* I, q. 3, Aquinas considers divine simplicity in several respects, four of which are particularly consequential for our consideration.[11]

---

10. The divine names are ultimately always positive in signification, meaning that they denote something of what God truly is in himself. Radical apophaticism is excluded by Aquinas, against what he takes to be the excessive skepticism of Maimonides. See *De potentia Dei*, q. 7, a. 5: "The idea of negation is always based upon an affirmation: as evinced by the fact that every negative proposition is proved by an affirmative: wherefore unless the human mind knew something positively about God, it would be unable to deny anything about him. And it would know nothing if nothing that it affirmed about God were positively verified about him. Hence following Dionysius [*Divine Names*, c. 12], we must hold that these terms signify the divine essence, albeit defectively and imperfectly" (Translation from Aquinas, *On the Power of God*, trans. English Dominican Province (Westminster, MD: Newman, 1952). I explore this topic in greater detail in Thomas Joseph White, *Wisdom in the Face of Modernity: A Study in Thomistic Natural Theology*, ch. 8 and appendix 2.

11. The summary offered here of Aquinas on divine simplicity is a succinct echo of two longer treatments. See White, "Divine Simplicity and the Holy Trinity"; "Nicene Orthodoxy and Trinitarian Simplicity," *American Catholic Philosophical Quarterly* 90, no. 4 (2016): 727–50.

First, St. Thomas affirms that God does not have a body.[12] There is no hylomorphic composition in God of form and matter. Consequently, he is not complex in the way any material body is complex, nor can the divine essence be represented physically or sensibly. Furthermore, our conceptual notions of natures are all drawn by abstraction from sensate individuals, but God is not a sensate individual, and so none of our abstract concepts could be perfectly adequate for thinking about what God is essentially. Aquinas's reflection on this point is evidently radically apophatic.

Second, there is no distinction of individuality and natural form in God.[13] For example, every human being, orange tree, or diamond is one individual of a given kind, within a larger set of natural kinds composed of a plurality of individuals (many human beings, orange trees or diamonds). However, God is not an individual of a given kind, a god among gods, or one kind of thing among others. Rather, God is outside every species and genus of being, as he who gives being to all that exists (across all genera and species) and who himself transcends every particular realization of created existence. God is the only God, and God is his own deity. There is no larger generic set of beings that he could be thought to be included within.

Third, there is in God no distinction of essence and existence.[14] He does not receive his being from another, nor can he fail to exist. Consequently, he does not participate in existence and is not measured or comprehended by another. In this sense, he is wholly unlike realities that are ontologically contingent or that have a potency for non-existence. Furthermore, because God is the author of all that exists, he cannot be conceived of as something within the transcendental range of being, a member of the total set of created beings (what Aquinas calls *ens commune*[15]). Transcendental notions do not signify God directly.[16] He is only intelligible for us as the origin and author of

---

12. *ST* I, q. 3, aa. 1–2.
13. *ST* I, q. 3, a. 3.
14. *ST* I, q. 3, a. 4.
15. See, for example, *ST* I, q. 3, a. 4, obj. 1 and ad 1, and *SCG* II, c. 54, para. 10.
16. See the argument of *ST* I, q. 4, a. 3, echoes Aquinas's presentation of the science

all that falls within the transcendental range of being and not as that which is ontologically common to all created being.

Fourth, there exists in God no distinction of substance and properties (or "accidents").[17] This is due to the fact that properties always actuate a latent potency in a substantial being. For example, the human capacity for violin playing is a potency in human nature that is not actuated in most people, but that is actuated over time by a person developing the actual property of that artistic skill. There is nothing like this in God, who (on Aquinas's account) does not become more perfect ontologically through his initiatives in regard to creation, but who is the unilateral giver of being to all that is created. Nor does God self-perfect by generating his own developmental properties over time. God simply is and is perfect eternally. Consequently, we can of course say that God is wise, good, or beautiful, but we should also add that whatever God is, God is his wisdom, goodness, or beauty. It would be metaphysically absurd for a human being to say, "I am wisdom," or "I am he who is," but in the case of God, these significations are rigorously correct, even if in saying this we still have no immediate knowledge of God in himself.[18] Such affirmations are true, and yet the inner mystery or essence of God remains numinous and incomprehensible for us.

How do these four considerations of divine simplicity affect our understanding of divine beauty? As noted above, divine names imply that God is the cause of perfections in creatures so that perfection

---

of metaphysics in the *proem.*, *In Meta.* He argues in both places that God is known only as the *cause* of the subject of metaphysics and does not fall under the subject of that study as its formal object. While metaphysics can consider *ens qua ens*, or being that is common to all created realities, it only approaches God as the transcendent cause of the subject matter of its study. Being itself in creatures is not reducible to a particular species or genus and can be known only analogically because it is present in every essential kind of thing, nor is it reducible to any essential kind. This is the case for the other transcendentals as well. But when we speak of what people call God we speak of the cause of all created being, and so there is another level of conceptual remove entailed. God is known by analogical significations due to the ontological similitude between creatures that have being, unity, goodness, etc. and God who is the origin of these features of reality.

17. *ST* I, q. 3, a. 6.
18. *ST* I, q. 13, aa. 3–5.

names like beauty can rightly be attributed to God. All that exists is beautiful, and beauty is in some way an expression of the splendor of a formal determination or nature. Consequently, the divine nature or essence may be said to be beautiful as the transcendent, hidden cause of the beauty present in all things. However, we must remove from perfection terms attributed to God any notion of ontological imperfection (by way of negation) so as to posit them of God in a super-eminent way. Furthermore, beauty was defined in creatures by recourse to three notions: integrity of form, proportionality or harmony, and splendor or radiance. However, in light of the metaphysics of divine simplicity, we clearly cannot attribute the modalities of beauty we find in creatures directly to God. What might we say, then, about the beauty of God when employing Aquinas's Dionysian framework for divine naming?

First, God is not a body or a hylomorphic subject, composed of matter and form. But beauty as we experience it in physical realities always emerges in a material form, with its own integrity, quantitative and sensibly qualitative proportions, as well as physical splendor. By contrast, if God is beauty, his beauty is literally hidden from view. There is no icon of God, no sensate representation of the ineffable divine essence. Nor can the formal beauty of God be conceived after the pattern of a nature or essence abstracted by us from a material subject, like the beauty of a human being, a star, or an orange tree. The immaterial beauty of God transcends all our abstract conceptual notions.

Second, God is not an individual of a common kind, nor is he a member of a larger genus. Therefore, the beauty of God is not that of a particular *kind* of reality.[19] Rather, it is the uniquely transcendent beauty that is the cause of all else that exists, the beauty that gives being to the world.[20]

---

19. *In Divinis Nominibus*, c. IV, lec. 5, para. 345.

20. Aquinas makes this point quite clearly in *In Div. Nom.*, c. IV, lec. 5, para. 343 (Marietti): "Excessus autem est duplex: unus in genere, qui significatur per comparativum vel superlativum; alius extra genus, qui significatur per additionem huius praepositionis: super [...]. Et licet iste duplex excessus in rebus causatis non simul conveniat,

Third, God does not receive his existence from others and is not a member of the transcendental set of all created beings (*ens commune*). Therefore, the beauty of God is not a part of the transcendental range of beauty found in all existence. Rather, this beauty is known only by analogy as the unique total cause of all created existence, as the beauty that gives being to all else that is beautiful. Nor can God be alienated from this attribute because God is not contingently beautiful. Rather, this property must be attributed to him eternally and in ontological distinction and independence from the whole created order.

Finally, there is no composition in God of substance and properties, and so one must also say that God is his own beauty and that, in God, beauty is identical in some way with being, goodness, wisdom, and power.[21] These divine names are appropriately drawn from

---

tamen in Deo simul dicitur et quod est pulcherrimus et superpulcher; non quod sit in genere, sed quod ei attribuuntur omnia quae sunt cuiuscumque generis." "But excess is twofold: one in genus, which is signified through the comparative or superlative; the other outside of genus, which is signified through the addition of the preposition 'super' [outside] [...]. And although this twofold excess in caused things does not come together simultaneously, nevertheless it is said in God simultaneously both that God is most beautiful and super beautiful [beyond all created beauty], not that God is in a genus, but since all things which are in any genus are attributed to God."

21. *In Div. Nom.*, c. IV, lec. 5, para. 345–47: "sed Deus quoad omnes et simpliciter pulcher est. Et omnium praemissorum assignat rationem, cum subdit quod ipse est pulcher *secundum seipsum*; per quod, excluditur quod non est pulcher secundum unam partem tantum, neque in aliquo tempore tantum, neque in aliquo loco tantum; quod enim alicui secundum se et primo convenit, convenit et toti et semper ubique. Iterum, Deus est pulcher in seipso, non per respectum ad aliquod determinatum et ideo non potest dici ad aliquid sit pucher et ad aliquid non pulcher et neque quibusdam pulcher et quibusdam non pulcher. Iterum, est *semper* et uniformiter pulcher, per quod excluditur primus defectus pulchritudinis, scilicet variabilitas. Deinde, cum decit: *et sicut omnis* [...] ostendit qua ratione dicatur Deus superpulcher, in quantum in seipso habet excellenter et ante omnia alia, fontem totius pulchritudinis. In ipsa enim *natura simplici et supernaturali* omnium *pulchrorum* ab ea derivatorum praeexistunt *omnis pulchritudo et omne pulchrum*, non quidem divisim, sed *uniformiter* per modum quo multiplices effectus in causa praeexistunt." "But God is beautiful in every respect and simply. And he [Dionysius] designates the reason of all the foregoing, when he adds that God is beauty in himself; through which it is excluded that God's beauty is not according to one part alone, nor in some time alone, nor in some place alone; for what is befitting to something according to itself and first, befits it wholly and always and everywhere. Moreover, God is beauty in himself, not with respect to something determinate [according to a finite form], and

distinct features of created reality to denote by analogy something that is mysteriously one in God himself.

If we return to the three-fold definition, we can consider the apophatic character of God's supereminent beauty. There is *integritas* in God because the divine essence is one, albeit of a wholly other order than anything we can conceive of directly. If this form of God's very being is identical with God's eternal truth and goodness, then surely we may say by analogy that God's divine form is splendid and eternally beautiful.

May we attribute a beauty of proportionality or harmony to the divine essence? In a human being, spiritual properties may emerge progressively that are complex and beautiful in nature due to their proportionate arrangement. A discursive philosophical argument may be beautiful due to its integrity as expressed through a complex, proportionate chain of reasoning, attaining to a kind of intellectual splendor or nobility in its true conclusions. But in God, divine knowledge is of a higher order that is non-compositional. In a human being, a spiritual moral virtue like charity or justice may emerge over time and appear beautiful in its diverse, complex, and proportionate expressions. But God is eternally charitable and just, and these properties are in some way indicative of the divine essence as such. Therefore, the beauty of God's truth and goodness are simply identical with what God eternally is.

We may conclude then that there is no compositional proportionality of quantity or quality in God and, therefore, no strict analogy of beauty between creatures and God in this particular sense. However, the beautiful proportions of complex created things, both

---

for this reason neither can it be said that in some respect God is beautiful and in some respect he is not nor that in some ways God is beautiful and in some ways not beautiful. Again, God is always uniformly beautiful, through which is excluded the first defect of beauty, namely of variability. Then when he says "and as of all beautiful etc." he shows why God is called "beyond" the beautiful. And he says that God is excellently and before all others the fountain of all beauty. For in God's simple and supernatural nature itself all beauty and every beauty of all beautiful things derived from it preexist, not indeed dividedly, but uniformly through the mode in which multiple effects preexist in a cause" (Marsh translation, p. 661, here slightly modified).

within themselves and among themselves (as diverse realities related to one another), are beautiful by virtue of the existence and formal determinations that God has given them. Therefore, they are expressive in their created complexity of what must exist in God in a wholly other, higher, and utterly simple way. The wisdom of God is eternally beautiful, and he expresses this wisdom within the complexity of creation by giving radiantly intelligible forms that are truly beautiful to so many diverse and complementary beings. The goodness of God is eternally beautiful, and he expresses this goodness within the complexity of creation by giving spiritually and sensibly attractive forms to so many diverse and complementary beings. The wisdom and goodness of God's beauty are expressed outwardly by the giving of existence to the created world, in its attractive intelligibility, and in the splendor of its diverse and manifold created forms.

CREATED ORDER AS CONCEALMENT AND MANIFESTATION OF DIVINE BEAUTY

By considering God as he who is simple, unchangingly eternal, good, wise, and beautiful, we can begin to perceive a certain kind of "creation mysticism" that arises from thinking about the Creator. As the cause of all that exists, God is he who sustains all things in being, and so he is immanently present to all that exists or is "omnipresent." In the words of Dionysius the Areopagite, "God is all things insofar as he is the cause of all things," and in the words of Augustine, "God is closer to us than we are to ourselves."[22] At the most intimate interior level of all that exists, God is hidden but utterly present as he who gives existence to all that is.

This also means that realities that spring from God and that are more manifest to us are a kind of visible expression or natural

---

22. Dionysius, *The Divine Names* V, 4 (PG 3:817). My translation is based on Aquinas's Latin rendering of the phrase in *S.Th.* I, q. 4, a. 2: "omnia est, ut omnium causa." Augustine, *Confessions* III, 6, 11: "interior intimo meo et superior summo meo" (more interior to my innermost and higher than my highest self).

"sacrament" (sign and instrument) of the presence of God. The beauty and complexity of nature, its immense, intricate order, and vast history are visible expressions of the infinite hidden wisdom of God. His divine eternity and wisdom are manifest in the unfolding effects of time and creaturely history. The creation is the written tableau on which God expresses his being outwardly.

So too, the human soul is the special expression of the mystery of God because the human being possesses intellectual understanding and moral freedom. Whereas God is infinitely wise and good, the human soul is capable of becoming progressively wiser and better. The soul is an image of God, then, a created reality that reflects in a special way the hidden presence of the omnipresent God who creates the spiritual soul and upholds it in being. God sustains us in being and is present in the most intimate depths of our soul, beckoning to us as rational creatures by the natural attraction of his uncreated truth and goodness. We are naturally able to think about God and search for him, he who is hidden in the very depths of our being.

How does this monotheistic vision of creation relate to the question of created beauty? From what we have argued, it follows that the created world is a kind of iconostasis of God. On the one hand, it serves to manifest, however imperfectly, the hidden beauty of God. The creation is not God, but God is omnipresent within all things, more interior to them than they are to themselves, as the inward cause of their very being. Consequently, their beauty is an expression of God's eternal wisdom. On the other hand, the world of finite beings is so utterly unlike God and wholly disproportionate to God ontologically that it cannot communicate any direct knowledge of what God is in himself. Therefore, the same beauty that is present in all that exists also conceals God. He remains hidden from sight as the unknown ground of creation.

The world that God has created is beautiful in diverse ways, and a deeper reflection on that beauty is helpful as a means of reflecting on the strangeness and transcendence of divine wisdom, the origin of all created beauty. Based on Aquinas's three-fold definition of beauty, we can note that each thing that exists is beautiful by reason of its inherent form: its integral wholeness, its manifold proportionate properties, and its expressive splendor. As already noted, such formal beauty in things reflects, in however faint a way, the transcendent beauty of God and relates each individual reality, however seemingly insignificant, directly to God as the primary author of its beauty. However, there is also an integrity of order *between* diverse individual forms of created reality and a corresponding proportionality and splendor that emerges from the order that exists between them. From collective order, natural beauty emerges on a much larger scale. Beauty is not only in individuals, then, but also in common goods or in variously arranged, holistic groups of beings, be they non-living, living, or properly intellectual in kind.[23] Most especially, the ultimate teleological order that exists between hierarchically differentiated goods (non-living being, living beings, and rational, human beings) forms a kind of collective common good that has emerged over a vast time and which is itself beautiful in its proportionate diversity. The universe in its hierarchical dimensions, set against the backdrop of a vast temporality, reflects the unfolding

---

23. *In Div. Nom.*, c. IV, lec. 5, para. 340: "est autem duplex consonantia in rebus: prima quidem, secundum creaturarum ad Deum et hanc tangit cum dicit quod Deus est causa consonantiae, *sicut vocans omnia ad seipsum*, inquantum convertit omnia ad seipsum sicut ad finem, ut supra dictum est et propter hoc pulchritude in Graeco callos dicitur quod est a vocando sumptum; secunda autem consonantia est in rebus, secundum ordinationem earum ad invicem; et hoc tangit cum subdit, quod congregat omnia in omnibus, ad idem. Et potest hoc intelligi, secundum sententiam, Platonicorum, quod superior sunt in inferioribus, secundum participationem; inferior vero sunt in superioribus, per excellentiam quamdam et sic omnia sunt in omnibus; et ex hoc quod omnia in omnibus inveniuntur ordine quodam, sequitur quod omnia ad idem ultimum ordinentur." "But there is a twofold consonance in things: first according to the order of creatures to God; and he touches upon this when he says that God is the cause of consonance, just insofar as he calls all things to himself insofar as God converts all things to himself to an end, as was said above, and because of this beauty in Greek is called "*kallos*" which is taken from calling. But the second kind of consonance is in things according to their order to each other; and he touches upon this when he adds that God can be understood according to the statement of the Platonists that superior things are in inferior things by participation but the inferiors are in the superiors through a certain excellence, and thus all things are in all things. And because in all things are found in a certain order, it follows that all things are ordained to the same end" (Marsh trans. p. 359, slightly altered).

effects of an eternal wisdom, an uncreated beauty, which lies hidden behind the ontological "narrative" of finite being as its unseen composer.

The notion of the world of existents as an orderly, beautiful, and ontologically interdependent system of beings is very ancient in western philosophy. Perhaps the most seminal text in Hellenistic philosophy is found in Aristotle's *Metaphysics* XII, c. 10, where the philosopher discusses the goodness of diverse realities in terms of final causality and addresses the way in which their mutually coordinated activities can be understood as a kind of imitation of God, who is pure actuality, and the primary cause of their being. In this passage, Aristotle famously compares the world metaphorically to an army that is arranged under a general, in which all are pursuing a collective end, but in various ways that are mutually complementary, so that each reality can achieve its own end only in interdependence upon the others, within a larger collective whole. Just as the soldiers act in conformity with the governing idea of the general, so by similitude, the beings in the world act in such a way as to imitate the goodness of the transcendent God who is perfect in actuality. The image is interesting because it suggests not only that all things can come to their perfection in distinct ways, but that they can do so only because they depend upon one another non-competitively, and that, in doing so, they also approach most ultimately the transcendent perfection of the primary cause, God.

Aquinas uses this idea of collective final causality in the universe to reinterpret Dionysius on the topic of creation and efficient causality. Dionysius speaks of God communicating being out of the resources of his own goodness.[24] Here, the ontology of goodness is understood primarily in terms of efficient causality. God loves his own infinite goodness, and from the perfection of this love, he wills to freely give being to other realities as a sheer gift, not to somehow develop his own potential, but as a free expression of divine wisdom and goodness. Where Dionysius emphasizes God as the

24. Dionysius, *The Divine Names* IV, 7 (PG 3, 700).

transcendent efficient cause, Aristotle emphasizes the final causality of God: all things imitate God's perfection in their own limited way but do so also in mutual reliance upon one another. Aquinas joins these two ideas together.[25] God gives being to a world in which all that exists is in some way good and beautiful. This gift of being is the expression of God's uncreated wisdom, goodness, and beauty. Ultimately, God's activity of creation (his transcendent efficient causality) is most intelligible in light of God's own final causality. God's eternal knowledge of himself and his eternal love of his own infinite goodness are the ground of all creation. Creation is a diffusion of divine goodness, having its deeper ground in God's own perfect actuality. Created realities themselves, in turn, act to imitate God or even, in a sense, return toward God by operating in accord with the innate structures of their being.[26] Each form is like God in a given way. Creatures come to be perfect over time and do so through mutually dependent forms of collective existence, or in the context of created "common goods" where they can only flourish in ontological societies of reciprocal causation. However, the whole common good of the universe exists ultimately for God himself, the uncreated common good. God is the ultimate end of all things because all things exist and act to perfect themselves in some real sense in virtue of God's wisdom and in view of God's ontological intentions for the universe. This notion of God as a transcendent common good is inclusive. There is no rivalry between the final ends of creatures and the final end of God as the common good of the universe. Things that pursue their own particular ends (such as human beings or animals, to take evident examples) become what God intends them to be as they attain their own intrinsic perfections, often in mutual dependence upon other realities that, in turn, act according to intrinsic

25. See in particular *ST* I, q. 5, a. 4, which comments on the text of Dionysius explicitly, and *In Div. Nom.* c. 4, lec. 5, para. 352 (on the efficient causality of divine beauty) and para. 353 (on the final causality of divine beauty).

26. On the beauty of God as the exemplary cause of creation, see *In Div. Nom.* c. 4, lec. 5, para. 354–55, which follow upon the consideration of efficient and final causality in the two previous paragraphs.

natural operations or perfections which characterize them in their being as well.

Aquinas accepts the basic understanding of created reality as hierarchically differentiated that one finds in classical neo-Platonic authors, Christian and non-Christian alike.[27] There are realities that have being and are physical in kind but that are not alive. There are realities that are physical and living but that do not have knowledge. There are realities that are living and have sensate knowledge but have no rational knowledge or deliberate freedom. And there are beings that are alive and are characterized not only by sensate knowledge, but also by intellectual understanding and the capacity to love by means of deliberate freedom. Each of these *kinds* of realities reflects something unique about the beauty of God.[28] At the same time, each of these *kinds* of realities can contribute to the good of the others, but in a hierarchically differentiated way. Aquinas thinks that it is possible for living things to emerge ontologically from non-living things, but he also argues that even if such emergence takes place, the specific form of living things is different in kind from that of non-living realities.[29] Non-living things exist principally to

27. See, for example, *SCG* III, c. 22, where this metaphysical view of the ontological hierarchy of being is clearly presented.

28. The physical non-living universe does not need living beings in order to reflect something of the governing wisdom, grandeur, and power of God. Its physical magnitude, vastness, intricacy, intelligible historicity, and temporal order all seem to reflect something of the divine beauty. But this also is refracted amidst the physical contingency, ontological fragility, and sheer material and accidental arbitrariness that characterize much of its internal order. Living beings are unlike non-living things and like God in virtue of the fact that they are alive, but of course, their life is physical in its realization and not spiritual or everlasting. Consequently, they can be said to imitate the eternal life of God primarily by reproduction and self-propagation, a form of ontological persistence through time that resembles the unchanging eternity of God in an ontologically faint and imperfect but real way. Ecosystems of living creatures depend upon one another even when their inhabitants prey on one another or, especially in such cases, and evolutionary systems suggest that the realization of new differentiations among various living things occurs in great part in reaction to and thus ontological dependence upon the pressures brought to bear from the operations of other living and non-living things in a shared environment.

29. St. Thomas thinks that it is possible, at least in principle, for living things to arise historically from non-living material bodies, even if life represents a principle not merely

create a context or setting in which living things can emerge. Plants exist for the sake of animals, and plants and animals exist for the sake of human beings. Human beings exist for the sake of life in community with one another and ultimately for God. The visible cosmos exists so that human beings may live in pursuit of union with God by grace, in friendship and society with one another, and in harmony with the wider created order.[30]

The interdependent hierarchy that emerges from differentiated kinds of beings gives rise to a larger overarching order, one that implies all three notes of beauty. This cosmic and ontological order has its own relative *integrity, proportionality* or *harmony* between distinct kinds of beings, and *splendor* that is present in the ontological "mystery" of the universe. Distinct kinds of beings are characterized by distinct operations, and therefore they pursue distinct ends.[31] Nevertheless, the distinct kinds of beings we find in the universe can be seen as profoundly complementary, set within a larger cosmic and

---

reducible to material parts and their quantitative arrangement (*ST* I, q. 69, a. 2; q. 71, a. 1, ad 1; q. 73, a. 1, ad 3; q. 118, a. 1, *sed contra*). Consequently, Aquinas is able to situate a differentiated hierarchy of being (from non-living beings to plants to animals) within a gradated ontological spectrum that allows for the progressive emergence of higher forms from lower ones. See on this topic with regards to evolution, Lawrence Dewan, "The Importance of Substance," in *Form and Being: Studies in Thomistic Metaphysics*, 96–130.

30. *SCG* III, c. 22, para. 8–9: "And since a thing is generated and preserved in being by the same reality, there is also an order in the preservation of things, which parallels the foregoing order of generation. Thus, we see that mixed bodies are sustained by the appropriate qualities of the elements; Plants, in turn, are nourished by mixed bodies; animals get their nourishment from plants: so, those that are more perfect and more powerful from those that are more imperfect and weaker. In fact, man uses all kinds of things for his own advantage: some for food, others for clothing [...]. Other things man uses for transportation [...]. And, in addition to this, man uses all sense objects for the perfection of intellectual knowledge. Hence it is said of man in the Psalms (8:8) in a statement directed to God: "You have subjected all things under his feet." And Aristotle says, in the *Politics* I [5: 1254b 9], that man has natural dominion over all animals. So, if the motion of the heavens is ordered to generation, and if the whole of generation is ordered to man as a last end within this genus, it is clear that the end of celestial motion is ordered to man as an ultimate end in the genus of generable and mobile beings."

31. Aquinas's understanding of natural end is analogical and quite flexible, modest enough to accommodate even the operations of atoms or minerals as realities having intrinsically oriented and statistically predictable agency that stems from their intrinsic forms.

ecological framework. This physical world capable of supporting the existence of living things is capable of becoming a theatre for human rationality and freedom, where specifically human communities can flourish. This overarching ontological order is beautiful in its own way, even if it is strange and vast, and seemingly impersonal in many respects. The detection of its deeper purpose can seem elusive or enigmatic to the human mind.

Aquinas's hierarchical understanding of reality is inclusive in character, so that an order of political and religious ethics derives from the natural order of beauty. The world's natural beauty ought to be respected and preserved in ways that acknowledge the intrinsic ontological integrity of all lesser realities but also their inclusion within an order that sustains rational creatures and their reference to the divine. How might we think in this respect about the moral orientation of the human person to the larger world of non-living things and non-human living things? Four succinct points of consideration are in order. First, it is legitimate for human beings to make use of non-living realities and non-human living things in view of the good of the human community. Human beings have an ontological dignity and nobility that is greater than that of all other created realities due to the existence in them of the spiritual soul. Society is rightly warranted to protect human life at all stages, from conception to natural death, and this protection includes the obligation to make good use of natural resources (including non-human animals) for the flourishing of the human community. To deny the hierarchical differentiation of human beings in relation to non-human creatures does nothing to advance the cause of respect for other forms of life or being. The free conquest of nature by intelligent animals of science and industry can only be understood and brought into measured employment by the right use of the philosophical and moral faculties of this same intelligent creature. The denial that this spiritual element of reality exists in man does nothing positive to advance the project of a harmonious existence for human beings within the wider context of their physical and living cosmos.

Second, all this being said, human beings can acknowledge reasonably and freely the deeper order of the cosmos and its beauty and should act accordingly in ways that respect the relative integrity, order, and beauty of non-human realities. This ontological integrity in non-human realities is intrinsic to what they are, not merely instrumental or anthropocentric. That is to say, non-human realities do not have an ontological meaning or purpose only insofar as they are useful to human beings or susceptible to arrangement within a human order. They have being, goodness, and beauty in themselves from God the Creator that exists independently of the human community and that could, in principle, continue to exist once that community ceases to be. A theocentric and religious understanding of cosmic order and an intrinsicist metaphysical account of the inherent integrity and dignity of non-human nature are not rival understandings but are mutually reinforcing ideas.

Third, human beings should acknowledge the ontological integrity of non-human physical and living beings for distinctly religious reasons, above all, insofar as these realities truly reflect in their very being something about God, his uncreated wisdom and beauty. To destroy a given species of non-human animal, for example, due to reasons of economic and industrial expediency, is to destroy something that has developed through time as an emanation and expression of uncreated wisdom. It is broadly morally impermissible to extinguish once and for all any irreducibly distinct species of living thing since each natural kind stems ultimately from the uncreated *Logos* of God and is in some way a distinctive finite expression of God's infinite uncreated beauty.[32] Likewise, to destroy a large-scale ecosystem through deliberate negligence is, in some cases, to harm the common good of the created order in a longstanding and seriously deleterious way.

---

32. I am not asserting that the extinction of a given species must always be an intrinsically evil act. If the last of a species of venomous serpents were threatening a helpless human child, it would be morally licit to kill the serpent in order to save the child and perhaps in given circumstances even morally incumbent. But as a more general principle, the preservation of species types seems morally warranted as approaching human responsibilityy toward the natural environment.

God is closer to all created realities than they are to themselves and sustains them in being as outward expressions of himself so that if a large interdependent network of natural beings is irreversibly damaged or eradicated, one acts implicitly upon the very integrity of God's creation and his expressions of divine wisdom.

Fourth, non-human creatures do exist for human beings in some real sense, to sustain them in being, but also as the mediating format through which human beings can discover God and live in community with other human persons. To destroy aspects of the non-human creation irresponsibly then can affect the human community itself in two significant ways. First, it can do long-term harm to the environment that sustains the human community, not only physically and materially, but also intellectually and spiritually. In this sense, an ascetical use of environmental resources forms part of the way in which one generation of human beings justly prepares a place for the next generation. Second, negligent destruction of the environment can also disfigure those who act against lesser non-human realities themselves, teaching us, in turn, to misperceive what we ourselves are as human animals. For example, the purposefully cruel mistreatment of non-rational animals by a human being (through abuse or torture) entails a cruelty toward what is animal not only in another but also by implication in ourselves. By acting to inflict pain without just cause, a human agent acts by violence not only against another but also against his own animality. In doing so, however, he also acts, in turn, inevitably against his own rationality, since the kind of rational agent he is is animal in kind. This specific example points toward a wider generic point. The person who callously disfigures the natural world acts also in an implicitly destructive way against the ends and aims of contemplative rationality and responsible human freedom precisely because the person acts against the native context (the natural environment) in which our distinctively human and embodied (non-angelic) rationality and freedom are meant to flourish.

Finally, there is a fundamentally aesthetic point we should make regarding the moral value of the cultural admiration of beauty for its own sake. The transcendentals co-exist in the world with their privations: being and non-being, unity and multiplicity, good and evil, truth and falsehood. Where there is real beauty in the world, then there is also the possibility of ugliness. The world is beautiful and is also suggestive of the possibilities of distinctly human forms of artificial beauty. The natural environment of human beings is a setting in which human art can develop, as human beings educe artefactual beauty from the natural forms and qualities they find pre-existing them in the world. The pursuit of humanly formed beauty takes place against the backdrop of what is naturally given. But the natural order and its beauty can also be rendered ugly, as can the world of human artifacts. Magnificent forests can be destroyed unnecessarily and unreflectively to produce a collectively tolerated form of social suffering that is termed by euphemism "modern architecture." The modern world is, in many respects, a world of terrific ugliness. Modern moral theory is not typically given to arguing for or against human actions on the basis of the ugliness or beauty that they produce, but this suggests a serious failure and perhaps obsolescence on the part of typical modern moral theory, not a problem with aesthetic arguments. Those who make the universe or the human culture of art into a sphere of ugliness act in ways that are in some way inhumane and unethical, in the sense that they act against the beauty that is present in the world, or that might be present in human society, and because they diminish the degree of overall goodness that is present in the world and that is possessed by the common good. A certain kind of respect of nature entails a respect of natural beauty and an acknowledgement of its inherent value against those who would trivialize its importance or adopt an instrumentalist approach to the use of nature to its aesthetic detriment. A rightly ordered sense of the common good should seek to integrate the order of artistic beauty and efficiency into the natural order of beauty and vice versa. Human beauty can adorn nature, and natural beauty can exist at the heart of human civilization. The religious acknowledgement of God in community should take account of both these aspirations.

CONCLUSION

Ultimately, a theocentric understanding of beauty interprets the created world ontologically in light of God. An anthropocentric account of the centrality of the human community within the larger cosmos sees the beauty of the world as being in some way of utility to the flourishing of the human community. These two visions are not opposed to one another. Nor is either of them opposed to a metaphysical and ethical vision of beauty in non-human creatures, one that acknowledges their intrinsic ontological worth and purposes apart from human beings. The hierarchy of being is inclusive. Human beings should acknowledge the order of nature that pre-exists them precisely so as to live in the midst of nature with wisdom and aesthetic moderation. God's creative action gives being to all things, so they can never rightly be understood to exist in ontological or moral rivalry with God himself. Rather, God, who is the unseen and naturally unknown giver of all that exists and of all beauty that is present in the world, sustains creatures in being precisely in their most noble operations of flourishing and self-realization. In one respect, God has created the vast, beautiful cosmos and the strange and wondrous development of living creatures in view of the emergence of human beings, in whom the created world becomes self-aware and capable of spiritual love. In another respect, God has created all things in view of himself, his own eternal goodness. Human beings, insofar as they are metaphysicians, can learn to acknowledge, then, not only the beauty and dignity of the creation that pre-exists them and their own hierarchical status within creation, but also especially the Creator, the uncreated beauty from whence all things come forth, and to which they all inevitably return.

A Brief Christological Epilogue

The analysis I have offered here emphasizes the apophatic character of our knowledge of God, who is simultaneously manifest (imperfectly) and concealed (in great part) from human understanding by the beauty of the world. This approach leaves out one key idea: that God might cross the ontological threshold that distinguishes him from his own creation and manifest himself intelligibly and visibly in created form. That is to say, God can express his own essential and eternal beauty outwardly by taking on the form of a human nature, by becoming man. The Christian confession of the Incarnation claims that God has made himself known in a particular way first in the election of the people of Israel and ultimately in the person of Jesus of Nazareth, who is God made human. That mystery is itself beautiful by a kind of integrity, proportionality and splendor that are of a higher order. The human form of Christ—his human life, actions, teachings, sufferings, execution, resurrection—are all discretely beautiful, and they, in turn, both manifest and conceal his divine form. The divinity of Christ is revealed through his human agency and his human suffering, which are both obscure and luminous, plain but also splendid. This theological postscript is important for thinking about all we have said previously on the subject of divine beauty and created beauty. There is a third kind of beauty present in the world that we can know about only in light of revelation: beauty that is both divine and human, existing in one person. The metaphysics of the Incarnation exists not as an extraneous supplement to our reflection on the beauty of creation but as its deepest element. It is in Christ and the Church that created beauty begins actively to ascend into the sphere of the divine. Grace does not destroy nature, but heals and transforms it. Everything that rises must converge. But that is a reflection for another day.

7

Thomas Aquinas and Karl Barth
on the Analogy of Being

INTRODUCTION

Karl Barth was critical throughout his life of the notion and practice of natural theology, a term he used to designate the human aspiration to natural knowledge of God by way of philosophy or religious anthropology.[1] He was also critical of what he called the Catholic "*analogia entis*," a term he used to denote Catholic philosophical claims to knowledge of God (exemplified by Thomas Aquinas) but also other Catholic ideas.[2] The latter have to do with instances of human cooperation with God by nature, even under grace, as in the use of the notion of cooperative habitual grace, the theology of saints, Mariology, and the Church's magisterial infallibility. All of these typically Catholic theological ideas imply that human nature can cooperate with grace in stable and unfailing ways. As such, they represent for Barth something like the notion of natural theology: the idea that

Originally published in *Doctor Communis* 4 (2020): 112–41.

1. See the study of Keith L. Johnson, *Karl Barth and the Analogia Entis* (London and New York: T&T Clark, 2011), who argues convincingly that Barth maintains a consistent if evolving critical stance of philosophical knowledge of God, or "natural theology," throughout the course of his theological career.

2. See, for example, Karl Barth, *CD* I:1, xiii, 41, 119, 168–73, 243–47; *CD*, I:2, 35–44,138–47.

we can ascend to God and his grace by our own means and power, even alongside or in addition to the solitary initiative and action of the Holy Spirit. In reaction to the Catholic "both-and" of grace and nature, Barth wishes to posit consistently what he sees as a distinctively Protestant "either-or" of God's solitary action or our unwarranted human presumption to act by our own power.

In this chapter, I would like to detail one set of criticisms Barth makes of the use of analogy in Catholic theology, pertaining to the theology of creation and causality, from *Church Dogmatics* III:3.[3] Then I will consider Barth's counter-alternative, his distinctively theological notion of an *analogia relationis*, or *analogia operationis*. The likeness of God and the world is revealed, for Barth, uniquely by God's initiative of grace in Jesus Christ, and there is also an ontological likeness between God and creation constituted by God's free initiative of election toward the human race in creation, and in the Incarnation and redemption. Consequently, the freedom of God to relate to humanity in Christ is revelatory of what God is and constitutive of the relation of God to creatures and of creatures to God. I will argue that this notion is consequential in Barth's thinking and that his own thought, as a consequence, runs into some of the very problems he is worried about initially in his criticisms of the *analogia entis* and of Aquinas, or what he takes Aquinas's thought to be. Ironically, Aquinas's own theory of analogy helps one avoid some of the very problems Barth's theology falls into. Far from being a source of intellectual idolatry or projection onto God, Aquinas's notions of analogy and causality allow one to speak of the mystery of the Trinity so as carefully to avoid excessively univocal and, in effect, anthropomorphic conceptions of God of the kind Barth wishes to avoid, but in fact does effectuate himself on multiple occasions.

---

3. *CD* III:3, 90–154: the section is entitled, "The Divine Accompanying."

CRITICISMS OF THE *ANALOGIA ENTIS*
IN *CD* III:3

Barth has several important treatments of the topics of natural theology and analogy in the course of the *Church Dogmatics* as well as in other loci. The treatment of *CD* III:3 is of particular interest because Barth is seeking there to understand and treat the Christian doctrine of creation as it applies to created causality and human freedom. In doing so, he wishes to distance himself unambiguously from conceptions of causality and creation that are found in Roman Catholic theology, namely in Aquinas, but also in the First Vatican Council, insofar as these rely considerably on classical philosophy and on medieval metaphysical theories of being. Thus, he is seeking to be consistent with his earlier criticisms of the metaphysics of being (*analogia entis*) from *CD* I:1 and II:1, framed in the context of his early debates with Erich Przywara.[4]

In analyzing this section of text from *CD* III:3, we can introduce a helpful initial distinction. When Barth discusses the conditions of an authentic theological notion of creative causality, he appeals to both epistemological criteria and ontological criteria. The two are deeply interrelated and logically so. On the one side, there are epistemological stipulations for any right consideration of causality in Christian theology. Such considerations must stem uniquely from the medium of divine revelation, namely Scripture, as indicating God's causality of the world as the Father of the Son and as he who sends the Son and the Holy Spirit into the world. The only way to understand creation is in light of the Trinity, the Incarnation, and the redemption, and thus, in light of God's election of the human race

---

4. It also should be noted that the polemic of this section of the *CD* is directed primarily at Protestant scholasticism and at forms of modern German philosophy of religion, both of which Barth thinks contributed to the mid-20th century acceptance by some Protestant theologians in Germany prior to World War II of National Socialism as an expression of natural religious activity. See, however, the unambiguous connection he draws to Aristotle and Aquinas on causality at *CD* III:3, 98.

in Jesus Christ.[5] This epistemological criterion is underscored over and against the notion of a purely or even partially philosophically informed vision of creation, derivative from a theory of being and of being as caused by God, who communicates being to all things.[6]

The ontological content of this claim is naturally interrelated in Barth's mind. The likeness between God and the world established in Christ is one that can only be perceived in light of the Trinitarian creation of the world revealed in the New Testament, itself inextricably related to election, Incarnation, and redemption.[7] One might suspect here that Barth is making a point that most Catholic theologians could easily consent to: that the creation of the world by God is, in fact, ontologically, only ever a Trinitarian activity and that the mystery of created being, in the actual existential order we experience, is always already bound up with the mystery of grace, Incarnation, and redemption, in one cohesive existential order.[8] Nevertheless, Barth seems to be making a stronger claim, namely that the inner ontological content of God's creative causality of the world is only ultimately discernible for us in light of its exemplary manifestation in Jesus Christ. Because God causes his own human nature to

---

5. CD III:3, 100: Barth claims that the traditional Catholic and Protestant theological notion of *causa* "missed completely the relationship between creation and the covenant of grace. In its whole doctrine of providence it spoke abstractly not only of the general control of God over and with the creature, but of the control of a ... neutral and featureless God, an Absolute.... It separated between world history and salvation history. And the result was that when the dogmaticians came to speak of the *causare* of the *causa prima* and the *causae secundae*, neither in the one case nor in the other had it any specifically Christian content."

6. See CD III:3, 98–101.

7. CD III:3, 105: "If the causal concept is to be applied legitimately, its content and interpretation must be determined by the fact that what it describes is the operation of the Father of Jesus Christ in relation to that of the creature ... God, the only true God, so loved the world in His election of grace that in fulfillment of the covenant of grace instituted at the creation He willed to become a creature, and did in fact become a creature, in order to be its Saviour."

8. This is a point Hans Urs Von Balthasar makes in seeking *rapprochement* with Barth in his work. See his *Karl Barth: Darstellung und Deutung seiner Theologie* (Cologne: Verlag Jakob Hegner, 1951); English translation: *The Theology of Karl Barth*, trans. Edward Oakes (San Francisco: Ignatius Press, 1992).

exist in relation to his divine nature and so relates himself freely to his creation in the human nature of Christ, we can thus perceive truly that a real relation exists between God and the world and between the world and God more generally.[9] Exemplary causality and Christology elide here in a surprisingly strong way since it is only because God has elected to be human (by election from all eternity as a Trinitarian event) that creation can exist universally in relation to God, and so all of creation is marked ontologically from within by a Christological orientation toward Christ and in Christ toward the mystery of God.[10] I will return to this point in greater detail below, but first, we should note why Barth considers the Catholic notion of creation, informed by the *analogia entis*, to be unsustainable.

Barth's criticisms of what he takes to be a typically Catholic, as well as Thomistic theology of creative causality, based on a metaphysics of being, are sevenfold and can be stated succinctly. First, such notions of causality tend toward a conceptual reification of God by natural human understanding. In this sense, the metaphysics of creative causality and analogy treat God as a thing, among other things, and fail to recognize the ontological transcendence and epistemological incomprehensibility of God with respect to human nature.[11]

Second, metaphysical accounts of being, unity, and causality that

9. *CD* III:3, 102: Barth goes as far as to say that the notion of God as cause of creation outside of the Biblical concept of the creative causality effectuated in the election of Christ bears no similitude whatsoever to the New Testament notion of causality. In *CD* III:1, 3–41 he affirms unambiguously that all knowledge of God as Creator and thus of the world as created is made possible only in virtue of the knowledge faith yields of the person and mystery of Jesus Christ, and that therefore all knowledge of creation as such is Christological in origin.

10. This way of reading Barth in *CD* III:3 seems logically coherent with his exploration of the doctrine of election in *CD* 2:2. See, for example, *CD* 2:2, 145–94, where Barth claims that the Trinitarian election by God of the human race in Christ both expresses God's innermost being and forms the inward structure of creation, so that in election in Jesus Christ (alone) we perceive simultaneously who God is in himself as Trinity and what the creation is as coming forth from God for the possibility of relation to God by grace in Jesus Christ. See also *CD* III:1, 228–329, "The Covenant at the Internal Basis of Creation."

11. *CD* III:3, 101.

embrace the consideration of God as Creator treat God in his "unity" as one being within a larger collection of numeric beings that are quantifiable. So too then, God is problematically quantified and is treated as merely one being within a system of ontological quantities, whom one appeals to in order to explain the rest.[12]

Third, metaphysical accounts of creative causality place God and creatures within a common genus of "causality" and of "being" so that God is conceived of in creaturely terms and reduced in his mystery to the level of a creaturely genus.[13]

Fourth, Thomistic notions of analogical causality fail to recognize adequately the absolute dissimilitude between God and creatures and between creatures and God.[14]

Fifth, Thomistic notions of causality portray God as a being that is necessarily relative to creatures.[15]

The sixth and seventh objections are each epistemological and go together. The theology of St. Thomas, Barth states, seeks to understand God in purely philosophical terms as Creator and cause of being, and in doing so, inevitably projects merely human notions derived from creatures onto God, understanding God anthropomorphically in light of features of the world.[16] Likewise, Thomistic theology brings concepts into theology that derive from non-Biblical sources and, in doing so, fails to recognize adequately a distinctly and uniquely biblical and Trinitarian conception of divine creation and causality, communicated to us by grace in the mystery of Jesus Christ and God's election of the human race.[17]

---

12. CD III:3, 102 and 104. This sounds somewhat parallel to Martin Heidegger's concept of classical metaphysics as onto-theology. (See "The Onto-theo-logical Constitution of Metaphysics," in *Identity and Difference*, trans. J. Staumbaugh (New York: Harper and Row, 1969), 42–74.) Eberhard Jüngel explicitly seeks to make the conceptual connection between these two systems of criticism in his work *God as the Mystery of the World*, trans. D. Guder (Grand Rapids, MI: Eerdmans, 1983), 277–80.

13. CD III:3, 102–4.

14. CD III:103.

15. CD III:3, 103: "The divine *causa*, as distinct from the creaturely, is self-grounded, self-positing, self-conditioning and self-causing [*causa sui*]."

16. CD III:3, 104.

17. CD III:3, 105.

As I have argued elsewhere in some detail, almost all of these characterizations are factually inaccurate when considered simply in terms of a textually responsible characterization of Aquinas's positions.[18] For example, Aquinas's doctrine of analogy, as pertaining to divine causality, is intended at least (whether it achieves its aims or not) to preserve and manifest the transcendence of God to creation, and it is developed precisely so as to avoid theologically reductive thinking of God in terms of created modes of being, or merely human concepts. This is precisely why Aquinas's notion of causality and of being is analogical rather than univocal.[19] The claim that Aquinas has quantified the unity of God seems untenable in light of the fact that his theory of divine unity in the *Summa Theologiae* overtly seeks to do the opposite, as Aquinas notes that quantitative unity (which pertains to quantity and numeric measure) and transcendental unity (which pertains to *esse*) are not identical and that only the latter is a foundation for speaking of divine unity, albeit analogically.[20] Likewise, Aquinas derives his theory of analogical predication of God precisely so as to make clear that God's mystery is not reducible to any species or genus of being, and he maintains that God is not subject in his essence or life to any division or composition of species and genus, as creatures are.[21] So, the claim that Aquinas treats God as if he were in a same genus with creatures is clearly erroneous. Perhaps Barth could argue that all thinking about God is necessarily quasi-generic or univocal, in a qualified Scotistic sense, and then argue that all such thinking is nonviable.[22] However, he

18. See White, *The Incarnate Lord*, 171–202. Indeed, most of them, considered conceptually as positions, are also incompatible with notions of creation found in other noteworthy Catholic authors, other than Aquinas.

19. As he notes in *ST* I, q. 4, a. 3, as well as I, q. 13. Speaking of divine causality and non-generic resemblance, Aquinas notes, "... if there is an agent not contained in any 'genus,' its effect will still more distantly reproduce the form of the agent, not, that is, so as to participate in the likeness of the agent's form according to the same specific or generic formality, but only according to some sort of analogy ..."

20. See the important analysis in this regard of *ST* I, q. 11, a. 1, ad 1.

21. *ST* I, q. 3, a. 5.

22. Consider in this respect Pannenberg's thesis on univocity in Scotus in Wolfhart Pannenberg, "Analogie und Offenbarung" (Habilitationsschrift, Heidelberg, 1955),

has not done this, which makes his considerations seem somewhat incoherent. Is Barth claiming that the Scotistic defense of a certain kind of univocal discourse is present in Aquinas even while Scotus claims the opposite? Who is right about Aquinas: Barth or Scotus? To give an account of Aquinas that elides him with Scotus, on a point that Thomists and Scotists have disagreed about for centuries, one must indeed make an argument from textual information. And if, in fact, Aquinas is implicitly "Scotist" and the Scotistic project is unworkable and marked by conceptual idolatry, one must consider arguments of Thomists and Scotists alike who maintain that the two projects of Aquinas and Scotus differ.[23]

Indeed, Barth does not even seem to be aware that Aristotle and virtually all medieval scholastics treat the categorial modes of being (substance, quantity, quality, relation) as genres of being and that instead, they treat the transcendentals as analogical modes of being, not reducible to any species or genus.[24] Once one realizes this *historical fact*, the logic of Barth's position begins to unravel as it is simply untenable as a characterization of tendencies in medieval Catholic metaphysics.

Finally, we may note that in Aquinas's doctrine of creation as a "mixed relation," he claims that all creatures are wholly relative to God in all they are as being caused by him, while God is in no way relative to creatures in the sense that he is not ontologically caused or determined by them in his inner life and essence.[25] In fact, he also sustains this notion of non-reciprocal causality in his Christology in

---

published in an altered version as *Analogie und Offenbarung: Eine kritische Untersuchung zur Geschichte des Analogiebegriffes in der Lehre von der Gotteserkenntnis* (Göttingen: Vandenhoeck & Ruprecht, 2007) and the analysis of Reinhard Huetter in "Attending to the Wisdom of God—from Effect to Cause, from Creation to God: A *Relecture* of the Analogy of Being according to Thomas Aquinas" in *The Analogy of Being: Invention of the Antichrist or the Wisdom of God?*, 209–45.

23. See in this regard the interesting analysis of the historian of Scotistic metaphysics, Olivier Boulnois, "Quand commence l'onto-théo-logie? Aristote, Thomas d'Aquin et Duns Scot," *Revue Thomiste* 95 (1995): 85–108; and his work *l'Être et représentation*.

24. On the analogical, non-generic understanding of being, see Aristotle, *Metaphysics*, IV, 1–2, 1003a26–34; *Nicomachean Ethics* I, 6, 1196a23–29.

25. *ST* I, q. 45, aa. 2–3.

ST III, qq. 2–6, where he notes that in the hypostatic union, in the very person of the Incarnate Word, the humanity of Jesus is wholly relative to the deity and person of the Son, while the Son in his deity and person is not determined by or re-configured ontologically by the Incarnation or in virtue of what occurs to the Son actively or passively in virtue of his humanity.[26] Far from making God merely impassible to the events of the life of Christ, this doctrine acknowledges that, indeed, it is God himself in his life and essence who is present at the heart of all of Christ's human actions and sufferings. While it is not the deity in its eternal identity (the Trinitarian life of God itself) that undergoes change or suffering in Christ, it is indeed the person of the Son in his deity, in union with his Father and the Spirit, who is present personally as one of us, in concrete human life, action, and suffering, in human death and resurrection.[27] Consequently, we must say, in keeping with Christian orthodoxy, that God truly suffered, died, and rose from the dead, all in his human nature, that is to say, that the very person of the Son and Word suffered, died, and was buried.[28] Indeed, the Son suffered and died personally as man in such a way as to manifest his innermost identity to us, as the eternally begotten Son of the Father, and as the eternal origin with the Father of the Holy Spirit. The visible missions of the Son in his human life among us and of the Spirit sent forth in time from the Father and the Son at Pentecost reveal the inner life of the Trinity and the eternal processions of the Son from the Father and of the Spirit from the Father and the Son.[29]

Independent of the inaccuracies of Barth's thought regarding Aquinas, one can consider what Barth is opposed to more generally,

26. See, especially *ST* III, q. 2, aa. 7–8.
27. *ST* III, q. 16, a. 1.
28. See Aquinas, *SCG* IV, c. 34.
29. See on this constellation of ideas, Bruce D. Marshall, "The Unity of the Triune God: Reviving an Ancient Question," *The Thomist* 74, no. 1 (2010): 1–32; Gilles Emery, "*Theologia* and *Dispensatio*: The Centrality of the Divine Missions in St. Thomas's Trinitarian Theology," *The Thomist* 74, no. 4 (2010): 515–61; Legge, *The Trinitarian Christology of St. Thomas Aquinas*; White, *The Trinity: On the Nature and Mystery of the One God*.

as well as what he is aiming to produce. Clearly, what Barth is opposed to is any kind of univocal discourse regarding God that aims to identify what God is from appeal to concepts derived philosophically from creatures. That Aquinas's approach to the metaphysics of creation is analogical and non-univocal and is allied to his Christological understanding of God is somewhat beside the point. Barth considers, in an *a priori* way, based on his commitments to what he believes about Reformed theology in its essential distinction from Roman theology, that all philosophical appeals to being are, in some way, human projections and inaccurate. Barth seems to take all merely human, philosophical thinking about the being of God to be inevitably univocal and projective in nature, just as he considers all philosophical notions of divine unity to be merely quantitative ones. All philosophical notions of causality are derived from the empirical sphere and denote God, then, in inter-created causal terms.[30] How does Barth know this? Such positions are, in fact, derived more or less directly from David Hume and Immanuel Kant, or resemble their positions as loose interpretations of them.[31] However, Barth denies that he has knowledge of God's philosophical non-intelligibility *from philosophy as such*.[32] His theologi-

---

30. This is the view of Kant in his *Critique of Pure Reason*, and his view seems to anticipate Barth's own, although Kant does think that insofar as one may conceive of God speculatively and hypothetically *for practical purposes* (as the condition for practical reason in the pursuit of just outcomes of human action), one can justly employ an analogical conception of God, not wholly different from that of Cajetan, who based his views on Aquinas's treatment on the topic in *De Ver.* q. 2, a. 11. See on this point Immanuel Kant, *Prolegomena to Any Future Metaphysics*, trans. P. Carus and J. Ellington (Indianapolis and Cambridge: Hackett Publishing, 1977), Sections 57–60.

31. Kant's restriction of thinking about causality to the immanent sphere of the empirical is clearly inspired in part from Hume, who awoke him from his dogmatic slumber. See *The Critique of Pure Reason*, A 609/B 637, 511: "We find [in the cosmological argument] the transcendental principle whereby from the contingent we infer a cause. This principle is applicable only in the sensible world; outside that world, it has no meaning whatsoever. For the mere intellectual concept of the contingent cannot give rise to any synthetic proposition, such as that of causality. The principle of causality has no meaning and no criterion for its application save only in the sensible world."

32. See *CD* I:1, 167, 179–83. The motivations of Barth's position are meant to be uniquely theological, based on the conditions of knowledge of God made known in

cal self-association with these modern criticisms of metaphysics is motivated principally by his own rather innovative interpretation of the Protestant notion of justification by faith alone and of creaturely finitude and sinfulness. He holds that, in light of revelation, we can ascertain that the only criteria of knowledge of God comes from revelation itself and not from human activity of philosophical reflection and that our human nature is incapable in its finite stature of attaining to God, and, in light of its sinfulness, seeks misguidedly to project onto God notions drawn from creatures, apart from and over and against revelation.[33] In this respect, Barth's thought does tend toward an ontological and epistemological dialectic against any Catholic notion of ontological and epistemological analogy.[34]

However, in his treatment of Christ, as indicated already above, Barth makes a noteworthy exception, and one that has universal consequences, in his view. As noted above, we can perceive the relation of God to creation and of creation to God only because we first perceive Christ, in whom God has determined from all eternity by

---

Jesus Christ, in light of which all other positions are understood as subject to specifically theological critique.

33. See the comments on this topic in his famous book written against the Reformed proposals providing a positive appraisal of natural theology by Emil Brunner in his book *Nature and Grace*, to which Barth responded in his work *No!* C.f.: *Natural Theology* by Emil Brunner and Karl Barth, trans. P. Fraenkel (Eugene, OR: Wipf and Stock, 2002), 102–4. Barth makes clear there that the early Reformers (Luther and Calvin, for example) saw through clearly to the implicit Pelagianism of a works righteousness scheme in medieval Catholic theology insofar as it affected the *moral domain* of the human relation to God, but that they did not take the insight of the Reformation as far as they might have in the *epistemological domain* pertaining to the total and real conditions for the *knowledge* of God. This task, Barth suggests, falls to the generation of Protestant theologians of a later time, a task he is taking up in confrontation with the half-hearted and superficial move backward toward Catholic thinking evinced by Brunner's positions.

34. I am siding with Bruce L. McCormack *and* Hans Urs von Balthasar on the characterization of Barth's earlier thought. They differ on Barth's more mature thought from *CD* III onward as Balthasar claims that Barth moves toward analogy in his Christology and that this affects all of his thinking generally, while McCormack underscores that a dialectical relation of the world of grace and nature remains perpetually in the thought of Barth until the end of his writing career. See Bruce L. McCormack, *Karl Barth's Critically Realistic Dialectical Theology: Its Genesis and Development, 1909–1936* (Oxford: Clarendon Press, 1995); Balthasar, *The Theology of Karl Barth*.

election to relate to his creation and determined as well from all eternity that creation should relate to him. It is this mystery that Barth denotes as the *analogia relationis* or *analogia operationis*, the analogy of relation or operation.[35] The analogy or similitude in question is clearly ontological and not merely epistemological, and it is established in an exemplary way in Christ himself, in the relation of his deity to his humanity and of his humanity to his deity. But what precisely does it consist in?

A comprehensive answer to this question lies beyond the scope of this essay, but I would like here to indicate briefly four important loci in Barth's work that I think help greatly to answer this question. We might characterize these four loci as related by a collective assembly of related ideas. All of them have in common that they treat God's free decision to relate to the world in Christ as (1) in some way reflective of who God is in himself as Trinity and (2) as effectuating the likeness of creation to God, and thus also of God to creation in the person of Christ. They also all suggest (3) that God's eternity is in some way characterized by the free decision to self-relate to creation and that creation is constituted ontologically by the orientation of all things toward relation to God in Christ. This third idea (of God relating to creation and creation to God) is deeply coordinated in logical coherence with (4) Barth's late treatment of the communication of idioms in *CD* IV, 1 and 2, where the human actions and sufferings of Jesus are indicative of eternal interpersonal Trinitarian relations in God.

To explore this set of claims, I would like to focus briefly on four ideas that correspond to the four interrelated ideas mentioned above: the distinction of persons of the Trinity composed through revelation in *CD* I:1, the notion of Trinitarian election as reflective of

---

35. Barth, *CD* III:3, 102–4. Speaking of the *analogia relationis et operationis* between God and creatures, Barth states on p. 103: "The divine *causa*, as distinct from the creaturely, is self-grounded, self-positing, self-conditioning and self-causing. It causes itself … in the triune life which God enjoys as Father, Son and Holy Spirit, and in which He has His divine basis from eternity to eternity. This is how God is a subject. And this is how he is a *causa*."

who and what God is in *CD* II:2, the notion of divine freedom able to react from and assimilate to human freedom from *CD* III:3, and the notion of the human nature of Christ as indicative of divine Sonship and deity in *CD* IV:1 and 2.

The first of these ideas occurs in *CD* I:1 in the wake of Barth's criticisms of natural theology and his positing in its place of a so-called *analogia fidei*, that is to say, of a similitude between God and the world made known in Christ alone.[36] In pursuing this idea further in the volume, Barth attempts to articulate his own original and modern recovery of the classical Reformed idea that the doctrine of the Trinity is the first and foremost principle of theology as a science of God, that is to say, a form of study of divine revelation conducted for the Church's life of preaching.[37] What is significant for our purposes is that when Barth elaborates what would become a massively influential treatment of Trinitarian revelation, he takes the distinction of persons to unfold from and have its identity for us in light of the specific actions of the three in the domain of divine revelation.[38] The Father is known to us as the one Revealing, the Son as the one Revealed by way of the Incarnation and paschal mystery, and

36. See *CD* I:1, 12, 243–47, 437, 457. See likewise Barth, *CD* II:1, 221–27, where he claims that theology must make systematic use of the notion of analogy (in a distinctively theological, not philosophical, way), and *CD* 4:2, 97–98, where Barth notes that the two essences of Christ, divine and human, must bear a resemblance to each other. The term *analogia fidei* is used differently here by Barth than it is in 19th and early 20th century Catholic theology, in which the term refers to the nexus of mysteries in their likenesses and distinctiveness. See on this Thomas Joseph White, "The *analogia fidei* in Catholic Theology," *International Journal of Systematic Theology* 22, no. 4 (2020): 512–37.

37. *CD* I:1, 5–11, 275–87. Barth approvingly cites *ST* I, q. 1, a. 5 on p. 5 regarding the subordination of all sciences to the truth of theology but goes on to express his ambivalence about the medieval notion of theology as a science, if such science is to be understood by a likeness with natural human forms of understanding.

38. See especially Barth, "The Root of the Doctrine of the Trinity," in *CD* 1:1, 304–33, where he formulates the notion of the immanent Trinity as an economic Trinity in revelation, a passage that no doubt influenced Karl Rahner. P. 333: "Our concepts of unimpaired unity and unimpaired distinction, modes of being to be distinguished in this essence, and finally the polemical assertion ... that God's triunity is to be found not merely in His revelation but, because in His revelation, in God Himself, and in Himself too, so that the Trinity is to be understood as 'immanent' and not just 'economic' ..."

the Spirit as the one Revealing the Son and Father to us interiorly in the historical economy.[39] We know God not only *through* but also *as* his activity of self-revelation and so in and from his relationships to us in the economy. On this view, the persons of the Trinity are not known *in se* (in virtue of their eternal relations to one another) through recourse to the famous "psychological analogy" of the Son as Logos and the Spirit as Love.[40] Instead, the economic actions of the Trinitarian persons provide the interpretive key that allows us to identify the proper distinctions that obtain between them eternally. I have written elsewhere about ways in which this schema suggests that there may be differing actions of distinct persons rather than common actions *ad extra* of all three persons, and I have presented some criticisms of Barth's view.[41] The key thing for us to note at this juncture is that Barth clearly is defining the persons *relationally* by analogy to human subjects who act in history. The persons of God are intelligible for us insofar as they *actively or operatively relate* to the creation in self-disclosure to the human race, specifically through the life, death, and resurrection of Christ. This idea of Barth's would eventually give rise, in an altered form, to Karl Rahner's famous understanding of the immanent Trinity as an economic Trinity or as a Trinity always, already *for* self-communication to creatures, specifically through the Incarnation.[42] Therefore, the *analogia fidei*, or analogy between God and the world, comes about because of the decision of God to reveal God's self as Trinity to the world, but that decision of God to relate to creation is also in some way revelatory of or expressive and perhaps eternally constitutive of what God is in

39. *CD* 1:1, 306: "According to Scripture God's revelation is God's own direct speech which is not to be distinguished from the act of speaking and therefore is not to be distinguished from God Himself ... in God's revelation God's Word [in which God actively reveals himself] is identical with God Himself."

40. See *CD* I:1, 337–47, where Barth effectively explains that theology today should not seek to have recourse to the analogy from acts of the human mind (or the psychological analogy) when speaking about the Trinity, that is to say, by the similitude of knowledge and love in the human soul.

41. See White, *The Trinity*, ch. 31.

42. Rahner, *The Trinity*, 22.

himself.[43] This idea seems clearly to foreshadow Barth's later, more formal notion of the *analogia relationis* from *CD* III:3.

A second instance is found in *CD* II:2, where Barth formulates his rather lengthy and innovative doctrine of election.[44] Though there are many facets of his thought one might appeal to, the most pertinent for our argument has to do with the notion of election as expressive of the very eternity and life of God as Trinity. Barth's notion that Jesus Christ, as true God but also true man, forms the *subject* of election as well as object suggests that the Trinity is expressing or formulating itself from all eternity to all eternity in such a way as to encompass and include in its identity as Trinity, a relation to the economic events of creation and Incarnation.[45] God is eternally "for" the Incarnation as the subject of election in Jesus Christ.[46] Likewise, Barth's idea in *CD* II:2 that the election is conducted in view of the perfect expression of what God is as Trinity is an interestingly ambiguous notion.[47] Does the elective choice in question

---

43. In my way of interpreting Barth here, I am suggesting a kind of internal tension that emerges in his early work that stands in need of resolution or that at the very least always is poised on a kind of knife edge that can fall in one of two competing and opposed directions, of God as sovereign and transcendent of election, creation, and Incarnation in his Trinitarian perfection, and of God as in some sense constituted by his eternal relationality to creation. The latter reading of Barth has been common for some time and can be found as the normative view of Barth held by thinkers like Pannenberg (who agrees with it) and Kasper (who distances himself from it in part) in the context of their subsequent writings on God and Christology. See Wolfhart Pannenberg, *Systematic Theology*, vol. 2, trans. G. W. Bromiley (Grand Rapids, MI: Eerdmans, 1994), 368; Walter Kasper, *Jesus the Christ*, trans. V. Green (London: Burns & Oates, 1976), 172.

44. *CD* II:2, 76–194.

45. *CD* II:2, 115–17, 145–58.

46. *CD* II:2, 156–58.

47. *CD* II:2, 156: "The eternal will of God which is before time is the same as the eternal will of God which is above time, and which reveals itself as such and operates as such in time ... Revealing to us the fullness of the one God, it discloses to us not only what the will of God is, but also what it was and what it will be." P. 158: "God's glory overflows in this the supreme act of his freedom ... The Son of God determined to give Himself from all eternity. With the Father and the Holy Spirit He chose to unite Himself with the lost Son of Man. This Son of Man was from all eternity the object of the election of the Father, Son and Holy Spirit." P. 161: "The eternal will of God in the election of Jesus Christ is His will to give Himself for the sake of man as created by Him and fallen from Him."

of God's decision to create, incarnate, and redeem function to reveal God "merely" as an efficient and exemplary cause so that all that comes from the Trinity in the election is expressive of what God is? Or does the election also function as a kind of quasi-eternal final cause, an immanent moment in the eternal life of God whereby the eternal identity of God as Trinity is anticipated prior to the economy and then, in turn, actuated or recapitulated? In the latter case, the relation to creation in God expressed by election is a kind of condition of possibility for God's self-constitution as Trinity or at least God's self-enrichment through recapitulation.[48] The Trinity becomes itself more deeply through election.

A third instance occurs in *CD* III:3, in logical continuity with the passages on divine causality in creation that we examined earlier. Here, Barth is considering Calvinist notions of *concursus* in dialogue with the famous *de Auxiliis* controversy that pitted Augustinian and Thomist predestinationists (who Barth thinks have some similarities to Calvin) against Molinists. As is often the case with Barth, he claims that neither side found perfectly adequate measures to treat the topic of divine and human freedom, and though he sides with the Reformed treatment of the topic, he also suggests that, in fact, no previous analysis has yet been fully adequate.[49] Barth seeks to overcome the seeming "antimony of reason" of the reconciliation of divine and human freedom by appealing to a notion of divine freedom that is di-polar, that is to say, characterized by the freedom to experience two modes at once, only seemingly opposed but ultimately reconciled in God's transcendent love. God can remain the free cause of his creatures who is ontologically and causally sovereign over them and their free choices in time, and God can simultaneously deploy his sovereignty so as to accompany and receive from his creatures their initiatives and weave these into his divine economy.[50] Both classical Thomistic and Calvinist views and classical

---

48. Bruce L. McCormack explores a version of this reading of Barth in his *The Humility of the Eternal Son* (Cambridge: Cambridge University Press, 2021).

49. *CD* III:3, 115–54, 185–95.

50. He speaks of this antinomy, for example, in *CD* III:3 on p. 187.

Molinist and Arminian views are true simultaneously under different aspects, when re-centered in Christology, because Christ is both the transcendent agent and historical subject of divine governance. In Christ, we see that God, in his divine freedom, can choose to relate in his own essence to creaturely freedom, as both cause and recipient, within one unified providence and one historical economy.[51] Again here, we see that God's freedom to become or relate to the creation by his election of love for humanity in Jesus Christ is allied closely with the idea that when God does freely relate to the creation he also always expresses and is faithful to what he is immutably and eternally, in his divine essence.

Finally, we can note that in *CD* IV:1, Barth develops a highly original conception of divine kenosis expressed in the Incarnation, dereliction, and crucifixion.[52] He does so against the backdrop of Gottfried Thomasius's 19th century Lutheran theology of kenosis and partially in response to it, behind whom we can identify the influence of Hegel.[53] Whereas Hegel attributed human properties of Christ to the divinity of Christ (God in his mode of being as Son is temporal, finite, subject to death, etc.), Barth posits a similitude or analogy between the human operations of Christ and his divine operations.[54] If Christ lives in obedience unto death in time as a human, this is indicative of an analogous divine obedience that transpires eternally in God, in his deity, between the Son and the Father, and that is constitutive of the Son in his eternal life as God.[55]

---

51. See, for example, *CD* III:3, 151 153; 185–88.

52. *CD* IV:1, 180–210.

53. *CD* IV:1, 182–83.

54. See Hegel, *Lectures on the Philosophy of Religion*, vol. 3, "The Consummate Religion," 310–27, compared with *CD* IV:1, 184–95, 201–4. See also *CD* IV, 2, 76–87.

55. The idea is stated especially clearly in *CD* IV, 1, on pp. 202–4. See also *CD* IV:1, 177: "Who the true God is, and what He is, i.e., what is His being as God ... his divine nature ... all this we have to discover from the fact that as such he is very man and a partaker of human nature, from His becoming man ... For, to put it more pointedly, the mirror in which it can be known (and is known) that He is God, and of the divine nature, is His becoming flesh and His existence in the flesh ... From the point of view of the obedience of Jesus Christ as such, fulfilled in that astonishing form, it is a matter of the mystery of the inner being of God as the being of the Son in relation to the Father."

To state things succinctly but clearly, the relational obedience of the Son to the Father in eternity can encompass the relational obedience of the Son's human nature to the Father in time and express itself in the latter. Here, especially, we see the perfection of human freedom coordinated with divine freedom in mutual relationality that we mentioned in the last point. In the person of Christ himself, the human features of relationality to God perfect the creation in its relation to God, *qua* creation, even as the Son in his eternal relation to God as Father expresses God's eternal relation to creation that comes to be through election, incarnation, and the obediential death of the Son.[56]

While I have described each of these notions only very briefly, and they are associated conceptually in a somewhat intuitive way by Barth himself (that is not always fully transparent in its implied logical consequences), there seems to be a great deal of consistency in Barth's thought across time. We can perceive this consistency from *CD* I:1 on the distinction of the divine hypostases as conceived principally in virtue of their activity of revelation to his treatment of divine election in *CD* II:2, where the election of God is a Trinitarian act by which God manifests his own distinction of Father, Word, and Spirit in the event of Christ as the elected one on behalf of the human race, to his treatment of the *analogia relationis* in *CD* III:3 where he claims that God is eternally characterized by his relations to the creation in election and the integration of human freedom to God's eternal action, to his treatment of the obedience and dereliction of Christ in *CD* IV:1 where the Son's human relation to the Father is indicative of an eternal divine relationality of the Father toward the Son by which he commands the Son and the Son obeys the Father,

56. In *CD* IV:2, p. 84, Barth writes: "We must begin with the fact that what takes place in this address is also and primarily a determination of divine essence: not an alteration, but a determination. God does not first elect and determine man but Himself. In His eternal counsel, and then in its execution in time He determines to address Himself to man, and to do so in such a way that He Himself becomes man. God elects and determines Himself to be the God of man. And this undoubtedly means ... that He elects and determines Himself for humiliation."

a seeming precondition for the Son's obedient journey into the far country of the Incarnation, cross, and resurrection. In all these instances, we see both that the persons of the Trinity are distinguished by their relation to creation (in revelation, election, creation, and redemption) and that the relations that are intra-Trinitarian, therefore, take on their intelligibility principally in light of God's activity manifest to us in the economy. However, we also see that the creation resembles God by its relationality to God, eventually manifest above all in the human nature of the person of the Son, Jesus Christ. In a certain sense, all of this is contained and indicated in a concentrated form in Jesus Christ, in whom both the electing God and elected human are revealed, and in which both the divine essence and the human essence are manifest in their similitude or analogy. The latter is an analogy of relations: of the relation of the obedient, kenotic Son to the Father in eternity, with that of the man Jesus in his obedience and suffering unto God on behalf of the human race.

BARTH'S CHRISTOLOGICAL ANALOGY OF BEING: SOME EVALUATIONS

In light of the considerations presented above, we can now make some initial critical inquiries. Barth has articulated several concerns about the deficits of a Catholic, and indeed, a Thomistic account of the "analogy of being." However, there are reasons to ask whether he has avoided in his own conception of Christological analogy of being some of the problematic issues he attributed (questionably in my opinion) to the thought of Aquinas. Furthermore, Aquinas's own form of inquiry seems destined to achieve distinct outcomes from that of Barth, and arguably preferable ones, precisely due to his alternative and more classical form of reflection on analogy and God's unique divine causality of existence, especially as it has bearing upon Christology.

Let us consider three examples.

First, there is Barth's concern that Aquinas's notion of analogy conceives of God anthropomorphically under the rubric of a concept derived from creatures and applicable accurately in reality only to creatures, not to God. It is worth considering in this context that Barth's key concepts of relation, operation, and election are all generic notions applicable univocally primarily to human experiences, insofar as human beings may acquire properties of relation to others by operations of freedom that they undertake by choice, or "electively."

Has Barth rightly understood the analogy of God's free decision to relate to creatures operatively in its similitude and dissimilitude to human being, event, and action (particularly evidenced in Christ's human being, life, and self-offering for us to God)? To regulate the theologically responsible use of such an analogy, one would need to clarify the terms of the use of the two analogates so as to specify why and under what conditions relation and operation/action are applicable to God in terms distinct from those of creatures, lest one fall into a distinctly univocal and generic use of the terms in question.[57] Barth, to my understanding, has not adequately specified the conditions of such use. This is not to say that he could not or that

57. On categories of relation and action/operation as generic, see Aristotle, *Categories*, ch. 7 (6a37–8b24) and ch. 9 (11b1–5). Aristotle derived the categories precisely to distinguish what is predicated univocally and generically (always in the same sense, despite specific differences) from what is predicated across genera, non-generically, or "transcendentally." Concepts such as nature, quantity, quality, action, and passion are predicated univocally or generically, while notions such as being, unity, truth, and goodness are predicated in an analogical, non-generic mode. This is why it is an error for Plato to speak of a form of the good since this would imply that goodness is a common genus or species of thing, which it is not. All things that exist are in some way good, just as they all in some way exist, are one, and are intelligible. So goodness is not reducible to a species or form (including a generic form). See *Nic. Ethics* I, 6 (1096a12–29): "Clearly the good cannot be something universally present in all cases and single; for then it would not have been predicated in all the categories but in one only." Election, for Aquinas as for virtually all Western philosophers prior to the 20th century, is a moment in the act of freedom, commonly denoted as "choice." (On "*electio*," see *ST* I-II, q. 13) As a species of human action, it follows within the genus of action. If we claim that God is characterized by election, we are technically prescribing a generic term of action to God. How may such a term denote a distinct and dissimilar version of election in God that does not fall into a univocally generic category with human elective choice? Or does it fall within a generic category of "action" just as any other univocal generic term would?

the analogies of relation and operation are unworkable or inherently problematic, but it does seem like a clear advantage of Aquinas's thought that he considers such a question directly and provides a way of solution to the problem that Barth's thought creates.[58]

Aquinas makes clear, in fact, in ST I, q. 13, aa. 3–5 that terms such as "wisdom," which are indicative of qualities that can be specified of human beings according to genus or species (univocally), are indicated of God only by analogical predication so as to underscore the inherent unlikeness or dissimilitude that is maintained when speaking of God the Trinity, who is the transcendent Creator revealed in Scripture.[59] The regulated analogical ascription of such terms is based on an underlying theory of existence as communicated by God to creatures in such a way that no essential or accidental properties in creatures may be said to subsist in God, at least in the form that they are present in creatures, due to the fact that God does not cause or receive being in himself, but simply is, in a wholly other and transcendent way.[60] This is also why we can say that, in a sense, God does not exist, at least in the way anything else exists, and that God is all things, insofar as he is the cause of all things, without being

58. If Barth were to treat this question in depth, he would need to make use of qualifications for attribution of "action" concepts to God of a kind very similar to Aquinas if he wanted to avoid falling into the very kind of univocity of genus he wishes to criticize. But does he avoid such univocity himself, precisely when speaking of election as characterizing God's inner life? See on this point John Bowlin, "Barth and Aquinas on Election, Relationship, and Requirement," in *Thomas Aquinas and Karl Barth: An Unofficial Catholic-Protestant Dialogue*, ed. B. L. McCormack and T. J. White (Grand Rapids, MI: Eerdmans, 2013), 237–61.

59. *ST* I, q. 13, a. 5: "Thus when any term expressing perfection is applied to a creature, it signifies that perfection distinct in idea from other perfections; as, for instance, by the term 'wise' applied to man, we signify some perfection distinct from a man's essence, and distinct from his power and existence, and from all similar things; whereas when we apply it to God, we do not mean to signify anything distinct from His essence, or power, or existence. Thus, also this term 'wise' applied to man in some degree circumscribes and comprehends the thing signified; whereas this is not the case when it is applied to God; but it leaves the thing signified as incomprehended, and as exceeding the signification of the name. Hence, it is evident that this term 'wise' is not applied in the same way to God and to man. The same rule applies to other terms. Hence no name is predicated univocally of God and of creatures."

60. See *ST* I, q. 13, a. 11.

identified with anything that is.[61] Every created nature (such as human nature) and every created quality (such as wisdom or love in human beings) is unlike the divine nature and the divine qualities, which are somehow incomprehensively identical with the divine existence and are thus subsistent.[62] Individual human natures are not identical with their existence because there is a real distinction of essence and existence in every created reality. Otherwise, each individual created reality would exist by nature or essentially (necessarily) and would be identical with the plenitude of being (what is essential to being).[63] God, meanwhile, exists "essentially" or by nature, and his nature contains the plenitude of what we mean when we speak of things existing.[64] Creation adds nothing to his incomprehensible plenitude but derives from it.[65] Meanwhile, individual human beings have qualities that are mere properties, while God's individual nature is identical with his perfect mystery of activity in wisdom and love. His "properties" are subsistent.[66] For these various reasons, there are regulatory alterations of our use of words for God we must make use of when ascribing to him "univocal" or generic properties otherwise found in creatures. To the extent that Barth aspires to develop a genuinely analogical (non-univocal) *theological* mode of speaking of God, his intent and aims converge with those of Aquinas. But his attempts would also potentially be aided and made more coherent by deeper engagement with Aquinas's actual theory, which seems to be more highly developed and more theologically intricate than Barth's, and certainly something that eluded Barth's own comprehension as concerns its actual historical, textual, and conceptual substance.

A second example is the criticism Barth raised having to do with

61. Aquinas explores this idea in *In Div. Nom.*, c. 1, lect. 1, in commenting upon the language of Dionysius the Areopagite.
62. *ST* I, q. 3, a. 5.
63. *ST* I, q. 3, a. 3.
64. *ST* I, q. 3, a. 4.
65. *ST* I, q. 44, aa. 1 and 3.
66. *ST* I, q. 29, a. 4.

unity. He argued that Aquinas assimilates God to a system of quantities. I will not treat the issue of Aquinas's position here since I have written about this elsewhere,[67] but leave it to say that Barth misunderstands or at least misrepresents what Aquinas actually believes about divine unity, which Aquinas underscores quite clearly as a mystery that cannot be quantitative or mathematical in nature.[68] What I would like to underscore here is that Barth's own theory of relational operation in God toward creatures raises real and very interesting questions about divine unity. We can underscore this in a two-fold way.

First, Barth posits that God can freely relate to creation by election, in himself, acting in such a way as to be revealed and, in a sense, ontologically defined by what he does in relating to creation. This idea is clearly expressed in Barth's idea that the persons of the Trinity are distinguished by their distinct activities in God's divine self-revelation as well as his notion of God revealed as who he is in election, and by his notion of God's self-determination as God for and from our activity of freedom in history, and finally by his notion of God's essential self-determination for incarnation, and redemptive suffering in Christ.[69] But here, one can ask a pertinent question: does this conception of God's activity entail a composition in God of act and potency so that God's essence is ontologically complex and develops in virtue of his relation to creation? Most Barth interpreters seem to think so. Some treat the potency in question as an active potency that God has eternally so that the "events" of God creating, electing, and incarnating reflect an ever deeper pre-existent "event" in

---

67. See White, *The Incarnate Lord*, ch. 4.

68. As already noted, in *ST* I, q. 11: a. 1, ad 1; a. 3, ad 2; a. 4, ad 2.

69. On the last idea, see *CD* IV, 2, 84–86. P. 85–86: "If we ... try to think of the Godhead of God in biblical rather than pagan terms, we shall have to reckon, not with a mutability of God, but with the kind of immutability which does not prevent Him from humbling Himself and therefore doing what He willed to do and actually did do in Jesus Christ, i.e., electing and determining in Jesus Christ to exist in divine and human essence in the one Son of God and Son of Man, and therefore to address His divine essence to His human, to direct it to it ... What, then, is the divine essence? It is the free love ... of the Father, Son and Holy Spirit.... The Father, He Himself, gives Himself up. This offering is, therefore, elected and determined by His own majesty—the majesty of the divine Subject."

the dynamism of God's eternal being and life. In this case, God does not develop historically *per se*, but his engagement with creaturely history is the occasion of an outward expression by God in his creation of an ongoing eternal dynamic in God that has "always already existed." Namely, there seems to be a cycle of potential action and active action present in the life of the persons of the Trinity that transcends creation and is expressed within it. The other option is also found in Barth-interpretation: to see the potency in God as passive, so that God is actuated or enriched in some way by his engagement with creation, and in this sense, has a kind of co-historicity within himself that emerges by his relations with creatures. This interpretation seemingly sets Barth one step closer to the ontology of Hegel.

For our purposes, the important thing is not to argue which of these interpretations is advantageous for reading Barth. The main point is that Barth seems committed by his discourse to some form of ontological composition of dynamic activity from potency to act in the being of God.

A second problem arises when we consider another example, namely, the fact that the persons of the Trinity are understood by Barth (in *CD* IV:1) in light of the relations of command (of the Father) and obedience (of the Son). The notion of divine freedom, which we have noted is so central to Barth's thought, here is differentiated as a freedom composed of two states or as distinguished in two subjects. The command of the Father is one active moment or expression of divine freedom, while the obedience of the Son is another active moment or expression of divine freedom.[70] This idea harmonizes nicely with the one just explored above. If the dynamic of act and potency characterizes the essence of God, as Barth seems to intimate, then we can specify how this event ontology unfolds or is illustrated, precisely in the act-potency relationships of the Father

70. *CD* IV:1, 202: "As we look at Jesus Christ we cannot avoid the astounding conclusion of a divine obedience. Therefore we have to draw the no less astounding deduction that in equal Godhead the one God is, in fact, the One and also Another, that He is indeed a First and a Second, One who rules and commands in majesty and One who obeys in humility. The one God is both the one and the other."

and the Son, who are differentiated for Barth precisely by such compositions.

Three key questions about divine unity arise from these considerations. First, is God's divine essence in any way simple or does it undergo change, and if it does undergo change, what does it undergo change in relation to? Does the eternal dynamic of change in God's essence occur in relation to itself alone, cyclically and eternally, or also in relation to others? If God's divine essence undergoes dynamic change only in relation to itself eternally and if this change is expressed in distinct natural properties of God present in distinct persons (in a dynamic of mutual command and obedience, or self-emptying under diverse states), then there would seem to be distinct natural properties in the persons that differentiate them, at least "at times" in the eternal cycle or dynamic. Then, the persons are precisely not perfectly one in unity of nature, and in fact, they must *not* be united perfectly in nature, at least under some aspects, precisely *so that* they can be differentiated dynamically across diverse natural states. In this case, it is difficult to see how the persons are truly one in being or united in nature (both senses of *homoousios*). If, by contrast, God's divine essence does actuate dynamically in relation to creation, is this through the *analogia relationis et operationis*? If so, then it seems that the Trinity in some real sense becomes Trinity or at least becomes more itself as Trinity, in function of its relation to creation. In this case, does the Creator create the creation, or does the creation not also in some way create the Creator? Barth has not, to my mind, worked out this issue sufficiently.

Aquinas's theology does not suffer from the ambiguities that Barth's theology does on this frontier, notably because of his theology of divine simplicity, which is deeply interrelated to Aquinas's theology of divine causality and his theory of analogy. I have written about this issue elsewhere and have compared Aquinas and Barth on this score.[71] Here, we might only note in passing that Aquinas argues

---

71. White, "Divine Simplicity and the Holy Trinity."

that the Trinity is characterized by a unity of essence (following the Nicene definition of God as *homoousios* or consubstantial.) Therefore, the persons are not differentiated by diverse *essential* or *natural* characteristics (such as command and obedience), but instead, each possesses the plenitude of divine life and being, equally and identically, so that each person is truly the one God. They are differentiated only by relations of origin and are themselves characterized *qua* persons as "subsistent relations."[72] Barth's theology of divine inter-relationality seems to echo elements of the tradition and to preserve a relational conception of God's Trinitarian life, in part. However, by his decision to introduce act-potency composition into the essence of God and into the differentiation of the persons, he seems to compromise in a serious way the Church's traditional confession of biblical faith in the *unity* of the Trinity and in the consubstantiality of the persons, based on their identical and equal possession of the divine nature. I take it that this is not "merely" a conciliar issue having to do with the Nicene creed, which functions effectively to unite orthodox Christians down through time, but indeed also a biblical issue, having to do with the scriptural revelation of the unicity of God, to which all who claim allegiance to the scriptures should render themselves docile in obedience to the living Word of God.

Our third example has to do with election and relation. Barth criticized the Catholic notion of causality of creation and analogy by claiming that it could not acknowledge sufficiently the mutual relationality of God and creation. God is relational in his way of being toward creation, and creation is related to God, as it is unveiled to us in Jesus Christ. However, there are questions that arise from the way Barth treats this issue systematically in his work. Consider here Barth's notion of election in Christ as revelatory of who and what God is in himself. If Christ is the subject of election as well as the object, then it would seem that God's self-determination to be human for our salvation is something that is internal to the divine essence

---

72. See *ST* I, q. 29, a. 4.

in such a way that God is only ever God by relating to his creation in Christ. This means that God is eternally actuating himself for the election and that this act is constitutive of God. Furthermore, this act places God from all eternity in an ontological stance of real relationality to creation. The final causality of divine action terminating in creation enters back up into the ontology of God's eternal identity as a potential nexus of divine life already, always anticipated by God in his developmental becoming. So, God is really relative to creation and is constituted in part by his historical being as man. Without creation, God could not be God.

Perhaps it is not necessary or even textually permissible to read Barth this way. However, there are ambiguities in texts of Barth that seem to suggest the possibility of such an interpretation, and in this sense, his work is ambiguous. If Barth is seeking to say that in God's dealings with us (a) we come to know really who God is in himself eternally and (b) how God acts with us depends upon and is expressive of who God is in himself eternally, then his views coincide significantly with those of Aquinas.

However, Aquinas's theology seems to maintain a better balance and clarity of self-expression in maintaining these two ideas.

It does so first and foremost because of Aquinas's doctrine of "mixed relations," or as I prefer to signify it, his doctrine of "non-reciprocal relationality." For Aquinas, God truly does know and love creation in Jesus Christ and, in acting, expresses who he is. But in doing so, God is not made relative ontologically to or dependent upon creation so as to be in any way constituted or caused by creatures in some facet of his being. Rather, God is the unilateral giver of existence and nature, for and in all that is, but is not himself adequately or fully disclosed in that created gift. His creation is unlike and like him due to the limitations and diversified properties of creatures that emerge continuously from him in the ongoing communication of existence to all things. God himself cannot be envisaged (univocally) as really relative to creation the way creatures are really relative to one another, ontologically. The divine otherness of

God is underscored by Aquinas precisely by appeal to the notion of non-reciprocal relational dependency.[73] All in creation is derived from God and given existence by him, and not the inverse.

This first notion is enriched further by Aquinas's treatment of the non-reciprocity of relationality in the two natures of Christ. The human nature of Jesus is wholly relative to his person and divinity and so is expressive of that mystery, but the second person of the Trinity is not relative ontologically to or defined as God in his Trinitarian life by his historical existence among us as human.[74] God can exist as one who is human and be truly human, suffer, and die as man without being re-defined as God or rendered ontologically relative to creation in his deity. The Incarnation and paschal mystery truly reveal who God is, but they do so in the human nature of God, which is analogically similar and dissimilar to his divine nature. The two natures of Christ resemble one another, or better stated, the human nature of Christ resembles his incomprehensible divine nature, such that the Son and Word in his unity with the Father and the Spirit is truly revealed in his human life, action, and suffering, even as his deity remains in part hidden or concealed by his human nature.

A second idea of Aquinas that harmonizes with the notion of non-reciprocal relations in Christology is his distinction between the eternal processions of the Trinitarian persons and their temporal missions.[75] The eternal processions simply are who and what God is eternally by the Father's eternal generation of the Word and his spiration of the Spirit with the Word. According to Aquinas, the visible

---

73. See in this respect *ST* I, q. 13, a. 7 read in concert with *ST* I, q. 44, a. 1, *ST* I, q. 45, a. 1, *ST* I, q. 13, a. 11, and *ST* I, q. 12, a. 8.

74. *ST* III, q. 2, a. 7: "The union of which we are speaking is a relation which we consider between the Divine and the human nature, inasmuch as they come together in one Person of the Son of God. Now, as was said above, every relation which we consider between God and the creature is really in the creature, by whose change the relation is brought into being; whereas it is not really in God, but only in our way of thinking, since it does not arise from any change in God. And hence we must say that the union of which we are speaking is not really in God, except only in our way of thinking; but in the human nature, which is a creature, it is really."

75. See *ST* I, q. 43.

missions of the Trinity, exemplified by the Incarnation of the Word and the visible sending of the Spirit at Pentecost, are the eternal processions with the addition of a temporal effect. In other words, the missions are activities of grace by which God the Holy Trinity renders the eternal immanent Trinity present and manifest to humanity in the economy.[76] This idea is pertinent because it suggests that the human nature of Christ, which is not his divine nature, is wholly relative to his person and his deity in the Incarnation so that God can reveal himself and his Trinitarian life of processions (the eternal relations of the Father, Son, and Holy Spirit) to all of humanity, in the life, death, and resurrection of Christ (the visible mission of the Son). The Son's human life among us manifests the mystery of his eternal relation to the Father and to the Spirit, without thereby constituting such relations of the Trinitarian persons in virtue of the same humanity or in virtue of the homonization of the Word.

Much more could be said about these points, but our key argument here is that what Barth aspires to, in a somewhat ambiguous way, seems to be achieved in a differing form by Aquinas, in his doctrine of God as Creator, as well as in his reflections on the ontology of the hypostatic union and in his Trinitarian theology. Far from being a hindrance to a coherent theology of divine causality, Christological ontology, and Trinitarian activity in creation, the doctrine of analogy in Aquinas seems to function in a sophisticated way to allow one to speak of a spectrum of mysteries respectfully and non-anthropomorphically.

---

76. *ST* I, q. 43, a. 2, ad 3: "Mission signifies not only procession from the principle, but also determines the temporal term of the procession. Hence mission is only temporal. Or we may say that it includes the eternal procession, with the addition of a temporal effect. For the relation of a divine person to His principle must be eternal. Hence the procession may be called a twin procession, eternal and temporal, not that there is a double relation to the principle, but a double term, temporal and eternal."

CONCLUSION

A basic ambiguity in Barth's Trinitarian thought stems from his concept of divine freedom. He consistently emphasizes God's sovereign freedom as a constitutive element of divine identity, but freedom can be interpreted in a variety of ways. Interpreters of Barth who read him in continuity with the classical theological tradition emphasize what the Thomistic tradition terms God's active or perfect power, that is to say, the transcendent freedom of the Creator to act in light of his own wisdom and love in creation and redemption. The emphasis is on freedom as transcendent capacity for efficient causation stemming from love. Other interpreters read Barth on freedom as denoting final causality: what God acts *for* in creation and redemption is seen to constitute or characterize who God is eternally. For example, God is identified as one who *eternally* elects humanity by grace, who freely intends to become incarnate as the expression of his own being, who freely intends just in virtue of his eternal Sonship to obey the Father, eventually expressing this as man, in Christ. For these latter interpreters, the terminus of the freedom by which God relates himself to creation in the Son (Barth's *analogia relationis*) determines God's very identity from all eternity. God is free to love by allowing himself to be in a sense defined inwardly by the Incarnation and passion of Christ, on behalf of all of humanity.

For Aquinas, by contrast, God does not exist eternally in view of his relationship to creatures. Rather, the analogy to "final causality" in God is that of God's eternal freedom to love God's own eternal goodness. The mystery of God as a mystery of love is eternal and is identical with God in his own inner life of Father, Son, and Holy Spirit. God's incomprehensible love of personal communion is the mystery that antecedes all activity of creation and redemption, and that is the fundamental ground for all the outward works and expressions of God. The cross reveals the love of God but is not a condition for its possibility. In this case, there is no analogy of being as Barth understands it, an *analogia relationis* of freedom, whereby God can be somehow identified with his relational activities of election, creation, and Incarnation. These actions do truly manifest God's transcendent identity as Trinity and are revelatory of his eternal wisdom and love, but they do not constitute the distinction of persons in God as such nor alter his divine nature. Barth has his own analogy of being, then, based on freedom and derived more or less from his original theological appropriation of modern philosophical depictions of the freedom of human subjectivity in history. The question remains, however, whether this depiction of freedom is sufficiently refined in light of the advances of classical Christian theology and philosophy over pre-Christian pagan theology and philosophy so as to adequately convey the scriptural sense of divine transcendence. The classical approach arguably provides superior analogies for the divine essence, especially when speaking of final causality in God with regard to intellect and volition, and speaks in this light of God's eternal contemplation of his own essence and love of his own goodness. God exists primarily "for himself" in the eternal perfection of Trinitarian contemplation and love, and he creates and redeems the world out of this ineffable and transcendent perfection. As Aquinas notes, this inner life essentially is that of the eternal procession of the Word by generation and the procession of the Spirit as the mutual Love of the Father and the Son.[77] Everything is from the Trinity and for the Trinity. There is no other primacy than that of God.

77. *ST* I, q. 39, aa. 2–4.

PART II

On Christology

8

---:---

Is a Modern Thomistic
Christology Possible?

At the start of our study of Thomistic Christology, we might first ask: is there such a thing as a *modern* Thomistic Christology? Behind this question, there are a number of substantive issues. For example, what does it mean to be modern? What constitutes "Thomism"? What is the relation between Thomistic thought and characteristically modern philosophy and theology? These are, of course, immense topics. Without pretending to ignore their importance, however, it is permissible to narrow the scope of our inquiry if we refocus the initial question posed here in a twofold way by asking: what are the particular defining features of Christology as it is articulated in modernity, and what distinctive contributions or theories is Thomism able to provide within the context of the modern conditions of debate on this subject?

In the first half of this chapter, I would like to describe briefly what I take to be the two most important challenges of modern Christology and to examine, in turn, two typical conundra to which these challenges give rise. For the sake of this presentation, I will

Previously published in *The Incarnate Lord: A Thomistic Study in Christology* (Washington, DC: The Catholic University of America Press, 2015), prolegomenon, and under a different title in *Pro Ecclesia* 20, no. 3 (2011): 229–63.

employ examples from Friedrich Schleiermacher and Karl Barth, respectively, to illustrate diverse ways in which antinomies are present in modern Christology, conflicts or contradictions that remain (at times) unresolved or inadequately treated. In the second half of the chapter, I will sketch out what I take to be two ways that Aquinas's Christology, especially as read by some of his modern interpreters, provides a set of cathartic distinctions that can help us to resolve tensions in modern Christology, and to propose a potentially more complete treatment of the mystery of Christ taken on modern terms, or at least developed in response to modern challenges. These reflections help set the stage for the further chapters that ensue.

TWO MODERN CHALLENGES
TO CHRISTOLOGY AND TWO LINGERING
CHRISTOLOGICAL ANTINOMIES

Identifying Two Challenges of
Modern Christology

The classical Chalcedonian doctrine of faith affirms that Christ is one person, the Son of God, who subsists in two natures as both God and man. In essence, one can characterize the challenges of modern post-Enlightenment thought to classical Christology and Chalcedonian doctrine in a twofold way. On the one hand, at least since Hermann Reimarus and Gotthold Lessing, the modern theological interpretation of the person of Jesus Christ has repeatedly confronted the question of the relationship between the historical Jesus and the New Testament doctrinal presentation of Jesus as Christ, Son of God and Lord.[1] Lessing, for example, envisaged

---

1. See Hermann Samuel Reimarus, *Apologie oder Schutzschrift für die vernünftigen Verehrer Gottes*, ed. Gerhard Alexander, 2 vols. (Frankfurt-am-Main: Insel, 1972); Gotthold Ephraim Lessing, *Lessing: Philosophical and Theological Writings*, ed. H. B. Nisbet (Cambridge: Cambridge University Press, 2005). The argument that there is a profound discontinuity between the Jesus of history and the Christ of the New Testament was originally developed by Spinoza and the English deists, and subsequently formulated more explicitly by Reimarus and Lessing. See the historical discussion by Jonathan

the historical Jesus as primarily a moral sage, a precursor to Enlightenment philosophical doctrine. The New Testament projected back onto his historical life the theological overlay of Christological ontology and dogma. The unavoidable question such speculations raised subsequently was: what is the relationship between the Christ of the New Testament and subsequent Church dogma, on the one hand, and the modern historical reconstructions of the figure at the origin of the early Christian movement on the other? In one sense, this is to ask the question of whether naturalistic explanations of the origins of Christianity succeed in overturning the potential rational and historical intelligibility of classical doctrinal and creedal statements. How should classical Christianity defend itself "apologetically" with respect to its modern historicist critics? However, in another (and distinct) sense, to respond to this question is also to grapple with a more integrally theological question: what importance (if any) should the hypothetical construal of the historical Jesus have within a modern Christology that bases itself upon the New Testament understanding of the significance of Christ? How should modern theology speak of the life of Jesus, and particularly of revelatory events such as the transfiguration or the ascension, in which the very mystery and being of the person of Christ are unveiled? What are the historical-critical conditions for a *theological* rather than merely apologetic discussion of these events as revelatory of Christ?

Second, in light of Immanuel Kant's critique of classical metaphysics and the subsequent Hegelian and Heideggerian reformulations of ontology in a modern, historical mode, what is the importance of the longstanding metaphysical tradition that was employed classically to articulate the meaning of the Incarnation in theological terms: "one in being with the Father," "one person in two natures," "two wills and operations," and so on?[2] Do these expressions retain

---

Israel, *Radical Enlightenment: Philosophy in the Making of Modernity 1650–1750* (Oxford: Oxford University Press, 2001), 197–229, 447–76.

2. On Kantian and Heideggerian notions of classical metaphysics as "ontotheology"

the full weight of their classical expression in a post-metaphysical age, and if so, how can this be?[3] Are we invited or required in modernity to reinterpret Chalcedonian doctrine in a post-Kantian, post-ontotheological way, and if so, what shape should this interpretation take?[4] Correspondingly, what difference should Christ make to our modern contemporaries, who admittedly inhabit a culture of distinctly empiricist hue? In what sense is contemporary Christology obliged to salvage, or to radically reformulate, classical ontological definitions concerning the person and natures of Christ if Christianity is to present itself as an authentic knowledge of God in the modern world?

These are, of course, vast questions, and in this context, they are being asked only in order to paint a background in very broad brush strokes concerning two ways in which modern Christology has developed responses to these challenges, at least in two of its most important representatives: Schleiermacher and Barth (who admittedly cannot by any typological configuration be said to represent all modern

---

and the respective criticisms of classical metaphysics by these thinkers, see Boulnois, *L'Être et representation*; White, *Wisdom in the Face of Modernity*.

3. Is our age truly "post-metaphysical?" Certainly, contemporary analytic philosophy is quite concerned with metaphysical questions, classical and otherwise (consider Kripke, Plantinga, Searle, or Swinburne). However, such considerations do not contribute a normative form of discourse to the broader university culture the way that metaphysical references of thought did in the pre-modern age. In the broader academy, empiricism and postmodernism remain the prevalent modes of unifying philosophical discourse. Furthermore, whatever one makes of the contemporary revival of metaphysics in analytic philosophy, this development has affected post-Kantian Protestant and Catholic theology very little (while such theology has tended to adopt its central philosophical principles from continental philosophy).

4. Bruce McCormack, in *Karl Barth's Critically Realistic Dialectical Theology*, argues that the Kantian critique of metaphysics stands in the background of the development of much of Barth's early work. He develops this idea in relation to Barth's later work in "Karl Barth's Version of an 'Analogy of Being': A Dialectical No and Yes to Roman Catholicism," in *The Analogy of Being: Invention of the Antichrist or the Wisdom of God*. Alternative post-Kantian and "post-metaphysical" Christologies are developed by Eberhard Jüngel, *God as the Mystery of the World: On the Foundation of the Theology of the Crucified One in the Dispute between Theism and Atheism*, trans. D. L. Guder (Grand Rapids, MI: Eerdmans, 1983), and Moltmann, *The Crucified God: The Cross of Christ as the Foundation and Criticism of Christian Theology*.

Christological development).[5] My argument is that in both of these historically significant thinkers, there are contrasting options taken regarding the problems mentioned above, but the thought of each of them remains markedly inadequate in certain key ways. In fact, these inadequacies suggest commonalities between them—structures of thought—that are deeper than the contrasts and which merit to be challenged in turn by some Thomistic reflections.

Historical Jesus Studies: Alternative Solutions of Schleiermacher and Barth

Let us consider, then, two contrasting ways of being a modern theologian in light of the two challenges mentioned above. The first contrast between Schleiermacher and Barth concerns the way in which each articulates the relationship between historical Jesus studies and classical Christological doctrine. For the purposes of my argument, I am concerned primarily with the revelatory epistemology and theological method of each.

In Schleiermacher one sees the emergence of a methodology in modern German Christology that will, in turn, evolve within liberal Protestantism from thinkers like Albrecht Ritschl and Wilhelm Hermann to Adolf von Harnack.[6] Succinctly stated, Schleiermacher

5. In English-speaking scholarship, Schleiermacher and Barth are commonly treated as two distinct paths of negotiating modern theological problems. However, it is also frequently acknowledged that they share common premises. See in particular Hans Frei's *Types of Christian Theology*, ed. George Hunsinger and William C. Placher (New Haven, CT: Yale University Press, 1992), where Frei arranges the two thinkers—despite their differences—together under a common "type" of theology. An extensive list of works on the interrelations of the two thinkers can be found in the bibliography of Matthias Gockel, *Barth and Schleiermacher on the Doctrine of Election* (Oxford: Oxford University Press, 2006).

6. Friedrich Schleiermacher, *Der christliche Glaube* (Berlin: G. Reimer, 1821–22); *The Christian Faith*, 2 vols., ed. H. R. Mackintosh and J. S. Stewart (New York: Harper and Row, 1963); Albert Ritschl, *Die christliche Lehre von der Rechtfertigung und Versöhnung*, 3 vols. (Bonn: A. Marcus, 1870–74) and *Theologie und Metaphysik: zur Verständigung und Abwehr* (Bonn: A. Marcus, 1887); Herrmann, Wilhelm, *Die Religion im Verhältniss zum Welterkennen und zur Sittlichkeit: eine Grundlegung der systematischen Theologie* (Halle: M. Niemeyer, 1879); Adolf von Harnack, *Das Wesen des Christentums* (Leipzig: J. C. Hinrichs, 1900).

correlates post-Enlightenment studies of the history of Jesus with a decidedly post-Chalcedonian stance of interpretation regarding classical (pre-modern) Christological ontology. Fundamentally, he embraces a primitive version of the modern Enlightenment historical study of the Jesus of history (as distinct from the Christ of scripture) but claims against both German Lutheran orthodoxy and Enlightenment secular historians that the historical-critical method can be employed profitably to identify rationally the enduring *theological* significance of the historical figure of Jesus. Chalcedonian doctrine has to be radically reinterpreted theologically in light of modern historical studies. Behind this approach lies the presupposition that there exists no sharp differentiation between the natural world and the supernatural activity of grace. What is "given" in Christ ("by grace") is what is always already coming into being through the natural religious orientation of human nature: a perfection of human religious consciousness.[7] The true Jesus of history shows us what it means to be a perfectly religious human being.

The central concern of theology, then, must be to recapture through a *historical-critical discernment* the original religious consciousness and sentiments of the founder of Christianity in their unalloyed beauty, as distinct from the later overlay of scriptural and ecclesial symbols and doctrines, which are, in fact, "accidental" to a theological doctrine of Christ as such. In a qualified fashion, Schleiermacher numbers among such accidental features classical doctrines such as the virgin birth, the prophecies attributed to Christ in the New Testament, and at least some of his miracles, the

---

7. Schleiermacher, *The Christian Faith*, 1:64: "It must be asserted that even the more rigorous view of the difference between Him and all other men does not hinder us from saying that His appearing, even regarded as the Incarnation of the Son of God, is a natural fact. For in the first place: as certainly as Christ was man, there must reside in human nature the possibility of taking up the divine into itself, just as did happen in Christ ... But secondly: even if only the *possibility* of this resides in human nature, so that the actual implanting therein of the divine element must be purely a divine and therefore an eternal act, nevertheless the temporal appearance of this act in one particular Person must at the same time be regarded as an action of human nature, grounded in its original constitution and prepared for by all its past history, and accordingly as the highest development of its spiritual power."

resurrection, the ascension, and the final judgment.[8] This approach makes historical Jesus studies, in some real sense, *foundational* for the discernment of what constitutes (or does not constitute) properly theological knowledge of Christ. Historical judgments about the real Jesus are to be distinguished from later apostolic presentations of the mystery of Christ given in scripture. Schleiermacher is clear about this, at least with respect to basic discernments about what is essential to the Gospel as opposed to what is "accidental." For example, the reader of scripture is invited to determine for himself if the non-essential doctrines of the resurrection or ascension are to be considered historical (presumably through both modern exegetical study and theological pondering of their fittingness), and if so or if not, what underlying theological repercussions there might be for one's doctrine of Christ.[9] However, the answer to this particular question *cannot determine* as such the intrinsic content of a doctrine of Christ, which is integral with or without the belief in the historical and physical resurrection and exaltation of Jesus. The proper object of theological faith is recalibrated in critical dialogue with modern historical criticism, and this occurs in such a way that the latter defines the content of the mystery of faith at least negatively, if not constructively, in significant ways. On the other hand, for Schleiermacher, the Chalcedonian metaphysics of Christ as both God and man (one person subsisting in two natures) is reinterpreted in terms

8. Schleiermacher, 2:419–20: "Belief in these facts, accordingly, is no independent element in the original faith in Christ, of such a kind that we could not accept Him as Redeemer or recognize the being of God in Him, if we did not know that He had risen from the dead and ascended to heaven, or if He had not promised that He would return for judgment. Further, this belief is not to be derived from those original elements; we cannot conclude that because God was in Christ, He must have risen from the dead and ascended into heaven, or that because he was essentially sinless He must come again to act as Judge. Rather they are accepted only because they are found in the Scriptures; and all that can be required of any Protestant Christian is that he shall believe them insofar as they seem to him to be adequately attested." The judgment concerning proper attestation seems to permit a rational-historical inquiry to determine whether these are to be considered historically based doctrines. Yet their importance is already ancillary as they have, as doctrines, been shifted outside of the proper scope of the object of "the original faith in Christ."

9. Cf. Schleiermacher, *The Christian Faith*, 2:420.

of the "original experience" of God in Christianity, as first instantiated in the life of Jesus (in his God-consciousness), and as transmitted to his disciples, who in turn codified this experience in doctrinal terms.[10] Historical study of Jesus in what is presupposed to be a post-metaphysical age permits us to recover anew the truth of Christianity that lies behind the artifices of ontological doctrine, a truth foundational to the existence of authentic Christianity. Unsurprisingly, it is this same pre-doctrinal, primitive truth that is simultaneously most relevant to our post-doctrinal contemporaries.

Barth initially seems to be at the antipodes of this epistemological stance. His doctrine concerning the historical Jesus resembles in key respects the doctrine of Martin Kähler in his famous work of 1892, *The So-Called Historical Jesus and the Historical Biblical Christ*.[11] In that work, Kähler had proposed that modern "biographies" of the historical Jesus, if we judge them by the canons of modern historiography, are not really scientifically warranted works. They only serve, therefore, as a distraction to a proper understanding of the object of theology: the person of Christ as presented in Scripture and as interpreted in distinctly theological terms by the ecclesial community.[12]

10. Schleiermacher, 2:385–87.

11. Martin Kähler, *Der sogenannte historische Jesus und der geschichtliche, biblische Christus* (Leipzig: A. Deichert, 1892); *The So-Called Historical Jesus and the Historical Biblical Christ*, trans. Carl E. Braaten (Philadelphia: Fortress, 1964).

12. Kähler, *So-Called Historical Jesus*, 54–56: "Obviously we would not deny that historical research can help to explain particular features of Jesus' actions and attitudes as well as many aspects of his teaching. Nor will I exaggerate the issue by casting doubt on the historian's capacity to trace the broad outlines of the historical institutions and forces which influenced the human development of our Lord. But it is common knowledge that all this is wholly insufficient for a biographical work in the modern sense. Such a work is never content with a modest retrospective analysis, for in reconstructing an obscure event in the past it also wishes to convince us that its *a posteriori* conclusions are accurate. The biographical method likes to treat that period in Jesus' life for which we have no sources and in particular seeks to explain the course of his spiritual development during his public ministry. To accomplish that something other than a cautious analysis is required. Some outside force must rework the fragments of the tradition. This force is nothing other than the theologian's imagination—an imagination that has been shaped and nourished by the analogy of his own life and of human life in general. In other words, the biographer who portrays Jesus is always something of a dogmatician in the derogatory sense of the word."

The latter community is itself primarily subject by faith to knowledge of the resurrected and glorified Christ who is alive, rather than the questionable and always conjectural human reconstructions of historians concerning the "Jesus of history," a past figure whose real historical life now completely evades us.[13]

Like Kähler, Barth treats the problem of modern reconstructions of the historical Jesus by a creative reappropriation of the classical Lutheran adage: *Sola Fide; Solo Christo; Sola Gratia*. Modern Jesus of history studies are conjectures of mere human reason, hypothetical, inherently uncertain, and potentially deeply flawed.[14] The root of the epistemological problem is the failure to realize what kind of book the New Testament is: not one from which we justify the warrant of our own beliefs through historical-critical reconstructions of the figure of Jesus, but rather a book through which the Word of God is communicating itself, setting up *its own preconditions* in the hearer for an authentic knowledge of God in Christ.[15] Barth's methodological neutralization of the *theological* importance of the historical-critical life of Jesus studies is almost the inverted mirror

13. Kähler, 66–67: "The real Christ is the Christ who is preached. The Christ who is preached, however, is precisely the Christ of faith. He is the Jesus whom the eyes of faith behold at every step he takes and through every syllable he utters—the Jesus whose image we impress upon our minds because we both would and do commune with him, our risen, living Lord. The person of our living Savior, the person of the Incarnate Word, of God revealed, gazes upon us from the features of that image which has deeply impressed itself on the memory of his followers and which was finally disclosed and perfected through the illumination of his Spirit." See the similar, contemporary proposals of Luke Timothy Johnson, *The Real Jesus* (New York: Harper Collins, 1996).

14. Karl Barth: "Thousands may have seen and heard the Rabbi of Nazareth. But this 'historical' (*historisch*) element was not revelation. The 'historical' element in the resurrection of Christ, the empty tomb as an aspect of this event that might be established, was not revelation As regards the question of the 'historical' certainty of the revelation attested in the Bible we can only say that it is ignored in the Bible itself in a way that one can understand only on the premiss that this question is completely alien to us, i.e., obviously and utterly inappropriate to the object of its witness." CD 1:1 325.

15. CD 1: 1, 109: "The fact that God's own address becomes an event in the human word of the Bible is God's affair and not ours. This is what we mean when we call the Bible God's Word. If the word imposes itself on us and if the Church in its confrontation with the Bible thus becomes again and again what it is, all this is God's decision and not ours, all this is grace and not our work."

image of Schleiermacher (a logical contrary in the same genus). For Schleiermacher, modern historical reconstructions have the power to provide a more accurate portrait of Christ and to deliver us from overdependence on the historically outdated doctrinal scaffolding that covers over Jesus. For Barth, historical reconstructions stand outside of the proper object of Christology, and that object has an intrinsically doctrinal content that is, in turn, alien to all merely human speculation about Jesus based upon conjectural constructions by modern historians.[16]

While they are contrary to one another in a specific respect, generically, both these views share a common problem. Neither instructs us as to how, if at all, we might reasonably seek explicitly to integrate methodologically the content of modern studies of Jesus of Nazareth in his historical context with a modern defense of the classical doctrine of Chalcedon. In accord with what has been discussed above, this deficit can be characterized in a twofold fashion. Let us presume for the sake of argument (on the basis of theological faith) that Christ is truly God incarnate and that this historical and ontological mystery of the Son of God made man was in some real sense accurately portrayed and interpreted in the New Testament (under the influence of divine inspiration). How, then, should we respond to the doubts of Christians themselves concerning the claims to historicity when they are confronted with alternative narratives of Christian origins, specifically those that deny the historicity of the New Testament? Is an apologetic construal of the "Christ of history" a possible or even necessary element of a responsible modern

---

16. CD 1, 1, 399–406. See the criticisms of Bultmann and Dibelius (on page 402): "The essential understanding is threatened if one agrees with M. Dibelius (RGG2 Art. 'Christologie') in formulating the problem of the New Testament Christology as the way in which 'knowledge of the historical figure of Jesus was so quickly transformed into faith in a heavenly Son of God.' The question is whether one can presuppose that knowledge of a historical figure came first and a transforming of this into faith in the heavenly Son of God came second, so that we have then to ask in terms of the history of thought how this came about. We see no possibility of this road ending anywhere but in a blind alley."

Christology, even if reconstructions of the historical Jesus remain only conjectural and relatively probabilistic (or improbabilistic)? And in a related but distinct sense, when one presumes the historicity of the Incarnate Word and begins from the premises of faith in the basic historicity of the Gospel interpretation of Christ, what *constructive* theological meaning should questions of *how* the life of Christ unfolded in its historical context have? For surely it is one thing to expound a dogmatic theology of the mystery of the person of Christ and the significance of the redemption, and another thing to expound a conjectural, reconstructed web of theories of how Jesus could have expressed himself originally and been perceived historically within his cultural-linguistic context. But should we have to choose between these two objectives that seemingly are not intrinsically opposed, even if the two are clearly not identical? In fact, is the question of their possible harmonization not an unavoidable challenge set before modern Christology in the face of its Enlightenment critics?

Post-Kantian Ontology and Christology: Alternative Solutions of Schleiermacher and Barth

There are in Schleiermacher and Barth contrasting responses to the Kantian critique of the classical metaphysical heritage. And yet, simultaneously, their respective approaches to this issue are not altogether dissimilar. For Schleiermacher, as I have already noted, Chalcedonian ontology is reinterpreted radically with reference to Jesus's God-consciousness, his exemplary religious experience of God. Schleiermacher's theory depends upon a notion of pre-categorical awareness of God that precedes all creedal or doctrinal formulations in theology. This idea has been subject to intense criticism in light of Wittgenstein's philosophical notions of linguistic world-articulation.[17] George Lindbeck has argued against

17. See especially, George Lindbeck, *The Nature of Doctrine: Religion and Theology in*

the "experiential expressivism" of Schleiermacher that language and cultural contexts of interpretation are always intrinsic to the ways in which one understands experience and its meaning and that these explanations are even in some real sense generative of the latter experiences. In other words, doctrinal cognition precedes and gives an internal form to religious experiences of any kind. Given the reality of the societal character of most human knowing and its irreducibly linguistic mode of transmission, Schleiermacher's notion of a pietistic sentiment of absolute dependence that is pre-conceptual (and therefore pre-dogmatic) appears as naïve and philosophically problematic. Speaking in a more Thomistic vein, we could say that it is simply too anti-intellectual in that it denies any necessary conceptual "information" to the act of human judgment, an act which must be present in the heart of any spiritual experience, including the apprehension of one's ultimate dependence upon God.

However, for the purposes of my argument here, the criticisms of Lindbeck and others, true though they may be, are of secondary importance. The more fundamental issue pertains to the nature of the union of God and man in Christ. For Schleiermacher, in truth, abandons the *ontological* locus of divine-human union as it is conceived classically in Chalcedonian Christology. For him, the union of God and man in Christ no longer occurs in the personal subject as such (the hypostatic subject of the Son existing as man) but rather within the world of human consciousness and specifically within the human consciousness of Christ. Christ is united with God through his self-awareness. The problem is that, ontologically speaking, any process of human consciousness—while it truly exists or has being— cannot be said to be all that a person is, for it is only an "accidental" characteristic of a substantial human being, albeit a quite important characteristic.[18] This holds true also in the case of Christ. His

---

a *Post-Liberal Age* (Louisville, KY: Westminster John Knox, 1984); Fergus Kerr, *Theology after Wittgenstein* (Oxford: Blackwell, 1986); Bruce D. Marshall, *Trinity and Truth* (Cambridge: Cambridge University Press, 2000).

18. Were this not the case (were the operations of knowledge or consciousness *what*

thinking and willing, no matter how significant, are not all that he is, but are merely "accidental properties" of his subsistent, personal being. Consequently, such operations are not hypostatic and cannot adequately substitute as an authentic locus of divine-human unity in the Incarnation.

Here, we return, in fact, to classical Christological considerations. For the theology of the hypostatic union as it emerged historically (particularly in the theological writing of Cyril of Alexandria) was understood to concern the very substance of the man Jesus, his being as flesh and soul, and not simply his conscious self-awareness, consciousness of God, self-expression, or linguistic communication. God became man—that is to say, united a human nature to himself hypostatically—such that God subsists in the flesh as the man Jesus Christ.[19] For Aquinas, in particular, this theology of substantial union is what characterizes the understanding of the hypostatic union at the Councils of Ephesus and Chalcedon, in differentiation from Nestorian and *homo assumptus* forms of Christological

---

we are essentially), then the activity of knowledge or consciousness would have to be the unifying principle of all the other powers of the soul, acting in and through them. Biological digestion, then, would be an act of human knowledge, and would depend formally itself in some way upon an act of thinking. Clearly such is not the case. Again, consciousness would also have to serve as the unifying principle of the body (which is substantial in the human person). The simple act of being of the living human body would be an act of consciousness. But this too is plainly false, since we remain embodied persons even when unconscious. Instead, acts of knowledge and love are accidental properties of the embodied person, but are not themselves what the person is substantially. Meanwhile, God alone simply is his knowledge. Cf. *ST* I, q. 77, a. 1, corp. and ad 1.

19. St. Cyril of Alexandria, *On the Unity of Christ*, trans. John A. McGuckin (Crestwood, NY: St. Vladimir's Press, 1995), 80: "If, as they [the Nestorians] say, one [the Word] is truly the Son of God by nature, but the other [the man Christ] has the sonship by grace and came to such dignity because of the Word dwelling within him, then what more does he have than us? For the Word also dwells in us. And so if we have been granted the same dignity by God the Father, our position is in no way inferior to his. For we too are sons and gods by grace, and we have surely been brought to this wonderful and supernatural dignity since we have the Only Begotten Word of God dwelling within us." Although Schleiermacher does not hold to a traditional understanding of the distinction of persons in the Trinity (and therefore neither a pre-existent Logos nor a distinction of natures in Christ), the *kind* of union he proposes is analogous to the position Cyril is criticizing here.

interpretation.[20] The latter Christologies presuppose an accidental union of God and the human being Jesus through a coordination of the wisdom and will of God and the wisdom and will of the man Jesus. They inevitably reduce the union of God and man in Christ to one that is moral rather than substantial, and thereby undermine any capacity to speak in exacting terms of God "existing" or subsisting as a human being.[21]

Against the backdrop of classical theology, then, Schleiermacher's Christology introduces something novel and represents a rupture. He undertakes what amounts to a "transfer" of the locus of divine-human unity from the realm of the substantial to that of the accidental. The locus of divine-human unity in Christ is no longer conceived of primarily by appeal to Christ's substantial personhood and hypostasis (as ontological categories). Structurally, it is the consciousness of Christ that now becomes important for identifying the transforming power of his historical life, and this is evidently a theological decision that affects Christology at a more profound level than differing conceptions of *how* the accidental world of "consciousness" is construed or structured (pre- or post-Wittgenstein). In post-Cartesian philosophy, the last place of refuge for personal identity typically is consciousness, a locus intensified by Kant as introspective moral conscience. After Schleiermacher, it is the introspective moral conscience of Christ that retains an importance for us

---

20. *ST* III, q. 2, a. 6. The teaching of Aquinas on this matter has also recently been reexamined quite helpfully by Jean-Pierre Torrell, in *Le Verbe Incarné* I (Paris: Cerf, 2002), Appendix II, 297–339. I treat this issue in depth in *The Incarnate Word*, ch. 1.

21. *SCG* IV, c. 34, para. 3: "For, in that position, the Word of God was united to that man only through an indwelling by grace, *on which a union of wills follows*. But the indwelling of God's Word in a man is not for God's Word to be made flesh. *For the Word of God and God Himself have been dwelling in all the holy men since the world was founded.* And this indwelling, for all that, cannot be called Incarnation; otherwise, God would have repeatedly been made flesh since the beginning of the world. Nor does it suffice for the notion of Incarnation if the Word of God or God dwelt in that man with a fuller grace, for 'greater and less do not diversify the species of the union.' Since the Christian religion is based on faith in the Incarnation, it is now quite evident that the position described removes the basis of the Christian religion" (emphasis added).

in a scientific age after the collapse of the culture of traditional metaphysics. While this interpretation of Christ gave rise to the great "ethical" Christologies of nineteenth-century liberal Protestantism, they, in turn, have provided the basis for a transition into the Christologies of "religious pluralism" in the twentieth century, in which Christ's unity-of-consciousness with God (or "Ultimate Reality") is understood in terms of his capacity to articulate and symbolize within a particular culture and language the communion with God that he possessed in an exemplary way.[22]

Initially, it might seem that Barth's Christology is entirely different from that of Schleiermacher. First, Barth clearly rejected Schleiermacher's basic project through his sustained polemic and overt criticisms of "human religion" as conceived within liberal Protestantism. Correspondingly, he systematically refused to speculate on the nature of Jesus's religious and historical consciousness. Second, Barth is certainly post-Kantian in his theological methodology, but he understands the prohibition on metaphysics in modernity very differently from Schleiermacher.[23] Schleiermacher perceives the Kantian limitation of speculative reason as an opening for emphasis on religious experience, Christian ethical practices, and the religion of piety. Barth sees in this same speculative limitation the specter of fallen humanity, which is unable by its own powers to resolve basic questions about religion, the existence and nature of God, or the content and meaning of human nature and ethics. Christology emerges, therefore, dialectically over against the limitations of human philosophical knowledge. Rather than reinterpret Christ in

22. One can think here of thinkers like John Hick and Jacques Dupuis. I take up a consideration of their views in *The Incarnate Lord*, ch. 1.

23. Simon Fischer discusses the influences of Marburg neo-Kantianism on the development of Barth's thinking in his early, liberal phase in *Revelatory Positivism: Barth's Earliest Theology and the Marburg School* (Oxford: Oxford University Press, 1988). Bruce McCormack discusses Barth's Kantianism (formulated against neo-Kantian postulates that he considered excessively idealist) in the post-World War I, neo-Orthodox phase of his thought in *Karl Barth's Critically Realistic Dialectical Theology*, 43–49, 129–30, 155–62, 218–26, 245–62.

light of modern philosophical presuppositions, fitting him into the procrustean bed of rationalism, Barth seeks to reinterpret the enigma of the modern (post-Kantian) human subject from the perspective of revelation given in Christ. Kant's methodological agnosticism is maintained as a structural feature of Barthian anthropology, but this is now transposed into a higher, Christocentric key. The crisis of the identity of the modern subject is resolved only in and by the revelation given in the Lord.[24] Against Schleiermacher's anthropology, Barth posits a Christocentric theology.

Third and last, in differentiation from Schleiermacher, Barth pursues an overtly Trinitarian and Christological form of theological reflection that is distinctly ontological in character. He reintroduces Nicene and Chalcedonian themes into post-Kantian theology, not without influence from classical sources, as well as event-ontology that is marked by the influence of Hegel.[25] His mature work seeks to recover an ontology of the hypostatic union and of the distinct "essences" of Christ as one who is both divine and human.[26] This ontology is not one provided for by natural reason, but is made available to us uniquely through divine revelation as expressed in the New Testament.

Despite all of these differences, which are far from trivial, there are still important points of similarity between Schleiermacher and

24. CD 1:1, 236: "But as faith has its absolute and unconditional beginning in God's Word *independently of the inborn or acquired characteristics and possibilities of man*, and as it, as faith, never in any respect lives from or by anything other than the Word, so it is in *every respect* with the knowability of the Word of God into which we are now enquiring. We cannot establish it if, as it were, we turn our backs on God's Word and contemplate ourselves, *finding in ourselves an openness, a positive or at least a negative point of contact for God's Word.* We can establish it only as we stand fast in faith and its knowledge, i.e., as we turn away from ourselves" (emphasis added).

25. For a presentation of Barth that emphasizes the traditional character of his Christological ontology, see George Hunsinger, "Karl Barth's Christology: Its Basic Chalcedonian Character," in *The Cambridge Companion to Karl Barth*, ed. John Webster (Cambridge: Cambridge University Press, 2000), 127–42. On the influences of Hegelian ontology, however, see Bruce McCormack, "Seek God Where He May Be Found: A Response to Edwin Chr. van Driel," *Scottish Journal of Theology* 60 (February 2007): 62–79.

26. CD 4:2, 70–112.

Barth. As noted above, Barth adamantly rejects the liberal Protestant understanding of the human being as a historically religious entity and, in doing so, seeks to purge Christology of any dependence upon an "*a priorist*" human anthropology or natural theology. He does share with Schleiermacher, however, a common conviction concerning the Kantian critique of all possible speculative natural knowledge of God. Barth seeks (over against liberal Protestantism) to develop an ontological reflection on God in light of election (*CD* 2:2), to reflect Christologically upon the being of man (*CD* 3:1), and to reflect upon the being of Christ and his human and divine essences (*CD* 4:1 and 2). All along, however, he also insists that speech concerning the very being of God is only made possible Christologically and not naturally or philosophically. In other words, he retains with Schleiermacher a prohibition on the intellectual accessibility of God by way of speculative reason. It is significant and not merely accidental, then, that he continues to maintain persistent reservations concerning the Catholic *analogia entis* throughout his life.[27] Barth intends to fashion a theology to permit us to surmount the problem of the radical secularization of the human intellect in modernity. His own way of doing this is to re-read Kant's speculative agnosticism as something "normal" when one considers the fallen character of human knowledge outside of Christ. Barth revives the Lutheran critique of any possible *theologia gloriae*, or human speculative theology, in favor of a unique *theologia crucis*, of the unique revelation of God in Christ.[28]

The problem with this is that, as Schleiermacher rightly intuited, one cannot articulate a genuine Chalcedonian metaphysics without a simultaneous commitment to classical metaphysics in general.

---

27. See *CD* 1:1, 238–47 (and many other places in this volume); 2:1, 310–21 and 580–86; III, 3, 89–154. In *CD* 4:1 and 2 Barth develops in various ways the notion of a Christologically centered analogy between God and man, established through the graced event of Jesus Christ. I do not think this is meant to imply a reversal of any of his earlier positions. I attempt to show where and how Barth seriously misinterprets Aquinas's thought on the metaphysics of analogy in *The Incarnate Lord*, ch. 3.

28. See *CD* 1:1, 14–17 and 167–69.

Chalcedon must face the same fate as all other forms of pre-modern ontology. If the latter is defensible, then classical Christology may be as well. If it is not, then the traditional Christian doctrine of the Church is endangered. If this presupposition is true, then Barth fails to confront the deeper problem. How do we respond critically to the Kantian prohibition on speculative thinking about God in general? If we have no philosophical (natural) capacity for speaking about God's presence in the world generally, then a theological treatment of the ontology of Christ is prohibited as well.

Kant himself—in response to Hume—did attempt to leave adequate conceptual space for speculative consideration of the problem of God in distinction from empirical reality and did so by defending the possibility of an analogical concept of God derived from empirical realities. In this, he appealed to a theory of proportional analogy.[29] He also insisted, however—in logical consistency with his own epistemological principles—that any appearance of God *within history* would need to be interpreted in pure continuity with the forms of natural phenomena as they appear to us (strictly in terms of natural causality), or as existing in dialectical opposition to these forms (supernatural thinking as magical thinking). Any gratuitous "revelation" of God is either necessarily reducible to the sphere of pure rationality or, in fact, illusory.[30] If one loyally follows through to the consequence of such a prohibition of speculative thinking about God's presence in history, then the *transcendence* of God incarnate as it is understood *to be revealed in Christ* is, in fact, something the mind simply does not have the capacity to entertain intellectually. We can only conceive of the presence of the divine *in this world* univocally,

---

29. Immanuel Kant, *Prolegomena to Any Future Metaphysics*, §58 (357–61). Kant makes clear that he wishes to argue against Hume that the notion of God as a primary cause of the world is not unintelligible or literally inconceivable, but that this conception is only useful for our thinking about the world we encounter sensibly as potentially caused, and tells us nothing about God in himself

30. This is a major theme in *Religion within the Boundaries of Mere Reason*. See the edition translated and edited by Allen Wood and George di Giovanni (Cambridge: Cambridge University Press, 1998), especially 6:63–64 and 190. I address this issue in *The Incarnate Lord*, ch. 3.

in terms of the natural forms of our world. The reality of the deity of Christ present historically in the flesh is a truth which is inherently unintelligible given the constraints of Kantian reason.

Of course, if one adopts these epistemological presuppositions, there are serious consequences for Christology. Insofar as God is conceived in Christ, he is conceived in terms that are strictly naturalistic. Schleiermacher seems to undertake this kind of transposition in a fluid way: it happens through a reduction of the mystery of Jesus to the world of human religious feeling and ethics. What is important about Jesus is not the claim that he performed miracles, or the ontology of the Incarnation, or the historical event of the resurrection. Instead, it is the evolution of his religious consciousness. When human nature becomes most perfect in its own natural religious trajectory (in Jesus of Nazareth), then it is divine.

Barth seemingly rejects such an approach. However, he does not provide us with a satisfying alternative. For in his own way, Barth also seeks to understand the deity and being of Christ uniquely with recourse to intra-worldly categories based upon human actions and historical events. Here we see in a strange way the shadow of Kant: human thought cannot rise speculatively above a consideration of the forms of this world, and so God, by condescension, takes on the form of our being in his own deity as a way of showing us what God is in himself. Consider, for example, Barth's attempt (in *CD* 4:1) to interpret all Trinitarian theology and Christology in light of Christ's human act of obedience. On this account, we find God in history only in Christ's humanity and specifically in Christ's human actions of obedience. How can Christ's human actions reveal to us *what God is*? For Barth, God has created this world so that the human essence of Christ might reveal to us what the deity of God is from all eternity. Consequently, the event of Christ's obedience unto death is expressive of the very life of God the Son in its eternal constitution. What the cross reveals to us is that God the Son is eternally obedient to the Father.[31] The argument is then developed further: the event

31. *CD* 4:1, 200–201. Bruce McCormack has recently analyzed this section of the

of the passion in time is, in fact, an event in the life of God himself. God, in his very deity, obeys and suffers. The very deity of God can be subject to death and the regaining of eternal life. This, at least, is how disciples like Moltmann, Jüngel, and Jenson interpret Barth (arguably rightly), so as to present a historicized portrait of the deity of God.[32]

Such a perspective is clearly very different from that of Schleiermacher. The problem, however, is that it too fails to preserve a classical form of Chalcedonian thought. What does it mean to say that God personally "exists" as a human being among us? How should we understand the difference between Christ's human nature and his divine nature? Both these questions point us toward the need for a metaphysics of the analogy of being. In one case, hypostatic existence needs to be understood analogically: how is the existence of the person of the Word different from our own? In the other case, we must examine different senses of the word "nature": how is it attributed to Christ's human essence as distinct from his divine essence? In seeking to recover Chalcedonian ontology "after Kant" without a commitment to classical metaphysics, the Barthian "tradition" cannot answer these questions adequately. It has produced answers that are creative, but which are also of a highly ambivalent nature.

In keeping with this criticism, we can note that there is an irony to Barth's particular focus upon the human operations of Jesus as expressive of his deity. Barth clearly rejects the liberal Protestant conception of our human religious consciousness as the locus of the

---

CD very accurately. See Bruce McCormack, "Karl Barth's Christology as a Resource for a Reformed Version of Kenoticism," *International Journal of Systematic Theology* 8, no. 3 (2006): 243–51, as well as his essay "Divine Impassibility or Simple Divine Constancy? Implications of Karl Barth's Later Christology for Debates over Impassibility," in *Divine Impassibility and the Mystery of Human Suffering*, 150–86. I address this issue in *The Incarnate Lord*, ch. 7.

32. This is one of the points of Erich Przywara's critique of Barth's thought as "theopanism" that has recently been reemphasized by David Bentley Hart. See David Bentley Hart, "No Shadow of Turning: On Divine Impassibility," *Pro Ecclesia* 11 (Spring 2002): 184–206.

divine-human encounter, yet he also seeks to place the "site" of the hypostatic union in an odd location: the transcendent identity of God is revealed in a voluntary act of the human Christ (the free and willing submission of Christ to God). Therefore, as with Schleiermacher's pietistic God-consciousness (the sentiment of absolute dependence), an "accidental" feature of the human being of Christ (conscious self-determination in freedom) becomes the privileged locus of divine-human unity. Barth wants to retrieve a sense of the classical Christological ontology over against liberal Protestantism, but he arguably ends up projecting an element of created human life onto the deity anthropomorphically.

We might summarize the argument, then, in this way: Schleiermacher rejects metaphysics and resorts to consciousness, while Barth rejects human metaphysics and resorts to a sort of revealed Christological metaphysics. But Barth's strategy, seemingly designed to avoid falling into Schleiermachian reductionism, ends up (ironically) projecting human categories onto God after all and (even more ironically) these turn out to be categories of consciousness. One can avoid these problems by accepting the possibility of a natural capacity in human beings for metaphysical reflection, so long as this metaphysics is endowed with a sense of analogy so that divine things are not reduced to human ones.[33]

Classical Chalcedonian theology could respond, then, to both Barth and Schleiermacher by asking the following questions. Is the unity of God and man in Christ assured first and foremost by his actions of obedience or by something more fundamental: his personal identity as the Word made flesh? Does Christ obey and suffer in virtue of his divinity or uniquely in virtue of his humanity? In the divine nature, are there properties distinct from the divine essence that allow it to undergo a "history" of development through actions of obedience? Following the mainstream patristic and scholastic tradition, we could argue that Barth fails to recognize the doctrine of

---

33. I am greatly indebted to Michael Gorman for this summation of the argument.

the pure actuality of God.[34] God, in his incomprehensible deity, is not composed of potency and act. Therefore, he is not subject to accidental development or progressive enrichment.[35] Consequently, if we are to attribute accidental features of human thinking or willing to God (even licitly) these must be rethought analogically when ascribed to the eternal life of God, precisely in order to preserve a sense of the divine transcendence.[36]

In appealing to the doctrine of God as pure actuality, I am not presuming that Aquinas's metaphysics is necessarily correct or that a particular version of classical metaphysics must be embraced if any modern Christian theology is to succeed. I am only suggesting that despite their otherwise laudable intentions, neither Barth nor Schleiermacher settles adequately the issue of how or to what degree classical ontology is a necessary feature of any real commitment to Chalcedonian Christology. Can we really retrieve this tradition if we do not make use of traditional ontological categories and concepts to speak about God in just such a way that many a post-Kantian

---

34. Thomas Aquinas, *Scriptum super libros Sententiarum magistri Petri Lombardi episcopi Parisiensis* (vols. 1–2), ed. P. Mandonnet (Paris: P. Lethielleux, 1929) and vols. 3–4, ed. M. Moos (Paris: P. Lethielleux, 1933–47), d. 8, q. 4, a. 3 [hereafter "*In I Sent.*"]; SCG I, c. 23; *De potentia Dei*, q. 7, a. 4; ST I, q. 3, a. 6; *Theological Compendium*, c. 23.

35. SCG I, c. 23, para. 3: "Furthermore, what is present in a thing accidentally has a cause of its presence, since it is outside the essence of the thing in which it is found. If, then, something is found in God accidentally, this must be through some cause. Now, the cause of the accident is either the divine essence itself or something else. If something else, it must act on the divine essence, since nothing will cause the introduction of some form, substantial or accidental, in some receiving subject except by acting on it in some way. For to act is nothing other than to make something actual, which takes place through a form. Thus, God will suffer and receive the action of some cause—which is contrary to what we already established. On the other hand, let us suppose that the divine substance is the cause of the accident inhering in it. Now it is impossible that it be, as receiving it, the cause of the accident, for then one and the same thing would make itself to be actual in the same respect. Therefore, if there is an accident in God, it will be according to different respects that He receives and causes that accident, just as bodily things receive their accidents through the nature of their matter and cause them through their form. Thus, God will be composite. But, we have proved the contrary of this proposition above [c. 18]." In cc. 22 and 23, Aquinas cites as patristic testimony St. Hilary, *De Trinitate* VII, 11; Augustine *De Trinitate* V, 4, and Boethius, *De Trinitate* II.

36. ST I, q. 13, a. 5.

thinker would in fact reject? If the mystery of Christ must be understood in ontological terms, then perhaps modern Christology must retrieve in an overt way the right use of the "metaphysics of being" and the language of analogical predications ascribed to God, even if this stands over against the prohibitions of Kant.[37]

Such a reconsideration of the "analogy of being" allows us to overcome the problematic opposition that emerges in modern Christology between the excessively anthropological focus (represented typologically by Schleiermacher) and the uniquely Christological focus (represented by Barth). Aquinas's metaphysics proposes that the human mind is meant ultimately to transcend history, attaining its complete perfection only through the knowledge of God and the analogical consideration of the divine names.[38] This natural openness to the transcendence of God is seen as a *sign* that the human intellect is capable of being elevated gratuitously into the order of supernatural grace, even unto the beatific vision.[39] On such an account, there is no dialectical opposition between the Christological revelation of God the Trinity and our authentic anthropological fulfillment. Theology of the human person and Christocentric theology are not opposed methodologically but are related in a hierarchical way. God unveils who he is in Christ so that we might become like him through the contemplation of his mystery. In discovering God in Christ, we also find ourselves. "The Word of Life ... was made manifest and we saw it ... the eternal life that was with the Father ... It does not yet appear what we shall be, but we know that when he appears we shall be like him, for we shall see him as he is" (1 Jn 1:1–2; 3:2).

---

37. I make this argument in greater detail in *The Incarnate Lord*, ch. 3 and 4.
38. See, for instance, *ST* I, q. 12, aa. 1 and 12; I-II, q. 3, a. 2, ad 4; a. 6.
39. *ST* I-II, q. 3, a. 8.

THOMISTIC REFLECTIONS ON THE CONDITIONS OF MODERN CHRISTOLOGY

Two Thomistic Reflections

The first half of this chapter has been etiological, while the second half is meant to be prescriptive. In what follows, I would like briefly to consider two ways that Aquinas's Christology provides resources for avoiding the two speculative antimonies I have identified above, each of which tends to influence greatly modern Christological thought. To do so, I will take up key distinctions of Aquinas as they are interpreted by modern Thomists. First, then, I will consider the issue of the potential harmonization or integration of historical life of Jesus research and Chalcedonian doctrinal reflection. Second, I will consider Chalcedonian Christology and the metaphysics of being and divine naming. The reflections offered here are evidently very partial but are meant to designate distinctions found in St. Thomas Aquinas's writings that speak eloquently to the problems described above. They indicate ways that a Thomistic Christology can be envisaged under modern conditions.

The Historical Son Incarnate: Formal and Material Objects of Faith

To address the first question, then, let us appeal to a well-known Thomistic distinction (found, for example, in the *ST* II-II, q. 1. a. 1) between the "formal object" of faith and the "material object" of faith. Aquinas writes in this article:

> The object of every cognitive habit includes two things: first, that which is known materially, and is the material object, so to speak, and secondly, that whereby it is known, which is the formal aspect of the object. Thus in the science of geometry, the conclusions are what is known materially, while the formal aspect of the science is the means of demonstration, through which the conclusions are known.

In speaking of the epistemological act of faith, the material object is the reality we believe in by the grace of faith and that we tend toward in hope and love. That material object is, ultimately, God himself, in whom we believe and who has been made manifest to us in Christ. The formal object, meanwhile, is the medium through which or by which we have access to God and to Christ in the supernatural habit of faith. The formal object, simply speaking, is God revealing himself, the gift of knowledge of God that comes to us through the event of Christ and subsequently through the conveyance of divine truth in scripture, tradition, and the ecclesial magisterium.[40] In faith we know the Trinity and the Incarnate Word, who has lived a human life among us for our salvation. In faith we know this *by* the medium or formal object of God revealing himself.

In his *Commentary on Boethius's De Trinitate*, as well as in the *Summa theologiae*, Aquinas employs this distinction to explain how it is that we might know God both through the formal medium of revelation *and* through the distinct formal medium of philosophical speculation simultaneously.[41] The two forms of knowledge attain to the same material object (who is God), but they in no way conflict with one another, as they approach God in distinct ways (and in differing degrees of imperfection).[42] Even though the two forms of knowledge are distinct, however, they do not remain merely alien to

40. *ST* II-II, q. 1, aa. 9–10.

41. *Expos. de Trin.*, q. 2, a. 2; *ST* I, q. 1, a. 1, ad 2. See also *ST* II-II, q. 2, aa. 3–4; *SCG* I, cc. 4–5.

42. *Expos. de Trin.*, q. 2, a. 2: "Now the knowledge of divine things can be interpreted in two ways. First, from our standpoint, and then they are knowable to us only through creatures, the knowledge of which we derive from the senses. Second, from the nature of divine realities themselves, and although we do not know them in their own way, this is how they are known by God and the blessed. Accordingly, there are two kinds of science concerning the divine. One follows our way of knowing, which uses the principles of sensible things in order to make the Godhead known. This is the way the philosophers handed down a science of the divine, calling the primary science 'divine science.' The other follows the mode of divine realities themselves, so that they are apprehended in themselves. We cannot perfectly possess this way of knowing in the present life, but there arises here and now in us a certain sharing in, and a likeness to, the divine knowledge, to the extent that through the faith implanted in us we firmly grasp the primary Truth itself for its own sake." In *ST* II-II, q. 1, a. 5, ad 4 Aquinas speaks not of distinct "formal objects" but rather of the same object considered under distinct aspects (in reference to Aristotle's *Posterior Analytics* I, 33, 89b2), and applies this to the distinction between revealed and natural knowledge of God

one another. For, as Aquinas points out in the beginning of the *Summa theologiae*, knowledge of God by grace permits us to make use of the grammar of metaphysical reflection upon God—assimilating the truths of this discourse into a greater sapiential totality that is distinctly theological. Sacred doctrine can make use of philosophy to illustrate theological truths, just as (analogically) the science of politics can make use of military knowledge to defend the citizens and material goods of the state.[43] Human metaphysical reflection upon God's simplicity, goodness, unity, knowledge, or will, for instance, may be employed within a context that is specifically theological, serving therein to articulate in more profound and numinous terms the mystery of the triune God.[44]

This distinction between the two formal objects—attaining the same material object in two different ways—is the starting point for a modern development of Thomistic thought undertaken at the beginning of the twentieth century by the French Dominican Ambroise Gardeil. In response to the so-called modernist crisis, Gardeil applied Aquinas's analysis to the relationship between faith and history.[45] This was a reflection that he, in turn, passed on to his student, Yves Congar, and which we find presented anew in Congar's classic work *Tradition and Traditions*.[46] In the distinction between formal and material objects, Gardeil perceived the basis for several important claims concerning the relationship of faith to history.

43. *ST* I, q. 1, a. 5, corp. and ad 2.
44. *Expos. de Trin.*, q. 2, a. 3: "The gifts of grace are added to nature in such a way that they do not destroy it, but rather perfect it. So too the light of faith, which is imparted to us as a gift, does not do away with the light of natural reason given to us by God. Accordingly we can use philosophy in sacred doctrine in three ways. First, in order to demonstrate the preambles of faith, which we must necessarily know in [the act of] faith. Such are the truths about God that are proved by natural reason, for example, that God exists, that he is one, and other truths of this sort about God or creatures proved in philosophy and presupposed by faith. Second, by throwing light on the contents of faith by analogies, as Augustine uses many analogies drawn from philosophical doctrines in order to elucidate the Trinity. Third, in order to refute assertions contrary to the faith, either by showing them to be false or lacking in necessity."
45. See Ambroise Gardeil, *La crédibilité et l'apologétique* (Paris: J. Gabalda et Fils, 1928), and *Le donné révélé et la théologie*, esp. 196–223.
46. Yves Congar, *La tradition et les traditions*, 2 vols. (Paris: A. Fayard, 1960–63).

First, modern rational historical study, with its conjectural reconstructions concerning the historical Jesus or the winding paths
of past development of ecclesial doctrine, approaches the subject of
Jesus Christ or Church doctrine from a different vantage point (under a different objective formality) than does the scriptural and ecclesial deposit of faith as such. The former study, even when it takes
into account the claims of scriptural revelation or significant philosophical truths about man, proceeds on the basis of rational historical speculation that begins from empirical certitudes of historical
facts and attempts to infer from these facts probable connections of
cause and effect that explain historical developments.[47] The mystery
of Christ, as understood by scripture and the Church, meanwhile,
has a different objective formality. The subject of its study is no less
concrete in nature. (There is nothing more concrete than the Incarnation and resurrection of Christ.) However, this form of reflection
attains to depths of reality and to divinely caused historical occurrences at levels that the senses and mere empirical reason cannot
perceive and that the reconstructions of historical reason (no matter
how philosophically informed) can neither demonstrate nor verify.
The theological knowledge of the mysteries of faith is much closer to
the form of natural knowledge that is properly metaphysical or ontological than it is to mathematics or to the observational sciences. Being, essence, unity, and goodness are present throughout all created
reality, after all, but are not merely reducible to the objects of sense
experience. The mystery of God revealed in Christ is like this. We
cannot see the divinity of Christ with our eyes, but we can touch it
by way of an intellectual judgment. Formally speaking, this mystery
utterly transcends the domain of natural reason as such (including
metaphysical knowledge) and is properly supernatural. Therefore,
the methodology of modern historical-critical study of the life of Jesus cannot be employed to provide the foundations for accepting
the truth of the Christian faith as such. These foundations can only

---

47. Often only natural causes and effects

be received supernaturally by grace and understood in that light.[48]

We might note that the supernatural character of the "science" of theology is something Kähler and Barth both rightly understood and defended in conflict with liberal Protestantism's seeming attempt to derive foundational principles of Christology from the modern study of history. (Analogous criticisms were posited by the Catholic John Henry Newman against Anglo-Catholicism's attempt to derive the norms of Catholic doctrine from one's personal study of the history of doctrine).[49] However, the acceptance of such supernatural realism does not imply that the material object of faith (in this case, the mystery of Jesus Christ) cannot be also understood in complementary fashion with recourse to the "formal medium" of the historical study of Jesus, the historical study of the eventual formation of the New Testament canon, of ecclesial doctrine, etc. On the contrary, such forms of knowledge *might contribute* to a better understanding of the material object of consideration (Jesus of Nazareth himself) but only as enriching the original "givens" of divine revelation, *illustrative* of the principles of theological science

---

48. Gardeil, *La crédibilité et l'apologétique*, 221–22: "Tradition and Scripture alone contain the revelation and constitute the theological loci that are *fundamental*. The Church has no other role than to determine with an infallible authority what is contained in Tradition and Scripture. Logically speaking, the Church comes after Tradition and Scripture [and is subordinate to these]. If, then, one begins treating the theological loci with a consideration of the theological loci of the Church, this could be based on a decision of a practical order that is pedagogically useful but in no way necessary. But what one cannot do without acting against the proper character of the theological principles of faith as such is to attempt to *found* their authority upon the authority of the Magisterium of the Church *in so far as this authority results from rational proofs* of rational apologetics [such as historical-critical reasons in favor of the faith]. This is to interpret reductively the theological loci which are the foundation of theology and must be the starting points in faith from the beginning. Between these starting points and the goal pursued in a rational apologetical argument on behalf of the faith, there is a gulf that can only be crossed by the total and definitive adhesion to the Catholic faith, and with this the apologetical arguments are finished. There is a discontinuity between the science of rational defense of the credibility of faith and the science of theology. In the interval between the two is a psychological act of faith, free and supernatural ... It is the faith and not the conclusions of apologetics that stands at the origins of theology 'quae procedit ex principiis fidei.'" All translations from French are my own unless otherwise stated.

49. See Congar, *La tradition et les traditions*, 1:244, 268–70.

and not as *demonstrative* of these principles.[50] Historical study can serve after the fact, so to speak, in the service of theological faith to further research as to *how* the principles of faith were unveiled, given, or received in subsequent historical contexts.[51] Historical reflection can also render us more sensitive to dimensions of the life of Jesus of Nazareth, and such knowledge can, in turn, invite us to further theological reflection. The ontological mystery of the Incarnate Word has historical-cultural conditions as dimensions of its being

50. Aquinas teaches that arguments for the rational credibility of Christian faith (such as those based upon sound argumentation for the historicity of the Gospels) cannot procure the faith but do allow one to defend in a fashion the proper principles of faith, according to a mode that is distinctly rational. *ST* II-II, q. 1, a. 4, ad 2: "Those things which come under faith can be considered in two ways. First, in particular; and thus they cannot be seen and believed at the same time, as shown above. Secondly, in general, that is, under the common aspect of credibility; and in this way they are seen by the believer. For he would not believe unless, on the evidence of signs, or of something similar, he saw that they ought to be believed." In this sense, the arguments in question, insofar as they do enrich the intellect's apperception of the object, can rightly be said not only to have a genuine apologetic (rational defensible) value, but also to illustrate more deeply something of the truth of the material object under consideration. Such argumentation occurs, however, in formal distinction from revelation as such and ultimately only in the service of the mystery of faith. Gardeil's thought is influenced in part by the analysis of apologetics by Reginald Garrigou-Lagrange, in his *De Revelatione*, 2 vols. (Rome and Paris: Ferrari and Gabalda, 1921), 1:41–44.

51. Or, in the more nuanced formulation of Gardeil, historical or philosophical study of Christianity might demonstrate its reasonableness, even in a rationally compelling fashion, but such "apologetic argumentation" will not provide immediate access to the divine mystery itself. *Le Donné Révélé*, esp. 204–5: "A scientific faith [or belief] produced by the evidence of certain motives of credibility, or acquired faith [stemming from study of history], which is human and natural, provides a certain correspondence between [Christian] theology and the science of God [the knowledge that God has of himself], because such an apologetic demonstrates rigorously that God speaks in His Church and that all the dogmas of the Church are, from a human point of view, worthy of belief by divine faith. But it is clear that the certitude that these arguments give is only an incomplete certitude, a certitude in waiting, that is ordered towards the certitude of the divine faith itself ... A sub-alternated science has to be able to join back up with the principles that are its foundation, so as to participate fully in their certitude ... Yet the only means by which theological science as such can rejoin effectively the object known by divine science is ... supernatural faith, which allows us to believe, with an assurance caused directly in us by God, that which God himself knows and reveals to us." It should be noted that Gardeil here seems to reduce Aquinas's conception of *sacra doctrina* in *ST* I, q. 1, to "theology" as distinct from and exclusive of revelation, which is a problematic interpretation of Aquinas on this point, but this is immaterial to the argument at hand.

that can be studied rationally, and likewise, knowledge of the empirical, historical-cultural conditions of Christ can invite us to a deeper reflection about the mystery of the Incarnate Word. Ultimately, however, none of the conditions of Christ's life can be fully understood except by recourse to supernatural faith, for only at this level of reflection do we attain to the deepest ontological core of his person. Therefore, historical study as such cannot allow us to determine what is held in faith, even if it can help us to clarify what is and is not reasonable to believe concerning the *historical mode* in which a given mystery was unveiled historically.

Allow me to illustrate this argument by means of a brief Thomistic consideration of the theories of N. T. Wright concerning the "sacrificial intentionality" of the historical Jesus on the eve of his death.[52] As everyone knows well, the sacrificial system of Jesus's own time revolved around the application of Levitical and Deuteronomical precepts of physical sacrifice within the context of the Second Temple and its vast cultic, political, and economic sociology. And yet, within a generation after Jesus's death, Christians who composed the writings of the New Testament considered the death of Jesus a "sacrifice" of a unique and ultimate kind.[53] Using Old Testament sacrifice imagery to describe the significance of his death, they claimed that this event displaced in some way the economy of Temple sacrifices and had redemptive effects for the entirety of humanity. They also claimed (arguably) that the Eucharist both signified and rendered present the sacrificed body and blood of Christ.[54]

But even if all this is the case, can we simply remain content to develop a theology of sacrifice from the New Testament if Jesus of

---

52. See especially the discussion of Jesus's self-interpretation of his impending death in N. T. Wright, *Jesus and the Victory of God* (Minneapolis: Fortress, 1996), 540–611.

53. Albert Vanhoye offers a helpful study of the emergence of the early Christian concept of the priesthood of Christ in his *Old Testament Priests and the New Priest*, trans. Bernard Orchard (Petersham, MA: St. Bede's Press, 1986)

54. See the brief scriptural argument to this effect by Charles Journet in *The Mass: The Presence of the Sacrifice of the Cross*, trans. Victor Szczurek (South Bend, IN: St. Augustine's Press, 2008), 30–32.

Nazareth, himself a first century Jew, may never have conceived of his own death in sacrificial terms? Clearly, the formal object of the faith is the significance of the death of Jesus as it is presented and understood in faith and for faith as God has revealed through scripture. Furthermore, the New Testament attributes to Christ himself, in numerous instances, a willingness to offer his life "sacrificially" for the multitude. However, this does not render irrelevant the question of how we might explain the origin of this belief historically in the life of Jesus himself, within the context of Second Temple Judaism, or the question of how his own Jewish mode of self-expression in this historical context might have illustrated *his own conviction* of the "sacrificial" and soteriological significance of his death. It is this kind of probabilistic and conjectural argument that Wright, for example, provides through the formal medium of historical speculation, following scholars like Martin Hengel[55] and George Caird,[56] upon whom his work builds.[57]

If, for example, we can trace back the Eucharistic institution narrative to the earliest Jerusalem Christian community ("this is the blood of the covenant, which will be shed for the many"), then we have evidence of a primitive theology of the death of Jesus that can reasonably be seen (by recourse to historical-critical modes of argumentation) to have originated with Christ himself. This theology of Jesus of Nazareth itself, in turn, refers to the foundational covenant

55. Martin Hengel, *The Atonement: The Origins of the Doctrine in the New Testament,* trans. J. Bowden (Philadelphia: Fortress, 1981).

56. See C. B. Caird and L. D. Hurst, *New Testament Theology* (Oxford: Oxford University Press, 1994).

57. See, for instance, *Jesus and the Victory of God,* 257: "The crucial thing is that for Jesus this repentance, whether personal or national, *did not involve going to the Temple and offering sacrifice.* John's baptism, as we saw earlier, already carried this scandalous notion: one could 'repent,' in the divinely appointed way, down by the Jordan instead of up in Jerusalem! In just the same way, Jesus offered membership in the renewed people of the covenant god *on his own authority and by his own process.* This was the real scandal. He behaved as if he thought (a) that the return from exile was already happening, (b) that it consisted precisely of himself and his mission, and hence (c) that he had the right to pronounce on who belonged to the restored Israel." Likewise, see E. P. Sanders, *Jesus and Judaism* (Philadelphia: Fortress, 1985), 203, 206.

sacrifice of Exodus 24 (where the phrase "blood of the covenant" originates), and that is seen in Exodus to have established the twelve tribes in contractual communion with the Lord of Israel. If Jesus not only foresaw his death, but interpreted it in advance as a radical renewal and completion of the covenant of Exodus 24, even a universalization of the covenant "for the many" (cf. Is 53:10–12), and if he signified this for his followers by the prescription of a new mode of sacrifice that now takes place outside of the Temple, then we begin to understand how Christ in history was conscious of articulating the sacrificial character of his death in distinctly Jewish terms, and yet simultaneously interpreted his own life and mission as having an entirely singular, authoritative significance.[58]

A collage of such illustrations of Christ's self-consciousness could suggest in greater and richer depth *how* the Incarnate Word conceived of himself, his identity, and authority within the context of the first century Judaism of his time, even while suggesting plausibly how the words and gestures of the historical Jesus gave rise to the subsequent beliefs about him that were promulgated in the New Testament writings. Do such historical conjectures *determine* the content of the object of faith or prove its truthfulness? For example, if it can be shown merely from the principles of natural reason to be historically probable that Jesus of Nazareth interpreted his

---

58. I am leaving to one side N. T. Wright's account of how Jesus acquires the insights of his self-understanding. Wright believes that any attribution of higher prophetic illumination given to the human intellect of Christ that would account for Christ's extraordinary self-understanding would entail a form of theological docetism that undercuts a sufficient realism concerning Christ's historical, fully human consciousness. Does Wright believe then that Jesus's self-understanding was obtained only through natural causes? He suggests that Jesus knew something of his own deeper identity as the Son and agent of YHWH through an obscure faith in his own mission, without clear certitude, articulated only by recourse to the resources of contemporary Jewish symbols and traditions that he creatively reformulated (see *Jesus and the Victory of God*, 648–53). Is this degree of self-understanding sufficient soteriologically for the moral intention that Christ must have had in order to make the sacrifice of the cross a saving act by giving *his own life* on behalf of all? Despite the many advantages of his work, Wright's interpretation on this point seems to me to be based on naturalistic theological suppositions and to be problematic soteriologically.

oncoming execution in sacrificial terms, does this demonstrate that the death of Jesus should be considered theologically to have been a sacrifice? Of course not. Such knowledge is given to human beings by grace alone, by the activity of the Holy Spirit teaching us through the medium of scripture, tradition, and the living proclamation of the Church. Do such historical reflections permit us to envisage theologically *how* the historical life of God the Son *might* have unfolded in its historical context and to defend a plausible historical account of Jesus *apologetically* over and against secular historical constructions that would contradict the testimony of the New Testament doctrine itself? Yes, they do, or at least, yes, they can in principle. The historical science of modern rational historical investigation (more modest in certitude than many other sciences but capable of some demonstrative conclusions) can be placed in the service of the faith so as to attempt to decrypt a more perfect understanding of its material object, the Son made man, even while it remains clear that this historical study does not provide or obtain the radical access to the mystery of Christ that comes through faith alone, through the mediating formal object of faith. Schleiermacher's confusion or blending of the two formal objects obscures the supernatural mystery of Christ and confines his meaning to the reductionist speculations of historical-critical scholars and their conjectures. Barth expurgates (or at least severely curtails) the possibility of such conjectures being used meaningfully in the service of the object of faith as a form of historical reason in the service of revelation. Gardeil seeks to distinguish in order to unite. He acknowledges the distinct contribution of historical-critical reflection as a lesser science of reason, a science that can be assimilated sapientially to the superior (and irreducibly integral) science of divine revelation. It is from the latter science alone, however, that theology receives its first principles.

Chalcedonian Christology and Metaphysical Knowledge of God: Primary and Secondary Actuality

The second topic discussed above concerns the relationship between classical Chalcedonian ontology and the modern philosophical prohibition on speculative knowledge of God. Can we really articulate theologically the redemption of the modern human self either by an experience of absolute religious dependence or by a revelatory actualism that alone makes accessible an ontological reflection on the depths of God if, from the beginning, the human mind is always, already bound to consider transcendent realities only from within the scope of intra-worldly univocity? In other words, must all Christology be subject to the constraints of a post-Kantian philosophical naturalism?

I have intimated that a recovery of the metaphysics of being and of the divine names is an integral part of a renewed Chalcedonian Christology. Here, I would like to suggest two ways in which Thomistic reflection on the being of Christ invites our modern secularized intellects to a remedy; not a cure from Wittgenstein, but rather one from the Aquinate. That is to say, not a rethinking from ordinary language we already know, but a rethinking *from within Christology* about our *natural* capacities for knowledge of God. What does Christ himself teach us about ourselves and about the transcendent capacities and teleological meaning of the human mind? In answering to this question, let us consider first a point in response to Barthian concerns and then one in response to Schleiermacher.[59]

---

59. In making this argument, I am indebted in part to the thinking of Hans Urs von Balthasar in his seminal work *Karl Barth: Darstellung und Deutung Seiner Theologie*, trans. E. Oakes as *The Theology of Karl Barth: Exposition and Interpretation*, esp. 267–325. Balthasar makes the case that a natural ontology and metaphysical theology are possible and even necessary within the framework of a Christological doctrine of the God-world analogy and a Catholic consideration of the relations of nature and grace. I am suggesting here something potentially complementary but distinct, and more classically Thomistic: because an analogical ontology of creation and God are possible and necessary within Christology, therefore a natural theology is necessary that is distinguishable from

These two points can be elaborated around another central Thomistic distinction, this one not being epistemological, but metaphysical: the distinction Aquinas (following Aristotle) makes between primary actuality and secondary actuality.[60] Primary actuality, for Aquinas, pertains to the substantial being of a thing, its being in act as a certain whole with an essential determination.[61] To be in act, in this primary respect, is to exist, simply, as a unique being of a certain kind. For example, we may say that from the time she is conceived, an embryonic person is a new human being, and this being will eventually develop in various ways but retains continuity of substance over time. She always exists in act. The second mode of actuality, secondary act, pertains to operations, for example, operations of conscious knowledge and reflective reason, or of deliberation or choice that progressively develop and manifest themselves. Such operations occur in human persons in habitual ways that make their behavior predictable and subject to normative descriptions (for example, in the form of virtues and vices). These secondary acts of the person (such as operational acts of piety or obedience) are accidental properties of the substance, secondary acts relative to that primary act that is substantial.[62]

Christology. And without a distinct metaphysical reflection on God that is philosophical in kind, true Christological reflection becomes intrinsically impaired.

60. See, for example, Aquinas, *De Ver.*, q. 21, a. 5; *ST* I, q. 48, a. 5; q. 76, a. 4, ad 1; q. 105, a. 5; I-II, q. 3, a. 2; q. 49, a. 3, ad 1; *In IX Meta.*, lec. 5, 1828; lec. 9, 1870; *In de Anima* II, lec. 1, 220–24. The distinction is found originally in Aristotle, particularly in *Metaphysics* IX, 6, 1048b6–9, and 8, 1050b8–16. He specifically applies the distinction to operations of the soul as accidental properties of the substance ("second acts") in *On the Soul* II, 1, 412a17–29.

61. *ST* I, q. 48, a. 5: "Act is twofold; first and second. The first act is the form and integrity of a thing; the second act is its operation."

62. *In de Anima* II, lec. 1, 224: "The difference between accidental form and substantial form is that whereas the former does not make a thing simply be, but only makes it be in this or that mode—e.g., as quantified, or white—the substantial form gives it simple being [*facit esse actu simpliciter*]. Hence the accidental form presupposes an already existing subject; but the substantial form presupposes only potentiality to existence, i.e., bare matter. That is why there cannot be more than one substantial form in any one thing; the first makes the thing an actual being; and if others are added they confer only accidental modifications, since they presuppose the subject already in act of being."

It is important for our purposes, then, to consider the union of God with human nature according to these two respective modes of being in act. The Incarnation, in which God exists as a human being, takes place primarily in the first of these modes: God subsists personally as a human being. By contrast, *our union* with God takes place primarily in the second mode, through human operations. By the working of grace, we can come to know God and to love him so as to be united with him by our human actions.[63] The distinction is important, then, because it allows us to see clearly the true "locus" of the Incarnation that is particular to Christ. It does not take place in the human consciousness of Jesus or in his human operations of obedience. It takes place in the very substance of Christ's person.

According to Aquinas's way of stating this point, then, the union of God and man in Christ is substantial and not accidental. It takes place within the subsistent person of the Word and not in the accidental operations of the man Jesus. The Son unites to himself a human nature in his own person. Consequently, the man Jesus Christ is the second person of the Trinity.[64] Accordingly, the Word exists as man in such a way that his body and soul subsist by virtue of his very *esse* (the being in act of the Word himself). Or, to say the same thing slightly differently, the human nature of the Incarnate Word subsists in his person by virtue of his being in act as God.[65] There-

63. *ST* III, q. 6, a. 6, ad 1–2.
64. *ST* III, q. 2, aa. 2–3.
65. *ST* III, q. 17, a. 2: "Now being [*esse*] pertains both to the nature and to the hypostasis; to the hypostasis as to that which has being, and to the nature as to that whereby it has being. But the being which belongs to the very hypostasis or person in itself cannot possibly be multiplied in one hypostasis or person, since it is impossible that there should not be one being for one thing. If, therefore, the human nature accrued to the Son of God, not hypostatically or personally, but accidentally, as some maintained, it would be necessary to assert two beings in Christ—one, inasmuch as He is God—the other, inasmuch as He is Man [But] since the human nature is united to the Son of God, hypostatically or personally as was said above [*ST* III, q. 2, aa. 5–6], and not accidentally, it follows that by the human nature there accrued to Him no new personal being, but only a new relation of the pre-existing personal being to the human nature, *in such a way that the Person is said to subsist not merely in the Divine, but also in the human nature*" (emphasis added). In a late disputed question on the union of the Incarnate Word (*De Unione*, a. 4) Aquinas does consider the possibility of a human, created *esse* in Christ. Based on this

fore, all that occurs to Jesus by virtue of his human nature, from the time of his conception until the moment of his death, is properly ascribed to God himself, as when we say, for example, that the Son of God wept, or that the Son of God was crucified.[66] We can also say that God obeyed as man or that God suffered in his human nature. But if we do so, we are saying this due to the hypostatic subsistence of the Word in a human nature and not because of a transposition of human attributes onto the divine nature. If we locate the union of God and man in the hypostasis of the Son, we must still distinguish adequately the human and divine natures of Christ and his human and divine operations.

Notice, then, that being-in-act (*entelecheia*) is understood by Aristotle and Aquinas to be denoted analogically and to have similar but not identical modes of realization. We can be-in-act substantially, or accidentally-operationally.[67] Thus, we are speaking of an *analogia entis* or analogical realization of created human being that is distinct from the question of an analogical knowledge of God based upon natural knowledge of creatures (natural theology). Neither Barth nor Schleiermacher, however, grasps adequately this analogical distinction, and so both think *univocally* about the being-in-act of operations (Jesus's consciousness of religious dependence, Christ's human obedience) as in some way equivalent with or susceptible to signifying formally the being-in-act of substantial being (the subsistent person of Christ in his unity of being with the Father). This is what leads each of them, in two very different ways, to seek to locate the divine-human union in Christ in the human actions of Jesus. In

text, the twentieth-century Thomist Herman Diepen famously posited an "integration" theory of *esse* in Aquinas's thought. Even if one adopts Diepen's interpretation, the personal subsistence of Christ is one and its unity stems from his divine *esse* as the eternally existent Son. Consequently, what I am claiming here about the unity of Christ's personal divine existence has no direct bearing upon the truth or falsehood of Diepen's interpretation. See Herman Diepen, "La critique du baslisme selon saint Thomas d'Aquin,"; "La psychologie humaine du Christ selon saint Thomas d'Aquin."

66. *Theological Compendium.* I, c. 210.

67. Aristotle, *Metaphysics* IX, 6, 1048b6–9: "But all things are not said in the *same sense* to exist actually, but only by analogy—as A is in B or to B, C is in D or to D; for some are as movement to potentiality, and others as substance to some sort of matter."

addition, then, Barth does not identify accurately what distinguishes the operations of the divine and human natures of Christ. Human operations become direct windows into the operation of the deity itself as if the two were somehow equated, or very similar.

I have suggested above that the underlying problem that has to be confronted is whether Chalcedonian Christology depends in part upon our acceptance of some form of classical ontology. If we turn the question around, we might also ask whether a robust form of Chalcedonian Christology has implicit recourse to analogical thinking about God in metaphysical terms. Consider, for example, the discourse concerning "existence" that the Chalcedonian speculations of Thomas Aquinas entail. They require that we can say that Christ, this existent man, is God, and that God exists as this man.[68] This notion of the existence of the Word made flesh is assuredly only accessible to us within the mystery of faith and, again, through the medium of the formal object revealed in scripture. Nevertheless, since it requires of us to speak of a relation between the existence of God the Creator and that of his creation (for it is the *existent* Creator who *exists* as man), such language also implies that the concept of the Incarnation *is not itself wholly alien to our ordinary human way of knowing*. Knowledge of it does not fall naturally within our ordinary scope of understanding, and it has to be revealed to us, in faith and by scripture, but when this occurs, the truth is not something so extrinsic to our thought that it remains unintelligible. On the contrary, we can undertake a graced act of faith in an intellectually *intrinsic* way, in what we truly are as cognitive human beings. If this were not the case, we would be no more subject to receiving divine revelation than is a stone.

What this line of argument suggests is significant. From within the natural frontier of our ordinary human knowing, we are in the possession of a *way of thinking about existence* that is intrinsically open to God and open even to the possibility of speaking about God *existing* as one of us that does not fail to acknowledge at the same time that *God's existence* as the Creator of the world cannot be

68. *ST* III, q. 16, a. 9

univocally identified with our mode of existence, *even when God the Creator exists as human.* There is an analogy of being that is implicitly present within Christology, *pace* Kant, Schleiermacher, and Barth. The recognition of the presence of God's transcendence in Christ, even in the midst of his immanence as one of us, requires, then, that we as creatures are naturally open to reflection about the metaphysical transcendence of God and can relate to his existence through conceptual thinking that is analogical. This form of Christological thinking does not reduce our understanding of God to that of the world. The goodness of Christ as God is not identical with his goodness as man. His obedience as man is not identical with his divine willing as God. Such analogical thinking avoids the reduction of the deity of Christ to the naturalistic forms of this world. All of this suggests that if human beings *can* believe in the Incarnation (by grace), then they are also capable of natural, analogical thinking about the transcendent God. That is to say, Christology makes implicit use of natural theology.[69] If we believe in the Incarnation, we need to be committed to the retrieval of some form of classical metaphysics.

What should we say, then, about "secondary actuality"? Of what value are the operative actions of Christ as a revelation of the Son of God and as a revelation to us of what it means to be authentically human? Here, I wish to shift the point of emphasis from Barth to Schleiermacher. I have argued above that Barth wishes to recover a robust Chalcedonian ontology in modernity but that he fails to identify sufficiently the locus of divine human unity in Christ (in the subsistence of the Word made flesh). This is due in part to a mistaken rejection (or misuse) of the metaphysics of being. Schleiermacher, meanwhile, seeks to appeal to the human religiosity of Jesus as the model of our encounter with God, but substitutes this treatment of Christ for a Chalcedonian Christology. In a rightly ordered Christology, however, we should not be obliged to choose between an ontology of the hypostatic union and an anthropological theology that focuses upon the human actions of Christ.

69. I take up this argument in greater detail in *The Incarnate Lord*, ch. 4.

To illustrate this claim, I will appeal to a soteriological point made by Jacques Maritain in his work *On the Grace and Humanity of Jesus*.[70] Maritain's book contains an analysis of Christ's knowledge, and specifically of Christ's beatific vision in his earthly life, that is to say, of his immediate, intuitive knowledge of his own identity and of the Father and the Holy Spirit. As commentators on Aquinas such as Maritain have noted, according to Aquinas, the historical Jesus did not believe that he was God by faith but knew who and what he was by a kind of higher immediate insight.[71] And he knew as well that he had come into this world to save us. This is a classical Thomistic doctrine (and the teaching of the ordinary magisterium of the Catholic Church).[72] What Maritain points out in this respect is that there is a double referentiality, or we might say "relativity" to the human knowledge of Christ, to his "secondary acts" of consciousness, as extraordinary as they are.[73] On the one hand, the actual consciousness of Christ by which he knows of his own identity as the Son is relative to the being of the Son, the primary actuality just discussed. That is to say, Christ knows as man that he is one with the Father, and he wishes to communicate knowledge of this unity to his disciples, in and through the event of his passion and death (Jn 17:11). On the other hand, his consciousness reveals the final good of our human nature. Because we are intellectual creatures, we are made to see God face to face by the grace of the beatific vision, which alone can ultimately satisfy the human heart and its longing for ultimate truth and undiminished goodness (Jn 17:24).[74]

If we accept this twofold conception of the consciousness of Christ, we can overcome some of the difficulties in modern theology inherited from Schleiermacher's thought. Against the liberal

---

70. Jacques Maritain, *On the Grace and Humanity of Jesus* (New York: Herder and Herder, 1969).

71. *ST* III, q. 9, aa. 2–3.

72. See *CCC* 472–74.

73. See Maritain, *On the Grace and Humanity of Jesus*, 14–27, 52–53, 62–67.

74. This is why Aquinas will argue that it is necessary for Christ to have the beatific vision: in order as man to be the Savior, and not one who is himself saved (*ST* III, q. 9, a. 2).

Protestant tendency, a Thomistic Christology of the consciousness of Christ cannot absolutize the consciousness of Jesus as the unique locus wherein his unity with God is formed or measured. On the contrary, it sees the self-awareness of Jesus as itself measured by and as a witness to the deeper ontological ground of unity between Christ and the Father. Barth is rightly concerned that any theology which places an emphasis on the religious acts of Christ can entrap us within a reductive form of anthropocentricism, or a generic "philosophy of religious ethics." However, a Thomist account of the consciousness of Christ as "secondary action" avoids this danger and invites us to a theology of the human person that is theocentric in the most Trinitarian of manners. For according to Aquinas, Christ as man is aware in a human way of his own divine identity by virtue of the beatific vision. Consequently, he can reveal to us in his own human actions and teachings who God truly is. Moreover, if the vision of the triune God alone will ultimately satisfy and, in fact, redeem the human person, then Christ also reveals humanity to itself by possessing as man that immediate knowledge of God to which we are called. He has come to us in human nature to reveal to us the inner life of God the Trinity and to call us to himself in the eventual vision of the divine essence and in the direct unveiling of God to the human mind.

If what I have argued above is the case, then Thomistic theology invites us to overcome a problematic modern opposition between Christological ontology and the anthropological dimension of theology. Aquinas makes very clear in the questions on beatitude at the beginning of *Summa theologiae* I-II that we attain to complete happiness and thus become fully ourselves only through the vision of God, which is a form of knowledge that transcends all historical objects, and that we are naturally open to or capable of, but which we also cannot procure for ourselves.[75] This being-turned radically toward the Trinitarian God, into the vision of God, only occurs by the grace of God given in Christ. All things are centered, therefore,

75. *ST* I-II, q. 5, aa. 1 and 5.

on Jesus, who is the way to the Father and who is himself the eternal Word who proceeds from the Father, and who with the Father spirates the Holy Spirit. We are called to know God in the eschaton, in ecstatic joy, by which the intellect is taken out of preoccupation with itself and into the unique contemplation of the Trinity. St. Thomas insists that in charity, we love God for God's own sake, *only for the goodness of God's own self*, through a love and admiration of God that place him above every other good, even our own good of eternal happiness.[76] There is no rivalry, then, between a theology of the human person and a theocentric theology. Under grace, the redeemed human person can become conscious of his or her dependence upon God for salvation, but this is a salvation that comes through knowledge of the very being and life of the Incarnate Word who has dwelt among us, God himself living among us as a human being.

CONCLUSION

What has our argument in this chapter sought to establish? We began by considering a juxtaposition of two modern theologians, Schleiermacher and Barth. I have argued that despite their differences, they share in a common set of predicaments, as their ingenious theologies fail to answer adequately certain essential questions. Can the Council of Chalcedon be harmonized with a well-employed use of modern biblical studies regarding Jesus of Nazareth? Can the ontology of the Incarnation be understood rightly without recourse to core elements of the "pre-Kantian" metaphysical tradition? I have suggested that there are problems with the respective answers of Schleiermacher and Barth to these two central questions. One places the accent upon modern historical studies of Jesus and a post-Kantian philosophical anthropology. The other places the accent upon the biblical portrait of Christ and a uniquely theological ontology. As such, neither resolves sufficiently the question of how we might reconcile the biblical portrait of Christ and modern

---

76. See *ST* I-II, q. 3, a. 1; II-II, q. 27, a. 3.

historical studies of Jesus. Nor do they provide us with an adequate understanding of the relationship between Chalcedonian ontology and a realistic philosophical metaphysics that acknowledges our capacity for analogical discourse concerning the transcendent God.

One condition for a coherent modern Christology is that it promotes a Chalcedonian theology that is based fundamentally in the revelation of the scriptures and the dogmatic tradition, but which also makes judicious use of modern historical-critical approaches to the figure of Jesus. Another condition is that modern theology challenge the Kantian prohibition on speculative knowledge of God. Any sufficiently profound exploration of the person of Christ—of God existing among us in history—must make use of our human capacity to speak of the divine attributes of God. This metaphysical accent in theology is also necessary so that we might rightly identify in what way Christ is (and is not) to be understood as a model of human perfection in his human operations of knowledge and love, or, to use the modern terminology, in his "religious consciousness" of God. On my view, a Christology that takes seriously the metaphysical structure of the hypostatic union is fully compatible with one that seeks to acknowledge the human subjectivity and cultural experience of Jesus. In fact, these two dimensions of Christology should be considered in their inter-relatedness; one is helped in this modern enterprise by averting to the antecedent reflections on Christological principles by St. Thomas Aquinas.

9

On True Enlightenment
The Incarnation as a Manifestation of the Trinity

INTRODUCTION

From what we know of Valentinus's second century treatise *The Gospel of Truth*, the work is characterized by a key theme of enlightenment.[1] The human being lives out an existence marked by confusion and ignorance regarding God and bound by suffering. The purpose of the revelation of God in Christ is to deliver men from this situation. Of course, there are other quite striking elements of Valentinus's argument that depart from the teachings of the canonical books of the New Testament. The enlightenment in question is one of liberation from the constraints of material-corporeal living so that the truth of who Christ is implies dissociation from the material world.[2] Second, Valentinus seems to have embarked on a

---

Originally published in *Doctor Communis* 4 (2020): 223–41.

1. For a modern English translation of the *Gospel of Truth* from the Nag Hammadi Library, see the text in Robert M. Grant, *Gnosticism and Early Christianity* (New York: Harper and Brothers, 1961).

2. On the theology of Valentinus, see G. C. Stead, *In Search of Valentinus*, in *The Rediscovery of Gnosticism*, 2 vols., ed. B. Layton (Leiden: Brill, 2018), 73–102, who argues that his thought is marked by dualistic Platonic roots. See also Mark J. Edwards, *Christians, Gnostics, and Philosophers in Late Antiquity* (Oxford: Routledge, 2012), chapters IX and X, who thinks that Valentinus held somewhat distinct views from other so-called Gnostics, but who nevertheless notes Valentinus' rejection of the material world as irremediably evil.

complex theory of social theodicy, explaining the origins of evil in the world from a pre-existent fall or rupture that took place in the dyadic structures of the divinity, a Godhead marked by complexity, and ironically (as Origen pointed out) something like material constitution, subject to political unity, then eventual rupture, followed by reconciliation, and reconstitution.[3]

A central point of Valentius's argument seems to be the idea that material existence mitigates against the plausibility of God's singular Incarnation in history. If life in the body leads to suffering and limitation of knowledge, then it is in no way fitting that God should take on a material existence. It is precisely this that we hope he might deliver us from. We find the idea posed in contemporary theology but wed to almost contrary associative points. For Valentinus, enlightenment occurs only for the Gnostics whose pre-history marks them out for election but does not occur in those persons characterized by more world-bound or animalistic attitudes encased in material existence. It is not a universal phenomenon. By contrast, a figure like John Hick wishes to dissociate the saving work of enlightenment from the particularity of the Incarnation precisely so as to emphasize the universality of salvation.[4] Any distinctively Christian salvation is too materially particular, and so we stand in need of a post-Christian religious universalism that is not overly determined by the material conditions of any one religious tradition. Here, material particularity is not evil but it does delimit the possibility of universal truth and revelation by framing the knowledge of God within the constraints

3. Irenaeus describes Valentius's theory of pre-existing dyads and criticizes it for its anthropomorphic materialism in *Against Heresies* I, c. 11, in *Ante-Nicene Fathers*, vol. 1, trans. A. Roberts, J. Donaldson, A. C. Coxe (Buffalo, NY; Christian Literature Publishing Co., 1885). See the study by Khaled Anatolios, "Faith, Reason, and Incarnation in Irenaeus of Lyons," *Nova et Vetera* (English edition) 16, no. 2 (2018): 543–60. Origin argues for the eternal immaterial procession of the Word from the Father as God from God, and for his eternal agency in creation in contradistinction to the concepts of divinity found in the Valentinian school, which imply composition of essence or distinction of substance. See *Commentary on the Gospel of St. John*, II, c. 8, Trans. A. Menzies, *Ante-Nicene Fathers*, vol. 9, Christian Literature Publishing Co., (Buffalo, NY: Christian Literature Publishing Co., 1896).

4. See John Hick, "Jesus and the World Religions," in *The Myth of God Incarnate*, ed. John Hick (Philadelphia: Westminster, 1977), 167–85.

of a given time and historical place. The diverse religious traditions provide distinct paths up the mountain to God (or the Absolute), so to speak, but none of them in their historical singularity can be said to be a fully adequate sign or indication of the presence of God in history.[5] Likewise, if Valentinus posits a theodicy in God as a means of engagement with the problem of evil, modern religious pluralistic theory posits a form of theodicy characterized by speculative agnosticism. That is to say, there is no one way to address the problem of suffering and evil, and in the face of the enigmas of being, all theoretical systems fail. No word of address is final, but rather each religious tradition provides ideas that are provisional and hypothetical. Karma, Purgatory, Final Judgment, Nirvana, Beatific Vision, Cycles of Rebirth, Resurrection: these eschatological notions are not interchangeable but are mutually convergent in some respects, even as they diverge in other ways, showing the provisionality of each.[6]

Both the older Gnosticism, with its more distinctive mistrust of the ontological goodness of a material incarnation, and the newer non-incarnational theologies of religious pluralism demonstrate a shared concern that the singular event of the Incarnation is something other than truly enlightening and universal in its scope of illumination. Aquinas is, in fact, quite sympathetic to these concerns for at least two reasons. First, because of his engagement as a Dominican with Albigensianism and its Manichaean sources, in view of which Aquinas frequently addresses Manichaean and Gnostic ideas of various sorts directly. Why is it fitting that God should take on a human nature, including a physical body? Second, he was aware of the philosophical ramifications of the claim that the most universal science of the divine is provided ultimately by means of revelation,

5. See for example John Hick, *God Has Many Names* (Philadelphia, PA: Westminster, 1992); R. Pannikar, *The Jordan, The Tiber, and The Ganges: Three Kairological Moments of Christic Self-Consciousness*, in *The Myth of Christian Uniqueness*, ed. J. Hick and P. Knitter (Maryknoll, NY: Orbis, 1987), 89–116.

6. See, for example, the eschatological argument to this effect in John Hick, *An Interpretation of Religion: Human Responses to the Transcendent* (New Haven, CT: Yale University Press, 1989), 362–77.

not metaphysics. The Incarnation, crucifixion, and resurrection of Christ are contingent events of history that provide universal knowledge of the first cause as Trinity. The knowledge is universal in the sense that the cause revealed (the Holy Trinity) is the first origin of all that is, and knowledge of this cause casts a light upon all that proceeds in creation from God. If this is true, then because God has become human, we can come to know who God is in himself as Trinity. But by a kind of epistemological corollary, this entails that philosophy as such cannot procure perfect knowledge of God as first cause and must be able to admit its limitations and even its intrinsic openness to divine revelation from within.[7] In what follows, I would like to explore briefly two related ideas. Why, according to St. Thomas, did God become human, and how does the hominization of God reveal the Trinity as the ultimate explanatory truth about reality?

MOTIVES OF THE INCARNATION

When Aquinas begins his treatment of the motives of the Incarnation in the Sentences commentary, he initially asks whether it is possible for God to become human and then asks whether it is fitting.[8] The answer to both questions is affirmative, but it is significant that the framing of the analysis in this order of questioning suggests that the Incarnation is intelligible according to an order of wisdom. God became human not simply because he could do so voluntaristically (as a sheer expression of omnipotence) but precisely for a fitting motive. Consequently, there is an intrinsic intelligibility to the divine motives that the Church can consider theologically and explain in a universal format.[9] What is wise is characterized by intelligence.

---

7. *ST* I, q. 1, a. 1; q. 12, a. 1. On Aquinas's eudaemonist arguments from within the philosophical order of reflection for the natural openness of man to revelation, see White, "Imperfect Happiness and the Final End of Man: Thomas Aquinas and the Paradigm of Nature-Grace Orthodoxy."

8. *In III Sent.* d. 1, aa. 1–2.

9. In art. 1, Aquinas argues that the Christian doctrine of the Incarnation implies no

In *ST* III, q. 1, a. 1, objections 2 and 3, Aquinas considers two Gnostic objections to the fittingness of the Incarnation. One stems from a consideration of the reality of the divine infinity and the finitude of human flesh. God cannot fittingly join what transcends creation infinitely to what is merely finite. The other objection is straightforward: God is sovereignly good, and the flesh is, by comparison to God, a principle of evil or privation of the good, so God cannot wisely take on human flesh. Aquinas responds to these objections by referring to the intelligibility of the divine goodness. It is proper to the good to be diffusive of self, to communicate, or to give of its goodness to others.[10] But God is infinite goodness. God

---

ontological contradiction or mode of impossibility and, therefore, could occur given that God is omnipotent. In art. 2, he stipulates that "man is among the most noble of creatures" but that by falling into sin, he has lost his orientation toward beatitude, and consequently it is fitting that God would unite himself to human nature so as to make satisfaction for human sin and reorient the human race toward authentic beatitude. In his commentary on the *ST* I, q. 1, Reginald Garrigou-Langrage asks if the very question of "whether the Incarnation is possible for God" is rationalistic in orientation since the premise of the question might imply that the philosopher as such can integrate the concept of the Incarnation into an argument of philosophical provenance. The context he has in mind is the First Vatican Council (*Dei Filius*) condemnation of so-called Catholic rationalism of the 19th century represented emblematically by thinkers like Jakob Froschammer. Reginald Garrigou-Lagrange, *Christ the Savior: A Commentary on the Third Part of St. Thomas' "Theological Summa,"* trans. B. Rose (London: Herder, 1957), 34–43. Nevertheless, there are at least two ways in which the early Aquinas, in treating the question of a possible incarnation, is not transgressing the line of needed distinction between the order of reason and the order of faith. First, it is clear that from within the logic of *In III Sent.* d. 1, a. 1, Aquinas is arguing from theological grounds that if the Incarnation occurs it occurs in a way that implies no contradiction since the union of two natures within the one hypostatic person of the Son does not imply any confusion of the natures. Second, his biblical appeal to omnipotence does leave open the conceivability philosophically speaking of God acting in any way he wishes that is wise and good (that is to say fitting) and that does not imply any contradiction. Meanwhile, it is true to say that philosophical understanding cannot elaborate an a priori definition of the Incarnation, even nominally, for apologetic purposes, if this definition is meant to signify truly what Christians denote as the mystery of God's homonization.

10. *ST* III, q. 1, a. 1: "it belongs to the essence of goodness to communicate itself to others, as is plain from Dionysius (*On Divine Names*, c. 4). Hence it belongs to the essence of the highest good to communicate itself in the highest manner to the creature." On this principle in Dionysius and Aquinas's interpretation of it more generally, see Fran O'Rourke, *Pseudo-Dionysius and the Metaphysics of Aquinas* (Notre Dame, IN: Notre Dame University Press, 2005), 215–76.

communicates the truth of who he is as Creator precisely through the medium of visible creatures. Therefore, despite his transcendent dignity, it is not unfitting for him to communicate his divine life to us by becoming human, which is the most perfect way for God to manifest himself within the visible world. Furthermore, it is an error to characterize material existence in terms of the pure privation of evil. God creates all things in wisdom and in view of his own goodness so that the physical world and temporal existence in the body are inherently good. It is true that there are natural evils or privations of punishment that afflict us and are quite serious, but these forms of suffering fall within the scope of God's justice and mercy, or they stem from divine permissions that are reflections of his divine goodness.[11] Such punishments originate in response to the evil of creaturely fault, but these faults themselves, voluntary moral defects in men and angels, stem not from God himself but from the creature withdrawing from the order of justice and mercy, that is to say from the goodness of God.[12]

Aquinas then proceeds to explore the intrinsic intelligibility of the divine goodness manifest in the Incarnation, in q. 1, art. 2. When discussing the core motives of the Incarnation, he creates two tables, as it were, of analysis, one pertaining to the advancement of

11. *ST* III, q. 1, a. 1, ad 3: "Every mode of being wherein any creature whatsoever differs from the Creator has been established by God's wisdom, and is ordained to God's goodness. For God, who is uncreated, immutable, and incorporeal, produced mutable and corporeal creatures for His own goodness. And so also the evil of punishment was established by God's justice for God's glory. But evil of fault is committed by withdrawing from the art of the Divine wisdom and from the order of the Divine goodness. And therefore it could be fitting to God to assume a nature created, mutable, corporeal, and subject to penalty, but it did not become Him to assume the evil of fault"

12. *ST* I-II, q. 79, a. 1: "Now God cannot be directly the cause of sin, either in Himself or in another, since every sin is a departure from the order which is to God as the end: whereas God inclines and turns all things to Himself as to their last end, as Dionysius states (*On Divine Names*, c. 1): so that it is impossible that He should be either to Himself or to another the cause of departing from the order which is to Himself. Therefore He cannot be directly the cause of sin. In like manner neither can He cause sin indirectly. For it happens that God does not give some the assistance, whereby they may avoid sin, which assistance were He to give, they would not sin. But He does all this according to the order of His wisdom and justice, since He Himself is Wisdom and Justice: so that if someone sin it is not imputable to Him as though He were the cause of that sin."

men in the good and the other to their withdrawal from evil. The advancement occurs through divinization and the withdrawal from evil through atonement so that these are the two core aims of the redemption. God became human in order that men might be united to God and also so that God as man might reconcile the human race to himself by making fitting *satisfactio* for the sins of the human race, reordering us toward God in justice. Here, indeed, we see emerge the theme of the Incarnation as a distinctive form of universal enlightenment. The first reason Aquinas gives for the fittingness of the Incarnation in the order of the advancement toward the good is related to knowledge. Divinization is characterized, first and foremost, by our union with the divine truth. Aquinas cites Augustine (*City of God*, XI, 2):

> In order that man might journey more trustfully toward the truth, the Truth itself, the Son of God, having assumed human nature, established and founded faith.

The Incarnation enlightens us by making knowledge of the absolute truth of God more secure and trustworthy within history, a point we will return to below. Similarly, Aquinas argues that the love of God is made manifest in a more intensive way in virtue of the Incarnation of God. We see in the Christ child a most concrete expression of the love of God for men. This is a theme that evidently can be developed in referring to the passion and resurrection of Christ in turn. If God has made himself subject to suffering and death for our sake, then it is manifest that God loves the human race universally. Finally, Aquinas notes that in the life of Christ, it is God himself who provides us with an eminently human example of instruction in how to live in the light of grace, in view of God.

In treating the second "table" of reasons, the withdrawal of man from evil, Aquinas also appeals to themes of illumination. God became human to liberate man from the power of evil and to atone for human sin.[13] Working from within this Anselmian line of reflection,

---

13. Aquinas is clearly working from within an Anselmian line of thought though with some nuances and alterations of the basic argument of *Cur Deus Homo*. See on this point,

St. Thomas notes that the Incarnation teaches fallen human beings their dignity because God deigned to become human, so human existence is especially meaningful and worthy of respect. The superstition of excessive worship of and reference to angels is dispelled as men realize that they are directly related to God by a man, Jesus Christ, and not through subjugation to heavenly powers. The Incarnation also teaches us humility because he who incomprehensibly transcends all creation took the initiative of condescension to live in solidarity with us who are the frailest of spiritual beings. Those who are truly greatest help those who are weaker. And the Incarnation shows forth the justice of God as he can reorder or justify the human race from within by way of atonement so that the frailty of Christ crucified becomes the venue or place of the manifestation of creative restoration and the making of all things new. From God's human life among us we learn what both divine and human righteousness truly are.

My argument up to this point has been that the Incarnation is illuminative for Aquinas, precisely due to the ways God's human life can illustrate the divine goodness and its effects, principally by effectuating our union with God and our withdrawal from evil. The Incarnation has a motive then that is universally intelligible and wise, and that turns our gaze toward the goodness of God. In what follows, I would like to concentrate on the hypostatic union as such and consider various ways that the hominization of God provides the deepest form of illumination available to men regarding the inner identity of God as Holy Trinity.

Anselm, *Cur Deus Homo* I, cc. 11–25; II, cc. 6–7, especially as interpreted by Aquinas, *ST* III, q. 48, aa. 1–4, *SCG* IV, c. 55. See on this point, the helpful analysis of Jean-Pierre Torrell, *Le Christ en ses Mystères: La vie et l'oeuvre de Jésus selon saint Thomas d'Aquin*, Tome II, (Paris: Desclée, 1999) 381–448, esp. 396–408.

ONTOLOGY OF THE
HYPOSTATIC UNION AS REVELATORY
OF THE HOLY TRINITY

The apostolic teaching of the New Testament asserts that the eternal Son of God, who is the eternal *Logos* and Image of the Father, has become human in time.[14] In 431 AD at the Council of Ephesus, the Church identified the core mystery of the hominization of the Son to consist in what Catholic theology traditionally terms the hypostatic union: the union of the human nature of Jesus with his divine nature in the very person of the eternal Son made man.[15] There is one concrete personal subject in Christ, who is the Word made flesh. When you touch the hand of Christ, you literally touch the hand of God because this man is indeed the Word and Son of God, subsisting in a human nature, having a true human body and soul.[16]

When Aquinas reflects on the hypostatic union, he notes that formally speaking it is only the Son who has become human, not the Father or the Holy Spirit. Nevertheless, this hominization of the Son as such reveals the Holy Trinity in various ways. Let us consider some of these in turn. First, we might think of the Trinitarian motives for the Incarnation of the Son as such. It is true that Aquinas

14. John 1:1–14; Heb. 1–2; Phil. 2:2–12; Col. 1: 15–20.

15. "We do not say, in fact, that the nature of the Word underwent a transformation and became flesh or that it was changed into a complete man composed of soul and body. Rather, we say that the Word, hypostatically uniting to himself the flesh animated by a rational soul, became man in an ineffable and incomprehensible manner [...]. For this reason [*the holy Fathers*] have not hesitated to speak of the holy Virgin as the Mother of God, not certainly because the nature of the Word of his divinity had the origin of its being from the holy Virgin, but because from her was generated his holy body, animated by a rational soul, a body hypostatically united to the Word; and thus it is said that [the Word] was begotten according to the flesh," *Denzinger*, nn. 250–51. On Cyril's Christology of the hypostatic union, which provides the foundations for the Ephesus definition, see J. McGluckin, *Cyril of Alexandria and the Christological Controversy* (Yonkers, NY: St. Vladimir's Press, 2010).

16. On the Cyrillian communication of idioms, which Aquinas takes up in his own Christology, see P. L. Gavrilyuk, *The Suffering of the Impassible God: The Dialectics of Patristic Thought*, (Oxford: Oxford University Press, 2004), 135–71 and *ST* III, q. 16.

asks in *ST* III, q. 3, a. 5, whether one of the other Trinitarian persons could have become human instead of the Son and answers affirmatively. This has been much misunderstood in the wake of Karl Rahner's claim that this kind of hypothetical counterfactual Thomistic theology fails to see the essentially filial character of the Incarnation and of the creation more generally.[17] However, Rahner initiates a critical misreading of Aquinas on this point. In fact, as with the questions on the Incarnation of the *Sentences*, here Aquinas is considering the non-necessity of the Incarnation of the Son (something else was possible) so as to show in q. 3, a. 8 why the Incarnation of the Son is deeply fitting for Trinitarian reasons.[18] Nor is the question of the possibility of the Incarnation of another person merely a logical thought experiment. It is precisely because the Son is God that he is one with the Father and the Spirit, who being identically God in essence, are equally omnipotently capable of being human. If the Son were not God, then his Incarnation would not unite us to God as such but only to a created intermediary.[19] But if he is God, then

---

17. Rahner, *The Trinity*. Rahner argues, in effect, that creation and man in particular are what occur when God wishes to express himself in his Word, "outside of God." That is to say, though creation and humanity are not strictly necessary for God, they are in a sense merely the ordinary manifestation of the Triune God who wishes to communicate his own life outside of himself to the creation in his Word. And consequently, humanity was created for the Incarnation and the Incarnation is simply a form of self-expression of the Logos of God in history. Otherwise stated, God's self-revelation and self-communication to us in history entails that the Word is made human, unveiling the reason for human existence. *The Trinity*, 32–33: "Human nature in general is a possible object of the creative knowledge and power of God, because and insofar as the Logos is by nature the one who is "utterable" (even into that which is not God); because he is the Father's Word, in which the Father can express himself, and, freely, empty himself into the non-divine; because, when this happens, that precisely is born which we call human nature. In other words, human nature is not a mask [...] assumed from without, from behind which the Logos hides to act things out in the world. From the start it is the constitutive real symbol of the Logos himself. So that we may and should say, when we think our ontology through to the end: man is possible because the exteriorization of the Logos is possible."

18. See the helpful discussion of this issue in Rahner's thought by Legge in *The Trinitarian Christology of Thomas Aquinas*, 3, 123–28.

19. This is a thematic soteriological argument of Athanasius in *On the Incarnation*, cc. 3–10, seemingly applicable subsequently in response to Arian Christology. *Nicene and*

he is one with the other two persons who, as God, do have the power to become incarnate just because they also have the power to will the Incarnation of the Son. Otherwise stated, unless the Son is truly one in being (consubstantial) with the Father and the Spirit who precisely as God must have the power to incarnate, then he cannot truly be he who is both God and man, and so he cannot really unite divinity and humanity in his person.[20] Nor could the Father send the Son into the world unless the Father were God and therefore had the power to incarnate (or to will effectively the Incarnation of the Son).

Post-Nicene Fathers, vol. 4, ed. A. Richardson and C. Scribner, trans. J. H. Newman (New York: Christian Literature Publishing, 1903). Aquinas takes this argument up in the *SCG* IV, c. 54, para. 2: "The Incarnation of God was the most efficacious assistance to man in his striving for beatitude. For we have shown in Book III that the perfect beatitude of man consists in the immediate vision of God. It might, of course, appear to some that man would never have the ability to achieve this state: that the human intellect be united immediately to the divine essence itself as an intellect is to its intelligible; for there is an unmeasured distance between the natures, and thus, in the search for beatitude, a man would grow cold, held back by very desperation. But the fact that God was willing to unite human nature to Himself personally points out to men with greatest clarity that man can be united to God by intellect, and see Him immediately. It was, then, most suitable for God to assume human nature to stir up man's hope for beatitude. Hence, after the Incarnation of Christ, men began the more to aspire after heavenly beatitude; as He Himself says: "I have come that they may have life and may have it more abundantly" (John 10:10)."

20. Rahner's argument would seem strongest if it depends upon a Scotistic and Teilhardian inspired form of argumentation: God could have chosen not to create but if he does create, he will do so in view of creatures who are spiritual animals in whom he can become present by incarnation so as to bring the universe to its ontologically evolutionary omega point. However, it does also seem as if Rahner is making a stronger claim, not merely that the incarnation of the Son is the teleological end of any fitting creation, but that God can only express himself externally if he does so in the incarnation of the Word made flesh. This latter claim is somewhat ambiguous and unclear in scope, but it can be hardened (somewhat artificially) into the claim that God can only express his Trinitarian identity by self-exteriorizing in the gift of creation and the historical incarnation of the Son. Read in this way: the economic Trinity really is the immanent Trinity in the strong sense of the identification: God only is himself through the dynamic self-communication process that entails the Incarnation. Rahner does not develop his thinking to this point expressly, but many who voiced similar ideas in the 20th century did. Rahner's articulation of the *Grundaxiom* in *The Trinity* seems deeply and directly inspired by the arguments of Karl Barth in *Church Dogmatics* I:1, in this regard, and by the time he composed *CD* II:2, Barth was clearly leaning in the direction of a historical identity of the Trinity constituted through the inner Trinitarian event of the election of man in Christ. See *CD* I:1, section 8, esp. 306–33, and *CD* II:2, sections 32–33, esp. 99–102.

Aquinas gives three reasons of fittingness for the Incarnation of the Son as such.[21] One is Trinitarian: God the Father creates all things through his eternal Word and Wisdom, who is, as it were, the eternal pre-existent model and exemplar of all created being. So, it is fitting that the world should be recreated through the medium of the humanity of the Word made flesh so that the works of creation and redemption manifest a harmonious expression of the Trinitarian wisdom of God at work in all things.[22] Two other reasons are given on the side of human illumination. God illumines us in our minds through the Word of God and predestines us to become sons of God by grace in conformity with the transcendent model of the Son. It is fitting then that the eternal Word should enlighten us and act so as to accomplish our predestination to filial adoption in and through a human life among us.[23]

So far, we have considered very briefly the formal mystery of the Son made man as such: the Trinitarian implications of the filial mode of the Incarnation. However, we might also think in turn about

21. *ST* III, q. 3, a. 8.

22. *ST* III, q. 3, a. 8: "Now the Person of the Son, Who is the Word of God, has a certain common agreement with all creatures, because the word of the craftsman, i.e. his concept, is an exemplar likeness of whatever is made by him. Hence the Word of God, Who is His eternal concept, is the exemplar likeness of all creatures. And therefore as creatures are established in their proper species, though movably, by the participation of this likeness, so by the non-participated and personal union of the Word with a creature, it was fitting that the creature should be restored in order to its eternal and unchangeable perfection [...]. Moreover, He has a particular agreement with human nature, since the Word is a concept of the eternal Wisdom, from Whom all man's wisdom is derived. And hence man is perfected in wisdom (which is his proper perfection, as he is rational) by participating the Word of God, as the disciple is instructed by receiving the word of his master [...]. And hence for the consummate perfection of man it was fitting that the very Word of God should be personally united to human nature." On the Trinitarian character of creation in Aquinas more generally, see Emery, *The Trinitarian Theology of St. Thomas Aquinas*, 195–200, 338–59.

23. *ST* III, q. 2, a. 8: "it was fitting that by Him Who is the natural Son, men should share this likeness of sonship by adoption, as the Apostle says in the same chapter (Rom. 8:29): "For whom He foreknew, He also predestinated to be made conformable to the image of His Son." [...] [T]he first man sinned by seeking knowledge, as is plain from the words of the serpent, promising to man the knowledge of good and evil. Hence it was fitting that by the Word of true knowledge man might be led back to God, having wandered from God through an inordinate thirst for knowledge."

the Trinitarian origins of the Incarnation and its Trinitarian effects. With regard to the first topic, Aquinas notes that the Incarnation is a work of the whole Trinity.[24] We see this in the Annunciation scene in Luke 1:26–38, at least arguably in an implicit manner, since the one who is announced as the child of the Virgin is the Son of the Most High (implying paternity in the Godhead) and his Incarnation takes place when the Holy Spirit overshadows Mary. In fact, the idea that the three persons are equally the co-simultaneous or, more properly speaking, the eternal authors of the one event of the Incarnation follows logically from the Cappadocian axiom that all works of the Holy Trinity *ad extra* ("outside" of God) are works of all three persons.[25] Gregory of Nazianzus argued against the Neo-Arian theologians that if the Son and Spirit partake truly and consubstantially in the power of the unoriginate Father then all that the Father does occurs through the begotten Son and the spirated Spirit. There is nothing that the Father does in creation or salvation that is not done also by the Son and the Spirit precisely because they are each the one God.[26] But by the same measure, this also means that all works of the Holy Trinity *ad extra* reveal Trinitarian action as personal action, action of the one God engaged in by the three persons co-eternally in ways that manifest their real personal distinction in unity.[27] It is the Father who

24. *ST* III, q. 3, a. 2. Aquinas notes that the Incarnation is a work of the divine nature that has for its term the personal assumption of human nature by the Son. Consequently, it is a work of the Father, Son and Spirit in its divine origination.

25. Consider the brief but forceful statement of Gregory of Nyssa in *Not Three Gods* (*Letter to Ablabius*): "But in the case of the Divine nature we do not similarly learn that the Father does anything by Himself in which the Son does not work conjointly, or again that the Son has any special operation apart from the Holy Spirit; but every operation which extends from God to the Creation, and is named according to our variable conceptions of it, has its origin from the Father, and proceeds through the Son, and is perfected in the Holy Spirit. For this reason the name derived from the operation is not divided with regard to the number of those who fulfill it, because the action of each concerning anything is not separate and peculiar, but whatever comes to pass, in reference either to the acts of His providence for us, or to the government and constitution of the universe, comes to pass by the action of the Three, yet what does come to pass is not three things" (In *Nicene and Post-Nicene Fathers*).

26. Gregory of Nazianzus, *Oration* 30, cc. 9–11, 20 and *Oration* 31, cc. 10 and 26.

27. See the sustained argument to this effect based in the theology of Aquinas by Emery, "The Personal Mode of Trinitarian Action in Saint Thomas Aquinas."

sends the Son into the world in the visible mission of the Incarnation, but it is also the Son who wills freely as God to enter the world as man in the womb of the Virgin, as one sent by the Father. Likewise, it is the Spirit who wills the Son to become incarnate and who freely wills to be sent from the Father and the Son into the world as the Spirit of Jesus.[28] The visible missions of the Son and Spirit are manifestations of the distinct persons but are also works of the Holy Trinity acting in unity.[29] There is no opposition between these two ideas. It is absurd to say that either the three persons act in their personal singularity or that only the one God acts who is the Holy Trinity. On the contrary, the two ideas logically imply one another since God is three distinct persons who are one in being and essence, as well as one in will. What the persons of the Trinity do, they do always ever as distinct persons and they do always ever as the one God. To speak of the Incarnation of the Son in the terms of a coherent Trinitarian monotheism, then, is to speak of the Incarnation of the Son as a revelation of the Father and the Spirit, even as it is the Son alone who is made man.

The Trinitarian revelation of the Sonship of Christ has its most extensive implications, however, when we think about the operations of Christ as operations of the God-human.[30] Only the Son is human, and so only the Son acts in all his human life by operations that are both human and divine, so-called theandric actions.[31] The Father and the Spirit do not act in a distinctively human way; only the Word made flesh does so. But precisely because the Word is in the Father and the Spirit is in the Word, the operations that the Word made man performs as God he performs only ever with Father

---

28. See on this point *ST* I, q. 43, aa. 1, 3, 8.

29. See *ST* I, q. 42, aa. 2 and 6.

30. See the thematic exploration by Legge in *The Trinitarian Christology of Thomas Aquinas*.

31. See Aquinas's basic account of theandric action in *ST* I, q. 19, a. 1, where he alludes to the Dionysian source of his thinking in ad 1. See on this matter A. Hofer, "Dionysian Elements in Thomas Aquinas's Christology: A Case of the Authority and Ambiguity of Pseudo-Dionysius," *The Thomist* 72, no. 3 (2008): 409–42. Aquinas is also clearly influenced by John Damascene in *The Orthodox Faith*, III, cc. 3, 6, 9, 11, 18.

and the Holy Spirit.[32] In fact, as Aquinas notes rightly, the person of the Son incarnate is more closely united ontologically to the Father and the Holy Spirit than his human nature is to his divine nature, even though the human nature of Christ is truly united to his divine nature in his unique filial person.[33] The reason for this is simply that the unity that pertains to the Father, Son, and Holy Spirit is uncreated and exists due to the shared divine life and essence of the three, in its eternal immutable simplicity, while the union of the human and divine natures in Christ is an ontological *novum*, something that comes to be in history.[34] The new beginning of the Incarnation does not pertain to the divine essence as such, as if God had to be human in order to be or to become God.[35]

32. I have explored this idea further in White, "Dyotheletism and the Instrumental Human Consciousness of Jesus."

33. See *ST* III, q. 2, a. 9, ad 3, one of the rare occasions where Aquinas openly takes issue with Augustine, precisely on this point: "the human nature is not more in the Son of God than the Son of God in the Father, but much less. But the man in some respects is more in the Son than the Son in the Father—namely, inasmuch as the same suppositum is signified when I say 'man,' meaning Christ, and when I say 'Son of God'; whereas it is not the same suppositum of Father and Son." Aquinas points out that the union or unity of the divine essence shared by the Son and Father is eternal and of a higher perfection than the union of the humanity of Christ with his divine person, which is more perfect than any other created union, but which is not characterized by the same dignity and perfection as the divine essence itself.

34. *ST* III, q. 2, a. 7. There are implications to this idea that might affect the interpretation of the dereliction theology of Hans Urs von Balthasar, who posits that the moral separation of the Son from the Father in the descent into hell on Good Friday and Holy Saturday is emblematic or reflective of a pre-existent eternal diremption (separation) and self-emptying of the Father toward the Son and the Son toward the Father, as the expression of Trinitarian love. If in fact the unity of the divine essence is the more fundamental ground of the union of the human nature of Christ with his divine person (because the person as Son is one in being with the Father eternally prior to being truly human and existing as a subject of history) then it seems problematic to posit a diremption in God as a condition of possibility for the manifestation of the Trinity in the incarnate life of the Son. In fact, the contrary would seem to obtain. Because the Son and Father are perfectly one in being and in freedom, they are also "incapable" of being subject to the imperfection of ontological sundering in any meaningful sense of the term, but just because this is the case, there cannot take place in the Cross event any descent into absolute separation or alienation of the Son from the Father. The Cross is a revelation of the Trinity because of the underlying ground of unity.

35. Evidently here Aquinas differs notably from theologians like Robert Jenson and

The operations of Christ then not only reveal the operative activity of the Father and the Spirit but the order of the persons in their mutual relations and life. The Incarnate Word acts with the Father but also always from the Father, as his begotten Son. The Son works with the Spirit but also always in the Spirit. The Spirit proceeds from the Son as God, and the Spirit rests upon the Son as man and operates directly in him by inspiring his human actions.[36] Therefore, the operative life of the Trinity is manifest in and through the human actions and words of Jesus. When Jesus heals, it is the Father who heals through his Son and in his Spirit. When Jesus teaches divine truth, it is the Son of the Father who reveals the truth of the Father, with and from the Father, and who also teaches in the Spirit of his Father and who in doing so reveals the Spirit who proceeds from himself, the Spirit of truth.

From what we have considered above, we might conclude with three notions taken from Aquinas, regarding the revelation of the Trinity in the flesh of Christ. First, the union of God with human nature is indicative of who God is in his goodness and wisdom in a distinctive way unlike any other effect of God of nature or grace and consequently serves as a principle of universal enlightenment like nothing else in human history. Secondly, the flesh of Christ is important to this mystery. God unites himself to a soul and a body that are one natural human individual: this man here. Consequently, it is only if the body of Christ, his very flesh, is the flesh of God, that this man here can truly reveal in what he is individually (a human being), the very person of the Word. Otherwise said, only if the Word subsists in a truly human way can he reveal his very identity as the eternal Son in his human actions and gestures of human physicality as well as in his simple subsistence as an embodied human being. But if this is the case, then the flesh of the Lord not only reveals his

Eberhard Jüngel who posit a historicized divine life in God as a condition of possibility for the events of the Incarnation and passion of Christ. Historical flesh can truly become transparent to the eternal, for Aquinas, but is not identified with the divine life and essence of God. It pertains to the human nature of God.

36. See on this point, Legge, *The Trinitarian Christology of Thomas Aquinas*, 187–210.

person as the Son but also necessarily reveals his relation to the Father and the Spirit even in his very being as man as corporeal, since in so being he is ontologically always from the Father and with the Father "for" the spiration of the Spirit, even in his very flesh. This follows from the fact that the person of the Son is always related to the Father and the Spirit, even when he is human, and in all that he is as human. Therefore, all the actions and sufferings of Christ in the flesh have a mysterious Trinitarian dimension as the deepest truth about them, in what they themselves are, even in the physical body of Jesus and his gestures. Thirdly, the soul of Christ, which is the principle from which his human operations of knowledge and love emerge, is the embodied soul of the second person of the Trinity. Consequently, all that Christ does and accepts to undergo freely as man, he does in concert with his divine wisdom and agency and, therefore, in direct union with the Father and the Spirit. The human intelligence and decision making of the Son (operations of his spiritual soul) are indicative of the uncreated wisdom and loving will of the Holy Trinity. If these three points are true, then the human nature of Christ is an especially fitting instrument for the revelation of God the Holy Trinity. Far from being an obstacle to knowing God, the human nature of Christ is the uniquely privileged vehicle in all of human history for the manifestation of God's identity as Trinity.

THE TRUTH OF THE TRINITY IN THE FLESH OF CHRIST: RESPONSE TO OBJECTIONS

We noted above that two modern objections commonly circulate that echo in various ways the ideas of Valentinus, albeit with strong distinctive differences as well. One was the objection of John Hick that a concrete singular incarnation of God in history delimits unjustly and arbitrarily the scope of salvation for all persons and the possibility of a universal knowledge of God available in various forms and ways through distinct religious traditions. The second objection was taken from theodicy: the human life we live of suffering and death is sufficiently obscure that no one religious tradition can claim to give final meaning or explanation to the mystery of human suffering, and instead, the various traditions offer partially incompatible but partially convergent accounts of the final end of man and the eschatological resolution of the cosmos.

To the first point, we may say the following. The human being learns through immediate sensory contact with singular entities and abstracts universal concepts from them.[37] It is true to say, then, that universal knowledge takes place through abstraction from singular instances. However, each human person we relate to by knowledge and love is a singular entity encountered in the flesh and this is true as well of ourselves to all others: we are each a singular embodied instantiation of human nature, unique and like no other in our distinctive subsistence as persons. Friendships, for example, are instances of singular encounters or relationships of one person to another and characterized by the mutual virtuous affection and love of the singular persons in question. But what can be said of one person here is true of each human person and therefore true "universally": all human beings flourish concretely through relationships to other persons in their singularity, even as they also are all able to think abstractly in universal form. If the visible universe is, in a sense, crowned by human personhood as the most noble, spiritual, and complex entity in the visible world, and if human persons seek to come to know the unknown God who is the universal author of all of reality through the medium of our embodied experience of singular existents, then nothing could be more fitting for our knowledge of God than that he should take on a singular individual human nature so as to reveal who he is personally (in his divine personhood and identity) precisely in human flesh. This would entail that we could come to know God personally as we normally know one

37. See the arguments of Aristotle, *De Anima*, III, 5; Aquinas, *In III De Anima*, lec. 10; *Quaest. Disp. De Anima*, q. 4; SCG II, cc. 76–78.

another, as individual embodied subjects in time and place, in the flesh, in word, gesture, and touch. To hear God speak humanly to us, to watch the physical gestures of God, to touch the bleeding hands of God: there is nothing more dignified or noble or beautiful if this reality has truly come to pass.[38]

Secondly, regarding theodicy, we may, in a sense, concede the objector's central observation, at least under an aspect. The history of human wisdom traditions and religious practices and more ornate theoretical developments does concern itself, among other things, with responses to human suffering, death, and theodicy, as well as eschatology or narratives of cosmic resolution.[39] This rich patrimony, far from being disdained, should stand as a testimony to the natural human aspiration to understand our human condition in light of the absolute, whether this is an impersonal metaphysical ground of being, the gods, or the one and saving God. It also serves as a testimony to the human being's confusion, rightly recognized by Valentinus. We are beings who stand in need of illumination. What is tragic about modern religious agnosticism is the thought that the truth about the absolute is something we must either procure ourselves or

38. Such arguments seek to provide an alternative vision to that of Gotthold Lessing, who argues that "truths of history can never become the proof of necessary proofs of reason," and thus consequently a historically contingent incarnation of God can provide no warrant for universal truth that must obtain for all men. See *On the Proof of the Spirit and of Power*, in *Lessing's Theological Writings*, 53–54. This objection suggests that if God has become a subject of human history, he has done so in an "arbitrarily" concrete place and time, and not all places and times. Therefore, there is no universal criterion of empirical verification by which to approach the truth of his incarnation. The calling of Abraham in Aquinas (*ST* I-II, q. 98, a. 4) is seen as historically arbitrary in one sense, since it is an expression of divine gratuity, and gives us universal insight into the divine favor by that very measure. Lessing says in effect, "I cannot now know or experience the incarnate Christ as a binding universal truth." To this we might respond: "we are all individuals existing in contingency and this is a deep universal truth about us, that God himself assumed. We can know that this is the case only supernaturally but if it is the case, then it is also deeply meaningful existentially." Indeed, we also can know him now *supernaturally* even in his *physical singularity* by way of the Eucharistic species.

39. For a constructive example of this kind of inter-religious comparative work, in dialogue with Catholic theology, see, for instance, Carol Zaleski, *Life of the World to Come: Near-Death Experience and Christian Hope* (Oxford: Oxford University Press, 1996).

that cannot be procured since all appeals to revelation are in some way ruled out from the beginning. The first idea is presumptuous, while the second is despairing. The two attitudes typically coexist and self-reinforce. But it is more reasonable to conclude from a respectful consideration of the history of religions that we cannot provide a comprehensive explanation of the divine for ourselves and that it is precisely for this reason that we do stand in need of a determinate revelation, as the First Vatican Council rightly stated in response to the conundrums of Enlightenment skepticism. Only God can illumine us as to how to live through suffering and what its resolution might really entail. If God has done this in the Incarnation, however, then he has done so not only by taking human flesh, but by suffering in it as well, and by glorifying his own human soul and body in the resurrection, giving us an entry point from which to understand our own eschatological horizon. Final judgment, purgatory, heaven and hell: these mysteries point us toward a Trinitarian resolution of the cosmos, in which all human beings, in ways known to God, are invited into the communion of Trinitarian life.[40] The acknowledgment of this revelation constitutes a liberation for human reason, not a delimitation. In the end, we may conclude: the flesh of Christ is the flesh of the Son of God, the bodily flesh of the one who suffered and died and is raised from the dead. In this state of glorified life, he can reveal the Father and the Holy Spirit now and forever, drawing us toward a resolution of our human condition in mystery and enigma but also in bedrock truth. Salvation comes from the flesh of the Lord. It is that flesh that shines resplendent before all men, in the crib, on the cross, and in the life to come.

---

40. Consider in this respect the Second Vatican Council, *Gaudium et spes* (hereinafter *GS*), §22, as interpreted subsequently by John Paul II, *Redemptor hominis*, for example, in section 18.

10

Why Catholic Theology Needs Metaphysics

A Christological Perspective

INTRODUCTION

The communication of idioms pertains to the language we use in classical Catholic theology to speak about the Incarnation of God, just insofar as God the Son, the eternal Word of the Father, has become human, one hypostatic subject subsisting in two natures. Linguistic tropes (idioms) assigned to Jesus of Nazareth either in virtue of his humanity—his nature as man—or in virtue of his divinity—his nature as God—are attributed hypostatically only to one personal subject, that of the eternal Son and Word of the Father. So, for example, we say rightly that the Son of God personally suffered, died, and was buried, in virtue of his human nature in which he was subject to these experiences, or more simply that God died by Roman crucifixion, here employing the nature-term "God" (*a subject* who has a divine nature) to denote the person of the Word who died a human death. Likewise, we may say that the human being Jesus can raise the dead in virtue of his omnipotent power or that this man, in particular, is the author of the stars. The man in question

Originally published in *Teologia w Polsce* 13, no. 2 (2019): 41–62.

is the person of the Son and, therefore, we rightly attribute to him the divine characteristics that are proper to the God of Israel, whom the Nicene creed denotes as one in being with the Father and as the Creator "of all things visible and invisible."[41]

In this chapter, I wish to consider the ontological dimensions of this form of linguistic designation of the mystery of the Incarnation, and, more specifically, to delineate various metaphysical implications of classical Christology. Can we speak truly of Christ the person of the Son as both true God and true man if we are incapable of positive philosophical and natural discourse concerning both the divine nature and human nature, that latter being the essence in virtue of which we are each human, and in virtue of which God who became human is one in nature with us? In what follows, I will present a brief account of the inward form of the classical use of the communication of idioms in Neo-Chalcedonian Christology. Secondly, I will argue that the assignments we make of nature terms to Christ in virtue of his divinity and humanity respectively though based in divine revelation specifically and associated with a central mystery of the faith, also require implicitly that we are naturally capable of thinking out philosophically what it means coherently to speak of the divine and human natures metaphysically. Were we unable to do this, we would, in turn, be unable to think about the hypostatic union and the core mystery of Christianity in a constructive fashion. In a final section of the chapter, I will consider some of the consequences of the distinctively Catholic view of the Incarnation I am defending in relation to metaphysics and consequently as an exemplification of the relationship between supernatural faith and natural knowledge, theology and philosophy, within the one cultural life of the Church.[42] I will argue that the intellectual heri-

41. Denzinger 125.

42. For the purposes of this chapter, I am employing the term "metaphysics" to refer to the study of being, in classical philosophy and in the Catholic intellectual tradition. Employed in this sense the term has a slightly narrower sense than "ontology" which can refer to the being of things themselves, whether or not it is apprehended and discussed philosophically and theologically. I also presume that philosophical metaphysics may

tage of divine-human synergy that fully acknowledges the ineffable transcendence and unique immanence of the Creator to creation in the Incarnation has a philosophical correspondent in the tradition of Catholic perennial philosophy and that these two together form the singular heritage of the Christian intellectual tradition, one that is essential to the health of the Church and human culture.

THE BASIC VIEW: CHALCEDONIAN CHRISTOLOGY AND THE ONTOLOGY OF THE COMMUNICATION OF IDIOMS

Single-subject Christology is derived from and enshrined in the basic givens of the New Testament as apostolic teaching. Christ is one person subsisting in two natural modes of being. A case in point is to be found in Phil. 2:6–11, where the pre-existence of Christ is affirmed as the Son who, "though he was in the form of God," "took the form of a servant," and as man became obedient unto death, even so as to be exalted in the resurrection. The mystery of the descent of the pre-existent Son into humanity and subsequent exaltation in resurrection culminates in the acknowledgement by the nations of his divine identity. He is given the name above every other name by the nations—"Lord" or "Yahweh"—who recognize in him the God of Israel denoted by the Tetragrammaton of Ex. 3:14–15. The fact that "every knee will bend" in adoration of him suggests that the prophecies of Is. 45:5–23, concerning the universal recognition of God by all gentile nations, is coming to pass in the recognition of Jesus of Nazareth as Lord, that is to say, as one who is both God and man, a man who was crucified and resurrected so as to reconcile the human race to the Father.[43]

---

and should be employed within and in the service of theology (*sacra doctrina*) in the service of the conceptual depictions of mysteries of the faith, as I shall mention below. I take this conceptual use of the term metaphysics to overlap significantly with the depiction of the term present in the papal encyclical *Fides et ratio* (1998) of Pope John Paul II.

43. See the pertinent analysis of the text on this point by Richard Bauckham, *God Crucified: Monotheism and Christology in the New Testament* (Grand Rapids, MI:

Evidently, already in this primal confession of Christological faith we perceive the nucleus of the classical use of the communication of idioms as expressive in turn of the ontology of what would eventually be confessed in dogmatic conceptual form 400 years later at the Council of Chalcedon. Christ is a singular subject of Pauline ascription to whom are attributed characteristics associated both with God (signified here by the "form" of God, the name of YHWH, and being a subject of worship) and those of a human being (signified here by being the Suffering Servant, practicing intentional obedience, subjection to death as the separation of body and soul, physical resurrection and glorification). There is, of course, a correspondence between this linguistic pattern of ascription and the ontology it implies. Only if Christ is a single person who is both God and man can formulations such as this one make sense. The person in question is pre-existent and divine in the Pauline logic since "he" exists in union with the Father prior to his historical experience of being human, but the person in question is also the singular bearer of traits derived from each nature or "form" of being, as Lord and as man.

It is significant to note that the Council of Chalcedon specifically chose to denote and interpret the "forms" of Paul's Philippians 2:6–11 in distinctively ontological terms of nature or *physis*, having echoes in Hellenistic metaphysics.[44] The impetus for this, historically speaking, is not simple and can be traced back in part to the influences of Athanasius, Gregory of Nazianzus's critique of Apollinarius, and the "letter of peace" written by John of Antioch in the wake of the Council of Ephesus. Nonetheless, the proximate inspiration for

---

Eerdmans, 1998), 44–54. Bauckham does not seek to derive a primal theology of the two natures of Christ from this text (an interpretative claim found in the patristic tradition but contested by many modern exegetes). However, he does argue convincingly that the Hebraic logic of the passage, which echoes the theology of Second Isaiah, co-simultaneously attributes to Jesus as a subject both the Lordship of the God of Israel and the human traits of the suffering servant.

44. Denzinger. 300: "... and it [i.e., the doctrine of the Church] resists those who imagine that there is mingling or admixture in the two natures of Christ and drives off those who foolishly believe that the 'form of a slave' taken by him from us is of heavenly or some other nature and it anathematizes those who invent the myth of two natures of the Lord before the union but imagine there was only one after the union."

the pronounced emergence of this pattern of interpretation was the famous Tome of Leo, his letter 28 to Flavian. Therein Leo does two things theologically that are of capital importance for the subsequent history of Christology. First, he interprets the "form of God" and the "form of a servant" in terms of the Latin notion of *natura* (or *essentia*) and, in so doing, also notes that the two natures are neither separate nor confused, but are united and distinct.[45] This language is clearly ontological in implication and would enter into the Council's formulations themselves, suggesting that God has become human without ceasing to be God and without abolishing, altering or, in any way, doing violence to what it is to be human.[46] On the contrary, God is the

---

45. Tome of Leo (letter 28 to Flavian), c. 3: "Without detriment therefore to the properties of either nature and substance which then came together in one person , majesty took on humility, strength weakness, eternity mortality: and for the paying off of the debt belonging to our condition inviolable nature was united with passible nature, so that, as suited the needs of our case , one and the same Mediator between God and men, the Man Christ Jesus, could both die with the one and not die with the other. Thus in the whole and perfect nature of true man was true God born, complete in what was His own, complete in what was ours. And by ours we mean what the Creator formed in us from the beginning and what He undertook to repair ... He took the form of a slave without stain of sin, increasing the human and not diminishing the divine: because that emptying of Himself whereby the Invisible made Himself visible, and Creator and Lord of all things though He be, wished to be a mortal, was the bending down of pity, not the failing of power. Accordingly He who while remaining in the form of God made man, was also made man in the form of a slave. For both natures retain their own proper character without loss: and as the form of God did not do away with the form of a slave, so the form of a slave did not impair the form of God."

c. 4: "In a new order, because being invisible in His own *nature*, He became visible in ours, and He whom nothing could contain was content to be contained: abiding before all time He began to be in time: the Lord of all things, He obscured His immeasurable majesty and took on Him the *form of a servant*: being God that cannot suffer, He did not disdain to be man that can, and, immortal as He is, to subject Himself to the laws of death. From the mother of the Lord was received *nature*, not faultiness: nor in the Lord Jesus Christ, born of the Virgin's womb, does the wonderfulness of His birth make His nature unlike ours. For He who is true God is also true man: and in this union there is no lie, since the humility of manhood and the loftiness of the Godhead both meet there." [Trans. C. L. Feltoe; Ed. P. Schaff and H. Wace, *Nicene and Post-Nicene Fathers*, vol. 12 (Buffalo, NY: Christian Literature Publishing Co., 1895).]

46. Council of Chalcedon, Denzinger 302: "We confess that the one and the same Lord Jesus Christ, the only begotten Son, must be acknowledged in two natures (*en duo phusesin*), without confusion or change, without division or separation. The distinction between the natures was never abolished by their union but rather the character proper

most human of all of us. This idea suggests that there is not only no concurrence or rivalry of divine and human natures in Christ but, in fact, a kind of simultaneous plenitude of complementarity, of immanence and transcendence simultaneously. The more God is present in our human nature, even by personal union with our nature, the more naturally human we are, as is perceptible in Christ.

Second, Leo attributes activity to both natures, suggesting that each has its own integrity of operation.

> "For each "form" does the acts which belong to it, in communion with the other; the Word, that is, performing what belongs to the Word, and the flesh carrying out what belongs to the flesh; the one of these shines out in miracles, the other succumbs to injuries."[47]

As we know, this was to be the most controversial aspect of the letter. Although it was itself incorporated into the acts of the council, there would be subsequent contestation of its contents precisely on this point. In the sixth century, Severus of Antioch argued that the Tome's formulations were Nestorian precisely because they denote that there are natures that operate as grammatical subjects and, therefore, as distinct natural individuals or personal subjects.[48] This line of thinking became common in monophysitism and monoenergism and would be condemned by the formal precisions of the Third Council of Constantinople, where the teachings of Maximus the Confessor were, in effect, made normative.[49] There, we see that

---

to each of the two natures was preserved as they came together in one Person and one hypostasis."

47. Leo the Great, Letter 28, c. 4.

48. See Severus Ant., *Ep. I ad Sergium,* CSCO 120, 60, 33–61, 9, esp. in Aloys Grillmeier, *Christ in Christian Tradition,* vol. 2, pt. 2 (London: Mowbray; Louisville: Westminster John Knox, 1995), 165. I have discussed this point in greater depth in "Dyotheletism and the Instrumental Human Consciousness of Jesus."

49. Referring back to Leo's Tome as a traditional *auctoritas,* the council affirms "two natural principles of action in the same Jesus Christ," and cites in this respect Leo's statement from the Tome in Greek so as to make clear that "each form does (*morphe energeï*)" that which is proper to it, in concord with the other. In addition, the document goes on to state that "each of the two natures wills and performs what is proper to it in communion with the other. Thus, we glory in proclaiming two natural wills and actions concurring together for the salvation of the human race." Denzinger 553, 558.

the distinct natural operations of God and man, of the God-man, work in distinction and symphony, with instrumental subordination of the human actions to the divine operation.

From this settlement of orthodox Christology, a mature Christian vision of the communication of idioms developed. It is one we find present in Damascene's *The Orthodox Faith*, for example, a work translated into Latin in the Middle Ages.[50] The perspective of Damascene was, in turn, self-consciously adopted and re-articulated by Thomas Aquinas in the *Summa Theologiae, Tertia pars*. Aquinas effectively notes four rules that govern the right application of the communication of idioms, each of which has an ontological correspondent, with significance for our consideration of philosophical metaphysics.[51]

50. See in particular *The Orthodox Faith* III, cc. 4–19. See *ST* III, c. 16 on the communication of idioms, and q. 19, a. 1 in his critique of Severus and his defense of dyotheletism. Damascene provides a clear analysis of the traditional use of the communication of idioms in *The Orthodox Faith*, III, c. 4. "When, then, we speak of His divinity we do not ascribe to it the properties of humanity. For we do not say that His divinity is subject to passion or created. Nor, again, do we predicate of His flesh or of His humanity the properties of divinity: for we do not say that His flesh or His humanity is uncreated. But when we speak of His subsistence, whether we give it a name implying both natures, or one that refers to only one of them, we still attribute to it the properties of both natures. For Christ, which name implies both natures, is spoken of as at once God and man, created and uncreated, subject to suffering and incapable of suffering: and when He is named Son of God and God, in reference to only one of His natures, He still keeps the properties of the co-existing nature, that is, the flesh, being spoken of as God who suffers, and as the Lord of Glory crucified [1 Corinthians 2:8], not in respect of His being God but in respect of His being at the same time man. Likewise also when He is called Man and Son of Man, He still keeps the properties and glories of the divine nature, a child before the ages, and man who knew no beginning; it is not, however, as child or man but as God that He is before the ages, and became a child in the end [of the ages]. And this is the manner of the mutual communication [of idioms]. . . . Accordingly we can say of Christ: 'This our God was seen upon the earth and lived among men,' and 'This man is uncreated and . . . uncircumscribed [i.e., in virtue of his divinity].'"

51. See the study of Aquinas's use of Damascene on this point by Corey L. Barnes, *Christ's Two Wills in Scholastic Thought: The Christology of Aquinas and its Historical Context* (Toronto: Pontifical Institute of Mediaeval Studies, 2015). In *ST* III, q. 19, a. 1, when treating of Leo and Severus, Aquinas follows Damascene's interpretation of the Third Council of Chalcedon found in *The Orthodox Faith*, III, c. 16. He then proceeds to defend Leo's Tome against its monenergist critics (corp. and ad 4): "The human nature has its proper operation distinct from the divine and conversely. Nevertheless, the divine nature makes use of the operation of the human nature, as of the operation of its instrument

First, Aquinas notes that all attributes of the divine nature and of the human nature of Christ pertain to the single personal subject of the Incarnate Word.[52] That is to say, whether we speak of the eternal generation of the Son or his human birth in time as man, we attribute such characteristics only to Jesus Christ, the eternal Son of the Father. He was born before all ages of the Father and born in time of the Virgin Mary. He is the author of creation and the giver of eternal life, but is also subject to human torture, suffering, and death.

Second, the attributes of the two natures are not rightly predicated of each other and should not be confused. They remain ontologically distinct.[53] The divine nature of Christ is eternal, not temporal, immutable, not subject to alteration, impassible, not subject to suffering, all-knowing, not subject to nescience. The human nature of Christ is present in time and place, not subject to omnipresence, finite, not subject to infinity, temporal, not subject to conditions of eternal pre-existence. The human nature of Jesus then is not omnipresent or pre-existent or eternal, while the divine nature is not a historically contingent process, subject to generation, or redetermined in identity through the impact of created realities.[54]

... Being and operation belong to the person by reason of the nature; yet in a different manner. For being belongs to the very constitution of the person, and in this respect it has the nature of a term; consequently, unity of person requires unity of the complete and personal being. But operation is an effect of the person by reason of a form or nature. Hence plurality of operations is not incompatible with personal unity."

52. *ST* III, q. 16, a. 4 and ad 1: "since there is one hypostasis of both natures, the same hypostasis is signified by the name of either nature. Thus whether we say 'man' or 'God,' the hypostasis of Divine and human nature is signified. And hence, of the Man may be said what belongs to the Divine Nature, as of a hypostasis of the Divine Nature; and of God may be said what belongs to the human nature, as of a hypostasis of human nature.... It is impossible for contraries to be predicated of the same in the same respects, but nothing prevents their being predicated of the same in different aspects. And thus contraries are predicated of Christ, not in the same, but in different natures."

53. An idea enunciated clearly by Damascene in *The Orthodox Faith*, III, c. 4, cited above.

54. *ST* III, q. 16, a. 5, corp. and ad 1, and ad 3: "What belongs to one cannot be said of another, unless they are both the same; thus 'risible' can be predicated only of man. Now in the mystery of Incarnation the Divine and human natures are not the same; but the hypostasis of the two natures is the same. And hence what belongs to one nature cannot be predicated of the other if they are taken in the abstract.... [T]hus we say that

Third, all nature terms (divine or human) can be employed grammatically as subject terms if and only if they denote the personal subject considered under the aspect of a nature. For example, we can rightly say that "God gestated in the womb of the Virgin," "God was born in poverty," "God suffered personally on the Cross," or "God truly died on the Cross." These are all necessary statements and are orthodox because the term God is a nature term denoting a specific person, the Second Person of the Son. This means it is not true to say "the divine nature was born, suffered, died, etc." or "the Father or the Holy Spirit suffered," but only "the Son who is God and man was born, suffered and died, as a divine person who is truly human like us," and therefore "God truly was born, suffered and died." Likewise, we may say that "this man created the world," indicating Jesus Christ, without implying that his human nature was an instrument of the creation, or we may say that "God was obedient in order to save us" without implying that his human obedience is constitutive of his eternal generation from the Father as the eternal Son.[55]

Fourth, one may ascribe actions to the natures of Jesus Christ as such so long as one is clear that this does not imply that these natures

---

the Son of God is born, yet we do not say that the Divine Nature is born; as was said in *ST* I, q. 39, a. 5. So, too, in the mystery of Incarnation we say that the Son of God suffered, yet we do not say that the Divine Nature suffered.... What belongs to the Divine Nature is predicated of the human nature—not, indeed, as it belongs essentially to the Divine Nature, but as it is participated by the human nature. Hence, whatever cannot be participated by the human nature (as to be uncreated and omnipotent), is nowise predicated of the human nature. But the Divine Nature received nothing by participation from the human nature; and hence what belongs to the human nature can nowise be predicated of the Divine Nature."

55. *ST* III, q. 16, a. 5: "Now concrete words stand for the hypostasis of the nature; and hence of concrete words we may predicate indifferently what belongs to either nature—whether the word of which they are predicated refers to one nature, as the word 'Christ,' by which is signified "both the Godhead anointing and the manhood anointed"; or to the Divine Nature alone, as this word 'God' or 'the Son of God'; or to the manhood alone, as this word 'Man' or 'Jesus.' Hence Pope Leo says (Letter 74): 'It is of no consequence from what substance we name Christ; because since the unity of person remains inseparably, one and the same is altogether Son of Man by His flesh, and altogether Son of God by the Godhead which He has with the Father.'" See also *ST* III, q 16, aa. 7 and 9.

are individual persons.[56] We may say, for example, as Leo does, that the "divinity performs miracles," while "the humanity suffers" because he indicates that the operations of the two natures are of the one person of the Son incarnate. This does not mean that the divinity is a personal subject distinct from the humanity but only that we abstractly signify the two natures by referring to the operations that are proper to each in the one person. It is in virtue of his divinity that Christ has the active potency to perform miracles and in virtue of his humanity that he has the capacity to suffer. Meanwhile, if we say that "the infinite lay in a crib" or "the humanity breathed its last on the cross," we refer to the nature substantively rather than operationally but we do so by prescribing implicitly these substantive features of nature to the one personal subject of the Word. "He who is infinite lay in a crib," "He who is human died on the cross."

It should be noted that these four principles help us delineate the shape of a mystery in human language. They are not meant to render the mystery of the Incarnation, life, suffering and death, and resurrection of Christ fully transparent to human reason, nor do they simply leave these features of his existence unintelligible or opaque. They serve rather to help us identify the inward region and boundaries of the mystery of the faith and exclude erroneous or counterfeit formulations. It seems to me, in turn, we can identify three important ontological features that emerge from this inscape of mystery,

---

56. *ST* III, q. 19, a 1, ad 3 and ad 5: "To operate belongs to a subsisting hypostasis; in accordance, however, with the form and nature from which the operation receives its species. Hence from the diversity of forms or natures spring the divers species of operations, but from the unity of hypostasis springs the numerical unity as regards the operation of the species: thus fire has two operations specifically different, namely, to illuminate and to heat, from the difference of light and heat, and yet the illumination of the fire that illuminates at one and the same time is numerically one. So, likewise, in Christ there are necessarily two specifically different operations by reason of His two natures; nevertheless, each of the operations at one and the same time is numerically one, as one walking and one healing ... The proper work of the Divine operation is different from the proper work of the human operation. Thus to heal a leper is a proper work of the Divine operation, but to touch him is the proper work of the human operation. Now both these operations concur in one work, inasmuch as one nature acts in union with the other."

rightly to be thought of as Christological truths, that in turn also have implications for philosophical metaphysics (without being reducible to the latter). I will return to these below.

The first ontological feature of the mystery pertains to the person of the Son: he can begin to subsist as man (by hominization in the womb of the Virgin Mary) without ceasing to be truly God. Consequently, precisely as one who is God personally, he can also become subject to all that is human, including birth, suffering, and death, which he truly experiences personally without ceasing to be "immutably, impassibly" divine and one of the Holy Trinity. There are various soteriological aspects to this mysterious truth. For example, God truly shows his divine solidarity with us by freely identifying with our human limitations, and he can unite his ineffable, perfect divinity and saving power to us even in the worst darkness of our human suffering. Everything we have as human becomes his so that everything he has as God can become ours, even in the most trying moments of our condition. Behind this soteriological claim, we confront the mystery of God's gratuitous freedom: it is grounded in his mysterious activity and eternal identity. The mystery from before the foundations of the world is personal, good, wise, and loving.

Second, the two natures of Christ are not confused or mixed, but they also are not competitive rivals or mutually exclusive. Christ does not have to cease being God in order to be human or take on a truncated or artificial human nature in order to be God.[57] There are

---

57. Consider in this respect the alternative views on the communication of idioms by Sergius Bulgakov in *The Lamb of God*. Bulgakov develops a coherent critique of John Damascene's use of the communication of idioms, based on the idea that the latter permits the divine essence of Christ to influence the human essence (through divinizing grace) but does not understand the divine essence to conform to or become subject to alteration by the human essence as an ontological condition of the Incarnation (see especially 209–10, 258–59). The proposed alternative of Bulgakov (which has its proximate origins in Gottlieb Thomasius and which resembles proposals of Karl Barth that we will examine below) is that the divine essence freely accommodates itself kenotically to the lowliness of the human state of Christ by adopting human characteristics of temporality and suffering into the godhead (the divine nature) as a condition of possibility for the mystery of the Incarnation. Interestingly, in the start of the book (pp. 2–19) Bulgakov begins his Christology with a defense of the Christological ontology of Apollinarius

profound metaphysical implications to this claim. God is not a rival to his creation, seemingly because God is in no way exterior to his creation as Creator, but is more intimate to created being than it is to itself, or most interior to the effect of the Creation (the *esse commune* of created being) without being identical with that creation as such.[58] This means that God can "step out onto the stage" of creation and enter the drama of created history without either ceasing to be God or doing violence to human nature. As noted above, the traditional Christian claim is that no one is more human than Christ, who is also truly God.[59] Furthermore, the human nature of Jesus can

of Laodicia, who he claims was the first truly to acknowledge the impossibility of the co-existence of two fully autonomous principles of nature (divine and human) in Christ co-existing in unity, without the problem emerging of rivalry. Whereas Apollinarius ultimately resolved the question problematically by denying the complete humanity of Christ, Bulgakov will ultimately attempt to resolve the problem otherwise by positing the self-delimitation and kenotic dynamism of the divinity of Christ. But whether one chooses one solution or the other (Apollinarius or Bulgakov) the problem is found in the fundamental premise (as elaborated by Bulgakov) of a necessary rivalry of natures unable to co-exist in a unity without the self-delimitation of one or the other. It is precisely this kind of erroneous principle (perhaps derivative remotely from the nominalist heritage) that Damascene avoids and rejects from the start. Far from being a hindrance to a dynamic Christology of divinization and a residue of Byzantine scholasticism that "did not go far enough," Damascene is a theologian who points us in the right direction, precisely on this point in question.

58. See on this point, *ST* I, q. 4, a. 2, and the study of Martin Bieler, "'Analogia entis' as an expression of love according to Ferdinand Ulrich," in *The Analogy of Being: Invention of the Antichrist or the Wisdom of God?*, ed. Thomas Joseph White (Grand Rapids, MI, Eerdmans, 2011), 314–37.

59. A point underlined in the Second Vatican Council, in *GS* §§22 and 45. In Chapter 22 where it is said that Christ is "perfect man," appeal is made in the footnote precisely to Chalcedonian Christology. (Denzinger 4322): "Council of Constantinople II (553), can. 7: '... without either the Word being transformed into the nature of the flesh or the flesh being translated into the nature of the Word,' cf. also Council of Constantinople III (681): '... for just as his most holy and immaculate flesh, animated by his soul, has not been destroyed by being divinized but remained in its state and kind'. Cf. Council of Chalcedon (451): '[the same Lord Jesus Christ] ... must be acknowledged in two natures, without confusion or change, without division or separation.' Perceiving the conceptual unity and organic development of thought across time expressed by these four Councils of the Catholic Church, one is reminded of John Henry Newman's notes pertaining to the identification of genuine development of doctrine in the Church. In fact, all seven notes would apply readily to this development from the affirmation of the two natures of Christ (Chalcedon) to the underscoring of the immutability and perfection of each nature (Constantinople II) to the affirmation of the two activities and wills

be subordinate to and the instrument of his divine person (the humanity of the Word) without in any way being diminished as human. On the contrary, the human nature of Jesus, his human actions of knowledge and love as man, are now expressive of his personal identity as God, the Son, who manifests his eternal life and presence in and through his epitomal human actions, words, gestures, teachings, sufferings, and miracles.[60] It is God the Son who shines forth radiantly in the most human life of Jesus, from the child in the crib to the crucified of Golgotha.

Third, we can infer from the third and fourth of our rules of predication above an ontological mystery first identified by the Cappadocian fathers. All works of the divine persons are works conducted through the medium of a nature. All works of a nature are works conducted by a personal subject.[61] The one is a principle "from which," while the other is a principle "through which." Persons are those "from whom," and natures are that "through which." The Father, Son, and Holy Spirit operate by virtue of or in and through the

---

(Constantinople III), to the emphasis on the reality, integrity and exemplary perfection of the Lord's humanity (Vatican II). We can perceive here preservation of type, continuity of principles, assimilative power, logical sequence, anticipation of the future developments in the early principles, conservationist action on the past principles by later affirmations, and chronic vigor. See *An Essay on the Development of Christian Doctrine* (London: Longmans, Green and Co., 1909), esp. ch. 5.

60. I have explored this idea further in *The Incarnate Lord*, ch. 1.

61. In fact, the principle that "a nature is never found except within a hypostasis" was employed by anti-Chalcedonian monophysites of the sixth century in order to argue for the singularity of the nature in Christ. Dyophysites responded by adopting the same principle and reinterpreting it in light of the distinction between the operation *of a* person and operation *through* (or by means of) a nature. This way of thinking has its origins in earlier Trinitarian debate. The distinction between the nature common to a plurality of persons and the particular personal subject in which this nature exists originates with Basil in his *Epistle to Terentius* (PG 32, 798 A). It was developed Christologically in the context of dyothelete disputes by John the Grammarian and Leontius of Byzantium. (See, for example, *Contra Nestorianos et Euthychianos*, PG 86,1280 A, by the latter.) John Damascene notes that the principle is essential to a right understanding of the practice of the communication of idioms as pertaining to the Incarnation, in *The Orthodox Faith* III, c. 4, 5, 9, 11, and 12. Aquinas's own thought offers a close parallel to Damascene in *ST* I, q. 39, a. 5, III, q. 3, a. 4, ad 1 and *ST* III, q. 19, a. 1: nature is the principle *through which* a subject or hypostasis acts, but it is always the subject *who* acts.

medium of their shared divine nature and life, as God, while the Son alone operates also by virtue of or in and through the medium of his human life as man. There are two significant features to this third idea. First, evidently, from a Christian and, therefore, Trinitarian point of view, all things are ultimately personal in origin. The divine nature that has given rise to all things and that providently governs human history in view of salvation is a reality that is personal in nature. The universe exists from persons, and in view of personal existence as the summit of created being, namely, our personal life, along with that of the angels, created meaningfully in view of communion with God in Christ. Second, in personal realities, all nature terms must be interpreted in a way that is in conformity with but also not in opposition to personal identity, and vice versa. Negatively speaking, it is a great mistake to oppose natural identity (being human or being a biological animal, for example) with personal identity, as if one must either advocate for an ontology of persons or an ontology of natures. One way to make this error is to claim that a serious study of human nature does away with personhood and personal dignity as a mere folklore concept from pre-modern culture. The other way to do so is to claim that the acknowledgement of human personhood and personal freedom requires that we delimit or deny the reality of nature as a normative concept for free human action or thought as if the personal agent could invent or at least mutate his nature in a plastic fashion in the service of his personal creative freedom or will to power. In reality, all personal acts of knowledge and love are eminently natural acts stemming from the natural principles of human knowledge and free will.[62] This is true in Christ's own human knowledge and freedom, which are reflective, in turn, of his uncreated divine life, his eternal natural wisdom and love as God.

---

62. See the Thomistic argument to this effect offered by Jacques Maritain in his *Court Traité de l'Existence et de l'Existant. Oeuvres Complètes*, vol. 9 (Fribourg and Paris: Éditions Universitaires and Éditions St. Paul, 1990), originally published in 1947 in response to the voluntarist ontology of Jean Paul Sartre.

THE NATURAL GROUNDS OF MYSTERY:
THE CHRISTOLOGICAL PRESUPPOSITION OF A
PHILOSOPHICAL METAPHYSICS

In light of the ontology implied by the classical use of the communication of idioms, we rightly should affirm that Chalcedonian Christology (and therefore a fortiori all Catholic theology) presupposes and needs to make use of various principles of classical metaphysics. Why is this the case, and in what sense? Here, I succinctly will demarcate basic principles contained implicitly within the Christology elaborated above, while still maintaining that philosophical reflection is formally distinct as such from theological or dogmatic reflection on the revelation of Christ.[63]

The first principle to be noted is that the identification of the form of metaphysical realism incumbent upon Catholic theologians for a right exercise of their own science can appear only consequent to and in a sense from within theology as such, and yet as a formally distinct subject area. Here, I mean simply that it is antecedently probable—in a world affected by the wounds of ignorance and human self-will—that in pre-Christian cultures, the natural human intellect may not take account of or realize all of its innate possibilities

---

63. Erich Przywara's characterization of the "analogia entis" as the fundamental form of Catholic theology seems to me to run the risk of identifying properly philosophical objects of reflection with those pertaining to divine revelation, so that theology is overly determined "from the bottom up" by metaphysical reflection culminating in Christology (one might think in this respect of Rahner's transcendental anthropology) or philosophical reflection is overly determined "from the top down" as essentially a dimension of Christology (analogous to Barth's Christological ontology). On this idea, see *Analogia Entis; Metaphysics: Original Structure and Universal Rhythm*, trans. J. Betz and D. B. Hart (Grand Rapids, MI: Eerdmans, 2014), Part II, ch. 2, "The Scope of Analogy as a Fundamental Catholic Form," pp. 348–99. Balthasar identifies this problem in Przywara's thought, rightly it seems to me. See his critical remarks in *Theo-Logic* II, 94–95, n. 16, and the logically congruent observations on p. 273, n. 109. My own views on the distinction and interaction of the "analogia fidei" and the "analogia entis" are akin to those of Gottlieb Söhngen, "The Analogy of Faith: Likeness to God from Faith Alone?," *Pro Ecclesia* 21, no. 1 (2012): 56–76 and "The Analogy of Faith: Unity in the Science of Faith," *Pro Ecclesia* 21, no. 2 (2012): 169–94, trans. K. Oakes.

or may have doubt about the latter. To affirm that there is such a thing as philosophical metaphysics follows from the distinction between nature and grace, and between natural knowledge and the revelation obtained in virtue of the grace of faith. The affirmation of natural knowledge is the necessary corollary to a theology of grace and revelation. This does not entail, however, that one must hold that a pristine, deeply developed natural metaphysical reflection must precede the exploration of the ontology of Christ in time either for any individual or for human culture more generally. Such may be the case in fact, but my argument here does not require that it be so. As a matter of hypothesis, one might posit that all Christian philosophy develops only after Christ, but even if this is the case, it still develops as philosophy, in the service of faith, and as logically entailed by the predications we make to Christ of the divine and human natures.

The second important principle to observe is that when we speak of the divine nature or the human nature of Christ, we must qualify that we are speaking of a theological mystery, not a mere truth of philosophical reasoning. Even if we do know something of what human nature is and how to speak rightly of the divine nature philosophically in distinction from or prescinding from divine revelation as such, the divine and human natures of Christ are *formally* mysteries approached primarily with the help of divine revelation. The nature in virtue of which Christ is one with the Father and the Holy Spirit pertains to the essence of the Trinity. The essence in virtue of which he is one with us designates our human nature redeemed and sanctified in the New Adam, subject to atoning death and eschatological exaltation. This is why *Gaudium et Spes* para. 22 rightly notes that the *mystery* of what it means to be human is only ultimately resolvable by reference to Christ, in whom are present the plenitude of grace and the perfection of human nature by and within the life of that grace.[64]

---

64. *GS* §22: "The truth is that only in the mystery of the Incarnate Word does the

Having provided these two primary warnings against a naïve form of theological rationalism, we can now proceed to a third and more essential point. The mysteries of Christ's divine nature and human nature are literally unthinkable or conceptually inaccessible for us unless we are also capable of some form of natural reflection regarding the nature of God the Creator (conceived by way of analogy), as well as regarding the structure of human nature (univocally denoted in universal fashion). The reasons for this should be obvious. Let us consider the divine and human natures in turn.[65]

If the human being cannot think naturally about the existence of God and the nature of God as Creator (however indirectly, apophatically or analogically), then the very idea of the Incarnation, as proposed in Chalcedonian terms, is literally unthinkable. This is the case because the very idea of Jesus as a personal subject possessing the divine nature and having its "attributes" predicated of him would be thoroughly unintelligible. Even if the divine nature of the Son is a mystery of faith, one essence possessed in common with the Father and the Spirit and revealed to us supernaturally, its reception in human thought requires an analogue concept drawn from philosophical understanding that allows the human intellect to orient itself toward God. Were this not the case, the judgment of faith that "Christ possesses divine nature" or "is God" would stand completely outside

---

mystery of man take on light. For Adam, the first man, was a figure of Him Who was to come, namely Christ the Lord. Christ, the final Adam, by the revelation of the mystery of the Father and His love, fully reveals man to man himself and makes his supreme calling clear." What is at stake is clearly the supernatural truth regarding the human being, revealed in the person of Christ and his human nature.

65. For the sake of what follows below, I am referring to natural knowledge of God as "analogical" in the broad sense so as to indicate that no species or genus of category we use for a created entity or feature of being can be predicated of God in precisely the same sense, without qualification. Presumably this kind of definition permits one to include, for the sake of argument, various Scotistic forms of predication, that are not the subject of criticism or consideration in this essay. Similarly, when speaking of the "univocal" predication of human nature to all human beings, I mean to suggest simply that we can and must denote all human beings as being essentially the same kind of reality, and not members of distinct species, independently of their property characteristics such as age, race, or sexuality.

the ambit of the natural capacities and range of human knowing. In this case, the gift of faith would be so extrinsic to the human intellect as to be literally inassimilable. Positive knowledge of the divine nature is a natural requirement if the human person is to be in "obediential potency" to the gift of grace that permits him to know and affirm that Christ is God.[66] This means that only if there is a metaphysical range of knowledge that can affirm the existence of God coherently and demonstrably as a truth of reason is it possible to develop a reasoned account of the intellectual possibility of faith and, in turn, also an intellectually self-conscious dogmatic theology. Dogmatic reflection on Christ without metaphysics would be, in this respect, an insincere act of the mind by which the activity of faith would orient the mind towards an end purely extrinsic to any conditions of human thought, leaving the latter (human reason) immanent to itself without intrinsic reference to divine truth, even despite the presence of the grace of faith.

To give precision to this notion, we can clarify what must be the case for there to be a natural capacity for faith in the mind without there being a purely rational derivation of the object or act of supernatural faith (epistemological Pelagianism). On the one hand, there must be a specification of human thinking by conceptual reason and contemplative judgment that allows human beings to think about God the Creator in truth by means of natural or philosophical reflection. This specification is not identical with that of supernatural faith, which orients human intelligence toward the awareness and understanding of God as Holy Trinity and eventually may terminate in the beatific vision of God, all of which is made possible only by grace. But the former natural specification is taken up into, preserved, and made use of within the activity of faith, even if it can

66. In employing the notion of obediential potency I am suggesting that we have no natural intellectual inclination to know of the Trinity as such, and its essential unity, but that we do have a natural inclination to think about God analogically, and about the divine nature, that can be elevated by grace so as to be placed in the service of reflection on the mystery of Trinitarian unity as such.

in no way produce or initiate the latter supernatural act. Under grace and within grace, however, the natural capacity to think about God is taken up into the act of faith and moved within this act toward God, as known both supernaturally and naturally.[67] The reason that the natural pre-disposition is essential is not because it causes the faith but because without it, faith would be so alien as to be violent to the human intellect, and nature would be unable to move itself under grace and within grace toward God.[68] The natural and supernatural specifications of the human intellect remain distinguishable but in no way extrinsic to one another. They function in harmony, hierarchical coordination, and instrumental subordination. The revelation of God addresses the natural human desire for perfect knowledge of God (the desire to see God) but elevates this inclination of nature to a higher plane and provides it with new life and dynamic specification.[69]

Likewise, the basic theological commitment to Chalcedonian Christology requires a metaphysics of human nature that permits us to identify a structure of human nature attributed univocally to all human beings. That is to say, there is an essence of human nature, one adopted by God in the Incarnation, that is present universally by way of identity of kind in all human beings. Note at least two reasons this must be the case, for theological motives. First, if we cannot in any way identify the essential nature of man in its universal specification, making use of the instruments of natural human reason, then we also cannot understand coherently what it means to say that God became a human being having a human nature in solidarity

67. This is why there will always be a *De Deo Uno* treatise of divine attributes or names within and for a *De Deo Trino*, in no matter what age of the world or in whatever philosophical register, be it Neoplatonic, Aristotelian-scholastic, Kantian, Hegelian, Analytic, etc.

68. Parallels exist in the world of the will. Only if there is a natural desire for God distinct from the grace-inspired inclination toward God by way of infused hope and charity can the latter grace be received into the human person in an immanent and humane way, and yet still be a gratuitous grace. See my argument to this effect in White, "Imperfect Happiness."

69. See on this point, *ST* I-II, q. 62, aa. 1–3.

and plenary identification with us. If this were the case, the universal soteriological significance of the Incarnation would be eclipsed. What does it even mean to say that God became truly human if there is no human race (a group of entities that share a common nature and destiny)? A merely extrinsic Christological designation of human nature (cf. Karl Barth) is not possible because we would not be able naturally to identify what a human being is as distinct from something having mere accord of phenomenological appearances.[70] Christ's divine "attempt" to draw the so-called human race into unity would be ineffective necessarily if we cannot ourselves even recognize what human nature is, even after redemption. Grace can heal or sharpen the capacities of natural intellect to identify the essence of man, and the Church's philosophical and natural law traditions serve to do just this, but they can only do so because there already exists in each human being a pre-disposition or natural capacity to think realistically about human identity in its essential constituents.

Second, on this front, we cannot understand the perfection of Christ's human nature in its modal realization under grace and internal to the hypostatic union if we cannot understand the essence of man as such. For example, we cannot understand the mode of perfection present in Christ's human obedience, in love, humility, and sinlessness if we cannot understand something of human reason and freedom, more generally, human obedience and the virtues. Likewise, we cannot appreciate the supernatural mystery of Christ's suffering out of love for the human race in the crucifixion if we cannot understand something of the philosophical conundrum of human

70. Barth famously argues that we can only accede to a genuine knowledge of human nature in light of Christ, and from the perspective of divine revelation. Taken to its logical conclusion, however, this position would suggest that the very notion of "nature" or "human nature" is so alien to us intellectually (at least in our fallen state) that it cannot be employed in any meaningful way. Insofar as we do think actively in conceptual forms, even in response to Christ and under the influences of his grace, we must make use of some conceptual forms of knowledge to orient ourselves toward the objects of faith, which is only possible if there is some way to identify them (in part) under naturally intelligible idioms, as when we say, for example, that Jesus of Nazareth was "a man" or "a human being" having the same identity as us in the order of nature.

suffering, and the distinctions of body and soul, as well as the enigma of death and the natural evil it represents. Examples could be multiplied, but the principal point is clear. Catholic theology must be committed to a metaphysical realism concerning the nature of the human being as a presupposition for any rigorous commitment to Christological orthodoxy.

A final philosophical principle concerns the philosophical notion of personhood. Evidently, Christianity depends upon and, in turn, interprets the basic claim of the Torah that the human being is made in the image of God. This view contains several essential components. There is a hierarchy of beings where non-living things exist in some sense not only for God, but for living things, and this, in turn, can be said of living things in relation to the human community.[71] The person is differentiated in a specific way by his immaterial powers of intelligence and deliberating love or free will. These features of personal existence emerge from the spiritual soul as the form of the human body. That the rational animal has a spiritual soul is indeed a truth of human reason, also maintained dogmatically by the teaching of the Catholic Church, based on a discerning interpretation of the givens of scriptural revelation.[72] It is because we are spiritual animals that we are persons and have in common with God and the angelic community, the features of existence that make personal communion possible with other spiritual realities.[73]

This means that there is a teleological end to human personhood that must also be maintained by Catholic theology for Christological purposes. Human beings are immanently inclined by their spiritual

---

71. See Aquinas's argument to this effect in *SCG* III, c. 22.

72. Catechism of the Catholic Church, para. 366: "The Church teaches that every spiritual soul is created immediately by God—it is not 'produced' by the parents—and also that it is immortal: it does not perish when it separates from the body at death, and it will be reunited with the body at the final Resurrection." Unambiguous authoritative clarifications on this point are found, for example, in Paul VI, Credo of the People of God; Pius XII, *Humani Generis*, and Lateran Council V (1513).

73. See the helpful Thomistic study of this topic by Francois Daguet, *Finis Omnium Ecclesia: Théologie du Dessein Divin chez Thomas D'Aquin* (Paris: Vrin, 2003).

powers toward the pursuit of the knowledge of the truth and the desire for happiness by way of love of the authentic good. It is worth mentioning in keeping with our theme that Christ cannot be the exemplar and indeed the savior of human existence in any meaningful way if he, as man in his human soul, does not teach us and realize in our human nature these features of human existence. Christ is a man who knows and expresses the most important truths of all of human history and who manifests in the redemptive event of his own human life the plenary realization of human happiness: the possession of God by the beatific vision and by the fullness of charity. This is, of course, a mystery of grace, but if human beings are not capable of any natural philosophical understanding of the spiritual vocation of the intellect of man for the truth and for the possession of personal happiness in God, then they are also incapable of seeing the inner intelligibility of the gift of salvation realized in Christ.[74] This claim does not imply that one must have philosophical understanding of any developed kind as a propaedeutic to acknowledging salvation in Christ but rather the converse: reception of the mystery of Christ in grace addresses, stimulates, rejuvenates, heals, and elevates the human capacity to seek the universal truth and to seek authentic and profound happiness in God.

CONCLUSION: CHRISTOLOGICAL COSMOPOLITANISM AND THE "METAPHYSICAL APOSTOLATE" OF THE CHURCH

We can conclude this chapter with two brief observations, one regarding what the vision it promotes implicitly excludes and one concerning the open horizon of what it can include. The first of these topics is easy to treat by noting positions of either theology or philosophical metaphysics that contradict the basic principles noted above. We can exclude either a theological totalism that refuses

---

74. See Aquinas's arguments regarding basic human inclinations in *ST* I-II, q. 94, a. 2.

in principle the possibility of a perennial metaphysics for theological reasons (represented in sophisticated fashion by Barth) or a rationalist evidentialism that might seek to demonstrate the truths and inward content of the mysteries of Christianity by recourse to principles of philosophical reason (cf. features of the project of Richard Swinburne).

The claim made above regarding philosophical knowledge of both divine and human natures remains in some fundamental incompatibility with the axiomatic speculative agnosticism of Kant, rearticulated in creative fashion by Heidegger in his later work. Arguably, it is also opposed to elements of Hegel's ontology insofar as the latter identifies the developmental life and evolution of God with the intra-created processes of history. The philosophical notion of a universally identifiable human nature also stands in contrast to ambient forms of nominalism that arise most typically in modern naturalism and which tend to see human identity as a mere bundle-configuration of atomic or cellular traits, or which interpret human identity only by reference to genetic codes and therefore interpret human nature ultimately in materialistic and quasi-individualistic terms. Mainstream contemporary naturalism is also opposed to the principle regarding personhood. Both the idea of a hierarchy of being within nature of grades of being and the idea of human beings as spiritual animals find no place within much of contemporary analytic philosophy when the latter seeks to explain human identity merely by reference to biological findings of the modern sciences and the material constitution of human mental activity. In such a world, human personal dignity and trinitarian mystery both become increasingly unintelligible. To speak of Christ in our own age, then, is also to speak metaphysically and incisively of God and human nature.

What does this Catholic advocacy of metaphysics permit or encourage? Thomism is, of course, a usual candidate in this regard. Aquinas's metaphysics of natural realities, his analogical discourse concerning the incomprehensible God, his commitment to a profound investigation of the nature of the human person, and his hylomorphism, as well as his metaphysics of creation and the real distinction of *esse* and *essentia*: all of this can be seen as a vast expression of spiritually enlightened Christian philosophy developed from within the folds of *sacra doctrina*. But this remains only one among many possibilities, classical and modern, from Irenaeus, Augustine, and Maximus to Bonaventure, Aquinas, and Scotus, to Pascal, Newman, Scheeben, and Ratzinger. In fact, just to the extent that all of these major figures think from within the form of understanding under consideration, they also speak to one another and, therefore, to those who take inspiration intellectually from their pluriform heritage within the Church.

Reflection on Christology and philosophical reflection on metaphysics both take place within a singular history, in which they are integrated in a singular (multivalent) Christian culture of faith and reason. This life of reflection on Christological ontology occurs for the Church first and foremost to clarify her confession of faith and in order to communicate it evangelically. But by that very measure, it also takes place for the world at large since it seeks to explain reality philosophically in light of Christ and in relation to God's existence among us as a human being. If the Incarnation has a universal horizon of meaning and intelligibility (so that all things are explained in light of Christ), then there must also be a way in the Church and in culture at large to think about all that is, philosophically in light of God, and to think about the place of human nature within the larger framework of the existence of the world God has made. Where this is impossible (on the natural level), we would be incapable of "taking every thought captive to obey Christ" (2 Cor. 10:5) on the supernatural level. For these same reasons, the universal proclamation of the mystery of Christ requires not only a theoretical Christology but also a metaphysical apostolate as a dimension of Christology. In concrete history, the stimulus may often come first from the side of the grace of the Holy Spirit, but to live this grace in an integral fashion, the Church must learn to confess Christ as both true God and true man as the basic truth of all reality, and in every generation. In doing so, she also learns to speak of God and man naturally and philosophically, in every generation—perennially—in sure ways, for the service of the Gospel and as a dimension of her own evangelical mandate. This is the only orthodox Christology that there is.

11

---:---

Divine Perfection and the
Kenosis of the Son

INTRODUCTION: KENOSIS AND THE
COMMUNICATION OF IDIOMS

Several scriptural passages from the New Testament suggest that
Christ, the Son of God, was subject to self-emptying or kenosis.[1] The
most evident of these is Phil. 2:7, which attributes kenosis to the Son,
who though he was in the form of God, took on the form of a servant, and became subject to suffering unto death, so that God has exalted him in the resurrection, and made him recognizable as Lord to
all the nations (Phil. 2:10–11; Isa. 45:22–24). Whether kenosis in this
passage pertains to a pre-existent subject who becomes human and
whether it signifies only the taking on of a human form (i.e., the Incarnation) or also designates the obedient suffering-unto-death are
disputed questions. I take it that the pre-existence and divinity of the
Son are implicitly denoted by this passage because the Son is said to

---

Originally published in *Kenosis*, ed. Paul T. Nimmo and Keith L. Johnson (Grand
Rapids: Eerdmans, 2022), 137–56. Reprinted by permission of the publisher.
1. This chapter is dedicated to Bruce L. McCormack in thanksgiving for his friendship and contribution to theological conversation. Bruce might not agree with all that
I argue below, but the argument is a reflection of ecumenical engagement with themes
that he has helped me to consider more closely.

be in the form of God prior to Incarnation and that the kenosis in question includes not only the Son's Incarnation, but also his obedience, suffering, and death, which all follow from his being human. Whether these interpretations are warranted or not, what is uncontroversial is that these various attributes of self-emptying, obedience, suffering, and death are attributed to the subject of the Son, to his person. Furthermore, they are said to contribute, along with his resurrection and exaltation, to the revelation of his Lordship and to the fact that he has received the name above every other name (Phil. 2:10), presumably the divine name, Lord or YHWH, "He who is." (Ex. 3:14–15) The kenosis of God is revelatory of his Lordship.[2]

The attribution of divine and human properties to the one person of the Son is historically denoted under the conceptual rubric of the "communication of idioms," or the attribution of names. In its traditional use, as exemplified in figures as diverse as Cyril of Alexandria, Leo the Great, John Damascene, and Thomas Aquinas, three main regulatory principles emerge for the right use of the communication of idioms. First, there is only one person in Christ (one hypostatic subject), as noted by the Council of Ephesus. Consequently, any property of the divine nature or of the human nature of the Son is attributed personally only to one subject, who is the eternal Son of God.[3] It is the Son and Word of God who created all things, with the Father and with the Spirit. It is the Son and Word who took flesh, suffered, and died. One of the Trinity has been crucified.[4] Historically we can associate this insight with the theology of Cyril.[5]

2. See the exegetical argument of Richard Bauckham, *Jesus and the God of Israel*, 1–59.

3. Consider in this respect the affirmations of the council of Ephesus taken from the 2nd letter of Cyril of Alexandria to Nestorius, and the 3rd and 4th anathemas, taken from his 3rd letter. Cf. Denzinger, para. 250–63. 250: "...we say that the Word, hypostatically uniting to himself the flesh animated by a rational soul, became man in an ineffable and incomprehensible manner..."

4. See in this regard the assessment of the Scythian monks' phrase, "one of the Trinity has suffered," made by Pope John II, letter *Olim quidem*, 534 AD, Denzinger, 401–4: "God suffered in the flesh."

5. Aquinas associates himself with Cyril's use of the communication of idioms in *ST* III, q. 16, a. 4.

Second, there are two natures in Christ that are truly distinct, united, not separated, unmixed, and unconfused, as noted by the Council of Chalcedon.[6] Therefore, the properties of the two natures are not attributed directly to one another. We cannot conclude from the Incarnation, for example, that the eternity of God has become temporal, that the divine nature suffers, or that the human nature of God is omnipresent or omnipotent.[7] However, we may say that God, who is all-powerful, has taken on human weakness, the eternal one has entered time, and the impassible God has truly suffered. These are not contradictory remarks since the properties attributed to the one person of the Son are ascribed to him in virtue of personal subsistence in distinct natures. Historically we can associate this insight with the theology of Leo.

Third, the two natures of Christ do have distinct operations, as noted by the Third Council of Constantinople.[8] Consequently, we can ascribe operations of Christ as either God or human to his person, signified by his nature taken not in the abstract but in the concrete.[9] For example, we can call Jesus the person, either "man" or "God," denoting him with these nature terms as a personal subject. In this case, it is true to say, for example, that this man created the world or that God suffers. The latter phrase indicates that one who is

6. See the Letter to Flavian (tome) of Leo the Great, Denzinger 290–95, and the Council of Chalcedon, Denzinger 300–4. 302: "...one and the same Lord Jesus Christ ... must be acknowledged in two natures, without confusion or change, without division or separation." Tome, 293: "The character of each nature, therefore, being preserved and united in one person, humility was assumed by majesty, weakness by strength, mortality by eternity..."

7. See the argument by Aquinas, who appeals to previous arguments of Leo the Great and John Damascene, in ST III, q. 16, a. 5.

8. See the Third Council of Constantinople, Denzinger 550–59. 556: "We likewise proclaim in him, according to the teaching of the holy Fathers, two natural volitions or wills and two natural actions, without division, without change, without separation, without confusion."

9. See the argument of Aquinas in ST III, q. 16, a. 1 and a. 9. A. 9: "... when we say 'this man,' pointing to Christ, the eternal suppositum is necessarily meant, with whose eternity a beginning in time is incompatible. Hence this is false: 'This man began to be.' Nor does it matter that to begin to be refers to the human nature, which is signified by this word 'man'; because the term placed in the subject is not taken formally so as to signify the nature [in this case], but is taken materially so as to signify the suppositum."

God truly experiences human suffering, death, and bodily resurrection. God was born in a cave. God suffered and died on a cross. God was raised from the dead and glorified.

If we approach the mystery of the kenosis of God with this background in mind, it is possible to attribute kenosis to God in three ways: first, as to his person; second, keeping in mind the distinction of the two natures of the Son; third, with respect to his operative actions in the kenosis, as attributed to one who is God and Lord. In the first sense, we can say that it was truly the Son of God who emptied himself and that all that pertains to the kenosis of the Son is attributed rightly to his person. In the second sense, we can say that the kenosis pertains to the Son principally in virtue of his human form and is carried out through his human life of obedience, suffering, and free acceptance of death.[10] Preceding death, he experiences agony, and in death, he experiences the separation of body and soul, events that can be considered dimensions of his kenosis. All of this is attributed to the Son in virtue of his human nature, not in virtue of his divine nature. Does it affect or change his divine nature so as to newly determine the identity of God? Does it indicate by analogy what is *already always*, i.e., eternally, the nature of God, or does it indicate by analogy the personal properties of the Son that pertain to him eternally? I will return to these questions below and argue that the kenosis of the Son pertains to him personally in virtue of his human nature and that it does not change or alter his divine perfection.

10. See Aquinas, *Commentary on St. Paul's First Letter to the Thessalonians and the Letter to the Philippians*, trans. F. R. Larcher and M. Duffy (Albany, NY: Magi, 1969), on Phil. 2:7, p. 80: "He says, therefore, He *emptied himself*. But since He was filled with the divinity, did He empty Himself of that? No, because He remained what He was; and what He was not, He assumed. But this must be understood in regard to the assumption of what He had not, and not according to the assumption of what He had. For just as He descended from heaven, not that He ceased to exist in heaven, but because He began to exist in a new way on earth, so He also emptied Himself, not by putting off His divine nature, but by assuming a human nature. How beautiful to say that He *emptied himself*, for the empty is opposed to the full! For the divine nature is sufficiently full, because every perfection of goodness is there. But human nature and the soul are not full, but capable of fulness, because it was made as a slate not written upon. Therefore, human nature is empty. Hence, he says, He *emptied himself*, because He assumed a human nature." [Emphasis in the original.]

It does, however, indicate by created similitude (in his human action of self-offering) something of his personal property as Son, that is, as one who is from the Father, and for the Father, in the spiration of the Holy Spirit as their mutual love. In the third sense of the communication of idioms, we can say that it is truly God who is subject to kenosis, in virtue of his hominization, suffering, and death. Whether this entails an alteration of the divine nature is an open question, as I have indicated. I will argue below that the kenosis of God does not entail any diminishment, alternation, or abandonment of God's perfection, but, in fact, stems from his inalienable perfection and is an epiphany of the splendor of divine love.

ONTOLOGICAL AND SOTERIOLOGICAL PRINCIPLES FOR THINKING ABOUT DIVINE KENOSIS

How might we pursue this line of inquiry regarding the perfection of the Son, who is subject to kenosis? What is this divine perfection, and what does it entail? To respond to these questions, it is helpful to recall fundamental points of orientation in Christology, regarding both the ontology of the Incarnation and its soteriological consequences, as indeed the topics of who Christ really is and of what he truly accomplishes for human beings are deeply interrelated ones.

Christ is One with the Father, True and Perfect God

We may begin by noting a classical principle drawn from the Council of Nicaea, based upon the Church's common reading of the New Testament, placed in opposition to the famous claim of Arius that the Son of God is a creature. That council stipulated against this idea, that Jesus is God, the eternal Son of God become human, God from God, light from light, true God from true God, consubstantial (i.e., *homoousios*: one in being and essence) with the Father.[11]

---

11. Cf. The Council of Nicaea, Dengzinger 125–26, and the study by Khaled Anatolios, *Retrieving Nicaea*.

The Nicene principle is obviously important ontologically, for it entails the claim that the Son of God, while distinct from the Father personally, is also one with the Father in being and essence, and so too, in light of a Trinitarian reading of the New Testament, is one in being and essence with the Holy Spirit. The kenotic ascriptions we have made in the previous section above presuppose this ontological set of claims so that we may say that the Son who emptied himself by Incarnation, suffering, and death was truly God, one in being with the Father and the Spirit, and also personally distinct from the Father and the Spirit. Therefore, the things we say of him in virtue of the kenosis are truly ascribed to him as a subject, not to the Father or Spirit per se but they are ascribed to one who is truly God. However, to say just this is also to affirm that the one subject to kenosis, because he is truly God and is one in being and essence with the Father and the Spirit, truly contains in himself as God the plenitude of the divine perfection. It is the ineffable and transcendent *God* who is incarnate, suffers, and is crucified, not a creature or some other subordinate entity. To be God, however, is to possess certain divine and inalienable perfections, which Christ must retain if it is truly God who is with us in the mystery of the Incarnation and the crucifixion and not an impostor or a creature we have projected divinity upon by error, as to one we merely mistake for God.

Soteriological consequences follow from these ontological considerations. One of them concerns divinization or union with God. Only if Christ is truly God has God united himself hypostatically to our human nature. A common patristic argument stipulates that God's Incarnation in human nature indicates a soteriological intent on the part of God. He has united himself to our nature so that we may realize that God intends to unite us to his deity by the adoptive life of grace.[12] As Aquinas restates the argument, if God does something ontologically greater or more magnificent in becoming human

---

12. See Athanasius, *On the Incarnation*, 54: "He indeed assumed humanity that we might become God."

himself, why should we fail to believe that he intends and is capable truly of uniting us to himself in the grace of the beatific vision and the universal resurrection?[13]

A second soteriological consideration concerns solidarity. Only if Christ is truly God can we say that God was crucified and died in solidarity with us in our suffering. Friedrich Nietzsche famously depicts Christianity as the culmination of a tradition of ancient Judaic grievance culture in which the sacerdotal class of an oppressed people created a fictive narrative of a vengeful God who would vindicate the poor and oppressed. This fictive account of divinely approved goods and evils, based on a suppressed will to power (*ressentiment*) on the part of the ancient prophets, functioned culturally to sustain their people by promising eventual triumph and, in doing so, also purported to subjugate other cultures to a Judaic standard of measure eschatologically.[14] The narrative of divine pity, centered on the absolute reference of God, was appropriated and intensified by Jesus of Nazareth in his own life of mercy and, after his death, was employed by the paragons of primitive Christianity to subject the noble, beautiful, and stronger cultures of Europe and the near Middle East to a diseased religious culture of morality by which the weak could emerge as triumphant over the strong. Contemporary narratives of liberation theology often underscore the idea of God's solidarity with us manifest in the mystery of the Incarnation of God and the crucifixion of Jesus and seek to explore the ethical and political implications of this mystery. However, any such soteriological exploration can only have a claim to our credence if God himself has truly become human so that the liberation or moral exemplarity we appeal to has a basis in reality and is not merely the arbitrary human construction of an aggrieved social class seeking to instrumentalize the lingering cultural influence of the New Testament narrative for expedient political purposes, which are ultimately built on untenable

13. Aquinas, *SCG* IV, c. 54, para. 2.

14. See the argument of Friedrich Nietzsche, *On the Genealogy of Morality*, trans. C. Diethe (Cambridge: Cambridge University Press, 2006).

philosophical foundations, or the intellectually uncompelling stances of a frustrated morality of resentment.

A third soteriological consideration has to do with the atonement. It matters for the purposes of our redemption whether the man Jesus, in his obedience and free acceptance of suffering on behalf of the human race, is himself also the Lord and God of Israel. The New Testament suggests that the voluntary suffering of Christ crucified is meritorious of our redemption.[15] The "merit" of Christ as one who is human pertains to the proportionate satisfaction of love and obedience he offers to God in reparation for human disobedience and sin so as to reconcile us with God justly or in authentic righteousness.[16] However, even if this righteousness of Christ pertains to him formally insofar as he is human, the deity of God present in Christ is also a factor of fundamental importance in the mystery of the atonement: "... in Christ, God was reconciling the world to himself ..." (2 Cor. 5:19) Aquinas places emphasis here on the infinite dignity accrued to the humanity of Christ in his passion, in virtue of his deity. The one who obeyed, suffered, was crucified, and died was truly God, and as a consequence, there is an infinite personal dignity to his human suffering and death, one that makes the holiness of his death unfathomable, and the righteousness of his human self-offering immeasurable.[17] Even if one holds, as Aquinas does, that God did not need to embark on the Incarnation and self-offering of the crucifixion to atone for our sins, it is still the case that God's elective decision to atone for human sin in this way is indicative of his wisdom and goodness.[18] This divine wisdom and

---

15. This is the logic of Phil. 2:9: Christ's resurrection was merited by his obedience and suffering. See, analogously, Rom. 3:25, Rom. 5:17; 1 Cor. 1:30; 2 Pet. 1:1, all of which intimate a correspondence between the intrinsic excellence of Christ in his human life and the grace of God given to humanity in virtue of Christ's free action.

16. See the argument of Anselm, "Why God Became Man," in *Anselm of Canterbury: The Major Works* esp. II, 7, where Anselm notes the relation between Chalcedonian Christology and his understanding of the substitutionary righteousness of the God-human.

17. See *ST* III, q. 48, a. 2.

18. See *ST* III, q. 1, a. 2, and q. 46, aa. 1–3, esp. q. 46, a. 2, ad 3.

goodness are manifest in his desire to express his mercy toward the human race precisely by communicating to us a perfect righteousness or justification, built solely on the grace of God, founded in the infinite perfection of Christ, who is God crucified.

The Son's Perfection as the Creator

The New Testament not only teaches that the Son is God crucified but also that the Son is a principle of creation, he through whom God created all things.[19] Within the context of Second Temple Judaism, it is significant that he is depicted as one who is at the origin of creation, the giver of being, and as one to whom worship is rightly directed. These are prerogatives traditionally associated with the God of Israel, which the New Testament newly extends so to include Christ, as the alpha and omega of all things, as he from whom all things come, and as he to whom worship and adoration is owed, now and in the eschaton.[20]

The centrality of this Judaic feature of New Testament Christology is of significance for our reflection on the perfection of the Son. If we read the Old and New Testaments together as a canonical text of inspired origin and thus as a unified source of divine revelation, we should acknowledge that it is God alone who has created all things and who actively sustains all things in being as Creator. In virtue of God's identity as Creator and his ongoing activity of creation, we can and indeed must also logically posit other attributes to God. He is truly the one who communicates being to all things, "He Who Is," the "I AM," who does not exist as we do but who transcends all we can comprehend of existence. He gives being to things not compulsively or arbitrarily by blind will but in wisdom, goodness, and freedom. As such, he is not ontologically dependent on his creation such that his identity should be determined and derived from creatures, but rather, the contrary is the case: he is the unilateral giver of being to all that is. He alone has the power to create, to author existence

---

19. See, for example, John 1:1–3; Col. 1:16; Heb. 1:3.
20. Rev. 5:8; 5:13; 7:11; On Christ as the alpha and omega, see 1:8; 21:6; 22:13

into being, and he alone has the power to save, to redeem the world, and to raise the dead. As such, his eternity as the living God encompasses and fills place and time from within, and his infinite perfection as God is present within the inner depths of creatures, more interior to them than they are to themselves, precisely insofar as he gives all things being.

If Christ is truly God, then these inalienable features that pertain to God alone as Creator are present in him, even within his filial kenosis of Incarnation and obediential suffering unto death. It is truly the Lord God who has suffered, he who is rightly given the name above every other name (Phil. 2:9, cf. Isa. 45:22–24), he who is rightly worshiped as only the Lord God of Israel can and should be. This reservation of worship to God alone is logically justified based on the reality of his infinite perfection, goodness, and creative power, in virtue of which he alone can providentially govern all things to their end effectively. Such worship is also indicative of the Church's recognition of God's unique soteriological power since only one who has the power to create, to sustain in being, and to providentially govern all things truly is one who also has the power to give grace, justify, sanctify, glorify, and save truly. Furthermore, that power to save is manifest in the resurrection and glorification of Christ, not only because God the Creator has raised Jesus from the dead, as a proleptic anticipation of the glorification of all creation, but also because Jesus has in himself the power to raise the dead and to redeem the creation.[21] He is not only the exemplary cause of the new creation as man, but also its efficient cause as God.[22]

It follows from the line of argument offered above that God cannot not be the Creator. He alone gives being to the world and cannot transmit this power to another (since it entails an omnipotence or infinite power that only he has as God).[23] He alone sustains in being all things actively and governs them providentially, activities he does

---

21. John 5:21–22; John 10:18. Rev.10:17 suggests the divine power of Christ resurrected.
22. ST III, q. 56, a. 1–2.
23. See the arguments of ST I, q. 45, aa. 1, 5, and 6, as well as ST I, q. 25, aa. 1–3.

not and cannot suspend if he intends to save and redeem the creation in the life of the resurrection. Consequently, God being God, God is always Creator. By that same measure, since the Son is true God, he is always the Creator with the Father, the Word through whom "all things were made" (John 1:3), even when he is the Word "made flesh" (John 1:14). The *Logos ensarkos* is the *Logos* of the Father who was in the beginning, he through whom the Father speaks so as to create the heavens and the earth. The God of Israel, then, who is the Creator of all things, has become genuinely human, been crucified, suffered, and died. "None of the rulers of this age understood this; for if they had, they would not have crucified the Lord of glory" (1 Cor. 2:8). We cannot divorce the New Testament Lordship of the Son from the Old Testament Lordship of the God of Israel. Consequently, if we wish to enunciate a doctrine of the kenosis of the Son, we must simultaneously maintain his pre-existent Lordship as the Creator of all that is. This entails that he possesses those perfections that are attributable to the Son precisely in virtue of his deity, perfections that are inalienable even in the Incarnation and crucifixion. As I have intimated above, these include the perfection of divine wisdom, goodness, love, mercy, justice, holiness, eternity, omnipotence (infinite power), and omnipresence. Truly, it is God who has become one of us.

The Son possesses all that the Father possesses as God, in a Filial Mode

It follows from the two principles mentioned above (the Son is truly God, God is truly the Creator) that the Son does not become God or develop as God as a consequence of his engagement with creation. That is to say, the Incarnation and crucifixion, and indeed the kenosis of the Son in history, is not something that gives being to the Creator. If one were to claim that it did so, this would lead inevitably in some fashion to the denial or obscuring of the scripturally revealed order of derivation: the creative Trinity communicates the plenitude of being to all things in creation out of the plenitude of perfection that the Trinity possesses ontologically prior to creation, and creation does not communicate being or perfection to God. The two are not part of a larger system in which each depends upon the other to contribute to the ongoing processes of the whole as if God were the living soul of the world. His utterly transcendent freedom to give (a dimension of his omnipotence) is a component of his communication of being in and through all time and in and through all instances, even as he freely begins to sustain creation in being forever in the mystery of the resurrection.

It follows from this idea that the Trinity cannot be perfected naturally or according to the plenitude of perfection of the divine essence in virtue of creation, Incarnation, kenosis, and resurrection. The mystery of God does not become internally more perfect, infinite, wise, or loving as a result of a developmental or evolutionary process in which God depends upon his relations in creation so as to self-perfect or self-enrich. The giving of God to creation and to human beings that is revealed initially to Israel and brought to fulfillment in Christ is of a wholly other order. God gives to us out of his immeasurable love and, in doing so, reveals who he is eternally in Christ. "God is love" (1 John 4:8). He can freely make himself subject to kenosis by becoming human because of the eternal power of his love, and in being truly human, suffering and dying, he can reveal to us that he is eternally perfect love. He does not undertake kenosis so as to develop as God in a divine life, that is, to become more loving, more powerful, or more perfectly self-improved. Likewise, the persons of the Trinity do not self-constitute in their eternal relations in virtue of the Son's temporal mission in the economy of taking on a human form. The economy of the Son's descent into our conditions is not constitutive of the relations that constitute the eternal processions of the persons from one another. The Son does not proceed eternally from the Father because of his kenotic Incarnation. The Father does not become the Father of the Son in virtue of the temporal kenosis of the Son, and the Spirit does not become the Spirit of the Lord Jesus in virtue of the kenosis of the Son. Rather, the eternal processions of the Son from the Father by way of generation and of the Spirit from the Father and the Son by way of spiration are the transcendent ontological presupposition of the economy, and these processions are made manifest in the temporal missions of the Son and the Spirit.[24] It is because God is eternally Triune in transcendent perfection of his creation that he can freely manifest himself to us and communicate to us a participation in his divine life by grace, precisely in the kenosis and exaltation of the Son.

The Fourth Lateran Council drew out an important facet of this teaching in 1215 in response to the Trinitarian theology of Joachim of Fiore, the 12th century Cistercian. Joachim held, in opposition to Peter Lombard, that in addition to saying that the Father eternally begets and that the Son is eternally begotten, Christians ought also to say that the divine essence begets and is begotten.[25] As the council noted, this idea leads to the mistaken notion that the divine essence is possessed unequally by the three persons so that some natural features of the deity are found in one person while other natural features of the deity are found in others.[26] So, for example, one might posit that the Father alone is all-powerful, while the Son is not, or that the Spirit alone is the source of grace, while the Father and the Son are not. Instead, the council underscored the dissimilitude of the three persons when compared with three human persons who may have distinct natural qualities and who are certainly three distinct individual beings. The Holy Trinity is one in being and essence, and each person possesses the plenitude of the divine essence, the deity in all its perfection. Consequently, each person is the one God, and there

---

24. ST I, q. 43. See the study of this issue by Gilles Emery, "*Theologia* and *Dispensatio*: The Centrality of the Divine Missions in St. Thomas's Trinitarian Theology."

25. See the analysis of Joachim's position in Gilles Emery, *The Trinitarian Theology of St. Thomas Aquinas*, 145–48.

26. See the Fourth Lateran Council in Denzinger, 800–820, esp. 803–4. 804: "This reality [the divine essence] is neither generating nor generated nor proceeding, but it is the Father who generates, the Son who is generated, and the Spirit who proceeds." 805: "One cannot say that he [the Father] gave him [the Son] a part of his substance and retained a part for himself, since the substance of the Father is indivisible, being entirely simple. Nor can one say that in generating, the Father transferred his substance to the Son, as though he gave it to the Son in such a way as not to retain it for himself . . ."

are not three gods. All that is in one person is in the other two, according to the origin of processional relations. The Father is the fontal origin of Trinitarian life from whom all comes forth, including the eternal divine life of the Son and the Spirit. The Son is the eternally begotten one, the *Logos* of God who receives all that he has and is as God eternally from the Father, God from God. The Spirit is the eternally spirated love of the Father and the Son, who proceeds from each as from one principle and as the mutual love of each. All that is in the Father that pertains to his deity is communicated to the Son by generation and all that is in the Father and the Son is communicated to the Holy Spirit by way of spiration. Consequently, when each of them acts personally in any work of creation or sanctification, it is also always all three who act personally and essentially, as God. The Son, in his kenosis, as one who is human, acts, lives, and dies among us, crucified, but in doing so, he also acts as the crucified Lord, one who can communicate grace to the world, even in his death, in virtue of his divine identity. Consequently, he acts with the Father, as one who proceeds eternally from the Father, as Lord. He acts also with the Spirit of the Lord, the Holy Spirit who proceeds from him and from the Father, as from one principle, who is sent upon the world from the cross and in the resurrection. Even in the kenotic life of the Son, then, it is all three persons who act to save and redeem. This claim must, in fact, absolutely be maintained if we wish to affirm that the Trinity is revealed in the cross of God. It is only if and because the three persons act concordantly and in their divine unity as God in the mystery of the self-emptying and crucifixion of the Son that we can, in turn, say that they are each revealed in the event of the crucifixion, in their real personal distinctness and in their divine unity.

We can conclude this line of argument by noting that just because the Son acts always with the Father (John 5:17), there is a modal distinction of personal action that should be acknowledged when we speak about the life of the Trinity.[27] The Father creates all

27. My argument on this point is influenced by Gilles Emery, "The Personal Mode of Trinitarian Action in Saint Thomas Aquinas."

things as the fontal origin of trinitarian life. However, he also only creates through the Word (John 1:1–3) and in his Spirit of holiness. The relations of origin of the three persons constitute the way in which each of them subsists, as innascible, generated, or spirated.[28] As Aquinas notes, the Son is truly God and has *in himself* the fullness of the divine power and will, but he does not have this *from himself* but only ever eternally from the Father.[29] He is also only ever "for" the spiration of their mutual love, just as the Holy Spirit is only ever the mutual gift of the Father and the Son, one who joyfully has all that he is from them and, in being so, eternally knows and loves all that is in the Father and the Son. These eternal relations in God are revealed to us by the missions of the Son and the Spirit. While the modal differences of the persons are not constituted or fashioned by the temporal missions of the persons, they are instantiated or rendered concretely present in these missions. The way the Son is God with us in his visible mission of Incarnation, then, is distinctively filial in mode or character. All that Jesus of Nazareth does and suffers as a human agent is obliquely indicative of his hidden identity as Son and so, also pertains to his filial way of being. Jesus of Nazareth is one who is always from his Father, and for the Father in all that he does and is as a person.[30] His life of human lowliness is lived for the

---

28. C.f. *ST* I, q. 29, a. 4.

29. See the argument to this effect in *SCG* IV, c. 8, para. 9: "The saying also, then, 'the Son cannot do anything of Himself,' [John 5:19] does not point to any weakness of action in the Son. But, because for God to act is not other than to be, and His action is not other than His essence … so one says that the Son cannot act from Himself but only from the Father, just as He is not able to be from Himself but only from the Father. For, if He were from Himself, He would no longer be the Son. Therefore, just as the Son cannot not be the Son, so neither can He act of Himself. However, because the Son receives the same nature as the Father and, consequently, the same power, although the Son neither is of Himself nor operates of Himself, He nevertheless is through Himself and operates through Himself, since just as He is through His own nature received from the Father, so He operates through His own nature received from the Father. Hence, after our Lord had said: 'the Son cannot do anything of Himself,' to show that, although the Son does not operate of Himself, He does operate through Himself, He adds: 'Whatever He does'— namely, the Father—'these the Son does likewise.'"

30. I have explored this idea in greater depth in *The Incarnate Lord,* ch. 5, and in *The Trinity,* part IV.

Father, and in view of the communication of the Holy Spirit of his Father, to all of humanity. "I came to cast fire on the earth" (C.f. Luke 12:49 and Acts 2:3). Likewise, the Spirit who is active in the corporate life of the Church is always only the Spirit of the Son and the Father, who alerts us to the reality of the Son present among us in the resurrection, and who in doing so turns us toward the Father of Jesus Christ by way of an adoptive life of grace in the Son.

THE KENOSIS OF THE SON AS A REVELATION OF THE TRINITY

In light of these considerations, how might we think about the kenosis of the Son more specifically as a revelation of the Trinity? Some options that have been excluded by the line of argument given above deserve mention in this context.

G. W. F. Hegel developed an original Christological ontology in light of his innovative interpretation of the use of the communication of idioms.[31] Prior to Hegel, there were significant pre-existing strata of debate in the Lutheran tradition regarding the communication of idioms. Luther famously had appealed to the notion of the omnipresence of Christ's humanity in debates regarding the Eucharist so as to maintain the affirmation of the presence of the risen Christ in the Lord's supper.[32] His appeal to this idea of a natural omnipresence of the humanity of the Son was disavowed by Calvin, as it was also by influential Catholic theologians.[33] The Lutheran Giessen and Tubingen schools of theology subsequently disputed ways

31. See in particular Hegel, *Lectures on the Philosophy of Religion, The Lecture of 1827*, Vol. 3, "The Consummate Religion," 452–69.

32. See Martin Luther, *Confession Concerning Christ's Supper* (1528), trans. R. H. Fisher, in *Luther's Works* vol. 37, ed. R. H. Fisher and H. T. Lehmann (Philadelphia: Fortress, 1961), 232–33; 276–81, and *Brief Confession Concerning the Holy Sacrament*, trans. M. E. Lehmann in *Luther's Works* vol. 38, ed. H. T. and M. E. Lehmann (Philadelphia: Fortress, 1971), 306–4.

33. See, for example, John Calvin, *Institutes of the Christian Religion*, IV, ch. 17, 16–31, esp. section 30, where Calvin claims that the attribution of ubiquity to the humanity of Christ violates a right usage of the practice of the communication of idioms.

in which natural properties of the deity might be communicated to the humanity of Christ and either surrendered or concealed for the duration of his visible life in the world as human.[34] Again, this debate presupposed that, contrary to the principles we have enunciated above, one might attribute various properties of the divine perfection, such as omnipresence or omnipotence, to the human nature as such. The innovation of Hegel was to invert the perspective so as to ascribe the human attributes to the deity rather than the inverse. In becoming human, God freely adopts finitude, temporality, historical development, experience of evil, death, and nothingness into his own being and nature.[35] On this view, the very nature of God is constituted developmentally by God becoming human. Hegel's new metaphysics of divine reason depicts the historical world as an unfolding of the divine life, happening in time and history.[36]

34. See the analysis in Wolfhart Pannenberg, *Jesus God and Man*, 2nd ed., trans. L. L. Wilkins, D. A. Priebe (Philadelphia: Westminster Press, 1968), 307–23.

35. See Hegel, *Lectures on the Philosophy of Religion*, Vol. 3, "The Consummate Religion," 452–69. Pp. 468–69: "'God himself is dead,' it says in a Lutheran hymn, expressing an awareness that the human, the finite, the fragile, the weak, the negative are themselves a moment of the divine, that they are within God himself, that finitude, negativity, otherness are not outside of God and do not, as otherness, hinder unity with God. Otherness, the negative, is known to be a moment of the divine nature itself. This involves the highest idea of spirit.... this is the explication of reconciliation: that God is reconciled with the world, that even the human is not something alien to him, but rather that this otherness, this self-distinguishing [of the divine nature through diremption], finitude as it is expressed, is a moment in God himself..." On historical aspects of the communication of idioms in the Tübingen school, see also Walter Kasper, *The Absolute in History: The Philosophy and Theology of History in Schelling's Late Philosophy*, 459–65.

36. Hegel, *Lectures on the Philosophy of Religion*, Vol. 3, "The Consummate Religion," 417–37. Pp. 417–18: "... we consider God in his eternal idea, as he is in and for himself, prior to or apart from the creation of the world, so to speak ... But God is the creator of the world; it belongs to his being, his essence, to be the creator.... His creative role is not an *actus* that 'happened' once; [rather,] what takes place in the idea is an *eternal* moment, an eternal determination of the idea.... Specifically, the eternal idea is expressed in terms of the holy *Trinity*: it is God himself, eternally triune. Spirit is this process, movement, life. This life is self-differentiation, self-determination, and the first differentiation is that spirit *is* as this universal idea itself." As Karl Barth rightly notes in his critical appraisal in *CD* IV:1, 179–83, God can only acquire his humanity, for Hegel, by voiding or foregoing divine prerogatives and suspending the activity of his divine attributes, at least in his personal mode of being as the Son of God.

From the point of view of the argument presented above, we may say that Hegel's proposal fails to recognize sufficiently the real distinction of the divine and human natures of Christ, which are truly united in the person of Christ, mysteriously, yet without confusion.[37] As a consequence, Hegel forfeits an adequate theology of God's transcendence and fails to acknowledge sufficiently God in his incomprehensible nature as Creator. Instead of being the one who freely communicates being to all that is, actively present in all things in history as the giver of being, Hegel's God is a process of reason and freedom that develops on the conditional basis of a created history. Likewise, the Trinity is constituted for Hegel by the Son's kenotic human life among us, a view that is inadequate to divine revelation. The history of God as incarnate is not a moment within the development of God's intra-trinitarian personhood, such that the processions of the persons would be subject to definition or alteration in virtue of the Incarnation, passion, death, and resurrection of Christ.[38] Needless to say, we also cannot know of the Trinity by a mere process of philosophical reasoning, something Hegel's philosophy seems to intimate.

Karl Barth perceived a number of the problems with Hegel's proposal and sought to save his novel proposal regarding the communication of idioms by placing it on a different footing.[39] Barth affirms

37. A point helpfully emphasized by Bruce L. McCormack in "Karl Barth's Christology as a Resource for a Reformed Version of Kenoticism."

38. Hegel's metaphysics is one in which the freedom of God is supreme among all divine attributes such that God can choose to self-identify with his seeming contrary and deploy his nature in a plastic way, to be eternal or temporal, impassible or suffering, omnipotent or powerless, existent or non-existent, Father or Son. The nature of God is defined then by an all-inclusive process of rational freedom that assimilates and transcends contraries passing through them as historical moments of self-development. This ontology is, however, alien to the biblical notion of God's freedom as something that stems from his nature and from the Trinitarian mystery of the Father, Son, and Spirit. The divine freedom does not continually re-define God's nature, like a liquid subject submitted to historical process or voluntary whim. Instead, the divine freedom is expressive of God's enduring *Logos*, and of his eternal goodness and love, manifest in the work of his Spirit. The Trinity communicates being to and saves the creation, and not the inverse.

39. CD IV:1, 179–210. CD IV:1, 182–83: "... according to the teaching of Thomasius,

that features of the Son's kenotic life are attributable to his eternal nature as Son, namely his humility, lowliness, obedience, and (arguably also) his suffering, but these features of the Son's natural life as God are not acquired by him in virtue of the kenosis of the Incarnation. Rather, they pertain to him in a higher way as God from all eternity, as the precondition for the temporal kenosis. There is a divine self-emptying in God eternally that functions as the transcendent ontological precondition of the temporal kenosis of the Son in time.[40] The human obedience and suffering unto death of the Son as

the *kenosis* consisted in the fact that in the Incarnation the divine Logos renounced the attributes of majesty in relation to the world (omnipotence, omnipresence, etc.), in order that in the man Jesus, until His exaltation, He might be God only in His immanent qualities, His holiness and love and truth. In Gess ... we are told that 'a change took place in the Son of God.' In the Incarnation He ceased to be actually God, in order to become conscious of Himself as God with the developing self-consciousness of Jesus, undergoing an 'evolution' in His identity with the man Jesus and finally being clothed again with the glory which He had had before in His exaltation.... They wanted to clear away the difficulties of the traditional teaching and make possible a 'historical' consideration of the life of Jesus. But they succeeded only in calling in question that 'God was in Christ' and in that way damaging the nerve of a Christology oriented by the Old and New Testaments. There are many things we can try to say in understanding the christological mystery. But we cannot possibly understand or estimate it if we try to explain it by a self-limitation or de-divinisation of God in the uniting of the Son of God with the man Jesus. If in Christ—even in the humiliated Christ born in a manger at Bethlehem and crucified on the cross of Golgotha—God is not unchanged and wholly God, then everything that we may say about the reconciliation of the world made by God in this humiliated One is left hanging in the air."

40. *CD* IV:1, p. 209: "The One who in this obedience is the perfect image of the ruling God is Himself-as distinct from every human and creaturely kind-God by nature, God in His relationship to Himself, that is, God in His mode of being as the Son in relation to God in His mode of being as the Father, One with the Father and of one essence. In His mode of being as the Son He fulfills the divine subordination, just as the Father in His mode of being as the Father fulfills the divine superiority. In humility as the Son who complies, He is the same as is the Father in majesty as the Father who disposes. He is the same in consequence (and obedience) as the Son as is the Father in origin. He is the same as the Son, that is, as the self-posited God ... as is the Father as the self-positing God ... The Father as the origin is never apart from Him as the consequence, the obedient One. The self-positing of God is never apart from Him as the One who is posited as God by God. The One who eternally begets is never apart from the One who is eternally begotten." Barth connects this eternal self-positing of God as Son to the determination of the divine essence for the mission-unto-dereliction of the Son in *CD* IV:2, p. 86: "No diminution comes to [the divine essence] by the fact that it is wholly directed and addressed to human essence in Jesus Christ, sharing its limitation and weakness and even

man, therefore, can be revelatory of an eternal divine obedience and self-surrender that exists in the deity prior to and independently of the creation.[41]

This idea is much closer to classical Trinitarian principles since it maintains a distinction of natures in Christ and does not entail the notion that the life of God is constituted by the historical economy or that the Trinity comes into being or undergoes internal development in virtue of the Incarnation. Nevertheless, Barth's position is surprisingly similar to that of Joachim of Fiore, mentioned above, in which it was said that the divine nature generates and is generated. By attributing command and obedience, paternal initiative, and filial kenosis to the deity of God itself (the divine nature), Barth posits a real distinction in God of natural attributes and ascribes some attributes of the divine essence to the Son and some to the Father. Various questions arise from this decision. For example, if the Son is truly one in being and essence with the Father, how may the Father

---

its lostness in the most radical and consistent way. But again, in this address, direction and participation, it does not acquire the increase of any alien capacity or even incapacity [i.e., in contrast with the views of Hegel, Thomasius, and Bulgakov noted above]. No difference at all is made. What then is the divine essence? It is the free love, the omnipotent mercy, the holy patience of the Father, Son and Holy Spirit. And it is the God of this divine essence who has and maintains the initiative in this event. He is not, therefore, subject to any higher force when He gives Himself up to the lowliness of the human being of the Son of God ... The offering is, therefore, elected and determined by His own majesty-the majesty of the divine Subject."

41. See CD IV:2, pp. 87–89. P. 87: "God is not only love ... but He loves, and He loves man-so much so that He gives Himself to him. He is not only gracious, but He exercises grace, and He does this by becoming the Son of Man as the Son of God, and therefore in the strictest, total union of His nature with ours. This does not take place at the expense but in the power of His divine nature. It is, however a determination which He gives it. It [the divine nature] acquires in man its *telos*. Directed and addressed to human nature it acquires a form, *this* form. This is why we cannot possibly maintain that the participation of the two natures in Jesus Christ is only one-sided, that of the human in the divine. In the first instance, indeed, it is that of the divine in the human." See also CD IV:1, pp. 208–10. Barth is clearly positing an *analogia relationis* by which God acquires his divine identity in both his nature as God and his personal mode of being as Son through the elective relationship he freely undertakes toward humanity, and the Incarnation, but this relationality has its precondition in God's self-determination for Sonship, in virtue of the eternal obedience of the Son toward the Father.

have natural capacities the Son does not have, and how may the Son have natural capacities that the Father does not have? If this is the case, each is perfect in various ways that the other is not, so that one may rightly ask whether there is a perfect unity of shared divine life. In fact, the position seems, despite protests to the contrary, to entail that each subject is finite, living within a larger (infinite?) process of becoming, seemingly one realized through the Son's submission to the Father. If this submission takes place at all, it must seemingly do so in the economy, in which case the economy is, in fact, essential to God's achievement of infinite life. Or likewise, if the Son and Father are constituted by distinct voluntary acts (rather than relations of origin, as is classically affirmed by seemingly all previous influential theological authors before Hegel and Barth), then there are distinct natural characteristics of willing present in the two subjects, and even it seems distinct wills. If this is the case, can we really speak of a divine unity of will in the Trinity exemplified in acts of creation and redemption, or as the authors of Lateran IV feared in regard to the thought of Joachim, are we not now dealing with a college of morally autonomous subjects who are not one in essence and will, but who decide to collaborate freely by a perennial repetition of mutually consensual decisions? Or if we say that Barth is merely signaling that the Son receives his eternal willing from the Father, and wills what the Father wills, but that the Son is constituted by this obedience to the Father's eternal willing, then are we not also committed to saying that the Son is constituted by willing what the Father wills, namely, the missions of the Son and Spirit into the world? In this case, the Son is constituted by willing to incarnate and so the temporal kenosis is in fact determinative of the eternal life of the Trinity and not the inverse.

While these options seem unworkable to me, I do think that they depend upon a resolve to argue that the kenosis of the Son in time is truly expressive of the intra-Trinitarian life of God. Of course, this must be the case in some way, so one is justified in asking what it would mean to affirm this while upholding the divine perfection of the Son in the way I have attempted to do in the arguments given above. By way of conclusion, then, I will suggest three ways I think that a theology of divine perfection can maintain and even emphasize rightly that the Holy Trinity is manifest to us, in a particularly intensive way, in the human kenosis of the Son.

First, on the view I have been exploring in this chapter, it should be said that kenosis pertains to the Son alone, not the Father or the Spirit, and that it pertains to him personally in virtue of his human nature, not his divine nature as such. It is only the Son who has become human, been crucified, died, and has risen from dead in a glorified human nature. We can and must say rightly that God himself underwent kenosis by becoming human and that God was crucified, and died in agony, but he did so as one who is truly human. The point of kenotic theology is not to submit the deity to becoming but to say that the transcendent God submitted to human becoming. Soteriologically, it matters that God retains his divine perfection, even in his crucifixion. It is the undying and infinite perfection of Trinitarian love that is manifest to us in the death of Christ crucified. The one who suffers in kenosis is the very one who alone can truly save us effectively in virtue of his hidden eternal power. He who suffered, died, and descended into hell as one of us is the one who can redeem all of us and, indeed, remake creation. Consequently, we must maintain a real distinction of natures in Christ, numinously present, even as we ascribe kenosis to God in virtue of the hominization of the Son.

Second, this kenosis, which stems precisely from God becoming human, is filial in mode. This is the case because Christ is the Son of God, and so all that he does as both God and man is emblematic of his person and expressed in a filial mode. Following Barth, then, we might think of the Gospel's depictions of the various human loves, desires, intentions, counsels, choices, and concrete initiatives of Jesus of Nazareth conducted in obedience to the divine will. Such human actions are not identical to the divine will as such. In his human willing, Jesus is submitted to the divine will of the Father, a will that mysteriously abides in him as Lord and that is fully present in the Spirit as well, who acts with Christ in his human mind and heart, inspiring him from within to conform his life inwardly to this divine will. Thus, the human decisions of Jesus transpire in harmony with the divine will and consequently are obliquely revelatory of the Father's designs, designs that the Lord Jesus Christ and the Spirit share in. If all this is true, then the obedience of the Son of Man is indicative of the shared life of Trinitarian communion and inter-personal love. His free acceptance of suffering, his decision to die by crucifixion, and his expiration in love on the cross indicate and manifest the hidden ground of love, the uncreated mystery of the Father, whose life he shares in fully as his transcendent Word, as the Lord of Israel crucified, spirating the Holy Spirit from the dereliction of the cross and sending that Spirit on mission to all creation as the Spirit of holiness and sanctification.

Third, even as we say rightly that the human self-emptying unto death of Christ can and does truly reveal intra-Trinitarian personal communion and the uncreated love of God as the fundamental ground of the world, we must preserve the analogical interval between the divine freedom of Christ as God and the human freedom of Christ as man, between the uncreated deity in its perfect power to remake all things and the fragile created nature in which God lives kenotically in solidarity with us in his perfect humanity, subject to suffering and death. Finitude is not a curse that God must reject for himself. It is merely the congenital sign of being a creation with the nobility and limitation that this entails, a finitude that invites us to turn upward in our restless minds and hearts toward a yet higher, infinite source for which we naturally yearn. The Son does not need to cede his deity of being in the form of God by an impossible alienation of his divine prerogatives in order to take on our finitude and to garner our loyalty. He was not jealous of his divine transcendence. Precisely because of the inalienable perfection of his love and power to redeem as God, he could become finite and humanly limited without ceasing to be infinitely perfect and divine. Consequently, in imitation of Christ, we should not be jealous of that transcendent perfection he alone has as a man who is God, as if we should require God to evacuate his perfection as Creator as a premise for his rendering himself present to us. Nor, however, should we ignore the distinctive perfection of Christ's humanity. It is a perfection achieved precisely in the lowliness of suffering and death and in surrender to the divine perfection of the Father, manifest in the obedience of love that characterized his human life. That human perfection was lived out among us in terms that have now become imitable by grace, as St. Paul tells us. (Phil. 2:5) We can, therefore, set out along the pathway of the Son who took on the form of a servant, and we may do so in the hope of the vision of his glory (1 Cor 13:12), a perfect glory of one who is eternally with and from the Father as Lord (John 17:5), in an eternal communion of life shared with the Holy Spirit. It is to that high place of eternal Trinitarian life that Jesus Christ is now exalted, and it is there that we hope to follow him.

12

The Voluntary Action
of the Earthly Christ and the Necessity
of the Beatific Vision

That Christ, in his earthly existence, possessed the beatific vision (or immediate knowledge of God) is a traditional affirmation of Christian theology.[1] However, this Christological theory is increasingly questioned by theologians deeply committed to the Catholic tradition, precisely on the grounds that they believe the theory, in fact, endangers more essential, traditional doctrines of Catholic belief. The latter include the patristic affirmations of the complete reality of Christ's historical human nature and the unity of subject in Christ's human actions.

Versions of this chapter were previously published in *The Thomist* 69 (2005): 497–534, and *The Incarnate Lord* (Washington, DC: The Catholic University Press: 2015), 236–76.

1. Medieval authors are mentioned below. For the recent Magisterium, see especially Pius XII, *Mystici Corporis* (DS 3812); *The Catechism of the Catholic Church*, n. 473; and John Paul II, *Novo Millennio Ineunte*, nn. 25–27. For recent Thomistic theological arguments in favor of the traditional teaching, see Romanus Cessario, "Incarnate Wisdom and the Immediacy of Christ's Salvific Knowledge," in *Problemi teologici alla luce dell'Aquinate*, Studi Tomistici 44:5 (Vatican City: Libreria Editrice Vaticana, 1991): 334–40; Jean-Miguel Garrigues, "La conscience de soi telle qu'elle était exercée par le Fils de Dieu fait homme," *Nova et Vetera* (French Edition) 79, no. 1 (2004): 39–51; Matthew Levering, *Christ's Fulfillment of Torah and Temple: Salvation According to Thomas Aquinas* (Notre Dame, IN: University of Notre Dame Press, 2002): 32–33; 39; 59–63; 73–75; Guy Mansini, "Understanding St. Thomas on Christ's Immediate Knowledge of God," *The Thomist* 59 (1995): 91–124.

In this chapter, I would like to present briefly two common objections against the classical theory and offer a response inspired by the Thomistic tradition. Both Jean Galot and Thomas Weinandy have argued that the doctrine of the beatific vision in the earthly life of Christ compromises the reality of the humanity of Jesus, on the one hand, and the unity of his filial personhood, on the other.

Having presented these claims, I will argue (against this perspective) that the affirmation of the beatific vision of the historical Christ was and is essential for maintaining the unity of his person in and through the duality of his natures, and most particularly in safeguarding the unity of his personal agency in and through the duality of his two wills (human and divine). This is not an argument Aquinas makes explicitly.[2] However, it is a conclusion that can be derived from his Christological principles. I will show this by referring to the studies of Herman Diepen, Jacques Maritain, and, more recently, Jean-Miguel Garrigues. They argue that in order for the created will of Jesus to be the instrument of his transcendent person, it must have a filial mode of being: it is expressive of the person who directs the human action of Christ, the Incarnate Son of God. This requires, in turn, that the human will of Christ conform to his divine personal will in all actions.

However, so that the exercise of the human will of Christ might be specified by the directives of his transcendent (divine) personhood and will, a higher knowledge concerning the divine will of the Son of God is necessary. This ultimately requires not only an "infused science" but also immediate knowledge of God present in the soul of Christ in and through all of his human actions. Having appropriated arguments from these thinkers on these points, I will conclude (with reference to Galot and Weinandy) that if the human action of Jesus is to be the personal action of the Son of God, it must be immediately subject to the activity of the divine will which

---

2. Aquinas's explicit arguments for the beatific vision of Christ are soteriological: Christ must have the vision so that he can communicate it to others. See *ST* III, q. 9, a. 2; *Comp. Theo.* c. 216.

it expresses. This requires that the human intellect of Jesus possess the vision of God.

Finally, I will show that only with this classical analysis of Christ's human vision of God can one understand the mystery of Christ's obedience and prayer without falling into either a confusion of the natures or a denial of the unity of his person. I will examine briefly Aquinas's treatment of both the obedience and the prayer of Christ as *human* manifestations of his *divine identity,* that is, as expressions of his intra-Trinitarian, filial relationship with the Father. Through both of these activities, which are proper to his created human nature, the man Jesus manifests *in his human acts* his personal, hypostatic mode of being as the eternal Son of God. As I will show, this is not possible without the presence in Christ of an immediate knowledge of his own filial nature and divine will. Therefore, without this traditional theological teaching, one cannot make adequate sense of the obedience and prayer of Jesus as revelatory of the Trinitarian persons. This being the case, the central objections to Aquinas's theory offered by Galot and Weinandy are unfounded. On the contrary, the classical theory of the immediate vision is necessary to safeguard the traditional Christology they wish to defend, as it is exemplified in the action of the earthly life of Christ.

CHALLENGES TO THE TRADITION[3]

Jean Galot, in an article in 1986, offered foundational contemporary criticisms to the traditional theory of the beatific vision in the

---

3. In this chapter, I offer no defense of the use of traditional Christological terms and conciliar definitions as applied to Jesus of Nazareth. All of the authors discussed below take their validity for granted (in differing ways) and employ them freely in this dispute. The presupposition here, then, is in favor of a certain kind of "Christology from above" that interprets Christ from within the classical Catholic tradition. Nevertheless, a complete treatment of the relationship between the historical Jesus, the early Church, New Testament literature, and the Hellenistic world of early Catholic dogma is essential to a coherent modern Christology. Valuable theological reflections on such issues are found in Walter Kasper, *Jesus the Christ*; and Gerald O'Collins, *Christology: A Biblical, Historical and Systematic Study of Jesus Christ* (Oxford: Oxford University Press, 1995).

earthly life of Christ.[4] His argument presents the most comprehensive and forceful criticism of the tradition in question and has since found favor with other authors.[5] More recently, Thomas Weinandy has developed criticisms that echo some of Galot's initial viewpoints.[6] In assessing the most pertinent challenges to the traditional teaching on this subject, I will briefly consider two of their criticisms, the first from Galot and the second from Weinandy. The accord between them on this subject gives a fair sense of the contemporary challenges to the tradition.

Jean Galot: Beatific Vision as Latent Monophysitism

Galot begins his argument with the claim that the doctrine of the immediate vision of God in the earthly life of Christ stems from an *a priori*, purely deductive reflection derived from the reasoning of medieval Scholastic theology without sufficient reference to the evidences of Scripture or the patristic theological heritage. He traces the teaching's historical origins from Candide (ninth century) to Hugh of St. Victor and from the latter to the *Sentences* of Lombard, from which it was developed into its classical form by Aquinas and other influential theologians of the High Scholastic period.[7] What all of these thinkers have in common is the appeal to an

---

4. Jean Galot, "Le Christ terrestre et la vision," *Gregorianum* 67 (1986), 429–50. Other related works include *La conscience de Jésus* (Paris: Duculot-Lethielleux, 1971); and *Vers une nouvelle christologie* (Paris: Duculot-Lethielleux, 1971).

5. See in particular Jean-Pierre Torrell, "S. Thomas d'Aquin et la science du Christ," in *Saint Thomas au XXe siècle*, ed. S. Bonino (Paris: Éditions St. Paul, 1994), 394–409.

6. Thomas Weinandy, "Jesus' Filial Vision of the Father," *Pro Ecclesia* 13 (2004): 189–201.

7. Galot, "Le Christ terrestre," 429–31; cf. Candide, *Epistola* 6 (PL 106:106); *Opusculum de Passione Domini* 17 (PL 106:95AB); Hugues of St. Victor, *De sapientia animae Christi* (PL 176:853AB); *De sacramentis christianae fidei* 2.1.6 (PL 176:388D-89B); Peter Lombard, III *Sent.*, d. 14, n. 2 (PL 192:783–84); *ST* III, q. 9, a. 4; III, q. 12, aa. 1 and 3. Galot writes ("Le Christ terrestre," 429 n. 3): "The patristic sources furnish no explicit testimony in favor of a beatific vision in the earthly life of Christ." However he does admit that the doctrine is evidently implicit in the affirmations of St. Fulgence (468–533), *Epist.* 14, q. 3, 25–34 (PL 65:415–24). (All translations from French sources into English are mine unless otherwise noted.).

argument based upon the necessary perfection of the human nature of Jesus. Because of the dignity of the hypostatic union, the humanity of Christ should be accorded the perfection of all human attributes from the time of his conception, excluding those which may act in some way as a hindrance to the realization of his soteriological mission, such as not being subject to emotional and physical suffering, as well as death. The vision of God must be included among such privileges. Therefore, Christ possessed the perfection of all human knowledge, and this would include, of course, not only the vision of God but also the infused science of prophetic *species,* by which he might know all that man could possibly come to know.[8]

Galot argues that, besides lacking sufficient reference to scriptural evidence of the earthly Christ, such a perspective, in fact, leads to an implicit denial of the real humanity of the earthly Christ, who was in his *created* humanity (like all intellectual creatures) subject to certain natural intellectual limitations. Among these would be the historically and culturally conditioned mode of his self-understanding, as well as social interdependencies for the exercise of his learning. The affirmation of this terrestrial vision, in fact, divinizes the earthly man Jesus in an unrealistic way. It is tantamount to a certain kind of Monophysitism in the epistemological realm:

> First of all, instead of referring to the testimony of the Gospels in order to discover the forms of knowledge which were manifest in the words and gestures of Jesus, the theological method proceeds in this case by positing an ideal of perfection from which is deduced all of the human knowledge of Christ. This a priori deduction leads to a maximum of perfection which itself impedes one from accurately taking account of the concrete conditions in which the human thought of

8. *ST* III, q. 9, a. 1: "Now what is in potentiality is imperfect unless reduced to act. But it was fitting that the Son of God should assume, not an imperfect, but a perfect human nature, since the whole human race was to be brought back to perfection by its means. Hence it behooved the soul of Christ to be perfected by a knowledge, which would be its proper perfection ... [namely, the beatific vision and the plenitude of infused science]." For further evidence of this "principle of perfection" see also *ST* III, q. 9, aa. 2 and 4; III, q. 11, a. 1; III, q. 12, aa. 1 and 3. I will argue below that Galot's treatment of Aquinas's thought is selective on this point, and fails to take sufficiently into account the "'economic'" character of Christ's extraordinary knowledge as St. Thomas understands it.

Jesus developed. This perfection attributed to Christ's knowledge is such that one no longer respects sufficiently the distinction between the divine nature and the human nature ... Human understanding is clothed with divine properties as regards the entire domain of knowledge. One can see immediately the risk of Monophysitism, and more precisely the difficulty in acknowledging the inherent limitations of human knowledge, a necessary recognition for avoiding all confusion with the perfection of divine knowledge.[9]

Furthermore, this affirmation has soteriological consequences. Galot argues if the earthly Christ possesses the vision of God and the consequent joy that follows from it (even if confined to the "heights" of the spiritual soul, as Aquinas affirms), then the true sufferings of his human life are attenuated in their salvific reality. They can no longer be true acts of human self-emptying (*kenosis*) in loving solidarity with our human condition, as portrayed by St. Paul in his Epistle to the Philippians.[10] The agony of the crucifixion and the cry of dereliction are not permitted their reality, and thus revelation is muted. In fact, the affirmation of such a vision of God obscures something of the epiphany of self-emptying love that God manifested through the event of the crucifixion and which the gospel writers wished to relate to us.

> A Jesus whose soul would have been continually immersed in the beatific vision would have only assumed the exterior appearances of our human life ... His resemblance to us would only have been a façade ... What would become of the sufferings of the passion? ... Not only does [the doctrine of the vision] put at risk the reality of the Incarnation, but also that of the redemptive sacrifice. How can we attribute to a Savior who is filled with heavenly beatitude these words: "My God, My God, why have you abandoned me?" ... The cry of Jesus on the cross makes manifest the depths of a suffering that is incompatible with the beatitude of the vision.[11]

---

9. Galot, "Le Christ terrestre," 431–32.

10. Phil 2:7–8: "He emptied himself, taking the form of a slave, coming in human likeness; and found human in appearance, he humbled himself, becoming obedient to death, even death on a cross."

11. Galot, "Le Christ terrestre," 434.

In place of these theological motifs, then, Galot proposes the existence in the historical Christ of a form of prophetic insight (infused science), by which he was endowed with a human awareness (albeit extraordinary) of his divine identity and soteriological mission. Certainly, Galot concedes, Christ did not know of his own identity by the theological virtue of faith. Yet his inspired conscious awareness of his own divine, filial identity was properly human, respecting the limitations of his created nature.[12] This more "sober" recognition of an extraordinary form of knowledge in the earthly Christ can account sufficiently for his privileged knowledge of his Father and his own filial identity, as well as his prophetic insights into salvation history, scriptural meaning, and the hidden thoughts of men's hearts. No recourse to the beatific vision is necessary.

Thomas Weinandy: The Vision of God in Jesus as a Nestorian Division of Subjects

Thomas Weinandy has published a great deal on the consciousness of Christ and is in part influenced by Galot. He has attempted to rethink the traditional understanding of the vision of God in Christ to emphasize the unity of the person of Christ and the Trinitarian character of Jesus' human knowledge of and relation to the Father.[13] Weinandy, following Galot, claims that in one respect, the affirmation of the vision of God in the earthly life of Christ denies Jesus his

12. Galot, 439–40: "It is certainly true that Jesus [as portrayed in the Scriptures] did not live in faith ... He knows the Father and he is conscious of being the Son. He does not believe in himself. He possesses the certitude of his own identity, by way of his personal consciousness. Others are invited to believe in him ... This consciousness implies an illumination received from above, an infused knowledge ... However, this infused knowledge that makes possible the conscious awareness of a divine 'I,' does not transform Jesus' human self-awareness into a vision. It implies neither a human vision of God, nor a heavenly beatitude. It respects the ordinary conditions of human consciousness, and accords with the historical development of the latter." See also Jean Galot, "Problèmes de la conscience du Christ," part 2, "La conscience du Christ et la foi."

13. See especially Weinandy, "Jesus' Filial Vision of the Father," but also Thomas Weinandy, Does God Change? (Still River, MA: St. Bede's Press, 1985); and Does God Suffer? (Notre Dame, IN: University of Notre Dame Press, 2000).

natural, human manner of knowing and therefore implies a kind of semi-Monophysitism as regards Christ's consciousness.[14] However, the central criticism of the Franciscan theologian is that the theory of the beatific vision falls *in a different respect* into the opposite Christological heresy of Nestorianism. Precisely in order to render Christ invulnerable to the limits of a human form of knowledge, traditional theology has claimed that he knows the divine essence immediately. But this seems to suggest that the man Jesus knows the divinity as a transcendent object, distinct from himself as subject. The soul of Christ is conceived in terms similar to that of any other creaturely person, but in Christ's case, he knows his transcendent Creator immediately by a special privilege. The latter idea of the man Jesus receiving a special knowledge of God implicitly imposes upon Christology a duality of personal subjects or Nestorianism.[15]

Weinandy argues that if Christ is to stand personally in relation to God intellectually, it must be as the Son who is *humanly aware* of the Father. Christ's filial awareness need not imply the beatific vision as classically conceived but could be understood instead in terms of a grace of filial insight (unique to Christ alone), unfolding in Jesus' consciousness progressively through the ordinary processes of human self-reflexivity.[16] He goes on to argue that an authentic

14. Weinandy, "Jesus' Filial Vision," 189–90.

15. Weinandy, "Jesus' Filial Vision," 192: "the subject (the 'who') of any vision of the Father is not a subject (a 'who') different from that of the divine Son, but *the divine Son himself* since it is actually the Son who *is* man. Since it is the Son who must be the subject of any such vision of the Father, his vision of the Father cannot be a vision of the divine essence as an object ontologically distinct from and over against himself. As traditionally asked and answered, the question concerning Jesus' beatific vision, by the very nature of the question, always necessarily posited another subject (another 'who') distinct from that of the Son who possessed an objective vision of God who was other than 'himself,' and it is this positing of another subject (or 'who') which is why this question of Jesus' beatific vision was necessarily asked and answered in a Nestorian manner." For a similar consideration, see also Galot, "Le Christ terrestre," 440. Weinandy and Galot claim that Aquinas falls into precisely such a Nestorian manner of conceiving of the earthly Christ in relation to God in *ST* III q. 10, aa. 2 ("Whether the soul of Christ knew all things in the Word?") and 4 ("Whether the soul of Christ sees the Word more clearly than any other creature?").

16. Weinandy, "Jesus' Filial Vision," 193: "While traditionally Jesus is said to have

admission of the unity of personhood in Christ entails only one center of consciousness in his earthly existence. This would be the self-awareness of Christ that is proper to his human nature *alone*. The man Jesus has a human awareness of being a divine person and this reality cannot be abridged or obscured by appeal to a grace such as the beatific vision, which would make God an object of knowledge extrinsic to his person.[17]

Summary

For the purposes of this chapter, two central criticisms can be culled from the arguments examined above. Galot and Weinandy claim, in effect, that the affirmation of the beatific vision in the earthly life of Christ implicitly denies the reality of the human nature of Christ in its historical mode of functioning and instead stems from an *a priori* deductive argumentation concerning the perfection of the humanity of Jesus. The latter idea lacks a sufficient grounding in Scripture and the most profound principles of patristic theology.

---

possessed the beatific vision, I would want to argue, in keeping with the above, that it is more properly correct, in accordance with the hypostatic union, to speak of a human 'hypostatic vision': the person (*hypostasis*) of the Son possessed as man, a personal human vision of the Father by which he came to know the Father as the Father truly exists. In coming to know the Father as truly Father, the Son equally became humanly conscious of himself as Son"; see also "Jesus' Filial Vision," 197: "As Jesus, as a young boy, studied the Scriptures and prayed the Spirit illumined his human consciousness and intellect with the vision of the Father such that he became hypostatically aware of the Father's glory and love, and within such an awareness he became conscious of his divine identity and so came to know that he was indeed the Father's eternal and only begotten Son."

17. Weinandy, "Jesus' Filial Vision," 195–96: "the Son as divine is conscious of himself as God within his divine 'I'. However, within his incarnate state I would not want to posit two 'I's'—one divine and one human—for within his incarnate state the one divine Son *is only conscious of himself as man*, within a human manner (as man he cannot be conscious of himself in a divine manner), and thus there is, as man, only one 'I' and that human. Therefore, I think it is better, for clarity's sake, to speak of a human 'I' of a divine person or subject (a divine 'who'), rather than confuse the issue by positing a second 'I' that is divine" (emphasis added). The question this raises (which I will return to below) is: what correspondence exists between this human knowledge Christ has of the Father and his own properly *divine* knowledge of himself as the Son? What rapport exists between the Son's eternal self-knowledge and will and his human knowledge, if any? Do they relate to each other in the human action of Jesus, and if so, in what way?"

Furthermore, this theology carries with it the danger of conceiving of Christ as a creaturely subject distinct from the Trinity of persons who are the object of such beatifying knowledge.

In response, I would like to examine the different but related question of the cooperation of wills (human and divine) in the earthly Christ. Both Scripture and the patristic tradition insist on the distinction and cooperation of the two wills in the one subject of the Son of God. I will argue that this cooperation can only take place in one unified activity due to the presence in the created soul of Christ of an immediate knowledge of his own personal, divine will, and divine essence. Referring to studies of Aquinas by Diepen, Garrigues, and Maritain, I will argue that it follows from Thomistic Christological principles, then, that only this immediate vision permits the human will and intellect of Christ to take on a particular hypostatic mode: that of the Son of God. In other words, this vision safeguards the unity of the personal actions of Christ in and through his two distinct natures and operations. It is after examining these points that I will respond to Galot's and Weinandy's respective concerns about the reality of Jesus' humanity on the one hand and the unity of his person on the other. I will show that the beatific vision of Christ if correctly understood, is filial in *mode* and thus is essential for there to be personal unity in the voluntary acts of the man Jesus (contrary to claims of Nestorianism). However, in its *nature,* this vision is accorded to the created intellect and will of the humanity of Christ, which it respects, even in their historical and human mode of functioning (contrary to claims of Monophysitism). After this, the examples of the obedience and prayer of Christ can be studied as concrete illustrations of this doctrine.

AQUINAS ON THE VOLUNTARY ACTION OF CHRIST

In what follows, I will make three brief points, relying in part on the insights of recent Thomistic commentors. First of all, as Aquinas rightly points out, due to the Incarnation, the human nature of Jesus must be understood first and foremost in *instrumental* terms, as subsisting in his divine person and as expressive of the latter.

Second, if Christ's humanity is the instrument of his divinity, then this intimately affects the way his human will cooperates with his divine will. As Jean-Miguel Garrigues has shown, Aquinas follows Maximus the Confessor and John Damascene in distinguishing between the specifically human character of the natural will of Christ and its hypostatic mode. This distinction helps explain how the man Jesus can manifest his identity as the Son of God through his human actions from within the *unity* of his person. Christ must personally will as man what he personally wills as God, such that the two operations remain distinct, but his human will acquires a filial mode or manner of exercise. The personal unity of Christ will only be adequately expressed if there is a perfect cooperation between his human will and his divine will in all his human actions.

Finally, if Christ's human will and consciousness must act as the instruments of his divine subject, then his human will must be specified at each instant by his divine will through the medium of human knowledge. For this to take place, Christ as man must have human knowledge of his own filial divine nature and will. The virtue of faith, or a uniquely prophetic knowledge (by infused species), is not sufficient. The unity of activity of the Incarnate Word requires, therefore, the beatific vision in the intellect of Christ so that his human will and his divine will may cooperate within one subject.

The Integrity of Christ's Human Nature and Its Filial Mode of Subsistence

At stake in this debate is the capacity of "beatific-vision" theology to make sense of the Incarnation as it is presented in Scripture and patristic tradition. A central concern of Galot is to recognize the human integrity of Christ's intellectual life in its historical setting. Ordinary human knowledge is subject to limitations and the conventional understandings and modes of expression of a cultural context. For Aquinas, however, the integrity of the human nature of Christ is first understood not in epistemological but in ontological terms and is seen as guaranteed by a classical scriptural principle: revelation teaches that God assumed in Christ a true and complete human nature.[18] Herman Diepen showed in an important series of articles that in this respect, Aquinas's Christology is directly inspired by the Greek patristic tradition (especially Cyril of Alexandria, the councils of Ephesus, Chalcedon, and Constantinople III, and John Damascene) and that Aquinas purposefully appropriated this tradition in continuity with his own metaphysics of *esse*.[19] In his

18. Cf. John 1: 14; Phil 2:7–8; Heb 4:15. The ontological Christologies of the patristic and medieval authors can be contrasted in approach with the subject-oriented Christologies of Schleiermacher and Harnack, who sought to circumvent the formulae of the traditional dogma of the Church. Should Christology begin from a reflection on the consciousness of Christ or from the revealed principles of the New Testament authors such as John and Paul concerning the identity and nature of the Son of God? A treatment of this question exceeds the goals of this essay. Speaking in summary fashion, one can say that the consciousness and ontology of Christ, when rightly understood, are mutually self-interpreting. Christ was certainly deeply psychologically integrated within his culture and historical epoch, but his self-awareness and discourse were also extraordinary. The consciousness of Christ manifests who he is (the Son of God), and the ontological mystery of Christ as the Incarnate Word is the source and root of his action and self-awareness. Neither pole (ontology/consciousness) can be abandoned without the risk of a reductive, one-sided Christology. However, in the very structure of personal being, ontology is more fundamental than consciousness. Self-awareness is only one dimension of human being and ultimately needs to be explained in terms of the latter. Consequently, in Christology, a hypostatic ontology is primary because it explains the principles of Jesus's filial consciousness. (If it fails to do so, it is insufficient.) The classical patristic and medieval approach, therefore, has more explanatory power because it begins from more fundamental starting points and can encompass the modern insistence on Jesus as a historical, existential subject without obscuring the realism of the dogmatic truths articulated by the Church's tradition.

19. Herman Diepen, "La critique du baslisme selon saint Thomas d'Aquin,"; "La psychologie humaine du Christ selon saint Thomas d'Aquin." In addition to the Latin translation of Damascene's *The Orthodox Faith*, Aquinas was familiar with these other sources from various medieval *florilegia* of the Greek fathers, such as the *Collectio Casinensis*. He probably consulted conciliar documents in the papal archives during his stay in Orvieto (1261–1265). See Ignaz Backes, *Die Christologie des hl. Thomas von Aquin und die griechischen Kirchenväter* (Paterborn: Ferdinand Schöningh Verlag, 1931), 192–212; Jean-Pierre Torrell, *St. Thomas Aquinas*, vol. I *The Person and His Work*, trans. R. Royal (Washington, DC: The Catholic University of America Press, 1996): 136–41. For Aquinas, creedal and conciliar formulations of faith act as "first principles" of theological reflection insofar as they denote explicitly and authoritatively the revelation transmitted by the apostolic

critique of the Scotist Christologist Paul Galtier, Diepen notes that the former argues from the autonomous human psychological consciousness of Christ to the necessity of a human subject in Christ distinct from that of the Word.[20] Galtier claimed that only the beatific vision could permit the human subject (Jesus) to be continually aware of the divine subject (the Word), so as to assure a unity of action on the part of these two component natures within the Incarnation.[21] This dualistic conception in fact closely approximates the kind of position that Galot and Weinandy are criticizing, and so Diepen's Thomistic response is significant. Noting the poignantly Nestorian tendency of this thought, Diepen points out that the unity of Christ's person for Aquinas follows first and foremost from the ontological subsistence of his humanity in the existent Word, the Son of God, and not from his intellectual assent to the will of God. Aquinas affirms this unity of personal subsistence in the Word made man and notes how it relates to the divine *esse* of the Word:

> Being (*esse*) pertains to both the nature and the hypostasis; to the hypostasis as that which has being, and to the nature as that whereby it has being. Now it must be borne in mind that if there is a form or nature which does not pertain to the personal being of the subsisting hypostasis, this being is said to belong to the person not simply but relatively ... [But] since the human nature is united to the Son of God hypostatically or personally, and not accidentally, it follows that by the human nature there accrued to Him no new personal being, but only a new relation of the pre-existing personal being to the human nature, in such a way that the person is said to subsist not merely in the Divine, but also in the human nature.[22]

---

deposit of faith. On the unity of the person in Christ as a first principle of Christological reflection (with explicit reference to both Cyril and certain of the above-mentioned conciliar decrees), see *STh* III q. 2, aa. 3 and 6; III, q. 3, a. 1, ad 1; III, q. 16, a. 4.

20. Diepen, "La psychologie humaine du Christ selon saint Thomas d'Aquin," 531.

21. See Paul Galtier, "Unité ontologique et unité psychologique dans le Christ," *Bulletin de littérature ecclésiastique* (Toulouse) 42 (1941): 161–75 and 216–32.

22. Aquinas, *ST* III, q. 17, a. 2. See also *ST* III, q. 2, aa. 2 and 3 and a. 6, ad 3; III, q. 16, aa. 7, 10, and 12; III, q. 18, aa. 1 and Aquinas shows a tendency in these articles to distinguish between the human nature in Christ and his *suppositum* or subject. Ontologically, the former denotes the essence of his created humanity, while the latter is related to his concrete existence (*esse*). This existence is communicated to his human nature

In effect, subsistence in the ontology of Aquinas pertains to a property of *esse*. It denotes both a separateness of existence and a certain mode or manner of being. That which has its own subsistence *exists apart from others* and has its *own mode of being* different from others.[23] For our purposes here, the central point of importance is that Aquinas's theology of the Incarnation (following John Damascene) distinguishes between the specific determinations of the complete human nature of Jesus and the unique hypostatic mode in which this nature subsists.[24] This human nature, by the mystery of the Incarnation, has no existence apart from its hypostatic union with the Word and thereby acquires a unique mode: it has the person of the Son as its unique subject.[25] As a consequence of this fact, as Diepen notes, there is not an autonomous "personality" in the humanity of Jesus, other than that of the hypostasis of the Son:

> There is certainly a human consciousness in Christ, but not the consciousness of a human self, either metaphysical or psychological. To say that the humanity knows, acts, is aware, these are different expressions which are certainly improper, because it is always the Word to whom these acts belong. It is he who is the proper and exclusive subject of their attribution ... He alone who possesses and exercises

from his person (hypostasis) and consequently causes his human nature to subsist in his divine person. In *ST* III, q. 2, aa. 3 and 4, Aquinas equates 'subsistence' with the Greek *hypostasis*. The one being of the person of Christ subsists in two natures. Subsistence thus pertains to the concrete person. A similar doctrine is found in John Damascene, *The Orthodox Faith* III, cc. 5–7.

23. Thus, Aquinas claims that the unique subsistence of each concrete personal subject gives his natural acts a particular manner of being, proper to that subject. See *ST* III, q. 2, aa. 2 and 3.

24. See for example John Damascene, *The Orthodox Faith*. III, cc. 15–17, 21. Damascene's distinction between the specifically human nature (*logos*) of Christ and its filial mode (*tropos*) was originally developed by Maximus the Confessor. See the study by Jean-Miguel Garrigues, "Le dessein d'adoption du créateur dans son rapport au fils d'après S. Maxime le Confesseur," in *Maximus Confessor*, ed. Felix Heinzer and Christoph Schönborn (Fribourg: Éditions Universitaires, 1982), 173–92.

25. *ST* III, q. 2. a. 3: "to the hypostasis alone are attributed the operations and the natural properties, *and whatever belongs to the nature in the concrete* Therefore, if there is any hypostasis in Christ besides the hypostasis of the Word, it follows that whatever pertains to man is verified of some other than the Word, e.g. that He was born of a Virgin, suffered, was crucified, was buried. And this ... was condemned with the approval of the Council of Ephesus (can. 4)" (emphasis added).

existence, the existant properly speaking, that is to say, the subject [*suppôt*] exerts operations ... The Son of God, by his human intelligence, is conscious of his human activity ... [but these acts] are perceived *as the acts of someone who is not simply a subsistent human nature on its own* ... These acts are perceived as acts that are not autonomous but dependent [on the subsistent Word].[26]

Consequently, the human nature of Jesus acts as an "assumed instrument" of his divinity. Because the Word subsists in a human nature, the humanity of Christ bears the mark of his divine identity and makes it manifest in and through all of his human activities.[27]

Speaking in broader terms than those of consciousness, then, Aquinas's theory of the Incarnation responds reasonably to the concerns of Galot and Weinandy. The integrity of human nature is preserved with respect to its specific determinations (vis-à-vis Galot). Yet through its manner of subsisting in the Word, this human nature assumed in Christ acquires a new mode, such that nothing in it falls outside of the divine subject of the Son (as Weinandy insists must be the case).[28] Thus, on this more fundamental, ontological level, we

---

26. Diepen, "La psychologie humaine," 531–32. Aquinas writes on the same subject: "Yet we must bear in mind that not every individual in the genus of substance, even in rational nature, is a person, but that alone *which exists by itself*, and not that which exists in some more perfect thing. Therefore, although this human nature [of Christ] is a kind of individual in the genus of substance, *it has not its own personality, because it does not exist separately, but in something more perfect, viz., in the person of the Word*" (ST III, q. 2, a. 2, ad 3; emphasis added).

27. Aquinas, ST III, q. 2, a. 6, ad. 4: "Not everything that is assumed as an instrument pertains to the hypostasis of the one who assumes, as is plain in the case of a saw or a sword; yet nothing prevents what is assumed into the unity of the hypostasis from being as an instrument, even as the body of man or his members. Hence Nestorius held that the human nature was assumed by the Word merely as an instrument, and not into the unity of the hypostasis. But Damascene held that the human nature in Christ is an instrument belonging to the unity of the hypostasis." As Theophil Tschipke and Diepen after him pointed out, Aquinas purposefully revived this Cyrillian insistence on the humanity of Christ as *organon* of the divinity, and used this to explain the way that his intellect and will, especially, could be the subservient instruments of his divinity. See Theophil Tschipke, *Die Menschheit Christi als Heilsorgan der Gottheit* (Freiburg im Breisgau, 1939), recently republished in French as *L'humanité du Christ comme instrument de salut de la divinité* (Fribourg: Academic Press Fribourg, 2003); and Herman Diepen, *Théologie d'Emmanuel* (Bruges, 1960), 275–93 on this point with respect to the nonautonomy of the psychological subject in Christ.

28. On this point Weinandy is in complete accord with Aquinas (i.e., it is actually

can see how the mode/nature distinction safeguards both the reality of the humanity of Christ and the unity of his person.

The Nature/Mode Distinction and the Two Wills of Christ

Having begun on the ontological level, I will now consider the personal actions of Christ. These, too, acquire a unique mode of being due to the fact that they subsist in the person of the Word. If the human will of Christ is the instrument of his person, it must express this hypostatic mode in its operations. Jesus must personally will as man what he personally wills as God. Only in this way can the singularity and unity of Christ's person be manifest in and through his human action. Furthermore, this cooperation between the human will of Christ and his divine will must be perfect and indefectible in all his human actions, precisely so as to express adequately his personal unity. How might we make this argument?

First, we should note that in the Christology of the *Summa*, Aquinas explicitly applies the nature/mode distinction discussed above directly to the particular spiritual faculties of intellect and will in the Incarnate Word.[29] In doing so, Aquinas is following the understanding of the "theandric acts" of Christ developed by Maximus the Confessor, which Aquinas assimilated through the writings of John Damascene.[30] This theology was developed in confrontation with Monothelitism precisely to affirm the Chalcedonian confession

---

the Son who *is* man), understanding the latter's metaphysics of the Incarnation as a true and careful expression of Chalcedonian orthodoxy. See Weinandy, *Does God Change?*, 82–88; *Does God Suffer?*, 206–8.

29. See Garrigues, "La conscience de soi telle qu'elle était exercée par le Fils de Dieu fait homme," 39–51; and "L'instrumentalité rédemptrice du libre arbitre du Christ chez saint Maxime le Confesseur," *Revue Thomiste* 104 (2004): 531–50. As will become clear, this section of my argument in particular is greatly indebted to the argument and perspective of these articles.

30. The notion of "theandric acts" originated with Dionysius (*Div. Nom.* 2), and was appropriated by Maximus and Damascene in a sense consistent with Chalcedon, against Monothelitism. Aquinas follows Damascene, denoting by the term the cooperation of the divine and human wills in Christ such that they form together the actions of a unique person; see *ST* III q. 19, a. 1, ad 1.

of the complete and real human nature of Christ (including his human will) while safeguarding (against the charge of Nestorianism) the Cyrillian confession of the singularity and unity of the person of the Incarnate Word. The distinction safeguards the fact that these operations are both fully human (in their nature) and expressive of Jesus' unique filial personhood (in their mode).

> The nature assumed by Christ may be viewed in two ways. First, in its specific nature, and thus Damascene calls it "ignorant and enslaved" (De Fide Orth. III, 21) Secondly, it may be considered with regard to what it has from its *union with the Divine hypostasis*, from which it has the fullness of knowledge and grace.[31]

In effect, as Garrigues shows in detail, the Greek fathers developed an understanding of the personal mode of the human will of Christ by distinguishing between the *logos* of this will and its *tropos*. "Logos" here signifies a distinct essence common to many who share a determinate nature, while "'tropos" signifies a 'manner of existing' particular to an individual hypostasis. In their essential specification, Christ's human will and intellect are identical with those of other men, but they acquire a unique mode because of the hypostatic union, through which they are appropriated *instrumentally* as the human expression of the person of God the Son.[32] Because they subsist in God the Son, the human will and intellect of Christ are

---

31. *ST* III, q. 15, a. 3, ad 1. See also *ST* III, q. 18, a. 1, obj. 4 and ad 4.

32. Maximus, *Disputatio cum Pyrrho* (PG 91:293A): "The fact of willing and the determined mode of willing are not identical, just as the fact of seeing and the determined mode of seeing are not either. For the fact of willing, like that of seeing, concerns the nature of a thing. It is common to all those who have the same nature and belong to the same kind. The determined mode of willing, however, like that of seeing, that is to say, to will to walk or not will to walk, to see what is at the right or at the left or high or below, or to look by sensual desire or in order to understand the essential principles in beings, all this concerns a mode of exercise [*tropos*] of willing or seeing. It concerns only him who exercises [these faculties of nature] and in so doing separates him from others according to particular differences" (translation mine). See Garrigues's analysis of this text and others in "L'instrumentalité," 542–50. As he points out, Aquinas also uses these same examples (eyesight, voluntary action) to denote the distinction between *specification* and *exercise* in De Malo, q. 6. Damascene reproduced this identical doctrine in *The Orthodox Faith* III, c. 14.

necessarily rendered relative to his divine intellect and will as the primary source of their personal operation.[33]

Aquinas develops this theological motif, interpreting it in light of the metaphysics of the Incarnation mentioned above. Because the personal existence of the Word gives the subsistent humanity of Christ its unique mode of being, the will of Christ also receives a unique mode of being. It is the human will of the divine person of the Son of God.

Damascene says (*De Fide Orth.* III, c. 14) that "to will this or that way belongs not to our nature but to our intellect, i.e., our *personal* intellect." When we say, "to will in a certain way," we signify a *determinate mode* of willing.

> Now a determinate mode regards the thing of which it is the mode. Hence since the will pertains to the nature, "to will in a certain way" belongs to the nature, not indeed considered absolutely, *but as it is in the hypostasis. Hence the human will of Christ has a determinate mode from the fact of being in a Divine hypostasis, i.e., it was always moved in accordance with the bidding of the Divine will.*[34]

Although the divine agency must always take the initiative in the human acts of Christ, Jesus is not, therefore, any less human than we are. On the contrary, his human nature is an "instrument" that operates itself in accordance with its own divine identity. Therefore, precisely because he has in his human intellect an immediate knowledge of his own personal divine goodness at all times, the judgments and practical choices of Christ are more and not less human than ours.

---

33. Damascene, *The Orthodox Faith* III, cc. 14–18. See for example, c. 17: "Wherefore the same flesh was mortal by reason of its own nature and life-giving through its union with the Word in subsistence. And we hold that it is just the same with the deification of the will; for its natural activity was not changed but united with His divine and omnipotent will, and became the will of God, made man. And so it was that, though He wished, He could not of Himself escape (Mk. 7: 24), because it pleased God the Word that the weakness of the human will, which was in truth in Him, should be made manifest. But He was able to cause at His will the cleansing of the leper, because of the union with the divine will."

34. *ST* III, q. 18, a. 1, obj. 4 and ad 4 (emphasis added).

Whatever was in the human nature of Christ was moved at the bidding of the divine will; yet it does not follow that in Christ there was no movement of the will proper to human nature. It is proper to an instrument to be moved by the principal agent, yet diversely, according to the property of its nature. And an instrument animated with a rational soul is moved by its will, the servant being like an animate instrument. And hence it was in this manner that the human nature of Christ was the instrument of the Godhead and was moved by its own will.[35]

This line of argument leads, then, to a second point. The singularity and unity of the person of Christ can only be sufficiently manifest in his human actions if his divine and human wills cooperate concretely in all of his personal actions. The human intentions and choices that Christ makes as a man are indicative of his divine personal will, intentions, and choices. It is this cooperation of the two wills that permits the human willing of Christ to take on its filial mode of expression.

We should note that it is not the case that the hypostatic unity of the person of Christ is *constituted* by the cooperation of his human and divine wills. However, this personal unity must be manifested adequately through the human actions of Jesus. This follows from the principles of the Incarnation. For the human actions of Jesus are actions of one person who is divine, and what the Son wills humanly is expressive of his personal identity. However, this person, the Son

---

35. *ST* III, q. 18, a. 1, ad 1 and 2. As Garrigues notes ("L'instrumentalité," 545–47), Aquinas differs from Maximus and Damascene insofar as these Greek Fathers denied the existence of an autonomous human moral deliberation and judgment in Christ, due to his superior knowledge of the good. Aquinas argues that moral deliberation and judgment are necessary to any human nature, and therefore existed in Christ, but were always inspired by a sense of the higher good of the divine will, which made the human choices of Christ freer and more pure. Colman O'Neill comments: "Christ was unique in that he had no choice [concerning the possible final end of man]; for with his human mind he saw God and his will was necessarily held by this Supreme Good (cf. *STh* III, q. 9, a. 2; q. 10). But anything less than God was powerless to compel his will. With respect to all created things he was supremely free for he could measure their value against his vision and possession of the divine good (III, q. 18, a. 4) … His obedience dedicated him to the will of his Father; far from restricting his liberty, it set him free from attachment to any created thing so that he could rise to the summit of human liberty and renounce his life for the sake of what his will held dearest." See "The Problem of Christ's Human Autonomy," appendix 3 in *ST*, 233–34.

of God, possesses a divine will, and it is impossible for the Son of God to act personally in such a way that his divine will should be absent from his personal action. The Incarnate Word, then, must be humanly conscious of his own divine will in all of his actions so that his human actions are indicative of his personal, divine willing as God.[36] This affirmation has a basis in sound Trinitarian doctrine as well. We might affirm, for example, that the Son incarnate must be humanly conscious of the divine will that he shares with the Father and the Holy Spirit. Why is this the case? Because all through his human life, the Son of God reveals in and through his human actions the will of the Father and the activity of the Holy Spirit. If the Son is going to adequately manifest the mystery of the Holy Trinity in his human decisions and choices, then he must be humanly aware of what the Father who sent him wills and of what he wills with the Holy Spirit, so that he can express this in his human actions and choices. He can only do this because he is conscious in his human decisions of the divine will that he shares with the Father and the Holy Spirit.

It follows from this line of reasoning that the conformity of the human will of Christ to the divine will of Christ cannot occur only in some of his human choices but must be something perfect and indefectible. This must be the case because the cooperation of the two wills stems from the hypostatic identity of Christ and is indicative of the unity of his person. This cooperation cannot, therefore, exist only at certain times in Christ's life. The man Jesus Christ is

36. Garrigues, "La conscience," 40, writes: "Certainly, in becoming man, [Christ] assumes in his human nature the same rational desire for the Good that is proper to spiritual creatures. But since his human soul exists within the very person of Him who, as God, is the Good as such, the rational desire of Christ need not search in and through a deliberation how to attain the ultimate Good by a moral progression transpiring through the choice of particular goods. The human will of Christ itself, while endowed naturally with the same free-will as us, nevertheless does not have an autonomous deliberation (gnome) characteristic of the mode of exercise found in created persons ... Fixed forever from the first instant of the Incarnation, by the hypostatic union, upon the supreme Good which is One of the Trinity, and by the plenitude of habitual grace which follows from this, the rational desire of the humanity assumed by the Son exists and is exercised in a unique mode, of perfect docility with respect to the divine will of the Trinitarian person who exercises this will as its subject."

always the Son of God, and so his human consciousness and free decision-making must always develop in active conformity with the operations of his divine will, expressing thereby who he is personally as the Son. This conformity has to be perfect and without defect, because Jesus's human actions are actions of his person, and the divine will of Christ is something intrinsic to his filial person. If Christ as man were able to make some choices in seeming oblivion of his own divine will, it would follow that he would be able to make choices in seeming oblivion of his own hypostatic identity. He would then make decisions in reference to what he (mistakenly) took to be an alternative personal identity: that of a created personal subject who is not one in will with the Father. On this model, Christ would be the Incarnate Word, but he might act as if he were a subject distinct from the Word because he would not be aware of sharing in one will with the Father. This is, of course, entirely unfitting, and so it is reasonable to affirm that there existed at all times a perfect conformity of the human, free actions of Jesus as man, with his divine activity as God.

The conclusion to be drawn from all this is that in at least one very important respect (that is, with regard to the divine will), Christ's human actions *must not* be characterized by ignorance or defectibility. What is at stake is not a principle of ideal humanity but the very unity of the operations of Christ in his practical actions. In order for Christ to be fully human, his psychological choices must be rational and natural (against Monophysitism), but for them to be the choices of his divine person, they must be unified with his divine will on the level of his personal action (against Nestorianism). The nature/mode distinction, as applied by Aquinas to the will of Christ, makes it possible to negotiate this theological challenge. The nature is respected but takes on a hypostatic mode, by which it accords always (instrumentally) with the divine, filial will of the Son. Thus, a perfect and continual correlation between the divine and human wills is essential for surmounting the dual Christological errors that Galot and Weinandy wish to combat. But how can this occur?

The Necessity of the Son's
Immediate Human Knowledge of
the Divine Will

The conclusion of the previous section is significant: in at least one important way, the absence of ignorance in the mind of Christ is not immediately related, for Aquinas, to the "principle of perfection" that Galot refers to, but rather, must exist for reasons *essential to the divine economy*. If Jesus is truly the Son of God and, therefore, a divine person, then his divine will is present in his person as the primary agent of his personal choices. This means that, necessarily, his human will, in its rational deliberation and choice making, must be continually subordinated to, informed by, and indefectibly expressive of his personal divine will in its human, rational deliberation and choice making. But of course, movements of human choice follow upon knowledge (apprehension of the good and deliberative judgments) informing the human intellect.[37] Here, then, I will introduce an argument that moves beyond Aquinas's explicit statements, to one which is homogeneous with his principles as they have been presented above. I will show that it is only if Christ's human intellect is continuously and immediately aware of his own divine will (by the beatific vision and not merely by infused knowledge and by faith) that his human will can act in immediate subordination to his divine will as the "assumed instrument" of his divine subject. Only such knowledge will assure the operative unity (in and through two distinct natures) of Christ's personal actions because it alone gives the mind of the man Jesus an evidential certitude of the will he shares eternally with the Father.

In order to present this argument, it is first necessary to make an important clarification. I have suggested above that only the immediate knowledge of God in the soul of Christ permits him to exert

---

37. *De Malo*, q. 6; *ST* I-II, q. 8, a. 1; I-II, q. 9, a. 1; I-II, q. 11, a. 1; I-II, q. 12, a. 1; I-II, q. 13, a. 1; I-II, q. 14, a. 1. On the intellect's role with respect to the exercise of the will as regards practical action, see the excellent study of Michael Sherwin, *By Knowledge and by Love* (Washington, DC: The Catholic University of America Press, 2005), especially 18–62.

his divine will in a human way through the activities of his human consciousness. However, the vision of God is not conceptual or notional, but immediate and intuitive.[38] Consequently, it cannot be "assimilated" by Christ's habitual, conceptual manner of knowing and willing in any direct fashion. As Aquinas and many Thomists after him have rightly insisted, then, the knowledge of Christ's vision is "communicated" to his ordinary human consciousness through the medium of a so-called infused, prophetic science.[39] The judgments and choices that inform the will of Jesus depend above all upon this "habitual" prophetic consciousness (which is, in some sense, abstract knowledge) rather than his immediate vision. Because of this, his knowing and obeying the Father "in a human way" (that is, in his human consciousness) would seem to depend *essentially* upon his prophetic science (or infused *species*). Why, then, might such a "prophetic light" in Christ not suffice *alone* without recourse to the vision of God? The latter does not add anything *necessary* to the human way of thinking and willing that characterizes the activity of the *earthly* Christ and, therefore, seems unnecessary for the purposes of his economic mission.[40]

In order to answer this objection, two things need to be kept in mind. First of all, in the absence of the immediate knowledge of vision, Christ would necessarily have to exercise the theological virtue of faith. The presence of a prophetic, infused knowledge cannot act as a substitute for faith, in the way Galot proposes. Galot claims that there is no faith in Christ, nor vision, but only a higher knowledge attained by prophecy. Yet, as Jean-Pierre Torrell has shown, prophetic or infused knowledge alone is only a mediate, *indirect* knowledge

38. *ST* I, q. 12, aa. 4, 5, and 9.
39. The basis for this position is found in *ST* III, q. 11, a. 5, ad 1. See its development by John of St. Thomas, *Cursus Theologicus*, vol. 8 (Paris: Vivès, 1886), d. 11, a. 2, especially n. 15, where he argues cogently that Christ had to possess infused science in order to receive the knowledge of the vision into his consciousness in a way that was connatural with his human nature.
40. The above paragraph contains an approximation of the argument presented by Torrell in "S. Thomas d'Aquin et la science du Christ," 394–409, influenced by Galot's perspective.

of God attained through the *effects* of God.[41] Necessarily, outside of the vision, all knowledge of God is through effects, and *only faith* permits a quasi-immediate contact with God, through love. Therefore, even infused knowledge requires faith in order to orient it toward God. This contact of faith, however, is obscure (nonevidential) and is therefore supported by a voluntary act of the will that believes in God by a free act of love. Without the vision, then, the intellect of Christ would not have "direct access to God" but would believe in his divinity and divine will through faith and in a free adherence of love.

Second, as Jacques Maritain has argued convincingly, the presumed presence or absence of this vision must alter profoundly the character of this infused knowledge in the consciousness of Christ.[42] Only if the vision is present in Christ's soul can such infused knowledge participate in the evidence of Christ's divine identity and will, which are immediately known by the vision.

> Insofar as viator, [Christ] knew himself God through his infused science,—finite and increasing under the state of way, but which under this state (in the here-below of the soul of Christ) participated in the evidence of the beatific vision ... And it is this participated evidence of the Vision which gave to the infused science of the Son of God *viator*

41. Torrell, 403–4: "If one renounces the beatific vision and if one follows the logic of the Thomistic perspective, it must be said that Christ had faith. The [bearer of prophecy] does not attain God in his experience [of infused science] but only expressive signs of the divine. He knows *that* God speaks to him, but *what* God says he can only believe. The grace of faith is another kind of supernatural gift ... a created participation in the life of God, it conforms the believer to the mystery itself (II-II, q. a. 2, ad 2.). In other words, with faith we are in the order of the supernatural *quoad essentiam*, while with prophetic knowledge we remain in the order of the supernatural *quoad modum* (*acquisitionis*). The two orders do not exclude one another, certainly, but the second is ordered to the first, and because the two are different kinds of realities, they must not be confused or made to play the role of one another. Concerning Jesus, then if we accord to him infused illuminations characteristic of the charismatic knowledge of revelation, he will be enabled for his role as a divine messenger, but he will still not have direct access to God, since these illuminations do not suffice as a replacement of faith." Aquinas makes related claims, denying that Christ is a prophet in the usual theological sense of the word, since he does not *believe* through an "obscure knowledge" the things he is given to reveal, but *knows* them in a more perfect, immediate way: see *In Joan.*, IV, lect. 6 (Marietti ed., n. 667).

42. See Jacques Maritain, *On the Grace and Humanity of Jesus*, 54–61, 98–125.

a *divinely* sovereign *certitude* with regard to all that which it knew, and especially with regard to the divinity of Jesus.[43]

In other words, because of the vision of God in the heights of Christ's soul, his intellect adheres immediately to his divine identity, and his human will is "informed" immediately by the knowledge of his divine will. The prophetic knowledge that informs his consciousness then acts in subordination to the immediate knowledge he has as man of his own identity and will as God, expressing this in and through his ordinary human consciousness.[44] By contrast, in the absence of the vision, the infused science of Christ would lack such immediate evidence and would need to be accompanied by faith. In this case, the prophetic awareness Christ had of his own divinity and will would have to be continuously accompanied by an autonomous decision of faith in the human heart of Christ and a repeated choice to welcome in trust this revelation *from his own divine self.* This would create, in effect, a kind of psychological autonomy in the man Jesus, distinct from the willing of his divine subject, resulting in a schism between the two operations of the Incarnate Word. Jesus as man would have to will to believe in his divine activity as God. He would not perceive it directly.

If we return to the theandric activity of Christ, then we can see that this point has significant consequences. Only due to the *immediate* knowledge of the vision can the human will of Christ be *directly* moved (or specified) by his divine will so as irremediably to correspond to its inclinations.[45] *Because of* the beatific vision, the

43. See the developed argument of Maritain in *On the Grace and Humanity of Jesus,* 54–61, 98–125, especially 101–2, 107.

44. For reflections on the relationship between this "supra-conscious" character of the vision, and its manifestation in consciousness, see *On the Grace and Humanity of Jesus,* 114–20.

45. In *ST* I-II, q. 4, a. 4 Aquinas shows that the *permanent and necessary* rectitude of the creaturely will in relation to the eternal goodness of God is dependent for man upon the *immediate* knowledge of the final end (the vision of the essence of God). John Damascene in *The Orthodox Faith* III, c. 14 suggests that the movement of the human will of the Word occurs by a direct specification of it by the divine will.

prophetic knowledge in Christ's consciousness is suffused by the evidence Christ has of the will he shares eternally with the Father. Thus, the human will of Christ acts "instrumentally," that is to say, through an immediate subordination to his divine will.[46] The infused science of Christ permits his ordinary consciousness to cooperate with this knowledge, which the vision alone provides. By it, Christ always knows immediately and with certitude who he is and what he wills in unity with the Father. His human will cooperates indefectibly with his divine will in the unity of one personal subject.

In the absence of the vision, by contrast, the infused knowledge of Christ would still be the medium by which the man Jesus would be conscious of his own divine will, but it would no longer participate in any evidential knowledge of that will. Consequently, the human mind of Christ could no longer be moved immediately influenced by the will of his divine person. Instead, the man Christ would continually need to make acts of faith in what he believed obscurely to be the divine will he shared (as God) with his Father. He would have to hope (as a man) that he was doing what his own transcendent identity (which he also believed in) willed for him. Christ would not know with luminous certitude, therefore, who he was and what he willed (as God) in each instant. Thus, his human operations of willing might subsist in the person of the Word, but in their operative exercise, they would work on a separated, "parallel track" to the operations of the Word without immediate influence in their mode of exercise. Both operations could subsist in one person, but they would not be immediately related to each other as the operations of one person. In this case, no true unity of subject is manifest in the actions of Jesus, and a kind of "operational dualism" results that has a semi-Nestorian quality.

---

46. I am employing the notion of "instrumentality" differently from Maritain here, so as to emphasize not only the instrumentality of the vision with regard to his infused knowledge, but the instrumentality of his entire human consciousness (with all of its forms of knowledge) as an expression of his divine personhood and will. Yet I follow him in holding that such a state of affairs depends upon the vision as a mediating principle.

Christ is one person having two natures and operations (as is maintained by Constantinople III). However, in the model we are considering, the actions of Christ as man do not reveal the will of God the Son, but only what Jesus as man hopes to be the will he shares in eternally with the Father. In fact, Christ would need to believe that God exists, that God is his Father, and that God has a concrete will regarding history for him to believe in. Such an idea is clearly dualistic since it prohibits the earthly Christ from being epistemologically proportioned so as to know immediately his own identity and will. It also does not permit him an adequate knowledge of the Father's will in each concrete circumstance, such that he can reveal this will to us in each of his human choices and desires. Theologians who wish to affirm uniquely an indirect knowledge of God (and therefore, also the existence of faith) in the historical Christ *and* the *real existence in him of a divine will and identity* must consider the question: how are these two phenomena capable of producing a unity of personal action that belongs to the Son of God as its principal source? How can such a theology maintain a unity of cooperation between the divine and human wills of the one Christ? How might it permit us to maintain that Jesus, in each of his concrete human actions, can manifest to us directly the revelation of the Father's will?[47]

Contrary to Weinandy's claim, then, Aquinas's discussion of the grace of the beatific vision in the soul of Christ—which has the

47. I do not believe that this dilemma is capable of positive resolution. One option I can see for avoiding a semi-Nestorian dilemma is to assert that the Son of God, in his incarnate state, does not know or will in his divine nature, but *only* in his human nature. See, for example, the proposals of Bernard Sesboüé in *Pédagogie du Christ* (Paris: Cerf, 1994), 160–61, following the ideas of Joseph Moingt. Such a kenotic theory of the person of Christ does surely safeguard the unity of his personhood (since he is aware of himself uniquely in a human way, without recourse to his own divine will), but this is attained at the expense of the duality of his natures and wills. Christ seemingly cedes the privileges of his divine nature and will for the interim of his temporal mission, and regains these at the resurrection. Such a kenotic theory implicitly breaks with the confession of faith of Chalcedon concerning the two natures of Christ, and with Constantinople III on the duality of wills. Moreover, it requires the direct negation of the divine aseity and therefore renders itself metaphysically irrational or "nontheistic."

Word (and the "divine essence") as its object—is important for a Chalcedonian theology of the hypostatic union. Aquinas recognizes that the human intellect of Christ is created and, as such, is infinitely removed from his divine essence. Due to this natural limitation, the humanity of Christ must be subject to an extraordinary grace so that his human spiritual operations adequately attain to his divine life and consequently bear its impressions in their own activity. So, in fact, it is the immediate vision that safeguards the unity of activity in the person of Jesus. This particular grace is the condition of possibility of an authentically unified filial consciousness, through which Christ expresses his intra-Trinitarian relationship with the Father and his true identity in his human actions.

Weinandy, however, is no doubt correct to insist on the unique character of this vision: it is indeed "filial." As Garrigues points out, not only the human nature but also the *graces* of the humanity of Christ *subsist* in the Word and thus have a filial *mode* as well. This grace of the vision of Christ, then, while analogous to that grace received in a human person or angel who sees God, is different insofar as it does not give the soul of Christ an awareness of the Trinity as a subject ontologically distinct from himself, but rather permits the Son to know *himself* "objectively" and to understand his own filial personhood in a certain and evidential way.[48]

THE OBEDIENCE AND PRAYER LIFE
OF THE SON OF GOD AS EXPRESSIONS OF HIS
FILIAL CONSCIOUSNESS

The Intra-Trinitarian Mode of the
Human Acts of Christ

Having considered above the principles of theandric cooperation in the action of Jesus, I will now move on to reflect on concrete

48. Garrigues, "La conscience," 43–46. By "objectively" I do not mean "notionally" (since the vision is an intuitive, *immediate* knowledge), but "pertaining to true knowledge of reality."

examples. The analysis can now be applied to actions characteristic of the human nature of the Incarnate Word in order to illustrate how these actions reveal his divine person. This is particularly evident with respect to Jesus' obedience and his prayer, two activities that do not occur between the uncreated persons of the Trinity *per se,* and that are proper to created nature, yet that in Christ express something of his filial identity through distinctly human acts.[49] This is only possible due to the correspondence between the human and divine wills of Christ within his *unified* personal action, effectuated by means of the beatific vision. Because the human will of Christ participates in the evidential certitude that he has of his own divine will, shared with the Father, his human acts of obedience and prayer express this certitude in gestures and words. The classical theory of the immediate vision, then, can be seen to be necessary in order to safeguard the personal unity of Christ's obedience and prayer as instrumental, *filial* actions, even while respecting the distinctly human character of these actions. By way of contrast, without this traditional theological teaching, one cannot make adequate sense of the obedience and prayer of Jesus as revelatory of the Trinitarian persons. This being the case, the central objections offered by Galot and Weinandy to the presence of the vision in Christ are unfounded. The Chalcedonian Christology they wish to defend is exemplified in the life and action of the historical Jesus, who obeys the Father and prays to the Father *because he knows immediately* the Father, and acts, even in his human nature, as the Son who proceeds from the Father.

The Obedience of Christ

To refer briefly to this dimension of the Incarnation, I will first mention certain aspects of Aquinas's treatment of the *divine* will of Christ in relation to the Father. As can be shown, obedience in

---

49. *ST* III, q. 20, preface. Aquinas notes here that the obedience, prayer, and priesthood of Christ, while being activities of his human nature, express his filial relation with respect to the Father.

Christ, for Aquinas, is the human expression of the divine will that he receives eternally from the Father. Consequently, his prayer life is also a tangible manifestation of the same relation of origination from the Father, expressed in a specifically human way.

On the one hand, as has been noted, Christ's human nature (including his intellect and will) takes on a particular mode because it is the human nature in which the Incarnate Word personally subsists. However, this nature/mode distinction is also applied by Aquinas in a different but related way to the subsistent hypostasis of the God the Son *as regards the divine nature*.[50] In a wholly different and higher way, the divine nature that God the Son receives eternally from the Father through the procession of begetting takes on a particular mode of being (of subsistence) in the person of the Son.

Therefore, the divine attributes that the Father and Son share in common (such as wisdom, goodness, eternity, etc.) are present in a unique way in each of the persons of the Trinity. In Jesus, this mode of being of the divine nature is that of the subsistent hypostasis of the Son and, consequently, is the same filial subsistence that informs the human nature of Christ assumed in the Incarnation. In other words, the mode of being of Christ's humanity is the very same as the mode of being of his divine nature (even though these two natures are utterly distinct).[51] So, for example, the Son subsists in divine eternity as God in a distinctly filial way (as eternally begotten of the Father), even as the Son subsists in his human historical

50. *ST* I, q. 29, aa. 2 and 4. Aquinas's treatment of subsistence in the Trinity is complex and exceeds the scope of this study. Gilles Emery in *Trinity in Aquinas* (Ypsilanti, MI: Ave Maria Press, 2002), 142–44 and 198–206 has examined this aspect of Aquinas's thought in detail. In "Essentialism or Personalism in the Treatise on God in St. Thomas Aquinas?," 534, he comments: "One cannot conceive of the person without the substance or without the nature belonging to the very *ratio* of the divine person, this latter being defined as 'distinct subsisting in the divine nature.'"

51. *ST* I, q. 39, aa. 1–3. *ST* III q. 2, a. 2, obj. 1 and 3, ad 1 and 3; III, q. 3, a. 3. This doctrine is also found in Damascene, and originates with Maximus the Confessor. See the study of Garrigues, "Le dessein d'adoption du créateur dans son rapport au fils d'après S. Maxime le Confesseur"; and the remarks of Christoph Schönborn, *The Human Face of God* (San Francisco: Ignatius Press, 1994): 113–16.

development as man in a filial way (due to the Incarnation).[52] But if this is the case with respect to attributes such as the divine eternity, then it is also the case for the divine will, which is an attribute of God's nature common to the three persons of the Trinity. The will of God is present in the person of the Son in a unique way. The Son subsists eternally, having in himself the unique divine will. However, he also has this divine will in a filial mode since all that he has (even as God) is received eternally through the begetting of the Father and stands in relation to the Father as its principle and source. Commenting on John 5:30 ("I am not seeking my own will, but the will of him who sent me"), Aquinas applies the saying to Christ's divinity:

> But do not the Father and the Son have the same will? I answer that the Father and the Son do have the same will, but the Father does not have his will from another whereas the Son does have his will from another, i.e., from the Father. Thus the Son accomplishes his own will as from another, i.e., as having it from another; but the Father accomplishes his own will as his own, i.e., not having it from another.[53]

Because Christ's human nature is united hypostatically to this divine will in its filial mode, the latter must exact upon this nature the expression of its own hypostatic identity: that of God the Son. Because of the union in one subsistent person, the created desires, intentions, and choices of Christ's human will must express the filial character of the divine will that is present in him *personally*.[54] Certainly, his obedience is proper to his created nature and does not reflect the uncreated relations of the Trinity *per se*.[55] Nevertheless, due

---

52. See *ST* I, q. 42, a. 4, ad. 2, concerning the divine attribute of dignity that the Son receives from the Father: "the same essence which in the Father is paternity, in the Son is filiation, so the same dignity which, in the Father is paternity, in the Son is filiation. It is thus true to say that the Son possesses whatever dignity the Father has." Similarly, *ST* I, q. 39, a. 5, ad 1 (wisdom); I, q. 42, aa. 1, 2, and 6 (power, perfection, greatness, and eternity).

53. *In Ioan.*, V, lect. 5 (Marietti ed., n. 798).

54. *ST* III, q. 18, a. 1, ad 1 and 2.

55. Aquinas insists on the irreducible distinction of natures in Christ. This is why, following Augustine (*De Trin.* 1.7), he claims that in a sense it is necessary to say that Christ "is subject to himself," i.e., subordinates his created will to his divine will (*ST* III, q. 20, a. 2). He does so, however, in invoking Cyril of Alexandria as a witness to the nonsubordination

to the hypostatic mode in which this obedience is exercised in the person of Christ, it can express through his specifically human acts his filial relativity toward the Father. This is only the case due to the fact that an absolute correspondence exists between the human and divine wills of Christ, a point Aquinas makes implicitly in his commentary on John 5:30:

> For there are two wills in our Lord Jesus Christ: one is a divine will, which is the same as the will of the Father; the other is a human will which is proper to himself, just as it is proper to him to be a man. A human will is borne to its own good, but in Christ, it was ruled and regulated by right reason, so that it would always be conformed in all things to the divine will. Accordingly, he says: "I am not seeking my own will," which as such is inclined to its own good, "but the will of him who sent me," that is, the Father ... If this is carefully considered, the Lord is assigning the true nature of a just judgment, saying: "because I am not seeking my own will." For one's judgment is just when it is passed according to the norm of law. But the divine will is the norm and the law of the created will. And so, the created will and the reason, *which is regulated according to the norm of the divine will,* is just, and its judgment is just.
>
> Secondly, this saying is explained as referring it to the Son of God ... Christ as the Divine Word showing the origin of his power. And because judgment in any intellectual nature comes from knowledge, he says significantly, "I judge only as I hear it," i.e., as I have acquired knowledge together with being from the Father, so I judge: "Everything I have heard from my Father I have made known to you (John. 15:5).[56]

The judgments of Christ's ordinary decisions are specified by his prophetic knowledge, such that he is mentally conscious of the will of God for him in a conceptual way. Yet, as I have discussed above, the judgment of Christ concerning the will he shares with the Father acquires its *evidential certitude* only through the beatific vision. This knowledge is an essential component, then, of the filial mode of the

---

of the hypostasis of Christ with respect to the Father. In *ST* III, q. 20, a. 1, ad 1 and 2 he notes that obedience as such pertains to Christ's human nature, but is not in him the act of a *creature*. Rather, it is an act of the hypostasis of the Son *in* his human nature.

56. *In Ioan.*, V, lect. 5 (Marietti ed., nn. 796–97) (emphasis added).

acts of Christ because it alone permits the Lord as man to know immediately his own divine will, being moved by it and cooperating with it at each instant. This, in turn, permits his human intellect and will to function *instrumentally* with his divine, personal will as the two wills of one subject. By the vision, the man Jesus knows immediately that he receives his divine will from the Father, and his human acts of obedience bear the imprint of this unique filial certitude. Nor can the human obedience of Christ have this same "instrumental mode" without recourse to this knowledge. Without the vision, the man Jesus—moved by faith—could only obey what he *believed and hoped* was *his own* divine will, but his acts would not stem from an evidential knowledge of this will. Consequently, the human obedience of Christ would function with a kind of independence, moved by the decision of faith. It would not manifest Christ's evidential certitude of his own divine will received eternally from the Father but would instead reflect an autonomous human desire to act in accordance with the unknown operative will of God (perceived obscurely and indirectly through the medium of prophecy). The human obedience and the divine will of Christ would, therefore, run on parallel tracks but never touch directly. His human operations could not be immediately moved by his divine operations in the unified cooperation of one subject. It follows that even though Christ as man would subsist in the Word, in his acts of obedience, he would seek in faith to obey himself in his divine nature.

We must conclude, then, that a Chalcedonian Christology, which wishes (following Cyril, Maximus, and John of Damascene) to affirm the instrumental unity of Christ's human actions with those of his divine will, should affirm the presence in his humanity of the beatific vision as well. The actions of his distinct, created nature are subordinate to and expressive of his divine personhood through the medium of his immediate knowledge of his divine filial will. In this way, his identity as the Son of God who is doing the work of the Father at all times (John 5:18–19) can be expressed in a filial mode through human voluntary submission to the paternal will.

The Prayer of Jesus to the Father

Analogous things can be said about the prayer life of Christ. Why does Christ pray if he already has the vision of God and knows that he and the Father will be "victorious over the world"?[57] First, as Aquinas makes clear, Christ's prayer is an expression of his created, dependent nature and does not pertain to his divine nature.[58] Consequently, it does not imply an eternal subordination or obedience within the uncreated Trinity. Yet this prayer is expressive of an inner-Trinitarian relation. It reveals to us the relation that the person of the Son has with respect to the Father: Jesus receives all that he is and has, both as God and man, from the Father as his origin.

> [B]eing both God and man [Christ] wished to offer prayers to the Father, not as though He were incompetent, but for our instruction ... *that He might show Himself to be from the Father*, hence he says (John. 11:42: "Because of the people who stand about I have said it [i.e., the words of the prayer], that they may believe that Thou has sent Me") ... Christ wished to pray to His Father in order to give us an example of praying; and also to show that His Father is the author [*auctor*] *both of His eternal procession in the Divine nature, and of all the good that He possesses in the human nature.*[59]

Significant in this respect is the fact that, in praying, Christ does not regard himself (the Word) as an object to whom he offers petitions. He does not adore the Trinity.[60] Rather, the scriptural evidence sug-

---

57. Cf. John 16:33.

58. *ST* III, q. 21, a. 1: "Prayer is the unfolding of our will to God, that He may fulfill it. If, therefore, there had been but one will in Christ, viz. the Divine, it would nowise belong to Him to pray, since the Divine will of itself is effective of whatever He wishes by it ... But because the Divine and the human wills are distinct in Christ, and the human will of itself is not efficacious enough to do what it wishes, except by Divine power, hence to pray belongs to Christ as man and as having a human will."

59. *ST* III, q. 21, a. 1, and a. 3, respectively (emphasis added).

60. I differ on this point from Matthew Levering (*Christ's Fulfillment of Temple and Torah,* 92–93, 143), who attributes to Aquinas the idea that Jesus adores the three persons of the Trinity in his human soul. To the best of my knowledge, there are no texts to support this view (which resembles Scotus's doctrine) in Aquinas's writings. Aquinas never ascribes either *adoratio* or *latria* to Christ as a subject, in relation to the Father as object, or to himself as object. It seems, rather, that devotion in Christ receives a peculiar mode that is hypostatic. It is a recognition by the Son *in his human nature* of having

gests that his prayer is directed to the Father: it is primarily, therefore, a human mode of expression of his intra-Trinitarian filial identity. It can only be this because of the perfection of the prayer of Christ: it mirrors the will of the Father due to the fact that Christ's heart is always "in the Father."[61] For Aquinas, then, Christ's exemplarity in prayer is not a kind of docetic play-acting, but a human expression and enactment of his eternal relation to the Father, meant to reveal to us that all things are received from the Father. His prayer initiates us into an analogous "Trinitarian" relationship as sons of the Father adopted by grace.

In light of what has been said above, however, it is clear that Christ as man could not prayerfully recognize his origin from the Father *with evidential certitude* without the beatific vision. Even though his prayer is conceptual, this conceptuality participates in the immediate knowledge of the Father's will imparted by the vision. This, in turn, permits his human intellect and will to cooperate instrumentally with his divine, personal will as the two wills of one subject. By the vision, the man Jesus knows who he is and what he wills as God, and his human acts of prayer bear the immediate imprint of this knowledge. As such, the prayer of Christ attains a unique, filial mode. It reflects through specifically human acts his personal recognition as the Son of God that he receives all things from the Father. This is why, even in praying for those things that his intercession would merit, Christ was acting in accordance with the plan he

---

the Father as the origin of his divine and human natures. As with obedience and prayer, therefore, it designates the procession of the Son from the Father in human terms and demonstrates that Christ receives the impetus of all acts of providence from the Father's will. H. Diepen ("La psychologie humaine du Christ selon saint Thomas d'Aquin," 540), also envisages the prayer of Christ as directed to all of the three persons as objects, citing as his authority Thomassin, *De Verbo Incarnato*, l. 9, c. 11, and in this respect resembles Levering. Diepen's inconsistency on this point with regard to his own teaching that there is no "psychological autonomy" (535–56) of a unique *human* subject in Christ is evident. In my opinion the positions of both Levering and Diepen justly incur the objections of Weinandy concerning an implicit Nestorianism by attributing to the human Christ an adoration of the Word.

61. John 14: 8–11.

foresaw in light of the Father's will, a will he shared in his divine nature.[62]

Could this form of "instrumental" revelatory prayer be possible uniquely by means of prophetic knowledge in the soul of Christ, lived out in faith? In this case, the man Jesus would lack evidential knowledge of the will he receives eternally from the Father. His prayer would, therefore, not be moved immediately by his filial will as the Son of God, but would express instead the desire in his human heart to do the will of God, which he only believed that he shared eternally with the Father. Therefore, his prayer would operate on a parallel track to his divine will without direct contact. It could no longer manifest to us an immediate awareness that he receives all things from the Father as Son. Instead of taking on this "Trinitarian form," then, the prayer of Christ would seemingly acquire a kind of human autonomy of operation, imploring in faith the divine activity of the Trinity that transcended the scope of its knowledge. It is difficult to resist the conclusion that Christ in his divine nature and activity would become an object of petition for Christ in his human nature and activity. Here again, then, the need for the vision of the divine will in the human soul of the Son is manifest: only this can bring into perfect accord the cooperation of the human and divine wills of Christ in his concrete agency as the Son of God.

The unity of the person of Jesus is manifest in his prayer because

---

62. *ST* III, q. 21, a.1, ad 3. Aquinas cites Damascene's *The Orthodox Faith* III, c. 24, agreeing with the latter that Christ did not "raise his mind to God" in the sense of progressively acquiring knowledge of God through prayer because he possessed the "blessed vision" of God. However, because of this grace, Christ's mind was always raised up to the contemplation of the divine nature, and was moved in accordance with the divine will. Christ therefore prayed for things that he knew would be merited by his prayer: *ST* III, q. 21, a. 1, ad 2. This does not mean, however, that his natural will and his human psychology (i.e., sensuality) were not revolted by the imminence of torture and death. On the contrary, Christ could overcome these natural reactions only by his "deliberate will," under the movement of the divine initiative in the heights of his soul (*ST* III, q. 21, a. 2; III, q. 21, a. 4, ad 1). The fact that his rational will was naturally repulsed by the prospect of death at Gethsemane does not imply a struggle of faith concerning the divine will, but a rational desire to overcome the natural fears of death that are proper to being human in order to obey the divine will (cf. *ST* III, q. 18, a. 5, especially corp. and ad 3).

this action reveals his immediate awareness that "all things come from the Father" (cf. John 13:3). This leads to a final objection: true prayer implies desire. But could Christ really have desired anything in his earthly state if he possessed the vision of God? Desire suggests an incompleteness, an absence, and therefore also broaches upon the problem of Jesus's true suffering and the privations imposed by his historical condition. As Galot poignantly objects, could a Jesus who possessed the immediate vision of God have suffered in reality in the ways that the Gospels themselves suggest? Could he truly have desired some state of affairs other than that to which he was immediately subject? Could a Jesus with the vision of God have implored the Father during his crucifixion?

As Jean-Pierre Torrell has demonstrated, Aquinas was innovative in rendering a theological account of the fully human character of the experiential knowledge of Christ, even against the tendencies of his theological age and environment.[63] This perspective was present in a particular way in his understanding of the existence of the beatific vision of the historical Christ. This vision, according to Aquinas, was a grace accorded to the humanity of Christ for the purposes of his soteriological mission. Consequently, it was regulated by a particular economy of grace, or *dispensatio,* proper to the earthly life of the Incarnate Son of God.[64] As Torrell shows, Aquinas explicitly applies this notion to *the way in which* the vision of God existed in the soul of Christ *in his earthly life.*[65]

---

63. Jean-Pierre Torrell, "Le savoir acquis du Christ selon les théologiens médiévaux," *Revue Thomiste* 101 (2001): 355–408.

64. Aquinas uses the term *dispensatio* as a Latin expression of the Greek concept of *oikonomia* (divine government). As is well known, Aquinas understands the redemption of fallen man as the teleological purpose of the Incarnation (see *ST* III q. 1, a. 1). This "redemptive" logic of divine government therefore effects not only *why* the Incarnation took place, but also *how.* For example, so that he could merit for humanity through the crucifixion, Christ assumed a human nature without sin but simultaneously capable of physical, emotional and spiritual suffering as well as corporeal death (see *ST* III qq. 14 and 15).

65. Cf. Torrell, "St. Thomas d'Aquin et la science du Christ," 400–401. cf. *ST* III, q. 14, a. 1, ad 2; III, q. 15, a. 5, ad 3; III, q. 45, a. 2; III, q. 46, a. 8

From the natural relationship which flows between the soul and the body, glory flows into the body from the soul's glory. Yet the natural relationship in Christ was subject to the will of His Godhead, and thereby it came to pass that the beatitude remained in the soul and did not flow into the body; but the flesh suffered what belongs to a passible nature.[66]

Far from deriving uniquely from a non-scriptural principle of perfection, then, this dimension of Aquinas's thought takes into consideration precisely the spiritual needs of the human Christ for the purposes of his saving mission. Among these is the need of the Son to know indefectibly in his human nature the will of the Father (which the Son receives eternally from him) so as to express it in a human way.[67] Yet this grace also coexists simultaneously with the natural possibility of experiential learning, as well as terrible physical and mental suffering.[68] This means that for Aquinas, what is denoted

66. ST III, q. 14, a. 1, ad 2.

67. Throughout this chapter I have emphasized the teachings of the Johannine theology of Christ. However, a number of texts from the Synoptic tradition also describe Christ referring (implicitly but evidently) to his divine will in his concrete human actions. See, for example, Matt 11:25–27 ("Yes Father such has been your gracious will. All things have been handed over to me by my Father"); Luke 10:18–20 ("I have given you the power to tread on scorpions"); Luke 13:34–5 ("Jerusalem, I yearned to gather your children together"). In all of these cases Jesus expresses, in his human desires, his divine identity and will. He does not have to ponder the nature of this will through a consideration of prophetic revelation. This can only be the case because, in the unity of his subjective action, he knows in an immediate human way his own divine power, identity, and will. The Synoptic miracle tradition is particularly eloquent in this regard: Matt 8: 2–3: "And then a leper approached, did him homage, and said, 'Lord, if you wish, you can make me clean.' He stretched out his hand, touched him, and said, 'I will do it. Be made clean'. His leprosy was cleansed immediately." See also Matt 9:27–29; Mark 2:5–12; Luke 8:22–24.

68. ST III, q. 19, a. 1. In ST III, q. 46, aa. 7 and 8, Aquinas follows Damascene (De Fide Orth., III, c. 19) in underscoring the economic mode of Christ's experience of the passion. Spiritual and physical agony were permitted to coexist with the pacifying beatitude of immediate knowledge of the Father and of the divine will. In counter-distinction from the beatific vision in the life of the glorified Christ and of the blessed, the mode of the beatific vision in the earthly life of Christ is such that it affects only the "heights of the soul," that is to say, uniquely the operations of intellect and will in their direct relation to the divine nature. This extraordinary knowledge presupposes, respects, and integrates the natural order of Christ's human thinking, feeling, and sensing without changing its essential structure. An excellent analysis of this point is made by Colman O'Neill ("The Problem of Christ's Human Autonomy," 234–37). See also Edouard-Henri Weber, Le Christ selon saint Thomas d'Aquin (Paris: Desclée, 1988), 179–98. Garrigues has extended this principle, showing

in contemporary parlance by the "psychology of Christ" (his imagination, emotions, ideas, etc.) is not structurally changed by Christ's extra-ordinary knowledge of his own divine identity, will, and mission. Once again, the human faculties of Christ are not affected in their natural *specification*, but only in their *mode of exercise*.[69] They are fully natural, but in their concrete exercise, they are organized from within by a higher spiritual awareness that Christ has of his transcendent identity, will, and mission. This means that they retain all of their natural vulnerability.

Consequently, for Aquinas, the prayer of Christ in a very real sense is a genuine expression of the historical character of his consciousness and of his real submission to the contingent circumstances of providence. Christ could and did hope for his own deliverance (through resurrection) from the terrible spiritual and sensible experiences of suffering and death. He also hoped for the future establishment of the Church among his followers and for their eventual earthly mission and heavenly glorification.[70] The fact that he foresaw these realities in the heights of his soul was not a substitute for his more ordinary human way of thinking and feeling about them: the latter coexisted with this higher knowledge.[71] Thus, his vision was not a consolation for the absence of the human experience of these specific objects of desire. In fact, it could be the source of an existential dissatisfaction: the desire for something known to be in the future but as yet unattained. This was particularly acute with respect to Christ's hope for the reconciliation of human persons with God.[72]

---

how it applies for Aquinas to the "infused science" of Christ, which is "habitual" and in potency to know all that can be known (*ST* III, q. 9, a. 3), but in act uniquely with respect to those things Christ must know for the sake of his mission (*ST* III q. 11, a. 5, obj. 2, corp. and ad 2). See Garrigues, "La conscience," 47–51. As Garrigues points out, this teaching is mirrored in the recent *CCC* 473–74, with reference to Mark 13:32 and Acts 1:7.

69. *ST* III, q. 19, a. 1, ad 3.

70. A point Aquinas makes clearly in analyzing the desires of Christ: *ST* III, q. 21, a. 3, corp., ad 2 and 3. See also III, q. 7, a. 4.

71. This is Aquinas's point in insisting on the simultaneous existence in Christ of both an immediate knowledge of God and an "experiential, acquired knowledge" of his human surroundings. Cf. *ST* III, q. 12, a. 2, where he notes his change of mind on this issue with respect to the earlier position of III *Sent.*, d. 14, a. 3.

72. Cf. Luke 13:34; 23:34; John 17:1, 5, 15–24. This principle is illustrated most acutely

What conclusion is to be drawn from these reflections concerning the claims of Galot and Weinandy? On the one hand, we see that St. Thomas's treatment of the human will of Christ permits us to take seriously the specifically human character of the willing of Jesus manifest in his obedience and prayer. On the other hand, it also accounts for the filial mode of this same voluntary activity in the human Christ. Therefore, it allows us to take seriously the historical contingency of the man Jesus in the limitations of his human historical state even while simultaneously insisting on the way in which this same human nature reveals intra-Trinitarian relations between Jesus and the Father. Only because of Aquinas's key distinction between the nature and mode of Christ's human activity is this insight available. At the same time, this operational correlation in Jesus between his human will and the will of the Father with whom he is in relation in his personal acts can itself only occur through the medium of an immediate knowledge of his own identity and divine will. Because this is the case, the Trinitarian intelligibility of the obedience and prayer of Christ requires that the immediate vision of God be present in Christ. Only this grace can effectuate the personal unity of the action of Jesus in and through a differentiation of natures so that the divine will of the Son of God is revealed to us instrumentally through Christ's human action. Only because of this grace do these activities in the consciousness of Christ appear in all of their "Chalcedonian" integrity. If we deny the existence of this grace in light of what has been said above, then we make the filial and instrumental character of the obedience and prayer of Christ unintelligible.

---

by John 17:24: "Father, I desire that they also, whom thou hast given me, may be with me where I am, to behold my glory which thou hast given me in thy love for me before the foundation of the world." The clear indication is that Christ actually beholds in his human nature the glory he has eternally from the Father, and that he simultaneously desires this glory to be shared in by his disciples. This prayer therefore both expresses a filial awareness of an identity received from the Father and an unfulfilled desire on behalf of the disciples, which motivates Christ to suffer the forthcoming passion.

CONCLUSION

In these brief observations I have argued (following a host of recent commentators) that Aquinas's theology of Christ bears within it significant resources for treating the contemporary challenge of a theological reflection on "the consciousness of Christ." Contrary to the claims of Galot and Weinandy, I do not believe that a Thomistic account of the presence of the beatific vision in Christ falls into the extremes of either Monophysitism or Nestorianism. On the contrary, the Thomistic understanding of this grace is central to an integral Christology that avoids either of these errors. The inner life of Jesus, as this argument has suggested following Herman Diepen, is to some extent irreducibly different from our own. There is no pure similitude between his self-awareness and ours due to the fact that his human self-awareness is that of the Incarnate Word. However, all that is human in Christ flourishes under the influence of grace, and his human actions are more perfect than our own precisely because of the presence in this humanity of the transcendent personhood of God. The immediate knowledge of God (or the beatific vision) is a necessary element of his humanity due to the duality of natures that are present in the life of the Son of God and their simultaneous cooperation in one personal subject. Only through this vision can the human actions of Jesus acquire their particular filial character as "instrumental" actions of the Son of God. Theologians who wish to reconsider this classical teaching of the Church must face the real challenge of explaining how, in the absence of this vision, the unity of the theandric acts of Christ may properly be maintained.[73]

73. I am grateful to Nicanor Austriaco, Jean-Miguel Garrigues, and Thomas Weinandy for their comments on earlier drafts of this argument, which helped greatly to improve its content.

13

Dyotheletism and the Human Consciousness of Jesus

The question of the consciousness of Christ has acted as a kind of lodestar for historical speculation and theological reflection in modern theology. From Schleiermacher and Harnack to Schweitzer and N. T. Wright, the question of Jesus's self-awareness had been debated with intensity by Protestant theologians of the modern epoch. Roman Catholic theology, meanwhile, has not stood aloof from this discussion, even if its initial approach to the question in the early twentieth century was marked above all by a Scholastic, metaphysical mode of inquiry. This methodology was on display, especially in the famous *homo assumptus* quarrels between Seiller, Deodat de Basly, Galtier, and Diepen, which terminated in the 1951 decree of Pius XII, *Sempiternus Rex*, criticizing the position of Seiller. Meanwhile, certain works of Lonergan, Rahner, Galot, and Maritain continued to develop this tradition both before and after Vatican II. More recent writings of Schillebeeckx, Kasper, and O'Collins have sought to identify elements of a Catholic "Christology from below" based on a more profound dialogue with the historical critical studies of modern exegesis.

Originally printed in *Pro Ecclesia* 17, no. 4 (2008): 396–422.

At the same time, this modern treatment of the human historical consciousness of Christ has tended to eclipse the classical theology of the two natures of Christ. Authors who concentrate on the former often regard the Chalcedonian formula as an excessively artificial, ahistorical abstraction superimposed upon the dynamic history of God present in Christ.[1] Consequently, there is a corollary tendency in modern Christology to emphasize the absolute unicity of Christ as a historical subject, the authentically human character of his consciousness, and the true historicity of God in Christ. One might consider this tendency a kind of "inverted Cyrillian" theology. It is Cyrillian insofar as it underscores the unicity of the subject of Christ, yet it is also "inverted" insofar as it places an acute emphasis on the historical nature of the Son as man rather than on his transcendent nature as Logos.

In a relatively recent issue of *Pro Ecclesia*, my friend and mentor Father Thomas Weinandy, OFM, Cap. offered a critique of the classical position of the Catholic Church concerning the presence of the beatific vision in the earthly life of the Son of God as a grace affecting his "filial consciousness" as man.[2] In short, Weinandy offered criticisms of Aquinas's doctrine on this point, claiming, in effect, that a certain kind of Nestorianism was present in St. Thomas's thinking. I have responded to Weinandy in *The Thomist* in defense of Aquinas's position, and recently he has, in turn, suggested in that same publication that my own Christological formulations are intrinsically semi-Nestorian.[3] This is unsurprising since my own formula-

---

1. For criticisms of the "two natures" theology as excessively abstract in its treatment of the historical mystery of God in Christ, see Wolfhart Pannenberg's very well formulated challenges in *Jesus: God and Man*, 307–64, which I will return to below. Likewise, consider Edward Schillebeeckx, *Jesus: An Experiment in Christology* (New York: Seabury, 1979), 650–69, esp. 655. Karl Rahner approaches the issue more moderately in his attempt to co-legitimate both a historical "Christology from below" and a Chalcedonian "Christology from above" in "The Two Basic Types of Christology," *Theological Investigations* Vol. 13, 213–2 (New York: Seabury, 1979).

2. See Thomas Weinandy, "Jesus' Filial Vision of the Father."

3. See my "The Voluntary Action of the Earthly Christ and the Necessity of the Beatific Vision," chapter 12 of this volume or *The Thomist* 69 (2005): 497–534; and

tions agree in many ways with those of John Damascene and Aquinas, with whom Weinandy begs to differ. At the heart of our debate are issues related to the topics mentioned above. In short, does the appeal to a classical theology of the "two natures" and "two wills" of Christ allow one to do justice to the unity of Christ as a person and to the authentically human character of his historical consciousness? If so, in what way can one speak rightly about this mystery?

In this chapter I would like to take a different tack toward the issue by exploring the patristic and Thomistic notion of the "instrumentality" of Christ's human operations of mind and will. In doing so, I will seek to delineate a patristic precedent for the modern Catholic magisterial affirmation that Christ, in his earthly life, enjoyed the "immediate vision" of God. I will do so in two stages. First, I will delineate Weinandy's chief criticism of my position: he claims that when I treat the human mind and will of Christ as *grammatical* subjects of action, my language implies that I am also treating the human operations of Christ as *ontological* "subjects," distinct from the Son of God. By way of response, I will demonstrate that this complaint has a precedent in the anti-Chalcedonian and monenergist positions of the sixth and seventh centuries, and I will discuss why and how it was refuted theologically by the sixth ecumenical council (Constantinople III), as well as the dyothelete teaching of John Damascene. Second, transposing the discussion into a modern format, I will briefly discuss two of the most important modern theological objections to usage of the theology of "two natures" and "two wills" with regard to the human consciousness of Christ. I will then delineate a way of speaking about the human consciousness of Christ as the "instrument" of his person in such a way that the Son incarnate is understood to act consciously as man in harmony with the divine life and will that operate in him by virtue of his divine nature. With these principles in place, I will argue that it is

_____

Weinandy's "The Beatific Vision and the Incarnate Son: Furthering the Discussion," *The Thomist* 70 (2006): 605–15.

necessary that the Incarnate Word possess some grace affecting his human mind and will such that the Word *as man* is aware of his own unity with the Father *and his divine will* shared with the Father. This grace is understood traditionally by recourse to the notion of the "immediate vision" of Christ, a teaching currently ensconced in official Catholic teaching. Considered from this perspective, there need be no intrinsic opposition between the classical dyothelete tradition and a modern theology of the consciousness of Christ. Rather, in principle, the two theological traditions could be considered in profound harmony with one another.

NATURES AS THE PRINCIPLES OF OPERATION AND CLASSICAL DYOTHELETISM

The majority of Weinandy's critique of my (rather traditional) use of incarnational language concerns expressions in which the human intellect and will of Christ are depicted as grammatical subjects of action.[4] In effect, in my own previous arguments, I have claimed that "Christ's will and consciousness *must act* as the instruments of his divine subject [or hypostasis]." In addition, "[t]he unity of activity of the Incarnate Word requires the beatific vision in the intellect of Christ, so that his human will and his divine will *may cooperate* within one subject." I have also stated that "[Christ's] human will *must be continually subordinate to* … his divine will in its [human] rational deliberation and choice making."[5] In all of these phrases, the *natural operations* of Christ's mind and will are treated as principles of activity, even as these transpire within the unity of his unique person, the Son of God. Because they can be identified as distinct principles of natural operations, they can also be treated as grammatical subjects of activity. Since they are the *grammatical*

---

4. See Weinandy, "Beatific Vision," sections I, II, and IV. Section III concerns the use of the communication of idioms, which I will return to below.

5. See White, "Voluntary Action," 507, 516.

subjects of predication, however, Weinandy suggests (with phrases of his own making) that I consider these to be *ontologically distinct* subjects of action.[6] In this way, he sees in such expressions a semi-Nestorian tendency to create a duality of subjects due to the attribution of actions to the distinct natures of Christ.

> White speaks of "Christ's human intellect" being "immediately aware of his divine intellect" and it is the beatific vision that ensures that "his human will can act in immediate subordination to his divine will" (516). But an "intellect" is not aware, nor does a "will" act; only a person knows and only a person acts and he does so through his will. Moreover, a "will" does not act apart from the one whose will it is, nor does a "will," as if it were an acting subject, subordinate itself to another will. Only persons subordinate their will to another person. *To say that one will subordinates itself to another will implies two persons.*[7]

Weinandy goes on from this "discovery" of dual-subject Christology to draw two relevant conclusions concerning my thoughts. First, he claims that my understanding of the cooperation of the two wills of Christ (which "act" in concord) requires that I understand the principle of unity in the Incarnation to stem from the beatific vision as the grace that permits the "taming" of the natural human will of Christ by his divine will. Without the vision, the human will would seemingly "run autonomously wild on its own" as something akin to a distinct subject.[8] The immediate vision of God is needed, then, to "unite" the two quasi-subjects of the two natural operations. Second, my use of the communication of idioms must in some way be

6. Weinandy, "Beatific Vision," 608: "[For White] the beatific vision mediates between the Son existing as God and the Son existing as man so as to ensure that the Son as God and the Son as man *are both* on the same page." Weinandy goes on to attribute Nestorianism to this phrase of his own making, but the phrase has no precedent in my own presentation or the dyothelete tradition to which I am appealing.

7. Weinandy, "Beatific Vision," 611 (emphasis added). One should note that I do not claim that the human will of Christ "subordinates *itself*" to his divine will, but only that the human will of Christ is subordinate to his divine will. As I will show below, it is not as if Leo, Damascene, Aquinas, or I myself think that the activity of the human will constitutes that will as a personal subject or "self." The real question at stake is whether such language inadvertently compromises the unity of Christ as a hypostatic subject.

8. Weinandy, "Beatific Vision," 609. Again, this is Weinandy's own phrase.

tainted by an implicitly Nestorian reading of the two-natures doctrine of Christ. To say, for example, that "the man Jesus comes to know that he is God" is illicit for Weinandy since such language would imply that the man Jesus is a distinct subject from God the Word. Instead, we should say that "the Son of God humanly comes to know that he is the Son of God."[9] To say that "Christ's will and consciousness must act as the instruments of his divine subject" is to fall into a semi-Nestorian usage of the communication of idioms since the treatment of the distinct activity of the human will as a grammatical subject implies that this activity is somehow an ontological subject distinct from the divine hypostasis of Christ.

Classical Objections to Leo's Tome and the Dyotheletism of the Ancient Church

It is necessary to note in the course of this discussion that these debates are not new ones. Father Weinandy's objection to my linguistic phrases has a clear precedent in the Cyrillian, anti-Chalcedonian thinkers of the sixth century AD, and chief among them Severus of Antioch, whose criticisms of Leo the Great were to influence the monenergists of the seventh century.[10] Severus appealed to certain formulations of Cyril of Alexandria in order to cast suspicion upon the Council of Chalcedon and specifically upon the Tome of Leo the Great as an "implicitly" Nestorian document. Chief among the objectionable phrases was Leo's famous statement in the Tome: "Agit enim utraque forma cum alterius communione quod

9. Weinandy, "Beatific Vision," 610.

10. The question of the *energeia* of Christ did not come to the forefront of Christological debate prior to the seventh century, when the monenergist position was developed by Sergius of Constantinople in order to attempt to attract anti-Chalcedonians back into a dialogue concerning the doctrine of the two natures of Christ. Severus himself foreshadows the formulation of "monenergist" theology, as the later movement was profoundly indebted to him, and its key positions were logically derived from the Cyrillian approach to the person of Christ that characterized anti-Chalcedonian sixth-century theology. (Sophronius and Maximus in turn believed that the problem with this position was that it was essentially Apollinarian in character.)

proprium est," or "each 'form' acts in communion with the other in accordance with what is proper to it." Contextually, Leo is speaking here about Christ as one subject being simultaneously "in the form of God" and the "form of a servant" (Phil 2:6ff.). The importance of the phrase, however, is that it treats the two natures of Christ as distinct principles of operation, or energies, and thus as distinct *grammatical* subjects. Severus, like members of the monenergist movement who came after him, objected to such language insofar as he believed that it implied a duality of *ontological* subjects. Writing against Leo's perspective, Severus states:

> For there is one who acts [*energesas*] that is the Word of God incarnate; and there is one active movement which is the activity [*energeia*], but the things which are done [the effects of Christ's action] are diverse ... And it is not the case that, because these things which were done were of different kinds, we say that conceptually *there were two natures which were effecting those things*, for as we have said, a single God the Word Incarnate performed both of them.[11]

In other words, it is illicit to speak (as Leo has) of the two natures as principles of action. Such actions can only be attributed to the Incarnate Word as the principle of their activity.

This position, while widespread in the sixth century, was not to carry the day in classical Christological orthodoxy, due in large part to the Christological writings of Leontius of Byzantium, Sophronius of Jerusalem, and Maximus the Confessor, who placed explicit

---

11. Severus Ant., *Ep. I ad Sergium*, CSCO 120, 60, 33–61, 9 (emphasis added). Translation by Aloys Grillmeier in his *Christ in Christian Tradition*, vol. 2, pt. 2, 165. Severus's position is subtle: there are truly two wills in Christ, but they are not distinct principles of action. On his critique and rejection of Leo's Tome on this point, see Roberta Chesnut, *Three Monophysite Christologies: Severus of Antioch, Philoxenus of Mabbug, and Jacob of Sarug* (Oxford: Oxford University Press, 1976), 25–36. See also Grillmeier's detailed discussion of Severus's doctrine on this point (Chesnut, *Three Monophysite Christologies*, 150–52, 162–67): "Severus could not tolerate conceding to the humanity of Christ ... an active principle of operation. Precisely in this natural ability to be the source of human acts, he sensed already the independence from the ultimate bearing subject ... Against this [singularity of operation] are contrasted the two activities of Leo, who in the eyes of Severus accepted with the two acting nature principles also two bearing subjects, that is, two persons" (151, 166).

emphasis on the two operations (energies) of Christ in contradistinction to the monenergist position. In particular, Sophronius and
Maximus defended the duality of wills in Christ as distinct principles of action, in controversy with monotheletes such as Sergius of
Constantinople and his successor Pyrrhus.[12] Their efforts were vin-
dicated by the ecclesial self-reflection of the sixth ecumenical council (Constantinople III, 680–681), in which the dyothelete position
was defined as a principle of universal Catholic doctrine. The council claims explicitly that there are "two natural principles of action
in the same Jesus Christ," and to this effect, cites Leo's famous statement from the Tome in Greek so as to make clear that "each *form
does (morphe energei)*" that which is proper to it, in concord with the
other. In addition, the document goes on to state that "*each nature
wills and performs the things that are proper to it* in a communion with
the other; [and] in accord with this reasoning, we hold that two natural wills and principles of action meet in correspondence for the
salvation of the human race."[13] Of course, it is significant that the linguistic subjects of such phrases are the "natures" of Christ, treated in

12. Much of the controversy concerned the rejection of Leo's Tome by the monotheletes and the acceptance and interpretation of it by the dyotheletes. See in this respect,
for example, the noted study of Christoph von Schönborn, *Sophrone de Jerusalem: vie monastique et confession dogmatique*, Theologie historique 20 (Paris: Beauchesne, 1972), esp.
199–224, where Schönborn shows multiple times the way in which Sophronius interpreted Leo's Tome. Sophronius perceived in Leo's theology an authentic delineation of the
two natures as veritable principles of operation and, following Leo, purposefully wrote of
the natures and wills (divine and human) as grammatical subjects of predication in order
to emphasize the reality of the distinction of the natures. This is interesting because, as I
will show below, the 1994 *Catechism of the Catholic Church* (edited by Schönborn) explicitly appeals to such a perspective and, following Sophronius and Constantinople, treats
the natural operations of Christ as grammatical subjects of actions. On Sophronius's and
Maximus's interpretations of the Tome in this regard, see the recent study of Demetrios
Bathrellos, *The Byzantine Christ: Person, Nature, and Will in the Christology of Saint Maximus the Confessor* (Oxford: Oxford University Press, 2004), 176–85. "Sophronius argued
that the formula of Leo is incompatible with Nestorianism for two reasons: first, because
the two natures worked not in separation from, but in communion with, each other; and
secondly, which perhaps follows from the first, because, despite the fact that there are
two working natures, there are not two, but only one, working person" (179).

13. This is the translation of Norman Tanner, *Decrees of the Ecumenical Councils*,
vol. 1 (London: Sheed & Ward; Washington, DC: Georgetown University Press, 1990),
129–30.

this instance as principles of operations. These were the very formulations the monothelete theologians would not accept.[14] Evidently, this document treats the natures as grammatical subjects, because the natures are themselves principles of operations or activities.

John Damascene and Thomas Aquinas on the Human Mind and Will of Christ

In order to further clarify the traditional basis for Aquinas's position, which I have sought to defend and develop, it is helpful to examine in particular John Damascene's work *The Orthodox Faith*, which itself influenced St. Thomas on this matter. Here, I would like to focus upon three ways in which Damascene interprets the teaching of Constantinople III with respect to the coordination of the acts of the two wills of Christ. His dyothelete position has in turn influenced Aquinas's position (and my own) concerning the points at issue.

First of all, following St. Sophronius and the sixth ecumenical council, Damascene places explicit emphasis upon the mind and will of Christ as principles of operations distinct from his divine knowledge and will. Writing against Severus, Damascene proposes the following:

14. The council makes quite explicit that the "forms" in question in Leo's Tome pertain to Christ's two *natures* (*duo physicas*), thus interpreting the Chalcedonian doctrine over and against the perspective of Severus. Maximus the Confessor in *Opusculum* 3 (PG91, 49C-52A) relates: "I remember when I was staying on the island of Crete, that I heard from certain false bishops of the Severan party who disputed with me, that 'we do not say, in accordance with the *Tome of Leo*, that there are two activities in Christ, because it would follow that there were two wills, and that would necessarily introduce a duality of persons, nor again do we say one activity, which might be regarded as simple, but we say, in accordance with Severus, that one will, and every divine and human activity proceeds from one and the same God and Word Incarnate.'" *Maximus the Confessor,* trans. Andrew Louth (London: Routledge, 1996), 195. See Aquinas's comment in *ST* III, q.18, a. 1 on the monothelete descendents of Severus: "Sergius of Constantinople and some of [his] followers held that there is one will in Christ, although they held in Christ there are two natures united in a hypostasis; because they believed that Christ's human nature *never moved with its own motion, but only inasmuch as it was moved by the Godhead*" (emphasis added).

When it is allowed by that which is more excellent [the divine will of Christ], the mind of Christ gives proof of its own authority [over his body], but it is under the dominion of and obedient to that which is more excellent, and *does those things* which the divine will purposes ... So, then, He had by nature, both as God and as man, the power of will. But *His human will was obedient and subordinate to His divine will,* not being guided by its own inclination, but *willing those things which the divine will willed* ... For when He prayed that He might escape death, it was with His divine will naturally willing and permitting it that He did so pray and agonize and fear, and again when His divine will willed that His human will should choose death, the passion became [humanly] voluntary to Him.[15]

Here, Damascene would seem vulnerable to the same criticisms Weinandy has proposed of my own reflections. Yet Damascene also uses a key qualification taken from his dyothelete forebears in order to evade the charge of Nestorianism: a nature is never found except *within* a hypostatic subject, and a hypostatic subject never acts except "in and through" a nature.[16] Therefore, Damascene asserts, if the natures are principles of operations ("the will acts," "the mind knows," etc.), this should not be construed as a kind of Nestorian dualism. Rather, these are the natural operations *through which the subject of the* Incarnate Word *acts.* It is in light of this distinction

15. *The Orthodox Faith* III, c. 6 and 18. See likewise, St. Sophronius' *Epist. Synod,* which uses similar language.

16. *The Orthodox Faith* III, c. 3, 9, 11. In fact, the principle that "a nature is never found except within a hypostasis" was employed by anti-Chalcedonian monophysites of the sixth century in order to argue for the singularity of the nature in Christ. Dyophysites responded by adopting the same principle and reinterpreting it in light of the distinction between the operation *of* a person and operation *through* (or by means of) a nature. This way of thinking has its origins in earlier Trinitarian debate. The distinction between the nature common to a plurality of persons and the particular personal subject in which this nature exists originates with Basil in his *Epistle to Terentius* (PG 32, 798 A). It was developed Christologically in the context of dyothelete disputes by John the Grammarian and Leontius of Byzantium. (See, for example, *Contra Nestorianos et Euthychianos,* PG 86, 1280 A, by the latter.) According to Andrew Louth, John of Damascus considers the nonacknowledgment of this distinction the central error of the monophysites. See his *St. John Damascene: Tradition and Originality in Byzantine Theology* (Oxford: Oxford University Press, 2002), 159. Aquinas's own thought offers a close parallel to Damascene in *ST* III, q. 3, a. 4, ad 1: nature is the principle *through which* a subject or hypostasis acts, but it is always the subject *who* acts.

between the hypostatic mode of Christ's filial action and the duality of the natural principles through which he, as an ontological subject, acts that Damascene interprets the Tome of Leo. Commenting directly on the document, Damascene states:

> For we hold that the two operations are not divided and that the natures do not act separately, but that each conjointly in complete community with the other acts with its own proper activity ... We speak sometimes of His two natures and sometimes of His one person: and the one or the two is referred to one conception. For the two natures are one Christ and the one Christ is two natures. Wherefore it is all the same whether we say "Christ acts according to either of His natures," or "either nature acts in Christ in communion with the other."[17]

Following Maximus, then, Damascene will distinguish between the personal *mode* (tropos) of the mental and voluntary activity of Christ and his distinct nature as man (logos)[18]. The natures are the principles of specifically human or divine operations in Christ, but these operations occur only in the unique hypostasis of the Son. Therefore, they exist only in a filial mode because they are always the natural operations of the Son of God made man.[19] Second, to qualify his distinction of the operations of the two natures such that it gives sufficient expression to the unicity of the subject of Christ, Damascene employs two notions developed within preceding patristic tradition. One of these, taken from Leontius and

---

17. *The Orthodox Faith*, III, c. 19 (translation slightly modified). The interpretation of Leo here is clearly indebted to Maximus's notion that by the Incarnation, the Son is "from the two natures, in the two natures and *is* the two natures."

18. *The Orthodox Faith*, III, c. 13.

19. It is significant to note that Aquinas follows Damascene quite closely here in *ST* III, q. 19, a. 1, where he cites Constantinople III against Severus. He then proceeds to defend the Tome against its critics (corp. and ad. 4): "The human nature has its proper operation distinct from the divine and conversely. Nevertheless, the divine nature makes use of the operation of the human nature, as of the operation of its instrument. Being and operation belong to the person by reason of the nature; yet in a different manner. For being belongs to the very constitution of the person, and in this respect it has the nature of a term; consequently, unity of person requires unity of the complete and personal being. But operation is an effect of the person by reason of a form or nature. Hence plurality of operations is not incompatible with personal unity." Similarly, Aquinas employs the hypostatic mode/nature distinction of Maximus and Damascene explicitly in *ST* III, q. 18, a. 1, ad 4.

Maximus, is that of the *perichoresis* or mutual indwelling of the two natures of Christ.[20] If the two operations of Christ as God and man are distinct, they are not, for this reason, separated. The divine nature indwells the human, such that the human operations of Christ are conduits for the operations and effects of his divine life. When Christ heals the blind man, he wills humanly to touch the man, yet the power of healing that proceeds forth from his hand emanates from the divine wisdom and power that are present in his person.[21] This means in turn that there is a hierarchical and instrumental character to the human acts of Christ. These latter are themselves subject to the activity of his person and work in concord with the operations of his divine nature. This is nowhere more true than with respect to the human mind and will of Christ. Since the latter are the human mind and will of God incarnate, they must operate according to their intrinsically natural principles, yet they are also altered as to their *mode* so as to function in concord with the *divine* life and will present within the Word.[22]

In what way, then, does this presence of divine life in Christ affect the character (or mode) of the operation of the human will of Christ? Weinandy has claimed that my presentation suggests a dichotomy of options. The human mind and will of Christ would (on

---

20. *The Orthodox Faith* III, c. 3.

21. *The Orthodox Faith* III, c. 15: "The power of miracles is the energy of His divinity, while the work of His hands and the willing and the saying 'I will, be clean,' are the energy of his humanity. And as to the effect, the breaking of the loaves, and the fact that the leper heard the 'I will,' belong to His humanity, while the multiplication of the loaves and the purification of the leper belong to his divinity." Likewise, see Aquinas, *STh* III, q. 19, a. 1.

22. *The Orthodox Faith* III, c. 15: "For through both, that is through the energy of the body and the energy of the soul, *He displayed one and the same, cognate and equal divine energy.* For just as we say that His natures were united and *permeate one another,* and yet do not deny that they are different but even enumerate them, although we know they are inseparable, so also in connection with the wills and the energies we know their union and we recognize their difference ... without introducing separation. For just as the flesh was deified without undergoing change in its own nature, in the same way also *will and operation are deified without transgressing their own proper limits.* For whether He is the one or the other, that is as God or as man, He is one and the same." (Emphasis added, translation slightly altered.)

my account as construed by Weinandy) be either "wild" without the grace of the immediate vision of God or "tamed" in the presence of such grace. This suggests some kind of innate tension between nature and grace in Christ since the will and intellect of Christ would naturally "run autonomously wild on their own"[23] without grace. In fact, since my own presentation is simply taken from Maximus and Damascene, the question is whether this dichotomous construal of their views is correct. Damascene, following Maximus, distinguishes between not two but three distinct modes in which the human will can subsist.[24] One mode does bear some similitude to what one might term a "wild" will. It pertains uniquely to persons in a fallen state of existence and is characterized by what the Byzantine theologian calls a "gnomic will." The will in this state is plagued by moral weakness, and the rational agent must consider alternatives between evil and good while subject to ignorance and inordinate passions. If the fallen agent defects from the sovereign good, his freedom thus "runs wild" in contradiction with the divine will. It can be "tamed" only by grace restoring the will in its rectitude toward God and its right relationship to the disordered passions. The second mode concerns the "natural will" of the created person. Since the will is created for God, it tends by its very nature toward the sovereign goodness of God as its ultimate term. Yet such a will cannot by nature know what the will of God is, at least as it applies to each historical circumstance or every prudential instance. It is, therefore, also deliberative and imperfect when it seeks to obey God, even if it is neither characterized by weakness nor sinful. Even an unfallen human being would have to live in opinion (rather than immediate certitude) concerning the proper good to pursue in contingent historical circumstances. Therefore, such a will (being "gnomic" in just this sense) could err in practical prudential judgment *without necessarily incurring moral fault*.[25]

---

23. Weinandy, *Beautific Vision*, 609.

24. For this discussion, see *The Orthodox Faith* II, c. 22 and III, c.14, following Maximus's *Dialogue with Pyrrhus*. See also *ST* III, q. 18, where Aquinas embraces this perspective.

25. In Roman Catholic tradition one would say as much of the Mother of Jesus in

This would be a will that is neither wild nor tame but rather "naturally good" yet only "imperfectly aware of or in communion with" the sovereign goodness of God. Were the Incarnate Word to be humanly unaware of the divine will of the Father in a given circumstance, *this* is the mode of the will he would share in, and not that which Weinandy claims I (and, by extension, John Damascene) would attribute to Christ.[26] The third mode, however, is that which is truly proper to the Son incarnate. It is "hypostatic" and "instrumental." Here (as in the former case), the will is ordered toward the sovereign good naturally such that it is not wild (passionately inclined toward sin) nor tame (reformed after sin). Yet, in addition, it is also informed by the knowledge of the will of God concerning contingent singular decisions. It is that mode of willing which is proper to the human nature of the divine person, whose human actions bear the imprint of his divine nature due to the cooperation of these human actions with the divine operations of the Son.[27]

This leads Damascene to an important conclusion: the operations of the divine and human wills in Christ must be coordinated in a unique way due to the hypostatic union. This is the classical dyothelete emphasis on the role of *synergy* in the life of Christ. True, Christ is not God and man because the two wills of Christ are coordinated. (Appeals to such a "moral union" would be absurd.) On the contrary, *because* Christ is God and man in one subsistent person, *therefore* there must be a coordination between his two wills *in all circumstances*.[28] Damascene argues that this occurs above all by a ten-

---

her "discovery" of the child Jesus in the temple in Lk 2:48, where she fails to understand the "prudence" of his behavior.

26. See in particular *The Orthodox Faith* II, c. 22, on this point.

27. *The Orthodox Faith* II, c. 22: "But in the case of our Lord Jesus Christ, since He possesses different natures, His natural wills, that is, His volitional faculties belonging to Him as God and as Man are also different. But since the hypostasis is one, and He who exercises the will is one, the object of the will, that is the gnomic will, is also one, His human will evidently following His divine will, and willing that which the divine will willed it to will."

28. It is important to acknowledge the radical disjunction between the Thomistically-inspired position of Herman Diepen, Bernard Lonergan, and Karl Rahner on this point, as contrasted with that of Leon Seiller, who, following Deodat de Basly,

dency proper to each will in Christ toward a common goal. Christ's divine and human will act in concord in each contingent historical circumstance in accordance with the wisdom of the divine economy. Likewise, there must be a *synergy* between the human mind of the Incarnate Son and the divine wisdom that dwells within him. When God the Son decides humanly to heal the blind man, his human decision and action occur in concord with the wisdom and action of his own divine will (which he shares with the Father). When he goes to Jerusalem to die, Jesus knows his human action corresponds in truth to the will of the Father. He knows this because he is aware in his human mind of the will of the Father in this contingent circumstance. "Father, let this cup pass from me" (Mk 14:36): the request presupposes knowledge of the divine will. He also knows that he shares in this will as the Son of the Father, who is one with the Father, and consequently can accept this will through his human deliberation. To follow the logic of Damascene (paraphrasing him quite closely), in the Son, the human will is subordinate at all times to the divine will, the divine will which he shares with the Father.[29] The Word expresses himself as a person in and through the cooperation of his two natures, operations and wills.

Third, Damascene develops a notion of the communication of

---

undertook to reinterpret Scotistic Christological ideas in an original, controversial way. Seiler seems to inadvertently locate the principle of unity in the Incarnation *within the beatific vision* such that in the absence of this grace, the man Jesus could seemingly function as an *ontologically* distinct subject from the Word. [Consider the perspectives of Seiller's *La psychologie humaine du Christ et l'unicité de personne* (Rennes and Paris: Vrin, 1949), 17–23.] One of the Thomistic responses of the above-mentioned thinkers to this quasi-Nestorian portrayal of Christ was to emphasize the distinction between "first act" and "second act" in Christ: between ontological constitution and psychological operation. In his fundamental act of being, the Incarnate Son is one being by virtue of the hypostatic union. However, precisely because of this fundamental principle of unity, the "second acts" of the Incarnate Son (his human psychological operations) are the acts of his person and must, therefore, operate in accord with his wisdom and will as God. Therefore, the cooperation of the two natures is an intrinsic *effect* of the hypostatic union, not its ontological premise.

29. See for the above-mentioned points, *The Orthodox Faith* III, c. 14. See also Aquinas, *ST* III, q. 19, a. 1, where commenting upon the sixth ecumenical council, he follows Sophronius and Damascene in claiming that the human will of Christ desired, willed, and acted in such a way so as to cooperate with and be in subordination to the divine will.

idioms consistent with the principles enunciated above.[30] As the Son incarnate is both man and God, so also his operations pertain to two natures. For Damascene (following such authors as Sophronius), it is theologically inappropriate to attribute the properties of the divine nature to the human nature (or vice versa). However, it is not only permissible but necessary to attribute the properties and operations of both natures to one subject, the Incarnate Word. Yet this same unique subject *can be designated,* John insists, by means of the attributes and operations of one of the natures so *long as these attributions make clear that the subject being designated is "this" particular subject, Jesus* (that is to say, the One we know to be the Incarnate Son).[31] So, for example, Damascene thinks that it is completely legitimate to say not only that "the Incarnate Word suffered in the flesh" but also that "this man is aware that he is God" or "the man Jesus is humanly aware of his hypostatic subject [i.e., that he is the Son of God]" since "this man" under consideration in both instances is the Incarnate Word. (Likewise, one might say that "the eternally impassible God suffered for the duration of his crucifixion.")

To speak in Thomistic terms once again, the "this" or the "his" in such grammatical instances correspond logically to the *suppositum* of Christ and therefore what they designate ontologically is the individuated matter of the object specified. They simply denote linguistically the "material individual" in question. In this case, the individual under consideration is clearly the Incarnate Word. The singular individuality of his matter (his "thisness") thus subsists in his person by virtue of the hypostatic union.[32] "This man" with "his" particular

---

30. *The Orthodox Faith* III, c. 4.

31. *The Orthodox Faith* III, c. 4: "When we speak of His divinity we do not ascribe to it the properties of humanity ... But when we speak of His hypostasis, *whether we give it a name implying both natures, or one that refers to only one of them, we still attribute to it the properties of both natures* ... Accordingly, we can say of Christ, 'this man is uncreated and impassible and uncircumscribed'" (emphasis added). See the congruent reflections of Aquinas, *ST* III, q. 16, aa. 7–9.

32. *ST* III, q.16, a. 9: "When we say; 'this man,' pointing to Christ, the eternal suppositum is necessarily meant, with whose eternity a beginning in time is incompatible. Hence this is false: 'this man began to be.' Nor does it matter that to begin to be refers

natural operations and characteristics *is* the incarnate person of the Son.[33] Consequently, when "this man" knows "his" hypostatic identity as the Son of God, he knows "who" he is in a human way. Correspondingly, we can say, pace Weinandy, that the "who" of God *is* human, not in the sense that the Son is a human person, but in the sense that the divine person of the Son is truly human and that, indeed, no one is more human than he.

Preliminary Conclusion

The mainstream tradition of the classical patristic and conciliar period is unambiguously dyothelete and therefore vindicates the use of the terms of Christ's natures in their respective operations as logical subjects of grammatical constructions. Christological formulations directly indebted to Leo, Sophronius, Maximus, Damascene, Aquinas, and the sixth ecumenical council, then, are in the doctrinal mainstream and in no way should be considered semi-Nestorian.[34] Yet to say all this is not necessarily to acknowledge the essential. Weinandy, like the venerable Cyrillian tradition that precedes him, is deeply sensitive to the question of the unicity of the subject of the Incarnate Word, particularly with regard to his historical life as man. It is this sensitivity to "single subject" Christology that is, in

---

to the human nature, which is signified by the word, 'man'; *because the term placed in the subject is not taken formally so as to signify the nature, but is taken materially so as to signify the suppositum*" (emphasis added). This is the distinction that, to my mind, Weinandy fails to accept in his critique of the use of the communication of idioms as employed by Aquinas. See also *ST* III, q. 16, a. 7, ad 4.

33. The ontological presupposition here is that the material individuality of the Word subsists by virtue of the hypostatic union and, in this respect, can be denoted linguistically as the ontological subject. When one touches the hand of Christ, one touches the hand of the Incarnate Word. "This hand here" is the hand of the Word. Yet by the same token, since this designation is made by reference to the material individuality of the Word, one can reflect conceptually upon the physicality of the Son, which is distinguishable from his (preexistent) hypostasis. Therefore, the *merely notional* difference between "this material man" and the "the Incarnate Word" is founded upon the logical distinction between the human nature of the Son as man and his divine identity. But *ontologically*, the two exist or subsist before us as the one person of the Incarnate Son.

34. This pattern of ascription is maintained most recently by the 1992 *Catechism of the Catholic Church*, which affirms (n. 475) that "Christ's human will does not resist or oppose but rather submits to his divine and almighty will."

many ways, at the heart of contemporary Christology. Is it not clear that the Son as man experienced the world and himself with a genuine human subjectivity? And consequently, should we not wish to moderate appeals to the classical tradition that might jeopardize an acknowledgment of the human, historical character of this personal subjectivity? Metaphysical appeal to the workings of an ahistorical "divine will" always impressing itself upon the human consciousness of Christ might seem inevitably to do just this, and so the more fundamental question may now be asked: of what relevance to contemporary Christology is the dyotheletist tradition of the two cooperative wills of Christ? Is it an aid or a hindrance for a modern reflection on the historical Christ? Does the classical paradigm of Byzantine and Scholastic Christology have intellectual import within the context of modern Christology?

MODERN TRANSPOSITION:
THE HUMAN CONSCIOUSNESS OF CHRIST
AND HIS DIVINE NATURE

Human Historical Consciousness, Subject Singularity, and Two-Nature Christology

At the heart of modern rearticulations of classical Christology, it is readily apparent that at least two fundamental concerns might put us on guard against an appeal to the "two will" theory of Christ's personal agency.[35] The first of these, and most poignant, is the modern concern with the historically derived, culturally locative character of the human consciousness of Christ.[36] Jesus was, according to

35. Both of these objections are adapted from Pannenberg, *Jesus: God and Man,* 307–64. I am not presuming that Thomas Weinandy would himself agree with either of the objections discussed below. His own modern "Cyrillian" Christology, however, bears some resemblances to that described in the first objection.

36. For the sake of this inquiry, it is helpful to appeal to Lonergan's reasonably succinct definition of consciousness: "Consciousness is an interior experience of oneself and one's acts, where 'experience' is taken in the strict sense of the word. 'Experience' may be taken in a broad or in a strict sense. Broadly speaking it is roughly the same as ordinary knowledge; strictly speaking it is a preliminary unstructured sort of awareness

virtually all modern considerations of the question, a human being living and reflecting within the epoch of Second Temple Judaism. If his self-understanding transcended in many ways the immanent cultural conceptual horizon of his time, nevertheless, such understanding found expression in and through the idioms and sentiments of his Judaic and Hellenistic thought-world. It is not strange, then, that a modern Christology concerned to preserve a crisp awareness of the historically situated character of Christ's self-understanding and self-expression as a man in time should also have great reserves concerning those conceptual constructions that seem to relativize or ignore his complete human reality with its inevitable limitations. The classical idea that the human will of Christ was always subordinate to his divine will seems to suggest that the former was being determined by an ahistorical, omniscient will independently of Christ's cultural history. Thinking this way would seem to obscure the fact that his human consciousness was immersed in the theological and political issues of his age, issues that, in fact, determined in some real way the aims and inward intentions of the historical Christ. Is the dyothelete viewpoint in any way compatible with an authentically modern "Christology from below"? It would seem that there is some kind of basic incommensurability between a theology that situates the aims of Jesus within the context of Second Temple Judaism and one that conceives of the coordination of his two wills in a metaphysical or "transcendental" sense.

Second, the modern concern with single-subject Christology is

---

that is presupposed by intellectual inquiry and completed by it." Bernard Lonergan, *The Ontological and Psychological Constitution of Christ, Collected Works,* vol. 7 (Toronto: University of Toronto Press, 2002), 157. It is important to note that consciousness here is understood not as the "perception of an object" (mere knowledge) but rather as an awareness of one's self as a subject. Consciousness, therefore, is more fundamental than thinking and is preconceptual, but it also is present as a dimension of "objective" thinking: the dimension of self-reflexivity, or self-awareness in thinking. Christ's linguistic and conceptual thinking as a first-century Jew pertains to his "consciousness," therefore, just as much as his "preconceptual" (affective, intuitive, and sensible) human experience of himself in the world. Yet the former is part of his consciousness *only* insofar as he is also *aware of himself as a subject in and through* his objective thinking about the world, himself, and the like. I will return to this issue below.

another source of anxiety concerning the classical dyophysite and dyothelete tradition. This can be explained succinctly in harmony with the previous concern. If modern Christology is to treat the historical Jesus as the Incarnate Son of God, it must respect not only the historical consciousness of the Son of God in time, but also insist that this man Jesus is the Son of God and that the Son of God is this man Jesus. Perhaps to do this most radically, however, is to maintain that it is the economy of birth, preaching, suffering, and Resurrection that reveals to us *what* God is. In the Incarnation, God has identified himself radically with our human historicity and finitude. The two-natures theology, in this respect, has seemed to some (particularly in the modern Lutheran tradition) to be, at the very least, an overly abstracted manner of conceiving of the revelation of God in Christ. It would suggest that an omnipotent, transcendent divine nature somehow accompanies all the historical human acts of Christ as the true agent of those acts. By projecting onto the single subject of the Son in time this overly metaphysical and ahistorical conception of the divine nature, one fails to acknowledge the radical identification of God in himself with our historical mode of being.[37] Since dyotheletism obscures in part the true perception of the very acts of the one Son incarnate in time, it becomes more of a hindrance to Christology than an aid.

Evidently, such proposals could elicit a variety of responses. In this context, I will offer two succinct critiques of the abovementioned reservations concerning two-nature Christology. First, it

37. See in particular in this respect, the analysis of Pannenberg, *Jesus: God and Man*, 319: "If God's self-humiliation to unity with a man is conceived only as manifestation of the divine glory and not as sacrifice of essential elements of the divine being, this expression does not help make the full humanity of Jesus in the Incarnation intelligible; for then Jesus would remain an almighty, omniscient, omnipresent man, even though he humbly hides his glory. Or he remains a dual being with two faces in which divine majesty and human lowliness live and work parallel to one another, but without living unity with one another." Likewise, consider the reserves of Robert Jenson in his *Systematic Theology* I, 127–38, and Jurgen Moltmann's more radical relativization of "two nature" Christology in *The Crucified God*, 244–47. A helpful commentary on this tendency in contemporary theology is offered by Bruce McCormack, "Karl Barth's Christology as a Resource for a Reformed Version of Kenoticism."

is readily apparent that however we may wish to construe the historically situated character of the human knowledge of Jesus, we must also take into account the extraordinary phenomena apparent in the words and deeds of Jesus on every page of the canonical Gospels. Classical Christian belief can readily accommodate the idea that the written portrayals of the historical Christ are later prisms through which his original light is recast or refracted in reference to subsequent historical situations. But it cannot abandon the principle that these later accounts do transmit faithfully a fundamentally reliable portrait of what Christ, who is God incarnate, said and did for the salvation of human beings. This being the case, it is evident that the actions of Christ *as portrayed by the New Testament* both conceal and manifest the hidden presence of a divine agency working *in and through* the words and actions of the man Jesus. Theandricism is a theologically axiomatic principle for the New Testament authors when they seek to portray the gestures of Christ: the spoken word of Christ forgives, prophesies, and judges; his touch restores physical life or cures blindness. Clearly, these are all to be considered signs of the coming kingdom of God. Christ is portrayed, then, as one who *is aware that he is able* to judge, forgive, cure, and raise the dead precisely because the one he calls his Father is bringing in the kingdom through his own actions. This is why *for the evangelists,* Christ himself can teach and act with authority. He is explicitly aware that the divine agency of the Father is working through him and at least *implicitly* aware that he shares in the divine identity of the Father.[38] In this sense, the narrative depictions of the historical and phenomenological activity of Christ send us back to the problem of his unity with the Father. To that extent, they bind us to the classical doctrinal concern with the two natures and wills of Christ. The theological

38. For further reflections in this respect, see the suggestive exegetical portrait of Ben Witherington III, *The Christology of Jesus* (Minneapolis: Fortress, 1990), 191–233, on the relation between Jesus's claim to inaugurate the kingdom and filial awareness, and that of N. T. Wright in *Jesus and the Victory of God,* 553–654, on the eschatological action of YHWH in the prophets, which Jesus seems to claim to "enact" by his own behavior.

problem of the conciliar tradition is grounded in the "objective" depictions of the primary accounts.

Second, an insoluble doctrinal difficulty results if we sever ourselves from the patristic admission of the unicity of the divine will and agency shared by the Father and the Son. We will be unable to specify in what sense (if any) the agency and being of the Father and the Son are truly one within the historical economy of the Incarnation. As Maximus and Damascene pointed out in their controversies with the monotheletes, willing pertains to a nature, and every hypostasis is intelligible only in relation to a given nature. If the Son is not one in will with the Father, then we cannot rightly say in what way he is one with him ontologically or how the personal activity of God present in him is one with the activity of the Father and the Holy Spirit. Otherwise, any construal of the tripersonal character of God would be emphasized in such a way as to eclipse the divine unity of the persons.

We can restate the matter, rephrased in less characteristically classical terms, in this way: if the action of God in Jesus is not truly the action of the Father, and if Christ is not able to act in concert with this action as man, then his "soteriological" pattern of living on behalf of human beings in fact has no intrinsically salvific value. But if God is, in fact, "in Christ reconciling the world to himself," then this activity is truly God the Father's, God the Holy Spirit's, and Christ's, and their activity is one. The dynamic actuality of the salvific work of the Father in and with the Son requires an ontological foundation. Indeed, this activity and work reveal and manifest a deeper ontological identity between the Father and the Son. Consequently, if we wish to affirm that the actions of the Son as a historical subject *reveal* who God is and, therefore, reveal the Father and the Holy Spirit (in the Son), then we must also admit that these actions correlate to that which the Father and the Holy Spirit are. But this is only the case if the Son incarnate himself, in his personal history, is also one with these others, such that his human actions manifest the divine life and will that he shares with the Father and the

Holy Spirit. And this requires that the divine life and will of the Son of God be present and (progressively) manifest in and through his human actions.

A succinct conclusion would follow from these arguments: there is a perennial need for an "instrumental" account of the hypostatic union with a two-nature Christology if we are to do justice to the narrative structure and doctrinal integrity of the New Testament portrayal of God. In what follows I would like to offer some brief but relevant reflections on the human consciousness and freedom of the Incarnate Word, keeping in mind the dyothelete account of the divine and human natures of Christ presented above.

"Instrumentality" and the Hypostatic Psychology of Christ

Thus far, I have argued that the dyothelete account of the two operations and wills of Christ is integral to classical doctrinal Christology and that it can and should be preserved as a way of speaking theologically about the theandric action of the God-human as he is presented in the canonical narratives of the Church. Yet this requires that we speak in turn about the nature of the instrumental consciousness of Jesus and the necessary correlation or cooperation between his human psychology as man and his divine nature as God. For this purpose, it is first of all helpful to make clear what an instrumental portrayal of the human consciousness is not. Talk about instrumentality in the hypostatic union does not primarily concern the action of one nature upon another (the divine upon the human) such that the human nature might be somehow considered the "instrument of the divine."[39] Rather, as the tradition makes

---

39. This is what Weinandy seems to understand me to be saying (see his "Beatific Vision," 611–12), but this is not the case. I have mentioned the idea of the human nature as the instrument of Christ's "person and will." Such an expression is admittedly ambiguous. However, as I will mention below, there is an ambiguity in the classical terminology: Maximus the Confessor does at times speak about the divine will of Christ "moving" the human will. But he does not claim (so far as I am aware) that the human will is the "organon" of the divine nature or will per se; Aquinas (ST III, q. 19, a. 1) does speak of the

clear, instrumentality is hypostatic. In the Incarnation of the Son, the human nature is the hypostatically conjoined instrument of the divine person of the Son. However, this person works through his divine nature and his human nature simultaneously. Therefore, the hypostatic union must result in a cooperation of the two natures of the Incarnate Word.

This point is made clearly by Bernard Lonergan in his reflection on "efficient causality" in the Incarnation.[40] On the one hand, he notes, it is illicit to claim that the Word "taken by himself" (without reference to his divine or human natures) exercises personal agency. This idea is consistent with what was mentioned above concerning the thought of Maximus and Damascene against monotheletism: the hypostasis is only active in and through its natures. Second, the divine nature of Christ can be said to exert influence upon the human nature of Christ, but this affirmation requires qualifications.

> Whatever is produced by a divine person by way of efficient causality is produced by divine power; this power is really identical with the divine essence, and the divine essence is common to all three persons. For this reason Catholic theology recognizes that all divine works produced outside the Godhead proceed in common from the three divine persons. Whatever, therefore, the Son as subsisting in the divine nature does by way of efficient causality is likewise and entirely the work of the Father and the Holy Spirit.[41]

And this is why the human nature of Christ could never be the instrument of his divine nature as such: the deity of the Trinitarian God acts in all works of creation and redemption, including those of the Incarnate Son. Were we to make the divine nature the source of the instrumentality, we would "hypostasize" the divine nature of Christ problematically and correspondingly eclipse the reality of the Trinitarian action of God in Christ. This leaves open, then, a

---

human nature of Christ as an "instrument" of his divine nature, but subsequently qualifies such language by referring to the humanity as the instrument of the Son.

40. Lonergan, *Ontological and Psychological Constitution of Christ*, 231.

41. Lonergan, 231. Lonergan himself does not employ the term "instrumentality" in his discussion of this dimension of the Incarnation, but his comments are consistent with the theology of Cyril, Damascene, and Aquinas, which make use of this notion.

unique possibility: the hypostasis of the Word is the one who expresses himself in Christ, yet it is through his human nature that he does so.

Ironically, it is only such an "instrumental" account of the human actions of Christ that allows us to take seriously the double concern of modern Christology outlined above. Christ's historical activity is true, human activity. Consequently, his historical consciousness, self-awareness, deliberation, and judgment, desiring and choosing are all truly human. Second, his human actions are truly those of a unique subject, the person of the Son. They are the actions of God the Son in history. Yet, as Lonergan goes on to point out, this means that there must be a "psychological unity" in Christ as one who is both God and human. "Christ as God knows himself to be this human being, and Christ as man knows himself to be the natural Son of God."[42] It is the principal subject, the Word, who is conscious as man. And the Word, as both God and man, is conscious of himself.[43] In other words, the Son is conscious of himself in and through his two natures, and thus in two distinguishable ways. The Son as God is "aware" in his divine nature that he is man, while the Son as man is aware in his human nature that he is God.

To illustrate this principle, the Jesuit theologian goes on to comment upon Leo's Tome as reread by Constantinople III ("each nature performs the functions proper to itself, yet in concert with the other nature").[44] The council requires, as he notes, that God the Son acts through his two natures and that these natures act in concert precisely because they are the natures through which one person

---

42. Lonergan, 243.

43. Lonergan is willing to speak about both a "divine consciousness" and a "human consciousness" in the person of Christ (191–230). I have avoided this terminology because of the questions this raises concerning the application of a notion of "consciousness" to the divine knowledge of the Son. However, Lonergan's own defense and explanation of his use of the "analogy" of consciousness when pertaining to the Trinitarian God (191–202) is sensitive to the classical tradition, conceptually well-measured, and extremely cogent.

44. Lonergan, *Ontological and Psychological Constitution of Christ*, 245. In this citation of the council, I have given Lonergan's own translation.

acts. This means that the Son of God as man (through his human operations of knowing) must be consciously aware that he is the Son of God; otherwise, the union would be effectuated in such a way that the Son as man would be entirely "unconscious" of his divine identity (which is theologically inane). In addition, he must be in some way conscious as man of the divine operations that are his as the Son of God. Otherwise, his human actions would not operate "in concert" with his divine actions (those actions through which he works as God). This would be patently unfitting, for in such a case, there would be an ontological unity of subject in the Incarnate Word, but his psychological unity (of operations) would not be preserved.

Consciousness versus Knowledge, Mediate versus Immediate Knowledge

The question we are led to by the previous reflections is this: what are the sufficient conditions required such that God as man might be humanly conscious of his divine identity as the Son and such that he might be conscious as man of the divine operations which he shares with the Father as the Son of God? The first thing to mention is that a theory of Christological "consciousness" may not be identified with a theory of Christological knowledge.[45] Knowledge relates to "objective" modes of understanding: the objective conceptualization of reality and the way this conceptualization permits us to know ourselves and others. Theories concerning the knowledge of Christ were developed by pre-modern theologians, and Aquinas, in particular, developed a plausible and profound theory of

45. The distinction between consciousness and knowledge was especially important in theological criticisms of Galtier's Christology in the 1950s. It was introduced by Angelo Perego, "II 'lumen gloriae' et l'unita psicologica di Cristo," *Divus Thomas* 58 (1955): 90–110, 296–310, and developed (problematically in my opinion) by Rahner in his "Dogmatic Reflections on the Knowledge and Self-Consciousness of Christ," *Theological Investigations* vol. 5, trans. K. H. Kruger (London: Darton, Longman & Todd, 1966), 193–215. Much of my discussion in this section, however, is directly influenced by Lonergan's use of the distinction in *Ontological and Psychological Constitution of Christ*, 157–68.

the "objective" media through which the human mind of the Word knows reality.[46] Christ acquired human knowledge through the senses and by means of his active intellectual nature. He also knew "the secrets of human hearts" as well as the deepest meanings of the divine economy by means of prophetic ideas. Finally, through the medium of the immediate vision of the divine essence (the beatific vision), he was intuitively aware of "what" he was as the Son of God.[47] All of this reflection is distinct, however, from a treatment of the consciousness of Christ.

Consciousness (in distinction from knowledge) has to do not with the objective media by which we know or what we know, but rather with the subject's experiential self-awareness in the process of knowing. This self-awareness is both prereflexive and reflexive. It is prereflexive in that it precedes objective knowing and yet is also reflexive insofar as it accompanies and is present within the activity of knowing. We are aware of ourselves (however dimly) as experiential

46. In my opinion Karl Rahner has seriously misrepresented this facet of Aquinas's thought in "Dogmatic Reflections on the Knowledge and Self-Consciousness of Christ," 207–9, and his error has been repeated somewhat uncritically by a host of contemporary thinkers. (See, for example, Pannenberg, *Jesus: God and Man*, 329–31.) In essence Rahner claims that if the Son as man knows himself "objectively" to be God through the graces received into his intellect (as Aquinas suggests), then he also knows himself as an "object." This in turn would imply that the man Jesus knows the Word as a distinct reality from himself, introducing a seemingly Nestorian dualism into the way Aquinas portrays the historical Christ. But here Rahner is unconvincing because in fact he inverts the medieval (and Thomistic) use of object and subject misleadingly. The ontological reality the Son as man knows humanly (for Aquinas) is his own personal *subject*. The epistemological manner in which he knows himself is intellectual, and therefore transpires through the medium of "informed" understanding. It is "objective" in just this sense. The "objectification" *through* which Christ knows himself is intentional (pertaining to his manner of knowing), not ontological (pertaining to a distinct subject). So just as a human person might know himself as a subject "intentionally" by thinking about himself, so the Word Incarnate knows "whom" he is as a subject "objectively" through the medium of his graced understanding.

47. This triple distinction in Christ's human manner of knowing is developed by Aquinas in *ST* III, q. 9–12. Christ has humanly acquired knowledge from experience, prophetically infused knowledge in view of his mission, and intimate, immediate knowledge of God, by which he knows the Father and the Spirit as well as his own identity as the Son. This classical view has recently been reaffirmed (in a slightly modernized but discernable idiom) by the magisterium of the Roman Catholic Church in the 1992, *CCC* 472–73.

subjects prior to knowing that such a thing is or what a thing is. (This is the case even in the life of young children.) And yet we are also present to ourselves as subjects in the act of knowing such or what a thing is, no matter how sophisticated or simple that objective knowledge is. In this sense, subjective consciousness accompanies all of our natural acts of knowing and all of our human development. It is a capacity that is proper to the human nature of a given person, but in its origin and term, it is an awareness of the personal subject by him or herself.[48]

The complexities that arise with regard to the human consciousness of the Son of God are manifold, but one that is important to note here concerns the way in which Christ as man must be aware or conscious that he is the Son of God. Evidently, in differentiation from other human beings, Christ is God the Son made human. As such, he must be conscious of who he is in a human way. Consequently, this requires both objective human knowledge of "what" he is and subjective psychological self-awareness.[49] His outright knowledge that he is God must pertain to his objective knowledge (he has to know "what" he is as the Son, in his human mind), while his subjective self-awareness is a facet of his human experiential presence-to-himself. Jesus is aware of himself as a person: when Jesus is aware of himself, the self he is aware of (his who) is the Son of God. In this sense, as Lonergan points out, Christ's human judgment that he is the Son is irreducibly complex. It requires an informed (objective) knowledge about "what" he is but also requires that this reflexive knowledge be referred to himself in his conscious

48. This paragraph is particularly indebted to the lengthier reflections of Lonergan, *Ontological and Psychological Constitution of Christ*, 161–69.

49. I am purposefully juxtaposing the terms "what" and "who." A human mind understands "quidditatively" in terms of thinking about what things or persons are. This is also the case when we think about ourselves: "my hand, mind, feelings," and so on. These are quidditative terms. Yet because of our prereflexive (affective, moral, intuitive) consciousness of ourselves and others, we are also able to experience *who* we ourselves and others are as singular subjects. Personhood is experienced in diverse ways: through conceptual thought about ourselves as persons and through a multifaceted (sensible, affective, intuitive) conscious awareness of ourselves and others as distinct singular subjects.

experience of himself. In short, this knowing is present in one who is aware of himself as a subject. Without the former "objective" knowledge, Christ would be unable to know that he is the Son of God. Without the latter human experience, he would be unable to be aware of himself as the subject who knows "objectively" that he is the Son of God.[50]

Yet what kind of "objective" knowledge is necessary in order for this subjective self-awareness to take place in God as man? Obviously, it is only possible for Christ to truly know that he is the Son of God if he has some "objective" intellectual knowledge of his own identity. The human mind cannot work otherwise. The person of the Son, however, can only be known by intellectual grace, and so this knowledge the Incarnate Son has of himself is a graced knowledge. Furthermore, this can occur in only one of two ways. It occurs by means of a knowledge of the truth that is either mediate or immediate, that is, through the medium of prophecy or by way of an intimate, direct awareness.[51] Mediated knowledge of Christ's divine identity in the Son's human mind would come about by way of prophetic insight. God, in his human consciousness, would then

---

50. See in particular Lonergan, *Ontological and Psychological Constitution of Christ*, 203–19. This theory is more suitable than that of Rahner in his "Dogmatic Reflections on the Knowledge and Self-Consciousness of Christ," 235–40. Rahner's account rightly emphasizes that the immediate, intuitive knowledge Christ has of his divine identity must allow him to be conscious of himself as the Son in a prereflexive, nonconceptual way. Yet it also evacuates from this graced form of knowing *any* specifying or *objective* content. Therefore, Christ (for Rahner) might well have had no "thematic" objective knowledge of his divine identity and yet still be aware of himself as the Son. Lonergan argues quite convincingly, however, that without some form of intuitive, "objective" intellectual knowledge of his own essence, the Son of God as man would be unable to be conscious of his own divine identity. See the criticisms of Rahner by Alois Grillmeier to the same effect (seemingly informed by Lonergan's views?) in *Fragen der Theologie heute*, ed. J. Feiner, J. Truesch, and F. Boeckle (Einsiedeln: Benzinger Verlag, 1957), 294–95. As Grillmeier notes rightly, Rahner's theory seems to leave us with the Son subsisting in a human nature which is illuminated only by the human awareness of "itself," and insufficiently *informed* as to "its" transcendent identity.

51. Jean-Pierre Torrell has, I think, argued for this binary alternative convincingly in his "S. Thomas d'Aquin et la science du Christ," in *Saint Thomas au XXe siecle*, 394–409, which I examine in my "Voluntary Action," 515–21. I differ from Torrell, however, in affirming the presence of the beatific vision in the soul of the earthly Christ.

be aware as man that he received revelation and would accept this revelation through actions of deliberated willing (what Damascene calls a "gnomic will" in a sinless person). The Christ thus depicted would have the theological virtue of faith: he would consciously believe in his prophetic knowledge. Jesus would believe in the Father, believe that he was God's Son, believe that he had an eschatological role to play in Israel's current history, and so on. He could, in theory, struggle in doubt with this revelation but might eventually (sinlessly) overcome his doubt so as to fulfill his role in the plan of history.[52]

Contrasted with this is the kind of self-awareness that would result from an "immediate knowledge" in the human mind of Christ, the so-called beatific vision. In this case, the kind of knowledge that results is not accepted *uniquely* through the mediation of an indirect revelation or prophetic awareness. Rather, it is also (and especially) known in an immediate way such that the Incarnate Word apprehends intuitively in his human mind what he is as the Son of God. Accordingly, he knows the Father and the Holy Spirit. Due to this intuition, the Son also has a knowledge of his hypostatic identity that is *evidentially certain* because it does not depend on a mediated knowledge of its intellectual "object."[53] Consequently, his knowledge

52. This explanation might offer a way of interpreting "Christologically" the historical reflections of N. T. Wright, who at times suggests that Jesus "believed" that he might be somehow one with God, or that he hoped (somewhat desperately, in Schweitzerian fashion) in an eschatological resolution of the mystery of Israel that he did not understand. See *Jesus and the Victory of God*, 593, 651–53.

53. Significantly, citing the above-mentioned *Catechism*, n. 473, the contemporary Catholic magisterium has recently reasserted this theological perspective and phraseology in the Vatican's *Notification on the Works of Fr. Jon Sobrino, SJ, Jesus the Liberator* (1991) *and Christ the Liberator* (1999) (issued November 26, 2006). Citing Jn 6:46, "Not that anyone has seen the Father except the one who is from God; he has seen the Father," the document goes on to state (n. 8): "The filial and messianic consciousness of Jesus is the direct consequence of his ontology as Son of God made man. If Jesus were a believer like ourselves, albeit in an exemplary manner, he would not be able to be the true Revealer showing us the face of the Father ... Jesus, the Incarnate Son of God, enjoys an intimate and immediate knowledge of his Father, a 'vision' that certainly goes beyond the vision of faith. The hypostatic union and Jesus' mission of revelation and redemption require the vision of the Father and the knowledge of his plan of salvation. This is what is indicated in the Gospel [text] cited above." Here the position is similar to that which I have mentioned above: if the Son as man does not have the immediate vision of God, then

of the Father's will is not believed in by the grace of faith *nor accepted* by an act of deliberated willing (the activity of a "gnomic will"). In knowing the Father, himself, and the Spirit "objectively," the Incarnate Word as man also has a mysterious understanding of his own divine nature, which he shares in with the Father and the Spirit. He has an intimate awareness of the activity of the Father and the Holy Spirit, with whom he knows that he acts as the Son.

Translated into the terms of human consciousness, this means that the Son of God made man would deliberate and think like any other historical human being, employing terms and concepts of his epoch. Yet he would also have a mysterious awareness of himself as the Son of God that was intuitive and that encompassed all of his natural psychological and conceptual development. It would allow for ordinary reflexive understanding and intellectual inquiry, and yet it would provide a stable form of self-awareness in the depths of Christ's human psyche. He would have a superior awareness of the activity of God the Father's will in particular contingent historical circumstances and would know that as the Son he shared in this activity. Such knowledge would not be merely conjectural or hypothetical but intuitive, experiential, and deliberative all at once.[54]

Filial Consciousness and the Freedom of Christ

This leaves us with a final question. What is the effect that this latter way of knowing would have on the theandric activity of Christ? How would the Son's intuitive human awareness of his divine agency (shared with the Father and the Holy Spirit) affect his experience

---

he has mediated knowledge of God, and in this case must have the theological virtue of faith, by which he believes that which is revealed to him mediately. Lonergan makes this same point, stressing that the Son as man can only be *perfectly aware* of his divine identity due to the vision (*Ontological and Psychological Constitution of Christ*, 265). Jacques Maritain has also argued for this point convincingly in *On the Grace and the Humanity of Jesus*, 54–61, 98–125.

54. This need not imply that Christ could not suffer acute agony spiritually in this human life. I will not treat here the question of the consolation or joy of the immediate vision of Christ in his historical life as man. This has been a subject of important debate in recent theology. For considerations on this subject, see my "Jesus' Cry on the Cross and His Beatific Vision," *Nova et Vetera* (English edition) 5 (2007): 525–51.

of free actions as man? Most especially, how would this conscious-ness contribute to his psychological unity as the Incarnate Word?

Here, we might return once again to the historically decisive for-mulation of the Third Council of Constantinople: "each nature wills and performs the things that are proper to it *in a communion with the other.*" Following Maximus, Damascene, and Aquinas, we must interpret this formula by keeping in mind at least two central qual-ifications. First, human action is a principle of nature *through which* the agent (the Son of God) acts. Therefore, if Christ acts as man, he does so by virtue of his human freedom, but the one who does so is the Son of God. Second, knowledge and choice-making are opera-tions proper to the human nature of Christ, and such action implies a "natural" autonomy of a person (not a personal autonomy!). In other words, Christ as man acts by means of natural human desires, deliberations, and choices: the will of Christ as a rational will moves by virtue of its own intrinsic structure.[55]

If Christ as man determines his action with regard to the will of the Father *by means of his free human deliberation,* then in all circum-stances in which he acts in accord with the Father's will, *he must be conscious of the Father's will.* His consciousness must be filial in this regard. Yet this requires at least two things in addition. First, as man, Christ must have knowledge of the Father's will *and* know that he shares in this will with the Father as the Son of God. Second, he must be conscious of himself as the Son of God. Without both of

---

55. Maximus the Confessor sometimes claims that the human will of Christ is "moved by his divine will" (Ops. 3, 48 A) and sometimes claims that the human will of Christ is "self-moving" (*autokinesis*) (*Ambigua* 1354). Bathrellos (*The Byzantine Christ,* 162–72) thinks that the first formulation seems excessively Alexandrian while the latter is perhaps excessively Antiochene. Another way to interpret Maximus on this point is to claim that the Son's human will is "self-moving," but that the "self" in question is the divine self (hypostasis) of the Son of God, who is acting in virtue of his human nature. Maximus clearly employs such an idea in his dyothelete interpretation of Christ's agony in Gethsemane (*Disputatio* 305 C-D): the Son as man, despite his natural frailty, moves himself freely toward the acceptance of the Passion in accord with what he knows to be his Father's will, a will he shares (as God) with the Father. See Damascene's similar treatment of the matter in *De duabus in Christo voluntatibus,* 27.9–13 (ed. Kotter, 209) and Aquinas's pertinent reflections in *ST III,* q. 18, aa. 3–5.

these conditions, *he will not be able to know that in his soteriological action, his action is united with that of the Father.*[56] It follows from this that *for Christ to have an authentically filial consciousness* that the eschatological kingdom of God is coming about *in and through his free human actions as the Son,* he must be mysteriously and intuitively aware as man of the will and operations he shares with the Father as God.

Let us conclude with some examples. According to Luke, it would seem that Jesus the Incarnate Son is aware as a human being that the Holy Spirit wills him to go out into the desert to fast for forty days.[57] He is also aware at Gethsemane that it is truly the will of the Father that he embrace the agony of Golgotha.[58] Yet he is also aware of being the unique Son of the Father, by whom and in whom the eschatological kingdom of God is coming.[59] Therefore, his human action seems to reflect the truth of a deeper, mysterious ontological unity. The Father reveals his identity and agency in the Son and in reciprocity with the Son. It is the human freedom that results from his knowledge of the Father's will which permits Christ to defy the temptations of the desert, to "empty himself" in obedience to the Father, to fulfill the Isaian type of the servant of YHWH, to embrace (despite its natural repulsiveness) the agony of the garden of Gethsemane, to bear in constancy and hope the torments of his executioners, and to surrender himself to the Father in the midst of his crucifixion and death. In all these instances, the New Testament portrait

---

56. Commenting on Jn 5:21, Aquinas writes: "The Father does not raise up and give life through the Son as through an instrument, because then the Son would not have freedom of power. And so to exclude this [Jesus] says, 'The Son grants life to those to whom he wishes,' i.e., it lies in the freedom of his power to grant life to whom he wills. For the Son does not will anything different than the Father wills: for just as they are one substance, so they have one will; hence Matthew (20:15) says: 'Is it not lawful for me to do as I will?'" *Comm. John,* [n. 761, Marietti ed.]. Aquinas's point here is well taken: if the Son incarnate does not share in the natural activity of the Father, then subordinationism results. Christ would become the instrument of the Father in his person and would not himself be free to do the works of the Father.

57. Lk 4:1–2.

58. Lk 22:42–46.

59. Lk 10:21–22; 11:20; 17:22–37; 20:9–18, 41–44.

of God is being unveiled: the history of the Son as man reveals to us the hidden unity he shares with the Father. But by this very fact, we must also say that Christ, in his filial consciousness according to Luke, is humanly aware that he can and should act in accord with the will of the Father and the Holy Spirit because he shares in their same activity as the unique Son. This knowledge renders the Incarnate Son *free* as man to do the will of the Father and the Holy Spirit in each circumstance. He can act dynamically as man in concert with the divine will he shares with the Father and the Holy Spirit as God because he is aware of this will.

Simultaneously, then, hidden within the historical Jesus and his conscious activities are his own divine nature and power. Correspondingly, his conscious human action also allows him to express his own divine operation as God in the world. Luke tells us that the poor man of Galilee can choose to resuscitate the dead son of a widow by compassion and that the crucified prisoner on the cross can offer paradise to his fellow prisoner with authority.[60] Matthew tells us that the Christ who preaches on the mountain reinterprets the precepts of Sinai in the place of the Lord of Israel and that his eschatological cry of suffering on Golgotha ushers in the eschaton.[61] Mark tells us that his human word can cast out demons, while his death gives saving faith to a pagan humanity.[62] John tells us that the Son of Man can say that he himself exists before Abraham, while the mortal piercing of his side on the cross communicates eternal life to "the world."[63] In all these instances, the divine essence of Christ is hidden but working, ever active even in the midst of his human weakness and voluntary self-emptying. God the Son as man is conscious of offering his life "as a ransom for the many" (Mk 10:45) in

60. Lk 7:14: "Young man, *I* say to you arise. And the dead man sat up and began to speak." 23:43: "Truly, *I* say to you, today you will be with me in paradise."

61. Cf. Mt 5:21–48; 27:50–54. Mt 5:43: "You have heard that it was said, 'you shall love your neighbor and hate your enemy.' [Lev 19:18] But *I* say to you, love your enemies and pray for those who persecute you."

62. Mk 5:1–13; 15:37–39.

63. Cf. Jn 19:34–37 and 8:58: "Before Abraham was, *I am.*"

humility and obedience, but he is also aware that by his own power as God, even in his death, "he and his Father are working" (Jn 5:17ff.) to give life to the world.

CONCLUSION

This chapter offers only a sketch of classical dyothelete doctrine and a brief reflection on what might be at stake in its contemporary rejection or rehabilitation. Nevertheless, it is clear that the classical doctrine of the two natures of Christ has undergone a kind of marginalization in mainstream modern and contemporary Christology. This might not be in every way to the advantage of a rigorous examination of the historical character of the biblical revelation. Ironically, it might also undermine a coherent confession of the unicity of the divine subject in Christ. If the New Testament revelation of the Son is to be understood as a revelation of God himself in history, then there must be some fundamental ways in which ontological claims of unity between the Son and the Father become manifest in the historical and personal life of Christ. And if this is the case, then the operations and will of God must also, in some way, be demarcated within and through the narrative of God's human life in time. Dyotheletism stands as a reminder of a classical tradition, which is full of insight into the mystery of the Gospels. But it also extends to us both a challenge and a resource for thinking more profoundly in the realm of modern Christology.[64]

64. I am grateful to Fr. Brian Daley, SJ, for comments on this chapter that greatly helped to improve its content. In particular, notes 10, 16, and 54 are heavily indebted to clarifying remarks he offered.

14

The Infused Science
of Christ, According to
Thomas Aquinas

Thomas Aquinas's theory of the knowledge of Christ may seem to
have little relevance for modern historical-critical study of the figure of Jesus of Nazareth.[1] In his mature work, represented emblematically by the third part of the *Summa Theologiae*, Aquinas presents
the knowledge of Christ in a four-fold descending perspective from
the highest forms of knowledge to the most basic. He begins from
the divine wisdom that Christ possesses as God and then examines
three modes of human knowledge: the immediate vision of God
that Christ possesses in his human soul, the infused science that Jesus possesses as the most perfect of the prophets, and the acquired
knowledge that Christ possesses as man, in virtue of the human
nature that he shares with us.[2] Aquinas's account stems originally
from the Chalcedonian principles of Christological doctrine. The

Originally published in *Nova et Vetera* (English edition) 16, no. 2 (2018): 617–41.
1. This chapter has benefited from the support of the John Templeton Foundation
grant "Virtue, happiness, and the Meaning of Life." An earlier version of it was given
at the Third International Conference on Thomistic Philosophy at Universidad Santo
Tomás, Chile, July 19–21 of 2016.
    2. *ST* III, qq. 9–12.

approach might be broadly characterized as a form of "descending Christology" insofar as the deity and divine wisdom of the Lord are presupposed, and his human acquired knowledge is affirmed just insofar as he is essentially human. Meanwhile, the beatific vision and infused science of Christ are interpreted as grace given to his human nature in view of his human actions on behalf of our salvation. It is due to his beatific vision and his infused prophetic knowledge, for example, that Christ as man is able to know perfectly who he is as the Son of God and who the Father and the Holy Spirit are, to reveal them to us, and to interpret scripture authoritatively, foretelling of his own passion and resurrection prophetically, and instituting the Church and the sacraments effectively.

In methodological contrast, the modern historical-critical study of the figure of Jesus of Nazareth makes use of a number of normative principles that stem from the Enlightenment era, among them a presupposition of the historical homogeneity of natural causes. That is to say, the causes of human experience and consciousness for all persons at the time of Jesus (including Jesus himself) should be understood against the backdrop of and in continuity with the language, concepts, and symbols of Second Temple Judaism.[3] These, in turn, should be understood in continuity with the predictable natural occurrences and causes that we experience in the modern scientific era. So, for example, apocalyptic elements in the culture of the Judaism of the time of Jesus should be employed to explain Jesus's imminent expectation of the "kingdom of God," but this need not mean that there is any such thing as an eschatological occurrence in reality.[4] Likewise, the New Testament portraits of the figure of Jesus should be understood as human literary artifacts and explained in

3. For an excellent example of a study of the historical Jesus conducted in this mode, see E. P. Sanders, *Jesus and Judaism*. The naturalistic explanation of the Gospels and of the figure of Jesus in particular arguably has its theoretical origins in the work of Baruch Spinoza, *Tractatus Theologico-Politicus*, 1690.

4. See, most famously, Albert Schweitzer, *Geschichte der Leben-Jesu-Forschung* (Tübingen: J.C.B. Mohr, 1913) and more recently, E. P. Sanders, *Jesus and Judaism*, 91–156, 334–40.

light of their cultural setting, the theological vantage points of their editors, and their intended uses for historically situated human communities.[5] This need not imply that they are inspired or that the portraits of Christ that they present must correspond to who Jesus of Nazareth really was ontologically. It follows from this that the portrait of Christ found in the Gospels might be very different from the "real" Jesus of history.

We might notice the contrasts these two methodological approaches represent. If Aquinas's presentation of the infused science of Christ seems to bespeak a knowledge derived immediately from God and therefore from "outside of time," the modern study of Jesus tends to construe his consciousness by ascetic reference uniquely to the immanent and limited horizon of his age. Pressed toward extremes, one account readily emphasizes the divine origin of Christ's message and its universality for all ages but does so to the potential exclusion of his historical particularity as a first century Jew, while the other account seeks to identify the historically particular and limited character of Jesus' aims and self-understanding within the context of Second Temple Judaism, but does so to the exclusion of his divine origin, and soteriological intensions which are universal in scope.

In this chapter, however, I will argue that these two approaches, while really distinct, need not be construed in opposition to one another. On the contrary, a nuanced appreciation of Aquinas's doctrine of the human knowledge of Christ may permit us to assimilate many of the legitimate aspirations of modern historical Jesus studies while still retaining a high doctrine of the infused knowledge of the Lord as the greatest of the prophets. To make this argument, I will advert to the Thomistic analysis of the knowledge of Christ. However, in order to engage the contemporary question of Jesus' historical self-understanding, we can invert the order of Aquinas's descending

5. The argument for this interpretive stance was crafted with great clarity by Gotthold Ephraim Lessing. See *Philosophical and Theological Writings* (Cambridge: Cambridge University Press, 2005).

perspective from higher to lower and proceed in the opposite direction. Beginning from a consideration of the acquired knowledge of Christ, I will seek to show that the historicity of the mode in which Christ learns and expresses himself as human is compatible with both implicit and explicit forms of universal reflection. In a second section, I will consider the habitual infused science of Christ within the context of his historically situated acquired knowledge. In the final section, I will consider his beatific vision as it relates to his infused science and acquired knowledge. My aim is to show the potential compatibility of a traditional theology of the infused science of Christ with what is best in contemporary historical studies regarding Jesus of Nazareth as set against the backdrop of his epoch. Ultimately, the balance of this Thomistic perspective is rooted in the realism of Biblical faith itself and the principles of Chalcedonian dogma, which affirm both the true historical humanity of God incarnate and his distinctive human graces and privileges as the man who is uniquely the Son of God.

ACQUIRED KNOWLEDGE: THE UNIVERSALITY OF HUMAN THOUGHT AND ITS HISTORICAL MODES

Aquinas is generally thought to have been the first 13th century scholastic doctor to posit the existence of naturally acquired human knowledge in Christ, as opposed to uniquely infused knowledge.[6] He did so based on the simple principle that Christ is fully human and that being human entails having an agent intellect by which we derive knowledge progressively from the senses, a claim that is, of course, derivative from Aristotelian philosophical anthropology.[7] This form of knowledge allows us to learn gradually of the very essences of things (such as what the human nature is that is

6. See ST III, q. 12, a. 2, where he notes his change of mind on this issue with respect to the earlier position of III Sent., d. 14, a. 3. See the historical reflections of Torrell, "Le savoir acquis du Christ selon les théologiens médiévaux."

7. See ST III, q. 9, a. 4, which appeals overtly to Aristotelian theories of human knowledge.

common to all men), but it also entails learning in and through a particular sensory mode, which stems from animality.[8] This animality is not only individual but also corporate. That is to say, we learn from and with others within a broader political community and culture, which we are typically deeply dependent upon for our education in various ways. Here, we should note some basic philosophical points that are pertinent to a theological consideration of Christ within his historical context.

First, while our acquired conceptual knowledge always pertains in some way to the universal, it is also always dependent upon the external and internal sense powers. The latter include the imaginative power (and sense memory), the synthetic "common" sense, which collates diverse phantasms from diverse senses, the passions and cogitative sense, which both entail affective reactions or attractions to objects of knowledge.[9] In other words, as we come to acquire knowledge of realities external to us, we simultaneously imagine sounds and words that act as phantasms of support for our spiritual insight and conceptual grasp of things.

Second, as Aristotle noted already in the *On Interpretation*, there is a kind of triangular reference of words to concepts and of concepts to things, insofar as the conventional significations of language denote the non-conventional, natural concepts of the mind, which themselves refer to the non-conventional, natural realities that language signifies.[10] At the same time, we can qualify this claim in two ways. First, we grasp reality largely through the stimulation of linguistic naming processes, through both the formal and informal methods by which our culture educates us. Language not only denotes but also draws our discriminating attention to various facets

---

8. See, for example, Aquinas's *In De Anima* III, lec. 12, on *De Anima* III, 7 (431a4–43lb19); *ST* I, qq. 78–79.

9. *ST* I, q. 78, a. 4; Mark Barker, "Experience and Experimentation: The Meaning of *Experimentum* in Aquinas," *The Thomist* 76, no. 1 (2012): 37–71; Mark Barker, "Aquinas on Internal Sensory Intentions: Nature and Classification," *International Philosophical Quarterly* 52, no. 2 (2012): 199–226.

10. Aristotle, *De Interpretatione* I, 1 (16a3–6).

of reality. Symbols, language, and names do not arise in us only "after" we perceive things and grasp them intellectually. Their cultural performance also initiates us to the act of grasping the things that they denote.

Third, the realities denoted are not only purely natural but also largely artifactual. Many external realities we perceive and name are themselves at least partially informed by processes of human ethical and artistic freedom (such as customs of religion and philosophy, politics and ethics, but also of art and artisanal objects). Many human symbols or forms of conventional reference are clearly understood only once one has a sufficient knowledge of the ambient culture and its references and functional symbols in a given time and place.[11]

Finally, even if we emphasize the reality of the knowledge of essences and the universal natural and ethical insights that are inevitably present in each human mind in every human culture, we must also recognize that there are cultures in which the *degree or intensity* of such insight differs in a given realm of understanding. And there are vastly different degrees of scientific, religious, philosophical, and moral insight (or ignorance) present in distinct cultures across time.

The point of my reflection to this point is not to suggest that all forms of knowledge are inherently *determined* by their cultural-linguistic setting (as if one could only learn what one was taught and never engage reality itself), but only that they are truly qualified or *conditioned* by it in a variety of ways both with regard to the *modes of acquisition* of that knowledge and to some extent the *objects* of knowledge that are readily available (or inaccessible) in a given culture. We should not expect to find first century Jews writing in symbolic logic or medieval Japanese calligraphy. Nor should we think they will be actively concerned with 6th century BC Confucian philosophy or the 20th century Einsteinian theory of general relativity.

11. See the argument to this effect by George Lindbeck, *The Nature of Doctrine: Religion and Theology in a Post-Liberal Age.*

This conditioning of our universal form of knowing is both culturally individuating and essentially (universally) human, just as material individuality, though distinctive to each person, is also (abstractly considered) an attribute of what it means for any human being to be human.[12] Like embodiment, the cultural mode of acquisition of our knowledge is not an effect of our fallen human condition (pace Origen and Plato), but simply characteristic of our animal nature with its distinctive mode of rationality, by which we learn spiritually through the senses, collectively, and across time and place.

What follows from this reflection theologically in our consideration of Christ? First, we may say that there is a certain culturally limited form of knowledge present in every human knower. Each of us speaks a particular language (or range of languages) and acquires knowledge within a given horizon of time and place in the context of the available patterns of reflection and debate that typically shape the thinking of a given culture. Christ is no exception to this general rule. If God truly became human, then in his human life, the Word Incarnate not only acquired knowledge but also spoke and thought through the medium of the language and symbols of his epoch, set against the complex Judaic and Hellenistic backdrop that such language and symbols presupposed. To be clear, I am not suggesting that Christ was unable to speak in clearly universalistic terms about the human condition or the meaning of all that exists, for clearly he was, as were his contemporaries and disciples, for that matter. But I am saying that there were delimiting features of human cognition that were part and parcel of the reality of the Incarnation. In the word of the Catechism of the Catholic Church: "This human soul that the Son of God assumed is endowed with a true human knowledge. As such, this knowledge could not in itself be unlimited: it was exercised in the historical conditions of his existence in space and time. This is why the Son of God could, when he became man, 'increase in wisdom and in stature, and in favor with God and man'

---

12. As Aquinas notes in *De Ente et Essentia*, c. 2.

(Luke 2:52), and would even have to inquire for himself about what one in the human condition can learn only from experience (Mark 6:38; 8:27; John 11:34). This corresponded to the reality of his voluntary emptying of himself, taking 'the form of a slave' (Phil. 2:7)."[13]

It follows from this perspective that we need not argue that the historical Christ, in virtue of his human perfection, must have been able to acquire natural knowledge of any possible intellectual subject matter available to any human person throughout time, such as knowledge developed in the 19th or 20th century through the experimental sciences. Christ did possess extraordinary insight into the human condition, in part from his infused science, and this, in turn, must have had reverberations upon the development of his acquired knowledge, as we will note further on. Likewise, due in part to the extraordinary grace that Christ enjoyed in his human intellect, we need not attribute any noetic error to the mind of Christ.[14] A limitation of knowledge by circumstances of time and place is not equivalent to and need not entail the presence of intellectual error. There is, therefore, a kind of perfection to the acquired knowledge of Christ. However, this perfection in its acquired mode should be understood as one that is culturally situated and that expresses itself intelligibly within the context and against the backdrop of the language and symbols of Second Temple Judaism.

Secondly, understood in a theological light, the culture in which Jesus of Nazareth lived was unique because it was in various respects the product of supernatural, prophetic revelation, originating in the Patriarchal and Mosaic epoch, following down through to the time

13. CCC 472.

14. This is a traditional assertion of Catholic theology, one that also is strengthened by the consideration that Christ is truth incarnate, himself the first truth, living a human life among us. Questions arise about Christ's interpretation of scripture: Does he treat Jonah as a historical figure, or Moses as the unique author of the Torah? If so, do these constitute errors of ignorance? My own interpretation is that Christ, as a first century Jew, frequently treats these figures as symbols of typology or authority according to the religious customs of his age and is not in every case attempting to assert a historical claim about particular Old Testament tropes of the kind modern biblical scholars characteristically engage in.

of the monarchy, the high prophets and post-exilic redaction of the Biblical texts. Biblical revelation is ultimately of divine origin but is also mediated through a vast mosaic of human authors, traditions, and interpreters, and thus makes use of precisely the fabric of human customs, language and symbols that we have alluded to above. This is of capital importance because Jesus of Nazareth clearly appealed to and actively interpreted the tradition of prophetic revelation that preceded him. What this means is that just as we can study the books of the Bible simultaneously as fonts of divine revelation and as products of human agency in a given time and place, so also we can analyze, for lack of a better term, the "theology" of the historical Christ insofar as it is an especially inspired, theologically ultimate *human* interpretation of the word of God.[15] Jesus is, after all, a human interpreter of the scriptures, as is Paul or John or the author of the Letter to the Hebrews. Modern Biblical scholars often examine in some great detail Jesus's interpretations of Jonah, or his reading of Second Isaiah, or of Daniel, or his particular eschatology, or his teachings on divorce, or his interpretations of the Psalms of David. They do so against the backdrop of the Judaism of his time, in part so as to underscore the originality of Jesus of Nazareth, the aims of his ministry, and his claims to authority. The point I am making is that this act of locating such teaching within a particular historical context is not opposed to the idea that Jesus is the Lord, God of Israel. If God became human, it is also normal that this man who is God should be himself an active human interpreter of the meaning of the Torah, the prophets, and the wisdom literature of the Hebrew Bible, and should, *as man in his human historical consciousness*, see himself indicated in Old Testament prophecy. That interpretation is aided and guided by the presence of infused science, to be sure, as we shall return to below. But the higher illumination of prophecy in the mind of Christ need not exclude the fact that he is a genuine

---

15. See for example, Witherington, *The Christology of Jesus*; Caird, *New Testament Theology*, ch. 9; N. T. Wright, *Jesus and the Victory of God*.

human agent, actively engaged with the living tradition of Judaism that he acquires knowledge of in and through his experiential life as a first century Jew.

Finally, we may conclude with the following observation. Rightly understood, a philosophy of the agent intellect allows us to understand that all modes of human thought have an overt degree of universality to them. Conceptual thought simply is universal in its signification and structure, no matter how provincial or limited the horizon of understanding may be in a given time and place. For this reason, theologically speaking, we may say that it is always impossible to demonstrate *apriori* (from philosophical premises of unaided natural reason) the impossibility of Biblical revelation simply by averting to the limitations of the historical context in which it was composed. If there is a particular culture that has become the receptive site or locus of revelation, that culture, just because it is human, will have individualizing features and limitations. At the same time, simply because it is a human culture, it is always potentially capable of signifying truths about God and humanity that are universal in scope. Christ is an ultimate revelatory figure in history, but he is so only ever within a given historical cultural setting. Jesus of Nazareth is a first century figure with a historical consciousness deeply conditioned by his distinctive culture, but he is also a universal revelation of the truth about God, humanity, and salvation. There is no inherent contradiction possible in the simultaneous affirmation of these twin facts.

INFUSED SCIENCE: ITS NATURE
AND ECONOMIC FUNCTION

There can be little doubt that the four canonical Gospels each ascribe extraordinary forms of knowledge to Jesus of Nazareth. In fact, these ascriptions are so prevalent, thematic, and intertwined throughout the narratives and instructions of the Gospels that their integrity and very narrative structures would appear virtually unintelligible or as mere fragments of texts were we to, by violence as it were, extract from them every instance of the appearance of such knowledge. Jesus reads hearts and can speak with accuracy of the faith or of the judgment present in a given person's mind (Mark 2:1–2; Luke 7:50). He interprets scripture not as one who is seeking its meaning but as its authoritative and final arbiter (Mark 12:1–12; Matt. 5:17–48; 12:38–45). He foretells the future, including his own rejection by the religious authorities of Israel, his public torture, death, and resurrection (Mark 8:31–32; 9:30–32; 10:32–34; 12:1–12; John 3:14; 8:28). He is aware that he has the power to perform miracles prior to the action of doing so (Matt. 8:3; John 11:4–11). He gives an account of the nature of the eschaton, the final judgment, and the life of the world to come (Matt. 24:3, 25:31–45; Luke 18:8). He chooses twelve disciples to prolong the spiritual effects of his kingdom and commands that they celebrate the sacraments, which he institutes for the future life of the Church (Mark 3:14; 14:22–24; John 6:26–59). More generally, he seems to know what the human being is, and to exhibit little surprise, scandal, or exertion of understanding in the face of human ignorance, weakness, or betrayal (John 2:25; 13:27; 19:11; Mark 14:18). In his intellectual and moral self-possession, he appears to remain somehow spiritually uncompromised by these features of fallen human existence (John 18:23; Mark 14:62).

It is, of course, possible that all of this knowledge gently exhibited by Christ as the Gospels depict him in his radiant holiness and majestic humility, is itself purely the product of post-paschal authors, and consists of retrospective projections cast back upon the historical Jesus artificially for theological reasons. Nevertheless, there are both historical-critical and distinctively theological reasons to reject this view. On the merely naturalistic level, we may note that there exist no very close literary parallels in ancient Judaic (or Graeco-Roman) literature to the figure of Jesus as he is portrayed in the four Gospels, insofar as he exhibits there a prophetic capacity that is not merely received from time to time (actualistically) but possessed habitually and exercised freely from his own person. This portrait has a basic originality that derives from within the early Christian community and not as a mimicking act of reference to a preexistent model. No pure parallel exists in the representation of a Jewish prophet either in the Hebrew scriptures or in the inter-testamental literature. Furthermore, the four canonical gospels are not merely the product of one person, nor the singular work of a group of redactors, but bear the marks of distinct literary origins, by individual authors, who conveyed authoritative traditions preserved in communities that pre-existed these authors or that they accompanied. Given the multiple attestations to the infused science of Christ from independent sources, their early origin and authority in the early Church, and their uniformity of theological content despite their heterogeneity of styles among the four evangelists, it is reasonable to conclude that accounts of the extraordinary knowledge of Christ date back to the earliest strata of Christian teaching and preaching, from the primitive apostolic age. Thoroughgoing skepticism regarding the reality of the infused science, therefore, is neither obligatory nor textually and historically warranted.

Furthermore, there are significant theological reasons for belief in the prophetic science of Christ during the course of his earthly life, prior to the resurrection. A first reason for this has to do with the identity and mission of Christ as the Son of God. If the visible mission of the Son is meant to reveal to us the mystery of the Father and to be the prelude to the sending of the Spirit, then the Son must be the self-conscious revealer of the Father and the Spirit, as well as of his own identity as the Son.[16] He must work in unity with the Father and the Spirit as the Lord, who is himself God, in his human actions of teaching and miracles, in his foretelling of his suffering, and in his institution of the apostolic college. But, of course, Christ can only be such a revealer, teacher, and redeemer *in his human life* among us if

16. See the argument to this effect in the 1985 document of the International Theological Commission, *The Consciousness of Christ Concerning Himself and His Mission*, especially regarding the four propositions concerning Christ's human knowledge that are requisite to any sound Catholic theology.

he enjoys *as man* the assistance of a particular supernatural knowledge of the mystery of God and of the economy of redemption.[17]

A second theological reason stems from principles of Biblical ontology. According to St. Paul, Jesus has been revealed to be the "new Adam" and the "perfect man." This claim is primarily soteriological in nature, but it also has ontological implications. Where the old Adam fell into ignorance, malice, and moral weakness, Christ exhibited wisdom, charity, and sinless obedience. Where the actions of the old Adam led the human race into death, the self-emptying of the new Adam has given rise to the re-creation and the resurrection (cf. Phil. 2:6–11).[18] If this is the case, then the historical Christ prior to his resurrection must have had the requisite moral insight to cooperate with the plan of salvation that was to be effectuated through his obedience unto death and his subsequent glorification. It is necessary, in this case, to ascribe to the historical Christ a particularly acute supernatural insight of mind into the life of the virtues under the movement of the Holy Spirit, as well as an inspired understanding of the divine economy.

A final theological reason pertains to the fact that the miraculous capacity of Christ to read hearts or foretell the future is evidently intended in the Gospels to produce repeated "signs" of the divinely sanctioned authority of Christ.[19] This is what the First Vatican Council called "reasons of credibility": miraculous signs given to natural human reason to suggest the presence of authentic divine revelation present in the historical figure of Jesus.[20] If the revelation itself suggests to us the credibility of supernatural belief in the

17. See *ST* III, q. 7, a. 1, where Aquinas presents similar arguments for the necessity of the presence of habitual grace in the human soul of Christ.

18. See on this theme, N. T. Wright, *The Climax of the Covenant: Christ and the Law in Pauline Theology* (Minneapolis: Fortress, 1993), 56–98.

19. C. H. Dodd identified the programmatic character of this theme in John's Gospel in his *The Interpretation of the Fourth Gospel* (Cambridge: Cambridge University Press, 1953), 297–89.

20. Vatican Council I, *Dei Filius*. See more recently the study of Mats Wahlberg, *Revelation as Testimony: A Philosophical Vatican Theological Study* (Grand Rapids: Eerdmans, 2014).

authority of Christ based upon his extraordinary forms of insight, we should not seek to extract or obscure this dimension of the New Testament, as if it were an embarrassment or an unwarranted addendum. On the contrary, the prophecy of Jesus of Nazareth is a feature of his existence that does make him distinctive in his own way within the broader context of the history of religions.

What, though, is the infused science of Christ, and how ought we best to understand its mode of exercise theologically? Here, Aquinas's treatment of the subject is characteristically helpful. Aquinas sees the infused science as a form of insight or intellectual understanding gained not through the ordinary natural process of the agent intellect acting through the senses but as received directly from God and as prophetic in character.[21] St. Thomas speaks here in Latin of infused *species* or higher concepts analogous to but not identical with angelic ideas.[22] These are forms of knowledge that provide the soul with intuitive understanding of things hidden from other human beings and that lie outside the scope of natural human reason, but that God might know, such as the hidden moral and intellectual dispositions of another human being, or future events. Such knowledge, for St. Thomas, does not do violence to ordinary human modes of understanding but integrates into our ordinary knowledge or happens from within the midst of it and is manifest through ordinary human speech or symbolic expression, as when the high prophets write about or enact through gesture in an 'ordinary' human way what they have been given to understand in a higher mode by infused science.[23]

Three key controversies ensue whenever one approaches this subject. One pertains to the *scope or extension* of the infused science, a second to its *actual occurrence* at any given moment in the life of Christ, and a third to its *compatibility* with the historical limitations of

---

21. *ST* II-II, q. 172, aa. 1–2.

22. *ST* II-II, q. 173, a. 2. See also q. 173, a. 4 on the extraordinary internal and external sensate forms that prophecy also can take.

23. This is implied of all prophets in *ST* II-II, q. 171, a. 5; Aquinas applies the principle to the case of Christ in a distinct way in *ST* III, q. 12, aa. 1–2 where he argues that Christ, as man, can and must have both infused and acquired knowledge.

Christ's acquired knowledge. We might characterize the maximalist perspectives here by the three-fold claim that (1) Christ as man knew through infused science all things possible for man to know, (2) that he knew them actually at every given moment, and (3) that he knew them in a way that transcended and was unconditioned by his historically acquired knowledge. If we follow this line of thought, we might conclude, for example, that Christ at every given moment of his life was aware by means of infused knowledge of every conclusion of geometry that might be possible, every philosophical truth, every law of physics, as well as every contingent fact of history, the grammar of every language, and that he had actual awareness of these realities at all times, albeit in a higher mode of awareness. Consequently, he was obliged in some sense to actively conceal or willfully mask massive portions of this knowledge in his ordinary life of engagement with others, even while revealing to them that limited portion of extraordinary knowledge that might pertain to their salvation and his mission as Redeemer. One might characterize this viewpoint as unhelpfully docetist, in that it suggests Christ's typically human behavior among us is slightly unreal or one given in appearance only.

Aquinas offers helpful principles for a more balanced treatment of this subject matter, especially by his characterization of the infused science of Christ as *habitual* in nature. The first observation to be made in this respect is that Christ is unique among the prophets, according to Aquinas, because he possesses the prophetic charism habitually and not merely actualistically.[24] That is to say, while other prophets receive revelatory insight passively by moment, at given times that are outside of their determination, Christ can turn freely at any given time to the extraordinary knowledge he possesses in a stable and habitual way. In this respect, Christ is not a prophet in the strict sense, according to Aquinas, but more than a prophet due to the habitual mode in which he possesses the infused science.[25]

24. *ST* III, q. 11, a. 5. Compare with *ST* II-II, q. 171, a. 2.
25. Aquinas, *In Ioan.*, IV, lect. 6, 667: "But was Christ a prophet? At first glance it seems not, because prophecy involves an obscure knowledge: 'If there is a prophet of the Lord among you, I will appear to him in a vision' (Nm 12:6). Christ's knowledge,

However, it also follows from this, in relation to the second controversy mentioned above, that according to Aquinas, Christ does not know all that he can know by infused science at any given instance, in an actualistic way, as if he were always to actively think about the weather in Tokyo in February of 1437 AD at each instant of his life. Rather, the power of Christ's extraordinary knowledge is actuated at given times, just as any habit lies in potency until it is actuated.[26] This is in keeping with the *human mode* of Christ's infused science. Human beings pass from potency to act in their vital activities, including the activity of thinking and deliberately choosing.[27] Christ's prophetic insights rise habitually within the horizon of his ordinary human way of knowing, and he has discrete prophetic insights regarding particular objects at distinct times and places.

This leads us back to the first point of controversy noted above: that of the extension or scope of the infused science in Christ. Here, Aquinas makes a two-fold assertion. On the one hand, Christ has the potency to know by infused science anything that can be known to human beings throughout time. On the other hand, the *actuation* of his habit occurs only with respect to those things that are of fitting importance for Christ's soteriological mission and for the sake of the

---

however, was not obscure. Yet he was a prophet, as is clear from, 'The Lord your God will raise up a prophet for you, from your nation and your brothers; he will be like me. You will listen to him' (Dt 18:15). This text is referred to Christ. I answer that a prophet has a twofold function. First, that of seeing: 'He who is now called a prophet was formerly called a seer' (1 Sam 9:9). Secondly, he makes known, announces; Christ was a prophet in this sense for he made known the truth about God: 'For this was I born, and for this I came into the world: to testify to the truth' (John 18:37). As for the seeing function of a prophet, we should note that Christ was at once both a 'wayfarer' and a "comprehensor," or blessed. He was a wayfarer in the sufferings of his human nature and in all the things that relate to this. He was a blessed in his union with the divinity, by which he enjoyed God in the most perfect way. There are two things in the vision or seeing of a prophet. First, the intellectual light of his mind; and as regards this Christ was not a prophet, because his light was not at all deficient; his light was that of the blessed. Secondly, an imaginary vision is also involved; and with respect to this Christ did have a likeness to the prophets insofar as he was a wayfarer and was able to form various images with his imagination."

26. *ST* III, q. 11, a. 5, ad 1.
27. *ST* III, q. 11, a. 5, corp.

revelation he wishes to communicate to the human race.[28] Both of these points are significant. The latter point is evidently pertinent because it allows us to understand why Christ's extraordinary knowledge that is manifest in the canonical Gospels is always related to the revelation of his identity, his saving mission, and the mystery of the Cross and the resurrection. This knowledge is actuated in view of divine revelation and the salvation of the human race. It does not contain anything extraneous to this purpose, such as the truths of geometry or manifest judgments about the philosophical errors of logical positivism. At the same time, it is significant that Christ is able, at least in potency, to have infused understanding of all that is human. This is of decisive importance eschatologically, in the resurrected and glorified state of Christ, where his infused science does *now* have a much broader extension of purpose of range. We should not say, for example, that a military scientist who is praying today to Christ in English about the moral decision of making a nuclear warhead is *unintelligible* to the risen Christ in his human mind. On the contrary, it must be precisely because Christ in his glory is able to assist such a person with the gift of his grace, not only divinely but also humanly, and in the light of his own understanding. We might conclude then that Aquinas's characterization of the habitual character of the infused science of Christ allows us to understand both why the exercise of his prophecy should be of a limited if utterly consequential kind during his human historical life among us and of a far more radiant extension in the mystery of the resurrection, as we see indeed in the New Testament itself, in the risen Lord's prophecies given to the seven churches of Asia in the book of Revelation (Rev. 2:1–3:22).

Finally, there remains the controversy of the congruity of the infused science of Christ with regard to his ambient culture and his own acquired knowledge. Was Christ obliged to hide from his auditors the vast majority of what he knew overtly and explicitly, even while behaving as a human being of his own historical epoch? In one

28. *ST* III, q. 11, a. 5, ad 2.

sense it should be stated directly that Christ in the Gospels clearly does know many things that he reveals to his disciples only partially and cryptically. Consequently, we should accept that Christ had extraordinary knowledge that he *did not* reveal in its fullness to the disciples (Acts 1:7; John 14:26). However, based upon the characterization we have offered, it should also be clear that the infused science of Christ is actuated only ever from within the context of the more foundational structure of his human acquired knowledge. Otherwise said, it was precisely as a first century Jew in the epoch of Second Temple Judaism with its particular cultural-linguistic tropes and symbols that God the Son made man acted as a prophetic figure in such a way as to teach the whole of the human race. His extraordinary knowledge was conveyed *to* his first century auditors and through them to us, and this knowledge was conveyed *through* the medium of the language and symbols of his epoch, including those of inspired scripture that were so deeply influential within his ambient culture. One may affirm that Christ knew many things that he did not tell the apostles. However, as Aquinas notes, charismatic graces are intended primarily to help those who they are directed to, not the one who possesses them.[29] This is true in the case of Christ's infused science: he communicates his higher prophetic insight in forms that those around him are capable of receiving (themselves enlightened by the grace of supernatural faith), in and through the idioms of the era.

This pattern continues in the later life of the Church: infused knowledge is a charism, and charisms are oriented to the common good of the ecclesial community. They are, therefore, culturally significant or corollary to the era and people they are given to. The revelations of Catherine of Siena, the elocutions of St. Teresa of Avila, or the confessional insights of St. Jean Marie Vianney are culturally situated in determinate ways and yet extraordinarily magnificent and miraculous. Jesus' miracles and teaching are signs meant to allow us to perceive his own identity, soteriological mission, and

29. *ST* I-II, q. 111, a. 1.

eschatological judgment of the world. They were given to the people of his time and embedded within the cultural-linguistic features of his historical epoch that we referred to above. In other words, the infused science is superior to but also exerted only from within and in a way at the service of the ordinary world of persons who learn by acquired knowledge and who are enlightened by the grace of faith.

THE INFUSED SCIENCE AS IT RELATES TO THE BEATIFIC VISION OF CHRIST

This brings us to our final topic, the question of how the infused science of Christ relates to that higher form of human knowledge that Aquinas identifies: the beatific or immediate vision of God in the human intellect of Christ. Here, we may first ask the evident question: why should we posit anything more than the infused prophetic knowledge of Christ and specify a distinct form of graced knowledge presence in his human intelligence? Does the infused knowledge mentioned above not suffice for a complete understanding of the special human knowledge of Christ as human in his earthly life?

The answer to this question can be posed in two stages. First, we might ask what difference it would make to affirm the beatific or immediate knowledge of God in the human mind of Christ as something distinct from his infused prophetic knowledge? Second, we might ask how the two relate in distinct ways to Christ's acquired knowledge.

Regarding the first question, the key insight to a treatment of the question comes from Jean-Pierre Torrell, who notes rightly that prophetic knowledge that is infused, however elevated it may be, is compatible with supernatural faith and is, in fact, "typically" received by persons who have such faith.[30] Old Testament prophets

30. Torrell, "S. Thomas d'Aquin et la science du Christ," 403–4: "If one renounces the beatific vision and if one follows the logic of the Thomistic perspective, it must be said that Christ had faith ... the [bearer of prophecy] does not attain God in his experience [of infused science] but only expressive signs of the divine. He knows *that* God speaks to him, but *what* God says he can only believe ... The grace of faith is another kind

and New Testament apostles as well as Catholic saints or friends of God who have received infused knowledge do so while abiding in faith and still live in the darkness of faith even while receiving such extraordinary revelation from God. The human nature of Christ is no different from theirs, such that if he had infused prophetic knowledge alone, in his human intellect, he too would live in faith. However, unlike the prophets, apostles, and saints, Jesus Christ is both true God and true man, a divine person subsistent in a human nature. He is also the unique savior of the human race. Traditionally, then, for various reasons, both the Catholic magisterium and classical Catholic theology have eschewed the attribution of supernatural faith to the Son of God made man.[31] We may note briefly three reasons for this affirmation. First, a reason given by Aquinas: Jesus is the Savior of the human race not only due to his divine nature (as the source of our grace) but also in virtue of his human nature. Christ as God communicates grace to us in unity with the Father and the Holy Spirit. Christ as man communicates grace to us instrumentally, through the medium of his human actions of deliberate willing, in concord with his divine will as God. Salvation for the human race consists, however, not only in redemption from sin but also in union with God, culminating in the beatific vision in which the soul knows God immediately and possesses God perfectly, without danger of loss. Therefore, if Christ did not possess this grace in his earthly life,

---

of supernatural gift. A created participation in the life of God, it conforms the believer ... to the mystery itself ... In other words, with faith we are in the order of the supernatural *quoad essentiam*, while with prophetic knowledge we remain in the order of the supernatural *quoad modum* (*acquisitionis*). The two orders do not exclude one another, certainly, but the second is ordered to the first, and because the two are different kinds of realities, they must not be confused or made to play the role of one another. Concerning Jesus, then if we accord to him infused illuminations characteristic of the charismatic knowledge of revelation, he will be enabled for his role as a divine messenger, but he will still not have direct access to God, since these illuminations do not suffice as a replacement of faith." (Translation by the author). See likewise on this question, *ST* I-II, q. 171, a. 5.

31. For the recent Magisterium, see especially Pius XII, Encyclical Letter *Mystici Corporis*, 75; *CCC* 473; John Paul II, Apostolic Letter *Novo Millennio Ineunte*, 25–27; Congregation of the Doctrine of the Faith, "Notification on the Works of Jon Sobrino, SJ," para. 8. See the recent study and defense of the traditional position by S. F. Gaine, *Did the Saviour See the Father? Christ, Salvation, and the Vision of God* (London: T&T Clarke, 2015).

then in a very real sense, Christ was not saved as of yet and lived in faith, awaiting the salvation or redemption of his human nature.[32] This is incongruent because it means that Christ, while in solidarity with us by virtue of his faith, would also be in solidarity with us in his awaiting redemption from another (the Father, for example). He would not be the savior but only one saved. That is to say, if Christ as the God-human is the active savior of the human race in and through his earthly life, then he is so in part by virtue of his immediate and perfect knowledge of God. He knows that he is one with the Father and does not merely discern or believe himself to be so, through the medium of faith as if through a mirror darkly.[33]

A second reason is that Christ as man should be able, as all human beings typically are, of grasping who he is as a person. But Christ, unlike all other human beings, is a divine person and one can only understand who a divine person is in an immediate way through the grace of the beatific vision. Therefore, for Christ to have an immediate grasp of who he is as the Son of God in his human self-awareness, it is necessary that he possess the beatific vision. The vision is, in other words, essential to his personal unity and integrity because Christ as a person is God subsisting as a human being.[34]

A final reason has to do with the salvific human will of Christ. Unlike other human beings, Christ is a person who has two wills: divine and human. His human will subsists in concord with and subordination to his divine will. If a person lives in supernatural faith, however, he or she cannot perceive immediately what the divine will is at any given moment. One must act prudently in hope of living in accord with the will of God, even in obscure moments of prudential discernment. If Christ as man lived in the faith (even with the infused science), he would be obliged to act in obscure hope of conforming his life to the divine will at each instance, something

32. See the argument in *ST* III, q. 9, a. 2.
33. I have offered a more developed version of this argument in White, *The Incarnate Lord*, ch. 8. I am indebted for this argument to conversations with Bruce D. Marshall.
34. See the arguments to this effect in D. Legge, *The Trinitarian Christology of Thomas Aquinas*, chap. 3.

that is commonplace to all ordinary believers. However, in Christ's case, he would be acting personally as man with the obscure hope of conforming himself to *his own will* as the eternal Son of God. That is to say, the life of faith would introduce a kind of moral bifurcation or dualism into the life of Christ as he would seek humanly *without certainty* to do what he himself willed himself to do divinely. Or he would will himself divinely to do things that humanly he could not be certain of, but that as man he only hoped he might be doing faithfully and failed to perceive clearly. This picture of things does not correspond accurately to the Gospels, however, which depict Christ as acting decisively with certain knowledge of his identity and mission as well as of contingent choices that the Father wills him to make and that he makes as man in conjunction with the Father and the Holy Spirit.[35]

For various reasons, then, it is fitting to attribute the beatific vision to Christ in his earthly life, albeit in such a way that this mysterious grace respects the human dimensions of acquired and infused knowledge that we have named above. How, then, does the beatific vision co-exist in Christ with his acquired knowledge, and how should we understand this co-existence in relation to the infused knowledge of Christ? The topic is very obscure, not in itself, but from our vantage point. It obliges us to consider the distinction and relationship of two forms of supernatural knowledge, each present within the human mind of Christ in the course of his human historical experience, and each of which is (in two different ways) superior to the grace of supernatural faith that we ourselves possess.

It is helpful to treat this difficult question by making a fundamental observation. Aquinas gives us reason to think that the beatific vision exists in the historical Christ in a way that preserves the ordinary structure of his human acquired knowledge and self-reflexive consciousness. He makes this point in at least two ways. First, he

---

35. I present this argument at greater length in White, *The Incarnate*, chap. 5. See also J-M. Garrigues, "La conscience de soi telle qu'elle était exercée par le Fils de Dieu fait homme," *Nova et Vetera* (French edition) 79, no. 1 (2004): 39–51.

notes that the beatific vision is present in the historical life and agency of Christ according to a particular *dispensatio* or economic exercise.[36] The Incarnation occurs in view of the redemption of the human race, and this mystery of the humanization of God entails God's
living in ontological solidarity with us. In Christ, God took upon
himself our actual human condition. Because Christ was subject to
the ordinary conditions of human existence (which include mental
and psychological suffering), Aquinas thinks that he possessed the
beatific vision in such a way that his lower powers (his corporeal and
sensate-psychological experience of reality) retained their ordinary
structure and vulnerability.[37] This state is to be distinguished from
that of the resurrection, where Christ in his glorified humanity enjoys the effects of the beatifying vision of God not only in the heights
of his soul but also in his corporeal-sensate subjectivity and is affected by this grace even in the very matter of his glorified human flesh.[38]

A second principle is analogous to the first. Not only does Aquinas stress that Christ possessed the beatific vision in the midst of
an ordinary human life of psychological and physical vulnerability.
He also stresses that the higher intuitive knowledge derived from
the vision did not impede or supervene upon the ordinary acquisition of knowledge that comes by way of human experience. Here,
Aquinas contrasts "higher reason" with "lower reason," not so as to
distinguish two faculties of the intellect or even two habits (such as
speculative and practical reason). Rather, he means to distinguish
two types of objects of knowledge.[39] With regard to the mystery of
God, Christ's human reason was always illumined from above by his
intuitive knowledge of the Father, of himself, and of the Holy Spirit.
With regard to temporal things, however, the vision did not supervene upon his acquisition of knowledge by way of direct experience.

Interpreters debate over the question of whether Aquinas might

36. See *ST* III, q. 14, a. 1, ad 2; III, q. 15, a. 5, ad 3; III, q. 45, a. 2; III, q. 46, a. 8.
37. *ST* III, q. 46, aa. 6–8.
38. *ST* III, q. 46, a.8; q. 54, a. 3.
39. *Compendium theologiae ad fratrem Reginaldum socium suum carissimum*, vol. 42 of
Sancti Thomae de Aquino opera omnia (Rome: Leonine Edition, 1979), I, c. 232.

think that the human intellect of Christ could "naturally" avail itself of knowledge from the vision of God and translate it into conceptual knowledge in an almost immediate way. John of St. Thomas thinks not, while modern interpreters like Marie-Joseph Nicolas and Simon Francis Gaine think so.[40] On one reading, then, Christ would know he is the Son of God by immediate vision, not by faith, but he would be able to actively cognize this knowledge humanly primarily through the medium of his infused science and only secondarily through his acquired knowledge. Since the beatific vision is non-conceptual and, therefore, in a sense, incommunicable, Christ would need the infused prophetic knowledge to 'translate' his vision into terms that he might conceptualize and represent for us in ordinary terms.[41] On the alternative reading, Christ would know he was God through the medium of the beatific vision and not by faith, but would also be able to understand something of the vision and articulate this knowledge directly, by way of his ordinary, acquired knowledge, without recourse to any special infused, prophetic knowledge. His agent intellect, in its ordinary human mode of operation, would have some form of access to the higher intuitive knowledge he possesses in virtue of the vision.[42]

We need not seek to resolve this dispute here, which is incidental to the argument of this chapter. For however one resolves the debate, a key distinction remains as regards the *natural character* of the two forms of knowledge: the immediate vision of God, and the grace of the infused science. Aquinas clearly affirms that the beatific vision affords a much higher form of knowledge than the infused science, since it allows the human nature of Christ to know the divine

---

40. See John of St. Thomas, *Cursus Theologicus*, vol. 8 (Paris : Vivès, 1886), q. 9, d. 11, a. 2, nn. 3–5; M-J. Nicolas, "Voir Dieu dans la 'condition charnelle,'" *Doctor Communis* 36 (1983): 384–94; Simon F. Gaine, "Is There Still a Place for Christ's Infused Knowledge in Catholic Theology and Exegesis?" *Nova et Vetera* (English edition) 16, no. 2 (2018): 601–15. In the arguments that follow, I am greatly indebted to Gaine's recent framing of the question, though I do not align with him on all points.

41. The text of Aquinas that comes closest to affirming this idea is found in ST III, q. 9, a. 3, corp. and ad 3, couples with q. 11, a. 5, ad 1.

42. For a text that seems to lean in this sense, see Aquinas, *De Veritate*, q. 20, a. 3 ad 4.

essence in a direct manner. However, it is also the form of knowledge that most directly fulfills the natural human longing for absolute knowledge of God.[43] The grace of the beatific vision is formally supernatural, of course, and is the highest and most naturally inaccessible of all forms of grace. But in its term or purpose, this grace is intrinsically human and epitomizes the maxim that grace does not destroy nature but brings it to completion. This is the case even as it co-exists in Christ with all that is proper to ordinary experience: his psychological sensate development and human vulnerability and suffering. This is congruent in key ways with life in the resurrection. There, one finds no suffering since it entails a transformed state. However, it is also the case that even in the resurrection, the grace of the beatific vision co-exists in Christ in perfect harmony with his ordinary sensate experiences and his acquisitional mode of animal reasoning. In other words, the beatific vision is a much higher form of knowledge but also a more 'ordinary' one, given that it effectuates the perfection of human beatitude.

By contrast, the infused knowledge is not ordinary from a natural point of view, either formally or in its teleological term, but extraordinary since it is knowledge that is not gained through the senses and the activity of the agent intellect, nor one that contributes essentially to the final fulfillment of the subject. Rather, it is particularly gratuitous in mode and consists in a charismatic form of knowing that is oriented primarily not toward the good of the individual but to the assistance of others. The prophet may express his knowledge in and through the ordinary language of his time and may employ symbols that everyone can understand, but even when he does this, he does so based upon a gift of knowledge that others do not have, and that is charismatic in kind. We can conclude from this that the beatific vision of Christ and the prophetic knowledge (infused science) of Christ are soteriological in two distinct ways. The first is soteriological in a more properly exemplary and universalistic

---

43. *ST* I-II, q. 3, a. 8; I have offered my own treatment of the famous "natural desire for God" question in White, "Imperfect Happiness."

way. The immediate vision of God is the perfection of noetic be-atitude for each human being.[44] Christ is the savior because he can communicate to us what he himself first possesses, the perfection of the knowledge of God that utterly and ultimately fulfills the human mind and heart. The second form of knowledge is soteriological be-cause it represents an extraordinary charismatic gift of prophecy that most do not receive and that no one other than Christ has in a habit-ual way. It is oriented toward the economy of revelation and allows Christ to teach others those received truths that are essential to the New Testament revelation so as to instruct them in the faith. It is true that the blessed, in the life to come, may well enjoy infused sci-ence as well as the beatific vision, even as the souls of the saints sep-arated from the body must possess some form of infused science in order to cognate, given the absence of the body.[45] Nevertheless, the infused science is not typically human and remains extraordinary for our human nature, while acquired knowledge and the beatific vi-sion are more typically human, the first by way of nature and the sec-ond by way of grace.[46] The latter is a highest and most extraordinary grace, but it fulfills what is deepest and most distinctively rational in human animals: the natural desire for the truth and the natural de-sire to know God immediately.

CONCLUSION

The modern rise of historical Jesus studies was conceived initially in opposition to classical dogmatic perspectives regarding the per-son of Christ.[47] It was thought by many that the historical-critical method could be employed to go back behind the portrait of Christ in the New Testament and the early Church to recover a more re-alistic vision of Jesus of Nazareth "before dogma." Although this

---

44. Cf. 1 Jn 3:2; 1 Co 13:12; Rev 22:4; *CCC* 1023–29; *ST* I, q. 12, a. 1.

45. *ST* I, q. 89.

46. We might contrast this with the case of angels, for whom infused knowledge is typical: *ST* I, q. 55.

47. See here the historical argument of Israel, *Radical Enlightenment*.

approach is still maintained by some, it is no longer associated with the use of the historical-critical method as such. On the contrary, the modern quest for the historical Jesus has increasingly been conducted in seeming congruity with classical dogmatic teaching, especially by some "Third Quest" representatives who emphasize Jesus' eschatological message within the context of Second Temple Judaism.[48] Many of these scholars argue that Jesus of Nazareth must have understood himself to be the definitive, eschatological emissary of God in history, one who was bringing the covenant of Israel to its definitive resolution.[49] Understood in this way, one may reconcile a modern appreciation of Jesus's historically contingent human consciousness (within the context of Second Temple Judaism) and the principles of Nicene Christology.

Nevertheless, the modern historical synthesis is also subject to a kind of theological Apollinarianism, not of the classical kind (in which the human mind of Christ was denied problematically in order to assert the reality of his divinity), but of an inverted kind. On this view, the divine wisdom of Christ as God is eclipsed kenotically for the duration of his incarnate life among us. Only the human historical consciousness of Christ appears in all its contingent ordinariness, and the graces of Christ's prophetic awareness and special knowledge of his own identity are construed as mere "post-paschal theologomena" added by the later Christian community in order to exalt the historical figure of Christ.[50] This theology is Nicene because it affirms the divinity of Christ, but it is not properly Chalcedonian due to a kenoticism that obscures the presence of divine operations in the historical Christ, thus failing to grapple with

48. See the argument of Stephen Neill and N. T. Wright, *The Interpretation of the New Testament 1861–1986* (Oxford: Oxford University Press, 1988).

49. See for example N. T. Wright, *Jesus and the Victory of God,* esp. ch. 8; James D. G. Dunn, *Jesus Remembered* (Grand Rapids: Eerdmans, 2003), esp. chs. 12, 15, and 16.

50. Most representative of this problem in systematic theology is the intriguing and historically influential work of Pannenberg, *Jesus: God and Man,* 307–64 where he offers systematic challenges to traditional dyotheletism. It seems to me that N. T. Wright's portrait of Jesus in *Jesus and the Victory of God* aligns closely (intentionally or not) with that of Pannenberg in significant ways.

authentic dyotheletism, in which the divine and human operations of Christ are each present and are coordinated hierarchically.[51] The infused science and beatific vision of Christ are graces that pertain to his human nature but they are graces that allow his human mind to cooperate actively with the divine wisdom that he possesses as God, with the Father and the Holy Spirit. The affirmation of these graces in the human mind of Christ is necessary in order to understand properly the real cooperation and coordinated harmony of Christ's divine wisdom and human understanding, his divine willing, and his human decision making. How then, might one accept the classical principles of dyotheletism, while also embracing the legitimate insights of modern historical-critical studies?

Return to a balance means acknowledging the acquisitions of the modern historical studies and the realism they imply about a historically situated Incarnation while also finding a way to acknowledge Christ's infused science as a key element in his historical mission. The extraordinary human knowledge of Christ is something integral to the New Testament and, therefore, a real element of the life of Jesus of Nazareth that can be subject to historical consideration. The early Christian community understood the earthly Jesus to be a person gifted with extraordinary knowledge of the divine economy, capable of foretelling key events that were to come, able to read hearts and minds, and uniquely aware of his own authority and identity as the Son of God.

Aquinas's treatment of the infused science and beatific vision of Christ provides needed balance for Christian theology because it helps us to understand the grace of the human mind of Christ, so as to explain how this grace is enrooted in his nature, and, therefore, in the context of his human acquired knowledge with its cultural-linguistic and temporally situated shape. Aquinas's affirmation of Jesus's human

---

51. Ratzinger has noted the need for a renewal of dyotheletist Christology within a modern context in *Behold the Pierced One* (San Francisco: Ignatius Press, 1986). On the prospects for dyotheletism in dialogue with modern objections, see White, "Dyotheletism and the Instrumental Human Consciousness of Jesus." For a helpful treatment of the historical sources of dyotheletism, see Bathrellos, *The Byzantine Christ*.

acquisition of knowledge allows us to understand how the Incarnate Word would have learned from his experience within the context of his surrounding culture. This temporal specificity of the knowledge and language of Christ need not mean Christ's mission has less universality. On the contrary, the Word became flesh in first century Galilee and from that particular flesh in that particular time and place, cast a light upon the whole world. As Jesus says prophetically about his own crucifixion as the privileged place of the revelation of his divine identity: "When you have lifted up the Son of Man, then you will know, that I AM" (John 8:28). Jesus could think about the meaning of the divine name of Ex. 3:14–15 based on his natural, acquired knowledge, as a first century Jew. By virtue of his vision and his infused science, he also knew that he could apply this name to himself as one who is one in being with the Father (John 10:30). Christological realism requires that we hold the two affirmations together in unity, just as we must affirm both the true divinity and the true humanity of Christ. In this aspiration, the theological vision of the knowledge of Christ offered by Thomas Aquinas is of essential help for the future of a sound modern Christology.

15

The Two Natures of Christ
in the Crucifixion: The Cross as a
Revelation of Divine Love

INTRODUCTION:
TWO CHARACTERISTICS OF MODERN
KENOTIC CHRISTOLOGY

In its general trends, twentieth-century Christology was animated by a concern to confront at least two pivotal difficulties. First, in
light of the development of modern historical-critical study of the
person of Jesus of Nazareth in his cultural context, modern theologians typically had to confront the question of how might one evaluate the classical Chalcedonian doctrinal understanding of Christ
in the Church's tradition. Is it reasonable to confess that the historical Jesus took himself to be the Lord and God of Israel? And re-
latedly, how might theologians evaluate or entertain the historical
reconstructions of modern historical exegetes in light of the dogmatic teaching of the tradition? Second, in a post-critical age skeptical of the accomplishments of pre-modern metaphysical thinking, how can theology today retain the classical idea of Christ as a

Originally published in *Angelicum* 97, no. 1 (2021): 121–51.

transcendent divine person subsisting in two natures, one human and one divine? Is such a notion even intelligible for us in the modern era? In the wake of the influence of the Enlightenment and modern philosophy (Kant, Hegel, Heidegger), alternative ontologies and philosophical anthropologies have become more culturally dominant. Should Christian theologians then seek to understand the divine nature of Christ not by appeal to pre-modern metaphysical arguments pertaining to the deity, but rather as a mystery of God's self-actualization of his inner life revealed in history, specifically in the event of Jesus crucified and resurrected? Can and should Chalcedonian Christology be restated in modern ontological terms, and if so, how is it best to do so? Diverse kenotic Christologies developed by seminal figures of the 20th century sought to offer constructive responses to both these challenges simultaneously in an integrated and original way. One can readily identify significant differences between the respective Christologies of Karl Barth, Sergius Bulgakov, Wolfhart Pannenberg, Jürgen Moltmann, and Hans Urs von Balthasar, for example. Nevertheless, there are also significant commonalities with respect to the ways in which they engage with the two-fold challenge mentioned above. In various ways, each of these thinkers understands the inner life of God (and thus the divine nature) as a kenotic process of freedom by which God is able to self-identify as God in his deity with the finitude of human creaturely modes of being, especially in virtue of the Incarnation.[1] Consequently, what we perceive in the human being Jesus Christ in his free human action, suffering, death, and bodily resurrection

---

1. See, for example, the kenoticism of Karl Barth in *CD* IV:1, section 57, pp. 157–357; Sergius Bulgakov, *The Bride of the Lamb*, trans. B. Jakim (Grand Rapids: Eerdmans, 2002), 3–124; Bulgakov, *The Lamb of God*, 89–212; Pannenberg, *Jesus God and Man*, 307–23; Pannenberg, *Systematic Theology*, 375–79; Moltmann, *The Crucified God*, 200–278; Hans Urs von Balthasar, *The Glory of the Lord: A Theological Aesthetics*, vol. 1: *Seeing the Form*, trans. E. Leiva-Merikakis (San Francisco: Ignatius Press, 1982), 478–80; von Balthasar, *Theo-Drama: Theological-Dramatic Theory*, vol. 3, 183–91, 521–23; von Balthasar, *Theo-Drama: Theological-Dramatic Theory*, vol. 4, *The Action*, 319–28; Hans Urs von Balthasar, *Theo-Drama: Theological Dramatic Theory V: The Last Act*, trans. G. Harrison (San Francisco: Ignatius Press, 1998), 236–39.

is indicative of the inner nature of God, now made accessible to us within the sphere of history, not transcendent of it. A Christological ontology of kenotic descent displaces the classical tradition of divine names, which would appeal to such notions as divine simplicity, perfection, or infinity and apply these in turn to the divine nature of Christ. Simultaneously, the man Jesus is understood as a figure who attains consciousness of himself in an ordinary human way, as a figure of his age and expresses himself within the linguistic and cultural delimitated norms of his time. God, in emptying himself to become human, became a human being of a distinctive epoch with its theological motifs and characteristic forms of human self-understanding. Therefore, we can situate Christ within history using modern methods of analysis and even acknowledge a profound self-limitation of understanding on his part subjectively as an apocalyptic preacher and miracle worker, while still retaining that he is the eternal, pre-existent Son who has freely identified with us in our limitations and finitude.[2] As a result of this stance, we can accept to have very limited ambitions in regard to any historical demonstration that Jesus maintained a high conception of himself. The matter becomes relatively less significant, in light of the realization of an ontological kenosis on the part of God, present in Christ's human finitude. The Church's realization of Jesus' divine stature is commonly taken to be accessible to us (and to the early Church) above all in the light of the resurrection as an eschatological event in

2. See the helpfully clear articulation by Pannenberg, *Systematic Theology*, 377: "In his form of life as Jesus, on the path of his obedience to God, the eternal Son appeared as a human being. The relation of the Son to the Father is characterized in eternity by the subordination to the Father, by the self-distinction from the majesty of the Father, which took historical form in the human relation of Jesus to God. This self-distinction of the eternal Son from the Father may be understood as the basis of all creaturely existence in its distinction from God, and therefore as the basis of the human existence of Jesus, which gave adequate embodiment in its course to the self-emptying of the Son in service to the rule of the Father. As the Incarnation of the Logos was the result of the self-emptying of the eternal Son in his self-distinction from the Father, so the self-humbling of Jesus in obedience to his sending by the Father is the medium of the manifestation of the Son on the part of his earthly life."

which the divinity of Christ is unveiled in faith.[3] In some cases, the two ideas meet up: God, who exists dynamically in history, emerges in his perfection only in the resurrection, the very place where we also come to know Jesus of Nazareth as God, in a post-paschal light.[4]

This idea of the revelation of the deity of God in the human life of Christ also affects the confessional treatment of the two natures of Christ. When we speak of the kenotic mission of the Son, we indicate God's decision to become present in a human life immanent to history, one that is itself expressive of the inner Trinitarian life of God. Consequently, the human life and death of Jesus lived in lowliness and historical facticity typically acts as a mirror or indication of the inner moment within God as Word and Son, that person or mode of subsistence in God whereby God is both posited within himself and expressed outside himself as self-emptying love. Here, a host of ambitious new analogies are developed that are meant to signal the mystery of eternal love in God the Holy Trinity. Barth speaks of the filial obedience of Jesus as man as indicative of the inner life of the Son as eternal obedience to the Father. Bulgakov argues that the suffering of Jesus in time corresponds to an eternal suffering love of the Father on behalf of humanity.[5] Moltmann posits the historical

3. See the development of this theme: Pannenberg, *Systematic Theology*, 325–95; and Balthasar, in *Theo-Drama IV*, 361–83.

4. See Balthasar, *Theo-Drama V*, 514–15: "'The fact that the Son returns to the Father richer than when he departed, the fact that the Trinity is more perfected in love after the Incarnation than before, has its meaning and its foundation in God himself, who is not a rigid unity but a unity that comes together ever anew in love, an eternal intensification in eternal rest' [...] We need not be shocked at the suggestion that there can be 'economic' events in God's eternal life. When the Father hands over all judgment to the Son, 'something happens in God.' When the risen Son returns to the Father, 'a new joy arises after the renunciation involved in the separation. This new joy [...] perfects the Trinity in the sense that the grace that is to be bestowed becomes ever richer, both in the world into which it pours forth and in God himself.'" [The inset quotes are from Adrienne von Speyr.] Moltmann offers analogous reflections in *The Trinity and the Kingdom*, 81–89.

5. Bulgakov, *The Lamb of God*, 98–99: "For the Father, begetting is self-emptying, the giving of Himself and of His own to the Other; it is the sacrificial ecstasy of all-consuming jealous love for the Other [...] The Son, as the Son, has Himself and His own not as Himself and His own but as the Father's, in the image of the Father.

becoming of the Son as man as indicative of the historical development of the deity itself through the Son's experience of death and
resurrection.[6] Balthasar sees in Jesus' human self-offering in surrender an indication of the infinite distance that exists eternally in God
between the Father and the Son as a dimension of their reciprocal
and free self-giving.[7] In light of each of these distinct but clearly related motifs, the crucifixion is an especially poignant manifestation
of divine love. For it is precisely in Jesus' dereliction on the cross
in human suffering, in which he is subject to agony, death, and

---

Spiritual sonhood consists precisely in the Son's depleting Himself in the name of the
Father. Sonhood is already *eternal kenosis* [...] The sacrifice of the Father's love consists
in self-renunciation and in self-emptying in the begetting of the Son. The sacrifice of the
Son's love consists in self-depletion in the begottenness from the Father, in the acceptance of birth as begottenness. These are not only pre-eternal facts but also acts for both
the one and the other. The *sacrifice* of love, in its reality is pre-eternal suffering [...] This
suffering of sacrifice not only does not contradict the Divine all-blessedness but, on the
contrary, is its foundation, for this all-blessedness would be empty and unreal if it were
not based on authentic sacrifice, on the reality of suffering. If God is love, He is also
sacrifice, which manifests the victorious power of love and its joy only through suffering."

6. Moltmann, *The Crucified God*, 202–4: "When the crucified Jesus is called the 'image of the invisible God,' the meaning is that *this* is God, and God is like *this* [...] The
nucleus of everything that Christian theology says about 'God' is to be found in this
Christ event. The Christ event on the cross is a God event [...] So the new christology
which tries to think of the 'death of Jesus as the death of God,' must take up the elements
of truth which are to be found in *kenoticism* [...] It cannot seek to maintain only a dialectical relationship between the divine being and human being, leaving each of these
unaffected [...] That means that it must understand the event of the cross in God's being
in both Trinitarian and personal terms. In contrast to the traditional doctrine of the two
natures in the person of Christ, it must begin from the totality of the person of Christ
and understand the relationship of the death of the Son to the Father and the Spirit [...]
From the life of these three, which has within it the death of Jesus, there then emerges
who God is and what his Godhead means. Most previous statements about the specifically Christian understanding of talk about 'the death of God' have lacked a dimension,
the Trinitarian dimension."

7. See Balthasar, *Theo-Drama IV*, 319–28. Balthasar follows Bulgakov in affirming an
analogy of kenosis, in which the eternal kenotic generation of the Son in the immanent
Trinity is the transcendent foundation for the temporal kenosis of the Son in the economy. *Theo-Drama IV*, 333: "If Jesus can be forsaken by the Father, the conditions for this
'forsaking' must lie within the Trinity, in the absolute distance/distinction between the
Hypostasis who surrenders the Godhead and the Hypostasis who receives it." Mutual
reciprocity of freedom, expressed through mutual kenotic love and surrender, is the constitutive feature of personal identity in the Trinity.

potential separation from God, that he is also expressive of an inward self-emptying *caritas* that pre-exists in the eternal life of God himself. The eternal Calvary on high is the transcendent condition of possibility for the temporal Calvary laid before our eyes in history.

JESUS CHRIST AS THE
CONCRETE *ANALOGIA ENTIS*:
THE CASE OF BALTHASAR

The late work of Balthasar provides an especially illustrative case of this form of reflection. In the second volume of the *Theo-Logic*, Balthasar claims that the Incarnation is the most concrete instantiation of the *analogia entis*, the likeness between God and humanity.[8] At face value, this idea is uncontroversial, at least from the perspective of Christian theology. The human nature of Jesus Christ, his individual humanity, actions, sufferings, understanding, and willing as man all bear some relation of similitude to his nature and identity as God, to his divine wisdom and willing, insofar as he is the Son and Lord, who is one with the Father and the Spirit. Consequently, once we begin to understand in the light of faith that Christ is the Lord, we begin to see how his humanity indicates by correspondence his divinity, the inner mystery of God, and the Trinitarian communion of persons.

Nevertheless, the way that Balthasar makes this argument is original and noteworthy. We can observe three key interrelated ideas.

8. See Balthasar, *Theo-Logic*, 94–95, 173–218, 273, n. 109. Likewise, see *Epilogue*, 89–90: "How can Jesus say of himself, 'I am the Truth'? This is possible only because all that is true in the world 'hold[s] together' in him (Col. 1:17), which in turn presupposes that the *analogia entis* is personified in him, that he is the adequate sign, surrender, and expression of God within finite being. To approach this mystery we must try to think: In God himself the total epiphany, self-surrender, and self-expression of God the Father *is* the Son, identical with him as God, in whom everything—even everything that is possible for God—is expressed. Only if God freely decides in the Son to bring forth a fullness of nondivine beings can the Son's essentially 'relative' and thus 'kenotic' act in God be seen as a personal act (*esse completum subsistens*) within the act of creation that gives to everything its real identity (*esse completum sed non subsistens*)"

First, in his treatment of the knowledge of God's nature provided in scripture or by way of philosophy, Balthasar minimalizes the knowledge we have outside of Christ. We may say philosophically that God exists, but saying what God is in himself is inconsistent with the prophetic literature of the Old Testament. In other words, we find in Balthasar on this point something very like the Lutheran criticism of the medieval divine attributes theology as *theologia gloriae*, which Luther contrasted with a *theologia crucis* unveiled in Christ alone, especially in the cross.[9] Likewise, this is a similitude here to the Barthian prohibition on the classical divine attributes of scholasticism as an anthropomorphic form of speculation fueled unhelpfully by "natural theology." In his treatment of the divine nature, Balthasar reads the Old Testament revelation of God's identity in highly apophatic terms so that the naming of God in his divine essence is rendered quasi-equivocal for human discourse.[10]

Secondly, then, the knowledge we have of God just in virtue of Christ's human life is seemingly maximized. Here, the revelatory locus of knowledge in the inner Trinity is especially given in the human nature of Christ that acts as a quasi-univocal depiction of the inner life of God. The human nature of Christ, its actions and sufferings, precisely due to its unity with the divine nature within the person of the Son of God, makes the inner mystery of God most intelligible to us. When Christ experiences separation from the Father in virtue of his mission as man, it is indicative of an eternal distance of freedom and love that exists in the persons eternally.[11] "What" God

9. In 1518 in his Heidelberg Disputation, Luther distinguished and contrasted what he called a *theologia gloriae* that seeks knowledge of God's nature from created effects with a *theologia crucis* that seeks to find God in his human suffering on the Cross. This treatise was to have an effect on the early work of Barth, who takes up the distinction in CD I:1, pp. 14–17 and 167–69. The echoes of this idea in Balthasar seem relatively clear if one reads him in parallel with Barth.

10. See Balthasar, *Theo-Logic II*, 65–70.

11. Balthasar, *Theo-Logic II*, 135–49, at 136: "No one doubts that, as the New Testament tells us, the Father's act of giving up the Son and the Spirit in the economy is pure love, as is the Son's and the Spirit's act of freely letting themselves be given up. But how could this fundamental claim about the economy of salvation have no foundation in any property of

is in nature turns out to be the eternal relationships of the Trinitarian persons. We might say that in the name of apophaticism Balthasar evacuates from his account a consideration of the nature of God that is common to the three persons (the depiction of God as simple, perfect, infinite, eternal). He substitutes in its stead, a Christological depiction of intra-Trinitarian relationships characterized by freedom. The "nature" of God is now not only characterized in highly personalistic terms but also in seemingly quite vivid voluntaristic terms, as a collaboration of personal agents who commune through always coordinated but essentially distinct acts of willing.

Third, the economy of Trinitarian activity does not constitute the persons per se, but it is in a sense the locus where the communion of persons is explored, enriched, and developed, especially through the paschal mystery. As a consequence, the knowledge of God by way of the *analogia entis Christi* is nowhere more manifest than in the crucifixion, for it is here that the drama of the intra-divine personal and free relations in God reaches its apogee. It is here, for example, that Jesus' self-emptying is most perfectly expressive of his personal communion with the Father, and his relationship to the Holy Spirit, so that the ground of reality that is Trinitarian is manifest as love precisely in Christ's human free self-surrender to the Father at Golgotha. In this sense, the Son's human suffering in time is an economic iteration of a pre-existent, eternal reality in God that makes it possible. In *Theo-Drama IV* when Balthasar describes what the obediential suffering and death of Christ indicate in God, he is beholden to both Bulgakov and Barth. The human kenosis of Christ in time, his mission of obedience unto death, indicates a more primary

---

the essence of the Triune God?" For Balthasar, if God is to be considered as pure love, the persons must be considered not as subsistent relations but as pre-constituted subjects who then chose freely and mutually to engage by self-surrender with one another. See 163–65 where Balthasar appeals to Bonaventure's notion of God the Father as pre-constituted in innascibility prior to the two processions of the Son and Spirit, and to Scotus's idea of the two processions as distinct natural and free acts of the Father. Balthasar adopts this more typically Franciscan position that understands the two processions in voluntaristic fashion, as acts of the Father, but reinterprets the processions so that they are expressed in the drama of the economy by freely mutual acts of love.

ontological mystery of kenosis that occurs in the persons of God. The Father self-empties as a condition for the eternal positing of the Son, who is begotten of the Father by a free self-abdication of the Father's will, so that the Son can respond to him in entire, unconditioned freedom. The Son, in turn, gives himself eternally in free self-emptying surrender to the Father, in an expression of love that is anticipatory and indicative of the Spirit, who proceeds as love from the Father through the Son, in their mutual acts of self-surrender. Consequently, the economy of the Son's self-offering at Golgotha has its deepest ground in the eternal kenotic mutual relations of the Trinitarian persons. The cumulative revelation is given in the Son's human dereliction on the cross, his descent into the state of alienation and damnation, condemned as the one who takes the sins of the world onto himself by love for humanity. Christ's own descent into hell, into the place of the greatest distance from the God and of solitude of abandonment by the Father, has its precondition ontologically in the eternal kenotic and infinite distantiation of the Son from the Father, in his anticipatory obedience to divine love, the Holy Spirit.

It is significant to note that for Balthasar, this Trinitarian kenosis undergirds and casts light not only upon the crucifixion, then, but upon the whole temporal economy. There can only be a creation, a created freedom in human beings, a possibility of sin and disobedience, a hell, but also a free decision for union with God by love and an acceptation of mission because there is, first of all, and before all else, a mutually reciprocal freedom for love shared between the Trinitarian persons. Freedom for love, we might say, is the transcendent condition for all other moments in the divine economy. To use a musical image that Balthasar does not, but that seems fitting given his musical sensibilities, we could say that there is the first opening dramatic movement of the symphony of the Trinity before there is every other movement within the symphony and every later movement is anticipated and, in a sense, contained by thematic anticipation within this first one.

We can circle back from this notion of Trinitarian freedom to the place we began: the revelation of the divine nature in the human nature of Christ. Precisely because God is a mystery of freedom for love, he is free to be in diverse and seemingly contrary states, that is to say, the love that the persons possess between them in freedom is so free as to be capable of being simultaneously both victoriously transcendent of suffering and subject to suffering essentially, so that God may render his own nature passible from love.[12] The love of the Trinity is immutable in perfection, as that greater than which nothing can be thought, but also subject to change for the sake of love, as Balthasar evinces in his famous notion of the Trinitarian inversion, in which the order of the persons undergoes fundamental alteration for the sake of the divine missions in time, wherein the Son is sent from the Father and the Spirit so that the procession of the Spirit from the Son is kenotically suspended for the duration of the earthly life of Christ.[13] God's love is eternal in identity but able to embrace and in a sense freely contain within itself temporal modes of being to enrich and express his eternity outwardly, so that God is changed by his own historical development in time.[14]

In presenting things this way, Balthasar has made several key breaks with the antecedent tradition of Catholic theology that should be noted. First, he has effectively bid farewell to any plenary development and use of the *de deo ut uno* treatise of classical Trinitarian theology: the treatment of God's simplicity, perfection, infinity, eternity, and so on. If he continues to assert some of these so-called divine attributes, we are not told in any systematic way, outside of brief intuitions, why or how they are to be understood

---

12. See Balthasar, *Theo-Drama V*, 212–46: "The pain of God."

13. See Balthasar, *Theo-Drama III*, 183–91 and 521–23, on the notion of an economic "Trinitarian inversion." The processions of the Son and the Spirit are supposedly inverted in the economy, due to this kenosis of the Son, as during the time of his Incarnation and prior to the resurrection, he proceeds from the Spirit and is utterly relative to him not merely in his human instincts of mind and heart (i.e., in virtue of Christ's capital grace), but rather in his very person and being as Son.

14. See, for example, the text cited above of Balthasar, *Theo-Drama V*, cit., 514–15.

ontologically or why their use is warranted epistemologically. Second, he has also bid farewell to the use of the classical psychological analogy common to both Eastern and Western Fathers, arguably founded in both the Johannine theology of the *Logos* and the Pauline identification of Christ with God's preexistent Wisdom.[15] This two-fold move away from the classical inheritance of scripture and tradition by both fathers and scholastics has for its effect that the self-differentiation of the persons must take place under different auspices. The classical tradition understands the relations of the Trinitarian persons primarily by means of relations of origin according to an analogy of spiritual processions of knowledge and love and by denotation of a shared common divine nature or essence proper to God in his eternity, the so-called *homoousios* formula. The Father begets the Son as his Word and, in so doing, communicates to him the plenitude of the ineffable divine nature, just as the Father and the Word (in the Augustinian tradition) are understood to spirate the Spirit as their shared mutual love and in so doing communicate to the Spirit the plenitude of the ineffable divine nature. Study of the divine nature (attributes of God common to the three persons), then, is not something adjacent to or outside of Trinitarian theology (a supposedly separate *de deo uno* treatise that in reality never existed). Rather, it is an essential part of the study of Trinitarian theology, since it helps us locate that in virtue of which the three persons are said to be one as God, the Creator and Redeemer of all things. If one does not avail one's self of the psychological analogy to understand the eternal processions in God allied with a study of the shared nature (the attributes of the one God), how can the distinction of persons be articulated? Only by reference to the roles of the three person in the economy. This is precisely why it is so important for Balthasar to narrate a drama of intra-divine engagement that takes place within the economy as the epistemological condition for understanding the distinction of persons in God.

15. See *Theo-Logic II*, 128–37, where Balthasar unambiguously questions the viability in Trinitarian theology of the use of the psychological analogy and then proposes an alternative conception of divine self-emptying love.

Third, then Balthasar has accepted a language of mutuality or duality of wills into the distinction of the persons, so that the intelligibility of personal self-differentiation depends in a sense upon freedom of self-effacement and surrender maintained by the Father and Son reciprocally. This makes the affirmation of a unity of divine will and a unity of divine essence itself ambiguous and does indeed suggest the possibility of a narrative drama occurring within God alongside or within the historical unfolding of the creation and redemption.

Finally, and perhaps most importantly, on this account, there is little or no real recourse made to the classical teaching of dyotheletism and the Third Council of Constantinople (680–681), that posits that there are two wills in Christ, human and divine.[16] Obviously, Balthasar does not deny the truth of this doctrinal teaching and its patristic roots. He famously wrote a major study of Maximus the Confessor, arguably the most important of the 20th century. However, in his mature work, Balthasar simply rarely alludes to the mystery of the two wills of Christ, and it plays no thematic role in his thinking. Or perhaps we could say that it is an idea subject to radical reinterpretation in light of a kenotic notion of the mission of Christ. Consequently, in the *Theo-Drama*, for example, the human willing of Christ in his temporal mission and obediential freedom is alone indicative, in a quasi-univocal way, of the inner life of the Trinitarian persons' relations. When the Son obeys the Father as man in time, we see into the self-surrendering love of the eternal Son as God and even see by a mirroring reciprocity the kind of kenotic love that the Father has for the Son from eternity. The human will of Christ is thus not depicted as distinct from and subordinate to his divine will

16. The council claims explicitly that there are "two natural principles of action in the same Jesus Christ," and to this effect, cites Leo's famous statement from his Tome (Letter to archbishop Flavian) in Greek so as to make clear that "each form does" that which is proper to it, in concord with the other. In addition, the document goes on to state that "each nature wills and performs the things that are proper to it in a communion with the other; [and] in accord with this reasoning we hold that two natural wills and principles of action meet in correspondence for the salvation of the human race." This is the translation of N. Tanner, *Decrees of the Ecumenical Councils*, vol. 1 (London: Sheed & Ward; Washington, DC: Georgetown University Press, 1990), 129–30.

in an instrumental fashion (as with Damascene, for example), nor is his divine will depicted as identical with that of the Father and the Spirit, as that of God (the three persons having one will that is identical with the divine nature).[17] Instead, we are presented with something like an inverted monophysistism, where the kenotic life of the Son in his identity with man manifests precisely only in his human nature as such what it is for him to be Son in his very person, eternally, as self-surrendering love.

Of course, Balthasar assents notionally to the whole doctrinal given of the tradition and understands its scope and depth in an exceptionally well cultured way. But one may rightly ask whether, despite this, he has adequately preserved essential elements of the tradition in his creative re-articulation of it. It should be evident from the tone and cursory character of my remarks that I am skeptical. But one should also understand that I take Balthasar's views to be relatively standard in modern Trinitarian theology and to resemble in various ways those of Barth, Bulgakov, Pannenberg, and to some degree Moltmann, on the various features indicated above briefly. If Balthasar is to be singled out, it is perhaps because he has developed the views mentioned above in a more coherent way than some of these colleagues and in deeper conversation with previous tradition.

---

17. John Damascene, *The Orthodox Faith*, 3, c. 6 and 18: "When it is allowed by that which is more excellent [the divine will of Christ], the mind of Christ gives proof of its own authority [over his body], but it is under the dominion of and obedient to that which is more excellent, and does those things which the divine will purposes [...] So, then, He had by nature, both as God and as man, the power of will. But His human will was obedient and subordinate to His divine will, not being guided by its own inclination, but willing those things which the divine will willed ... For when He prayed that He might escape death, it was with His divine will naturally willing and permitting it that He did so pray and agonize and fear, and again when His divine will willed that His human will should choose death, the passion became [humanly] voluntary to Him."

DYOTHELETIST CHRISTOLOGY: THE HUMAN ACTIVITY OF CHRIST AS ANALOGICALLY INDICATIVE OF ESSENTIAL AND PERSONAL LOVE IN GOD

In the second half of this chapter, I would like to explore the idea that the crucifixion is a manifestation of Trinitarian love. I will do so from a Thomistic perspective, having recourse, especially to principles of dyotheletism, the notion of there being two wills and activities in the one composite person of Christ, those that are human and those that are divine. These two activities of Christ are distinct but not separate so that the human agency of Christ is not identical with his divine agency but is truly subordinate to and indicative of it, in such a way that it reveals his personal identity as the Son of God, and manifests his divine agency. The love of Christ as man in the crucifixion is expressive of his divine identity as God and of the Trinitarian relations. The dyotheletist account is helpful not only because it allows one to speak of the similitude of the human nature to his divine nature, but also of the dissimilitude. We can speak here of an analogical interval between the divine nature of Christ and his human nature. Jesus' human nature not only manifests but also conceals the hidden presence of God, who is active in the Son's human actions, suffering, cadaveric death, and bodily glorification. The hiddenness of God in the crucifixion should be acknowledged as it indicates the irreducible distinction between the two natures and the real but limited character of the knowledge of the divine nature conveyed by God's human nature. This theology of the analogical interval also thereby leaves within Christology an important place for eschatological reserve regarding our knowledge in this world of God's inner life, even after the revelation of Christ's deity in the event of the cross. The teleological aspirations of our current knowledge point us toward a more perfect union we do not yet possess, and thus stand at a remove from and as a criticism of various univocal conceptions of the Trinitarian life of God based on Jesus's human actions and suffering. No Christology provides us with adequate univocal significations of the Godhead simply in virtue of a consideration of God's human state of being. How can we depict rightly, then, this "analogical interval" between the divine will and the human will of Christ crucified so that we think rightly about the manifestation and hiddenness of the Trinity as these are revealed in the crucifixion of the Son of God made man?

We may begin by noting three facets of Aquinas's dyotheletism, itself a recapitulation of themes found in Maximus the Confessor that Aquinas assimilated self-consciously from John Damascene.[18] The first idea in this regard is that the human activities of Christ, his ordinary human understanding and elective freedom, are formally identical with those of all other human beings.[19] They are characterized by an orientation toward the universal horizon of the truth and the desirable good, but also occur through the medium of abstraction and within the contextualized development of a historical consciousness. Jesus, as a human being, truly learned and reflected, thought and suffered within the context of a particular cultural setting, albeit one that was itself influenced deeply by divine inspiration and the presence of the prophetic knowledge of the God of Israel.[20] Second, these same activities in Christ, while authentically human in every regard, are also subordinate instrumentally to his divine knowledge and volition, in such a way that they are illuminated

---

18. See the study of Aquinas's use of Damascene on this point by Barnes, *Christ's Two Wills in Scholastic Thought*. In *ST* I, q. 19, a. 1, when treating of Leo and Severus, Aquinas follows Damascene's interpretation of the Third Council of Chalcedon found in *The Orthodox Faith*, 3, c. 16. He then proceeds to defend Leo's Tome against its monenergist critics (corp. and ad 4): "The human nature has its proper operation distinct from the divine and conversely. Nevertheless, the divine nature makes use of the operation of the human nature, as of the operation of its instrument [...] Being and operation belong to the person by reason of the nature; yet in a different manner. For being belongs to the very constitution of the person, and in this respect it has the nature of a term; consequently, unity of person requires unity of the complete and personal being. But operation is an effect of the person by reason of a form or nature. Hence plurality of operations is not incompatible with personal unity."

19. See *ST* III, q. 9, a. 4; q. 12, aa. 1–2; q. 18, aa. 1, 4, 5.

20. I have attempted to develop this line of thinking based on Aquinas's principles in "The Infused Science of Christ." *Nova et Vetera* (English edition) 16, no. 2 (2018): 617–64.

from within and inspired in concord with a hidden divine wisdom and will.[21] In Jesus's human thoughts and decisions, as a first century Jew who expresses himself within the context of Second Temple Judaism, we see the manifestation of the divine truth of the Son marked by the volitions of divine love, which pertain to the Father, the Word, and the Spirit.[22] What Christ chooses and what he suffers deliberately are instrumentally indicative of the presence, activity and eternal designs of divine love. Third, this manifestation of love in the human heart of Christ is interpersonal, so that his action

21. Aquinas distinguishes Christ's "will as sensuality" from his voluntary will, the former being the impulse of his animal sensitivity, which naturally shrinks from death, while the latter pertains to his natural faculty of voluntary desire and choice-making. The latter however can also be considered as natural versus deliberative, as Christ can naturally desire not to suffer but can choose to embrace the mystery of the Cross freely and reasonably in view of a higher good. *ST* I, q. 18, a. 5: "In Christ according to His human nature there is a twofold will, viz. the will of sensuality, which is called will by participation, and the rational will, whether considered after the manner of nature, or after the manner of reason. Now [...] by a certain dispensation the Son of God before His Passion allowed His flesh to do and suffer what belonged to it. And in like manner He allowed all the powers of His soul to do what belonged to them. Now it is clear that the will of sensuality naturally shrinks from sensible pains and bodily hurt. In like manner, the will as nature turns from what is against nature and what is evil in itself, as death and the like; yet the will as reason may at time choose these things in relation to an end, as in a mere man the sensuality and the will absolutely considered shrink from burning, which, nevertheless, the will as reason may choose for the sake of health. Now it was the will of God that Christ should undergo pain, suffering, and death, not that these of themselves were willed by God, but for the sake of man's salvation. Hence it is plain that in His will of sensuality and in His rational will considered as nature, Christ could will what God did not; but in His will as reason He always willed the same as God, which appears from what He says (Matthew 26:39): 'Not as I will, but as Thou wilt.' For He willed in His reason that the Divine will should be fulfilled although He said that He willed something else by another will."

22. Commenting on John 5:19 ("the Son cannot do anything of himself"), Aquinas writes [*Commentary on St. John's Gospel*, trans. J. Weisheipl (Albany, NY: Magi, 1993), V, lect. 3, n. 749]: ".".. he says, the Son cannot do anything of himself, for the Son's power is identical with his nature. Therefore the Son has his power from the same source as he has his being (*esse*); but he has his being (*esse*) from the Father: "I came forth from the Father, and I have come into the world" (Jn 16:28). He also has his nature from the Father, because he is God from God; therefore, it is from him that the Son has his power (*posse*). So his statement, the Son cannot do anything of himself, but only what he sees the Father doing, is the same as saying: The Son, just as he does not have his being (*esse*) except from the Father, so he cannot do anything except from the Father."

as man is not only expressive of the divine will but also of his personal filial identity. The Son does what he does from and for the Father and as the source of the Spirit. The Spirit proceeds from Jesus as Son and Lord, but also reposes upon and directs him inwardly as man.[23] How, then, do the personal actions of Christ as one who is both God and man manifest the presence and activity of the Holy Trinity? Only the Son of God is human, not the Father or the Spirit. The Son, however, is one in being and nature with the Father and the Spirit as God, and he proceeds from the Father personally, as his Word, just as the Spirit proceeds from the Father and the Son as their mutually shared love.[24] Consequently, when Jesus acts as both God and man, he acts with the Father and the Spirit in virtue of his divine agency, in the power of his deity, and does so in accord with the internal order of the processional persons. His divine action is truly his own as the Son, but it is also always, already from the Father from who he receives all things, and it is in the Spirit who proceeds from the Father and from him or through him. The human actions as such are proper to him alone, but they do indicate the divine authority and power present within him and the personal relations he possesses with the Father and the Spirit. Furthermore, his human actions as man are revelatory of his divine Sonship not only when he heals or teaches saving truth but also when he voluntarily suffers, insofar as his human sufferings freely consented to in obedient human love for the Father and the human race are indicative of a divine will to communicate Trinitarian life to the world precisely through the epiphany of the cross.

Aquinas provides us with two overlapping but irreducibly distinct ways to think about divine love in the Holy Trinity, as both

23. See *ST* III, q. 7, a. 13 on the habitual grace of Christ as the effect of the Spirit's activity in him, as well as q. 7, a. 5 on the fullness of the gifts of the Spirit in the man Jesus. See also the helpful study of this theme in Aquinas by Legge, *The Trinitarian Christology of St. Thomas* Aquinas, 187–210.

24. Here I follow Augustine and Aquinas on the procession of the Spirit as the mutual love of the Father and the Son, a point I will not argue for in this context. See however the arguments in White, *The Holy Spirit*, in *The Oxford Handbook of Catholic Theology*, ed. L. Ayres and M. A. Volpe (Oxford: Oxford University Press, 2019), 183–97.

essential and personal, based on the internal requirements of Trinitarian monotheism.[25] Essential terms pertain to that in virtue of which the Trinitarian persons are one in being and nature. If we can speak, for example, analogically of the wisdom and power of the Father, then we must also ascribe this identical divine wisdom and power to the Son and the Spirit, who are each the one God even in their distinctions of person. The Father communicates all that he has to the Son and Spirit so that each of these persons is all that we may speak of God being. If then there is one God and God is something we call love, then God is whatever this "love" is essentially, that is to say, in virtue of his nature.[26] Just because the Father, Son, and Holy Spirit are one in being and essence, as the council of Nicaea states, so too they are also one in love, not merely relationally or politically by communion but essentially and consubstantially. They are each the one God who is love in all that God is, just as they are also one in being, wisdom, goodness, power, and so forth.

However, Aquinas also rightly denotes that the Spirit is love not only in an appropriated sense, but by proper analogy. The Father is wise eternally and, in knowing himself, generates the Son as his begotten wisdom. The Father does not become wise in virtue of the generation of the Son but expresses his eternal wisdom in the begetting of the Logos.[27] Therefore, the Son can be wise essentially, having received all that he has from the Father, and he can be personally the begotten Word and Wisdom, in a way the Father and the Spirit are not.[28] This is because he receives immaterially all he is from the

---

25. See *ST* I, q. 39, aa. 1–3. *Commentary on St. John's Gospel*, V, lect. 3, n. 753, "In divine realities, love is taken in two ways: essentially, so far as the Father and the Son and the Holy Spirit love; and notionally or personally, so far as the Holy Spirit proceeds as Love."

26. See *ST* I, q. 20.

27. *ST* I, q. 34, a. 1, ad 2.

28. See *ST* I, q. 34, on the Son as Word and *SCG*, IV, c. 12. On the Son as Wisdom. *SCG* IV, c. 12: "Now, that there is wisdom in God must certainly be said by reason of the fact that God knows Himself; but, since He does not know Himself by any species except His own essence—in fact, His very act of understanding is His essence—the wisdom of God cannot be a habit, but is God's very essence. But from what has been said, this is clear: The Son of God is the Word and conception of God understanding Himself. It follows, then, that the same Word of God, as wisely conceived by the divine mind, is

Father and is the fruit of understanding, and so is properly denoted by the notion of the *Logos* or *Verbum*. The Holy Spirit is similar, however, in the order of love. The Spirit proceeds immaterially from the Father and the Son, and if this procession is from the Word and has an immaterial content, then the appropriate analogy is to the affection of love from the will.[29] The Father and the Son knowing and loving one another spirate the Holy Spirit. The Holy Spirit proceeds eternally from the Father and Son as their mutually spirated love. He receives all that he is from them as their personally subsistent love, even as he contains in himself all that is in the other two persons, including the essential or natural properties of God.[30]

---

properly said to be 'conceived or begotten Wisdom'; and so the Apostle calls Christ: 'the Wisdom of God' (1 Cor. 1:24). But the very word of wisdom conceived in the mind is a kind of manifestation of the wisdom of the one who understands, just as in our case all habits are manifested by their acts. Since, then, the divine Wisdom is called light (for it consists in the pure act of cognition, and the manifestation of light is the brightness proceeding therefrom) the Word of divine Wisdom is named 'the brightness of light.' Thus the Apostle speaks of the Son of God: 'Who being the brightness of His glory' (Heb. 1:3). Hence, also, the Son ascribes to Himself the manifestation of the Father. He says in John (17:6): 'Father, I have manifested your name to men.' But note: Although the Son who is the Word of God is properly called 'conceived Wisdom,' the name of 'wisdom' must, nonetheless, when taken absolutely, be common to the Father and the Son; since the wisdom resplendent by the Word is the Father's essence, as was said; but the Father's essence is common to Him and to the Son."

29. See *ST* I, q. 27, a. 4; q. 37, aa. 1–2. q. 37, a. 2: "... in God 'to love' is taken in two ways, essentially and notionally, when it is taken essentially, it means that the Father and the Son love each other not by the Holy Ghost, but by their essence. Hence Augustine says (*De Trin.* xv, 7): 'Who dares to say that the Father loves neither Himself, nor the Son, nor the Holy Ghost, except by the Holy Ghost?' The opinions first quoted are to be taken in this sense. But when the term Love is taken in a notional sense it means nothing else than 'to spirate love'; just as to speak is to produce a word, and to flower is to produce flowers. As therefore we say that a tree flowers by its flower, so do we say that the Father, by the Word or the Son, speaks Himself, and His creatures; and that the Father and the Son love each other and us, by the Holy Ghost, or by Love proceeding."

30. See on this point, *ST* I, q. 42.

THE ANALOGICAL REVELATION
OF TRINITARIAN LOVE IN THE CRUCIFIXION
OF THE SON

In the previous section of this chapter, I have argued that on Aquinas's account, first, the Son's human actions and sufferings manifest the divine life and will, as well as the communion of Trinitarian persons. Second, the love of the immanent Trinity can rightly be spoken of in two complementary and non-competitive ways, as essential and personal. The question we may then pose in light of these two considerations is how, from a Thomistic perspective, do the actions of Jesus in the crucifixion manifest the essential and personal dimensions of Trinitarian love?

Let us consider first the essential love of God present at Golgotha, hidden in the human actions and sufferings of Christ crucified. Aquinas notes that God essentially loves himself from all eternity and creates all things that emanate from him by giving them being freely as an expression of divine goodness from within the divine love God has for himself.[31] The redemption recapitulates this pattern. God loves his own eternal goodness and freely gives from this pre-existent wellspring the gift of grace and redemption, manifest especially in the Incarnation and the crucifixion. Christ's human decision to suffer death by crucifixion for us then is a human manifestation of the Son's divine desire to recreate the world in light of the Trinitarian goodness. "The Father so loved the world that he gave his only begotten Son" (John 3:16). The Son so loved the world that he gave his life humanly. The Spirit so loved the world that he gave all of humanity new filial life from the cross. This essential love is present in the crucifixion and in the resurrection, like complementary ontological diptychs. The essential love of the Trinity is revealed in the crucifixion in the Son's inalienable union of being and essence with the Father and the Spirit, which is unsunderable. "I am not alone for

---

31. *ST* I, q. 20, aa. 2–3.

the Father is with me" (John 16:32). "When you have lifted up the Son of Man then you will know that I Am" (John 8:28). The union of the Son with the Father as God is greater and more perfect than the union of Christ's human nature with his divine nature. The Son on the cross is grounded in the unalterable union of love with the Father and the Spirit by which they are in him, and he is in them. By the same measure, that love can be re-creative even from the cross, manifest in Christ's own explicit acts as man. In Luke's Gospel, he forgives his enemies and conveys grace to the good thief, just as in John's Gospel, as interpreted in the Catholic tradition, he denominates the Virgin Mary, the mother of the Church, and he voluntarily wills the salvation of the world, something he can effectuate and communicate in virtue of divine love. It is also true, however, that this same love is eclipsed and hidden in the crucifixion since the God who is love is silent in the suffering, death, and cadaveric burial of the Son. The dead body of Christ on the cross is the dead body of God (the Son who is God in his divine nature), and the divine person of the Son is truly present and subsistent in his dead body prior to his resurrection.[32] This hiddenness of God in our human death remains, after Christ's resurrection, an aspect of our own lives, in ongoing history prior to the eschaton. The power of God is present to us but veiled. The historical resurrection of the Son, meanwhile, manifests the victory of divine love that was formerly hidden and present in the cross. The flesh containing the hidden power of God is now glorified, alive, and life-giving, casting eschatological perspective upon all penultimate things.[33] God is able to make

32. See *ST* III, q. 50, aa. 2, 3, 6.

33. Aquinas points out in *ST* III, q. 53, a. 4 that just as Christ's divinity is present in his dead body, so too his divinity is active in the glorification of his body in the resurrection. ". . . in consequence of death Christ's Godhead was not separated from His soul, nor from His flesh. Consequently, both the soul and the flesh of the dead Christ can be considered in two respects: first, in respect of His Godhead; secondly, in respect of His created nature. Therefore, according to the virtue of the Godhead united to it, the body took back again the soul which it had laid aside, and the soul took back again the body which it had abandoned: and thus Christ rose by His own power. And this is precisely what is written (2 Cor. 13:4): 'For although He was crucified through our weakness, yet

all things new, and we, too, can hope to be recreated in Christ by the power of God. But this same resurrection is concealed from our ordinary perception and known principally in faith, standing at the horizon of all ordinary human experience. For now, it casts an ultimate light on the provisionality of every human accomplishment or intra-historical achievement.

The personal love of the Trinity we mentioned above is that which pertains to the Holy Spirit in his procession from the Father and the Son. How does the human activity of Christ crucified reveal the Holy Spirit? In one sense, his human actions and sufferings reveal the Spirit because he is moved by the Spirit inwardly as man to offer his life for the world.[34] We perceive indirectly from Jesus' human actions the hidden interior will of the Spirit who moves him. In this sense, Jesus as man is subordinate to the Spirit, who is Love and who collaborates with the Son in his visible mission. The theandric action of Jesus, then, is indicative of the transcendent work of the Holy Spirit as Love that unfolds in and through the work of Jesus of Nazareth, his teaching, miracles, suffering, and free acceptance of death.

We also can consider how Jesus crucified relates to the Spirit in virtue of the eternal processions of the persons, which are manifest in their visible missions in the world. Aquinas tells us a divine mission just is a procession with the addition of a new presence.[35]

He liveth by the power of God.' But if we consider the body and soul of the dead Christ according to the power of created nature, they could not thus be reunited, but it was necessary for Christ to be raised up by God."

34. In *ST* III, q. 47, a. 2 Aquinas underscores Jesus' human submission to the will of the Father in his passion, and this is also revelatory of Trinitarian relations. We can predicate his human will to suffer in subordination to the Father, to himself as Lord and to the Spirit in three distinct modes of appropriation. The human will to suffer in subjection to the Father's will denotes in a personal filial way his derivation from the Father as Son. His desire to suffer in subordination to his own divine will denotes that he is Lord and does as man what he does in view of the triumph of his Lordship, in union with his Father. His human subordination to the Spirit shows that he is moved inwardly by the Spirit who rests upon him as man and fills him with a plenitude of habitual grace, as the head of the Church who wills as man to share his grace with all of humanity. See *ST* III, q. 7, a. 12 and q. 8, a. 1–2.

35. *ST* I, q. 43, a. 2, ad 3.

The visible missions of the persons in the economy manifest the eternal processions of the persons and so follow their order. If the Son is sent into the world by the Father, this is ultimately because he proceeds eternally from the Father, and if the Spirit is sent into the world from the Father and the Son, this is ultimately because he proceeds eternally from the Father and the Son.[36] The missions of the Son and Spirit mirror or reflect the processions and, in doing so, reveal to us the life of the immanent Trinity.[37] Consequently, when the Father sends the Son into the world in a most distinctive way in the Incarnation, this is in view of the sending of the Holy Spirit, the love of the Father and the Son who proceeds from both of them. This latter sending of the Spirit in his visible mission takes place in a distinctive way in and through Jesus' crucifixion.[38] Having redeemed the world by his obedient suffering and death, Christ sends the Holy Spirit upon all of humanity in the wake of his passion. The eternal procession in which he is one with the Father spirating the love of the Spirit takes place immanently, or is rendered present within history, in the event of the crucifixion.

We have noted above that the theandric acts of Jesus manifest his personal relations, which are intra-Trinitarian. The man Jesus desires or accepts freely to live the mystery of the passion in accordance with the Father's will, revealing thereby that he is from the Father and acts with him. He also, however, manifests thereby his human desire to send the Spirit upon the world. It is as Lord and Son that he can send the Spirit, as he who is one with the Father. He is also able to send the Spirit as man, instrumentally, not in the sense that the

---

36. See the arguments to this effect in *ST* I, q. 43, aa. 1, 2, and 4. The temporal missions truly reveal the eternal processions and as such the missions imply the presence of the processions according to the order of relations of origin present in God from all eternity. If the Son proceeds from the Father from all eternity, this is made manifest in his mission from the Father. If the Spirit proceeds from the Father and the Son from all eternity, this is made manifest in his mission from the Father and the Son.

37. See the study of Emery, "*Theologia* and *Dispensatio*."

38. This can be said without denying the distinctive character of Trinitarian revelation in the conception of Christ, his baptism, transfiguration, resurrection, or at Pentecost.

Spirit proceeds from him eternally in virtue of his humanity, which is untrue, but in the sense that he as the Son can will both divinely and humanly to send the Spirit upon the whole human race. Jesus's human acceptation of the cross then is revelatory of the divine intention he has with the Father to send the Spirit, and thereby manifests truly, if obliquely, the intra-trinitarian order of processions in God.

It follows from this that in virtue of the event of the crucifixion and death of Jesus, the Spirit is sent on mission as the eternal procession of love now made present to us in a new way. Jesus tells us as much in the Gospel of John: "Unless I go [... to the Father], the Paraclete will not come to you" (John 16:7). "And I will ask the Father, and he will give you another advocate to help you and be with you forever" (John 14:16). In the Johannine portrait of the death of Christ, this distinctive sending of the Spirit from the cross is symbolized by the miracle of the outpouring of the water and the blood. The Spirit comes out from the side of the dead body of God, sent from him as Word made flesh, that is to say from the man Jesus, whose humanity is the instrument of his divine person. Jesus breathes his last: breathing the Spirit of love upon the world. The night of Easter in John 20 he also breathes again humanly, now alive, glorified, and spirates the Spirit upon the apostles, who are entrusted with the office of the forgiveness of sins.[39] The uncreated Gift who is the Spirit

---

39. John 20:20–23: "When he had said this, he showed them his hands and his side. Then the disciples were glad when they saw the Lord. Jesus said to them again, 'Peace be with you. As the Father has sent me, even so I send you.' And when he had said this, he breathed on them, and said to them, 'Receive the Holy Spirit. If you forgive the sins of any, they are forgiven; if you retain the sins of any, they are retained.'" Aquinas notes that this gesture signifies that the Son is giving the Spirit, which implies the missions of the two persons. However, this gesture is also that of the man Jesus who has his habitual grace from the Spirit signifying that he will share this life of grace with the Church by means of the sacraments, as administered by the apostles. On the procession of the Spirit from the Son implied by this gesture see *Commentary on St. John's Gospel*, trans. P. Larcher (Albany, NY: Magi, 1997), lect. 4, n. 2538: "Jesus makes them adequate for their task by giving them the Holy Spirit, 'God, who has qualified us to be ministers of a new covenant, not in a written code but in the Spirit' (2 Cor 3:6). In this giving of the Spirit, he first grants them a sign of this gift, which is, that *he breathed on them*. We see something like this in Genesis (2:7), when God 'breathed into his nostrils the breath of life,'

is now a gift to the Church, the uncreated soul of the Church, sent upon the apostles to live with them and within them, and from them in us, the mystical body of Christ, alive in the Spirit.[40]

FREE UNIVOCAL IDENTIFICATION OR ANALOGICAL SIMILITUDE? HEGELIAN AND THOMISTIC VARIATIONS IN THE USE OF THE PSYCHOLOGICAL ANALOGY

In the previous section, I argued that in light of the distinction between the divine and human wills of Christ and the distinction between the essential love of God and the processional Love of God as the Holy Spirit, we could consider the revelation of love in the crucifixion in two ways. In one sense, Christ's human love reveals the essential love of God present in the three persons in virtue of their shared Godhead, that love that is co-extensive with and, in fact, mysteriously identical with their essential wisdom and power, by which they have created the world and that has begun in Christ to remake the world. In another sense, Christ's human love is indicative of the Holy Spirit as Love, the Love that moves him as man to give his life for the world, and that Love that proceeds from him as Son, even especially in the cross, from which he as the God-human sends the Spirit upon the world, in the Spirit's visible mission to all human beings.

If what I am arguing is correct, then the classical psychological analogy of Word and Love is key to understanding the identity of God as love. This is especially true for the second feature just

---

of natural life, which the first man corrupted, but Christ repaired this by giving the Holy Spirit. We should not suppose that this breath of Christ was the Holy Spirit; it was a sign of the Spirit. So Augustine says, in *The Trinity*: 'This bodily breath was not the substance of the Holy Spirit, but a fitting sign that the Holy Spirit proceeds not just from the Father but also from the Son.' [*De Trin.*, 4, ch. 20]"

40. See *ST* I, q. 38, a. 1, ad 4 and a. 2, ad 2: Aquinas points out that the name "gift" pertains to the Spirit in one sense insofar as he is given to us, but in another sense as one who is the eternal Love of the Father and the Son who proceeds from both as Love and who is given to the world precisely as this eternal person who is uncreated Love.

mentioned above. The emitted love of the Spirit who is sent from the cross by the Father and the Son manifests the transcendent procession of the Spirit who eternally receives all that he is from the Father and the Word. The psychological analogy is in play here because it is employed in traditional Western Trinitarian theology to denote the relations of origin pertaining to the Son as Word and to the Spirit as Love, respectively. However, the account we are considering also makes overt use of the distinction of intellect and will as immaterial faculties in the human being, precisely so as to consider the human mind and will of Christ as instrumentally expressive of his divine person and divine nature. In this sense, the account offered above makes use of the immanent created term of the psychological analogy to analyze the human acts of Christ, that are said to be indicative of his divine nature, and makes use of the transcendent uncreated term of the psychological analogy to analyze the distinction and order of the eternal persons in God. On this account, the use of psychological analogy plays a key role in the way we understand Christ as the concrete *analogia entis*. This is the case because his human activities of knowledge and love are expressive of the nature of God residual in him and of the relations of the Trinitarian persons. Meanwhile, those latter relations can only be understood rightly according to their order of origination by recourse to a theology of processions, wherein the Son originates from the Father as Word and the Spirit originates from the Father and Son as Love.

In the first half of this chapter, we noted that Balthasar posits that Christ is the concrete *analogia entis* but that he does so in a relatively novel way that bids farewell to the use of the psychological analogy, the classical treatise of the attributes proper to the divine nature and overt use of the principles of dyotheletism. In the wake of these decisions, the distinctions of the persons are evinced principally from their role in the economy of salvation in a shared life of free exchanges. The human nature of Jesus obedient, suffering, and crucified provides a kind of concrete picture or quasi-univocal indicator of the distinction of persons that obtains in the eternal life of

God. In contrast to this portrait, I have offered indications of how one might depict the crucifixion as a revelation of intra-trinitarian love by making use of core elements of the classical tradition: the notion of the human acts of Christ as distinct from, subordinate to, and indicative of his divine person and agency, the notion of the essential love of God (pertaining to God in his unity of nature not in personal relations *per se*), and the notion of the Spirit as Love proceeding, in accordance with the psychological analogy.

This being said, there are many alternative ways to employ the psychological analogy in order to understand Trinitarian life, at least one of which is itself decidedly kenoticist. What would it mean to hold to a kenoticist understanding of the Word and the Spirit in their immanent processions in the life of God? Hegel offers us one way to think about this option, based on his understanding of divine freedom for diremption. According to Hegel's depiction of the Trinity in the *Lectures on the Philosophy of Religion* God is free in his very being to appear under his contraries, in time and death, and to develop historically as divine reason precisely through the medium of created human spirit. Here then, we find the idea of a procession of the Son from the Father as Word or Reason manifest in time, but now understood as identifying with human nature in its finitude and temporality so that the human nature of God is indicative of his internal ontology of divine becoming.[41] It is often said that theological problems arise from philosophical errors and some claim that Hegel has sought to translate Trinitarian theology into a new idiom of post-Enlightenment reason by way of a novel philosophical ontology. There is undoubtedly a line of truth to this characterization of Hegel as a modern philosopher. However, it would be a mistake to presume that his ideas are purely rationalistic or philosophical in origin since his Christological thinking also contains novel theological ideas as such. In fact, he creatively rearticulated a Lutheran notion

---

41. See the analysis of Samuel M. Powell, *The Trinity in German Thought* (Cambridge: Cambridge University Press, 2001), 104–41.

of the communication of idioms, wherein divine properties (such as omnipresence) are attributed to the human nature of Christ, an idea of Luther that was famously criticized by Calvin. Hegel inverts this theological paradigm and claims that the human attributes of Christ are attributable to the divine nature so that God's activity of self-definition as freedom is able to include and make itself manifest in human history by the Incarnation. The kenotic movement of the Son into history is a movement of God's divine rationality into our human rationality. Consequently, the supposedly "rationalist" side of Hegel's program also has a Christological warrant. In becoming human in time, the Reason of God has become accessible to human reason and indeed has become human so that our "merely" human understanding of history, through philosophy, can attain to absolute knowledge of God, in Christ.[42]

Behind this view, we see a collapse of the analogical interval between the divine and human natures of Christ. There is no longer an analogy between the two, in fact, so much as a free exploration

---

42. In the 1827 *Lectures on the Philosophy of Religion*, Hegel seems to invert, as it were, the perspective of the Tübingen school regarding the *genus majestaticum*. Whereas they speculated on how or in what way the attributes of the deity might be communicated to the humanity (omnipresence, omnipotence), Hegel speculates on how the attributes of the humanity might be communicated to the divinity. The condition for this is the capacity of the deity as spirit to self-identify with its ontological contrary by way of free, self-exploratory diremption. The most famous case is that pertaining to the human death of Christ, which Hegel posits as an ontological reality pertaining to the very being of God as spirit, who is subject to "death" in the divine nature. This occurs internal to a process of dialectical reconciliation in the very life of God, which is accomplished in the resurrection, wherein God as spirit is revealed to be and reaches self-actualization as love. Hegel, *Lectures on the Philosophy of Religion*, "The Consummate Religion," 326–27: "'God himself is dead,' it says in a Lutheran hymn, expressing an awareness that the human, the finite, the fragile, the weak, the negative are themselves a moment of the divine, that they are within God himself, that finitude, negativity, otherness are not outside of God and do not, as otherness, hinder unity with God. Otherness, the negative, is known to be a moment of the divine nature itself. This involves the highest idea of spirit [...] this is the explication of reconciliation: that God is reconciled with the world, that even the human is not something alien to him, but rather that this otherness, this self-distinguishing [of the divine nature through diremption], finitude as it is expressed, is a moment in God himself..." On historical aspects of the communication of idioms in the Tübingen school, see also Kasper, *The Absolute in History*, 459–65.

on the part of the deity of the possibilities of identification through univocal assumption of finite into infinite. The Church fathers typically employ the communication of idioms to attribute properties of each of Christ's natures to the one subject and person of the Word made human, but they do not attribute these properties of natures directly to one another. We may say, for example, that the child in the cave created the stars, and the God who is all-powerful suffers personally on the cross. These are true expressions. In keeping with the patristic heritage of the communication of idioms, however we may not say that the eternity of God—God in his nature and deity—becomes temporal by free, redemptive self-identification with the finite, or that the life of God is itself subject to death on Good Friday so that something in atheism is philosophically true in a dialectically qualified but nevertheless real way, for a moment in time.[43] Hegel then reformulates the use of the communication of idioms so that the human properties of Christ can be attributed to the divine nature, which is understandable if the divine nature is characterized primarily in terms of a divine reason that is free to explore its own internal development through finite becoming within history. Even if Hegel's unique form of kenotic modern Christology is problematic, it is true that he is attempting to discern ways that divine freedom is manifest in and through the culture of Christianity and the symbols of the New Testament, especially in the ontology of the Incarnation and crucifixion.

Aquinas provides us with an alternative vision of God's freedom in history that is more apophatic and eschatological. On his view, there is no redemptive identification of the divine and human. God is free in his love to become human, but when he does so, he remains truly and unchangeably the transcendent God even as he subsists truly and personally as one who is genuinely human. The two natures of the Lord and his two activities as God and man, respectively,

43. Hegel, *Lectures on the Philosophy of Religion*, 327–28: "It is said, 'Christ has died for all.' This is not a single act but the eternal divine history. It is a moment in the nature of God himself. It has taken place in God himself."

remain always distinct, even if also inseparable. This means that the Son expresses himself personally as Son and Lord by means of his human nature and its states. All that he does and suffers as one who is human like us is genuinely filial. It is indicative of his personal relation to the Father and to the Spirit. It also is indicative of the condescending love of God, a divine love fully present in him as Lord, even while he is fully human like us. However, the human actions and gestures of the Son are not univocally indicative of his divine nature or divine love as such. His human love indicates his divine love by similitude but is not identical with it formally or essentially, as if the Incarnation should mandate that the human actions of Christ should be ascribed directly to his divine actions.

CONCLUSION: ESCHATOLOGICAL CONSEQUENCES OF A DYOTHELETIST THEOLOGY OF THE CROSS

There are eschatological consequences that stem from the acknowledgment of this irreducibility. On Aquinas's account, who God is as Trinity immanently is indeed revealed to us in the crucifixion. In Christ crucified, we may come to know the Father, the Son, and the Spirit in faith by a form of knowledge that is both interpersonal and veridically propositional. We can say things that are true about the Trinity that correspond to what God is in himself, and we can know and love the persons of God in themselves by faith. Nevertheless, God also remains in many respects concealed and hidden from us in this life, even as we await a perfect knowledge of him in the eschatological life that is to come. One may, for example, wish to affirm that the unique revelation of God as Trinity made available to us in the crucifixion provides the ultimate and most perfect knowledge of God made available to human beings within the sphere of history. Indeed, Christians must confess that the human life, death, and resurrection of Christ are the privileged locus in which we are given truly to know God in himself, as Trinity. However, the eschatological reserve remains. In this life, "our knowledge is imperfect," as St. Paul reminds the Christian community at Corinth (1 Cor. 13:9). Even if we do know the Triune God in himself in faith and in the most perfect way possible in this life, we do not know the Triune God in the most perfect way possible as such since the grace of faith is itself ordered toward a yet more perfect vision of God in the life to come. "For now we see in a mirror dimly, but then face to face" (1 Cor. 13:12). The revelation of God in our human flesh is oriented toward a more perfect and immediate knowledge of God in himself, made possible by the beatific vision.

Second, then, as we noted above, if the natures are distinct and the human nature of the Son indicates to us truly but obliquely who God is as Trinity, then his human nature is not indicative univocally of his divine life. From what we have just stated about the eschatological horizon of faith, it would seem to follow that our attempts to indicate the divinity of Christ univocally by appeal to his human states and modes of action run the risk of problematically anticipating the eschatological consummation of knowledge. A certain kind of kenotic Christology seeks to immanentize God but, in so doing, may construe God's deity in an anthropomorphic fashion by appeal to the human traits of Christ. In doing so, it also can potentially turn the consideration of Christology away from its true final end: the union with God in the life to come. God's hominization is meant to lead human beings to their divinization by union with God in vision. This true teleological orientation of the Incarnation and cross of the Lord can be obscured if we begin to imagine that the purpose of the Incarnation and the crucifixion is to effectuate a development in the ontological nature of God or the relationships of the Trinitarian persons. In this latter case, the final purpose of the Incarnation and cross risks to become God's diremptive history of being with us rather than our being with God, through the reception of eternal life. A Christology of the two natures, however, reminds us that the mystery of God is not perfected or achieved within the immanent frame of human history, through a diremptive or developmental assimilation of the divine nature to our human mode of being. The two natures interpretation of Christ underscores that our future in God has been initiated in the paschal mystery and in the life of the Church of Christ and the Spirit. However, it has yet to make its plenary appearance. Jesus' theandric actions (the concrete *analogia entis*) now stand as a promise of eternal life beyond the horizon of temporal history and indicate a more plenary knowledge of God in the life to come. Jesus' human suffering and death do unveil already in this life the inner mystery of the Trinity, Father, Son, and Holy Spirit. However, the New Testament's corresponding teaching on the eschatological consummation of our knowledge of the Trinity also acts as a critique of the theological tendency toward univocal Christology, whether in the Balthasarian or Hegelian form, one that would depict the divine nature in overly human terms. In this respect, Aquinas's balanced account of the two natures of Christ invites us to rethink anew (in a perennially coherent way across time) the traditional confession of the faith: that God became truly human while remaining truly God, and that he did so that we might be united to the mystery of God in himself. The final destiny of human beings is initiated in God's human history with us, but it is consummated in eternal life by participation in the very mystery of the Trinitarian God.

16

The Universal Mediation of Christ and Non-Christian Religions

The modern magisterium of the Catholic Church, particularly at the Second Vatican Council, articulated in tandem two fundamentally interdependent principles, both of Biblical origin. First, Christ is the unique universal mediator of salvation for the entire human race (and with this, all salvation occurs through membership in the Catholic Church or by being ordered toward it).[1] Second, because Christ died for all human beings and does offer the possibility of salvation to all members of the human race, the practices and beliefs of non-Christian religions may contain elements of truth that the Holy Spirit may make use of for the purposes of the saving work of God in history.[2] Note the twofold conditional character of this second statement. There may be elements of truth, and God may employ them. In documents such as *Redemptoris Missio* and *Dominus Jesus*, the reflection on *Nostra Aetate* has been refined.[3] The

---

Originally published in *Nova et Vetera* (English edition) 14, no. 1 (2016): 177–98. An earlier version of this chapter was presented at the plenary session of the Pontifical Academy of St. Thomas Aquinas, Rome, June 19–21, 2015.

1. Second Vatican Council, *Lumen Gentium* (hereafter *LG*), §14–16.
2. *GS* §§22 and 45; Second Vatican Council, *Nostra Aetate*, §2.
3. John Paul II, *Redemptoris Missio* (hereafter *RM*), §§28–30, 55–57; Congregation for the Doctrine of the Faith (hereafter CDF), *Dominus Jesus* (hereafter *DJ*), §4.

sacred writings of other religious traditions are not to be considered inspired in the profound theological sense of the term.[4] Their rites are not sacramental (instrumental *ex opere operato* causes of grace).[5] Nor are their beliefs to be confused with the grace of supernatural faith.[6] Such beliefs and practices may contain important elements of error or superstition and may harm or delude the human person.[7] At the same time, some human religious traditions do contain profound elements of the truth and reflect, in many cases, the depths of the human search for God.[8] The Holy Spirit may work through elements of these traditions—including in their collective and historical nature—so as to communicate hidden forms of invitation to, or even habitual participation in, the grace of Christ.[9] Here we find something akin to a highly qualified version of sacramental occasionalism: God may, when he wishes, according to his wisdom and providence, make use of elements of the non-Christian religious traditions either to initiate, or even progressively to effectuate, the salvation of human beings who are not baptized and are not visible members of the Catholic Church.[10] The teaching of Thomas Aquinas regarding the headship or capital grace of Christ offers resources for thinking about this contemporary theological problem.

4. *RM*, §36; *DJ*, §8.

5. *DJ*, §21

6. *DJ*, §7.

7. *RM*, §55; *DJ*, §§8 and 21: "it cannot be overlooked that other rituals, insofar as they depend on superstitions or other errors (cf. 1 Cor 10:20–21), constitute an obstacle to salvation."

8. *RM*, §28–29; *DJ*, §§2 and 14.

9. *RM*, §28; *DJ*, §12.

10. See Benoit-Dominique de la Soujeole, "Etre ordonné à l'unique Eglise du Christ: L'ecclésialité des communautés non chrétiennes à partir des données oecuméniques," *Revue Thomiste* (2002): 5–41, in which he argues (at 33–37) that authentic truths and ethical practices embodied in the cultural forms of other religions may indeed be used in an "occasionalist" fashion by God's providence. God may employ them *when He wills* as stable natural dispositions to the operation of and cooperation with grace. Consequently, they may be sign-*expressions* of persons who are motivated by grace, without in any way being *ex opere operato instruments* of the supernatural order. The latter order is "mediated" instrumentally uniquely through Christ's sacred humanity, the sacraments, and through the mystery of the Church.

I would like here briefly to reflect on three elements: (I) the capital grace of Christ as it pertains to our human salvation, (II) the various ways, according to Aquinas, that all human beings are potentially receptive to the work of grace in virtue of their intrinsically religious nature, and (III) the qualifications that are in order when considering the effective work of grace present outside the visible economy of the Catholic Church and her sacramental life.

THE CAPITAL GRACE OF CHRIST

Aquinas famously considers the grace of Christ according to a tripartite distinction.[11] First, it is a "grace" for the individual human nature of Jesus that it should be the human nature of the Word Incarnate. This grace of the hypostatic union (or *grace of union*) is proper to Christ alone because he alone is God made man, the eternal Word subsisting in a human nature. Second, the *habitual grace* in Christ is that created grace that is present in his human soul, particularly manifest in his spiritual faculties of intellect and will, resulting in the plenary illumination of his human mind with supernatural wisdom and the influx of a plenitude of charity in his human heart.[12] By extension, Christ possesses as man the plenitude of the infused virtues and the gifts of the Holy Spirit.[13] Third, there is the *capital grace* of Christ, that of his headship, by which he communicates his grace to the entire Church, to all those who partake of his grace visibly or invisibly. Aquinas underscores that this grace is not ontologically or essentially distinct from the habitual grace of Christ but is distinguished only logically or notionally.[14] This point

---

11. Aquinas, *Super Ioan.* 2, lec. 6: "There is in Christ a three-fold grace: the grace of union (*gratia unionis*), the grace that is proper to him as distinct person, which is a habitual grace (*gratia habitualis*), and last of all, his grace as Head [of the Church] (*gratia capitis*), which is that of his grace of influence [upon others]. Each of these graces, Christ receives without measure." This is my own translation from no. 544 in *S. Thomae Aquinatis Super Evangelium S. Ioannis Lectura*, ed. R. Cai, 5th ed. (Turin/Rome: Marietti, 1952).

12. *ST* III, q. 7, a. 1.

13. *ST* III, q. 7, aa. 11–12.

14. *ST* III, q. 8, aa. 1 and 5.

is significant. The capital grace of Christ is his sanctifying grace *just insofar as it is shared with other members of the human race.* All who are given any participation in the life of God whatsoever participate in some way in the habitual grace of the Lord, who possesses this grace as the source or principle from which all human beings derive their salvation.

Here, we should make four subjacent points that are of essential importance. First, according to Aquinas, Jesus possesses a unique plenitude of habitual grace and is the head of the Church fundamentally due to the ontological reality of the hypostatic union.[15] As Jean-Pierre Torrell has observed, St. Thomas purposefully opposed himself to a common opinion held at his time (by Alexander of Hales, among others), according to which the habitual grace of Christ given to his individual human nature should serve as an ontological disposition to the hypostatic union.[16] It would be as if his humanity needed first to be proportioned by a grace *of the kind other human beings receive* so as to be capable of being united to the Word. Aquinas perceives there to be a relation between this idea and the *homo assumptus* Christologies that he labels quite strikingly as "Nestorian" in kind. These are theories of the hypostatic union derivative from the first theory of hypostatic union found in the Lombard. According to this theory, the human being Jesus is a man united to the Word by virtue of a habitual relation.[17] In fact, Alexander goes so far as to speak of two hypostases or concrete substances, the man assumed and the Word assuming. They are united in one person (*persona*), but this union occurs by the disposition of the habitual grace that

15. *ST* III, q. 7, aa. 1 and 13.

16. Alexander of Hales, *Glossa Alex* 3.7.27 (L), in *Magistri Alexandri de Hales Glossa in Quatuor Libros Sententiarum Petri Lombardi,* ed. PP. Collegii S. Bonaventurae, 4 vols. (Florence: Quaracchi, 1960). See Walter H. Principe, *Alexander of Hales' Theology of the Hypostatic Union* (Toronto: Pontifical Institute of Mediaeval Studies, 1967), 163–65 and 171–73. Philip the Chancellor holds this view even more overtly in *De Incarn.* 2.19; see Walter H. Principe, *Philip the Chancellor's Theology of the Hypostatic Union* (Toronto: Pontifical Institute of Mediaeval Studies, 1975), 116–17.

17. *ST* III, q. 2, a. 6. The teaching of Aquinas on this matter has also recently been reexamined quite helpfully by Torrell in *Le Verbe Incarné,* Appendix II, 297–339.

exists in the human nature of Christ.[18] The "person" in question is one who is constituted by a habitual relation between the Word acting upon the *suppositum* of the humanity and the humanity being illumined and inspired by the grace of the Word. Aquinas is concerned rightly that this form of union (based on a relation, and therefore accidental rather than substantial) cannot be understood as specifically distinct in kind from that which we might find in the saints, created human persons who receive habitual grace like Christ himself, but to a lesser degree. His reflection is of a striking pertinence since one finds positions analogous to the one he criticizes in contemporary theorists of religious pluralism. Often, such thinkers perceive in Jesus of Nazareth a figure of moral perfection, like other religious founders, differentiated from them more according to a degree of enlightenment (or "grace" equivocally speaking) than due to a distinction of personal identity insofar as Jesus alone is the God-man.[19] Aquinas posits, by contrast, then, that the human nature we possess does not require any grace to proportion it to personal union with the Word but is naturally open to the possibility of the Incarnation by virtue of our spiritual nature.[20] In principle, God could become incarnate in any individual human nature. The humanity of Christ therefore needs no dispositive habitual grace in order to make the hypostatic union possible. Indeed, no such grace would suffice for this purpose! No habitual grace, however intensive, could adequately dispose the created human nature in such a way that it could effectively receive the infinite, uncreated gift of the hypostatic union. Instead, the order must be inverted in order to be properly understood. *Because* Christ is the Word made flesh—God who subsists in

---

18. Principe, *Alexander of Hales' Theology of the Hypostatic Union*, 123. Principe shows how Alexander can consider the human nature of Christ to be a distinct hypostasis while not having a unique personhood, since the latter is a characteristic that the assumed humanity acquires from the divine hypostasis.

19. For prominent examples, see Schleiermacher, *Der christliche Glaube*, 2:385–424 (§94–99); and Jacques Dupuis, *Toward a Christian Theology of Religious Pluralism* (Maryknoll, NY: Orbis, 1997), 270–71, where the influence of Schleiermacher is apparent.

20. *SCG* IV, ch. 41, no. 13.

a human nature composed of body and soul—*therefore*, he possesses the plenitude of habitual grace as a proportionate *effect*.[21] God incarnate fittingly possesses the perfection of grace in himself *as man* due precisely to the fact that his humanity is the humanity of God. In turn, it is this grace that he can share with us as the head of the Church. Here, we rejoin the soteriological principle of Athanasius that Aquinas was quite familiar with. Christ alone, among all men, is the mediator of salvation because Christ alone is truly God. Since God has united himself to our human nature in Christ, we are assured the possibility of being united to God by grace.[22]

A second point concerns the relation of the habitual grace of Christ to atonement, which is accomplished especially by virtue of Christ's obedient suffering even unto death by way of crucifixion. When Aquinas considers the principles of the atonement (*satisfactio*) in article 2 of question 48 of the *tertia pars* of the *Summa*, it is interesting to note that he interprets Anselm's teaching in the *Cur Deus homo* in light of the mystery of Christ's capital grace. Aquinas gives three reasons that Christ's passion is meritorious of our salvation: first, due to the plenitude of charity by which he obeys the Father in our stead; second, due to the infinite dignity of the person who suffers; and third, due to the intensity of his suffering. Some commentators emphasize the second of these reasons as the essential reason for our salvation. Christ's merits of love and obedience are infinite in kind due to the fact that he is God.[23] Other commentators emphasize the first reason—Christ's habitual grace of charity is the formal principle of our salvation. [24]

---

21. *ST* III, q. 2, a. 10; q. 6, a. 6; q. 7, a. 13.

22. *SCG* IV, ch. 54, no. 2.

23. See, for example, Garrigou-Lagrange, *Christ the Savior*, 577–88; Jean-Hervé Nicolas, *Synthèse Dogmatique; de la Trinité à la Trinité* (Fribourg and Paris: Éditions universitaires Fribourg and Éditions Beauchesne, 1991), 363–66, 511–12, and 547–48. However, both Garrigou-Lagrange and Nicolas maintain the traditional Thomist view that habitual sanctifying grace in the human soul of Christ stems necessarily from the mystery of the hypostatic union.

24. See, for example, Torrell, *Le Verbe Incarné*, Appendix II, 396–409.

A balanced interpretation should insist on both principles but in a given order.[25] The Son of God crucified acts "formally," or essentially, as mediator of our salvation as man by virtue of his human obedience and love, which he "substitutes" for our actions of gracelessness and disobedience. Just because this is the case, we must say that the habitual grace of Christ (and particularly his actions of charity or love) is the formal principle by which he as man atones universally for all sins of the human race. However, this human action is rooted in the *person* who acts and whose dignity is infinite since the person is God the Word. This principle is not formal, but foundational, or hypostatic. Fundamentally, the subject who acts humanly to save us is God, and so his actions and sufferings are of a mysterious, infinite worth or dignity.[26]

Aquinas sometimes casts this mystery in terms of the *virtus divinitatis* of Christ. Because Christ is the Lord, his human self-offering is unique as an offering of reparation for human sin. Christ has the *power as the Lord incarnate* to communicate the fruits of his passion to all human beings.[27] Here, we see what Aquinas calls the *effective* dimension of Christ's saving mediation.[28] Christ as man is able to communicate effectively to all the members of the mystical body, the Church, the grace by which they might be conformed progressively from within to his Paschal mystery. He does this principally as God, of course, insofar as he is the author of grace with the Father and the

25. See in this respect the balanced analysis of Domingo Bañez, *Tertia partis divi Thomae Aquinatis commentaria*, q. 1, a. 2, nos. 16–27, in *Comentarios ineditos a la tercera parte de Santo Tomas*, vol. I, *De Verbo Incarnato (qq. 1–42)*, ed. V. Beltran de Heredia (Salamanca: Biblioteca de Teologos Españoles, 1951).

26. *ST* I, q. 48, a. 2, obj. 3, ad 3: "Christ did not suffer in His Godhead, but in His flesh. . .[However,] the dignity of Christ's flesh is not to be estimated solely from the nature of flesh, but also from the Person assuming it—namely, inasmuch as it was God's flesh, the result of which was that it was of infinite worth."

27. *ST* III, q. 49, a. 1, ad 2: "Passio Christi, licet sit corporalis, sortitur tamen quondam spiritualem virtutem ex divinitate, cuius caro ei unita est instrumentum. Secundum quam quidem virtutem passio Christi est causa remissionis peccatorum." This Latin text is from *Summa Theologiae* (Torino: Edizioni San Paulo, 1988). See also *ST* III, q. 48, a. 6, ad 2; and q. 56, a. 1, ad 3.

28. *ST* III, q. 48, a. 6.

Holy Spirit. However, he also does so instrumentally as man since the sacred humanity of the Word is the conjoined instrument of his divinity. The Lord wishes, in his human reason and will, to give grace to the world in accord with his sacred will as God, which he shares in with the Father and the Holy Spirit.

We may note two conclusions of contemporary significance that each derive from this last point. First, any work of grace that occurs within salvation history and that derives from the Holy Trinity is also a work of the man Jesus. When the Holy Spirit gives grace previous to the time of the Incarnation, this grace is given in view of the merits of Christ crucified.[29] When the Holy Spirit gives grace subsequent to the age of the Incarnation, this is always mediated instrumentally (according to Aquinas) through the human mind and heart of the incarnate Lord.[30] Second, the theory of the *virtus divinitatis* offers at least one profoundly reasonable way to respond to the famous objection of Gotthold Lessing: how can the contingent singular life of one figure in history (to whom we have no empirical access) be the basis for a universal science of explanatory knowledge and moral behavior that affects the whole human race?[31] Well, this is possible because that person alone is God, who is the transcendent universal cause of all reality and who, *by virtue of the divine power that resides within him*, is able not only to merit salvation for the whole human race *but also to communicate this grace of salvation to all effectively*, not

29. *ST* II-II, q. 2, a. 7; *ST* III, q. 26, a. 1, ad 2; q. 61, a. 3.

30. *ST* III, q. 22, a. 5; q. 26, aa. 1–2.

31. Lessing, "On the Proof of the Spirit and of Power," in *Lessing's Theological Writings*, 53–54: "If no historical truth can be demonstrated, then nothing can be demonstrated by means of historical truths. That is: *accidental* [i.e., contingent] *truths of history can never become the proof of necessary truths of reason*. It is said: 'The Christ of whom on historical grounds you must allow that he raised the dead, that he himself rose from the dead, said himself that God has a Son of the same essence as himself and that he is this Son.' This would be excellent! If only it were not the case that it is not more than historically certain that Christ said this. If you press me still further and say: 'Oh yes! this is more than historically certain. For it is asserted by inspired historians who cannot make a mistake.' But, unfortunately, that also is only historically certain, that these historians were inspired and could not err. That, then, is the ugly, broad ditch which I cannot get across, however often and however earnestly I have tried to make the leap."

only by virtue of his divinity, but also by virtue of his conjoined humanity.[32]

THE RELIGIOUS DISPOSITIONS
OF THE HUMAN PERSON

How does the capital grace of Christ come to non-Christian persons? In the second part of this chapter, let me simply note some principles offered by Aquinas.

Implicit Faith

Aquinas is well aware of the problem of salvation for non-baptized persons. His theology of the non-baptized Jews of the Old Testament serves as primary evidence of his belief that non-Christians can be saved and that their salvation orders them in various ways toward the mystery of Christ.[33] Here, the concept of *implicit faith* plays a central role. Those in the ancient covenant of Israel prior to the time of Christ who believed explicitly in the God of Israel by supernatural faith were oriented implicitly toward the mystery of the Lord incarnate as the culminating work of the God of Israel in history.[34] Aquinas extends this same line of thinking to those "holy pagans" mentioned in Heb. 11, who are given as exemplars of faith from former times: Abel, Enoch, Noah, and Rahab.[35] Interestingly, Heb. 11:6 states that "without faith it is impossible to please [God]. For whoever would draw near to God must believe that he exists and that he rewards those who seek him". Salvation comes by way of supernatural faith alone, but that supernatural faith, Aquinas notes, may be present in those who believe that God exists and who expect good to come from his universal providence.[36] There is clear-

---

32. See the argument to this effect in *ST* III, q. 48, a. 6, and q. 56, a.1, ad 3.
33. *ST* I-II, q. 100, a. 12; q. 102, a. 2.
34. *ST* II-II, q. 2, aa. 7–8.
35. *Super Heb.* 11, lec. 2; from *Commentary on the Epistle to the Hebrews*, trans. C. Baer (South Bend, IN: St. Augustine's Press, 2006), esp. nos. 575–79.
36. *Super Heb.* 11, lec. 2, esp. no. 576.

ly an overlap here with Aquinas's treatment of the *praeambula fidei*: there are basic truths of faith that may also be grasped in another way by natural reason.[37] The knowledge that there exists some kind of unitary transcendent cause of reality and that there exists some kind of universal providence is not something wholly inaccessible to human beings.[38] Aquinas thinks that natural knowledge of God is available to all ordinary people in an imperfect way.[39] Indeed, he even thinks this knowledge is available to children who attain the age of reason and that grace is offered to children who are aware of God even outside of the realm of sacramental baptism, grace that they can resist or refuse, as well as accept.[40] Inchoate stirrings of supernatural faith, then, *can* be at work in and through the imperfect religious perceptions of human beings. We find implicit faith in at least some non-Christians.

Aquinas gives several examples of this idea in his writings. One pertains to his treatment of the Magi discussed in Matthew 2:1–12. In his commentary on the *Gospel of Matthew*, Aquinas claims that these pagan sages did, in fact, possess the "zeal of faith" and that, when they found Christ, they adored him with proper worship, thus prefiguring the Gentile nations that eventually would be adopted by God into the new covenant of grace.[41]

A second example pertains to the Sybil, the supposed Roman prophecies of the birth of Christ, which were commonly taken to be authentic in the high middle-ages. What is striking about Aquinas's treatment of the question is that, although he does seem to prefer the theory of a prophetic inspiration to account for the Sybil, he clearly does not distinguish it very radically from pre-Christian religious traditions in which there was no authentic revelation. In fact,

---

37. *Super Boetium De Trinitate*, q. 2, a. 1; from *Commentary on Boethius' De Trinitate*.
38. *SCG* III, ch. 94.
39. *SCG* III, ch. 38.
40. *ST* I-II, q. 89, a. 6: the terminology employed strongly suggests that Aquinas is referring to people who are born in original sin and not baptized, who have the possibility of receiving the grace of justification once they reach the age of reason.
41. See *In Matt.*, II, lec. 2 and 3. These are nos. 176–204 in *S. Thomae Aquinatis Super Evangelium S. Matthaei Lectura*.

Aquinas suggests that, insofar as Gentile peoples predicted that God would intervene in some way for their future benefit through an appointed mediator, there might exist within this vague and perhaps opaque human religious hope a deeper instinct of grace at work in ways hidden from the ordinary sight of men.

> Many of the gentiles received revelations of Christ, as is clear from their predictions. Thus we read (Job 19:25): "I know that my Redeemer lives." The Sibyl too foretold certain things about Christ, as Augustine states (*Contra Faust.* 3.15). Moreover, we read in the history of the Romans that at the time of Constantine Augustus and his mother, Irene, a tomb was discovered wherein lay a man on whose breast was a golden plate with the inscription: "Christ shall be born of a virgin, and in Him, I believe. O sun, during the lifetime of Irene and Constantine, thou shall see me again." If, however, some were saved without receiving any revelation, they were not saved without faith in a Mediator, for, though they did not believe in Him explicitly, they did, nevertheless, have implicit faith through believing in Divine providence, since they believed that God would deliver mankind in whatever way was pleasing to him, and according to the revelation of the Spirit to those who knew the truth, as stated in Job 35:11: "Who teaches us more than the beasts of the earth."[42]

A third example pertains to Cornelius, the Roman centurion, found in Acts 10:1–2, who clearly professed faith in Christ prior to his baptism by the apostles. In article 4 of question 69 of the *tertia pars* of the *Summa*, Aquinas considers the question of whether baptism is necessary for salvation and gives, as an objection, the observation that grace and infused virtues were communicated by God to Cornelius prior to his baptism. His response is that "man receives the forgiveness of sins before Baptism insofar as he has Baptism of desire, explicitly or implicitly; and yet when he actually receives Baptism, he receives a fuller remission, as to the remission of the entire punishment. So also, before Baptism, Cornelius and others like him receive grace and virtues through their faith in Christ and their desire for Baptism, implicit or explicit: but afterward, when baptized, they receive a yet greater fullness of grace and virtues." We should

---

42. *ST* II-II, q. 2, a. 7, ad 3.

note that the reflection is not qualified by a temporal consideration. Aquinas seemingly believes this kind of dynamic to be at work in the actual dispensation of the divine economy after the coming of Christ. There are non-baptized persons drawn to Christ imperfectly but truly who are implicitly animated by the supernatural grace of faith, hope, and charity, as well as infused virtues.

Natural Religious Inclinations

This is not to say that human religiosity is something *supernatural* as such for Aquinas. Rather, he treats the virtue of religion as a potential part of the virtue of justice and, therefore, as something pertaining to human nature.[43] Furthermore, our human nature is fallen and subject to vices as well as virtue. Consequently, any theological consideration of non-Christian religion has to be qualified carefully.

On the one hand, it is clear that there are fundamental natural inclinations of the human intellect and will toward God as the first truth and cause of reality and as the sovereign good.[44] The human intellect is structured so that it may naturally desire to know the primary cause of all that is, and the human will is likewise made for love of the universal good that is God.[45] The inclinations toward natural knowledge and love of the Creator, then, are latent capacities of the human person.[46] These are not eradicated by the consequences of original sin in the human person. They are, however, seemingly weakened greatly.[47] Aquinas says as much. It is difficult for fallen human beings to come to know God rightly in any sophisticated fashion by the use of unassisted natural reason, and if persons do come to do so, it is after a long time; they are few in number, and their doing so is admixed with error.[48] More poignantly, Aquinas states baldly that the fallen human being cannot love God above all things

---

43. *ST* II-II, q. 81, a. 5.
44. *ST* I-II, q. 94, a. 2.
45. *ST* I, q. 12, a. 1.
46. *SCG* III, ch. 37; *ST* I-II, q. 109, a. 3.
47. *ST* I-II, q. 85, aa. 1–3.
48. *ST* I, q. 1, a. 1.

naturally by his own powers, though this would have been possible prior to original sin. To assure genuine love of God (and therefore authentic worship of God) in the fallen world, the healing activity of grace is required.[49] It is clear that St. Thomas thinks that to affirm otherwise is overtly Pelagian, as it would suggest that the fallen human being can observe the commandments of the Decalogue by his own powers without the healing work of grace.[50]

Human nature is wounded, then, by ignorance and malice (selfishness) in regard to God, and unsurprisingly we see the admission of this present in Aquinas's treatment of the vices that afflict human religion: superstition, idolatry, and religious indifference.[51] The human being finds itself in a liminal state: a fundamentally religious being by nature, it is unable to heal itself of the plights that maim or fragment its best religious inclinations and leanings. So, if there is a true religious foundation in man from which or in which grace may act, it does do so in a humanity torn in many ways by error and moral compromise, and this enters into the very composition of the non-Christian religions themselves.

Aquinas gives concrete examples. He speaks of sacrifice as a practice that pertains to the natural law as a dimension of justice and atonement for human sin.[52] However, when speaking of examples of religious actions as "natural" in the treatise on religion, he gives the example of human sacrifice practiced among the ancient Romans![53] The example is not intended ironically. It is meant to illustrate poignantly that while religion is natural to man, all religious acts need not spring from the work of charity in the human person and can be vitiated by superstition or error. Analogously, Aquinas can identify good aspirations present in the midst of erroneous religious doctrines of other religions. He spends a great deal of space in Book 2 of the *Summa contra gentiles* arguing that the theory of reincarnation

49. *ST* I-II, q. 109, a. 3.
50. *ST* I-II, q. 109, aa. 4–5.
51. *ST* II-II, q. 92–95.
52. *ST* II-II, q. 85, a. 1.
53. *ST* II-II, q. 82, a. 1. See also q. 81, a. 1.

is metaphysically incoherent and unreasonable.[54] However, he also notes that the theory, which he knows to be common in pre-Christian religion, hints opaquely at a deep truth: the need for reunion of soul and body. Reincarnation is not a feasible theory of human eschatology, but by its insistence on the fitting reconciliation of the separated soul with a physical body, it points negatively and obliquely toward the truth of the resurrection.[55] Only when the latter mystery is revealed can the truth and error of the pre-Christian theory be adequately discerned.

Sacraments of the Natural Law

Finally, we should say a word about the sacraments of the natural law. Aquinas distinguishes the sacraments of the Old Law from those of the New. The rites of the Torah are instituted by divine inspiration, but they do not communicate grace *ex opere operato*.[56] Rather, they are signs or expressions of supernatural faith present in their ancient Hebrew practitioners, and they signify a reality that is to come: the unique atoning sacrifice of Christ.[57] The sacraments of the New Law, by contrast, signify the mystery of Christ but also effectuate what they signify as instrumental causes of grace.[58] They communicate effectively the capital grace of Christ (or he

54. SCG II, ch. 83.

55. *Super I Cor.* 15, lec. 2: "If the resurrection of the body is denied, it is not easy, yea it is difficult, to sustain the immortality of the soul. For it is clear that the soul is naturally united to the body and is departed from it, contrary to its nature and *per accidens*. Hence the soul devoid of its body is imperfect, as long as it is without the body. But it is impossible that what is natural and *per se* be finite and, as it were, nothing; and that which is against nature and *per accidens* be infinite, if the soul endures without the body. And so, the Platonists positing immortality, posited re-incorporation, although this is heretical. Therefore, if the dead do not rise, we will be confident only in this life. In another way, because it is clear that man naturally desires his own salvation; but the soul, since it is part of man's body, is not an entire man, and my soul is not I; hence, although the soul obtains salvation in another life, nevertheless, not I or any man. Furthermore, since man naturally desires salvation even of the body, a natural desire would be frustrated" (trans. D. Keating, unpublished manuscript; from *In Omnes St. Pauli Apostoli Epistolas Commentaria*, vols. 1 and 2 (Turin: Marietti, 1929), no. 924).

56. *ST* III, q. 62, a. 6.

57. *ST* I-II, q. 101, a. 2.

58. *ST* III, q. 62, aa. 1–5.

communicates his grace through them) to all who partake of them with a genuine good will.

Aquinas needs to posit a third category, however: sacraments of the natural law.[59] Why so? In fact, this category is necessary in particular to talk about the religion of the patriarchs as well as that of the "holy pagans" mentioned above: Abel, Noah, and so on, who clearly perform non-covenantal religious actions and do so in ways pleasing to God.

Aquinas thinks these are something both unlike and like the ancient rites of the Old Law. They are unlike them because they are not instituted by God and bear within them no guarantee of a relationship to God. Rather, they are the products of natural human culture. After all, it is natural to be religious, and so human beings generate external rites of various kinds. Even in cases where grace may be at work, then, the rites in question are conventional and man-made. However, while such sacraments are not causes of grace in any way, they may be the *outward expressions of the inward work of grace* in the human person.[60] They *can* be signs or indications of the grace of God present in the world, acting in and through the human inclinations of human beings, purifying them and elevating them. St. Thomas mentions overtly the possibility of charity at work in the religious actions of persons outside the visible covenant who have offered their lives to God in authentic worship.[61] He is probably thinking of people like Abel, mentioned in the Roman canon of the Mass.

Aquinas clearly thinks that all grace is ecclesiologically oriented. This is evident in his consideration of the effects of the grace of the

---

59. *In IV Sent.* d. 1, q. 2, a. 6, qc. 3, corp.; *ST* I-II, q. 103, a. 1.

60. *In IV Sent.* d. 1, q. 2, a. 6, qc. 3, corp.: ".". . .illa sacramenta legis naturae non erant ex praecepto divino obligantia, sed ex voto celebrabantur, secundum quod unicuique dictabat sua mens, ut fidem suam aliis exteriori signo profiteretur ad honorem Dei, *secundum quod habitus caritas inclinabat ad exteriores actus; et sic dicimus de caritate, quod sufficit motus interior*; quando autem tempus habet operandi, requiruntur etiam exteriores actus. Ita etiam quantum ad adultos in lege naturae sufficiebat sola fides, cum etiam modo sufficiat ei qui non ex contemptu sacramenta dimittit; sed ipsa fides, quando tempus habebatur, instigabat ut se aliquibus signis exterioribus demonstraret" (emphasis added; 1856 Parma edition).

61. *ST* I-II, q. 103, obj. 1, corp. and ad 1.

Eucharist. He says that the Eucharistic sacrifice ultimately effectuates the mystical body of Christ, the Church, as its *res tantum*, or most inward purpose.[62] Thus, anyone who receives any grace whatsoever is oriented implicitly toward the Eucharist as the one saving sacrifice of Christ present at the heart of the Church and her communion. All salvation takes place in the Church or as ordered toward visible membership in her, including in her sacramental communion.[63]

GRACE AND JUSTIFICATION OUTSIDE THE VISIBLE CATHOLIC CHURCH

The reflections we have made up to this point have sought to maintain in harmony two core teachings of the Catholic Church. First, Christ is the unique universal mediator of salvation, the One who died for all human beings. Second, then, in some mysterious way, all human beings are offered the real possibility of participation in the redemptive economy of salvation. The grace of Christ may address humanity in its natural religion dimension. However, the work of grace is only ever implicitly ecclesiological in kind and causes its participants to tend, in however indirect or hidden a fashion, toward inclusion in the one mystical body of Christ, the Catholic Church.

Here, then, we should also specify that this participation in Christ by those who are non-Catholics or non-Christians takes place only under certain conditions. It, therefore, has to be understood by reference to various theological qualifications that are significant.

Operative Actual Grace and Cooperative Justifying Grace

The explicit distinction between operative and cooperative grace has its origins in the mature work of St. Augustine, who fashioned the distinction in order to respond to the Pelagian controversy.[64]

---

62. *ST* III, q. 73, a. 3. See on this subject, Gilles Emery, "The Ecclesial Fruit of the Eucharist," *Nova et Vetera* (English edition) 2, no. 1 (2004): 43–60.

63. Consider the treatment of this subject by Charles Journet in *L'Église du Verbe Incarné*, vol. VI: *Essai de théologie de l'histoire du salut* (Paris: Saint Augustin, 2004).

64. See, for example, Augustine, *On Grace and Free Will*, ch. 33, trans. P. Holmes and

Augustine sought to underscore the unequivocally Pauline New Testament teaching that grace is at work in the human person prior to conversion and as a precondition for the possibility of conversion. Furthermore, this initial work of "operative" grace that precedes all human efforts or merits is oriented toward the justification of the human being, a subsequent effect of grace that, in turn, permits the active cooperation of the human being with God. Such cooperation is itself a gift, and so one must posit a subsequent effect of grace that follows from justification, one that is "cooperative" in kind. Operative grace that is prevenient (prior to justification) leads the recipient toward justification and to cooperative grace, a process of sanctification that is subsequent to justification.

This distinction between operative and cooperative effects of grace was a theological commonplace in medieval and early modern Catholic theology. Aquinas employs the distinction meaningfully in order to suggest the universality of *operative grace* since all human beings may be offered a participation in the mystery of redemption.[65] However, one need not infer from this that the operative help of grace must lead necessarily into the justification, sanctification, and salvation of all. On the contrary, as Aquinas makes clear, operative grace can be refused, and indeed may be much of the time.[66] Such resistance to grace compounds the guilt of the recipient. Consequently, while it may be the case that many are called, it does not follow that many or all are justified or glorified (Mt 22:14; Rom 8:30). This perspective on grace emphasizes both the reality of the universal offer of salvation and the real threat (and seeming reality) of eternal loss. Such was the commonly transmitted teaching in modern Roman Catholic theology prior to the Second Vatican Council.[67]

R. Wallis, in *Nicene and Post-Nicene Fathers*, vol. 5, ed. Philip Schaff (Buffalo, NY: Christian Literature Publishing Co., 1887).

65. *ST* I-II, q. 111, aa. 2–3.

66. On the resistance to grace, see especially *SCG* III, chs. 161–62; *Super Ioan.* 15, lec. 5 (Marietti ed., no. 2055).

67. See the articulation of this view offered by Charles Journet, for example, in *The Meaning of Grace*, trans. A. V. Littledale (Princeton, NJ: Scepter, 1996).

Nevertheless, influential theories regarding the theology of grace that arose in the mid-twentieth century sought to re-envisage the subject without overt reference to the Augustinian paradigm that had been dominant in traditional western theology: prevenient operative grace, justification, and the subsequent cooperative grace of sanctification. Without disregarding the important questions raised by Henri de Lubac concerning the natural desire for God and the subsequent re-envisaging of his hypothesis by Karl Rahner in his theology of the "supernatural-existential," it must be stated that both of these theologies and that of their analysts and critics turned the subject of the study of grace away from any overt consideration of the topic of operative and cooperative grace.[68] As a result, that classical Augustinian way of analyzing the work of God in history, which is of clear biblical origin, has been largely eclipsed. This has the following result: where one affirms that grace is at work universally in all of humanity, it is frequently presumed (following what are, in fact, contestable interpretations of Rahner) that the grace in question must result in the justification and salvation of the person or community in question. The effects of grace are conceived of in rather univocal, virtually ahistorical terms. Accordingly, the affirmation of the universal offer of grace has frequently become confused with a vague, implicit presumption of soteriological universalism. Or the inverse of the equation is believed: if it is stated that there may be persons who are not saved or that particular non-Catholic or non-Christian religious communities are at an objective disadvantage with regard to those who know Christ explicitly and receive the sacraments, then God does not offer those outside the Catholic Church any authentic possibility of salvation. Once there is no longer any sufficient distinction of the analogically diverse effects of grace and the economic ordering among them, a dialectic tends to emerge between Jansenism and universal salvation. This follows

68. Henri de Lubac, *Surnaturel: Études historiques* (Paris: Aubier, 1946); Karl Rahner, "Nature and Grace," in *Theological Investigations* vol. 4, 165–88.

almost necessarily from the *absence* in recent Catholic theology of any effective employment of the distinction between operative and cooperative grace, or of the distinction between grace that is offered prior to justification and that offered posterior to it.

Justification by Hope, Charity, and Repentance of Grave Sin.

Consideration of the issue of the distinct effects of grace has direct bearing on a second one: the nature of justification and the need for effective repentance of grave sin as a condition for the possibility of salvation. As each one knows, the traditional Catholic theology of justification insists on the ontological requirement not only of supernatural faith (which affects the human mind) but also of supernatural hope and charity, infused virtues that transform the human will or heart.[69] This Catholic dogma has clear precedents in the teaching of Aquinas, who treats justification itself as an *operative habitual* grace, something God does in us through a unilateral gift on his part (though not without our consent). This particular gift of justifying grace moves the will to detach from grave sin effectively and to turn toward God under the influence of the infused habit of charity.[70] This is why justification is the proximate preparation for works of *cooperative grace*: it disposes the heart supernaturally to live habitually in friendship with God and to keep the commandments of Christ by the grace of charity (Jn 14:15).[71]

Of course, Aquinas recognizes that many baptized Christians sin gravely after Baptism and that they consequently forfeit the state of justification by destroying in themselves the habit of supernatural charity (and possibly that of hope or faith as well). The restoration of the state of grace normally can take place for any baptized Christian, then, only by recourse to the valid reception of the sacrament of

---

69. *CCC* 1987–1995; Council of Trent, Degree on Justification (1547): "Justification...is not only the remission of sins but the sanctification and renewal of the interior man through the voluntary reception of grace and of the gifts," Denzinger no. 1528.

70. *ST* I-II, q. 113, prologue and aa. 1–6.

71. *ST* I-II, q. 114, prologue.

reconciliation (confession).[72] This is the normative teaching not only of the medieval theologians but also of the Council of Trent and the modern magisterium of the Catholic Church.[73] Aquinas does consider the real possibility of repentance for sins that is merely intentional or internal and certainly affirms the possibility of making (by consent to the work of grace) a "perfect act of contrition" outside of the sacrament of confession, especially when the latter is not available.[74] However, the Catholic Church traditionally underscores that the person who understands the faith of the Church rightly must have recourse to the sacrament of confession at such time as he or she is able, even in the wake of the attempt to make a perfect act of contrition outside of or apart from the sacrament.

The reason all of this is significant for our discussion is that it suggests that the movements of grace that take place in Christians who are not Catholic, in monotheists who are not Christian, or in religionists who are not monotheists must all be oriented in some way toward participation in the habit of infused charity *if they are to be justifying and saving works of grace*. And yet, these same individuals or communities of persons do not possess the objective mean of reconciliation that is the sacrament of reconciliation.[75] Consequently, according to the inexorable logic of a Catholic and truly biblical doctrine of justification and of salvation, such persons (to be justified and eventually saved) must be transformed inwardly in their human hearts by grace to the point of renouncing grave sin and of repenting effectively of their attachment to it.

The relationship between the theoretical beliefs and moral decisions of non-Catholics and non-Christians and their possible inward

---

72. *ST* III, q. 84, aa. 5–6.

73. *CCC* 1425–70; Council of Trent, Decree on the Sacrament of Penance (1551) (Denzinger, nos. 1667–1693).

74. *ST* III, q. 86, aa. 1, 2, and 6.

75. I am leaving to one side here the consideration of the Eastern Rite non-Catholic Churches. Their practice raises a separate set of theological questions, since they do practice sacramental confession and have a validly ordained episcopate. On this topic, see the helpful reflections of Charles Journet, *L'Église du Verbe Incarné*. Vol I: *La hiérarchie apostolique* (Paris: Saint Augustin, 1998), 1025–30.

state of grace remains somewhat opaque due to the limitations of our human observational knowledge. In addition, there are difficult theoretical questions that remain. Can a person be in a state of grace and yet at the same time (due to the consequences of invincible ignorance) remain in an objective state of gravely morally deformed conduct? It would seem not. Might they have some partial awareness, however, of their need for mercy from God, over and above their own limitations of understanding? Most certainly they might. Is it possible for a person who decidedly believes that Christ is not the Incarnate Word to pray truly (if imperfectly) to the living God and to love God truly above all things *by virtue of a supernatural infused virtue of faith*? Perhaps this is so. However, even if we find a way to answer some or all of these questions positively by appeal to the possibility of inspired adherence to truths about God *imperfectly grasped*, there still remains the fact that the intellectual and moral errors of the person who is not Catholic mitigate (sometimes severely) against the plenary reception of the salvation and grace of Christ. One may rightfully hope that God's grace might progressively triumph in the lives of non-Christian persons, in and through their lives of moral and religious seeking and in their confrontation with God in death. However, this hope should not be confused with the presumption of universalism. History offers sobering illustrations of what seem to be clear counter-alternatives to the free acceptance of the Gospel.

The Real Possibility of Eternal Loss and the Ordinary Means of Salvation

This leads us to a third and final consideration. The Catholic tradition rightly insists theologically that the "ordinary means of salvation" are to be found in the Catholic Church alone. As John Paul II wrote in 1990 in the encyclical *Redemptoris Missio*,

> although the Church gladly acknowledges whatever is true and holy in the religious traditions of Buddhism, Hinduism and Islam as a

reflection of that truth which enlightens all people, this does not lessen her duty and resolve to proclaim without fail Jesus Christ who is "the way, and the truth and the life"…. The fact that the followers of other religions can receive God's grace and be saved by Christ apart from the ordinary means which he has established does not thereby cancel the call to faith and baptism which God wills for all people. Indeed Christ himself "while expressly insisting on the need for faith and baptism, at the same time confirmed *the need for the Church*, into which people enter through Baptism as through a door" (*Lumen Gentium*, §14). Dialogue should be conducted and implemented with the conviction that *the Church is the ordinary means of salvation* and that *she alone* possesses the fullness of the means of salvation (c.f. The Second Vatican Council's *Unitatis Redintegratio*, §3).[76]

This viewpoint is not based on any form of triumphalism but on a realistic acceptance of the plenary truth of the Gospel as proclaimed within the context of the Catholic tradition. Fidelity to divine revelation requires that one assert that the objective truth of divine revelation in its most explicit mode and the rightly oriented practice of the sacramental life operate together as the best and most preeminent guarantors of salvation, those established by God himself. It is the revealed truth and sacramental life of Christ in the Catholic Church that serve as the most effective vehicles for the transmission of the grace of eternal salvation.

What follows from this is not a despair regarding the possibility of salvation for non-Catholic persons but a sober realization of the imperative of evangelization as the correlate to the affirmation of the universal work of God's operative grace. Such grace, due to the fact that it is present in all the world and does orient human beings toward Christ and the Church, is answered or completed by the proclamation of the Gospel.

Understood in this context, theologies of *apokatastasis* do little to assist the Church as she is immersed in the trials of a distinctively secular age. The claim or expectation that all might be saved can function in practice as a form of denial of the sociological condition

76. RM §55.

of the Church in the current epoch. Theologians may understandably wish to assert the inevitable acceptance of Christ that is going to occur in each person's life, either in hidden ways in this world (by way of the secret workings of the supernatural-existential dynamic of grace) or in an eschatological epiphany that is reserved to the next (in a theology of Christ's descent into hell that serves by a kind of seeming inevitability to eventually conform all to Christ). Such universalism is attractive and even triumphalistic. However, it also poses great risks. Yes, the error of Jansenism—with its latent despair of the salvation of non-Catholics—is seemingly avoided, but that does not mean that despair as such has been evaded. Despair can also manifest itself under its contrary—that is to say, in a presumption that is spiritually complacent and that refuses (out of latent resignation) to confront with clarity the objective configurations of reality.

On the one hand, theologies of *apokatastasis* seemingly refuse to acknowledge the real possibility of enduring human tragedy and the fact that there are perennial consequences to human acts of personal evil. That is to say, that there is eternal loss. Instead, acts of personal evil are explained against the backdrop of a more determinate "fundamental option" for the good or in light of the eventual determination of God eschatologically to overcome each human reaction against the good. Accordingly, if salvation is lacking, this is seen to be primarily due to the absence of an initiative on the part of God (whose innocence now deserves to be questioned) and not due fundamentally to the responsibility of the spiritual creature. On the other hand, such theologies also function as a numbing salve on the conscience of the Church, one that lulls ecclesial members into resignation or complacency in the face of a non-Christian world. Our defeat in the face of the progress of secularization can be accepted with equanimity, given what we know about the reality of the eschaton. Behind the mask of soteriological universalism, we find the hidden face of our own spiritual *acedia*.

Hope is the virtue that guides the soul to persevere with true confidence in God, even in the midst of adversities, and to count on the promised assistance of the grace of God in all circumstances. To understand and cultivate this virtue, however, requires an adequate sense of real risk and of real responsibility. Our own age, marked by the progress of religious ignorance, is one laden with real risks and with real possibilities. Hope requires that we live the Gospel in this age in such a way that we are willing to accept the full demands of the Catholic faith ourselves and to find ways to communicate clearly to others its plenary truth. Hope in the capacity of God's grace to save one's self requires a habitual recourse to the "ordinary means" of salvation instituted by Christ in the Church, including the sacraments of baptism, reconciliation, and communion. Hope in the capacity of God's grace to save others requires that one seeks not only to respond to, but also to inaugurate the hidden work of operative grace in them through evangelization, by way of the outward proclamation of the Catholic faith in its plenary ecclesial form. For, God "desires all men to be saved and to come to the knowledge of the truth" (1 Tim 2:4). "But how are men to call upon him in whom they have not believed? And how are they to believe in him of whom they have never heard? And how are they to hear without a preacher?" (Rom. 10:14).

CONCLUSION

How may we conclude? What is the contribution of Aquinas's theology to the modern problem regarding Christ and non-Christian religions? We may summarize by thinking about the relationship of grace and nature from a twofold viewpoint. First, natural religious instincts do not suffice. Christ alone is the savior of our human religiosity, for he alone is God made man and possesses, accordingly, the fontal principle of sanctifying grace for the human race. This grace is the source of redemption of the religious dimension of the human person, and it is within the sphere of the Catholic Church that we find religion healed and elevated into its most noble and true form. Against all contemporary temptations to a neo-Pelagianism that would see in every religious instinct of man an intrinsic avenue toward salvation, we should say that natural religious activity outside of the sphere of the grace of Christ not only is not intrinsically salvific but can enter readily into the world of superstition and irrational fanaticism. The biblical and Christological critique of human religion should be deeper than that of secular liberalism.

On the other hand, the grace of Christ is universal in horizon. Against the modern error of Jansenism, classical Thomism and the modern magisterium affirm that the grace of God may be at work in the natural, social, and historical experiences of non-Christian humanity. God can indeed work graciously in more or less discreet ways, in and through the natural religious structures of human persons and societies. We see this most unambiguously when non-Christians seeking God find avenues from within their own religious traditions by which they arrive at the doorstep of the Church.

What results from this brief portrait is a complex vision. All salvation takes place from and through the mediation of Christ in his capital grace and from the unique atoning sacrifice of the Cross. Salvation has an ecclesiological character or horizon. Natural religious inclinations in human beings are not inimical to the work of salvation but integral to it. Other religious traditions can embody elements of profound truth in this regard, as well as serious falsehood.[77] We need to practice a careful discernment in the face of other religious traditions: one that is simultaneously philosophical, theological, and spiritual.[78] "By their fruits you will know them" (Mt 7:16). "We take

---

77. *DJ*, §14: "The Second Vatican Council, in fact, has stated that: 'the unique mediation of the Redeemer does not exclude, but rather gives rise to a manifold cooperation which is but a participation in this one source' (*Lumen Gentium*, §62). The content of this participated mediation should be explored more deeply, but must remain always consistent with the principle of Christ's unique mediation: 'Although participated forms of mediation of different kinds and degrees are not excluded, they acquire meaning and value *only* from Christ's own mediation, and they cannot be understood as parallel or complementary to his' (*RM*, §5). Hence, those solutions that propose a salvific action of God beyond the unique mediation of Christ would be contrary to Christian and Catholic faith."

78. See the helpful principles enunciated by the document of the International

captive every thought to make it obedient to Christ" (2 Cor 10:5). If we wish to follow these Dominical and Apostolic adages in the twenty-first century, we will profit greatly from recourse to the perennial wisdom of Thomas Aquinas.

Theological Commission, *Christianity and the World Religions* (Vatican City: Libreria Editrice Vaticana, 1997).

Bibliography

WORKS BY THOMAS AQUINAS

Compendium theologiae ad fratrem Reginaldum socium suum carissimum. Vol. 42 of *Sancti Thomae de Aquino opera omnia.* Leonine Edition. Rome: Editori di San Tommaso, 1979.

De ente et essentia. In *Opuscula Philosophica*, vol. 1. Edited by R. Spiazzi. Turin and Rome: Marietti, 1950.

De principiis naturae. In *Opuscula Philosophica.* Edited by R. Spiazzi. Rome: Marietti, 1954

De potentia Dei. Edited by P. M. Pession. In *Quaestiones disputatae*, vol. 2, edited by R. Spiazzi. Turin and Rome: Marietti, 1965.

De veritate. In *Sancti Thomae de Aquino opera omnia*, vol. 22. Leonine Edition. Rome: Editori di San Tommaso, 1975–76.

In Divinis Nominibus. Latin edition from *In Librum Beati Dionysii de Divinis Nominibus Expositio*, ed. C. Pera, Rome-Turin: Marietti, 1950.

In duodecim libros Metaphysicorum Aristotelis expositio. Edited by M. R. Cathala and R. M. Spiazzi. Turin and Rome: Marietti, 1964.

In Omnes St. Pauli Apostoli Epistolas Commentaria, vols. 1 and 2. Turin: Marietti, 1929.

Quaestiones disputatae de potentia Dei.

S. Thomae Aquinatis Super Evangelium S. Matthaei Lectura. Edited by R. Cai, 5th rev. ed. Turin/Rome: Marietti, 1951.

Scriptum super libros Sententiarum magistri Petri Lombardi episcopi Parisiensis (vols. 1–2), edited by P. Mandonnet (Paris: P. Lethielleux, 1929) and vols. 3–4, edited by M. Moos. Paris: P. Lethielleux, 1933–47.

Summa contra Gentiles. Vols. 13–15 of *Sancti Thomae Aquinatis opera omnia.* Leonine Edition. Rome: R. Garroni, 1918–30.

Summa theologiae. Vols. 4–12 of *Sancti Thomae Aquinatis opera omnia.* Leonine Edition. Rome: 1888–1906.

TRANSLATIONS OF WORKS BY THOMAS AQUINAS

Commentary on Aristotle's De Anima. Translated by K. Foster and S. Humphries. Notre Dame, Ind.: Dumb Ox Books, 1994.

Commentary on Aristotle's Metaphysics. Translated by J. P. Rowan. Notre Dame, Ind.: Dumb Ox Books, 1995.

Commentary on Boethius' De Trinitate. In *Thomas Aquinas: Faith, Reason and Theology,* translated by A. Maurer. Toronto: Pontifical Institute of Mediaeval Studies, 1987.

Commentary on the Book of Causes. Translated by V. Guagliardo, C. Hess, and R. Taylor. Washington, D.C.: The Catholic University of America Press, 1996.

Commentary on the Epistle to the Hebrews. Translated by C. Baer. South Bend, Ind.: St. Augustine's Press, 2006.

Commentary on the Nicomachean Ethics. Translated by C.I. Lintzinger. Chicago: Henry Regnery, 1964.

Commentary on the Gospel of St. John, vol. 2. Translated by J. Weisheipl. Albany, NY: Magi Press, 1980.

Commentary on the Gospel of St. John, vol. 2. Petersham, MA: St. Bede's Publications, 2000.

Commentary on St. Paul's First Letter to the Thessalonians and the Letter to the Philippians. Translated by F. R. Larcher and M. Duffy. Albany, NY: Magi, 1969.

Compendium of Theology, Translated by C. Vollert. St. Louis & London: Herder, 1947.

Cosmic Structure and the Knowledge of God: Thomas Aquinas' In Librum beati Dionysii de divinis nominibus expositio, Translation by H.C. Marsh. Ann Arbor, Mich.: UMI Diss., 1994.

Faith, Reason and Theology. Translated by A. Maurer. Toronto: PIMS, 1987

In Liber de Causis. Translated by Elizabeth Anne Collins-Smith. Austin, Tex.: UT-Austin Diss., 1991.

On the Power of God. Translated by English Dominican Province. Westminster, MD: Newman, 1952.

Summa contra Gentiles I. Translated by A. C. Pegis. Garden City, N.Y.: Doubleday, 1955.

Summa contra Gentiles II. Translated by J. Anderson. Garden City, N.Y.: Doubleday, 1956.

Summa contra Gentiles III. 2 vols. Translated by V. J. Burke. Garden City, N.Y.: Doubleday, 1956.

Summa contra Gentiles IV. Translated by C. J. O'Neill. Garden City, N.Y.: Doubleday, 1956.

Summa Theologica. Translated by the English Dominican Province. New York: Benziger Brothers, 1947.

Theological Compendium. Translated by Cyril Vollert. St. Louis, Mo.: B. Herder Book Co., 1947.

Thomas Aquinas: Selected Writings. Translated by R. McInerny. London: Penguin Books, 1998.

Truth. 3 vols. Translated by J. V. McGlenn, R. W. Mulligan, and R. W. Schmidt. Indianapolis, Ind.: Hackett, 1994.

CONCILIAR, MAGISTERIAL, AND PAPAL WORKS

Catechism of the Catholic Church. 2nd ed. Vatican City: Libreria Editrice Vaticana, 1997.

Congregation for the Doctrine of the Faith. *Dominus Jesus*. Declaration on the Unicity and Salvific Universality of Jesus Christ and the Church. August 6, 2000.

Congregation of the Doctrine of the Faith. *Notification on the Works of Jon Sobrino, S.J.* November 26, 2006.

Council of Trent, Decree on the Sacrament of Penance, 1551.

Decrees of the Ecumenical Councils. Edited by N. P. Tanner. Washington, D.C.: Georgetown University Press, 1990.

Denzinger, Heinrich. *Compendium of Creeds, Definitions, and Declarations on Matters of Faith and Morals*. 43rd ed. Edited by P. Hünermann, edited for English by R. Fastiggi and A. E. Nash. San Francisco: Ignatius Press, 2012.

John Paul II. *Fides et Ratio*. Encyclical Letter. September 14, 1998.

John Paul II. *Novo Millennio Ineunte*. Apostolic Letter. January 6, 2001.

John Paul II. *Redemptor hominis*. Encyclical Letter. March 4, 1979.

John Paul II. *Redemptoris Missio*. Encyclical Letter. December 7, 1990

Pius V. *Cum quorumdam hominum*. Apostolic Letter. August 7, 1955.

Pius XII. *Humani Generis*. Encyclical Letter. August 12, 1950.

Pius XII. *Mystici Corporis Christi*. Encyclical Letter. June 25, 1943.

Vatican Council I. *Dei Filius*. Dogmatic Constitution. April 24, 1870.

Vatican Council II. *Gaudium et Spes*. December 7, 1965.

Vatican Council II. *Lumen Gentium*. Dogmatic Constitution. November 21, 1964.

Vatican Council II. *Nostra Aetate*. Declaration on the Relation of the Church to Non-Christian Religions. October 28, 1965.

CLASSICAL AND MODERN WORKS

Aertsen, Jan. *Medieval Philosophy and the Transcendentals: The Case of Thomas Aquinas*. Leiden: Brill, 1996.

———. *Medieval Philosophy as Transcendental Thought. From Philip the Chancellor (c.a. 1225) to Francisco Suárez*. Leiden: Brill, 2012.

Alexander of Hales. "*Glossa Alex 3.7.27* (L)". In *Magistri Alexandri de Hales*

Glossa in Quatuor Libros Sententiarum Petri Lombardi, edited by PP. Collegii S. Bonaventurae, 4 vols. Florence: Quaracchi, 1960.

Anatolios, Khaled. *Athanasius*. London: Routledge, 1998.

———. "Faith, Reason, and Incarnation in Irenaeus of Lyons," *Nova et Vetera* (English edition) 16, no. 2 (2018): 543–60.

———. *Retrieving Nicaea: The Development and Meaning of Trinitarian Doctrine*. Grand Rapids, MI: Baker Academic, 2018.

Anselm. *Anselm of Canterbury: The Major Works*, edited by B. Davies and G. R. Evans. Oxford: Oxford University Press, 2008.

The Apostolic Fathers, with Justin Martyr and Irenaeus. Vol. 1 of *Ante-Nicene Fathers*, eds. A. Roberts, J. Donaldson, and A. C. Coxe. Buffalo, N.Y.: Christian Literature Publishing, 1885.

Aristotle. *The Complete Works of Aristotle*. Edited by J. Barnes. Translated by W. D. Ross. 2 vols. Princeton: Princeton University Press, 1984.

———. *Physics*. Translated by R. Waterfield. Oxford: Oxford University Press, 2008.

Athanasius. *On the Incarnation*. In *Nicene and Post-Nicene Fathers*, vol. 4, edited by A. Richardson and C. Scribner, translated by J.H. Newman. New York: Christian Literature Publishing, 1903.

Athanasius and Didymus. *Works on the Spirit: Athanasius's Letters to Serapion and Didymus the Blind's On the Holy Spirit*. Translated by Mark DelCogliano, Andrew Radde-Gallwitz, and Lewis Ayres. Crestwood, NY: St. Vladimir's Seminary Press, 2001.

Augustine. *On Grace and Free Will*. In *Nicene and Post-Nicene Fathers*, vol. 5, edited by P. Schaff, translated by A. H. Newman. Buffalo, N.Y.: Christian Literature Publishing, 1887.

———. *The Confessions*. Translated by M. Boulding. New York: Vintage Spiritual Classics, 1998.

———. *The Trinity*. Edited by J. E. Rotelle. Translated by E. Hill. Hyde Park, NY: New City Press, 1991.

Ayres, Lewis. *Augustine on the Trinity*. Cambridge: Cambridge University Press, 2010.

———. *Nicaea and its Legacy: An Approach to Fourth-Century Theology*. Oxford: Oxford University Press, 2004.

Backes, Ignaz. *Die Christologie des hl. Thomas von Aquin und die griechischen Kirchenväter*. Paterborn: Ferdinand Schöningh Verlag, 1931.

Balthasar, Hans Urs von. *The Glory of the Lord: A Theological Aesthetics*. Vol. 1: *Seeing the Form*. Translated by E. Leiva-Merikakis, San Francisco: Ignatius, 1982.

———. *Theo-Drama: Theological-Dramatic Theory*. Vol. 3, *The Dramatis Personae: Persons in Christ*. Translated by G. Harrison. San Francisco: Ignatius Press, 1992.

———. *Theo-Drama: Theological-Dramatic Theory*. Vol. 4, *The Action*. Translated by G. Harrison. San Francisco: Ignatius Press, 1994.

———. *Theo-Drama: Theological-Dramatic Theory*. Vol. 5, *The Last Act*. Translated by G. Harrison. San Francisco: Ignatius Press, 1998.

——. *Theo-Logic: Theological Logical Theory*. Vol. 2, *The Truth of God*. Translated by A. Walker. San Francisco: Ignatius Press, 2004

——. *Karl Barth: Darstellung und Deutung Seiner Theologie*. Köln: Verlag Jakob Hegner, 1951. Translated by E. Oakes. *The Theology of Karl Barth: Exposition and Interpretation*. San Francisco: Ignatius Press, 1992.

Bañez, Domingo. *Scholastica Commentaria in Primam Partem Summae Theologiae S. Thomae Aquinatis*. Madrid: F.E.D.A., 1934.

Barker, Mark. "Aquinas on Internal Sensory Intentions: Nature and Classification," *International Philosophical Quarterly* 52, no. 2 (2012) 199–226.

——. "Experience and Experimentation: The Meaning of *Experimentum* in Aquinas," *The Thomist* 76, no. 1 (2012) 37–71.

Barnes, Corey L. *Christ's Two Wills in Scholastic Thought: The Christology of Aquinas and its Historical Context*. Toronto: Pontifical Institute of Mediaeval Studies, 2015.

Barnes, Michel René. 'Irenaeus' Trinitarian Theology', *Nova et Vetera* (English ed.) 7, no. 1 (2009): 67–106.

Barr, James. "Theophany and Anthropomorphism in the Old Testament," *Vetus Testamentum* Sup 7 (1959): 31–38.

Barth, Karl. *Church Dogmatics*. Edited by G. W. Bromiley and T. F. Torrance. 4 vols. Edinburgh: T. & T. Clark, 1936–75.

Bathrellos, Demetrios. *The Byzantine Christ: Person, Nature, and Will in the Christology of Saint Maximus the Confessor*. Oxford: Oxford University Press, 2004.

Bauckham, Richard. *God Crucified: Monotheism and Christology in the New Testament*. Grand Rapids, Mich.: Eerdmans, 1998.

——. *Jesus and the God of Israel: God Crucified and Other Studies on the New Testament's Christology of Divine Identity*. Grand Rapids, Mich.: Eerdmans, 2008.

Berti, Enrico. "Unmoved Mover(s) as Efficient Cause(s) in Metaphysics Λ 6." In *Aristotle's Metaphysics Lambdai*, edited by M. Frede and D. Charles, 181–206. Oxford: Oxford University Press, 2000.

Bonaventure, *Commentaria in quatuor libros Sententiarum*. 4 vols. (Ad Claras Aquas, Quaracchi: Prope Florentiam Ex Typographia Collegii S. Bonaventurae, 1882–89).

Bonino, Serge-Thomas. *Angels and Demons: A Catholic Introduction*, translated by M.J. Miller. Washington, D.C.: The Catholic University of America Press, 2016.

——. *Dieu, 'Celui Qui Est'* ; *De Deo ut Uno*. Paris: Parole et Silence, 2016.

——. *Les Anges et Les Démons : Quatorze leçons de théologie*. Paris: Parole et Silence, 2007.

Boulnois, Olivier. *Duns Scotus on God*. Aldershot and Burlington: Ashgate, 2005.

——. "La destruction de l'analogie et l'instauration de la métaphysique." In *Sur la connaissance de Dieu et l'univocité de l'étant*, Paris: Presses Universitaires de France, 1988.

——. *l'Être et representation: Une généologie de la métaphysique moderne à l'époque de Duns Scot (XIIIe–XIVe Siècle)*. Paris: Presses Universitaires de France, 1999.

———. "Quand commence l'onto-théo-logie? Aristote, Thomas d'Aquin et Duns Scot." *Revue Thomiste* 95 (1995): 85–108.

Bower, Jeffrey E. *Aquinas's Ontology of the Material World: Change, Hylomorphism, and Material Objects*. Oxford: Oxford University Press, 2014.

Bowlin, John. "Barth and Aquinas on Election, Relationship, and Requirement." In *Thomas Aquinas and Karl Barth: An Unofficial Catholic-Protestant Dialogue*, edited by B.L. McCormack and T.J. White, 237–61. Grand Rapids, MI: Eerdmans, 2013.

Brueggemann, Walter. *Theology of the Old Testament: Testimony, Dispute, Advocacy*. Minneapolis: Fortress, 2012.

Brunner, Emil and Karl Barth. *Natural Theology*. Translated by P. Fraenkel. Eugene, Ore: Wipf and Stock, 2002.

Bulgakov, Sergius. *The Bride of the Lamb*. Translated by B. Jakim. Grand Rapids, Mich.: Eerdmans, 2002.

———. *The Lamb of God*. Translated by B. Jakim. Grand Rapids, Mich.: Eerdmans, 2008.

Caird, C. B. and L. D. Hurst. *New Testament Theology*. Oxford: Oxford University Press, 1994.

Calvin, John. *Institutes of the Christian Religion*. 2 vols. Translated by F. Battles. Philadephia: Westminster Press, 1960.

Cessario, Romanus. "Incarnate Wisdom and the Immediacy of Christ's Salvific Knowledge." In *Problemi teologici alla luce dell'Aquinate*, Studi Tomistici 44, no. 5, 334–40. Vatican City: Libreria Editrice Vaticana, 1991.

Chadwick, Henry. *East and West: The Making of a Rift in the Church: From Apostolic Times Until the Council of Florence*. Oxford: Oxford University Press, 2003.

Chesnut, Roberta. *Three Monophysite Christologies: Severus of Antioch, Philoxenus of Mabbug, and Jacob of Sarug*. Oxford: Oxford University Press, 1976.

Congar, Yves. *La tradition et les traditions*, 2 vols. Paris: A. Fayard, 1960–1963.

Cross, Richard. *Duns Scotus*. Oxford: Oxford University Press, 1999.

———. *Duns Scotus on God*. Aldershot: Ashgate, 2005.

Cullen, Christopher. "Bonaventure on Nature Before Grace: A Historical Moment Reconsidered." *American Catholic Philosophical Quarterly* 85 (2011): 161–76

Cyril of Alexandria. *On the Unity of Christ*. Translated by John A. McGuckin. Crestwood, NY: St. Vladimir's Press, 1995.

Daguet, Francois. *Finis Omnium Ecclesia: Théologie du Dessein Divin chez Thomas D'Aquin*. Paris: Vrin, 2003.

De la Soujeole, Benoit-Dominique. "Etre ordonné à l'unique Eglise du Christ: l'ecclésialité des communautés non chrétiennes à partir des données oecuméniques," *Revue Thomiste* (2002): 5–41.

De Lubac, Henri. *Surnaturel: Études historiques*. Paris: Aubier, 1946.

Dewan, Lawrence. *Form and Being: Studies in Thomistic Metaphysics*. Washington, D.C.: The Catholic University of America Press, 2006.

Diepen, Herman. "La critique du baslisme selon saint Thomas d'Aquin." *Revue Thomiste* 50 (1950): 82–118 and 290–329.

———. "La psychologie humaine du Christ selon saint Thomas d'Aquin." *Revue Thomiste* 50 (1950): 515–62.

———. *Théologie d'Emmanuel.* Bruges: Desclée de Brouwer, 1960.

Dionysius. *Pseudo-Dionysius: The Complete Works.* Translated by C. Luibheid and P. Rorem. Mahwah, N.J.: Paulist Press, 1987.

Dodd, C. H. *The Interpretation of the Fourth Gospel.* Cambridge: Cambridge University Press, 1953.

Dodds, Michael J. *The Unchanging God of Love: Thomas Aquinas and Contemporary Theology on Divine Immutability.* Washington, D.C.: The Catholic University of America Press, 2008.

Dolezal, James E. *God without Parts: Divine Simplicity and the Metaphysics of God's Absoluteness.* Eugene: Pickwick Publications, 2011.

Duby, Steven J. *Divine Simplicity: A Dogmatic Account.* (London: Bloomsbury T&T Clark, 2016)

Dunn, James D.G. *Jesus Remembered.* Grand Rapids, MI: Eerdmans, 2003.

Duns Scotus, John. *Opera omnia.* Edited by C. Balić and others. Rome: Typis Polyglottis Vaticani, 1950–2013.

Dupuis, Jacques. *Toward a Christian Theology of Religious Pluralism.* Maryknoll, NY: Orbis, 1997.

Durand, Emmanuel. *La périchorèse des personnes divines: Immanence mutuelle, Réciprocité et communion.* Paris: Cerf, 2005.

Edwards, Mark J. *Christians, Gnostics, and Philosophers in Late Antiquity.* Oxford: Routledge, 2012.

Emery, Gilles. "The Ecclesial Fruit of the Eucharist," *Nova et Vetera* (English) 2, no. 1 (2004): 43–60.

———. "Essentialism or Personalism in the Treatise on God in St. Thomas Aquinas?" *The Thomist* 64, no. 1 (2000): 521–563.

———. 'La relation dans la théologie de saint Albert le Grand.' In *Albertus Magnus: Zum Gedenken nach 800 Jahren: Neue Zugänge, Aspekte und Perspektiven.* Edited by Walter Senner, O.P. Berlin: Akademie Verlag, 2001.

———. *La théologie trinitaire de saint Thomas d'Aquin.* Paris: Cerf, 2004

———. "The Personal Mode of Trinitarian Action in Saint Thomas Aquinas." *The Thomist* 69, no. 1 (2005): 31–77.

———. "*Theologia* and *Dispensatio*: The Centrality of the Divine Missions in St. Thomas's Trinitarian Theology," *The Thomist* 74, no. 4 (2010): 515–61.

———. *The Trinitarian Theology of St. Thomas Aquinas.* Translated by F. Murphy. Oxford: Oxford University Press, 2010.

———. *Trinity in Aquinas.* Ypsilanti, Mich.: Ave Maria Press, 2002.

G.R. Evans. *Bernard of Clairvaux.* Oxford: Oxford University Press, 2000.

Fabro, Cornelio. *Participation et Causalité selon Thomas d'Aquin.* Louvain / Paris: Publications Universitaires de Louvain / Éditions Béatrice-Nauwelaerts, 1961.

Feser, Edward. *Aquinas: A Beginner's Guide.* Oxford: Oneworld Press, 2009.

———. "Swinburne's Tri-Theism". *International Journal for Philosophy of Religion* 42, no. 3 (1997): 175–84.

Fischer, Simon. *Revelatory Positivism: Barth's Earliest Theology and the Marburg School*. Oxford: Oxford University Press, 1988.

Frei, Hans. *Types of Christian Theology*. Edited by G. Hunsinger and W. C. Placher. New Haven, Conn.: Yale University Press, 1992.

Friedman, Russell L. *Medieval Trinitarian Thought from Aquinas to Ockham*. Cambridge: Cambridge University Press, 2010.

Gaine, Simon Francis. *Did the Saviour See the Father? Christ, Salvation, and the Vision of God*. London: T&T Clarke, 2015.

———. "Is There Still a Place for Christ's Infused Knowledge in Catholic Theology and Exegesis?", *Nova et Vetera* 16 no. 2 (2018): 601–615.

Galot, Jean. *La conscience de Jésus*. Paris: Duculot-Lethielleux, 1971.

———. "La conscience du Christ et la foi." *Esprit et vie* 92 (1982): 145–52.

———. "Le Christ terrestre et la vision," *Gregorianum* 67 (1986): 429–50.

———. *Vers une nouvelle christologie*. Paris: Duculot-Lethielleux, 1971.

Galtier, Paul. "Unité ontologique et unité psychologique dans le Christ." *Bulletin de littérature ecclésiastique* (Toulouse) 42 (1941): 161–75 and 216–32.

Gardeil, Ambroise. *La crédibilité et l'apologétique*. Paris: J. Gabalda et Fils, 1928.

———. *Le donné révélé et la théologie*. 2nd ed. Paris: Cerf, 1932.

Garrigou-Lagrange, Reginald. *Christ The Savior: A Commentary on the Third Part of St. Thomas' "Theological Summa"*, Translated by B. Rose. London: Herder, 1957.

———. *De Deo Uno*. Paris: Desclée et Brouwer, 1938.

———. *De Revelatione*. Rome: Ferrari and Gabalda, 1921.

Garrigues, Jean-Miguel. "La conscience de soi telle qu'elle était exercée par le Fils de Dieu fait homme", *Nova et Vetera* (French Edition) 79, n. 1 (2004) 39–51.

———. "Le dessein d'adoption du créateur dans son rapport au fils d'après S. Maxime le Confesseur." In *Maximus Confessor*, edited by Felix Heinzer and Christoph Schönborn, 173–92. Fribourg: Éditions Universitaires, 1982.

———. *L'Esprit qui dit 'Pere'*: L'Esprit-Saint dans la vie trinitaire et le probleme du filioque. Paris: Tequi, 1981.

———. "L'instrumentalité rédemptrice du libre arbitre du Christ chez saint Maxime le Confesseur," *Revue Thomiste* 104 (2004): 531–50.

Gavrilyuk, Paul L. *The Suffering of the Impassible God: The Dialectics of Patristic Thought*. Oxford: Oxford University Press, 2004.

Gilbert of Poitiers. "Expositio in Boecii de Trinitate." In *The Commentaries on Boethius by Gilbert of Poitiers*, edited by N. Häring. Toronto: PIMS, 1966.

Gilson, Étienne. *Elements of Christian Philosophy*. New York: Doubleday, 1960.

Gockel, Matthias. *Barth and Schleiermacher on the Doctrine of Election*. Oxford: Oxford University Press, 2006.

Grant, Robert M. *Gnosticism and Early Christianity*. New York: Harper and Brothers, 1961.

Gregory of Nazianzus. "Orations 29 & 31" in *Nicene and Post-Nicene Fathers*, vol. 7. Edited and translated by C. G. Browne and J. E. Swallow. Peabody, MA: Hendrickson Publishers, 1994.

———. *On God and Christ. The Five Theological Orations and Two Letter to Cledonius.* Translated by Frederick Williams and Lionel Wickham. Yonkers, NY: St. Vladimir's Seminary Press, 2002.

Gregory of Nyssa. *Life of Moses.* Translated by A. Malherbe and E. Ferguson. New York: Paulist Press, 1978.

———. *On "Not Three Gods": To Ablabius* and *"Against Eunomius".* In *Letters and Select Works,* vol. 5 of *Nicene and Post-Nicene Fathers, Second Series,* edited by P. Schaff and H. Wace, translated by H.A. Wilson. Buffalo, NY: Christian Literature Publishing Co., 1893

Gregory Palamas. *The Triads.* Translated by N. Gendle. Mahwah: NJ: Paulist Press, 1983.

Grillmeier, Aloys. *Christ in Christian Tradition,* vol. 2, pt. 2. London: Mowbray; Louisville: Westminster John Knox, 1995.

———. *Fragen der Theologie heute,* ed. J. Feiner, J. Truesch, and F. Boeckle. Einsiedeln: Benzinger Verlag, 1957.

Haddad, Robert M. "The Stations of the Filioque." *St. Vladimir's Theological Quarterly* 46, no, 2 (2002): 209–268.

Harnack, Adolf von. *Das Wesen des Christentums.* Leipzig: J.C. Hinrichs, 1900.

Hart, David Bentley. *The Beauty of the Infinite: The Aesthetics of Christian Truth.* Grand Rapids, Mich.: Eerdmans, 2003.

———. "No Shadow of Turning: On Divine Impassibility," *Pro Ecclesia* 11 (Spring 2002): 184–206.

Hasker, William. "Is Divine Simplicity a Mistake?", *American Catholic Philosophical Quarterly* 90, no. 4 (2016): 699–725.

———. *Metaphysics and the Tri-Personal God.* Oxford: Oxford University Press, 2013.

Hegel, Georg W. F. *Lectures on the Philosophy of Religion, The Lectures of 1827.* 3 vols. Edited by P. C. Hodgson. Translated by R. F. Brown, P. C. Hodgson, J. M. Stewart. Berkeley, Cal.: University of California Press, 2006.

———. *The Phenomenology of Spirit.* Translated by T. Pinkard (Cambridge: Cambridge University Press, 2018).

Heidegger, Martin. *Identity and Difference.* Translated by J. Staumbaugh. New York: Harper & Row, 1969.

Hengel, Martin. *The Atonement: The Origins of the Doctrine in the New Testament.* Philadelphia: Fortress, 1981.

Herrmann, Wilhelm. *Die Religion im Verhältniss zum Welterkennen und zur Sittlichkeit: eine Grundlegung der systematischen Theologie.* Halle: M. Niemeyer, 1879.

Herrara, Juan José. *La simplicidad divina según santo Tomás de Aquino.* Salta, Argentina: Ediciones de la Universidad del Norte Santo Tomás de Aquino, 2011.

Hick, John. *An Interpretation of Religion: Human Responses to the Transcendent.* New Haven, Conn.: Yale University Press, 1989.

———. "Jesus and the World Religions," In *The Myth of God Incarnate,* edited by John Hick, 167–85. Philadelphia: Westminster, 1977.

———. *God Has Many Names.* Philadelphia, PA: Westminster, 1992.

Hochschild, Joshua P. *The Semantics of Analogy: Rereading Cajetan's De Nominum Analogia*. Notre Dame: Notre Dame University Press, 2010.

Hofer, Andrew. "Dionysian Elements in Thomas Aquinas's Christology: A Case of the Authority and Ambiguity of Pseudo-Dionysius." *The Thomist* 72, no. 3 (2008): 409–442.

Hoyum, John W. "Luther and Some Lutherans on Divine Simplicity and Hiddenness." *Lutheran Quarterly* 34, no. 4 (2020): 390–409.

Hughes, Christopher. *On a Complex Theory of a Simple God: An Investigation in Aquinas' Philosophical Theology*. Ithaca and London: Cornell University Press, 1987.

Humbrecht, Thierry-Dominique. *Théologie négative et noms divins chez Saint Thomas d'Aquin*. Paris: J. Vrin, 2005.

———. *Trinité et création au prisme de la voie négative chez Saint Thomas d'Aquin*. Paris: Parole et Silence, 2011.

Hunsinger, George. "Karl Barth's Christology: Its Basic Chalcedonian Character." In *The Cambridge Companion to Karl Barth*, edited by John Webster, 127–42. Cambridge: Cambridge University Press, 2000.

Hurtado, Larry W. *Lord Jesus Christ: Devotion to Jesus in Earliest Christianity*. Grand Rapids, Mich.: Eerdmans. 2003.

International Theological Commission. *Christianity and the World Religions*. Vatican City: Libreria Editrice Vaticana, 1997.

———. *The Consciousness of Christ Concerning Himself and His Mission*. Vatican City: Libreria Editrice Vaticana, 1985.

Irenaeus. *Against Heresies*. In *Ante-Nicene Fathers*, vol. 1, edited by A. Roberts and J. Donaldson. Peabody, MA: Hendrickson Publishers, 2004.

Israel, Jonathan. *Radical Enlightenment: Philosophy in the Making of Modernity 1650–1750*. Oxford: Oxford University Press, 2001.

Jenson, Robert. *Systematic Theology I*. Oxford: Oxford University Press, 1997.

John Damascene, *The Orthodox Faith*. In *Nicene and Post-Nicene Fathers, Second Series*, vol. 9. Edited by P. Schaff and H. Wace, translated by E. W. Watson and L. Pullan. Buffalo, N.Y.: Christian Literature Publishing, 1899.

John of St. Thomas. *Cursus Theologicus*. Vol. 8. Paris: Vivès, 1886.

Johnson, Keith L. *Karl Barth and the Analogia Entis*. London and New York: T&T Clark, 2011.

Johnson, Luke Timothy. *The Real Jesus*. New York: Harper Collins, 1996.

Journet, Charles. *L'Église du Verbe Incarné*. Vol I. *La hiérarchie apostolique*. Paris: Saint Augustin, 1998.

———. *L'Eglise du Verbe Incarné*. Vol. II. *La structure interne de l'Eglise: Le Christ, la Vierge, l'Esprit Saint*. Paris: Saint Augustin, 1999.

———. *L'Église du Verbe Incarné*. Vol. VI. *Essai de théologie de l'histoire du salut*. Paris: Saint Augustin, 2004.

———. *The Mass: The Presence of the Sacrifice of the Cross*. Translated by Victor Szczurek. South Bend, Ind.: St. Augustine's Press, 2008.

——. *The Meaning of Grace.* Translated by A.V. Littledale. Princeton, NJ: Scepter, 1996.

Jüngel, Eberhard. *God as the Mystery of the World: On the Foundation of the Theology of the Crucified One in the Dispute between Theism and Atheism.* Translated by D.L. Gouder. Grand Rapids, Mich.: Eerdmans, 1983.

Kähler, Martin. *Der sogenannte historische Jesus und der geschichtliche, biblische Christus.* Leipzig: A. Deichert, 1892. English translation by Carl E. Braaten. *The So-Called Historical Jesus and the Historical Biblical Christ.* Philadelphia: Fortress Press, 1964.

Kant, Immanuel. *The Critique of Pure Reason.* Translated by N.K. Smith. London: Macmillan, 1990.

——. *Prolegomena to Any Future Metaphysics.* Translated by P. Carus and J. Ellington. Indianapolis and Cambridge: Hackett Publishing, 1977.

——. *Religion within the Boundaries of Mere Reason.* Translated and edited by Allen Wood and George di Giovanni. Cambridge: Cambridge University Press, 1998.

Kasper, Walter. *The Absolute in History: The Philosophy and Theology of History in Schelling's Late Philosophy.* Translated by K. Wolff. New York: Paulist Press, 2018.

——. *Jesus the Christ.* Translated by V. Green. London: Burns & Oates, 1976.

Keating, James F. and Thomas Joseph White, eds. *Divine Impassibility and the Mystery of Human Suffering.* Grand Rapids, Mich.: Eerdmans, 2009.

Kerr, Fergus. *Theology after Wittgenstein.* Oxford: Blackwell, 1986.

Kretzmann, Norman. *The Metaphysics of Theism: Aquinas's Natural Theology in "Summa Contra Gentiles I".* Oxford: Oxford University Press, 1997.

Legge, Dominic. *The Trinitarian Christology of St. Thomas Aquinas.* Oxford: Oxford University Press, 2017.

Leo the Great. "Tome of Leo." In *Nicene and Post-Nicene Fathers,* Vol. 12. Translated by C.L. Feltoe; eds. P. Schaff and H. Wace. Buffalo, NY: Christian Literature Publishing Co., 1895.

Lessing, Gotthold Ephraim. *Lessing's Theological Writings,* Translated by H. Chadwick. Stanford, Calif.: Stanford University Press, 1957.

——. *Philosophical and Theological Writings.* Edited by H.B. Nisbet. Cambridge: Cambridge University Press, 2005.

Levering, Matthew. *Christ's Fulfillment of Torah and Temple: Salvation according to Thomas Aquinas.* Notre Dame, Ind.: University of Notre Dame Press, 2002.

Lindbeck, George. *The Nature of Doctrine: Religion and Theology in a Post-Liberal Age.* Louisville, Ky.: Westminster John Knox Press, 1984.

Lonergan, Bernard. *The Ontological and Psychological Constitution of Christ.* In *Collected Works,* vol. 7. Translated by Michael G. Shields. Toronto: University of Toronto Press, 2002.

Lossky, Vladimir. *The Mystical Theology of the Eastern Church.* Yonkers, NY: SVS Press, 1997.

Louth, Andrew. *St John Damascene: Tradition and Originality in Byzantine Theology.* Oxford: Oxford University Press, 2002.

Louth, Andrew, trans. *Maximus the Confessor*. London: Routledge, 1996.

Luther, Martin. *Brief Confession Concerning the Holy Sacrament*. In *Luther's Works*, vol. 37. Edited by R.H. Fisher and H.T. Lehmann. Translated by H. Fisher. Philadelphia: Fortress, 1961.

———. *Confession Concerning Christ's Supper* (1528). In *Luther's Works*, vol. 37. Edited by R.H. Fisher and H.T. Lehmann. Translated by H. Fisher. Philadelphia: Fortress, 1961.

McCormack, Bruce L. *The Humility of the Eternal Son*. Cambridge: Cambridge University Press, 2021.

———. "Karl Barth's Christology as a Resource for a Reformed Version of Kenoticism," *International Journal of Systematic Theology* 8, no. 3 (2006): 243–51.

———. *Karl Barth's Critically Realistic Dialectical Theology: Its Genesis and Development, 1909–1936*. Oxford: Clarendon Press, 1995.

———. "Seek God Where He May Be Found: A Response to Edwin Chr. van Driel," *Scottish Journal of Theology* 60, no 1 (2007): 62–79.

McGluckin, John. *Saint Cyril of Alexandria and the Christological Controversy*. Yonkers, NY: St. Vladimir's Press, 2010.

MacIntyre, Alasdair, *After Virtue*. South Bend, Ind.: Notre Dame University Press, 1981.

Mansini, Guy. "Can Humility and Obedience be Trinitarian Realities?". In *Thomas Aquinas and Karl Barth: An Unofficial Catholic–Protestant Dialogue*, edited by B.L. McCormack and T.J. White, 71–98. Grand Rapids, Mich.: Eerdmans, 2013.

———. "Understanding St. Thomas on Christ's Immediate Knowledge of God," *The Thomist* 59 (1995): 91–124.

Marion, Jean-Luc. *Being Given. Toward a Phenomenology of Givenness*. Translated by J. L. Kosky. Stanford: Stanford University Press, 2002.

———. "De la 'mort de Dieu' au noms divines: l'itinéraire théologique de la métaphysique." In *l'Être et Dieu*, ed. D. Bourg. Paris: Cerf, 1986.

———. *God without Being*. Translated by T. A. Carlson. Chicago and London: University of Chicago Press, 1991.

———. *The Idol and the Distance*. Translated by T. A. Carlson. New York: Fordham University Press, 2001.

———. "Saint Thomas d'Aquin et l'onto-théo-logie." *Revue Thomiste* 95, no. 1 (1995): 31–66.

Maritain, Jacques. *Art and Scholasticism with Other Essays*. Translated by J.F. Scanlan. New York: Scribner's, 1939.

———. *Court Traité de l'Existence et de l'Existant, Oeuvres Complètes*, vol. 9. Fribourg and Paris: Éditions Universitaires and Éditions St.-Paul, 1990.

———. *On the Grace and Humanity of Jesus*. New York: Herder and Herder, 1969.

Marshall, Bruce D. *Trinity and Truth*. Cambridge: Cambridge University Press, 2000.

———. "The Unity of the Triune God: Reviving an Ancient Question," *The Thomist* 74, no. 1 (2010): 1–32.

Maurer, Armand. "St. Thomas on the Sacred Name 'Tetragrammaton,'" *Mediaeval Studies* 34 (1972): 275–86.

Miller, Patrick D. *The Religion of Ancient Israel*. (Louisville: Westminster John Knox, 2000).

Moltmann, Jürgen. *The Crucified God: The Cross of Christ as the Foundation and Criticism of Christian Life*, Translated by R. A. Wilson and J. Bowden. San Francisco: Harper and Row, 1974.

———. *God in Creation: A New Theology of Creation and the Spirit of God*. Minneapolis, Minn.: Fortress, 1993.

———. *The Trinity and the Kingdom: The Doctrine of God*. Translated by M. Kohl. San Francisco: Harper and Row, 1981.

Montagnes, Bernard. *La doctrine de l'analogie de l'être d'après saint Thomas d'Aquin*. Louvain: Éditions Peeters, 1963.

Neill, Stephen and Tom Wright. *The Interpretation of the New Testament 1861–1986*. Oxford: Oxford University Press, 1988.

Newman, John Henry Cardinal. *An Essay on the Development of Christian Doctrine*. London: Longmans, Green & Co., 1909.

Nicolas, Jean-Hervé. *Synthèse Dogmatique; de la Trinité à la Trinité*. Fribourg and Paris: Éditions universitaires Fribourg and Éditions Beauchesne, 1991.

Nicolas, Marie-Joseph. "Voir Dieu dans la 'condition charnelle'," *Doctor Communis* 36 (1983) 384–94.

Nietzsche, Friedrich. *On the Genealogy of Morality*. Translated by C. Diethe. Cambridge: Cambridge University Press, 2006.

Novak, David. *The Natural Law in Judaism*. Cambridge: Cambridge University Press, 2008.

———. *Talking with Christians: Musings of a Jewish Theologian*. Grand Rapids, Mich.: Eerdmans, 2005.

O'Collins, Gerald. *Christology: A Biblical, Historical and Systematic Study of Jesus Christ*. Oxford: Oxford University Press, 1995.

Oderberg, David S. *Real Essentialism*. London: Routledge, 2008.

———. "No Potency without Actuality: The Case of Graph Theory." In *Contemporary Aristotelian Metaphysics*, edited by T.E. Tahko, 207–28. Cambridge: Cambridge University Press, 2012.

O'Regan, Cyril. *The Heterodox Hegel*. Albany, NY: State University of New York Press, 1994.

O'Rourke, Fran. *Pseudo-Dionysius and the Metaphysics of Aquinas*. Notre Dame, Ind.: University of Notre Dame Press, 2005.

Owens, Joseph. *The Doctrine of Being in the Aristotelian Metaphysics: A Study in the Greek Background of Mediaeval Thought*. Toronto: PIMS, 1951.

Pannenberg, Wolfhart. "Analogie und Offenbarung." Heidelberg: Habilitationsschrift 1955. Published in an altered version as *Analogie und Offenbarung: Eine kritische Untersuchung zur Geschichte des Analogiebegriffes in der Lehre von der Gotteserkenntnis*. Göttingen: Vandenhoeck & Ruprecht, 2007.

———. *Jesus: God and Man*. 2nd ed. Translated by L. L. Wilkins and D. A. Priebe. Philadelphia: Westminster, 1968.

———. *Systematic Theology*. Vol. 2. Translated by G. W. Bromiley. Grand Rapids, Mich.: Eerdmans, 1994.

Pannikar, Raimon. "The Jordan, The Tiber, and The Ganges: Three Kairological Moments of Christic Self-Consciousness." In *The Myth of Christian Uniqueness*, edited by J. Hick and P. Knitter. Maryknoll, NY: Orbis, 1987.

Papademetriou, George C. *Introduction to St. Gregory Palamas*. Brookline, MA: Holy Cross Orthodox Press, 2004.

Perego, Angelo. "Il 'lumen gloriae' et l'unita psicologica di Cristo," *Divus Thomas* 58 (1955): 90–110, 296–310.

Peter Lombard, *The Sentences*. Translated by Giulio Silano. Toronto: Pontifical Institute of Mediaeval Studies, 2007–10.

Plantinga, Alvin. *Does God Have a Nature?* Milwaukee, Wisc.: Marquette University Press, 1980.

Plato. *Complete Works*. Edited by J. M. Cooper. Translated by G. M. A. Grube. Indianapolis, Ind.: Hackett, 1997.

Plotinus, *Enneads*. Translated by G. Boys-Stones, J. M. Dillon, L. P. Gerson, R. A. H. King, A. Smith, and J. Wilberding. (Cambridge: Cambridge University Press, 2019).

Porro, Pasquale. *Thomas Aquinas: A Historical and Philosophical Profile*. Translated by J. Trabbic and R. Nutt. Washington, D.C.: The Catholic University of America Press, 2016.

Powell, Samuel M. *The Trinity in German Thought*. Cambridge: Cambridge University Press, 2001.

Principe, Walter H. *Alexander of Hales' Theology of the Hypostatic Union*. Toronto: Pontifical Institute of Mediaeval Studies, 1967.

———. *Philip the Chancellor's Theology of the Hypostatic Union*. Toronto: Pontifical Institute of Mediaeval Studies, 1975.

Przywara, Erich. *Analogia Entis: Metaphysics: Original Structure and Universal Rhythm*. Translated by J. Betz and D. B. Hart. Grand Rapids, Mich.: Eerdmans, 2014.

Rahner, Karl. *Theological Investigations*. Vol. 4. Translated by K. Smith. London: Darton, Longman & Todd, 1966.

———. *Theological Investigations*. Vol. 5. Translated by K.-H. Kruger. London: Darton, Longman & Todd, 1966.

———. *Theological Investigations*. Vol. 13. New York: Seabury, 1979.

———. *The Trinity*. Translated by J. Donceel. London: Continuum, 2001.

Ratzinger, Joseph. *Behold the Pierced One*. San Francisco: Ignatius Press, 1986.

Reimarus, Samuel. *Apologie oder Schutzschrift für die vernünftigen Verehrer Gottes*. Edited by Gerhard Alexander. Frankfurt-am-Main: Insel, 1972.

Richard of St. Victor. *On the Trinity*. Translated by C. P. Evans. In Coolman and Coulter, *Trinity and Creation*.

Ritschl, Albert. *Die christliche Lehre von der Rechtfertigung und Versöhnung.* 3 vols. Bonn: A. Marcus, 1870–74.

———. *Theologie und Metaphysik: zur Verständigung und Abwehr.* Bonn: A. Marcus, 1887.

Sanders, E. P. *Jesus and Judaism.* Philadelphia: Fortress, 1985.

Scheeben, Matthias. *Handbook of Catholic Dogmatics,* vol. II: *Doctrine about God or Theology in the Narrower Sense.* Translated by Michael J. Miller. Steubenville, OH: Emmaus Academic, 2022.

———. *The Mysteries of Christianity.* Translated by C. Vollert. New York: Crossroad, 2006.

Schillebeeckx, Eduard. *Jesus: An Experiment in Christology.* New York: Seabury, 1979.

Schleiermacher, Friedrich. *Der christliche Glaube.* Berlin: G. Reimer, 1821–1822. *The Christian Faith.* 2 vols. Edited by H. R. Mackintosh and J. S. Stewart. New York: Harper and Row, 1963.

Schönborn, Christoph. *Sophrone de Jerusalem: vie monastique et confession dogmatique.* Théologie historique 20. Paris: Beauchesne, 1972.

———. *The Human Face of God.* San Francisco: Ignatius Press, 1994.

Schweitzer, Albert. *Geschichte der Leben-Jesu-Forschung.* Tübingen: J. C. B.Mohr, 1913.

Seiller, Leon. *La psychologie humaine du Christ et l'unicité de personne.* Rennes and Paris: Vrin, 1949.

Sesboüé, Bernard. *Pédagogie du Christ.* Paris: Cerf, 1994.

Sherwin, Michael. *By Knowledge and by Love: Charity and Knowledge in the Moral Theology of St. Thomas Aquinas.* Washington, D.C.: The Catholic University of America Press, 2005.

Smith, Mark. *The Origins of Biblical Monotheism: Israel's Polytheistic Background and the Ugaritic Texts.* Oxford: Oxford University, 2003.

———. *Where the Gods Are.* New Haven: Yale University, 2016.

Söhngen, Gottlieb. "The Analogy of Faith: Likeness to God from Faith Alone?" in *Pro Ecclesia* 21, n. 1 (2012): 56–76. Translated by K. Oakes.

———. "The Analogy of Faith: Unity in the Science of Faith," *Pro Ecclesia* 21, n. 2 (2012): 169–94. Translated by K. Oakes.

Soloveitchik, Joseph B. *Halakhic Man.* Philadelphia: The Jewish Publication Society, 1983.

———. *The Halakhic Mind.* New York: The Free Press, 1986.

Spinoza, Baruch. *Ethics: Proved in Geometrical Order.* Translated by M. Silverthorne. Cambridge: Cambridge University Press, 2018.

Stăniloae, Dumitru. "The procession of the Holy Spirit from the Father and his relation to the Son, as the basis of our deification and adoption." In *Spirit of God, Spirit of Christ,* edited by L. Vischer, 174–86. London/Geneva: SPCK/World Council of Churches, 1981.

Stead, G.C. "In Search of Valentinus." In *The Rediscovery of Gnosticism,* 2 vols, edited by B. Layton, 72–102. Leiden: Brill, 2018.

Stump, Eleonore. *Aquinas.* London: Routledge, 2006.

———. *The God of the Bible and the God of the Philosophers.* Milwaukee: Marquette University, 2016.

———. "Simplicity and Aquinas's Quantum Metaphysics." In *Die Metaphysik des Aristoteles im Mittelalter: Rezeption Und Transformation,* edited by Gerhard Krieger, 191–210. Berlin: De Gruyter, 2016.

Swinburne, Richard. *The Christian God.* Oxford: Clarendon Press, 1994.

———. *The Coherence of Theism.* Rev. ed. Oxford: Clarendon Press, 2010.

———. *Revelation.* Oxford: Clarendon Press, 1992.

Tanner, Norman. *Decrees of the Ecumenical Councils.* Vol. 1. London: Sheed & Ward; Washington, D.C.: Georgetown University Press, 1990.

Te Velde, Rudi. *Aquinas on God.* Aldershot: Ashgate, 2006.

Torrell, Jean-Pierre. *Le Christ en ses Mystères: la vie et l'oeuvre de Jésus selon saint Thomas d'Aquin.* Vol. 2. Paris: Desclèe, 1999.

———. "Le savoir acquis du Christ selon les théologiens médiévaux," *Revue Thomiste* 101 (2001): 355–408.

———. *Le Verbe Incarné.* Paris: Cerf, 2002.

———. "S. Thomas d'Aquin et la science du Christ." In *Saint Thomas au XXe siècle,* edited by S.-T. Bonino. Paris: Éditions St. Paul, 1994.

———. *St. Thomas Aquinas.* Vol. 1 *The Person and His Work.* Translated by R. Royal. Washington D.C.: The Catholic University of America Press, 1996.

Tschipke, Theophil. *Die Menschheit Christi als Heilsorgan der Gottheit.* Freiburg-im-Breisgau, 1939, republished in French as *L'humanité du Christ comme instrument de salut de la divinité.* Fribourg: Academic Press Fribourg, 2003.

Vanhoye, Albert. *Old Testament Priests and the New Priest.* Translated by Bernard Orchard. Petersham, Mass.: St. Bede's Press, 1986.

Vidu, Adonis. *The Same God Who Works In All Things: inseparable Operations in Trinitarian Theology.* Grand Rapids, MI: Eerdmans, 2021.

Wahlberg, Mats. *Revelation as Testimony: A Philosophical Vatican Theological Study.* Grand Rapids, Mich.: Eerdmans, 2014.

Weber, Edouard-Henri. *Le Christ selon saint Thomas d'Aquin.* Paris: Desclée, 1988.

Weinandy, Thomas. "The Beatific Vision and the Incarnate Son: Furthering the Discussion." *The Thomist* 70 (2006): 605–15.

———. *Does God Change?* Still River, Mass.: St. Bede's Press, 1985.

———. *Does God Suffer?* Notre Dame, Ind.: University of Notre Dame Press, 2000.

———. "Jesus' Filial Vision of the Father." *Pro Ecclesia* 13 (2004): 189–201.

White, Thomas Joseph ed. *The Analogy of Being: Invention of the Anti-Christ or Wisdom of God?* Grand Rapids, Mich.: Eerdmans, 2011.

———. "The *analogia fidei* in Catholic Theology," *International Journal of Systematic Theology* 22, no. 4 (2020): 512–37.

———. "Divine Simplicity and the Holy Trinity." *International Journal of Systematic Theology* 18, no. 1 (2016): 66–93.

———. "Dyotheletism and the Instrumental Human Consciousness of Jesus", *Pro Ecclesia* 17, no. 4 (2008) 396–422.

Bibliography

———. "The Holy Spirit." In *The Oxford Handbook of Catholic Theology*, edited by L. Ayres and M.A. Volpe, Oxford: Oxford University Press, 2019.

———. "How Barth Got Aquinas Wrong: A Reply to Archie J. Spencer on Causality and Christocentrism," *Nova et Vetera* (English Edition) 7, no. 1 (2009): 241–70.

———. "Imperfect Happiness and the Final End of Man: Thomas Aquinas and the Paradigm of Nature-Grace Orthodoxy," *The Thomist* 78 (2014): 247–89.

———. *The Incarnate Lord: A Thomistic Study in Christology*. Washington, D.C.: The Catholic University of America Press, 2015.

———. "The Infused Science of Christ." *Nova et Vetera* (English Edition) 16, no. 2 (2018): 617–64.

———. "Jesus' Cry on the Cross and His Beatific Vision." *Nova et Vetera* (English Edition) 5 (2007): 525–51.

———. "Kenoticism and the Divinity of Christ Crucified," *The Thomist* 75, no. 1 (2011): 1–42.

———. "Nicene Orthodoxy and Trinitarian Simplicity," *American Catholic Philosophical Quarterly* 90, no. 4 (2016): 727–50.

———. *Principles of Catholic Theology*: Book 1: *On the Nature of Theology*. Washington, D.C.: The Catholic University of America Press, 2023.

———. "Thomas Aquinas and the Paradigm of Nature-Grace Orthodoxy." *The Thomist* 78, no. 1 (2014): 247–89.

———. *The Trinity: On the Nature and Mystery of the One God*. Washington, D.C.: The Catholic University of America Press, 2022.

———. "The Voluntary Action of the Earthly Christ and the Necessity of the Beatific Vision," *The Thomist* 69 no. 1 (2005): 497–534

———. *Wisdom in the Face of Modernity: A Study in Thomistic Natural Theology*. Naples, Fla.: Sapientia Press, second edition, 2011.

William of Ockham. *Opera theologica*. Vols. 1–10. St. Bonaventure, N.Y.: Franciscan Institute Publications, 1967–86.

Wippel, John. *Metaphysical Themes in Thomas Aquinas II*. Washington, D.C.: The Catholic University of America Press, 2007.

———. *The Metaphysical Thought of Thomas Aquinas*. Washington, D.C.: The Catholic University of America Press, 2000.

Witherington III, Ben. *The Christology of Jesus*. Minneapolis, Minn.: Fortress, 1990.

Wright, N. T. *The Climax of the Covenant: Christ and the Law in Pauline Theology*. Minneapolis, Minn.: Fortress, 1993.

———. *Jesus and the Victory of God*. Minneapolis, Minn.: Fortress, 1996.

Zaleski, Carol. *Life of the World to Come: Near-Death Experience and Christian Hope*. Oxford University Press, Oxford 1996.

Person Index

Subject Index